Goldmine

Christmas Record

Price Guide

Tim Neely

Published by

 **krause publications**

700 E. State Street • Iola, WI 54990-0001
Telephone: 715/445-2214

Please call or write for our free catalog.
Our toll-free number to place an order or obtain a free catalog is 800-258-0929
or please use our regular business telephone 715-445-2214
for editorial comment and further information.

Library of Congress Catalog Number: 97-073028
ISBN: 0-87341-524-8
Printed in the United States of America

Table of Contents

Happy Holiday!

An Introduction to the *Goldmine* Christmas Record Price Guide

Ah yes, Christmas. The time of year for peace on earth, good will toward men, chestnuts roasting on an open fire, decking the halls with boughs of holly, Santa Claus coming to town, and Grandma getting run over by a reindeer.

You get the idea. The last month of the year has inspired a wide variety of music, from the profound to the profane... and much of it is collectible.

In the past few years, the growth of Christmas music collecting has been obvious. Many used record stores never remove their holiday offerings from sight; many collectors' catalogs offer Christmas records all year, not just in October, November and December. And those department-store and tire company compilations aren't as omnipresent in thrift stores as they once were. Now, here is the first guide to collecting holiday music on vinyl, complete with current values.

New Christmas singles are usually available for a short time and usually don't sell as many copies as an artist's regular releases. For example, many a Beach Boys collector has struggled to find original copies of their holiday singles, "Little Saint Nick," "The Man with All the Toys" and especially "Child of Winter."Christmas albums can be available for decades. Nonetheless, most of the copies that enter the market seem to be reissues. Many older LPs are replaced in personal libraries with newer copies and the originals are thrown out.

Finally, there are the much-maligned, yet often worthwhile, special-products compilations. It's generally known that some Christmas various-artists sets contain tracks unavailable anywhere else. But what is not as well known is that sometimes these are by prominent artists such as Simon and Garfunkel, Barbra Streisand, Petula Clark, Mark Lindsey and Gary Puckett. Finding those records has been a hit-and-miss proposition – until now.

This book has two features never before seen in a price guide. First, included under each artist is a listing of their songs that appear on various-artists LPs. Second, the various-artists LPs in the last 40-50 pages of the book list, whenever possible, the complete contents in order on each side, and not just the artists included on the records. You can now find out which compilations have the rare Simon and Garfunkel song "The Star Carol" or which ones have Glen Campbell or Mormon Tabernacle Choir recordings.

The listings are exhaustive, as you will see, but they certainly are not complete. At the end of the introduction, I'll tell you how you can help make them even more complete.

What's In Here, What's Not

Any 45, 7-inch extended play single, 12-inch single or album that we could find that had some relation to the holiday season is in here. Technically, such songs as "Jingle Bells" and "Winter Wonderland" are not Christmas songs, they are winter songs, but they are closely associated with that time of the year.

Genre is irrelevant. In this book you'll find orchestras and choirs, Bing and Sting, Kate Bush and Kate Smith, Bob Seger and Pete Seeger. Classical, rock, pop, easy listening, jazz, novelty, children's, contemporary Christian, heavy metal, rap, punk, New Wave...all kinds of music are here.

We've also included listings for hundreds of various-artists collections, most of which have never been so fully documented. We've been able to obtain copies of almost all the Goodyear, Firestone, Grants and True Value Hardware LPs, plus some from Zenith, A&P, B.F. Goodrich, JCPenney, Amway, Avon, Philco and Beneficial Finance, to name a few, and that data is here.

We've had to make a few judgment calls, though, on the songs we list.

We have included songs for New Year's Day, such as "Auld Lang Syne" and "What Are You Doing New Year's Eve?" But "New Year's Day" by U2, which really isn't about New Year's Day, isn't here. (In 1995 it actually appeared on a Christmas compilation CD, though.)

"My Favorite Things," one of the songs from *The Sound of Music,* often is recorded on Christmas albums. But we don't include it in here unless its appearance is in that context. The same is true of several other songs, such as "Baby It's Cold Outside," "I've Got My Love to Keep Me Warm," and "Snowbird," the Anne Murray hit which appears on a Christmas compilation but isn't really a Christmas song.

Finally, while excerpts of the works are included, we've included no listings of entire performances of Christmas-related classical pieces such as George Frederick Handel's *Messiah.*

Otherwise, I can't think of any restrictions we've placed on the listings.

Selling Your Records

Remember, as you read this book, two key things, and you'll have much less frustration when you try to buy or sell.

1. This book is only a guide! This is not meant to be a bible. As will often happen in a first-time guide, some of the values will be way off, either too high or too low. Prices, too, can depend on geography (New York prices are generally higher than those in the South, for example), the venue (records in a used record store should usually sell for more than those at a flea market, for example), and with holiday music, even the time of year (Christmas records may sell for less in July than in November).

2. The prices in here are retail! In other words, if you were to go to a show or collector's shop, you might pay something close to these prices for the record. If you are trying to sell your records to a dealer, expect to get no more than half, and more likely much less than half, of the values for a Near Mint record. If that sounds like a rip-off, well, consider the costs a dealer has to cover through sales: Rent, employees, shipping, postage, utilities, phone service (business lines cost more than residential lines), taxes, and many other sundry items, not to mention the costs of maintaining and obtaining inventory. With all that, you can see why a dealer can't buy at the same prices he or she sells!

To get prices close to what this book suggests, the best way is to sell directly to the consumer -- in essence, to become a dealer yourself, albeit temporarily. (Many dealers became dealers by starting with their own collections and finding they enjoyed the selling.)

The best way is to place an advertisement in *Goldmine* magazine. *Goldmine,* published every other week, is the world's largest marketplace for collectible music of all kinds and eras. The magazine has advertising salespeople who will help you put your ad together for maximum impact.

To see what *Goldmine* is about, pick up a copy. *Goldmine* magazine is available at Tower Records, Blockbuster Music and a couple other major music chains; Barnes & Noble, Borders and other larger booksellers; and many independent music shops. If you still can't find a copy, call 1-800-258-0929.

A Grading Primer

The most important thing to remember is this:

Condition is (almost) everything!

That is the maxim to remember when buying (and selling) records. If an item is unusually rare or desirable, it may be acceptable in any condition, as you might never see it again. But even with those items with a three- and four-figure value, the better condition a record (or sleeve), the more money it will fetch.

The grading system established by *Goldmine* magazine many years ago, with the occasional refinement, has become the most widely accepted in record collecting.

Visual or Play Grading? In an ideal world, every record would be played before it is graded. But the time involved makes it impractical for most dealers, and anyway, it's rare that you get a chance to hear a record before you buy through the mail. Some advertisers play-grade everything and say so. But unless otherwise noted, records are visually graded.

How to Grade

Look at everything about a record — its playing surface, its label, its edges — under a strong light. Then, based on your overall impression, give it a grade based on the following criteria:

Mint (M): Absolutely perfect in every way -- certainly never played, possibly even still sealed. (More on still sealed under "Other considerations.") Should be used sparingly as a grade, if at all.

Near Mint (NM or M-): A nearly perfect record. Many dealers won't give a grade higher than this, implying (perhaps correctly) that no record is ever truly perfect.

The record should show no obvious signs of wear. A 45 RPM or EP sleeve should have no more than the most minor defects, such as almost invisible ring wear or other signs of slight handling.

An LP jacket should have no creases, folds, seam splits or any other noticeable similar defect. No cut-out holes, either. And of course, the same should be true of any other inserts, such as posters, lyric sleeves and the like.

Basically, an LP in Near Mint condition looks as if you just got it home from a new record store and removed the shrink wrap.

Near Mint is the highest price listed in this price guide. Anything that exceeds this, in the opinion of both buyer and seller, is worth significantly more than the highest value in here.

Very Good Plus (VG+): Generally worth 50 percent of the Near Mint value.

A Very Good Plus record will show some signs that it was played and otherwise handled by a previous owner who took good care of it.

Record surfaces may show some slight signs of wear and may have slight scuffs or very light scratches that don't affect one's listening experience. Slight warps that do not affect the sound are OK.

The label may have some ring wear or discoloration, but it should be barely noticeable. The center hole will not have been misshapen by repeated play.

Picture sleeves and LP inner sleeves will have some slight ring wear, lightly turned-up corners, or a slight seam split. An LP jacket may have slight signs of wear also and may be marred by a cut-out hole, indentation or corner indicating it was taken out of print and sold at a discount.

In general, if not for a couple minor things wrong with it, this would be Near Mint. All but the most mint-crazy collectors will find a Very Good Plus record highly acceptable.

Very Good (VG): Generally worth 25 percent of the Near Mint value.

Many of the defects found in a VG+ record will be more pronounced in a VG disc.

Surface noise will be evident upon playing, especially in soft passages and during a song's intro and fade, but will not overpower the music otherwise. Groove wear will start to be noticeable, as will light scratches (deep enough to feel with a fingernail) that will affect the sound.

Labels may be marred by writing, or have tape or stickers (or their residue) attached. The same will be true of picture sleeves or LP covers. However, it will not have all of these problems at the same time, only two or three of them.

Very Good is the lowest value we list in here. This, *not* the Near Mint price, should be your guide when determining how much a record is worth, as a dealer will rarely pay you more than 25 percent of its Near Mint value. (He/she has to make a profit, after all.)

Good (G), Good Plus (G+): Generally worth 10-15 percent of the Near Mint value.

Good does not mean Bad! A record in Good or Good Plus condition can be put onto a turntable and will play through without skipping. But it will have significant surface noise and scratches and visible groove wear (on a styrene record, the groove will be starting to turn white).

A sleeve or jacket will have seam splits, especially at the bottom or on the spine. Tape, writing, ring wear or other defects will start to overwhelm the object.

If it's a common item, you'll probably find another copy in better shape eventually. Pass it up. But if it's something you have been seeking for years, and the price is right, get it...and keep looking to upgrade.

Poor (P), Fair (F): Generally worth 0-5 percent of the Near Mint price.

The record is cracked, badly warped, and won't play through without skipping or repeating. The picture sleeve is water damaged, split on all three seams and heavily marred by wear and/or writing. The LP jacket barely keeps the LP inside it. Inner sleeves are fully seam split, crinkled, and written upon.

Except for impossibly rare records otherwise unattainable, records in this condition should be bought or sold for no more than a few cents each.

Other considerations: Most dealers give a separate grade to the record and its sleeve or cover. In an ad, a record's grade is listed first, followed by that of the sleeve or jacket.

With **Still Sealed (SS)** records, let the buyer beware, unless it's a U.S. pressing from the last 10-15 years or so. It's too easy to re-seal one. Yes, some legitimately never-opened LPs from the 1960s still exist. But if you're looking for a specific pressing, the only way you can know for sure is to open the record. Also, European imports are not factory-sealed, so if you see them advertised as sealed, someone other than the manufacturer sealed them.

Making Sense of the Listings

Now that we've told you about the book, and how to figure out how to sell your records, here's how to figure out the individual entries.

The artist's name is in bold, ALL CAPITAL LETTERS. They are mostly alphabetized the way our computer did. I think we caught most of the way-out things, but if not, let us know and we'll get 'em the next time.

Under some artists are cross-references, where other records involving that performer can be found.

The records are grouped in this order: 12-inch singles; 45 rpm singles; 7-inch extended play records; albums. Within each type of record (45s, EPs, albums), we have listed them alphabetically, not chronologically, by record label. Because most artists have only one or two Christmas releases, we didn't group by record label as in the 45 rpm and British Invasion books. Individual listings are in numerical order, ignoring prefixes (except in the case of RCA Victor singles), They have the label and number, the title (or A-side/B-side), year of release, and values in Very Good, Very Good-Plus and Near Mint.

For many listings, you'll see a letter or two before the title. These designate something special about the listing as follows:

DJ: some sort of promotional copy, usually for radio stations, and not meant for public sale.

EP: a 12-inch extended play record, usually from the 1980s or later.

M: a mono record.

P: for LPs, a record listed as stereo has some tracks in true stereo and some tracks in rechanneled stereo. The stereo or the rechanneled tracks are often listed below.

PD: picture disc (artwork is actually part of the record).

PS: for 45s and some EPs, a picture sleeve (this is the value for the sleeve *alone*; combine the record and sleeve value to get an estimated worth for the two together).

R: for LPs, a record listed as stereo is entirely rechanneled stereo.

S: for any record pressed in both mono and stereo, a stereo record. Either the entire record is known to be true stereo or we don't know whether it's all stereo.

10:    a 10-inch LP, generally from the early 1950s.

(x)   where x is a number: the number of records in a set.

In some cases, the VG and/or the VG+ columns have dashes in them. That indicates that the item in question goes for under $2 in that condition. A few items have dashes in all three columns. There is usually a good reason, and that is explained in the line below the listing.

Some items have lines in italics following them. That defines something about the item listed above, such as who also is on the record, or a color of label or vinyl.

Finally, unique to this book is a section titled "On Various-Artists Collections." This lists all the tracks by a particular artist that we have been able to document as appearing on one of the compilations listed in the back of the book. These are alphabetical by song title; in the second column is an alphabetical list of those records on which the song is known to appear. For more information on those LPs, check the listings in the back of the book.

Various-artists records have their own sections after the letter Z. Within three categories – "Original Cast Recordings," "Soundtracks" and "Various Artists Collections" – they are arranged first by format (singles, 7-inch EPs, then LPs), then alphabetically *by record title*. As often as possible, we also list the contents of each side in the order the songs appear on the record (another unique feature). Otherwise, the listings are similar to those in the rest of the book.

Acknowledgments

This book would be a much lesser product without substantial help from many *Goldmine* magazine and price guide readers.

Foremost is Tim Sewell, whose outstanding Christmas 45 rpm collection is prominent throughout, both in the listings and in some of the photos of picture sleeves. Without his help, the singles listings would not be as complete as they are. I also thank him for his patience as I questioned him and asked for clarifications on the more unusual items. Tim has helped Rhino Records put together several Christmas compilations, and I am flattered he would help us, too.

At first, it appeared as if the album listings would include only my own collection. But many people came through when I asked for information in my regular *Goldmine* column, "Platter Chatter." Much thanks to Bill Hamilton, who continued to add to the LP information right up until my deadline and even beyond. James Scharnott and James Dittoe also contributed dozens of previously undocumented albums. And the LP listings would not be so thorough without Don Mahaffey, Ben Rogers, Richard Lump, Ed Cummings, Steven Annan, Fred Heggeness, Sue and Ed Turchick, and Weird Harold's Records in Davenport, Iowa. And to those who may have told me about one or two records but whose name I didn't mention, thank you and I apologize for missing you.

Many of my compatriots at Krause Publications assisted with contributions from their own collections, both for listings and for photographs. Among them are Steve Ellingboe, Maggie Thompson, Joyce Greenholdt, Michael Dean, Greg Loescher, John Diser and George Cuhaj.

Thanks are in order to more Krause Publications people: Greg Loescher (again) and Pat Klug, for giving this project the go-ahead; to Ross Hubbard for his wonderful cover art; to Chris Pritchard for the design of the color pages, the first to grace a *Goldmine* price guide; to Don Gulbrandsen, book division managing editor, for guidance and reality checks; Bonnie Tetzlaff and Gena Pamperin for production advice; and as always, the crack proofreading staff.

Thanks, too, to my parents, William and Judy Neely. Their purchase of *A Very Merry Christmas* in 1967 helped spark a six-year-old's interest in "grown-up" Christmas music. Also thanks to everyone from Enrico Caruso to the Vandals for recording the music. And finally, thanks to all that has influenced holiday music, from mistletoe to Santa Claus to the Christ child. (Can't forget Him, you know!)

Tim Neely
Iola, Wisconsin
July 1997

How You Can Help

This is the most complete book of Christmas recordings ever published. But it's not 100 percent complete; we know that, and you'll know that once you search the listings.

Many average collectors contributed to this edition. It's likely that at some point a second edition will become warranted, and we'd like to make that one even better. Here are some of the things we're seeking:

1. **Missing years.** Many of the 45s in here were independent or private issues, and a lot of them had no copyright date on them. You'll see many dates with one or two question marks. We need more information on these.

2. **Early 45s.** We're sure that some records first released on 78s later saw release on 45s, but we couldn't find copies to confirm this. We have lists of some of these, and we suspect many of them came out on 45s, but we omitted them because of our lack of proof.

3. **Extended-play records.** We are missing some titles and contents of some EPs; information on those is always welcome.

4. **Contents of LPs.** An unfinished project is to list the contents of not only the various-artists LPs, but of the single-artist LPs. We've got many of them in our database, but there are many we don't have.

5. **Absent various-artists LPs.** We know that there was a *Happy Holidays, Volume 10,* for example, but we couldn't find a copy of it, and thus we know neither its catalog number nor its contents. There must be dozens, if not hundreds, more similar albums we couldn't find in time for this edition.

6. **Anything else that might be of help** that I have failed to mention.

Anyone who contributes will be mentioned in the next edition, unless you don't want to be. You may contact me...

> by mail: **Tim Neely**
> **Goldmine Christmas Record Price Guide**
> **700 E. State Street**
> **Iola, WI 54990**
> or by phone: **(715) 445-4612, extension 782**
> or by e-mail: **neelyt@krause.com**

Please include a weekday, daytime phone number or e-mail address in case I have any questions or want more information.

I can also be reached via fax at (715) 445-4087, but I'd prefer you reach me by one of the other three methods before you fax me any large submissions.

Label, Number		Title (A Side/B Side)	Year	VG	VG+	NM

A

A-STRINGS, THE
45s

Warner Bros. 27784		The Christmas Song/Sleigh Ride	1988	—	2.00	4.00

— *A-side with Kathy Mattea*

Albums

Warner Bros. 25759		Home for Christmas	1988	2.50	5.00	10.00

On Various-Artists Collections

Jingle Bells	Christmas Tradition, A, Volume II (Warner Bros. 25762)	

AABERG, PHILIP
On Various-Artists Collections

Gift, The	Winter's Solstice II, A (Windham Hill WH-1077)
High Plains	Winter's Solstice, A (Windham Hill WH-1045)
(Christmas on the High-Line)	

AARON, CHARLIE
45s

Triple A 7870		Christmas Is The Best/Summertime Love	19??	—	2.00	4.00

ABBA
45s

Atlantic PR 390	DJ	Happy New Year	1980	3.00	6.00	12.00

— *One-sided promo*

ABBEY CHOIR, THE
Albums

Diplomat X-1709	M	The Little Drummer Boy	196?	3.00	6.00	12.00

— *Contents are the same as the Parade record, but in a new order and with one extra track*

Diplomat SX-1709	S	The Little Drummer Boy	196?	3.00	6.00	12.00
Parade XSP 415	M	The Abbey Choir Sings Christmas	195?	3.75	7.50	15.00

ABBOTT, JERRY
45s

Elliott 100/101		Christmas Is A Whispering Time Of The Year/Jing-A-Ling	197?	2.00	4.00	8.00

ABBOUD, MONA
45s

Phonograph 100180		The Pretty Little Dolly/I Should've Left The Lites On For Santa	1980	2.00	4.00	8.00

ABEL, ALAN
45s

MGM 11898		The Story of Santa Claus/Santa and the Doodle-Li-Boop	1954	5.00	10.00	20.00

AC/DC
45s

Atco 8886		Mistress For Christmas/Moneytalks	1990	—	3.00	6.00
Atco 8886	PS	Mistress For Christmas/Moneytalks	1990	—	3.00	6.00

— *Record and sleeve are U.K. imports*

Albums

Atco 91413		The Razors Edge	1990	3.75	7.50	15.00

— *Contains one Christmas song:* Mistress for Christmas

ACCELERATORS, THE
12-Inch Singles

Dolphin DPRO 72756		Blue Christmas/Terminal Café	19??	2.00	4.00	8.00

ACE, CHARLIE
45s

Logan 446		Jingle Bells Cha-Cha/I Was Lucky	195?	2.50	5.00	10.00

Label, Number		Title (A Side/B Side)	Year	VG	VG+	NM
ACEY, JOHNNY & ESQUIRES LTD.						
45s						
Smog City 744		Christmas Keeps On Coming (Part 1)/ Christmas Keeps On Coming (Part 2)	19??	—	3.00	6.00
ACKERMAN, WILL						
On Various-Artists Collections						
New England Morning		Winter's Solstice, A (Windham Hill WH-1045)				
Abide the Winter		Winter's Solstice II, A (Windham Hill WH-1077)				
AD LIBS, THE						
45s						
Johnnie Boy 01		Santa's On His Way/I Stayed Home (New Year's Eve)	19??	2.00	4.00	8.00
ADAMS, BOB						
45s						
(no label) ERK-0853		Merry Christmas To Me/Into My Life	19??	—	2.50	5.00
ADAMS, BRYAN						
45s						
A&M 2798		Christmas Time/Reggae Christmas	1985		*Unreleased*	
A&M 8651		Christmas Time/Reggae Christmas	1985	—	2.00	4.00
— *Green vinyl*						
A&M 8651	PS	Christmas Time/Reggae Christmas	1985	—	2.50	5.00
— *"Package" sleeve*						
A&M 8651	PS	Christmas Time/Reggae Christmas	1986	—	2.00	4.00
— *Sleeve with winter scene*						
On Various-Artists Collections						
Run Rudolph Run		Very Special Christmas, A (A&M SP-3911)				
ADAMS, DAVE, AND JUDIE COCHILL						
45s						
Pioneer 2900		An Old Fashioned Christmas (same on both sides)	19??	—	2.00	4.00
ADAMS, J.T.						
45s						
Republic 7020		Christmas Time Is the Best Time/It's Christmas Time	1952	10.00	20.00	40.00
ADAMS, JOHNNY						
45s						
Hep Me 138		Please Come Home For Christmas/I Only Want To Be With You	197?	—	2.50	5.00
Hep Me 163		Silent Night/The Lord's Prayer	197?	—	2.50	5.00
ADDOTTA, KIP						
45s						
Laff 024		I Saw Daddy Kissing Santa Claus (same on both sides)	1984	2.00	4.00	8.00
ADORNO, PEPI, MAMBO BAND						
45s						
Rainbow 267		Santa Baby Mambo/East of the Sun Mambo	1954	3.75	7.50	15.00
AEOLIAN KAMMERCHOR						
On Various-Artists Collections						
Den die Hirten Lobten Sehre		Joyous Music for Christmas Time (Reader's Digest RD 45-M)				
Es Ist ein Ros' Entsprungen		Joyous Music for Christmas Time (Reader's Digest RD 45-M)				
Heiligste Nacht		Joyous Music for Christmas Time (Reader's Digest RD 45-M)				
Ihr Kinderlein Kommet		Joyous Music for Christmas Time (Reader's Digest RD 45-M)				
Nun Singet und Seid Froh		Joyous Music for Christmas Time (Reader's Digest RD 45-M)				
O Du Frohliche, O Du Selige		Joyous Music for Christmas Time (Reader's Digest RD 45-M)				
O Tannenbaum		Joyous Music for Christmas Time (Reader's Digest RD 45-M)				
Stille Nacht, Heilige Nacht		Joyous Music for Christmas Time (Reader's Digest RD 45-M)				
Vom Himmel Hoch Da Komm Ich Her		Joyous Music for Christmas Time (Reader's Digest RD 45-M)				
Wie Schon Leuchtet der Morgenstern		Joyous Music for Christmas Time (Reader's Digest RD 45-M)				
AGEE, RAY						
45s						
Celeste 616		Merry Christmas My Love/Po-Lee The Polar Bear	1964	2.50	5.00	10.00
Celeste 616		Merry Christmas My Love/I Want You	1964	2.50	5.00	10.00

Label, Number	Title (A Side/B Side)	Year	VG	VG+	NM

AIR SUPPLY
45s

Arista 9659	The Eyes of a Child/The Christmas Song-Winter Wonderland	1987	—	2.00	4.00

Albums

Arista AL-8528	The Christmas Album	1987	2.50	5.00	10.00

AKIN & THE TEDDY VAN PRODUCTION COMPANY
45s

Simtone 2001	Santa Claus Is A Black Man/A Natural Santa	197?	—	2.00	4.00

AL AND DICK CHILDREN'S CHORUS, THE
45s

Coral 62157	We Wish You a Merry Christmas/Santa Cwuz	1959	3.00	6.00	12.00

AL' OF US
On Various-Artists Collections

Happy Time, The   Ten Tunes of Christmas (Candee 50-50)

ALABAMA
45s

RCA 5051-7-R	Christmas in Dixie/Tennessee Christmas	1986	—	—	3.00
RCA PB-13358	Christmas in Dixie/Christmas Is Just a Song for Us This Year	1982	—	2.50	5.00
— B-side by Louise Mandrell and R.C. Bannon					
RCA PB-13664	Christmas in Dixie/Never Be One	1983	—	2.00	4.00
RCA PB-14213	Thistlehair the Christmas Bear/ Santa Claus (I Still Believe in You)	1985		*Unreleased*	
RCA PB-14219	Joseph and Mary's Boy/Santa Claus (I Still Believe in You)	1985	—	2.00	4.00
RCA 62643	Angels Among Us/Santa Claus (I Still Believe in You)	1993	—	—	3.00
RCA 64436	Christmas in Dixie/Thistlehair the Christmas Bear	1995	—	—	3.00

Albums

RCA Victor ASL1-7014	Christmas	1985	3.00	6.00	12.00
— Original copies have gold embossed letters on cover					
RCA Victor ASL1-7014	Christmas	1986	2.50	5.00	10.00
— Later copies have white non-embossed letters on cover					

On Various-Artists Collections

Christmas in Dixie	Best of Christmas, The (RCA Victor CPL1-7013)
	Country Christmas (Time-Life STL-109)
	Country Christmas, A (RCA CPL1-4396)
	Country Christmas, A, Volume 2 (RCA AYL1-4809)
	Country Christmas, A, Volume 3 (RCA CPL1-5178)
	60 Christmas Classics (Sessions DVL2-0723)
	Time-Life Treasury of Christmas, The (Time-Life STL-107)
Happy Holidays	Family Christmas Collection, The (Time-Life STL-131)
	Happy Holidays, Vol. 21 (RCA Special Products DPL1-0739)
Homecoming Christmas	Happy Holidays, Vol. 22 (RCA Special Products DPL1-0777)
Santa Claus (I Still Believe in You)	Celebrate the Season with Tupperware (RCA Special Products DPL1-0803)
	Mistletoe and Memories (RCA 8372-1-R)
Tennessee Christmas	Country Christmas (Time-Life STL-109)
	Time-Life Treasury of Christmas, The, Volume Two (Time-Life STL-108)

ALABAMA CHRISTIAN MOVEMENT FOR HUMAN RIGHTS CHOIR
45s

TCF 2	Do You Hear What I Hear?/The Virgin Mary	1963	3.00	6.00	12.00

ALAMO, TONY
45s

MGM 11390	Merry Christmas Darling/It's Christmas Time	1952	5.00	10.00	20.00

ALARM, THE
45s

I.R.S. S7-19353	Happy Xmas (War Is Over)/ All I Want for Christmas Is My Two Front Teeth	1996	—	—	3.00
— B-side by Dread Zeppelin					

ALBERGHETTI, ANNA MARIA
On Various-Artists Collections

Caroling, Caroling	Great Songs of Christmas, The, Album Five (Columbia Special Products CSP 238M)
Star Carol, The	Great Songs of Christmas, The, Album Five (Columbia Special Products CSP 238M)

Label, Number		Title (A Side/B Side)	Year	VG	VG+	NM
ALBERT THE ALLEY CAT						
45s						
Key K1002		Santa's Helper/Send Me A Bit Of Home For Christmas	19??	—	3.00	6.00
ALBERT, EDDIE						
45s						
Cadence ZTSP 66814	DJ	Edgar Guest's On Going Home For Christmas/ (B-side unknown)	195?	2.50	5.00	10.00
ALCOA SINGERS, THE						
Albums						
Alcoa 44-4184-J		Old-Fashioned Christmas, An	1979	3.00	6.00	12.00
ALDEN, BUD, AND THE BUCKAROOS						
45s						
Four Star 1685		Rudolph the Red-Nosed Reindeer/Alaskan Christmas	1955	5.00	10.00	20.00
ALDRICH, RONNIE						
Albums						
London LL 3383	M	Christmas with Ronnie	1964	2.50	5.00	10.00
London SP 44051	S	Christmas with Ronnie	1964	3.75	7.50	15.00
On Various-Artists Collections						
Have Yourself a Merry Little Christmas		Magic of Christmas, The (Columbia Musical Treasury P3S 5806)				
White Christmas		Magic of Christmas, The (Columbia Musical Treasury P3S 5806)				
ALEXANDER, BEN						
On Various-Artists Collections						
Reminder Spot		For Christmas Seals…A Matter of Life and Breath (Decca Custom Style E)				
ALEXANDER, SCOTTY						
45s						
Grand Prize 5202		Santa Lives At Our House/(B-side unknown)	19??	—	3.00	6.00
ALEXANDRIA, LOREZ						
45s						
Pzazz 017		Santa Is Here/Nonchalantly	19??	—	3.00	6.00
ALGAE AFTERBIRTH						
45s						
Black & Blue (no #)		Santa Claus Is Dead/GG's Xmas Song	198?	2.50	5.00	10.00
— B-side by GG Allin						
Black & Blue (no #)	PS	Santa Claus Is Dead/GG's Xmas Song	198?	2.50	5.00	10.00
— B-side by GG Allin						
ALLAN & THE FLAMES						
45s						
Campbell 225		Winter Wonderland/Till The End of Time	1960	12.50	25.00	50.00
Colonial 7006		Winter Wonderland/Till The End of Time	1960	12.50	25.00	50.00
ALLEN & THE LADS						
45s						
Beaver 7695		Ghost On Christmas Eve/Angel On The Tree	19??	—	2.00	4.00
ALLEN, BARRY						
45s						
Dot 16799		Pretty Paper/Hurry, Santa, Hurry	1965	5.00	10.00	20.00
ALLEN, DEBORAH						
45s						
RCA JK-13904	DJ	Rockin' Little Christmas (same on both sides)	1984	—	2.00	4.00
RCA PB-13904		Rockin' Little Christmas/It's a Good Thing	1984	—	2.00	4.00
On Various-Artists Collections						
Rockin' Little Christmas		Country Christmas, A, Volume 3 (RCA CPL1-5178)				

Label, Number		Title (A Side/B Side)	Year	VG	VG+	NM
ALLEN, JIMMY, AND TOMMY BARTELLA						
45s						
Al-Brite 1300		When Santa Comes Over The Brooklyn Bridge/ What Would You Like To Have For Christmas?	1959	10.00	20.00	40.00
ALLEN, RANCE, GROUP						
45s						
Truth 3218		White Christmas/(Instrumental)	1975	—	2.50	5.00
ALLEN, REX						
45s						
Decca 28933		Where Did My Snowman Go?/Why Daddy?	1953	3.75	7.50	15.00
Decca 88161		Where Did My Snowman Go?/Why Daddy?	1953	3.00	6.00	12.00
Decca 88161	PS	Where Did My Snowman Go?/Why Daddy?	1953	5.00	10.00	20.00
ALLIN, GG						
45s						
Black & Blue (no #)		GG's Xmas Song/Santa Claus Is Dead	198?	2.50	5.00	10.00
— B-side by Algae Afterbirth						
Black & Blue (no #)	PS	GG's Xmas Song/Santa Claus Is Dead	198?	2.50	5.00	10.00
— B-side by Algae Afterbirth						
ALLISON, FRAN						
45s						
RCA Victor 47-3938		The Christmas Tree Angel/Christmas in My Heart	1950	3.75	7.50	15.00
ALLISON, JACK						
45s						
Mica 206		Santa's Tag-A-Long/Whispering Spirit Of Christmas	19??	—	2.00	4.00
ALPERT, HERB, AND THE TIJUANA BRASS						
45s						
A&M 1001		My Favorite Things/The Christmas Song	1968	—	3.00	6.00
A&M 1001	PS	My Favorite Things/The Christmas Song	1968	2.50	5.00	10.00
A&M 1237		The Bell That Couldn't Jingle/Las Mañanitas				
Albums						
A&M SP-3113		Christmas Album	198?	2.00	4.00	8.00
— Reissue of SP-4166						
A&M SP-4166		Christmas Album	1968	3.00	6.00	12.00
On Various-Artists Collections						
Herb Alpert and the Tijuana Brass Show, The		For Christmas Seals…A Matter of Life and Breath (Decca Custom Style F)				
Jingle Bell Rock		Something Festive! (A&M SP-19003)				
Winter Wonderland		Magic of Christmas, The (Columbia Musical Treasury P3S 5806) Something Festive! (A&M SP-19003)				
ALPHA OMEGA						
45s						
WJS 1322		Christmas Day/One Time Of The Year	19??	—	2.00	4.00
ALVIN AND THE CHIPMUNKS – See THE CHIPMUNKS.						
ALVIN, JOHNNIE						
45s						
Warner Bros. 5024		Santa Claus Wrecked My 'Lectric Train/ Rudolph, the Red-Nosed Reindeer	1958	3.75	7.50	15.00
AMBASSADORS, THE						
45s						
Cuca 1022		Christmas Polka/Little Drummer Boy	1960	3.00	6.00	12.00
AMBROSIAN CHILDREN'S CHOIR						
On Various-Artists Collections						
It's Christmas Again		Santa Claus The Movie (EMI America SJ-17177)				
Making Toys		Santa Claus The Movie (EMI America SJ-17177)				
Thank You, Santa		Santa Claus The Movie (EMI America SJ-17177)				

Label, Number		Title (A Side/B Side)	Year	VG	VG+	NM

AMBROSIAN SINGERS
On Various-Artists Collections

Once in Royal David's City		Old Fashioned Christmas, An (Reader's Digest RDA 216-A)	
Patch, Natch!		Santa Claus The Movie (EMI America SJ-17177)	

AMECHE, JIM
45s

Deltone 5016		First Christmas Tree (Part 1)/First Christmas Tree(Part 2)	1964	2.50	5.00	10.00
Ric 137		The First Christmas Tree (Part 1)/The First Christmas Tree (Part 2)	1964	2.50	5.00	10.00
Ric 137	PS	The First Christmas Tree (Part 1)/The First Christmas Tree (Part 2)	1964	3.00	6.00	12.00

AMELING, ELLY
Albums

| CBS Masterworks M 36677 | | Christmas with Elly Ameling | 1980 | 3.00 | 6.00 | 12.00 |

AMERICA'S CHILDREN
45s

| Audition 6106 | | Swingin' Christmas/The Star | 1965 | 2.50 | 5.00 | 10.00 |

AMES BROTHERS, THE
Also see ED AMES.

45s

Coral 60267		The Twelve Days of Christmas/Wassail Song	1950	3.75	7.50	15.00
Coral 60268		Silent Night/Adeste Fideles	1950	3.75	7.50	15.00
Coral 60269		Hark! The Herald Angels Sing/It Came Upon a Midnight Clear	1950	3.75	7.50	15.00
Coral 60270		Oh, Little Town of Bethlehem/God Rest Ye Merry Gentlemen	1950	3.75	7.50	15.00
Coral 60572		Jolly Old St. Nicholas/Ting-a-Ling-a-Jingle	1951	3.75	7.50	15.00
Coral 60861		Sing a Song of Santa Claus/Winter's Here Again	1952	3.00	6.00	12.00
RCA Victor WY 491		There'll Always Be a Christmas/I Got a Cold for Christmas	1954	2.50	5.00	10.00

— *From the "Little Nipper" children's series*

| RCA Victor WY 491 | PS | There'll Always Be a Christmas/I Got a Cold for Christmas | 1954 | 3.00 | 6.00 | 12.00 |
| RCA Victor 47-5929 | | There'll Always Be a Christmas/I Got a Cold for Christmas | 1954 | 2.50 | 5.00 | 10.00 |

7-Inch Extended Plays

| Coral 83010 | DJ | Sing A Song Of Santa Claus/Winter's Here Again// Let's Have An Old Fashioned Christmas/I've Got The Christmas Spirit | 195? | 3.75 | 7.50 | 15.00 |

— *B-side by Don Cornell*

| RCA Victor EPA 1-1541 | | Silver Bells/The Christmas Song// Jingle Bells/There'll Always Be a Christmas | 1957 | 3.75 | 7.50 | 15.00 |
| RCA Victor EPA 1-1541 | PS | There'll Always Be a Christmas, Vol. 1 | 1957 | 3.75 | 7.50 | 15.00 |

Albums

Coral CRL 56014	10	Sing a Song of Christmas	1950	12.50	25.00	50.00
Coral CRL 56080	10	Merry Christmas	1952	12.50	25.00	50.00
Coral CRL 57166		Sounds of Christmas Harmony	1957	7.50	15.00	30.00
RCA Victor LPM-1541	M	There'll Always Be a Christmas	1957	7.50	15.00	30.00
Vocalion VL 73788	R	Christmas Harmony	196?	3.00	6.00	12.00

— *Reissue of some Coral tracks*

On Various-Artists Collections

Adeste Fideles		Thank You for Opening Your Christmas Club with Us (Decca 34211)
Christmas Song, The		Christmas Festival of Songs and Carols, Volume 2 (RCA Victor PRM-195)
Deck the Halls		Joyous Noel (Reader's Digest RDA-57A)
Good King Wenceslas		For a Musical Merry Christmas (RCA Victor PR-149A)
		Gift from Your RCA Victor Record Dealer, A (RCA Victor SP-45-35)
		Happy Holidays, Vol. 21 (RCA Special Products DPL1-0739)
		Time-Life Treasury of Christmas, The, Volume Two (Time-Life STL-108)
I Got a Cold for Christmas		Merry Christmas And A Happy New Year (Modern Radio 102)
Jingle Bells		Family Christmas Collection, The (Time-Life STL-131)
Jolly Old St. Nicholas		Christmas Through the Years (Reader's Digest RDA-143)
Santa Claus Is Comin' to Town		For a Musical Merry Christmas, Volume 3 (RCA Victor PRM-221)
		Joyous Noel (Reader's Digest RDA-57A)
		RCA Victor Presents Music for the Twelve Days of Christmas (RCA Victor PRS-188)

AMES, ED
Also see THE AMES BROTHERS.

45s

| RCA Victor SP-45-188 | DJ | The Ballad Of The Christmas Donkey/ Let It Snow! Let It Snow! Let It Snow! | 1968 | 2.00 | 4.00 | 8.00 |
| RCA Victor 47-9682 | | Away in a Manger/Carry the Lord to Jerusalem | 1968 | | *Unreleased* | |

Albums

| RCA Victor LPM-3838 | M | Christmas with Ed Ames | 1967 | 3.75 | 7.50 | 15.00 |
| RCA Victor LSP-3838 | S | Christmas with Ed Ames | 1967 | 3.00 | 6.00 | 12.00 |

Label, Number		Title (A Side/B Side)	Year	VG	VG+	NM

On Various-Artists Collections

Away in a Manger	Christmas Through the Years (Reader's Digest RDA-143)
	Old Fashioned Christmas, An (Reader's Digest RDA 216-A)
	Time-Life Treasury of Christmas, The (Time-Life STL-107)
Ballad of the Christmas Donkey, The	Very Merry Christmas, A, Volume 5 (RCA Special Products PRS-343)
Christmas Is the Warmest Time of the Year	Happy Holidays, Volume 18 (RCA Special Products DPL1-0608)
	Henry Mancini Selects Great Songs of Christmas (RCA Special Products DPL1-0148)
Do You Hear What I Hear	60 Christmas Classics (Sessions DVL2-0723)
	Time-Life Treasury of Christmas, The, Volume Two (Time-Life STL-108)
First Noel, The	Family Christmas Collection, The (Time-Life STL-131)
I Heard the Bells on Christmas Day	Very Merry Christmas, A, Volume VI (RCA Special Products PRS-427)
Joy to the World	Brightest Stars of Christmas, The (RCA Special Products DPL1-0086)
Let It Snow! Let It Snow! Let It Snow!	Christmas in California (RCA Victor PRS-276)
	Christmas in New York Volume 2 (RCA Victor PRS-270)
	60 Christmas Classics (Sessions DVL2-0723)
O Come All Ye Faithful	Time-Life Treasury of Christmas, The, Volume Two (Time-Life STL-108)
Silent Night	Happy Holidays, Vol. III (RCA Victor PRS-255)
What Child Is This	Christmas in New York (RCA Victor PRM-257)'Very Merry Christmas, A, Volume VII (RCA Special Products DPL1-0049)

AMOS 'N' ANDY
45s

Label, Number		Title (A Side/B Side)	Year	VG	VG+	NM
Columbia 42623	DJ	The Lord's Prayer/Little Bitty Baby	1962	2.00	4.00	8.00
Columbia 48002		The Lord's Prayer/Little Bitty Baby	1962	2.00	4.00	8.00
Columbia 48002	PS	The Lord's Prayer/Little Bitty Baby	1962	2.50	5.00	10.00

ANDERSON, BILL
45s

Label, Number		Title (A Side/B Side)	Year	VG	VG+	NM
Decca 32417		Po' Folks' Christmas/Christmas Time's a-Coming	1968	—	3.00	6.00
Decca 32417	PS	Po' Folks' Christmas/Christmas Time's a-Coming	1968	2.00	4.00	8.00

ANDERSON, JON
45s

Label, Number		Title (A Side/B Side)	Year	VG	VG+	NM
Elektra 69580		Easier Said Than Done/Day of Days	1985	—	2.00	4.00
Elektra 69580		Easier Said Than Done/Day of Days	1985	2.00	4.00	8.00
— Green vinyl						

Albums

Label, Number		Title (A Side/B Side)	Year	VG	VG+	NM
Elektra 60469		3 Ships	1985	3.75	7.50	15.00

ANDERSON, LEROY
45s

Label, Number		Title (A Side/B Side)	Year	VG	VG+	NM
Decca 28429		Sleigh Ride/Saraband	1952	5.00	10.00	20.00

7-Inch Extended Plays

Label, Number		Title (A Side/B Side)	Year	VG	VG+	NM
Decca ED 2315		Angels In Our Fields Abiding/Pastores A Belén/ O Come, O Come, Emmanuel/I Saw Three Ships// It Came Upon a Midnight Clear/The Coventry Carol/March of the Kings	195?	2.00	4.00	8.00
Decca ED 2315	PS	(title unknown)	195?	3.00	6.00	12.00

Albums

Label, Number		Title (A Side/B Side)	Year	VG	VG+	NM
Decca DL 8193	M	Christmas Festival	1955	5.00	10.00	20.00
Decca DL 8925	M	Christmas Festival	1959	3.00	6.00	12.00
Decca DL 78925	S	Christmas Festival	1959	3.75	7.50	15.00

On Various-Artists Collections

Sleigh Ride	Old-Fashioned Christmas, An (Longines Symphonette LS 214)
	Popular Christmas Classics (Capitol Special Markets SL-8100)
	12 Hits of Christmas (United Artists UA-LA669-R)

ANDERSON, LIZ
45s

Label, Number		Title (A Side/B Side)	Year	VG	VG+	NM
Hobby House CSA-1	PS	Christopher, The Christmas Seal	196?	2.00	4.00	8.00
Hobby House CSA-1	DJ	Christopher The Christmas Seal (same on both sides)	196?	2.00	4.00	8.00
RCA Victor 659G-2446	DJ	The Spirit Of Christmas/Promos	196?	2.50	5.00	10.00

ANDERSON, LYNN
45s

Label, Number		Title (A Side/B Side)	Year	VG	VG+	NM
Columbia AE7 1056	DJ	Frosty The Snowman/Don't Wish Me Merry Christmas	1972	—	3.00	6.00
Columbia 45251		Don't Wish Me Merry Christmas/Ding-a-Ling the Christmas Bell	1970	—	3.00	6.00
Columbia 45251	PS	Don't Wish Me Merry Christmas/Ding-a-Ling the Christmas Bell	1970	2.00	4.00	8.00
Columbia 45527		Don't Wish Me Merry Christmas/Ding-a-Ling the Christmas Bell	1971	—	2.50	5.00
Mercury 872 154-7		The Angel Song (Glory to God in the Highest)/When a Child Is Born	1988	—	—	3.00
— With Butch Baker						

Label, Number	Title (A Side/B Side)	Year	VG	VG+	NM
Albums					
Columbia KC 30957	Christmas Album	1971	3.00	6.00	12.00
Columbia 3C 30957	Christmas Album	198?	2.00	4.00	8.00
— *Reissue of above LP*					
On Various-Artists Collections					
Ding-a-Ling the Christmas Bell	Blue Christmas (Welk Music Group WM-3002)				
Don't Wish Me Merry Christmas	Christmas Greetings from Nashville (Columbia PC 39467)				
Frosty the Snowman	Magnavox Album of Christmas Music (Columbia Special Products CSQ 11093)				
	We Wish You a Country Christmas (Columbia Special Products P 14991)				
I Saw Mommy Kissing Santa Claus	Merry Christmas (Columbia Musical Treasury 3P 6306)				
Jingle Bell Rock	Country Style Christmas, A (Columbia Musical Treasury 3P 6316)				
Mr. Mistletoe	Christmas Greetings, Vol. 3 (Columbia Special Products P 11383)				
	Country Style Christmas, A (Columbia Musical Treasury 3P 6316)				
Rockin' Around the Christmas Tree	Joyous Christmas, Volume 6 (Columbia Special Products C 11083)				
Rudolph, the Red-Nosed Reindeer	Happy Holidays, Album 8 (Columbia Special Products C 11086)				
Soon It Will Be Christmas Day	Country Christmas Favorites (Columbia Special Products C 10876)				
	Country Style Christmas, A (Columbia Musical Treasury 3P 6316)				
	Down-Home Country Christmas, A (Columbia Special Products P 14992)				
	Joy of Christmas, The, Featuring Marty Robbins and His Friends				
	(Columbia Special Products C 11087)				
	Nashville's Greatest Christmas Hits, Volume II (Columbia PC 44413)				
	RFD Christmas (Columbia Special Products P 15427)				
Spirit of Christmas, The	Country Style Christmas, A (Columbia Musical Treasury 3P 6316)				

ANDERSON, MARIAN
On Various-Artists Collections

Angel's Song	Joyous Noel (Reader's Digest RDA-57A)				
Ave Maria (Schubert)	Joyous Noel (Reader's Digest RDA-57A)				
Silent Night	Christmas in New York (RCA Victor PRM-257)				
We Wish You a Merry Christmas	For a Musical Merry Christmas (RCA Victor PR-149A)				
	Music to Trim Your Tree By (RCA Victor PRM 225)				
	We Wish You a Merry Christmas (RCA Victor PRS-277)				

ANDERSON, RANDY
45s

Comstock 1959	It's Christmas (I Wish You Were Here)/(B-side unknown)	198?	—	2.00	4.00

ANDREWS SISTERS, THE
Also see BING CROSBY.
45s

Capitol F3583	A Child's Christmas Song/Silver Bells	1956	3.75	7.50	15.00
Decca 23722	Christmas Island/Winter Wonderland	1950	3.75	7.50	15.00
— *With Guy Lombardo and His Royal Canadians; lines label*					
Decca 23722	Christmas Island/Winter Wonderland	1955	3.00	6.00	12.00
— *With Guy Lombardo and His Royal Canadians; star label*					
Decca 23722	Christmas Island/Winter Wonderland	1960	2.50	5.00	10.00
— *With Guy Lombardo and His Royal Canadians; color bars label*					
Decca 24748	Merry Christmas Polka/Christmas Candles	1950	3.75	7.50	15.00
— *With Guy Lombardo and His Royal Canadians; 78 released in 1949, may not exist on 45*					
Decca 27251	I'd Like to Hitch a Ride with Santa Claus/	1950	3.75	7.50	15.00
	(Sweet Angie) The Christmas Tree Angel					
Decca 27310	Sleigh Ride/Telephone Song	1950	5.00	10.00	20.00
MCA 65020	Christmas Island/Winter Wonderland	1973	—	2.00	4.00
— *With Guy Lombardo and His Royal Canadians; black label with rainbow*					
MCA 65020	Christmas Island/Winter Wonderland	1980	—	—	3.00
— *With Guy Lombardo and His Royal Canadians; blue label with rainbow*					
Albums					
Decca DL 5282	10	Christmas Cheer	1950	10.00	20.00	40.00
On Various-Artists Collections					
Christmas Island	Billboard Greatest Christmas Hits, 1935-1954 (Rhino R1 70637)				
Winter Wonderland	Happy Holidays, Vol. 23 (MCA Special Products 15042)				
	Time-Life Treasury of Christmas, The, Volume Two (Time-Life STL-108)				

ANDREWS, JULIE
45s

USA 600		The Sound of Christmas/O Come, All Ye Faithful	19??	—	2.00	4.00
USA 600	PS	The Sound of Christmas/O Come, All Ye Faithful	19??	—	2.00	4.00
Albums						
RCA Victor LPM-3829	M	A Christmas Treasure	1967	3.75	7.50	15.00
RCA Victor LSP-3829	S	A Christmas Treasure	1967	3.75	7.50	15.00
On Various-Artists Collections						
Angels from the Realm of Glory	Firestone Presents Your Favorite Christmas Music, Volume 5 (Firestone MLP 7012)					
	Happy Holidays, Vol. 21 (RCA Special Products DPL1-0739)					

Label, Number		Title (A Side/B Side)	Year	VG	VG+	NM
Away in a Manger		Family Christmas Collection, The (Time-Life STL-131)				
		Firestone Presents Your Favorite Christmas Music, Volume 5 (Firestone MLP 7012)				
		Happy Holidays, Vol. 22 (RCA Special Products DPL1-0777)				
Bells of Christmas, The		Family Christmas Collection, The (Time-Life STL-131)				
		Firestone Presents Your Favorite Christmas Music, Volume 4 (Firestone MLP 7011)				
		Firestone Presents Your Favorite Christmas Music, Volume 5 (Firestone MLP 7012)				
Christmas Song, The		Firestone Presents Your Favorite Christmas Music, Volume 4 (Firestone MLP 7011)				
Deck the Halls		Christmas Treasury of Classics from Avon, A (RCA Special Products DPL1-0716)				
		Firestone Presents Your Favorite Christmas Music, Volume 5 (Firestone MLP 7012)				
		Happy Holidays, Volume 16 (RCA Special Products DPL1-0501)				
God Rest Ye Merry, Gentlemen		Firestone Presents Your Favorite Christmas Music, Volume 5 (Firestone MLP 7012)				
		60 Christmas Classics (Sessions DVL2-0723)				
		Time-Life Treasury of Christmas, The (Time-Life STL-107)				
		Very Merry Christmas, A, Volume VII (RCA Special Products DPL1-0049)				
Irish Carol		Firestone Presents Your Favorite Christmas Music, Volume 5 (Firestone MLP 7012)				
		Henry Mancini Selects Great Songs of Christmas (RCA Special Products DPL1-0148)				
		Time-Life Treasury of Christmas, The, Volume Two (Time-Life STL-108)				
It Came Upon the Midnight Clear		Firestone Presents Your Favorite Christmas Music, Volume 5 (Firestone MLP 7012)				
		It's Christmas Time! (Columbia Special Products P 14990)				
Jingle Bells		Brightest Stars of Christmas, The (RCA Special Products DPL1-0086)				
		Firestone Presents Your Favorite Christmas Music, Volume 5 (Firestone MLP 7012)				
		Happy Holidays, Volume 13 (RCA Special Products DPL1-0319)				
		We Wish You a Merry Christmas (RCA Victor PRS-277)				
Joy to the World		Firestone Presents Your Favorite Christmas Music, Volume 5 (Firestone MLP 7012)				
		Happy Holidays, Volume 19 (RCA Special Products DPL1-0689)				
		Time-Life Treasury of Christmas, The, Volume Two (Time-Life STL-108)				
O Come All Ye Faithful		Christmas Trimmings (Columbia Special Products P 12795)				
		Many Moods of Christmas, The (Columbia Special Products P 12013)				
		Ronco Presents A Christmas Gift (Columbia Special Products P 12430)				
Rocking (Little Jesus, Sweetly Sleep)		Firestone Presents Your Favorite Christmas Music, Volume 4 (Firestone MLP 7011)				
Secret of Christmas, The		Christmas Greetings, Vol. 4 (Columbia Special Products P 11987)				
See Amid the Winter Snows		60 Christmas Classics (Sessions DVL2-0723)				
Silent Night		Christmas Is... (Columbia Special Products P 11417)				
		Great Songs of Christmas, The, Album Three (Columbia Special Products CSP 117)				
		Silent Night... (Columbia Special Products P 14989)				
		Very Merry Christmas, A, Volume IV (Columbia Special Products CSS 1464)				
Sunny Bank (I Saw Three Ships)		Firestone Presents Your Favorite Christmas Music, Volume 5 (Firestone MLP 7012)				
		Happy Holidays, Volume 15 (RCA Special Products DPL1-0453)				
		60 Christmas Classics (Sessions DVL2-0723)				
Wexford Carol		Family Christmas Collection, The (Time-Life STL-131)				
		Firestone Presents Your Favorite Christmas Music, Volume 5 (Firestone MLP 7012)				
What Child Is This?		Carols and Candlelight (Columbia Special Products P 12525)				

ANGEL
45s

Label, Number		Title	Year	VG	VG+	NM
Casablanca 903		Winter Song/Can You Feel It	1977	—	2.50	5.00
Casablanca 903 DJ	DJ	The Winter Song/The Christmas Song	1978	—	3.00	6.00

Albums

| Casablanca NBLP 7085 | | White Hot | 1977 | 3.00 | 6.00 | 12.00 |

— *Contains one Christmas song:* Winter Song

ANGELIC GOSPEL SINGERS, THE
45s

| Gotham 675 | | Jesus Christ Is Born/Glory, Glory to the Newborn King | 195? | 3.75 | 7.50 | 15.00 |
| Nashboro 946 | | Glory to the New Born King/Father, I Stretch My Hands | 1968 | 2.00 | 4.00 | 8.00 |

ANGELOS, GAIL
45s

| Jimbo 5854 | | Hello Santa (same on both sides) | 198? | — | — | 3.00 |
| Jimbo 5854 | PS | Hello Santa (same on both sides) | 198? | — | — | 3.00 |

ANGER, DAROL, AND MIKE MARSHALL
On Various-Artists Collections

Bach Bourée (from the French Suite)   Winter's Solstice, A (Windham Hill WH-1045)

ANIMALS, THE
On Various-Artists Collections

We're Gonna Howl Tonight   Dangerous Christmas of Red Riding Hood, The (ABC-Paramount 536)

ANKA, PAUL
45s

ABC-Paramount 10163		Rudolph, the Red-Nosed Reindeer/I Saw Mommy Kissing Santa Claus	1960	6.25	12.50	25.00
ABC-Paramount 10169		It's Christmas Everywhere/Rudolph, the Red-Nosed Reindeer	1960	4.00	8.00	16.00
ABC-Paramount 10169	PS	It's Christmas Everywhere/Rudolph, the Red-Nosed Reindeer	1960	6.25	12.50	25.00

Label, Number	Title (A Side/B Side)	Year	VG	VG+	NM
Albums					
ABC-Paramount ABC 360 M	It's Christmas Everywhere	1960	7.50	15.00	30.00
ABC-Paramount ABCS 360 S	It's Christmas Everywhere	1960	10.00	20.00	40.00

ANN-MARGRET
On Various-Artists Collections

Christmas Greetings	Christmas Greetings From RCA Victor And Groove Recording Artists (RCA Victor SP-45-128)
New Year's Greetings	Christmas Greetings From RCA Victor And Groove Recording Artists (RCA Victor SP-45-128)

ANN-MARGRET, ALISON DOWLING AND OLIVER REED
On Various-Artists Collections

Christmas	Tommy (Polydor PD 2 9502)

ANTHONY, MARK
45s

La Belle 779	Mama's Twistin' With Santa/Music From Studio "D"	1962	3.00	6.00	12.00

ANTHONY, RAY
45s

Capitol F1196	A Marshmallow World/Where Do I Go from You	1950	3.75	7.50	15.00

ANTON, BARBARA, SINGERS
45s

Godsong 13	Jolly Cholly/The Candles Of St. Lucia	19??	—	2.00	4.00

ANTONY, MARK
45s

Duke 465	Christmas Together (Part 1)/Christmas Together (Part 2)	1970	—	3.00	6.00

APAKA, ALFRED
45s

Decca 31331	Medley: Mele Kalikimaka (Merry Christmas)-Jingle Bells/Silent Night (Polai E)	1961	3.00	6.00	12.00

APOLLONIA
On Various-Artists Collections

Holiday I.D. (English)	Winter Warnerland (Warner Bros. PRO-A-3328)
Holiday I.D. (Spanish)	Winter Warnerland (Warner Bros. PRO-A-3328)

APPERSON, BOB
45s

Arrow 3002	Christmas In My Town/Christmas Bells	19??	—	2.00	4.00

ARGENT
45s

Epic S EPC 1243	Christmas For The Free/God Gave Rock & Roll To You	1973	—	3.00	6.00
— U.K. release					
Epic 10972	God Gave Rock and Roll To You/Christmas for the Free	1973	—	2.50	5.00

ARKENSTONE, DAVID
On Various-Artists Collections

I Saw Three Ships	Narada: The Christmas Collection (Narada N-63902)

ARLENE, BESS
On Various-Artists Collections

Rejoice Greatly (from Messiah)	Joyous Christmas, Volume 4 (Columbia Special Products CSS 1485)

ARMSTRONG, BILLY, AND THE GENERAL STORE
45s

Hillside 8107	Christmas Is Bigger In Texas/Tater Pie	19??	—	3.00	6.00

ARMSTRONG, BRICE, AND THE AMERICAN GHOULS
45s

Duchess 1020	The Fright Before Christmas/Happy Ghoul Tide	1962	5.00	10.00	20.00

Label, Number		Title (A Side/B Side)	Year	VG	VG+	NM

ARMSTRONG, LOUIS
45s

Amsterdam 85017	DJ	Here Is My Heart For Christmas/His Father Wore Long Hair	1970	2.50	5.00	10.00
Brunswick 55534		'Twas the Night Before Christmas/(B-side unknown)	1976	2.00	4.00	8.00
Continental 1001		The Night Before Christmas/When the Saints Go Marching In	1971	—	2.50	5.00
Continental 1001	PS	The Night Before Christmas/When the Saints Go Marching In	1971	—	2.50	5.00
— With sticker: "Only 25 cents with purchase" of one of four brands of cigarette						
Continental 1001	PS	The Night Before Christmas/When the Saints Go Marching In	1971	—	3.00	6.00
— With sticker: "Free with purchase" of six-pack of Fresca						
Decca 28443		White Christmas/Winter Wonderland	1952	3.75	7.50	15.00
Decca 28943		'Zat You, Santa Claus?/Cool Yule	1953	3.75	7.50	15.00
Decca 29710		Christmas Night in Harlem/Christmas in New Orleans	1955	3.75	7.50	15.00

On Various-Artists Collections

Christmas in New Orleans	Stash Christmas Album, The (Stash 125)
Cool Yule	Stash Christmas Album, The (Stash 125)
Night Before Christmas, The	Stash Christmas Album, The (Stash 125)
'Zat You, Santa Claus?	Stash Christmas Album, The (Stash 125)

ARNGRIM, STEFAN
45s

Jerden 916		Where Has Christmas Gone?/Cooper's Lagoon	1968	—	2.50	5.00

ARNOLD, EDDY
45s

RCA Victor 47-5905		Christmas Can't Be Far Away/I'm Your Private Santa Claus	1954	5.00	10.00	20.00
RCA Victor 47-9027		The Angel and the Stranger/The First Word	1966	—	3.00	6.00
RCA Victor 47-9387		Jolly Old St. Nicholas/This World of Ours	1967	2.00	4.00	8.00
RCA Victor 48-0127		C-H-R-I-S-T-M-A-S/Will Santa Come to Shanty Town	1949	12.50	25.00	50.00
— Originals on green vinyl						
RCA Victor 48-0127		C-H-R-I-S-T-M-A-S/Will Santa Come to Shanty Town	1949	6.25	12.50	25.00
— Second pressings: Green label, black vinyl						
RCA Victor 48-0390		White Christmas/Santa Claus Is Comin' to Town	1950	12.50	25.00	50.00
— Originals on green vinyl						
RCA Victor 48-0390		White Christmas/Santa Claus Is Comin' to Town	1950	6.25	12.50	25.00
— Second pressings: Green label, black vinyl						

Albums

RCA Victor LPM-2554	M	Christmas with Eddy Arnold	1962	5.00	10.00	20.00
RCA Victor LSP-2554	S	Christmas with Eddy Arnold	1962	6.25	12.50	25.00

On Various-Artists Collections

C-H-R-I-S-T-M-A-S	Country Christmas (Time-Life STL-109)
	Joyous Noel (Reader's Digest RDA-57A)
	Old Fashioned Christmas, An (Reader's Digest RDA 216-A)
Christmas Greetings	Christmas Greetings From RCA Victor And Groove Recording Artists (RCA Victor SP-45-128)
I Heard the Bells on Christmas Day	Christmas with Eddy Arnold/Christmas with Henry Mancini (RCA Special Products DPL1-0079)
It Came Upon a Midnight Clear	Christmas with Eddy Arnold/Christmas with Henry Mancini (RCA Special Products DPL1-0079) Family Christmas Collection, The (Time-Life STL-131)
Jingle Bell Rock	Family Christmas Collection, The (Time-Life STL-131)
Jolly Old St. Nicholas	Christmas with Eddy Arnold/Christmas with Henry Mancini (RCA Special Products DPL1-0079) Family Christmas Collection, The (Time-Life STL-131) Old Fashioned Christmas, An (Reader's Digest RDA 216-A) RCA Victor Presents Music for the Twelve Days of Christmas (RCA Victor PRS-188)
New Year's Greetings	Christmas Greetings From RCA Victor And Groove Recording Artists (RCA Victor SP-45-128)
O Little Town of Bethlehem	Christmas with Eddy Arnold/Christmas with Henry Mancini (RCA Special Products DPL1-0079)
Santa Claus Is Comin' to Town	Very Merry Christmas, A, Volume 5 (RCA Special Products PRS-343)
Silent Night	Christmas with Eddy Arnold/Christmas with Henry Mancini (RCA Special Products DPL1-0079) Happy Holidays, Volume 17 (RCA Special Products DPL1-0555)
Up on the House Top	Christmas with Eddy Arnold/Christmas with Henry Mancini (RCA Special Products DPL1-0079) Time-Life Treasury of Christmas, The, Volume Two (Time-Life STL-108)
Winter Wonderland	Country Christmas, A, Volume 2 (RCA AYL1-4809) Country Style Christmas, A (Columbia Musical Treasury 3P 6316)

ARNOLD, EDDY & JO ANN
45s

RCA Victor 490		A Present For Santa Claus/Sittin' On Santa Claus' Lap	195?	—	2.50	5.00
RCA Victor 490	PS	A Present For Santa Claus/Sittin' On Santa Claus' Lap	195?	—	2.50	5.00

ARNOLD, LEE
45s

Kirshner 4268		A Trucker's Christmas/That Good Old Gospel Music	1976	—	2.50	5.00

ARPAIA, WILLIAM HOWARD
45s

Vandalia 112		The Mistletoe March/Me As Jack And You As Jill	19??	—	2.00	4.00
Vandalia 117		The Christmas March/I'm A Catastrophe	19??	—	2.00	4.00

Label, Number		Title (A Side/B Side)	Year	VG	VG+	NM

ARRIGO, BEN
45s

| GP 527 | | An Old Fashioned Christmas/Christmas Time Is Here | 19?? | — | 2.00 | 4.00 |

ARTIES, WALTER, CHORALE
45s

| Atlantic 7569 | | All He Wants Is You/Christmas Medley | 196? | 2.00 | 4.00 | 8.00 |

— Green label "Religious Series" release

ARTS MUSICALE SINGERS
45s

| Four Jays 100 | | I Wonder Where I'll Be Next Christmas/Come Home | 1988 | — | — | 3.00 |
| Four Jays 100 | PS | I Wonder Where I'll Be Next Christmas/Come Home | 1988 | — | — | 3.00 |

ASTAIRE, FRED
45s

| DC 201 | DJ | Once A Year Night (same on both sides) | 1979 | — | 3.00 | 6.00 |

ASTROS, THE
45s

| Party-Time 4591 | DJ | Little Oscar The Astrodeer/Silent Night | 196? | 2.00 | 4.00 | 8.00 |

ATCHER, BOB
45s

| Capitol F1258 | | Blue Christmas/Christmas Island | 1950 | 3.75 | 7.50 | 15.00 |

ATKINS, CHET
45s

| Columbia AE7 1776 | DJ | East Tennessee Christmas/Winter Wonderland | 1983 | — | 2.00 | 4.00 |
| RCA Victor 47-5995 | | Silver Bells/Old Spinning Wheel | 1954 | 5.00 | 10.00 | 20.00 |

— With Hank Snow

| RCA Victor 47-6314 | | Christmas Carols/Jingle Bells | 1955 | 3.75 | 7.50 | 15.00 |
| RCA Victor 47-7971 | | Jingle Bells/Jingle Bell Rock | 1961 | 3.00 | 6.00 | 12.00 |

Albums

| Columbia PC 39003 | | East Tennessee Christmas | 1983 | 2.50 | 5.00 | 10.00 |
| RCA Victor ANL1-1935 | S | Christmas with Chet Atkins | 1976 | 2.00 | 4.00 | 8.00 |

— Reissue with same contents as LSP-2423

| RCA Victor LPM-2423 | M | Christmas with Chet Atkins | 1961 | 3.75 | 7.50 | 15.00 |
| RCA Victor LSP-2423 | S | Christmas with Chet Atkins | 1961 | 5.00 | 10.00 | 20.00 |

On Various-Artists Collections

Blue Christmas	Blue Christmas (Welk Music Group WM-3002)
Deck the Halls	Country Style Christmas, A (Columbia Musical Treasury 3P 6316)
Do You Hear What I Hear	Nashville's Greatest Christmas Hits (Columbia PC 44412)
East Tennessee Christmas	Christmas Greetings from Nashville (Columbia PC 39467)
I Heard the Bells on Christmas Day	Christmas Eve with Colonel Sanders (RCA Victor PRS-256)
Jingle Bell Rock	Christmas with Colonel Sanders (RCA Victor PRS-291)
	Country Christmas (Time-Life STL-109)
	Time-Life Treasury of Christmas, The, Volume Two (Time-Life STL-108)
Jingle Bells	October '61 Pop Sampler (RCA Victor SPS-33-141)
Jolly Old St. Nicholas	Happy Holidays, Volume IV (RCA Victor PRS-267)
	Time-Life Treasury of Christmas, The, Volume Two (Time-Life STL-108)
Let It Snow, Let It Snow, Let It Snow	Nashville's Greatest Christmas Hits, Volume II (Columbia PC 44413)
Little Drummer Boy	Christmas Festival of Songs and Carols, Volume 2 (RCA Victor PRM-195)
	For a Musical Merry Christmas, Volume 3 (RCA Victor PRM-221)
	Happy Holidays, Vol. III (RCA Victor PRS-255)
	Merry Christmas (RCA Victor PRM-168)
Medley: Coventry Carol/God Rest Ye Merry, Gentlemen	Music to Trim Your Tree By (RCA Victor PRM 225)
	Very Merry Christmas, A, Volume VI (RCA Special Products PRS-427)
O Come, All Ye Faithful	Christmas Eve with Colonel Sanders (RCA Victor PRS-256)
Winter Wonderland	Country Christmas (Time-Life STL-109)

ATLANTA SYMPHONY ORCHESTRA (SHAW)
Also see ROBERT SHAW CHORALE.

Albums

| Telarc DG-10087 | | Many Moods of Christmas, The | 1983 | 2.50 | 5.00 | 10.00 |
| Vox/Turnabout QTV-S 34639 | | Christmas with Robert Shaw Conducting the Atlanta Symphony Orchestra and Chorus | 1976 | 3.00 | 6.00 | 12.00 |

On Various-Artists Collections

Adeste Fideles	Home for the Holidays (MCA MSM-35007)
Hallelujah Chorus	Home for the Holidays (MCA MSM-35007)

Label, Number		Title (A Side/B Side)	Year	VG	VG+	NM

ATOMIC 61
45s

Label, Number		Title (A Side/B Side)	Year	VG	VG+	NM
Sympathy for the Record Industry 198		White Christmas/Blue Christmas	1991	—	2.00	4.00
— 500 copies on blue vinyl						
Sympathy for the Record Industry 198		White Christmas/Blue Christmas	1991	—	2.00	4.00
— 500 copies on white vinyl						
Sympathy for the Record Industry 198	PS	White Christmas/Blue Christmas	1991	—	2.00	4.00

ATWELL, WINIFRED
45s

Label, Number		Title	Year	VG	VG+	NM
Columbia 43472		Snow Bells/Flea Circus	1965	—	3.00	6.00

AUGUST, JAN
45s

Label, Number		Title	Year	VG	VG+	NM
Mercury 1245		The Christmas Song/White Christmas	195?	3.00	6.00	12.00

Albums

Label, Number		Title	Year	VG	VG+	NM
Mercury MG 20160	M	Christmas Favorites	1955	6.25	12.50	25.00

AUGUSTANA CHOIR, THE
On Various-Artists Collections

Greensleeves	Family Christmas Collection, The (Time-Life STL-131)
In the Bleak Midwinter	Family Christmas Collection, The (Time-Life STL-131)

AULD, GEORGIE
45s

Label, Number		Title	Year	VG	VG+	NM
Coral 60558		The Christmas Ball/It Ain't Snowin' Outside	1951	3.75	7.50	15.00

AUTRY, GENE
45s

Label, Number		Title (A Side/B Side)	Year	VG	VG+	NM
Challenge 1010		Rudolph the Red-Nosed Reindeer/Here Comes Santa Claus	1957	3.00	6.00	12.00
— Re-recordings of originals on Columbia						
Challenge 59030		Rudolph, the Red-Nosed Reindeer/Here Come Santa Claus	1958	3.00	6.00	12.00
Challenge 59030	PS	Rudolph, the Red-Nosed Reindeer/Here Come Santa Claus	1958	5.00	10.00	20.00
Columbia 4-56 (90049)		Rudolph, the Red-Nosed Reindeer/If It Doesn't Snow on Christmas	1951	5.00	10.00	20.00
— Yellow-label Children's Series issue						
Columbia 4-56 (90049)	PS	Rudolph, The Red-Nosed Reindeer/If It Doesn't Snow On Christmas	1951	6.25	12.50	25.00
Columbia 4-75 (90072)		Frosty the Snow Man/When Santa Claus Gets Your Letter	1951	5.00	10.00	20.00
— Yellow-label Children's Series issue						
Columbia 4-75 (90072)	PS	Frosty the Snow Man/When Santa Claus Gets Your Letter	1951	6.25	12.50	25.00
Columbia 4-84 (90088)		Here Comes Santa Claus/He's A Chubby Little Fellow	1951	5.00	10.00	20.00
— Yellow-label Children's Series issue						
Columbia 4-84 (90088)	PS	Here Comes Santa Claus/He's A Chubby Little Fellow	1951	6.25	12.50	25.00
Columbia 4-121 (90135)		Thirty-Two Feet — Eight Little Tails/ (Hedrock, Coco and Joe) The Three Little Dwarfs	1952	5.00	10.00	20.00
— Yellow-label Children's Series issue						
Columbia 4-121 (90135)	PS	Thirty-Two Feet — Eight Little Tails/ (Hedrock, Coco and Joe) The Three Little Dwarfs	1952	6.25	12.50	25.00
Columbia 4-122 (90136)		Poppy the Puppy/ He'll Be Coming Down the Chimney (Like He Always Did Before)	1952	5.00	10.00	20.00
— Yellow-label Children's Series issue						
Columbia 4-122 (90136)	PS	Poppy the Puppy/ He'll Be Coming Down the Chimney (Like He Always Did Before)	1952	6.25	12.50	25.00
Columbia 4-150 (90172)		Merry Texas Christmas, You All!/ The Night Before Christmas (In Texas, That Is)	1953	5.00	10.00	20.00
— Yellow-label Children's Series issue						
Columbia 4-150 (90172)	PS	Merry Texas Christmas, You All!/ The Night Before Christmas (In Texas, That Is)	1953	6.25	12.50	25.00
Columbia 4-176		Santa Claus Is Comin' To Town/Up On The Housetop (Ho! Ho! Ho!)	1954	3.75	7.50	15.00
— Yellow-label Children's Series issue						
Columbia 4-176	PS	Santa Claus Is Comin' To Town/Up On The Housetop (Ho! Ho! Ho!)	1954	5.00	10.00	20.00
Columbia 1-375		Rudolph, the Red-Nosed Reindeer/If It Doesn't Snow on Christmas	1949	10.00	20.00	40.00
— Microgroove 33 1/3 rpm single						
Columbia 6-375		Rudolph, the Red-Nosed Reindeer/If It Doesn't Snow on Christmas	1950	6.25	12.50	25.00
— Reissue on 45 of a single originally on 33 1/3 Microgroove single						
Columbia 1-742		Frosty the Snow Man/When Santa Claus Gets Your Letter	1950	10.00	20.00	40.00
— Microgroove 33 1/3 rpm single						

Label, Number		Title (A Side/B Side)	Year	VG	VG+	NM
Columbia 6-742		Frosty the Snow Man/When Santa Claus Gets Your Letter	1950	5.00	10.00	20.00
Columbia 20377		Here Comes Santa Claus (Down Santa Claus Lane)/	1950	5.00	10.00	20.00
		An Old-Fashioned Tree				
— Reissue on 45 of a single originally on 78						
Columbia 38610		Rudolph, the Red-Nosed Reindeer/If It Doesn't Snow On Christmas	1951	3.75	7.50	15.00
— Second 45 issue of this song						
Columbia 38907		Frosty The Snowman/When Santa Claus Gets Your Letter	1951	3.75	7.50	15.00
— Second 45 issue of this song						
Columbia 39461		Frosty the Snow Man/An Old-Fashioned Tree	1951	3.00	6.00	12.00
Columbia 39462		When Santa Claus Gets Your Letter/He's a Chubby Little Fellow	1951	3.00	6.00	12.00
Columbia 39463		Rudolph, the Red-Nosed Reindeer/	1951	3.00	6.00	12.00
		Here Comes Santa Claus (Down Santa Claus Lane)				
Columbia 39464		Santa, Santa, Santa/If It Doesn't Snow on Christmas	1951	3.00	6.00	12.00
Columbia 39542		Poppy the Puppy/	1951	3.75	7.50	15.00
		He'll Be Coming Down the Chimney (Like He Always Did Before)				
Columbia 39543		Thirty-Two Feet — Eight Little Tails/	1951	3.75	7.50	15.00
		(Hedrock, Coco and Joe) The Three Little Dwarfs				
Columbia 39876		The Night Before Christmas Song/Look Out the Window	1952	3.75	7.50	15.00
— With Rosemary Clooney						
Columbia 40092		Where Did My Snowman Go?/Freddie the Little Fir Tree	1953	3.75	7.50	15.00
Columbia 40135		I Wish My Mom Would Marry Santa Claus/Sleigh Bells	1953	3.75	7.50	15.00
Columbia 40589		Round, Round the Christmas Tree/Merry Christmas Tree	1955	3.75	7.50	15.00
Columbia 40790		Everyone's a Child at Christmas/You Can See Old Santa Claus	1956	3.75	7.50	15.00
Columbia Hall of Fame 33165		Rudolph, the Red-Nosed Reindeer/	1970	—	2.50	5.00
		Here Comes Santa Claus (Down Santa Claus Lane)				
— Red and black label						
Columbia Hall of Fame 33165		Rudolph, the Red-Nosed Reindeer/	198?	—	—	3.00
		Here Comes Santa Claus (Down Santa Claus Lane)				
— Gray label						
Cricket CX-6		Rudolph, the Red-Nosed Reindeer/Tinker Town Santa Claus	196?	3.00	6.00	12.00
— B-side by the Cricketones						
Mistletoe 801		Rudolph, The Red-Nosed Reindeer/Up On The House Top	196?	2.00	4.00	8.00
Republic 326		Rudolph the Red-Nosed Reindeer/Here Comes Santa Claus	1976	—	2.00	4.00
Republic 1405		Rudolph the Red-Nosed Reindeer/Here Comes Santa Claus	1969	2.00	4.00	8.00
Republic 2001		Nine Little Reindeer/	1959	3.00	6.00	12.00
		Buon Natale (Means Merry Christmas)				
Republic 2001	PS	Nine Little Reindeer/	1959	3.00	6.00	12.00
		Buon Natale (Means Merry Christmas)				
Republic 2002		Santa's Comin' in a Whirlybird/Jingle Bells	1959	3.00	6.00	12.00
Albums						
Columbia CL 2547	10	Merry Christmas with Gene Autry	1954	30.00	60.00	120.00
— "House Party Series" release						
Columbia CL 6137	10	Merry Christmas	1950	37.50	75.00	150.00
Grand Prix KX-11	M	Gene Autry Sings	1959	3.75	7.50	15.00
Grand Prix KS-X11	S	Gene Autry Sings	1959	5.00	10.00	20.00
Gusto 1038		Christmas Classics	19??	2.50	5.00	10.00
Harmony HL 9550	M	The Original Rudolph the Red-Nosed	1964	6.25	12.50	25.00
		Reindeer and Other Children's Christmas Favorites				
Harmony HS 14450	R	The Original Rudolph the Red-Nosed	1964	3.00	6.00	12.00
		Reindeer and Other Children's Christmas Favorites				
Republic RLP 6018	M	Christmas with Gene Autry	1976	3.00	6.00	12.00

On Various-Artists Collections

Frosty the Snowman	Merry Christmas (Columbia Musical Treasury 3P 6306)
	Santa's Hit Parade (Columbia Record Club D-17)
He'll Be Coming Down the Chimney	First Christmas Record for Children (Harmony HS 14554)
Here Comes Santa Claus	Billboard Greatest Christmas Hits, 1935-1954 (Rhino R1 70637)
	Country Christmas (Time-Life STL-109)
	Merry Christmas from… (Reader's Digest RD4-83)
	12 Hits of Christmas (United Artists UA-LA669-R)
Rudolph, the Red-Nosed Reindeer	Best of Christmas (Mistletoe MLP-1209)
	Billboard Greatest Christmas Hits, 1935-1954 (Rhino R1 70637)
	Child's Christmas, A (Harmony HS 14563)
	Christmas Greetings from Nashville (Columbia PC 39467)
	Country Christmas (Columbia CS 9888)
	Country Christmas (Time-Life STL-109)
	Home for Christmas (Columbia Musical Treasury P3S 5608)
	Home for Christmas (Realm 2V 8101)
	Merry Christmas from… (Reader's Digest RD4-83)
	Popular Christmas Classics (Capitol Special Markets SL-8100)
	Santa's Hit Parade (Columbia Record Club D-17)
	60 Christmas Classics (Sessions DVL2-0723)
	Time-Life Treasury of Christmas, The (Time-Life STL-107)
	12 Hits of Christmas (United Artists UA-LA669-R)
Up on the House Top	Best of Christmas (Mistletoe MLP-1209)

(Top left) The picture sleeve for Herb Alpert and the Tijuana Brass' "My Favorite Things," their version of which has a stop-and-start arrangement similar to their biggest hit, "Taste of Honey." (Top right) Jon Anderson's *3 Ships* LP, which often is not recognized as a Christmas record. (Bottom left) Atomic 61's "Blue Christmas"/"White Christmas" single was pressed in an edition of 500 on blue vinyl and 500 on white vinyl. (Bottom right) The first regular 45 rpm pressing of Gene Autry's "Rudolph, the Red-Nosed Reindeer," No. 2 in all-time Christmas record sales. This version, Columbia 6-375, came out in 1950, a year after the 78 and the 33 1/3 microgroove single did.

Label, Number		Title (A Side/B Side)	Year	VG	VG+	NM
AVALON, FRANKIE						
45s						
Chancellor 11FX 1		Christmas Holiday/Dear Gesu Bambino	196?	5.00	10.00	20.00
Albums						
Chancellor CHL 5031	M	Frankie Avalon's Christmas Album	1962	7.50	15.00	30.00
Chancellor CHLS 5031	S	Frankie Avalon's Christmas Album	1962	10.00	20.00	40.00
AVALON, FRANKIE, AND ANNETTE FUNICELLO						
45s						
Pacific Star 569		(Together We Can Make a) Merry Christmas/ The Night Before Christmas	1981	—	2.50	5.00
— Red vinyl						
Pacific Star 569	PS	(Together We Can Make a) Merry Christmas/ The Night Before Christmas	1981	—	2.50	5.00
AVELLANET, CUCHO						
45s						
United Artists 50241		Jingle Bells (Cascabel)/Joy To The World (Gloria A Jesus)	1967	2.00	4.00	8.00
AVERN, HARVEY, BAND						
45s						
Fania 551	DJ	Let's Get It Together This Christmas/Christmas Song	19??	—	2.00	4.00

B

Label, Number		Title (A Side/B Side)	Year	VG	VG+	NM
B. BOYS CHRISTMAS						
12-Inch Singles						
B-Boy BB-102187		My Christmas Bells/My Christmas/Elf Dub/Happy Holiday/ Happy Holiday (Instrumental)//My Christmas Bells (Hard Call)/ Who Needs Real Drums/Funky Fresh Xmas	1987	2.00	4.00	8.00
B. Bumble and the Stingers						
45s						
Rendezvous 166		Nut Rocker/Nautilus	1962	3.75	7.50	15.00
B.G.O.T.I.						
On Various-Artists Collections						
O Holy Night		Christmas on Death Row (Death Row/Interscope INT2-90108)				
B.G.O.T.I. AND 6 FEET DEEP & GUESS						
On Various-Artists Collections						
Silent Night		Christmas on Death Row (Death Row/Interscope INT2-90108)				
BABBITT, HARRY						
45s						
Coral 60271		Frosty the Snowman/Rudolph the Red-Nosed Reindeer	1950	3.75	7.50	15.00
Coral 60272		Here Comes Santa Claus (Down Santa Claus Lane)/ (All I Want for Christmas Is) My Two Front Teeth	1950	3.75	7.50	15.00
Coral 60554		Twas the Night Before Christmas (Part 1)/ Twas the Night Before Christmas (Part 2)	1951	3.75	7.50	15.00
Coral 60555		Thirty-Two Feet — Eight Little Tails/ Hard Rock, Coco and Joe (The Three Little Dwarfs)	1951	3.75	7.50	15.00
BABIT, HI						
45s						
Bi Music 132		Dear Mister Santa Claus/It Makes No Never Mind	1973	—	2.50	5.00
BABY JANE						
45s						
Whitch 112		You Trimmed My Christmas Tree/(B-side unknown)	19??	—	2.50	5.00
BABY'S FIRST CHRISTMAS						
7-Inch Extended Plays						
Fission BFX002		Christmas/Walk With A Winner/Building Up Speed// Purple/Midnight Hour/Frontier	1985	—	3.00	6.00
Fission BFX002	PS	Christmas/Walk With A Winner/Building Up Speed// Purple/Midnight Hour/Frontier	1985	—	3.00	6.00

Label, Number		Title (A Side/B Side)	Year	VG	VG+	NM
BACHARACH, BURT						
45s						
A&M 1004		The Bell That Couldn't Jingle/What the World Needs Now Is Love	1968	—	3.00	6.00
On Various-Artists Collections						
Bell That Couldn't Jingle, The		Something Festive! (A&M SP-19003)				
BACKUS, JIM						
45s						
Dico 101		I Was a Teenage Reindeer/The Office Party	1959	5.00	10.00	20.00
Jubilee 5351		Cave Man/Why Don't You Go Home for Christmas	1958	3.00	6.00	12.00
BAD MANNERS						
45s						
Blue Beat 010		Christmas Time Again/Skinhead Love Affair	198?	2.00	4.00	8.00
Blue Beat 010	PS	Christmas Time Again/Skinhead Love Affair	198?	2.50	5.00	10.00
— Both record and sleeve are U.K. imports						
BAD NEWS						
12-Inch Singles						
EMI 12EM 36	PS	Cashing In On Christmas (Let's Bank Mix)//	1987	3.00	6.00	12.00
		Bad News/Cashing In On Christmas (7" Version)				
— U.K. import						
45s						
EMI EM 36		Cashing In on Christmas/Bad News	1987	—	3.00	6.00
EMI EM 36	PS	Cashing In on Christmas/Bad News	1987	—	3.00	6.00
— Sleeve and record are U.K. imports						
EMI EMG 36	PS	Cashing In on Christmas/Bad News	1987	2.50	5.00	10.00
— Christmas card poster pack sleeve (U.K. import)						
BAEZ, JOAN						
45s						
Vanguard 35046		Little Drummer Boy/Cantique de Noel	1966	2.50	5.00	10.00
Albums						
Vanguard VRS-9230	M	Noel	1966	3.00	6.00	12.00
Vanguard VSD-79230	S	Noel	1966	3.75	7.50	15.00
BAGDASARIAN, ROSS						
Real name of David Seville, who "led" THE CHIPMUNKS.						
45s						
Mercury 70254		Let's Have a Merry, Merry Christmas/Hey Brother, Pour the Wine	1953	6.25	12.50	25.00
BAH HUMBUG SINGERS, THE						
45s						
Playback BH-1		Discount Sales (Jingle Bells)/O Christmas Tree	1986	—	—	3.00
BAILEY, PEARL						
45s						
Roulette 4206		Jingle Bells (Cha Cha Cha)/Five Pound Box of Money	1959	5.00	10.00	20.00
BAILEY, RAZZY						
45s						
RCA PB-13359		Peace on Earth/Let It Snow, Let It Snow, Let It Snow	1982	—	2.00	4.00
— B-side by Charley Pride						
On Various-Artists Collections						
Peace on Earth		Country Christmas, A (RCA CPL1-4396)				
BAILLARGEON, HELENE						
Albums						
Folkways FW 829	10	Christmas Songs of French Canada	195?	12.50	25.00	50.00
Folkways FC 7229		Christmas Songs of French Canada	195?	12.50	25.00	50.00
BAILLIE AND THE BOYS						
On Various-Artists Collections						
In a Manger		Mistletoe and Memories (RCA 8372-1-R)				

Label, Number		Title (A Side/B Side)	Year	VG	VG+	NM
BAIN, BARBARA/MARTIN LANDAU						
On Various-Artists Collections						
Reminder Spot		For Christmas Seals. . .A Matter of Life and Breath (Decca Custom Style E)				
BAJA MARIMBA BAND, THE						
Also see JULIUS WECHTER AND THE BAJA MARIMBA BAND.						
45s						
A&M XMAS 1	DJ	The 12 Days Of Christmas/My Favorite Things	1968	3.00	6.00	12.00
— B-side by We Five						
A&M XMAS 1	PS	The 12 Days Of Christmas/My Favorite Things	1968	3.75	7.50	15.00
BAKER, "WEE BONNIE"						
45s						
Kahill 1017		Send A Christmas Card To Joe/A Stretch Sock For Santa	19??	—	3.00	6.00
BAKER, CHET						
On Various-Artists Collections						
Winter Wonderland		Yule Struttin' — A Blue Note Christmas (Blue Note 1P 8119)				
BAKER, KENNY						
45s						
Decca 23671		O Little Town Of Bethlehem/It Came Upon A Midnight Clear	1950	3.75	7.50	15.00
BAKER, WALTER						
On Various-Artists Collections						
Adeste Fideles		Life Treasury of Christmas Music, The (Project/Capitol TL 100)				
Hark! The Herald Angels Sing		Life Treasury of Christmas Music, The (Project/Capitol TL 100)				
Joy to the World		Life Treasury of Christmas Music, The (Project/Capitol TL 100)				
BAKER, WARREN						
45s						
Warner Bros. 5118		Midnight in Bethlehem/Little Bitty Baby	1959	3.00	6.00	12.00
BAKKE, BRONI						
45s						
Calypso 8101		Almost Time For Santa Claus/Christmas Present For Santa	19??	—	2.00	4.00
BALL, LUCILLE, AND CAST						
On Various-Artists Collections						
We Need a Little Christmas		Mame (Warner Bros. W 2773)				
BALLARD, HANK, AND THE MIDNIGHTERS						
45s						
King 5729		Christmas Time for Everyone But Me/Santa Claus Is Coming	1963	3.75	7.50	15.00
BALLEW, JIM						
45s						
Wynn-Ballew (no #)	DJ	Holy Is The Day/Holy Is The Day (Instrumental)	19??	—	—	3.00
BAND AID						
12-Inch Singles						
Columbia 05157		Do They Know It's Christmas? (2 versions)/Feed the World	1984	3.75	7.50	15.00
45s						
Columbia 04749		Do They Know It's Christmas?/Feed the World	1984	—	2.50	5.00
Columbia 04749	PS	Do They Know It's Christmas?/Feed the World	1984	—	2.50	5.00
BAND AID II						
New version of Band Aid single, unreleased in U.S. for legal reasons.						
45s						
Polydor FEED 2		Do They Know It's Christmas?/(Instrumental)	1989	—	2.50	5.00
Polydor FEED 2	PS	Do They Know It's Christmas?/(Instrumental)	1989	—	2.50	5.00
BANFIELD, KRISTIN						
45s						
UPG 007		The Christmas Song/Baubles, Bangles and Beads	19??	2.00	4.00	8.00

Label, Number	Title (A Side/B Side)	Year	VG	VG+	NM

BANJO BARONS, THE
45s
| Columbia 42244 | I Saw Mommy Kissing Santa Claus/ | 1961 | 2.50 | 5.00 | 10.00 |
| | Have Yourself A Merry Little Christmas-Santa Claus Is Comin' To Town | | | | |

BARE, BOBBY
On Various-Artists Collections
| Christmas Greetings | Christmas Greetings From RCA Victor And Groove Recording Artists (RCA Victor SP-45-128) |
| New Year's Greetings | Christmas Greetings From RCA Victor And Groove Recording Artists (RCA Victor SP-45-128) |

BAREFOOT MAN
45s
| NSD 113 | Santa Got A Sunburn/Grandpa's Christmas Fiddle | 1981 | — | 2.50 | 5.00 |

BARKDULL, WILEY
45s
| Allstar 7275 | Merry Christmas To You/Jingle Bells | 19?? | — | 2.50 | 5.00 |

BARKER, JEFF
45s
| Jo-Lyn 28385 | The Birthday Of A King/The Ringing Of The Bells | 19?? | — | — | 3.00 |

BARON, SANDY
45s
| Gulf 028 | Swingin' Santa/Back Home | 19?? | 2.50 | 5.00 | 10.00 |

BARREL, VIC
45s
| Atlantic 2083 | White Christmas/Footing | 1960 | 3.00 | 6.00 | 12.00 |

BARRIE, DON
45s
| Tiara 663 | Christmas Is For Giving/Christmastime | 19?? | — | 2.00 | 4.00 |

BARRON KNIGHTS, THE
45s
| Epic 9070 | | Never Mind The Presents/The Swindon Cowboy | 1980 | — | 2.00 | 4.00 |
| Epic 9070 | PS | Never Mind The Presents/The Swindon Cowboy | 1980 | — | 2.00 | 4.00 |
— Sleeve and record are U.K. imports

BARRON, BLUE
45s
MGM 10523	Christmas Time/Santa Claus Is Coming To Town	1949	5.00	10.00	20.00
MGM 10781	Red Cheeks & White Whiskers/Jolly Jolly Jingle	1950	5.00	10.00	20.00
MGM 11375	Santa Claus Lullaby/The Little Match Girl	1952	5.00	10.00	20.00

BARRY AND THE HIGHLIGHTS
45s
| Airmaster 700 | Christmas Bell Rock/Chil-E Baby | 1960 | 12.50 | 25.00 | 50.00 |
| Baye 511 | Christmas Bell Rock/Chil-E Baby | 1960 | 12.50 | 25.00 | 50.00 |

BARRY AND THE TOTS
45s
| Fury 1058 | Christmas Each Day of the Year/ | 1961 | 3.00 | 6.00 | 12.00 |
| | I'm a Happy Little Christmas Tree | | | | |

BARRY, KEN
On Various-Artists Collections
| Reminder Spot | For Christmas Seals...A Matter of Life and Breath (Decca Custom Style E) |

BARRY, LEN
45s
| Amy 11047 | The Child Is Born/Wouldn't It Be Beautiful | 1968 | — | 3.00 | 6.00 |

Label, Number		Title (A Side/B Side)	Year	VG	VG+	NM
BARRYMORE, LIONEL						
45s						
MGM 30258		A Visit From St. Nicholas/No Room In The Inn	1950	3.75	7.50	15.00
Albums						
MGM CH 112	10	A Christmas Carol	1952	10.00	20.00	40.00
On Various-Artists Collections						
Christmas Carol, A		Christmas Carol, A/Music of Christmas (MGM E3222)				
BART, LIONEL						
45s						
London 9505		Give Us A Kiss For Christmas/How Now Brown Cow	1961	3.00	6.00	12.00
BART, TEDDY						
45s						
Centaur 102		Christmas Fills My Heart/Moody	19??	—	2.00	4.00
BARTON, EILEEN						
45s						
Coral 60880		The Night Before Christmas Song/The Little Match Girl	1952	3.75	7.50	15.00
7-Inch Extended Plays						
Coral 83011		The Little Match Girl/The Night Before Christmas// Christmas In The Air/Christmas Is A Time	195?	3.75	7.50	15.00
— B-side by Johnny Desmond						
BARTON, LARRY, AND THE FREEBEES						
45s						
Musitron 1061		Seymour, The Beatnick Elf/Crazy Sleigh Ride	19??	3.00	6.00	12.00
BARTOO, MARION						
45s						
Fable 531		Mrs. Santa's Party/Jingle Bill	19??	—	3.00	6.00
— Red vinyl						
BASEMENT 5, THE						
12-Inch Singles						
Island 12WIP 6654		Last White Christmas/Paranoia Claustrophobia (Part 2)	1980	2.50	5.00	10.00
— U.K. import						
BASHAM, JOE						
45s						
Icon 1101		Santa's Southern Visit/The Dickens Christmas Carol	19??	—	2.00	4.00
BASIE, COUNT						
45s						
Capitol S7-57888		Jingle Bells/Let It Snow! Let It Snow! Let It Snow!	1992	—	2.00	4.00
— B-side by Lena Horne						
Roulette 4465		Basie's Jingle Bells/Lullabye of Birdland	1962	2.50	5.00	10.00
On Various-Artists Collections						
Jingle Bells		Philco Album of Holiday Music, The (Columbia Special Products CSM 431) Yule Struttin' — A Blue Note Christmas (Blue Note 1P 8119)				
BASKERVILLE HOUNDS, THE						
45s						
Tema 131		Christmas Is Here (But Not For Long)/Make Me Your Man	1966	3.75	7.50	15.00
Tema 131	PS	Christmas Is Here (But Not For Long)/Make Me Your Man	1966	12.50	25.00	50.00
BASSETTE, JOHN						
45s						
Tinker Too 7720		The Christmas Season/Every Day Is Christmas From Now On	19??	2.50	5.00	10.00
BAXTER, LES						
45s						
Capitol F2275		Santa Claus' Party/Hang Your Wishes on the Tree	1952	3.00	6.00	12.00
Reprise 0243		How Shall I Send Thee/Have Yourself a Merry Little Christmas	1963	5.00	10.00	20.00
— B-side by Frank Sinatra						

Label, Number		Title (A Side/B Side)	Year	VG	VG+	NM

On Various-Artists Collections

Hang Your Wishes on the Tree		Christmas to Remember, A, Vol. 3 (Capitol Creative Products SL-6681)				
		Happy Holidays, Album 6 (Capitol Creative Products SL-6669)				
		Sound of Christmas, The, Vol. 3 (Capitol Creative Products SL-6680)				
Medley: Go Tell It On the Mountain/		Have Yourself a Merry Little Christmas (Reprise R 50001)				
How Shall I Send Thee/						
Carol of the Bells/Joy to the World						
Santa Claus' Party		Happy Holidays, Album 6 (Capitol Creative Products SL-6669)				

BAXTER, TERRY
On Various-Artists Collections

For Unto Us a Child Is Born		Magic of Christmas, The (Columbia Musical Treasury P3S 5806)				
Out of the East		Merry Christmas (Columbia Musical Treasury 3P 6306)				

BAXTERS, THE
45s

E Ticket 004		Racing Homer / Crickets Ice Soda & More//	19??	—	2.50	5.00
		Christmas With Kieslowski In Red				
— Red vinyl						
E Ticket 004	PS	Racing Homer / Crickets Ice Soda & More//	19??	—	2.50	5.00
		Christmas With Kieslowski In Red				

BAYS, DENE & TOM BAKER
45s

Globe 109		Christmas Time (Is Here)/'Twas The Night Before Christmas	1971	—	2.50	5.00

BEACH BOYS, THE
45s

Brother/Reprise 1321		Child of Winter (Christmas Song)/Susie Cincinnati	1974	12.50	25.00	50.00
Brother/Reprise 1321	DJ	Child of Winter (Christmas Song) (mono/stereo)	1974	6.25	12.50	25.00
Capitol 5096		Little Saint Nick/The Lord's Prayer	1963	5.00	10.00	20.00
— Orange and yellow swirl label						
Capitol 5096		Little Saint Nick/The Lord's Prayer	1969	4.50	9.00	18.00
— Red and orange "target" label						
Capitol 5096		Little Saint Nick/The Lord's Prayer	1972	3.75	7.50	15.00
— Orange label with "Capitol" at bottom of label						
Capitol 5096		Little Saint Nick/The Lord's Prayer	1978	—	2.50	5.00
— Purple label						
Capitol 5096		Little Saint Nick/The Lord's Prayer	1982	—	2.50	5.00
— Black label with colorband						
Capitol 5312		The Man with All the Toys/Blue Christmas	1964	5.00	10.00	20.00
Capitol S7-18205		Merry Christmas, Baby/Santa's Beard	1994	—	2.00	4.00
— Green vinyl						
Capitol S7-57886		Frosty the Snowman/Little Saint Nick	1992	—	2.50	5.00
— Originals on black vinyl						
Capitol S7-57886		Frosty the Snowman/Little Saint Nick	1993	—	2.00	4.00
— Second pressing on green vinyl						

Albums

Capitol T 2164	M	The Beach Boys' Christmas Album	1964	10.00	20.00	40.00
Capitol ST 2164	S	The Beach Boys' Christmas Album	1964	10.00	20.00	40.00
— "Merry Christmas, Baby" is longer on this LP than on the mono version						
Capitol SM-2164		The Beach Boys' Christmas Album	197?	2.50	5.00	10.00
Capitol DKAO 2945	P	The Best of the Beach Boys, Vol. 3	1968	3.75	7.50	15.00
— Black label with colorband. Contains one Christmas song: Frosty the Snowman						
Capitol DKAO 2945	P	The Best of the Beach Boys, Vol. 3	1969	5.00	10.00	20.00
— "Starline" label						

On Various-Artists Collections

Blue Christmas		Blue Christmas (Welk Music Group WM-3002)				
Christmas Day		Christmas Day (Pickwick SPC 1010)				
		Time-Life Treasury of Christmas, The, Volume Two (Time-Life STL-108)				
I'll Be Home for Christmas		I'll Be Home for Christmas (Pickwick SPC-1009)				
Man with All the Toys, The		Jingle Bell Rock (Time-Life SRNR-XM)				
Merry Christmas, Baby		Christmas Rock Album, The (Priority SL 9465)				
Santa Claus Is Coming to Town		Christmas Songs, The (Capitol SLB-57074)				
Santa's Beard		Time-Life Treasury of Christmas, The (Time-Life STL-107)				
We Three Kings of Orient Are		Christmas Songs, The, Volume II (Capitol SL-57065)				
		Magic of Christmas, The (Capitol SWBB-93810)				

BEALE STREET BOYS, THE
45s

OBA 101		Next Christmas/There's Nothing Greater Than A Prayer	1960	15.00	30.00	60.00

Label, Number		Title (A Side/B Side)	Year	VG	VG+	NM

BEATLES, THE
Also see GEORGE HARRISON, JOHN LENNON, PAUL McCARTNEY.

45s

Label, Number		Title (A Side/B Side)	Year	VG	VG+	NM
Apple 58497		Free as a Bird/Christmas Time (Is Here Again)	1995	—	2.00	4.00
— *Small center hole; all with large hole were "dinked" somewhere other than when manufactured and have little, if any, value*						
Apple 58497	PS	Free as a Bird/Christmas Time (Is Here Again)	1995	—	2.00	4.00
Beatles Fan Club (1964)		Season's Greetings from the Beatles	1964	75.00	150.00	300.00
— *Tri-fold soundcard*						
Beatles Fan Club (1965) Lyntone 948e		Beatles Third Christmas Record	1965	20.00	40.00	80.00
— *Flexi-disc*						
Beatles Fan Club (1965) Lyntone 948	PS	The Beatles Third Christmas Record	1965	25.00	50.00	100.00
Beatles Fan Club (1966)		Everywhere It's Christmas	1966	37.50	75.00	150.00
— *Postcard*						
Beatles Fan Club (1967)		Christmastime Is Here Again	1967	37.50	75.00	150.00
— *Postcard*						
Beatles Fan Club (1968) H-2041		The Beatles 1968 Christmas Record	1968	15.00	30.00	60.00
— *Flexi-disc*						
Beatles Fan Club (1968) H-2041	PS	The Beatles 1968 Christmas Record	1968	17.50	35.00	70.00
Beatles Fan Club (1969) H-2565		Happy Christmas 1969	1969	10.00	20.00	40.00
— *Flexi-disc*						
Beatles Fan Club (1969) H-2565	PS	Happy Christmas 1969	1969	15.00	30.00	60.00
Vee Jay (no #)	PS	We Wish You a Merry Christmas and a Happy New Year	1964	20.00	40.00	80.00
— *Used with any Vee Jay or Tollie Beatles single in 1964-65 holiday season*						

Albums

Label, Number		Title (A Side/B Side)	Year	VG	VG+	NM
Apple SBC-100	M	The Beatles' Christmas Album	1970	100.00	200.00	400.00

BEAU, BILLY
45s

Label, Number	Title (A Side/B Side)	Year	VG	VG+	NM
Dot 16281	Hey Daddy (I'm Gonna Tell Santa On You)/Santa's Coffee	1961	10.00	20.00	40.00

BEAUMONT, RICHARD
On Various-Artists Collections

Beautiful Day, The	Scrooge (Columbia Masterworks S 30258)

BECK, BECKY LEE
45s

Label, Number	Title (A Side/B Side)	Year	VG	VG+	NM
Challenge 59272	I Want a Beatle for Christmas/Puppy Dog	1964	5.00	10.00	20.00

BEE BEE TWINS, THE
45s

Label, Number	Title (A Side/B Side)	Year	VG	VG+	NM
Liberty 55173	The Night Before Christmas/Yuletide Tango	1958	3.75	7.50	15.00

BEE, MOLLY
45s

Label, Number	Title (A Side/B Side)	Year	VG	VG+	NM
Capitol F2285	I Saw Mommy Kissing Santa Claus/ Willy Claus (Little Son of Santa Claus)	1952	3.75	7.50	15.00

BEECHAM, SIR THOMAS
On Various-Artists Collections

Hallelujah Chorus	Very Merry Christmas, A, Volume VII (RCA Special Products DPL1-0049)

BEERS FAMILY, THE
45s

Label, Number	Title (A Side/B Side)	Year	VG	VG+	NM
Columbia 43916	Three Little Drummers/The Peace Carol	1966	—	3.00	6.00

Albums

Label, Number		Title (A Side/B Side)	Year	VG	VG+	NM
Biograph BLP-12033		The Seasons of Peace — A Great Family Sings	1971	3.00	6.00	12.00
— *Evelyne and Bob Beers; Martha and Eric Nagler; Bill, Janet, Susan, Joe, Becky and John Boyer (all related).*						
Columbia Masterworks ML 6335	M	Christmas with the Beers Family	1966	3.00	6.00	12.00
Columbia Masterworks MS 6935	S	Christmas with the Beers Family	1966	3.75	7.50	15.00

BEGINNING OF THE END, THE
45s

Label, Number	Title (A Side/B Side)	Year	VG	VG+	NM
Alston 4605	Gee Whiz, It's Christmas/Surrey Ride	1971	—	2.00	4.00

Label, Number		Title (A Side/B Side)	Year	VG	VG+	NM

BELAFONTE, HARRY
45s

RCA Victor 47-6735		Mary's Boy Child/Venezuela	1956	3.00	6.00	12.00
RCA Victor 47-6735	PS	Mary's Boy Child/Venezuela	1956	6.25	12.50	25.00
RCA Victor 47-7425		I Heard the Bells on Christmas Day/Mary, Mary	1958	2.00	4.00	8.00
RCA Victor 47-7425	PS	I Heard the Bells on Christmas Day/Mary, Mary	1958	3.75	7.50	15.00

Albums

RCA Victor LPM-1402	M	An Evening with Belafonte	1957	6.25	12.50	25.00
— Contains one Christmas song:		Mary's Boy Child				
RCA Victor LSP-1402(e)	R	An Evening with Belafonte	1960	3.00	6.00	12.00
— Dog on top						
RCA Victor LSP-1402(e)	R	An Evening with Belafonte	1969	2.50	5.00	10.00
— Orange label						
RCA Victor LPM-1887	M	To Wish You a Merry Christmas	1958	6.25	12.50	25.00
RCA Victor LSP-1887	S	To Wish You a Merry Christmas	1958	10.00	20.00	40.00
RCA Victor LPM-2626	M	To Wish You a Merry Christmas	1962	5.00	10.00	20.00
— Reissue of LPM-1887 with new cover and "Mary's Boy Child" added						
RCA Victor LSP-2626	S	To Wish You a Merry Christmas	1962	6.25	12.50	25.00

On Various-Artists Collections

Christmas Is Coming	Very Merry Christmas, A, Volume 5 (RCA Special Products PRS-343)
Gifts They Gave, The	Time-Life Treasury of Christmas, The, Volume Two (Time-Life STL-108)
I Heard the Bells on Christmas Day	Time-Life Treasury of Christmas, The, Volume Two (Time-Life STL-108)
Mary's Boy Child	Billboard Greatest Christmas Hits, 1955-Present (Rhino R1 70636)
	Christmas Through the Years (Reader's Digest RDA-143)
	Christmas with Colonel Sanders (RCA Victor PRS-291)
	Happy Holidays, Volume 15 (RCA Special Products DPL1-0453)
	Joyous Noel (Reader's Digest RDA-57A)
	Time-Life Treasury of Christmas, The (Time-Life STL-107)
Silent Night	Carols and Candlelight (Columbia Special Products P 12525)
	Gift from Your RCA Victor Record Dealer, A (RCA Victor SP-45-35)
Star in the East, A	Christmas in California (RCA Victor PRS-276)
	Christmas in New York Volume 2 (RCA Victor PRS-270)
	Christmastime in Carol and Song (RCA PRM-271)
	Family Christmas Collection, The (Time-Life STL-131)
Twelve Days of Christmas, The	Happy Holidays, Volume 18 (RCA Special Products DPL1-0608)
	Joyous Noel (Reader's Digest RDA-57A)
	Very Merry Christmas, A, Volume VI (RCA Special Products PRS-427)

BELL TONE TRIO
45s

Kentucky 4-550		Oh Little Town Of Bethlehem/Joy To The World	19??	—	2.00	4.00

BELL, EDDY
45s

Versa 101		Twinkletoes/Because It's Xmas	19??	2.50	5.00	10.00

BELL, WILLIAM
45s

Atlantic 13154		Everyday Will Be Like a Holiday/Winner	197?	—	2.00	4.00
— Oldies Series reissue						
Stax 237		Everyday Will Be Like a Holiday/Ain't Got No Girl	1967	2.00	4.00	8.00

BELLAMY BROTHERS, THE
45s

Warner Bros. 49875		It's So Close to Christmas/Let Me Waltz Into Your Heart	1981	—	2.00	4.00

BELLETTO
45s

White Cliffs 206		Have A Merry Christmas/Have A Happy, Happy New Year	19??	—	2.50	5.00

BELLOWS, BOB
45s

Iris 1002		Your Special Christmas Angel/Hey, Mister Santa Claus	1961	2.50	5.00	10.00

BELVIN, JESSE
45s

Modern 1005		Goodnight My Love (Pleasant Dreams)/ I Want You With Me at Christmas	1956	10.00	20.00	40.00

Label, Number		Title (A Side/B Side)	Year	VG	VG+	NM

BENATAR, PAT
45s
| Chrysalis S7-18913 | | Please Come Home for Christmas/True Love | 1995 | — | — | 3.00 |

BENEFICIAL SINGERS, THE
On Various-Artists Collections
Joyous Christmas — Joyous Christmas, Volume 4 (Columbia Special Products CSS 1485)
Joyous Christmas, Volume V (Columbia Special Products C 10398)
Joyous Christmas, Volume 6 (Columbia Special Products C 11083)
Toyland — Joyous Christmas, Volume 4 (Columbia Special Products CSS 1485)

BENEKE, TEX
"In the Glenn Miller Style" with Ray Eberle and the Modernaires.
45s
| Columbia JZSP 111917/8 | DJ | And The Bells Rang/Merry Christmas, Baby | 1965 | 2.00 | 4.00 | 8.00 |
| MGM 11098 | | Santa Claus Parade/Root'n Toot'n Santa | 1951 | 5.00 | 10.00 | 20.00 |
Albums
| Columbia CL 2392 | M | Christmas Serenade | 1965 | 3.00 | 6.00 | 12.00 |
| Columbia CS 9192 | S | Christmas Serenade | 1965 | 3.75 | 7.50 | 15.00 |
On Various-Artists Collections
Christmas Song, The — Many Moods of Christmas, The (Columbia Special Products P 12013)
Jingle Bells — It's Christmastime! (Columbia Special Products CSM 429)
Snowfall — Happy Holidays, Volume II (Columbia Special Products CSM 348)

BENNETT, ANN
45s
| Bertlen 101 | | Another Christmas Rolls Around Again/Chrissy The Christmas Tree | 19?? | — | 2.50 | 5.00 |

BENNETT, LINDA
45s
| Mercury 73750 | | An Old Fashioned Christmas/Daddy Cursed the Day | 1975 | — | 2.50 | 5.00 |

BENNETT, TONY
45s
| Columbia 07658 | | White Christmas/All of My Life | 1987 | — | — | 3.00 |
| Columbia 07658 | PS | White Christmas/All of My Life | 1987 | — | — | 3.00 |
Albums
| Columbia CS 9739 | | Snowfall: The Tony Bennett Christmas Album | 1968 | 3.00 | 6.00 | 12.00 |
On Various-Artists Collections
Christmas Song, The — Best of the Great Songs of Christmas (Album 10) (Columbia Special Products CSS 1478)
Christmas Album, A (Columbia PC 39466)
Christmas Trimmings (Columbia Special Products P 12795)
Great Songs of Christmas, The, Album Seven (Columbia Special Products CSS 547)
Magic of Christmas, The (Columbia Musical Treasury P3S 5806)
WHIO Radio Christmas Feelings (Sound Approach/CSP P 16366)
Christmasland — Many Moods of Christmas, The (Columbia Special Products P 12013)
Have Yourself a Merry Little Christmas — Very Merry Christmas, A, Volume IV (Columbia Special Products CSS 1464)
Medley: I Love the Winter Weather/I've Got My Love to Keep Me Warm — Carols and Candlelight (Columbia Special Products P 12525)
Great Songs of Christmas, The, Album Eight (Columbia Special Products CSS 888)
Magnavox Album of Christmas Music (Columbia Special Products CSQ 11093)
Medley: We Wish You a Merry Christmas/Silent Night/O Come, All Ye Faithful/Jingle Bells — Joyous Christmas, Volume V (Columbia Special Products C 10398)
Medley: We Wish You a Merry Christmas/Silent Night/O Come All Ye Faithful/Jingle Bells/Where Is Love — Christmas Greetings, Vol. 3 (Columbia Special Products P 11383)
My Favorite Things — Collection of Christmas Favorites, A (Columbia Special Products P 14988)
Happy Holidays, Album 8 (Columbia Special Products C 11086)
Merry Christmas (Columbia Musical Treasury 3P 6306)
Santa Claus Is Coming to Town — Christmas Is... (Columbia Special Products P 11417)
Great Songs of Christmas, The, Album Seven (Columbia Special Products CSS 547)
Ronco Presents A Christmas Gift (Columbia Special Products P 12430)
60 Christmas Classics (Sessions DVL2-0723)
Tony Bennett Show, The — For Christmas Seals...A Matter of Life and Breath (Decca Custom Style F)
What Child Is This — Great Songs of Christmas, The, Album Eight (Columbia Special Products CSS 888)
When Lights Are Low — Happy Holidays, Volume II (Columbia Special Products CSM 348)
White Christmas — Christmas Greetings, Vol. 4 (Columbia Special Products P 11987)
Home for Christmas (Columbia Musical Treasury P3S 5608)
Home for Christmas (Realm 2V 8101)
Jazzy Wonderland, A (Columbia 1P 8120)
60 Christmas Classics (Sessions DVL2-0723)
Winter Wonderland — Joyous Songs of Christmas, The (Columbia Special Products C 10400)
60 Christmas Classics (Sessions DVL2-0723)

Label, Number	Title (A Side/B Side)	Year	VG	VG+	NM

BENOIT, DAVID
On Various-Artists Collections

Carol of the Bells	GRP Christmas Collection, A (GRP 9574)				

BENSON, RICHARD, AND HIS ORCHESTRA
On Various-Artists Collections

Christmas Suite for Orchestra	Joyous Music for Christmas Time (Reader's Digest RD 45-M)				

BENTON, BROOK
45s

Cotillion 44141	Soul Santa/Let Us All Get Together with the Lord	1971	2.00	4.00	8.00
Mercury 30101	Merry Christmas, Happy New Year/This Time Of The Year	196?	2.00	4.00	8.00
— Reissue					
Mercury 71554	This Time of the Year/Nothing in the World	1959	3.75	7.50	15.00
Mercury 71558	This Time of the Year/How Many Times	1959	3.75	7.50	15.00
Mercury 71730	This Time of the Year/Merry Christmas, Happy New Year	1960	3.00	6.00	12.00
Mercury 72214	This Time of the Year/You're All I Want for Christmas	1963	2.50	5.00	10.00
RCA Victor 47-9031	Our First Christmas Together/Silent Night	1966	3.00	6.00	12.00

Albums

HMC 830 724	Beautiful Memories of Christmas	1983	3.00	6.00	12.00

On Various-Artists Collections

This Time of the Year	Best of Christmas (Mistletoe MLP-1209)				
You're All I Want for Christmas	Best of Christmas (Mistletoe MLP-1209)				

BERNSTEIN, LEONARD
Also see NEW YORK PHILHARMONIC.
On Various-Artists Collections

O Come All Ye Faithful	Carols and Candlelight (Columbia Special Products P 12525)				

BERRY, CHUCK
45s

Chess 1714	Run Rudolph Run/Merry Christmas Baby	1958	7.50	15.00	30.00
Collectables 3437	Run Rudolph Run/Merry Christmas Baby	199?	—	—	3.00

On Various-Artists Collections

Merry Christmas Baby	Happy Holidays, Vol. 23 (MCA Special Products 15042)				
	Have a Merry Chess Christmas (Chess/MCA CH-25210)				
	Rockin' Little Christmas (MCA 25084)				
Run Rudolph Run	Have a Merry Chess Christmas (Chess/MCA CH-25210)				
	Jingle Bell Rock (Time-Life SRNR-XM)				
	Rockin' Little Christmas (MCA 25084)				

BERRY, CLEVELAND, QUINTET
45s

Discovery (# unknown)	Christmas Bum/Good Morning Miss Lady	19??	—	3.00	6.00

BERRY, JOHN
45s

Capitol Nashville S7-18910	O Holy Night/O Come Emmanuel	1995	—	—	3.00

BERT AND ERNIE
On Various-Artists Collections

Have Yourself a Merry Little Christmas	Merry Christmas from Sesame Street (CRA CTW 25516)				

BERT/ERNIE/PRAIRIE DAWN/HERRY MONSTER/GROVER/COOKIE MONSTER
On Various-Artists Collections

Christmas Pageant, A	Merry Christmas from Sesame Street (CRA CTW 25516)				

BERTRAM, BOB
45s

Bertram International 201	A Christmas Aloha for You/I Don't Need a Thing for Christmas	1958	3.75	7.50	15.00

BERU REVUE, BUNNY DRUMS, DA PLIARS, PRETTY POISON, THE HOOTERS & THE VELS
45s

Half Track 914	Hang Up Your Stockings/Sleigh Ride	1984	—	2.50	5.00

BETRO, DOM
45s

(no label) 101281	Merry Christmas Darling/I'll Be Home For Christmas	197?	—	2.00	4.00

Label, Number		Title (A Side/B Side)	Year	VG	VG+	NM
BEULAH						
45s						
Beulah 11181		Christmas America Is Proud of Nixon/Santa Claus Kissed Me	197?	2.50	5.00	10.00
BEVEL, CHARLES						
45s						
A&M 1481		Black Santa Claus/Making A Decision (Bring On Sunshine)	1973	—	3.00	6.00
A&M AM-8725		Black Santa Claus/Sally B. White	199?	—	—	3.00
— Reissue						
BEVERLY						
45s						
Deram 7502		Happy New Year/Where The Good Times Are	1966	2.50	5.00	10.00
BEVERLY SISTERS, THE						
45s						
London 1862		The Little Drummer Boy/Strawberry Fair	1958	3.00	6.00	12.00
BEVIS, J. S. & GENO WHITE						
45s						
Christmas Club 111287		Kringle Jingle/Santa Goes Surfing	196?	2.50	5.00	10.00
BICKEL, BILL, TRIO						
45s						
Coral 60307		The Christmas Tree Angel/Christmas Island	1950	3.75	7.50	15.00
BIG BEN BANJO BAND, THE						
45s						
Buena Vista 439		Jolly Holiday/Mary Poppins Medley	1964	3.00	6.00	12.00

BIG BIRD/SUSAN AND GORDON/BOB/GROVER
On Various-Artists Collections

It's Beginning to Look a Lot Like Christmas Medley		Merry Christmas from Sesame Street (CRA CTW 25516)				

BIG MAYBELLE						
45s						
Savoy 1541		White Christmas/Silent Night	1958	3.75	7.50	15.00
BIG MOUTH						
45s						
Atlantic 89024		X-mass Rapp/Big Mouth	1988	—	—	3.00
Atlantic 89024	PS	X-mass Rapp/Big Mouth	1988	—	—	3.00
BIGGS, E. POWER						
Albums						
Columbia Masterworks ML 5567	M	Joyeaux Noel: Twelve Noels by Louis Clark Daquin	1960	3.75	7.50	15.00
Columbia Masterworks MS 6167	S	Joyeaux Noel: Twelve Noels by Louis Clark Daquin	1960	5.00	10.00	20.00

On Various-Artists Collections

Deck the Halls	Merry Christmas from... (Reader's Digest RD4-83)
Der Tag, Der Ist So Freudenreich	Very Merry Christmas, A (Columbia Special Products CSS 563)
Good King Wenceslas	Magic of Christmas, The (Columbia Musical Treasury P3S 5806)
Holly and the Ivy, The	Home for Christmas (Columbia Musical Treasury P3S 5608)
	Joy to the World (30 Classic Christmas Melodies) (Columbia Special Products P3 14654)
	Magnavox Album of Christmas Music (Columbia Special Products CSQ 11093)
Joy to the World	Happy Holidays, Album Nine (Columbia Special Products P 11793)
Medley: Merry Christmas/ Dame, Get Up and Bake Your Pies/ Christmas Is Coming	Joyous Christmas, Volume 6 (Columbia Special Products C 11083)
Noel We Sing	Joy to the World (30 Classic Christmas Melodies) (Columbia Special Products P3 14654)
O Tannenbaum	It's Christmastime! (Columbia Special Products CSM 429)
Unto Us a Child Is Born	Merry Christmas (Columbia Musical Treasury 3P 6306)
We Three Kings of Orient Are	Joy to the World (30 Classic Christmas Melodies) (Columbia Special Products P3 14654)

BIGGS, RICHARD KEYS						
Albums						
Capitol T 9013	M	Christmas Bells	1954	5.00	10.00	20.00

Label, Number		Title (A Side/B Side)	Year	VG	VG+	NM
BIKEL, THEODORE						
On Various-Artists Collections						
Sweetest Dreams Be Thine		Very Merry Christmas, A (Columbia Special Products CSS 563)				
BILL & "SHAKEY"						
45s						
WHN Sounds 71284		Woodolph (The Petrified Red-Nosed Reindeer)/Santa's Helper	19??	—	—	3.00
WHN Sounds 71284	PS	Woodolph (The Petrified Red-Nosed Reindeer)/Santa's Helper	19??	—	—	3.00
BING & BOWIE – See DAVID BOWIE.						
BINKLEY, CAROLYN						
45s						
Columbia 43468		I Want A Baby Brother For Christmas/	1965	2.50	5.00	10.00
		All I Want For Christmas Is My Two Front Teeth				
Columbia 43468	PS	I Want A Baby Brother For Christmas/	1965	3.75	7.50	15.00
		All I Want For Christmas Is My Two Front Teeth				
Columbia 43918		I Want a Baby Brother for Christmas/Mister Pilot	1966	2.50	5.00	10.00
BISHOP, BOBBY						
45s						
Goldisc 3027		Santa Claus (Don't Pass Me By)/Ann Marie	1961	5.00	10.00	20.00
BISHOP, ELVIN						
45s						
Capricorn 0248		Silent Night (Vocal Version)/	1975	—	3.00	6.00
		Silent Night (Instrumental Version)				
On Various-Artists Collections						
Silent Night		Christmas Rock Album, The (Priority SL 9465)				
BITE THE WAX GODHEAD						
45s						
Flying A 19763		Lookin' For Santa/(I'll Be Glad When) Christmas Is Over	1988	—	2.50	5.00
— *B-side by the Hungry Dutchmen; red vinyl*						
Flying A 19763	PS	Lookin' For Santa/(I'll Be Glad When) Christmas Is Over	1988	—	2.50	5.00
— *B-side by the Hungry Dutchmen*						
BLACK, CLINT						
45s						
RCA 3709-7-R		'Til Santa's Gone (I Just Can't Wait) (same on both sides)	1990	—	2.00	4.00
RCA 64442		Life Gets Away/The Kid	1995	—	—	3.00
— *A-side is not a Christmas song*						
BLACK, PABLO						
On Various-Artists Collections						
Silent Night		Reggae Christmas, A (Real Authentic Sound RAS 3101)				
BLACKGIRL						
45s						
RCA 64227		Give Love on Christmas Day/Where Did We Go Wrong	1994	—	2.00	4.00
BLACKHAWK						
45s						
Arista Nashville 13060		We Three Kings (Star of Wonder)/Rudolph the Red-Nosed Reindeer	1996	—	—	3.00
— *B-side by Alan Jackson*						
BLACKWELLS, THE						
45s						
Jamie 1146		The Christmas Holiday/Little Match Girl	1959	5.00	10.00	20.00
Jamie 1173		The Christmas Holiday/Little Match Girl	1960	3.75	7.50	15.00
BLAIR, PAMELA, ET AL.						
On Various-Artists Collections						
Hard Candy Christmas		Best Little Whorehouse in Texas, The (MCA 3049)				

Label, Number	Title (A Side/B Side)	Year	VG	VG+	NM
BLAKE, RICK / GARY KEKEL					
45s					
Keynote 16820	Santa's Christmas Song/Empty Stocking	1986	—	2.00	4.00
BLANC, MEL					
45s					
Capitol F1853	I Tan't Wait Till Quithmuth/Christmas Chopsticks	1951	7.50	15.00	30.00
Capitol F2619	Ya, Das Ist Ein Christmas Tree/I Tan't Wait Till Quithmuth	1953	7.50	15.00	30.00
Capitol F3902	The Hat I Got for Christmas Is Too Beeg/Pancho's Christmas	1959	6.25	12.50	25.00
Warner Bros. 5129	Tweety's Twistmas Troubles/I Keep Hearing Those Bells	1959	6.25	12.50	25.00
BLAND, BOBBY					
45s					
MCA 52508	You Are My Christmas/New Merry Christmas Baby	1984	—	—	3.00
BLANK, CHAPLAIN DICK, & TRIO					
7-Inch Extended Plays					
Canterburry 5006	Deck The Halls/God Rest Ye Merry Gentlemen// What Child Is This?/Good King Wenceslas	19??	—	2.00	4.00
Canterburry 5006 PS	Deck The Halls / God Rest Ye Merry Gentlemen// What Child Is This?/ Good King Wenceslas	19??	—	2.00	4.00
BLANTON, LOY					
45s					
Soundwaves 4744	Christmas At The Jersey Lily Lounge/Ghost Story	1980	—	2.00	4.00
BLAZONCZYK, EDDIE'S, VERSATONES					
45s					
Bel-Aire 2960	All I Want For Christmas Is You/White Christmas	19??	—	2.00	4.00
BLEVINS, CHUCK					
45s					
Foxie 7006	Sleigh Bell Rock/(B-side unknown)	1959	5.00	10.00	20.00
BLOCH, RAY					
45s					
Coral 60767	Adeste Fideles/Cantique de Noel	1952	3.00	6.00	12.00
Coral 60768	Here We Come a-Caroling-The First Nowell- God Rest Ye Merry Gentlemen/Joy to the World- Good King Wenceslas-Angels We Have Heard on High	1952	3.00	6.00	12.00
Coral 60769	Silent Night/Deck the Halls-Away in the Manger- Hark The Herald Angels Sing	1952	3.00	6.00	12.00
Coral 60863	The Christmas Song/White Christmas	1952	3.00	6.00	12.00
— With Monica Lewis					
Coral 60864	Santa Claus Is Comin'/Let It Snow	1952	3.00	6.00	12.00
Coral 60865	Jingle Bells/Rudolph the Red-Nosed Reindeer	1952	3.00	6.00	12.00
BLONDIE CO-STARRING FREDDIE					
On Various-Artists Collections					
Yuletown Throw Down (Rapture)	(untitled) (Flexipop 15)				
BLOW, KURTIS					
12-Inch Singles					
Mercury MDS-4009	Christmas Rappin'/(B-side unknown)	1979	3.00	6.00	12.00
45s					
Mercury DJ 562 (MDS-4009) DJ	Christmas Rappin' Part 1/Christmas Rappin' Part 2	1979	2.00	4.00	8.00
— 45 promo of 12-inch single					
Mercury 76194	Christmas Rappin'/Daydreamin'	1982	—	2.50	5.00
Mercury 810 324-7	Christmas Rappin' Part 2/The Breaks	1983	—	2.00	4.00
BLOWFLY					
12-Inch Singles					
T.K. Disco 453	Blowfly's Christmas Party/Blowfly's New Year's Party	1980	2.00	4.00	8.00
45s					
Collectables 363	Christmas Party/New Years Party	199?	—	—	3.00
— Reissue					

Label, Number	Title (A Side/B Side)	Year	VG	VG+	NM

BLUE BAND, THE
45s
Hot Fudge 104612-1S	Santa's Messin' With The Kid (B-side unknown)	198?	—	2.50	5.00

BLUE CHIPS, THE
45s
Laurel 1026	The New Year's In/Double Dutch Twist	1961	5.00	10.00	20.00

BLUE NOTES, THE
45s
Collectables 1113	Winter Wonderland/O Holy Night	198?	—	2.00	4.00
— *Reissue*					
Val-Ue 215	O Holy Night/Winter Wonderland	1960	12.50	25.00	50.00

BLUE RIDGE QUARTET, THE
Albums
Mark IV 1118	Another Christmas with the Blue Ridge Quartet	197?	2.50	5.00	10.00
Mark IV 21027	Christmas with the Blue Ridge Quartet	197?	2.50	5.00	10.00

BLUES MAGOOS, THE
45s
Mercury 72762	Jingle Bells/Santa Claus Is Coming to Town	1967	2.50	5.00	10.00

BLYTHE, ARTHUR, QUARTET
On Various-Artists Collections
Christmas Song, The	God Rest Ye Merry, Jazzmen (Columbia FC 37551)

BOB B. SOXX AND THE BLUE JEANS
On Various-Artists Collections
Bells of St. Mary's, The	Christmas EP (Philles X-EP)
	Christmas Gift for You from Phil Spector, A (Philles PHLP-4005)
	Phil Spector's Christmas Album (Apple SW 3400)
	Phil Spector: Back to Mono 1958-1969 (Phil Spector/Abkco 7118-1)
Here Comes Santa Claus	Christmas Gift for You from Phil Spector, A (Philles PHLP-4005)
	Phil Spector's Christmas Album (Apple SW 3400)
	Phil Spector: Back to Mono 1958-1969 (Phil Spector/Abkco 7118-1)

BOBBIE & BOOBIE
45s
Dice 480	Cool, Cool Christmas/Teenage Party	195?	50.00	100.00	200.00

BOBBY THE POET – See SENATOR BOBBY.

BOCK, FRED
Albums
Impact R 3479	Upon a Midnight Clear	1977	3.00	6.00	12.00

BOGGUSS, SUZY
45s
Capitol B-44503	Mr. Santa/I'm at Home on the Range	1989	—	2.50	5.00
Capitol Nashville S7-19349	Two-Step Around the Christmas Tree/	1996	—	—	3.00
	I Heard the Bells on Christmas Day				
— *Slightly altered A-side title from original on Liberty*					
Liberty S7-17650	I'll Be Home for Christmas/Mr. Santa	1993	—	2.00	4.00
— *Green vinyl*					
Liberty S7-56805	Two-Step 'Round the Christmas Tree/	1992	—	2.50	5.00
	I Heard the Bells on Christmas Day				

On Various-Artists Collections
First Noel, The	Christmas for the 90's, Volume 2 (Capitol Nashville 1P 8118)
I'll Be Home for Christmas	Christmas for the 90's, Volume 1 (Capitol Nashville 1P 8117)

BOGIE, COLONEL DOUG
45s
ABC 12148	Away in a Manger/Cokey Cokey	1975	—	2.50	5.00

Label, Number		Title (A Side/B Side)	Year	VG	VG+	NM
BOLDEN, LULA						
45s						
Lanor 611		Old Time White Christmas/A Change Is Gonna Come	19??	—	2.00	4.00
— B-side by Mighty Blasters						
BOLGER, RAY						
45s						
Armour 7799		Li'l Elfy/Frosty The Snowman	1963	2.50	5.00	10.00
Armour 7799	PS	L'il Elfy/Frosty The Snowman	1963	5.00	10.00	20.00
BOLTON, MICHAEL						
45s						
Columbia 74798		Reach Out I'll Be There/White Christmas	1992	—	2.00	4.00
— A-side is not a Christmas song						
BON JOVI						
45s						
Jambco 864 432-7		Keep the Faith/I Wish Everyday Could Be Like Christmas	1992	—	—	3.00
— A-side is not a Christmas song						
Mercury JOV 8		Keep The Faith/I Wish Everyday Could Be Like Christmas	1992	—	2.50	5.00
Mercury JOV 8	PS	Keep The Faith/I Wish Everyday Could Be Like Christmas	1992	2.00	4.00	8.00
— A-side is not a Christmas song; record and sleeve are U.K. imports						
Mercury 884 299-7		Price of Love/Silent Night	1986	—	2.00	4.00
— A-side is not a Christmas song						
On Various-Artists Collections						
Back Door Santa		Very Special Christmas, A (A&M SP-3911)				
BONAIRS, THE						
45s						
Dootone 325		It's Christmas/I'm Alone Tonight	1953	37.50	75.00	150.00
— B-side by Ernie Tavares Trio						
BONAPARTE, GONZALES						
45s						
Madison 142		Why Is There Christmas/Christmas Medley	1960	3.75	7.50	15.00
BOND, JOHNNY						
45s						
Columbia 20756		I Wanna Do Something For Santa/Jingle Bell Boogie	1950	5.00	10.00	20.00
Columbia 40080		Santa Got Stuck in the Chimney/I Said a Prayer for Santa Claus	1953	3.75	7.50	15.00
— With Jimmy Boyd						
BONDS, GARY U.S.						
45s						
Legrand 1045		Call Me for Christmas/Mixed Up Faculty	1967	3.00	6.00	12.00
BONEY M						
45s						
Sire 1036		Mary's Boy Child-Oh My Lord/Dancing in the Street	1978	—	2.50	5.00
Sire 49144		Mary's Boy Child/Oh My Lord//He Was a Steppenwolf	1979	—	3.00	6.00
BONNIE LOU						
On Various-Artists Collections						
Christmas Is Gettin' Mighty Close		Ten Tunes of Christmas (Candee 50-50)				
It's Christmas-Time Again		Ten Tunes of Christmas (Candee 50-50)				
BONNIE SISTERS, THE						
45s						
Rainbow 328		I Saw Mommy Cha Cha Cha with You Know Who?/Cry Baby	1955	5.00	10.00	20.00
BONO, SONNY & LITTLE TOOTSIE – See SONNY.						
BOOGIE KINGS, THE						
45s						
PIC 1 128		Last Christmas Eve/(Sing Along) Last Christmas Eve	196?	5.00	10.00	20.00

Label, Number		Title (A Side/B Side)	Year	VG	VG+	NM

BOOKENDS, THE
45s

Capitol 4667		Christmas Kisses/Let Me Walk with You	1961	3.75	7.50	15.00

BOOKER T. AND THE MG'S
45s

Stax 203		Jingle Bells/Winter Wonderland	1966	3.00	6.00	12.00
Stax 236		Silver Bells/Winter Snow	1967	3.00	6.00	12.00

Albums

Stax ST-713	M	In the Christmas Spirit	1966	100.00	200.00	400.00
— Fingers and piano keys cover						
Stax STS-713	S	In the Christmas Spirit	1966	100.00	200.00	400.00
— Fingers and piano keys cover						
Stax ST-713	M	In the Christmas Spirit	1967	50.00	100.00	200.00
— Santa Claus cover						
Stax STS-713	S	In the Christmas Spirit	1967	50.00	100.00	200.00
— Santa Claus cover						

On Various-Artists Collections

Jingle Bells	Jingle Bell Rock (Time-Life SRNR-XM)

BOONE, PAT
45s

Buena Vista 487		Little Green Tree/The Sounds of Christmas	1973	—	3.50	7.00
Dot 16547		Santa's Coming in a Whirleybird/Oh Holy Night	1963	2.50	5.00	10.00
Lamb & Lion 818		It's OK to Be a Kid at Christmas/Don't Let the Season Pass You By	1979	—	2.50	5.00

7-Inch Extended Plays

Dot DEP 1062		White Christmas/Silent Night//	1957	7.50	15.00	30.00
		Jingle Bells/Santa Claus Is Comin' to Town				
Dot DEP 1062	PS	Merry Christmas	1957	7.50	15.00	30.00

Albums

Dot DLP 3222	M	White Christmas	1959	6.25	12.50	25.00
Dot DLP 25222	S	White Christmas	1959	7.50	15.00	30.00
MCA 15028	S	White Christmas	198?	2.50	5.00	10.00
— Reissue of Dot LP						
Pickwick SPC 1024		White Christmas	197?	2.50	5.00	10.00

On Various-Artists Collections

Christmas Waltz	Many Moods of Christmas, The (Columbia Special Products P 12013)
Joy to the World	12 Days of Christmas, The (Pickwick SPC-1021)
Sweetest Song, The	Wonderful World of Christmas, The, Album Two (Capitol Special Markets SL-8025)

BOONE, PAT, FAMILY
On Various-Artists Collections

Hark the Herald Angels Sing	Home for the Holidays (MCA MSM-35007)
Silent Night	Home for the Holidays (MCA MSM-35007)

BOONES, THE
On Various-Artists Collections

Gift of Love	On This Christmas Night (Songbird MCA-3184)

BORESON, STAN
45s

Golden Crest 575		Christmas In Seattle/	19??	—	2.00	4.00
		The Most Beautiful Time Of the Year Is Christmas				

BORESON, STAN, AND DOUG SETTERBERG
Albums

Golden Crest CR 31021		Yust Go Nuts at Christmas	197?	3.00	6.00	12.00

BOSTICK, CALVIN
45s

Chess 1530		Christmas Won't Be Christmas Without You/Four-Eleven Boogie	1952	37.50	75.00	150.00

BOSTON CAMERATA, THE
Albums

Nonesuch H-71315		A Medieval Christmas	1975	3.00	6.00	12.00
Nonesuch H-71354		Sing We Noel: Christmas Music from England and Early America	1978	3.00	6.00	12.00

Label, Number		Title (A Side/B Side)	Year	VG	VG+	NM

BOSTON POPS ORCHESTRA (FIEDLER)
Also see ARTHUR FIEDLER.

45s

Label, Number		Title (A Side/B Side)	Year	VG	VG+	NM
RCA Victor 49-0515		Sleigh Ride/Serenata	1949	7.50	15.00	30.00
— Originals on red vinyl						
RCA Victor KO7W-1589	DJ	White Christmas/(B-side unknown)	1959	3.75	7.50	15.00

Albums

Label, Number		Title (A Side/B Side)	Year	VG	VG+	NM
Deutche Grammophon 419 414-1		White Christmas	198?	2.50	5.00	10.00
Polydor PD 5004		A Christmas Festival	1970	2.50	5.00	10.00
RCA Gold Seal AGL1-3436		Pops Christmas Party	1979	2.50	5.00	10.00
— Reissue of LSC-2329						
RCA Red Seal LSC-2329	S	Pops Christmas Party	1959	20.00	40.00	80.00
— Original copies have "shaded dog" with small "RCA Victor" logo						
RCA Red Seal LSC-2329	S	Pops Christmas Party	1964	7.50	15.00	30.00
— Second editions have "white dog" with large "RCA Victor" logo						
RCA Red Seal LSC-3324		Pops Goes Christmas	1972	2.50	5.00	10.00
— Compilation of older Christmas recordings						

On Various-Artists Collections

Christmas Festival, A (Medley)	Christmas Eve with Colonel Sanders (RCA Victor PRS-256)
	For a Musical Merry Christmas (RCA Victor PR-149A)
	For a Musical Merry Christmas, Volume 3 (RCA Victor PRM-221)
	Happy Holidays, Volume IV (RCA Victor PRS-267)
	Very Merry Christmas, A, Volume VI (RCA Special Products PRS-427)
	RCA Victor Presents Music for the Twelve Days of Christmas (RCA Victor PRS-188)
	60 Christmas Classics (Sessions DVL2-0723)
	October Christmas Sampler 59-40-41 (RCA Victor SPS-33-54)
Dance of the Sugar Plum Fairy/ Dance of the Toy Flutes	Very Merry Christmas, A, Volume IV (Columbia Special Products CSS 1464)
Hansel and Gretel: Overture/Dream Pantomime	American Family Album of Favorite Christmas Music, The (RCA Red Seal VCS-7060)
Medley: Here We Come a-Caroling/ O Christmas Tree/ I Saw Three Ships	Happy Holidays, Volume 13 (RCA Special Products DPL1-0319)
	Time-Life Treasury of Christmas, The (Time-Life STL-107)
Nutcracker, The: Christmas Tree Scene/Dance of the Sugar-Plum Fairy	American Family Album of Favorite Christmas Music, The (RCA Red Seal VCS-7060)
Nutcracker, The: Dance of the Sugar-Plum Fairy	Family Christmas Collection, The (Time-Life STL-131)
Nutcracker, The: Overture/ Dance of the Sugar Plum Fairy	Christmas Festival of Songs and Carols, Volume 2 (RCA Victor PRM-195)
Overture; Marche (from The Nutcracker)	Merry Christmas (RCA Victor PRM-168)
Parade of the Wooden Soldiers	American Family Album of Favorite Christmas Music, The (RCA Red Seal VCS-7060)
Rudolph, the Red-Nosed Reindeer	American Family Album of Favorite Christmas Music, The (RCA Red Seal VCS-7060)
	Christmas in New York (RCA Victor PRM-257)
	Christmas Programming from RCA Victor (RCA Victor SP-33-66)
Santa Claus Is Comin' to Town	American Family Album of Favorite Christmas Music, The (RCA Red Seal VCS-7060)
	Happy Holidays, Volume 15 (RCA Special Products DPL1-0453)
Sleigh Ride	American Family Album of Favorite Christmas Music, The (RCA Red Seal VCS-7060)
	Brightest Stars of Christmas, The (RCA Special Products DPL1-0086)
	Celebrate the Season with Tupperware (RCA Special Products DPL1-0803)
	Christmas in California (RCA Victor PRS-276)
	Christmas in New York Volume 2 (RCA Victor PRS-270)
	Christmas Through the Years (Reader's Digest RDA-143)
	Christmas with Colonel Sanders (RCA Victor PRS-291)
	Christmastime in Carol and Song (RCA PRM-271)
	For a Musical Merry Christmas, Vol. Two (RCA Victor PRM 189)
	Happy Holidays, Vol. III (RCA Victor PRS-255)
	Magic of Christmas, The (Columbia Musical Treasury P3S 5806)
	Merry Christmas (Columbia Musical Treasury 3P 6306)
	Music to Trim Your Tree By (RCA Victor PRM 225)
	60 Christmas Classics (Sessions DVL2-0723)
	Time-Life Treasury of Christmas, The, Volume Two (Time-Life STL-108)
	Very Merry Christmas, A, Volume 5 (RCA Special Products PRS-343)
Sleigh Ride (Mozart)	American Family Album of Favorite Christmas Music, The (RCA Red Seal VCS-7060)
	Happy Holidays, Volume 18 (RCA Special Products DPL1-0608)
White Christmas	American Family Album of Favorite Christmas Music, The (RCA Red Seal VCS-7060)
	Happy Holidays, Volume 19 (RCA Special Products DPL1-0689)
	60 Christmas Classics (Sessions DVL2-0723)
Winter Wonderland	American Family Album of Favorite Christmas Music, The (RCA Red Seal VCS-7060)
	Happy Holidays, Volume 14 (RCA Special Products DPL1-0376)
	Very Merry Christmas, A, Volume VII (RCA Special Products DPL1-0049)

BOSTON POPS ORCHESTRA (FIEDLER) WITH AL HIRT
On Various-Artists Collections

Toy Trumpet, The	Time-Life Treasury of Christmas, The, Volume Two (Time-Life STL-108)

Label, Number		Title (A Side/B Side)	Year	VG	VG+	NM

BOSTON POPS ORCHESTRA (WILLIAMS)
Albums
| Philips 416 287-1 | | We Wish You a Merry Christmas | 198? | 2.50 | 5.00 | 10.00 |

BOTICELLI, ANTHONY
Albums
| Caroleer X 1702 | M | Christmas Favorites | 196? | 3.00 | 6.00 | 12.00 |
| Caroleer SX 1702 | S | Christmas Favorites | 196? | 3.75 | 7.50 | 15.00 |

BOTTOM 12
45s
| Apparition 001 | | Jingle Bells/Fuck Christmas//No Butt No Glove | 19?? | — | 2.50 | 5.00 |
| Apparition 001 | PS | Jingle Bells/Fuck Christmas//No Butt No Glove | 19?? | — | 2.50 | 5.00 |

BOUCHER, PEGI
45s
| Hiback 101 | | The Christmas Clock/Christmas Tree Heaven | 1966 | 2.00 | 4.00 | 8.00 |
| Hiback 101 | PS | The Christmas Clock/Christmas Tree Heaven | 1966 | 3.75 | 7.50 | 15.00 |

BOWENS, PRIVATE CHARLES
45s
| Rojac 111 | | Christmas In Viet Nam/(B-side unknown) | 196? | 15.00 | 30.00 | 60.00 |

BOWERS, GEORGE
45s
| NTM 001 | | Christopher the Christmas Tree/Lonely Christmas | 1971 | 2.00 | 4.00 | 8.00 |
| Paramount 0139 | | Christopher the Christmas Tree/Lonely Christmas | 1971 | — | 3.00 | 6.00 |

BOWERS, KENNY
45s
| Columbia 41049 | | Weach For The Wafter, Santa/
An Ax, An Apple And A Buckskin Jacket | 1957 | 3.75 | 7.50 | 15.00 |

BOWIE, DAVID
12-Inch Singles
| RCA Victor BOWT 12 | | Dialogue (Peace On Earth)/Peace On Earth/
Little Drummer Boy//Fantastic Voyage | 1982 | 5.00 | — | 20.00 |

— *A-side with Bing Crosby; U.K. import*

45s
| B&B Records 100 | | Little Drummer Boy/Heroes | 197? | 12.50 | 25.00 | 50.00 |

— *As "Bing & Bowie"; full-length version with spoken intro; bootleg*

| RCA PH-13400 | | Peace on Earth-Little Drummer Boy/Fantastic Voyage | 1982 | — | 2.50 | 5.00 |

— *A-side with Bing Crosby*

| RCA PH-13400 | PS | Peace on Earth-Little Drummer Boy/Fantastic Voyage | 1982 | 2.50 | 5.00 | 10.00 |

— *A-side with Bing Crosby*

BOWLING, SHELL
45s
| Soundwaves 4690 | | Christmas Time Is Coming/Born On Christmas Day | 1980 | — | 2.00 | 4.00 |

BOWMAN, JIMMY
45s
| Soma 1152 | | Big Red And Cool Yule/Portrait Of Jenny | 1960 | 5.00 | 10.00 | 20.00 |

BOY CHORISTERS OF THE CHURCH OF THE TRANSFIGURATION (NY)
On Various-Artists Collections
| Rocking Carol | | Life Treasury of Christmas Music, The (Project/Capitol TL 100) | | | | |

BOYD, BILL
45s
| RCA Victor 48-0129 | | Jingle Bells/Up on the House Top | 1949 | 12.50 | 25.00 | 50.00 |

— *Originals on green vinyl*

| RCA Victor 48-0129 | | Jingle Bells/Up On The House Top | 1950 | 6.25 | 12.50 | 25.00 |

— *Later issues on black vinyl*

Label, Number		Title (A Side/B Side)	Year	VG	VG+	NM
BOYD, CHARLIE						
On Various-Artists Collections						
First Noel, The		Home for Christmas (Realm 2V 8101)				
BOYD, JIMMY						
45s						
Columbia 4-152 (90174)		I Saw Mommy Kissing Santa Claus/Thumbelina	1952	5.00	10.00	20.00
— Yellow-label Children's Series issue						
Columbia 4-152 (90174)	PS	I Saw Mommy Kissing Santa Claus/Thumbelina	1952	6.25	12.50	25.00
Columbia 4-183		Santa Got Stuck In The Chimney/I Said A Prayer For Santa Claus	1953	3.75	7.50	15.00
— Yellow-label Children's Series issue						
Columbia 4-183	PS	Santa Got Stuck In The Chimney/I Said A Prayer For Santa Claus	1953	5.00	10.00	20.00
Columbia 39871		I Saw Mommy Kissing Santa Claus/Thumbelina	1952	3.75	7.50	15.00
Columbia 40070		I Saw Mommy Kissing Santa Claus/Santa Claus Is Coming to Town	1953	3.00	6.00	12.00
Columbia 40071		Winter Wonderland/Here Comes Santa Claus	1953	3.00	6.00	12.00
Columbia 40072		Silent Night, Holy Night/Frosty the Snowman	1953	3.00	6.00	12.00
Columbia 40073		The Little Match Girl/Rudolph, the Red-Nosed Reindeer	1953	3.00	6.00	12.00
Columbia 40080		Santa Got Stuck in the Chimney/I Said a Prayer for Santa Claus	1953	3.75	7.50	15.00
— With Johnny Bond						
Columbia 40365		I Saw Mommy Do the Mambo (With You Know Who)/Santa Claus Blues	1954	3.75	7.50	15.00
Columbia 40601		Reindeer Rock/A Kiss for Christmas	1955	5.00	10.00	20.00
Underground 1110		I Saw Mommy Kissing Santa Claus/It's A Sin To Tell A Lie	198?	—	—	3.00
— Canadian import, widely distributed in U.S.; B-side by Somethin' Smith and the Redheads						
7-Inch Extended Plays						
Columbia B-1913		I Saw Mommy Kissing Santa Claus/Jingle Bells//I Said A Prayer For Santa Claus/Santa Got Stuck In The Chimney	195?	3.00	6.00	12.00
Columbia B-1913	PS	Jimmy Boyd	195?	3.75	7.50	15.00
On Various-Artists Collections						
I Saw Mommy Kissing Santa Claus		Billboard Greatest Christmas Hits, 1935-1954 (Rhino R1 70637)				
		First Christmas Record for Children (Harmony HS 14554)				
		Merry Christmas from... (Reader's Digest RD4-83)				
		12 Hits of Christmas (United Artists UA-LA669-R)				
BOYD, LIONA						
Albums						
CBS FM 37248		A Guitar for Christmas	1981	3.00	6.00	12.00
BOYER, DAVE						
Albums						
Word 8612		Christmas with Dave Boyer	198?	2.50	5.00	10.00
BOYS FROM INDIANA						
45s						
Old Heritage 8812	PS	Santa Got Picked Up For A D.U.I./Christmas Time	1988	—	2.50	5.00
Old Heritage 8812		Santa Got Picked Up For A D.U.I./Christmas Time	1988	—	2.50	5.00
BOYS NEXT DOOR, THE						
45s						
Atco 6455		Christmas Kiss/The Wildest Christmas	1966	2.50	5.00	10.00
BOYZ II MEN						
45s						
Motown 2218		Let It Snow/Silent Night	1993	—	—	3.00
BRADLEY, HAL, ORCHESTRA						
45s						
Delhi 0770		Space Age Santa Claus/When Christmas Bells Are Ringing	196?	2.00	4.00	8.00
BRADLEY, JAN						
45s						
Hootenanny 1		Christmas Time (Part 1)/Christmas Time (Part 2)	1962	3.00	6.00	12.00
BRADLEY, OWEN						
45s						
Coral 60273		Silent Night/Oh Holy Night	1950	3.75	7.50	15.00
Coral 60274		The First Nowell/Joy to the World	1950	3.75	7.50	15.00
Coral 60275		Deck the Halls/Ring Out the Bells	1950	3.75	7.50	15.00
Coral 60276		O Come All Ye Faithful/The Birthday of the King	1950	3.75	7.50	15.00

Label, Number		Title (A Side/B Side)	Year	VG	VG+	NM
Coral 60564		Uncle Mistletoe/Merry Christmas Rhumba	1951	3.75	7.50	15.00
Coral 60594		Santa Claus Looks Like My Daddy/Uncle Mistletoe	1951	3.75	7.50	15.00
Coral 60836		O Come All Ye Faithful/Blest Be the Tie That Binds	1952	3.00	6.00	12.00
Albums						
Coral CRL 56012	10	Christmas Time	1950	20.00	40.00	80.00
Decca DL 8652	M	Joyous Bells of Christmas	1957	7.50	15.00	30.00
On Various-Artists Collections						
Medley: Joy to the World/		Decca 38170 (title unknown) (Decca DL 38170)				
God Rest Ye Merry, Gentlemen/Away in a Manger						

BRADY BUNCH, THE
45s

Paramount 0062		Frosty the Snowman/Silver Bells	1970	3.00	6.00	12.00
Paramount 0062	PS	Frosty the Snowman/Silver Bells	1970	5.00	10.00	20.00
Albums						
Paramount PAS-5026		Merry Christmas from the Brady Bunch	1971	20.00	40.00	80.00
On Various-Artists Collections						
Jingle Bells		Home for the Holidays (MCA MSM-35007)				

BRADY, DAPHNE
45s

Ref-O-Ree 714		Christmas Across The Tracks (Part 1)/	19??	—	2.50	5.00
		Christmas Across The Tracks (Part 2)				

BRAND, OSCAR
Albums

Caedmon TC 1658		Singing Is Believing: Songs of the Advent Season	1980	3.00	6.00	12.00

BRANDO, HUB
45s

Teardrop 3008		Jingle Bells/Eskimo Walk	1962	3.00	6.00	12.00

BRANDON, JOHNNY
45s

Laurie 3042		Santa Claus Jr./Theme from Santa Claus Jr.	1959	3.00	6.00	12.00

BRANDON, PATTI
45s

Vik 0245		Christmas Prayer/Fairyland	1956	3.75	7.50	15.00

BRANDYWINE CHORALE, THE
45s

Coral 62434		Christmas Is Here Now/The Old Bell Ringer	1964	2.00	4.00	8.00
Coral 98126	DJ	Christmas Is Here Now/The Old Bell Ringer	1964	2.50	5.00	10.00
Coral 98126	PS	Christmas Is Here Now/The Old Bell Ringer	1964	3.00	6.00	12.00
— 1964 Christmas Seals promotional record						

BRATTLES, THE
On Various-Artists Collections

Christmas Song, The		(untitled) (Flexipop 15)				

BRAUN, BOB
Albums

United Artists UAS 6664		Christmas in Your Heart	1968	3.00	6.00	12.00
On Various-Artists Collections						
Sing a Song of Christmas		Ten Tunes of Christmas (Candee 50-50)				

BRENNAN, WALTER
45s

Liberty 55518		White Christmas/Henry Had a Merry Christmas	1962	3.00	6.00	12.00
Liberty 55518	PS	Henry Had A Merry Christmas/White Christmas	1962	5.00	10.00	20.00
Albums						
Liberty LRP-3257	M	'Twas the Night Before Christmas Back Home	1962	5.00	10.00	20.00
Liberty LST-7257	S	'Twas the Night Before Christmas Back Home	1962	6.25	12.50	25.00

BRENT, RANDY, AND THE HIGHWAY SERENADERS
45s

Highway 1007	DJ	What I Want For Christmas, Is Christmas/Candles In Heaven	19??	—	2.50	5.00

Label, Number		Title (A Side/B Side)	Year	VG	VG+	NM
BRETTON, ELISE						
45s						
Plaza 5004	PS	Christmas Without You/Give Your Love For Christmas	19??	—	2.50	5.00
Plaza 5004		Christmas Without You/Give Your Love For Christmas	19??	—	2.50	5.00
BREWER, SPENCER						
On Various-Artists Collections						
Ukrainian Carol		Narada: The Christmas Collection (Narada N-63902)				
BREWER, TERESA						
45s						
Coral 61078		I Saw Mommy Kissing Santa Claus/Ebenezer Scrooge	1953	3.00	6.00	12.00
Coral 61079		I Just Can't Wait Till Christmas/Too Fat for the Chimney	1953	3.00	6.00	12.00
Coral 62058		Jingle Bell Rock/I Like Christmas	1958	2.50	5.00	10.00
Coral 69039		Too Fat For The Chimney/I Just Can't Wait Till Christmas	1953	3.75	7.50	15.00
— Maroon label with silver print						
Teresa Brewer TB-1	DJ	Take a Message to Jesus (same on both sides)	198?	—	2.00	4.00
7-Inch Extended Plays						
RCA ZE-11882		Jingle Bells/Santa Claus Is Comin' To Town- The Christmas Song//Deck The Halls/Away In A Manger	1979	2.50	5.00	10.00
— Name of EP is "Merry Christmas From Teresa Brewer"; picture label, no PS						
Albums						
Columbia PW 40113		At Christmas Time	1985	2.50	5.00	10.00
Coral CRL 57144	M	Teresa Brewer At Christmas Time	1957	7.50	15.00	30.00
BRIGGS, LILLIAN						
45s						
Epic 9138		Rock and Roll-y Poly Santa Claus/Can't Stop	1955	7.50	15.00	30.00
BRIGGS, RICK						
45s						
Rockin' 2934		Christmas Tears/Christmas Everywhere	19??	—	2.50	5.00
BRIGHT, DICK, YOUTH CHORALE						
45s						
Ambition 102		(What's So Funny 'Bout) Peace, Love and Understanding/ Xmas In The Hot Tub	1980	3.00	6.00	12.00
— B-side by Little Roger and the Goosebumps						
BRINE, MARK						
45s						
Society 103		The Christmas Carol No One Listens For/(B-side unknown)	19??	2.00	4.00	8.00
BRITO, PHIL						
45s						
MGM 10779		White Christmas/Ave Maria	1950	3.75	7.50	15.00
BRITT, ELTON						
45s						
Decca 31568		Christmas in November/Jingle Bell Polka	1963	3.00	6.00	12.00
RCA Victor 47-4988		Merry Texas Christmas/Christmas Will Be Here	1952	5.00	10.00	20.00
BROCK, WAYNE						
45s						
Fable 533		Santa Claus Has A Secret/Too Late To Shed A Tear	19??	2.50	5.00	10.00
BROGGS, PETER						
On Various-Artists Collections						
Twelve Days of Christmas		Reggae Christmas, A (Real Authentic Sound RAS 3101)				

BROGGS, PETER/DON CARLOS/FREDDIE MCGREGOR/ SMILEY/ MICHIGAN/GLENICE

On Various-Artists Collections						
We Wish You a Merry Christmas		Reggae Christmas, A (Real Authentic Sound RAS 3101)				
BROOKMEYER, BOB, QUINTET						
45s						
Pacific Jazz 642		Santa Claus Blues/Sweet Like This	1956	3.75	7.50	15.00

Label, Number		Title (A Side/B Side)	Year	VG	VG+	NM
BROOKS, ALBERT						
45s						
Asylum XMAS 1	DJ	A Daddy's Christmas (mono/stereo)	1974	12.50	25.00	50.00
Asylum XMAS 1	PS	A Daddy's Christmas (mono/stereo)	1974	25.00	50.00	100.00
BROOKS, DONNIE						
45s						
Yardbird 8010		Tree Trimming Time/(Instrumental)	1968	—	3.00	6.00
BROOKS, GARTH						
45s						
Liberty S7-17649		Silent Night/White Christmas	1993	—	2.50	5.00
— Red vinyl						
Liberty S7-57892		God Rest Ye Merry Gentlemen/White Christmas	1992	—	—	3.00
Liberty S7-57893		The Old Man's Back in Town/Santa Looked a Lot Like Daddy	1992	—	—	3.00
Liberty S7-57894		Go Tell It on the Mountain/The Friendly Beast	1992	—	—	3.00
On Various-Artists Collections						
God Rest Ye Merry, Gentlemen		Christmas for the 90's, Volume 1 (Capitol Nashville 1P 8117)				
Silent Night		Christmas for the 90's, Volume 2 (Capitol Nashville 1P 8118)				
BROOKS, GILBERT						
45s						
Whirl 4539		Christmas Round Up/Calypso Santa	19??	—	2.00	4.00
BROOKS, LILLIAN						
45s						
King 4999		Merry Christmas To Michael/Twinkle Twinkle Christmas Star	1956	5.00	10.00	20.00
Newport 105		Twinkle Toes/Nina Non	196?	3.00	6.00	12.00
BROOKS, RON						
45s						
Twin 010		Little Boy's Christmas Prayer/What Christmas Means To Me	19??	—	2.50	5.00
BROOKSHIRE, GLENN						
45s						
Kangaroo 17		Christmas, Come Back To Me/Searchin' For Contentment	19??	2.00	4.00	8.00
BROTHER EYE						
45s						
Futurist 9086		Black Christmas/Jesus' First Cavity	19??	—	2.50	5.00
— Red vinyl						
Futurist 9086	PS	Black Christmas/Jesus' First Cavity	19??	—	2.50	5.00
BROTHERS CAZIMERO, THE						
45s						
Blue Water 1832		Aloha Kalikimaka/Little Drummer Boy	196?	2.00	4.00	8.00
BROTHERS FOUR, THE						
45s						
Columbia 42235		What Child Is This/Christmas Bells	1961	2.50	5.00	10.00
Columbia 43919		I'll Be Home for Christmas/'Twas the Night Before Christmas	1966	2.00	4.00	8.00
On Various-Artists Collections						
Go Tell It on the Mountain		Great Songs of Christmas, The, Album Four (Columbia Special Products CSP 155M)				
God Rest Ye Merry, Gentlemen		Great Songs of Christmas, The, Album Four (Columbia Special Products CSP 155M)				
		Great Songs of Christmas, The, Album Seven (Columbia Special Products CSS 547)				
		Home for Christmas (Columbia Musical Treasury P3S 5608)				
		Home for Christmas (Realm 2V 8101)				
		It's Christmas Time! (Columbia Special Products P 14990)				
I'll Be Home for Christmas		Merry Christmas from... (Reader's Digest RD4-83)				
Mary's Little Boy Child		Great Songs of Christmas, The, Album Eight (Columbia Special Products CSS 888)				
'Twas the Night Before Christmas		Merry Christmas (Columbia Musical Treasury 3P 6306)				
What Child Is This		Great Songs of Christmas, The, Album Four (Columbia Special Products CSP 155M)				
		Joy to the World (30 Classic Christmas Melodies) (Columbia Special Products P3 14654)				
		60 Christmas Classics (Sessions DVL2-0723)				
BROWN, CHARLES						
45s						
Aladdin 3348		Merry Christmas, Baby/Black Night	1956	6.25	12.50	25.00
Blues Spectrum 17		Merry Christmas, Baby/Rockin' Blues	197?	—	3.00	6.00

Label, Number		Title (A Side/B Side)	Year	VG	VG+	NM
Bluesway 61031		Merry Christmas, Baby/Rainy, Rainy Day	1969	—	3.00	6.00
Charlena 001		Please Come Home For Christmas/Santa Claus Santa Claus	197?	—	2.00	4.00
Charlena 001	PS	Please Come Home For Christmas/Santa Claus Santa Claus	197?	—	2.50	5.00
EMI S7-18213		Please Come Home for Christmas/Merry Christmas Baby	1994	—	2.00	4.00
— Green vinyl						
Hollywood 1021		Merry Christmas Baby/Sleigh Ride	1954	5.00	10.00	20.00
— Charles Brown's first recording of the A-side, released on 78 on Exclusive 254 (1946); B-side by Lloyd Glenn; red label						
Hollywood 1021		Merry Christmas Baby/Sleigh Ride	196?	2.00	4.00	8.00
— B-side by Lloyd Glenn; color label						
Hollywood 1021		Merry Christmas Baby/Sleigh Ride	197?	—	2.50	5.00
— B-side by Lloyd Glenn; black label						
Imperial 5902		Merry Christmas Baby/I Lost Everything	1962	2.50	5.00	10.00
Jewel 814		Christmas in Heaven/Just a Blessing	1970	—	3.00	6.00
Jewel 815		Merry Christmas Baby/Please Come Home for Christmas	1970	—	3.00	6.00
Jewel 847		Please Come Home for Christmas/Christmas in Heaven	1974	—	2.50	5.00
Kent 501		Merry Christmas Baby/3 O'Clock Blues	1968	2.50	5.00	10.00
King 5405		Please Come Home for Christmas/Christmas (Comes But Once a Year)	1960	3.00	6.00	12.00
— B-side by Amos Milburn; original blue label						
King 5405		Please Come Home for Christmas/Christmas (Comes But Once a Year)	1970	—	3.00	6.00
— B-side by Amos Milburn; black label						
King 5530		Christmas in Heaven/It's Christmas All Year 'Round	1961	3.00	6.00	12.00
King 5726		It's Christmas Time/Christmas Finds Me Lonely	1963	2.50	5.00	10.00
King 5731		Christmas Questions/Wrap Yourself in a Christmas Package	1963	2.50	5.00	10.00
King 5946		Christmas Blues/My Most Miserable Christmas	1964	2.50	5.00	10.00
King 5947		Christmas Comes (But Once a Year)/Bringin' In a Brand New Year	1964	2.50	5.00	10.00
King 6194		Merry Christmas, Baby/Let's Make Every Day Christmas	1968	2.00	4.00	8.00
Liberty 1393		Merry Christmas, Baby/Silent Night	1980	—	2.50	5.00
— B-side by Baby Washington						
Liberty 5902		Merry Christmas, Baby/I Lost Everything	196?	2.00	4.00	8.00
— Reissue of Imperial 5902						
Swing Time 238		Merry Christmas, Baby/Lost In The Night	195?	6.25	12.50	25.00
— Originally released on 78, but a 45 does exist						
Teem 1008		Merry Christmas Baby/Christmas Finds Me Oh So Sad	19??	—	3.00	6.00
United Artists XW582		Merry Christmas Baby/(B-side unknown)	1974	—	2.50	5.00
Upside PRO 002		Santa Claus Boogie (one-sided)	1986	—	2.00	4.00
— Flexidisc						
Upside PRO 002	PS	Santa Claus Boogie	1986	—	2.00	4.00
Albums						
Big Town 1003		Merry Christmas Baby	1977	3.00	6.00	12.00
King 775	M	Charles Brown Sings Christmas Songs	1961	50.00	100.00	200.00
King KS-775	S	Charles Brown Sings Christmas Songs	1963	100.00	200.00	400.00
— Stereo copies (whether true stereo or rechanneled, we don't know) exist on blue labels with "King" in block letters (no crown).						

On Various-Artists Collections

Merry Christmas Baby		Merry Christmas Baby (Christmas Music for Young Lovers) (Hollywood HLP 501)				
		Merry Christmas Baby (Gusto/Hollywood K-5018-X)				
Please Come Home for Christmas		Billboard Greatest Christmas Hits, 1955-Present (Rhino R1 70636)				

BROWN, CRAIG
45s

Label, Number		Title (A Side/B Side)	Year	VG	VG+	NM
Pulse 1007		The Christmas Child (Bambino)/The Christmas Child (Bambino)	19??	—	2.00	4.00
— B-side by Maria Layna						

BROWN, HYLO
45s

Label, Number		Title (A Side/B Side)	Year	VG	VG+	NM
K-Ark 805		Daddy's Drinking Up Our Christmas/I Saw Christmas	197?	—	2.50	5.00

BROWN, JAMES
45s

Label, Number		Title (A Side/B Side)	Year	VG	VG+	NM
King 6064		The Christmas Song (Version 1)/The Christmas Song (Version 2)	1966	3.75	7.50	15.00
King 6065		Sweet Little Baby Boy (Part 1)/Sweet Little Baby Boy (Part 2)	1966	3.00	6.00	12.00
King 6072		Let's Make Christmas Mean Something This Year (Part 1)/Let's Make Christmas Mean Something This Year (Part 2)	1967	3.00	6.00	12.00
King 6203		Santa Claus Go Straight to the Ghetto/You Know It	1968	2.50	5.00	10.00
King 6205		Let's Unite the World at Christmas/In the Middle (Part 1)	1968	2.50	5.00	10.00
King 6277		It's Christmas Time (Part 1)/It's Christmas Time (Part 2)	1969	2.50	5.00	10.00
King 6340		Santa Claus Is Definitely Here to Stay/(Instrumental)	1970	2.00	4.00	8.00
King 6340	PS	Santa Claus Is Definitely Here to Stay/(Instrumental)	1970	7.50	15.00	30.00
Polydor 14161		Santa Claus Goes Straight to the Ghetto/Sweet Little Baby Boy	1972	—	3.00	6.00
Albums						
King 1010	M	Christmas Songs	1966	25.00	50.00	100.00
— Wreath on gray wall, no song titles on back						

Label, Number	Title (A Side/B Side)	Year	VG	VG+	NM
King KS 1010 S	Christmas Songs	1966	37.50	75.00	150.00
— *Wreath on gray wall, no song titles on back*					
King 1010 M	Christmas Songs	1967	20.00	40.00	80.00
— *Wreath on white wall, song titles are on back*					
King KS 1010 S	Christmas Songs	1967	25.00	50.00	100.00
— *Wreath on white wall, song titles are on back*					
King KS-1040	A Soulful Christmas	1968	20.00	40.00	80.00
Rhino R1 70194	Santa's Got a Brand New Bag	1986	2.50	5.00	10.00
— *Reissue of King material*					

BROWN, JIM ED, AND HELEN CORNELIUS
45s

RCA PB-11162	Natividad/Fall Softly Snow	1977	—	2.00	4.00

On Various-Artists Collections

Fall Softly Snow	Country Christmas, A (RCA CPL1-4396)
	Family Christmas Collection, The (Time-Life STL-131)

BROWN, JOYCE
45s

Drew-Blan 1017	Christmas In Vietnam/(B-side unknown)	196?	3.00	6.00	12.00

BROWN, JUDY
45s

Skyla 1122	Dear Santa/Christmas Wedding Day	1961	3.00	6.00	12.00

BROWN, JULIE
On Various-Artists Collections

Ways to Save Money at Christmas	Winter Warnerland (Warner Bros. PRO-A-3328)

BROWN, LES
45s

Coral 60820	Let It Snow, Let It Snow, Let It Snow/Rain	1952	3.75	7.50	15.00
Coral 62237	Silver Bells/The Stranger	1960	2.50	5.00	10.00

BROWN, PETER
On Various-Artists Collections

Winter Wonderland	We Wish You a Merry Christmas (Warner Bros. W 1337)

BROWN, RANDY
45s

Sound Town 0010	At Christmas Time/(Instrumental)	198?	—	2.00	4.00

BROWNS, THE
45s

RCA Victor 47-7820	Blue Christmas/Greenwillow Christmas	1960	3.00	6.00	12.00

On Various-Artists Collections

Scarlet Ribbons	60 Christmas Classics (Sessions DVL2-0723)

BRUBECK, DAVE, QUARTET
On Various-Artists Collections

Santa Claus Is Comin' to Town	Jingle Bell Jazz (Columbia PC 36803)

BRUCE, ED
On Various-Artists Collections

Christmas Started with a Child	Country Christmas, A, Volume 4 (RCA CPL1-7012)

BRUCE, VIN
45s

Swallow 10137	Christmas With A Broken Heart/Christmas On The Bayou	196?	3.00	6.00	12.00

BRUNO BEATS
7-Inch Extended Plays

Recca 2006	Wintergreen/Frosty The Snowman//	198?	—	2.00	4.00
	Cryin' On Christmas/Swingin' On A Star				
Recca 2006 PS	Wintergreen/Frosty The Snowman//	198?	—	3.00	6.00
	Cryin' On Christmas/Swingin' On A Star				

Label, Number		Title (A Side/B Side)	Year	VG	VG+	NM
BRYAN, DORA						
45s						
Fontana TF 427		All I Want for Christmas Is a Beatle/If I Were a Fairy	1963	6.25	12.50	25.00
— *U.K. pressing, one of the first Beatles novelties*						
BRYANT, ANITA						
45s						
Columbia 44341		Do You Hear What I Hear/Away in the Manger	1967	2.00	4.00	8.00
Columbia 44341	PS	Do You Hear What I Hear/Away in the Manger	1967	2.50	5.00	10.00
Albums						
Columbia CL 2720	M	Do You Hear What I Hear?	1967	3.75	7.50	15.00
Columbia CS 9520	S	Do You Hear What I Hear?	1967	2.50	5.00	10.00
On Various-Artists Collections						

Away in a Manger	Merry Christmas from... (Reader's Digest RD4-83)
	Wondrous Winter: Songs of Winter, Songs of Christmas
	(Columbia Special Products CSS 708/9)
Do You Hear What I Hear	Christmas Trimmings (Columbia Special Products P 12795)
	Country Christmas (Columbia CS 9888)
	Country Style Christmas, A (Columbia Musical Treasury 3P 6316)
	Merry Christmas (Columbia Musical Treasury 3P 6306)
First Noel, The	Gift of Christmas, The, Vol. 1 (Columbia Special Products CSS 706)
He's Got the Whole World in His Hands	Joyous Christmas, Volume 6 (Columbia Special Products C 11083)
It Came Upon the Midnight Clear	Happy Holidays, Album Nine (Columbia Special Products P 11793)
	Very Merry Christmas, A, Volume Two (Columbia Special Products CSS 788)
Keep Thy Faith, Children	Fenwick (Fenwick FLP-621)
Mary's Lullaby (Sleep Baby, Sleep)	Spirit of Christmas, The, Volume III (Columbia Special Products CSS 1463)
O Come All Ye Faithful	It's Christmas Time! (Columbia Special Products P 14990)
Our Winter Love	Happy Holidays, Volume II (Columbia Special Products CSM 348)
Silent Night, Holy Night	Have a Happy Holiday (Columbia Special Products CSS 1432)
	Home for Christmas (Columbia Musical Treasury P3S 5608)
	Home for Christmas (Realm 2V 8101)

Label, Number		Title (A Side/B Side)	Year	VG	VG+	NM
BRYANT, DON						
45s						
Southern Tracks 1048		I Couldn't Wait For Christmas/In Way Over My Heart	1985	—	2.00	4.00
Southern Tracks 1072		I Couldn't Wait For Christmas/The Only Thing Bad About Christmas	1986	—	2.00	4.00
BUCHANAN AND GOODMAN						
Also see DICKIE GOODMAN.						
45s						
Luniverse 107		Santa and the Satellite Part 1/Santa and the Satellite Part 2	1957	10.00	20.00	40.00
On Various-Artists Collections						

Santa and the Satellite	Dr. Demento Presents the Greatest Novelty Records of All Time
	Volume VI: Christmas (Rhino RNLP 825)
	Rockin' Christmas — The '50s (Rhino RNLP-066)

Label, Number		Title (A Side/B Side)	Year	VG	VG+	NM
BUCHANAN, ART						
45s						
Lost Gold LGRX-3		Santa Claus Is Comin' To Our Town/(B-side unknown)	198?	—	—	3.00
— *Red vinyl*						
BUCK, CHARLIE						
45s						
Tad 104		I Wish I Were A Christmas Tree/We Can't Miss This Christmas	1962	3.00	6.00	12.00
BUCK, TRUDY						
45s						
TBR & Co 101		Christmas Mouse/Blessed Baby Jesus	19??	3.00	6.00	12.00
BUFFETT, JIMMY						
45s						
MCA S45-17084	DJ	Christmas In The Caribbean (same on both sides)	1985	—	2.50	5.00
On Various-Artists Collections						

Christmas in the Caribbean	Tennessee Christmas (MCA 5620)
	Tennessee Christmas (MCA S45-17046)

BUFFETT, PETER
On Various-Artists Collections

What Child Is This	Narada: The Christmas Collection (Narada N-63902)

Label, Number		Title (A Side/B Side)	Year	VG	VG+	NM
BULLETBOYS						
On Various-Artists Collections						
Holiday I.D.		Winter Warnerland (Warner Bros. PRO-A-3328)				
BUNYUPS, THE						
45s						
Dancing Bunny 3670		Christmas Presents/The Tu Krang Krang Tu	198?	—	—	3.00
Dancing Bunny 3670	PS	Christmas Presents/The Tu Krang Krang Tu	198?	—	—	3.00
BURD FAMILY, THE						
45s						
Legend 113		When Santa Comes On Christmas Night/Just Peace And Love Will Do	19??	2.50	5.00	10.00
BURDEN, RAY						
45s						
Cullman 6407		Christmas Is Here At Last/Santa, Bring Me A Gal	1958	12.50	25.00	50.00
BURKE FAMILY SINGERS, THE						
On Various-Artists Collections						
I Saw Three Ships		Philco Album of Holiday Music, The (Columbia Special Products CSM 431)				
BURKE, SOLOMON						
45s						
Apollo 485		Christmas Presents/When I'm All Alone	1955	7.50	15.00	30.00
Atlantic 2369		Presents for Christmas/A Tear Fell	1966	3.00	6.00	12.00
MCI 712842		You're All I Want For Christmas/No Place Like Home	19??	2.00	4.00	8.00
— B-side by Rayne						
Pride 1022		All I Want for Christmas/I Can't Stop Loving You (Part 1)	1972	—	3.00	6.00
BURLAND, SASCHA & THE SKIPJACK CHOIR						
45s						
RCA Victor 47-8277		Have Yourself a Merry Little Christmas/ The Chickens Are in the Chimes	1963	7.50	15.00	30.00
RCA Victor 47-8277	PS	Have Yourself a Merry Little Christmas/ The Chickens Are in the Chimes	1963	10.00	20.00	40.00
BURNETT, BOBBY						
45s						
Topaz APL	PS	Christmas Time/Circles	1984	—	—	3.00
Topaz APL		Christmas Time/Circles	1984	—	—	3.00
BURNETT, CAROL						
On Various-Artists Collections						
Christmas Song, The		Christmas Greetings, Vol. 3 (Columbia Special Products P 11383)				
		Christmas Song, The, And Other Favorites (Columbia Special Products P 12446)				
		Joyous Songs of Christmas, The (Columbia Special Products C 10400)				
BURNETTE, SMILEY						
45s						
Capitol F32110		Rudolph The Red-Nosed Reindeer/The Swiss Boy	195?	5.00	10.00	20.00
— From "Album CASF-3160"						
BURRELL, KENNY						
45s						
Cadet 5555		The Little Drummer Boy/Silent Night	1966	2.00	4.00	8.00
BURT, ALFRED, CAROLS						
Also see THE COLUMBIA CHOIR.						
On Various-Artists Collections						
Bright, Bright the Holly Berries		Magic of Christmas, The (Columbia Musical Treasury P3S 5806)				
Come, Dear Children		Magic of Christmas, The (Columbia Musical Treasury P3S 5806)				
BURTON, WENDY						
45s						
Columbia 42624		Mommy's Daddy, Daddy's Daddy and Santa Claus/ 17 Million Bicycles	1962	2.50	5.00	10.00

Label, Number		Title (A Side/B Side)	Year	VG	VG+	NM
BUSH, KATE						
45s						
EMI 5121		December Will Be Magic Again/Warm And Soothing	1980	2.50	5.00	10.00
EMI 5121	PS	December Will Be Magic Again/Warm And Soothing	1980	3.75	7.50	15.00
— Record and sleeve are U.K. imports						
BUSHKIN, JOE						
45s						
Columbia 39172		Every Day Is Christmas/The Lady Is A Tramp	1951	3.75	7.50	15.00
BUSKIN, DAVID						
45s						
Epic 10817		Just for the Children/The Rest of the Year	1972	—	2.50	5.00
BUTLER, JEFF						
45s						
P.S. 104		I'm Gonna Celebrate The New Year/It's Christmas	198?	—	—	3.00
BUTLER, JERRY						
45s						
Mistletoe 803		Silent Night/O Holy Night	1974	—	2.50	5.00
Vee Jay 371		Silent Night/O Holy Night	1960	5.00	10.00	20.00
BUTLER, JIMMY						
45s						
Gem 222		Trim Your Tree/Cruelty For Kindness	1954	12.50	25.00	50.00
BUTTER						
45s						
Bookshop 782		Dimmi Di Si/(Instrumental)	1988	—	2.00	4.00
Bookshop 782	PS	Dimmi Di Si/(Instrumental)	1988	—	2.00	4.00
BUTTHOLE SURFERS						
45s						
Trance 30		Good King Wenceslas/The Lord Is A Monkey	198?	2.50	5.00	10.00
BUTTONS, RED						
45s						
Columbia 40384		Bow Wow Wants a Boy for Christmas/Little Johnny Snowball	1954	3.75	7.50	15.00
BYRD, CHARLIE						
45s						
Columbia 43942		It's Christmas Again, Jesus/It's Morning, Jesus	1966	2.00	4.00	8.00
— With Father Malcolm Boyd						

On Various-Artists Collections

Coventry Carol, The		Happy Holidays, Album 8 (Columbia Special Products C 11086)				
		Magic of Christmas, The (Columbia Musical Treasury P3S 5806)				
		Merry Christmas from... (Reader's Digest RD4-83)				
First Noel, The		Home for Christmas (Columbia Musical Treasury P3S 5608)				
God Rest Ye Merry, Gentlemen		Merry Christmas (Columbia Musical Treasury 3P 6306)				
Good King Wenceslas		Christmas Greetings (Columbia Special Products CSS 1433)				
Silent Night		Merry Christmas from... (Reader's Digest RD4-83)				
We Three Kings		WHIO Radio Christmas Feelings (Sound Approach/CSP P 16366)				
What Child Is This		Joy of Christmas, The (Columbia Special Products P 12042)				

Label, Number		Title (A Side/B Side)	Year	VG	VG+	NM
BYRNE, MARTHA						
45s						
RCA 62979		O Come All Ye Faithful/Joy to the World// Merry Christmas Wherever You Are	1994	—	—	3.00
— B-side by the Soaps and Hearts Ensemble						
RCA 62979	PS	O Come All Ye Faithful/Joy to the World// Merry Christmas Wherever You Are	1994	—	—	3.00
BYRNES, EDD						
45s						
Warner Bros. 5121		Yulesville/Lonely Christmas	1959	4.00	8.00	16.00
Warner Bros. 5121	PS	Yulesville/Lonely Christmas	1959	10.00	20.00	40.00

(Top left) *The Beach Boys' Christmas Album,* which featured the group's first recordings with strings, remains one of the most popular rock-related holiday releases. (Top right) "Christmas Time (Is Here Again)," a version of the song the Beatles made for their 1967 fan club record, was released as the B-side of the 1995 single "Free As A Bird." (Bottom left) The original cover for Harry Belafonte's *To Wish You a Merry Christmas* from 1958. Several years later, "Mary's Boy Child" was added and both the cover and the number were changed. (Bottom right) A sought-after Kate Bush 45, "December Will Be Magic Again," which to date has never been released in the US.

Label, Number	Title (A Side/B Side)	Year	VG	VG+	NM
On Various-Artists Collections					
Yulesville	We Wish You a Merry Christmas (Warner Bros. W 1337)				

BYRON, LORD DOUGLAS
45s

Dot 16685	Surfin' Santa/The Drink That Makes You Shrink	1964	7.50	15.00	30.00
On Various-Artists Collections					
Surfin' Santa	Rockin' Little Christmas (MCA 25084)				

BYU SYMPHONIC BAND, THE
45s

| Century 32396 | A Season For Remembering/A Season For Remembering | 19?? | — | 2.50 | 5.00 |

— B-side by Ron Clark and the Sweetbriar Trio

C

C-QUENTS, THE
45s

| Capetown 4027 | All I Want For Christmas Is You/Merry Christmas, Baby | 1962 | 5.00 | 10.00 | 20.00 |

CADILLACS, THE
45s

| Josie 807 | Rudolph the Red-Nosed Reindeer/Shack-a Doo | 1956 | 10.00 | 20.00 | 40.00 |

CAESAR, SHIRLEY
45s

| Rejoice 2895   DJ | Won't You Come A-Christmasing (same on both sides) | 198? | — | — | 3.00 |

CAFFERTY, JOHN, AND THE BEAVER BROWN BAND
45s

| Nard's 16880 | All Around the World/Welcome Home | 1986 | 2.00 | 4.00 | 8.00 |

— B-side by Mike Cavaliere

CAIOLA, AL
45s

| United Artists 50237 | Bossa Nova Noel/Holiday on Skis | 1967 | 2.50 | 5.00 | 10.00 |

— With Riz Ortolani

CALABRESE, JOANNE, AND DOC GALVEZ
45s

| Scepter 12238 | God Rest Ye Merry Gentlemen/(Instrumental) | 1968 | — | 3.00 | 6.00 |

CALDERAZZO, JOEY
On Various-Artists Collections

| God Rest Ye Merry Gentlemen | Yule Struttin' — A Blue Note Christmas (Blue Note 1P 8119) | | | | |

CALLOWAY, LAEL
45s

| ABC-Paramount 9761 | Dear Santa, Have You Had The Measles?/If Santa Was My Daddy | 1956 | 3.75 | 7.50 | 15.00 |

CAMBRIDGE, GODFREY
On Various-Artists Collections

| Reminder Spot | For Christmas Seals. . .A Matter of Life and Breath (Decca Custom Style E) | | | | |

CAMEOS, THE
45s

| Cameo 123 | Merry Christmas/New Year's Eve | 1957 | 37.50 | 75.00 | 150.00 |
| Cameo 123 | Merry Christmas/New Year's Eve | 197? | 2.50 | 5.00 | 10.00 |

— Reproduction of the original 1957 release

Label, Number	Title (A Side/B Side)	Year	VG	VG+	NM

CAMILLE
45s
EMI 5014	White Christmas/Snowbelle	1979	6.25	12.50	25.00
— U.K. import					

CAMPBELL, ARCHIE
45s
RCA Victor 47-9028	Christmas at the Opry/Christmas Eve in Heaven	1966	2.50	5.00	10.00

CAMPBELL, EDDIE C.
45s
Rooster Blues 46	Santa's Messin' With The Kid/King Of The Jungle	1981	3.00	6.00	12.00

CAMPBELL, GLEN
45s
Capitol 2336	Christmas Is for Children/There's No Place Like Home	1968	—	2.50	5.00
Capitol 3509	I Believe in Christmas/New Snow on the Roof	1972	—	2.00	4.00
Liberty S7-18214	Blue Christmas/Feliz Navidad	1994	—	2.00	4.00
— B-side on EMI Latin by Jose Feliciano; red vinyl					

Albums
Capitol ST 2978	That Christmas Feeling	1968	3.75	7.50	15.00

On Various-Artists Collections
Blue Christmas	Blue Christmas (Welk Music Group WM-3002)
	Let's Celebrate Christmas (Capitol Special Markets SL-6923)
	Time-Life Treasury of Christmas, The (Time-Life STL-107)
	Very Merry Christmas, A, Volume VIII (Capitol Special Markets SL-6954)
	Wonderful World of Christmas, The, Album Two (Capitol Special Markets SL-8025)
Christmas Is for Children	Best of Christmas, The, Vol. I (Capitol SM-11833)
	Sound of Christmas, The, Vol. 2 (Capitol Creative Products SL-6534)
	Time-Life Treasury of Christmas, The, Volume Two (Time-Life STL-108)
Christmas Song, The	Christmas for the 90's, Volume 1 (Capitol Nashville 1P 8117)
Have Yourself a Merry Little Christmas	All-Time Christmas Favorites (Capitol Special Markets SL-6931)
	Christmas Sounds of Music, The (Capitol Creative Products SL-6643)
	Holiday Magic (Capitol Creative Products SL-6728)
I'll Be Home for Christmas	Christmas Songs, The (Capitol SLB-57074)
	Christmas with Glen Campbell and the Hollywood Pops Orchestra (Capitol Creative Products SL-6699)
It Must Be Getting Close to Christmas	Christmas America, Album Two (Capitol Special Markets SL-6950)
	Christmas with Glen Campbell and the Hollywood Pops Orchestra (Capitol Creative Products SL-6699)
Little Altar Boy	Christmas, A Gift of Music (Capitol Special Markets SL-6687)
	Happy Holly Days (Capitol Creative Products SL-6761)
	Zenith Presents Christmas, A Gift of Music Vol. 4 (Capitol Creative Products SL-6687)
New Snow on the Roof	Wonderful World of Christmas, The, Album Two (Capitol Special Markets SL-8025)
Night Before Christmas, The	Christmas Sounds of Music, The (Capitol Creative Products SL-6643)
	Christmas with Glen Campbell and the Hollywood Pops Orchestra (Capitol Creative Products SL-6699)
	Magic of Christmas, The (Capitol SWBB-93810)
O Holy Night Silent Night	Christmas for the 90's, Volume 2 (Capitol Nashville 1P 8118)
	Christmas Sounds of Music, The (Capitol Creative Products SL-6643)
	Christmas with Glen Campbell and the Hollywood Pops Orchestra (Capitol Creative Products SL-6699)
	Popular Christmas Classics (Capitol Special Markets SL-8100)
There's No Place Like Home	Christmas America (Capitol Special Markets SL-6884)
	Christmas Carousel (Capitol SQBE-94406)
	Christmas Sounds of Music, The (Capitol Creative Products SL-6643)
	Christmas with Glen Campbell and the Hollywood Pops Orchestra (Capitol Creative Products SL-6699)
	Holiday Magic (Capitol Creative Products SL-6728)
	Merry Christmas (Columbia Musical Treasury 3P 6306)

CAMPBELL, JEANETTE
On Various-Artists Collections
La Volta	Christmas in San Francisco (Embarcadero Center EC-101)

CAMPBELL, JO ANN
45s
Gone 5049	Happy New Year Baby/Tall Boy	1958	7.50	15.00	30.00

CAMPBELL, SID
45s
K and B 101	Teardrops Falling In The Snow/Christmas Stocking	198?	—	—	3.00

Label, Number	Title (A Side/B Side)	Year	VG	VG+	NM

CANADIAN BRASS, THE
Albums
FM/CBS FM 39740	A Canadian Brass Christmas	1985	2.50	5.00	10.00
RCA Red Seal ARL1-4132	Christmas with the Canadian Brass	1981	2.50	5.00	10.00

On Various-Artists Collections
Holly and the Ivy, The	Family Christmas Collection, The (Time-Life STL-131)
I Wonder As I Wander	Happy Holidays, Vol. 21 (RCA Special Products DPL1-0739)
Medley: O Come, O Come Emmanuel/	Family Christmas Collection, The (Time-Life STL-131)
I Wonder As I Wander	
Medley: O Little Town of Bethlehem/	Time-Life Treasury of Christmas, The, Volume Two (Time-Life STL-108)
It Came Upon a Midnight Clear	

CANDLE-LIGHTERS, THE
45s
A.H.D. 324	Old Fashioned Christmas/Castle Of Dreams	19??	2.50	5.00	10.00

CANDY STORE, THE
Albums
Decca DL 75147	Turned-On Christmas	1969	6.25	12.50	25.00

CANNAN, JERRY
45s
CBM 998	Randolph The Brown-Nosed Reindeer/I Believe In Santa Claus	19??	—	3.00	6.00

CANNED HEAT
45s
Capitol S7-57890	Christmas Blues/Christmas Is the Time to Say "I Love You"	1992	—	2.00	4.00
— B-side by Billy Squier					
Liberty 56079	Christmas Blues/The Chipmunk Song	1968	6.25	12.50	25.00
— B-side with the Chipmunks					

CANNIBALS, THE
45s
Hit FREEBEE 2		Christmas Rock 'n' Roll/New Year's Eve Song	1980	2.50	5.00	10.00
Hit FREEBEE 2	PS	Christmas Rock 'n' Roll/New Year's Eve Song	1980	2.50	5.00	10.00
— Record and sleeve are U.K. imports						

CANNON, ACE
45s
Hi 2084		Blue Christmas/Here Comes Santa Claus	1964	2.50	5.00	10.00
Albums
| Hi HL 12022 | M | Christmas Cheer | 1964 | 5.00 | 10.00 | 20.00 |
| Hi SHL 32022 | S | Christmas Cheer | 1964 | 6.25 | 12.50 | 25.00 |

CANTERBURY CHOIR, THE
On Various-Artists Collections
Angels We Have Heard on High	Christmas Carol, A/Music of Christmas (MGM E3222)
Away in a Manger	Christmas Carol, A/Music of Christmas (MGM E3222)
Coventry Carol	Christmas Carol, A/Music of Christmas (MGM E3222)
God Rest Ye Merry Gentlemen	Christmas Carol, A/Music of Christmas (MGM E3222)
In the Bleak Mid-Winter	Christmas Carol, A/Music of Christmas (MGM E3222)
Medley: Deck the Halls/	Christmas Carol, A/Music of Christmas (MGM E3222)
I Saw Three Ships	
O Holy Night	Christmas Carol, A/Music of Christmas (MGM E3222)
What Child Is This?	Christmas Carol, A/Music of Christmas (MGM E3222)
While Shepherds Watched Their Flocks	Christmas Carol, A/Music of Christmas (MGM E3222)

CANTRELL, LANA
On Various-Artists Collections
I'll Be Home for Christmas	Christmas in California (RCA Victor PRS-276)
	Christmas in New York Volume 2 (RCA Victor PRS-270)
	Christmas with Colonel Sanders (RCA Victor PRS-291)
	Christmastime in Carol and Song (RCA PRM-271)
	Happy Holidays, Volume 14 (RCA Special Products DPL1-0376)
	60 Christmas Classics (Sessions DVL2-0723)
White Christmas	Happy Holidays, Volume 15 (RCA Special Products DPL1-0453)

CANUSO, CONNIE
45s
Applause 1246	Someone Painted Rudolph's Nose a Chocolate Brown/	196?	3.75	7.50	15.00
	Santa Claus And His Sleigh				

Label, Number		Title (A Side/B Side)	Year	VG	VG+	NM
Applause 1246	PS	Someone Painted Rudolph's Nose a Chocolate Brown/ Santa Claus And His Sleigh	196?	3.75	7.50	15.00

CAPELLA MUSICALE DELLA BASILICA DI SAN FRANCISCO IN ASSISI
On Various-Artists Collections

Alla Luce d'una Stella		Christmas in Italy (Capitol T 10093)				
Campane di Natale		Christmas in Italy (Capitol T 10093)				

CAPITOL SYMPHONY BAND
45s

Capitol F984		Sleigh Ride/Syncopated Clock	1949	3.75	7.50	15.00

CAPPS, JOHNNY
45s

K-Ark 1044		White Christmas/(B-side unknown)	198?	—	2.50	5.00

CAPRA, RENO
45s

United Artists 50242		Winter Song/Sancta Maria	1967	2.00	4.00	8.00

CAPTAIN & TENNILLE, THE
45s

Purebred 0001		Tahoe Snow/ Here Comes Santa Claus	198?	—	2.50	5.00
Purebred 0001	PS	Tahoe Snow/ Here Comes Santa Claus	198?	—	3.00	5.00

CAPTAIN KANGAROO – See BOB KEESHAN.

CARAVANS, THE
45s

Cuca 1017		Rock And Roll Christmas/Caravan	1960	3.75	7.50	15.00

On Various-Artists Collections

God Rest Ye Merry Gentlemen		Mahalia (Jackson) and Friends at Christmastime (Columbia Special Products P 11804)				

CARBONE, RAYMOND
45s

Star-X 502		My Christmas Problem/Rockin' On My Rockin' Horse	19??	2.50	5.00	10.00

CARDINI, GEORGE
45s

Skyway 110		Season's Greetings "A Cheerful Hello"/Christmas Kisses	1957	3.75	7.50	15.00

CARDWELL, DAMON
45s

Deuce 57		A Visit From Nick/Jerusalem Slim	19??	5.00	10.00	20.00

CAREY, MARIAH
45s

Columbia 661070		All I Want for Christmas Is You/Miss You Most (At Christmas Time)	1994	—	2.50	5.00
Columbia 661070	PS	All I Want for Christmas Is You/Miss You Most (At Christmas Time)	1994	—	3.00	6.00
— Record and sleeve are U.K. imports (not all records have sleeves)						

CARGILL, HENSON
45s

Monument 1178		Silver Bells/The Little Drummer Boy	1969	2.00	4.00	8.00

CARILLO, FRANK
45s

Brewery 1023		It's Christmas Again/(Christmas) Everyday	198?	—	—	3.00
Brewery 1023	PS	It's Christmas Again/(Christmas) Everyday	198?	—	—	3.00

CARL, SHARI
45s

Little Crow 680		Natividad/The Little Tiny King	19??	2.50	5.00	10.00

Label, Number		Title (A Side/B Side)	Year	VG	VG+	NM
CARLOS, DON, AND GLENISE SPENCER						
On Various-Artists Collections						
Jingle Bells		Reggae Christmas, A (Real Authentic Sound RAS 3101)				
CARLSON, KEN						
45s						
Gun 17980		Christmas And Dad/A New Year's Prayer	19??	—	—	3.00
CARLTON, LARRY						
Albums						
MCA 6322		Christmas at Our House	1989	2.50	5.00	10.00
CARLYLE, RUSS						
45s						
Mercury 5760		Santa Looks Like Daddy/Only You	1951	3.75	7.50	15.00
CARNEY, ART						
45s						
Columbia 40400		'Twas The Night Before Christmas/Santa And The Doodle-Li-Boop	1954	6.25	12.50	25.00
On Various-Artists Collections						
'Twas the Night Before Christmas		Child's Christmas, A (Harmony HS 14563)				
CARNEY, JACK, AND HARRY FENDER						
On Various-Artists Collections						
Santa's Clause		Christmas in Saint Louis ((no label) TS77-558/9)				
CARO, NYDIA						
45s						
Roulette 4588		Ask Me What I Want for Christmas/Hey Johnny What	1964	3.00	6.00	12.00
Roulette 4588	PS	Ask Me What I Want for Christmas/Hey Johnny What	1964	5.00	10.00	20.00
CAROL, LINDA AND CATHY						
45s						
United 216		Merry Christmas/I Don't Wanna Be Last On Santa's List	1957	5.00	10.00	20.00
CAROLEER SINGERS AND ORCHESTRA, THE						
Albums						
Diplomat X 1714	M	Frosty the Snowman	196?	2.50	5.00	10.00
Diplomat SX 1714	S	Frosty the Snowman	196?	3.00	6.00	12.00
CAROLEERS, THE						
45s						
Peter Pan X-1		Jingle Bells / Deck The Halls/Good King Wenceslas	196?	2.00	4.00	8.00
Peter Pan X-1	PS	Jingle Bells / Deck The Halls/Good King Wenceslas	196?	2.50	5.00	10.00
7-Inch Extended Plays						
Peter Pan X-25		Hark the Herald Angels Sing/O Little Town of Bethlehem/Deck The Halls//Joy to the World/ Away in the Manger/It Came Upon a Midnight Clear	196?	2.00	4.00	8.00
Peter Pan X-25	PS	Hark the Herald Angels Sing/O Little Town of Bethlehem/Deck The Halls//Joy to the World/ Away in the Manger/It Came Upon a Midnight Clear	196?	2.50	5.00	10.00
Peter Pan X-26		The First Noel/Carol Of The Bells// The 12 Days Of Christmas/Adeste Fidelis	196?	2.00	4.00	8.00
Peter Pan X-26	PS	The First Noel/Carol Of The Bells// The 12 Days Of Christmas/Adeste Fidelis	196?	2.50	5.00	10.00
CAROLERS, THE						
Albums						
Vanguard Cardinal VCS 10015		A Music Box of Christmas Carols	1967	3.00	6.00	12.00
— With Music Boxes from the Borland Collection...also see "Welch Chorale, The"						
CARPENTERS						
45s						
A&M 1236		Merry Christmas Darling/Mr. Guder	1970	—	3.00	6.00
— A-side vocal is different than later releases of this song						
A&M 1236	PS	Merry Christmas Darling/Mr. Guder	1970	2.00	4.00	8.00
A&M 1648		Santa Claus Is Coming to Town/Merry Christmas Darling	1974	—	2.50	5.00
A&M 1648	PS	Santa Claus Is Coming to Town/Merry Christmas Darling	1974	2.50	5.00	10.00

Label, Number		Title (A Side/B Side)	Year	VG	VG+	NM
A&M 1991		The Christmas Song/Merry Christmas Darling	1977	—	2.50	5.00
A&M 1991	PS	The Christmas Song/Merry Christmas Darling	1977	2.00	4.00	8.00
A&M 2700		Do You Hear What I Hear/Little Altar Boy	1984	2.50	5.00	10.00
A&M 8620		The Christmas Song/Merry Christmas Darling	1982	—	2.50	5.00
Albums						
A&M SP-3210		Christmas Portrait	198?	2.00	4.00	8.00
— Reissue of SP-4726						
A&M SP-3270		An Old-Fashioned Christmas	1984	2.50	5.00	10.00
A&M SP-4726		Christmas Portrait	1978	3.75	7.50	15.00

On Various-Artists Collections

Christmas Song, The	Time-Life Treasury of Christmas, The (Time-Life STL-107)
Have Yourself a Merry Little Christmas	Happy Holidays, Vol. 22 (RCA Special Products DPL1-0777)
Merry Christmas Darling	Christmas Is... (Columbia Special Products P 11417) Happy Holidays, Volume 19 (RCA Special Products DPL1-0689) Stars of Christmas, The (RCA Special Products DPL1-0842)
Santa Claus Is Comin' to Town	Henry Mancini Selects Great Songs of Christmas (RCA Special Products DPL1-0148)
Sleigh Ride	Happy Holidays, Vol. 20 (RCA Special Products DPL1-0713)

CARR, JOE "FINGERS", AND DALLAS FRAZIER
45s

Label, Number	Title (A Side/B Side)	Year	VG	VG+	NM
Capitol F2956	My Birthday Comes on Christmas/Jingle o' the Brownie	1954	3.75	7.50	15.00

CARR, ROBERTA, AND MARILYN MILLER
45s

Label, Number	Title (A Side/B Side)	Year	VG	VG+	NM
Epic 9642	Christmas in the Hills/No Man But a Snowman	1963	3.00	6.00	12.00

CARR, VIKKI
45s

Label, Number		Title (A Side/B Side)	Year	VG	VG+	NM
Columbia AS 85	DJ	It Came Upon A Midnight Clear/Wind Me Up	1971	—	2.00	4.00
Columbia AS 85	PS	It Came Upon A Midnight Clear/Wind Me Up	1971	2.00	4.00	8.00
Columbia 45403		Six Weeks Every Summer (Christmas Every Day)/ If You Could Read My Mind	1971	—	2.00	4.00

On Various-Artists Collections

It Came Upon a Midnight Clear	Christmas Greetings, Vol. 3 (Columbia Special Products P 11383) Silent Night... (Columbia Special Products P 14989) Sounds of Christmas (Columbia Special Products P 12474)
What Child Is This?	Christmas Greetings, Vol. 4 (Columbia Special Products P 11987) Christmas Is... (Columbia Special Products P 11417) Christmas Trimmings (Columbia Special Products P 12795) Ronco Presents A Christmas Gift (Columbia Special Products P 12430)

CARR, VIKKI, AND FIRESTONE CHORUS
On Various-Artists Collections

I Still Believe in Christmas	Firestone Presents Your Christmas Favorites, Volume 7 (Firestone CSLP 7015)
Medley: Jolly Old St. Nicholas/ Up on the House Top	Firestone Presents Your Christmas Favorites, Volume 7 (Firestone CSLP 7015)

CARRADINE, JOHN
On Various-Artists Collections

Gift of the Magi, The	O. Henry's The Gift of the Magi (E.F. MacDonald EFMX-62)

CARROLL, BOB
45s

Label, Number	Title (A Side/B Side)	Year	VG	VG+	NM
Ocean State DMS-3	Dreaming Of Christmas/I Want My Santa Claus	1982	—	2.00	4.00
— B-side by Lynn Roberts					

CARROLL, DAVID
45s

Label, Number	Title (A Side/B Side)	Year	VG	VG+	NM
Mercury 70759	My Christmas Carol/I'll Be Home for Christmas	1955	3.00	6.00	12.00

CARROLL, DIAHANN
On Various-Artists Collections

Do You Hear What I Hear	Great Songs of Christmas, The, Album Seven (Columbia Special Products CSS 547) Joyous Christmas, Volume V (Columbia Special Products C 10398)
Lo, How a Rose E'er Blooming	Great Songs of Christmas, The, Album Five (Columbia Special Products CSP 238M)
Some Children See Him	Great Songs of Christmas, The, Album Five (Columbia Special Products CSP 238M) Very Merry Christmas, A, Volume 3 (Columbia Special Products CSS 997)

Label, Number	Title (A Side/B Side)	Year	VG	VG+	NM
CARROLL, IRENE					
45s					
Arrow 712	It's Christmas/The "Let Me" Song	1956	3.75	7.50	15.00
CARROLL, JIMMY, ORCHESTRA					
45s					
Golden Star 616	Winter Wonderland/Mister Snow	19??	3.75	7.50	15.00
CARSON, KEN					
45s					
Capitol F1260	Gabby the Gobbler/Do You Believe in Santa Claus	1950	5.00	10.00	20.00
— B-side by Santa Claus					
CARSON, MARTHA					
45s					
Capitol F2969	Christmas Time Is Here/Peace On Earth (At Christmas Time)	1954	3.75	7.50	15.00
CARSON, MINDY					
45s					
RCA Victor 47-4316	Christmas Chopsticks/Doors That Lead to You	1951	5.00	10.00	20.00
CARTELL, LARRY					
45s					
Glenolden 150	Cowboy Santa/Little Drummer Boy	196?	2.50	5.00	10.00
CARTER, CARLENE					
45s					
Giant 18006	Rockin' Little Christmas/The Working Elf Blues	1994	—	2.00	4.00
— B-side by Daron Norwood					
CARTER, CLARENCE					
45s					
Atlantic 2576	Back Door Santa/That Old Time Feeling	1968	2.00	4.00	8.00
CARTER, GAYLORD					
45s					
Skyway 103	Season's Greetings (A Cheerful Hello)/ Season's Greetings (A Cheerful Hello)	1960	2.00	4.00	8.00
— B-side by Pete Pontrelli					
CARTER, ROMAN					
45s					
Jewel 794	There's Trouble Brewin'/Queen Bee	1968	—	3.00	6.00

CARTER, WILF – See MONTANA SLIM.

Label, Number	Title (A Side/B Side)	Year	VG	VG+	NM
CARTON, MARY					
45s					
Decca 27348	Christmas in Killarney/Did Santa Claus Come from Ireland	1950	3.75	7.50	15.00
CARTWRIGHT, PHILIP J.					
Albums					
Euterpe ER-103	The Christmas Story in Scripture and Song	1974	2.50	5.00	10.00

CARUSO, ENRICO
On Various-Artists Collections
Cantique de Noel (O Holy Night)   Joyous Noel (Reader's Digest RDA-57A)

CASALS, PABLO
On Various-Artists Collections
Jesu, Joy of Man's Desiring   Great Songs of Christmas, The, Album Six (Columbia Special Products CSM 388)

Label, Number	Title (A Side/B Side)	Year	VG	VG+	NM

CASAMENIT, AL
45s

Command 4107	Sleigh Ride/Jingle Bells	1967	—	3.00	6.00
— B-side by Toots Thielmans					

CASAZZA, JIMMY
45s

Atina 449	Little Drummer Boy/Carol Of The Drums (Disco '77)//	1977	—	2.50	5.00
	All I Want for Christmas Is My Two Front Teeth				

CASH, JOHNNY
45s

Columbia 41481	The Little Drummer Boy/I'll Remember You	1959	3.75	7.50	15.00
Columbia 45979	Christmas As I Knew It/That Christmasy Feeling	1973	—	2.50	5.00
— With Tommy Cash					

Albums

Columbia CL 2117	M	The Christmas Spirit	1963	6.25	12.50	25.00
Columbia CS 8917	S	The Christmas Spirit	1963	7.50	15.00	30.00
Columbia JC 36866		Classic Christmas	1980	3.00	6.00	12.00

On Various-Artists Collections

Blue Christmas	Christmas Greetings, Vol. 3 (Columbia Special Products P 11383)
Christmas Spirit, The	Christmas Greetings (Columbia Special Products CSS 1499)
I Heard the Bells on Christmas Day	Country Christmas (Columbia CS 9888)
	Country Style Christmas, A (Columbia Musical Treasury 3P 6316)
	Home for Christmas (Columbia Musical Treasury P3S 5608)
	Home for Christmas (Realm 2V 8101)
	Very Merry Christmas, A, Volume IV (Columbia Special Products CSS 1464)
	Very Merry Christmas, A, Volume Two (Columbia Special Products CSS 788)
	Wondrous Winter: Songs of Winter, Songs of Christmas
	(Columbia Special Products CSS 708/9)
Jingle Bells	Country Style Christmas, A (Columbia Musical Treasury 3P 6316)
	Merry Christmas (Columbia Musical Treasury 3P 6306)
Joy to the World	Christmas Greetings from Nashville (Columbia PC 39467)
	Nashville's Greatest Christmas Hits (Columbia PC 44412)
Little Drummer Boy, The	Country Christmas (Time-Life STL-109)
	Country Christmas Favorites (Columbia Special Products C 10876)
	Joyous Christmas, Volume 4 (Columbia Special Products CSS 1485)
Silent Night, Holy Night	Joy of Christmas, The, Featuring Marty Robbins and His Friends
	(Columbia Special Products C 11087)
	Ronco Presents A Christmas Gift (Columbia Special Products P 12430)
	Spirit of Christmas, The, Volume III (Columbia Special Products CSS 1463)
Spirit of Christmas, The	Down-Home Country Christmas, A (Columbia Special Products P 14992)

CASHMERES, THE
45s

Laurie 3078	I Believe in St. Nick/A Very Special Birthday	1960	10.00	20.00	40.00

CASSADY, LINDA
45s

Metro County 2010	Is Santa Claus A Hippie?/What Do You Do?	1969	—	3.00	6.00

CASSINI, DARIO
45s

Epic 9084	Santo Natale/O Holy Night	1954	3.75	7.50	15.00

CAST, THE (OF IRMA LA DOUCE)
On Various-Artists Collections

Christmas Child	Irma La Douce (Columbia Masterworks OS 2029)

CASTELLE, GEORGE
45s

Grand 118	It's Christmas Time/Over The Rainbow	1954	12.50	25.00	50.00

CASTELLES, THE
45s

Classic Artists 114	At Christmas Time/One Little Teardrop	1989	—	2.00	4.00

CASTELLUCCI, LOUIS
45s

Capitol F1620	Sleigh Ride/Syncopated Clock	195?	3.00	6.00	12.00
— Reissue of Capitol Symphony Band single (F984)					

Label, Number		Title (A Side/B Side)	Year	VG	VG+	NM
CASTOR, JIMMY, BUNCH						
45s						
Atlantic 3302		The Christmas Song (Chestnuts Roasting on an Open Fire)/ Merry Christmas	1975	—	3.50	7.00
CATES, GEORGE						
45s						
Coral 60302		Sleigh Ride/Tubby the Tuba Song	1950	3.75	7.50	15.00
Coral 60326		Silver Bells/Jing-a-Ling, Jing-a-Ling	1950	3.75	7.50	15.00
Coral 60556		Jingle Bells Around the World/The Winter Song	1951	3.75	7.50	15.00
7-Inch Extended Plays						
Coral EC 81076		Sleigh Ride/Jingle Bells Around The World// Silver Bells/Jing-A-Ling Jing-A-Ling	195?	3.00	6.00	12.00
Coral EC 81076	PS	Sleigh Ride	195?	3.00	6.00	12.00
CATHEDRAL ORGAN WITH CHIMES						
45s						
Capitol F95007		Silent Night/Adeste Fideles//Joy to the World/Silent Night	1951	2.50	5.00	10.00
— Part of album CDF-9013						
Capitol F95008		Cantique de Noel/It Came Upon a Midnight Clear	1951	2.50	5.00	10.00
— Part of album CDF-9013						
Capitol F95009		Ring Out, Wild Bells/O Little Town of Bethlehem// Hark, the Herald Angels Sing	1951	2.50	5.00	10.00
— Part of album CDF-9013						
7-Inch Extended Plays						
Capitol CDF-9013	(3)	Christmas Bells	1951	8.75	17.50	35.00
— Includes three records (F95007, F95008, F95009) and box						
CAULFIELD, SANDY						
45s						
Citation 110041		Christmas (Is The Happiest Time Of All)/Christmas (Instrumental)	19??	—	2.00	4.00
Citation 110041	PS	Christmas (Is The Happiest Time Of All)/Christmas (Instrumental)	19??	—	2.00	4.00
CAVALLARO, CARMEN						
45s						
Decca 24141		Silent Night/White Christmas	1950	3.00	6.00	12.00
— Reissue; 78 rpm released in 1947						
CAVANAUGH, MICHAEL						
45s						
Contrast 700		Merry Christmas, Baby/Christmas Tree	19??	2.50	5.00	10.00
CELIBATE RIFLES, THE						
45s						
Black AFTP001		Merry Xmas Blues/Splatterdance	1986	5.00	10.00	20.00
— B-side by the Saqqara Dogs						
CENTER, SANDY						
45s						
Ruby 260		Come On Baby, It's Christmas/For Me, No Christmas	1957	3.75	7.50	15.00
CESAR & SANDY						
45s						
Sanco 81787		(We Want A) Little Cowboy/White Country Christmas	1987	—	—	3.00
CETERA, PETER						
On Various-Artists Collections						
Holiday I.D.		Winter Warnerland (Warner Bros. PRO-A-3328)				
Silent Night		Winter Warnerland (Warner Bros. PRO-A-3328)				
CHABOT, MARIE						
45s						
Constellation 31590		Connecticut Christmas/My Christmas With You	198?	—	—	3.00
CHAMBERS BROTHERS, THE						
45s						
Columbia 45055		Merry Christmas, Happy New Year/ Did You Stop to Pray This Morning	1969	—	3.00	6.00

Label, Number		Title (A Side/B Side)	Year	VG	VG+	NM
Columbia 45518		Merry Christmas, Happy New Year/ Did You Stop to Pray This Morning	1971	—	3.00	6.00

CHAMPAGNE BROTHERS, THE
45s
| Teardrop 3046 | | Christmas Time Without You/Snow On The Old Bayou | 1964 | 3.00 | 6.00 | 12.00 |

CHAMPION, WAYNE
45s
| Invictus 7690 | | It's Xmas Time/Merry Yuletide Day | 196? | 2.50 | 5.00 | 10.00 |

CHANDLER, BARBARA
45s
| Kapp 575 | | A Lonely New Year/I'm Going Out With The Girls | 1964 | 2.50 | 5.00 | 10.00 |

CHANEY, LON
45s
| Tower 114 | | Monster's Holiday/Yuletide Jerk | 1964 | 6.25 | 12.50 | 25.00 |

CHANNING, CAROL
Albums
| Caedmon TC 1303
— Spoken-word recordings | | The Year Without a Santa Claus and Other Stories for Christmas | 1977 | 3.00 | 6.00 | 12.00 |

CHANT, THE
45s
| Safety Net NETMAS 16
— Red vinyl | | We Three Kings/Bullshit (Goin' On) | 198? | — | 2.00 | 4.00 |
| Safety Net NETMAS 16 | | We Three Kings/Bullshit (Goin' On) | 198? | — | 2.00 | 4.00 |

CHANTEURS DE LA VIERGE
On Various-Artists Collections
Bethlehem: Dans cette etable	Joyous Music for Christmas Time (Reader's Digest RD 45-M)
Ding, Dong	Joyous Music for Christmas Time (Reader's Digest RD 45-M)
Durreau la Duree	Joyous Music for Christmas Time (Reader's Digest RD 45-M)
Guillo Pron Ton Tambourin	Joyous Music for Christmas Time (Reader's Digest RD 45-M)
Marche des Rois	Joyous Music for Christmas Time (Reader's Digest RD 45-M)
Noel, Noel, Noel	Joyous Music for Christmas Time (Reader's Digest RD 45-M)
O Jesus, Nous Voici Comme Autrefois les Anges	Joyous Music for Christmas Time (Reader's Digest RD 45-M)
Quelle Est Cette Odeur Agreable?	Joyous Music for Christmas Time (Reader's Digest RD 45-M)
Sus! Qu'on Se Reveille	Joyous Music for Christmas Time (Reader's Digest RD 45-M)
Voici la Nouvelle	Joyous Music for Christmas Time (Reader's Digest RD 45-M)

CHANTS, THE
45s
| U.W.R. 4243 | | Rockin' Santa/Respectable | 1962 | 6.25 | 12.50 | 25.00 |

CHAPEL, BETTY
45s
| Kandy 104 | | It's Christmas Time/You Trimmed My Christmas Tree | 195? | 3.75 | 7.50 | 15.00 |
| Mercury 5549 | | Christmas in Killarney/Rainbow Gal | 1950 | 3.75 | 7.50 | 15.00 |

CHARACTERS, THE
On Various-Artists Collections
Home for Christmas	Stuff This in Your Stocking! Elves in Action (Veebltronics/Skyclad 68)

CHARLES, JIMMY
45s
Promo 1004		Santa Won't Be Blue This Christmas/ I Saw Mommy Kissing Santa Claus	1960	3.75	7.50	15.00
Promo 1004	PS	Santa Won't Be Blue This Christmas/ I Saw Mommy Kissing Santa Claus	1960	5.00	10.00	20.00
Promo 1005		Christmasville U.S.A./A Little White Mouse Called Steve	1960	3.75	7.50	15.00
Promo 1005	PS	Christmasville U.S.A./A Little White Mouse Called Steve	1960	5.00	10.00	20.00

Label, Number		Title (A Side/B Side)	Year	VG	VG+	NM
CHARLES, RAY						
45s						
Atlantic 3549	DJ	Christmas Time (same on both sides)	1978	—	3.00	6.00
— *May be promo-only*						
Albums						
Columbia FC 40125		The Spirit of Christmas	1985	2.50	5.00	10.00
CHARLES, RAY, SINGERS						
45s						
Command 4074		Christmas Is a Birthday/A Toy for a Boy	1965	2.50	5.00	10.00
MGM 12606		Let It Snow, Let It Snow, Let It Snow/You're My Girl	1957	3.00	6.00	12.00
CHARLIE, FRED						
45s						
Lanor 579		Merry Christmas To A Cajun/Casse	197?	—	2.50	5.00
CHARMAIN						
45s						
Allied Artists 72501		Christmas Is for Kids/(Instrumental)	19??	—	—	3.00
Allied Artists 72501	PS	Christmas Is for Kids/(Instrumental)	19??	—	—	3.00
CHARMETTES, THE						
12-Inch Singles						
Logarhythm LR-1004		Be My Christmas Love/Sleigh Ride	1986	—	3.00	6.00
CHARO						
45s						
Salsoul 2076		(Mamacita) Donde Est· Santa Claus?/(Instrumental)	1978	2.00	4.00	8.00
CHASE, CHARLIE						
45s						
Epic 77309		Christmas Is for Kids/My Wife	1993	—	2.00	4.00
CHEECH AND CHONG						
45s						
Ode 50499		Santa Claus and His Old Lady/Rudolph the Red-Nosed Reindeer	1977	2.50	5.00	10.00
Ode 66021		Santa Claus and His Old Lady/Dave	1971	2.00	4.00	8.00
Ode 66021	PS	Santa Claus and His Old Lady/Dave	1971	3.00	6.00	12.00
On Various-Artists Collections						
Santa Claus and His Old Lady		Dr. Demento Presents the Greatest Novelty Records of All Time Volume VI: Christmas (Rhino RNLP 825)				
CHEETAHS, THE						
45s						
Chunk 451		A Message To Santa Claus/That's Your Problem	19??	—	2.50	5.00
Chunk 451	PS	A Message To Santa Claus/That's Your Problem	19??	—	2.50	5.00
CHENIER, CLIFTON						
45s						
Bayou 712		It's Christmas Time/Time Of Crying	1964	2.00	4.00	8.00
CHERRY, DON						
45s						
Monument 45269		Six Weeks Every Summer, Christmas Every Day/Play Her Back to Yesterday	1978	—	2.50	5.00
CHESTERFIELD SINGERS, THE						
45s						
Chesterfield 69		Ho! Ho! Ho! A-Ho-Ho-Hoin' All The Way/It Was Christmas Eve On A Starry Night	19??	—	3.00	6.00
CHEVALIER, DON						
45s						
Tiara 1980		Christmas Is For Giving/Christmastime	1980	—	2.00	4.00

Label, Number	Title (A Side/B Side)	Year	VG	VG+	NM

CHEVALIER, MAURICE
On Various-Artists Collections

Jolly Old St. Nicholas	Great Songs of Christmas, The, Album Five (Columbia Special Products CSP 238M)				
Silent Night	Great Songs of Christmas, The, Album Five (Columbia Special Products CSP 238M)				

CHILDREN'S CHORAL GROUP, PERKINS SCHOOL FOR THE BLIND
45s

Columbia (none)	The Twelve Days Of Christmas	196?	2.00	4.00	8.00
— Cardboard disc					

CHILDREN'S CHORUS
On Various-Artists Collections

Jingle Bells	Disney's Christmas All-Time Favorites (Disneyland 1V 8150)				
Jolly Old Saint Nicholas	Disney's Christmas Favorites (Disneyland 2506)				
We Wish You a Merry Christmas	Disney's Christmas Favorites (Disneyland 2506)				

CHIP 'N' DALE AND DONALD DUCK
On Various-Artists Collections

Chipmunk Song, The	Disney's Christmas All-Time Favorites (Disneyland 1V 8150)				

CHIPMUNKS, THE
The later incarnation, headed by Ross Bagdasarian, Jr.
45s

Epic 77768	Rockin' Around the Christmas Tree/Rudolph the Red-Nosed Reindeer	1994	—	2.00	4.00
— As "Alvin and the Chipmunks"					
RCA PB-12354	The Chipmunk Song/Sleigh Ride	1981	—	2.00	4.00
Albums					
RCA Victor AQL1-4041	A Chipmunk Christmas	1981	3.75	7.50	15.00
— With booklet					

On Various-Artists Collections

Dialog and Songs/It's Beginning to	Happy Holidays, Volume 17 (RCA Special Products DPL1-0555)				
Look a Lot Like Christmas					

CHIPMUNKS, THE, DAVID SEVILLE AND
Also see ROSS BAGDASARIAN, CANNED HEAT.
45s

EMI S7-17645		The Chipmunk Song/Frosty the Snowman	1993	—	2.00	4.00
— Green vinyl						
Liberty 55168		The Chipmunk Song/Almost Good	1958	6.25	12.50	25.00
— Blue-green label						
Liberty 55168		The Chipmunk Song/Almost Good	1958	7.50	15.00	30.00
— Black label						
Liberty 55250		The Chipmunk Song/Alvin's Harmonica	1959	3.75	7.50	15.00
— Blue-green label, no horizontal lines						
Liberty 55250	PS	The Chipmunk Song/Alvin's Harmonica	1959	10.00	20.00	40.00
— Sleeve has Chipmunks depicted somewhat like real chipmunks						
Liberty 55250		The Chipmunk Song/Alvin's Harmonica	1961	3.00	6.00	12.00
— Blue-green label with horizontal lines						
Liberty 55250	PS	The Chipmunk Song/Alvin's Harmonica	1961	7.50	15.00	30.00
— Sleeve has Chipmunks depicted as the familiar cartoon characters						
Liberty 55289		Rudolph, the Red-Nosed Reindeer/Spain	1960	3.75	7.50	15.00
Liberty 55289	PS	Rudolph, the Red-Nosed Reindeer/Spain	1960	10.00	20.00	40.00
Liberty 55635		The Night Before Christmas/Wonderful Day	1963	3.75	7.50	15.00
Liberty 55635	PS	The Night Before Christmas/Wonderful Day	1963	7.50	15.00	30.00
Liberty 56079		The Chipmunk Song/Christmas Blues	1968	4.00	8.00	16.00
— With Canned Heat						
United Artists XW056		The Chipmunk Song/Ragtime Cowboy Joe	1973	2.00	4.00	8.00
— "Silver Spotlight Series" reissue						
United Artists XW057		Alvin's Harmonica/Rudolph, the Red-Nosed Reindeer	1973	2.00	4.00	8.00
— "Silver Spotlight Series" reissue						
United Artists XW576		The Chipmunk Song/Rudolph, the Red-Nosed Reindeer	1974	—	3.00	6.00
7-Inch Extended Plays						
Liberty LSX-1007		The Chipmunk Song/Ragtime Cowboy Joe//	1960	7.50	15.00	30.00
		Alvin's Harmonica/If You Love Me				
Liberty LSX-1007	PS	Let's All Sing with the Chipmunks	1960	12.50	25.00	50.00
Liberty LSX-1017		Wonderful Day/Christmas Time//	1963	5.00	10.00	20.00
		Deck The Halls/The Night Before Christmas				
Liberty LSX-1017	PS	Christmas with the Chipmunks, Volume 2	1963	12.50	25.00	50.00

Label, Number		Title (A Side/B Side)	Year	VG	VG+	NM
Albums						
Liberty LM-1070		Christmas with the Chipmunks	1980	2.00	4.00	8.00
— Reissue with two tracks omitted						
Liberty LRP-3132	M	Let's All Sing with the Chipmunks	1959	15.00	30.00	60.00
— Red vinyl; contains one Christmas song: Chipmunk Song, The						
Liberty LRP-3132	M	Let's All Sing with the Chipmunks	1959	7.50	15.00	30.00
— Same as above, but on black vinyl; original cover features "realistic" chipmunks and no reference to "The Alvin Show"						
Liberty LRP-3132	M	Let's All Sing with the Chipmunks	1961	5.00	10.00	20.00
— Same as above, but with second cover featuring the "cartoon" Chipmunks and a reference to "The Alvin Show"						
Liberty LRP-3170	M	Around the World with the Chipmunks	1960	10.00	20.00	40.00
— Original covers have "realistic" Chipmunks on and near a plane. Contains one Christmas song: Rudolph the Red-Nosed Reindeer						
Liberty LRP-3170	M	Around the World with the Chipmunks	1961	5.00	10.00	20.00
— Same as above, but with second cover featuring the "cartoon" Chipmunks on and near a camel						
Liberty LRP-3256	M	Christmas with the Chipmunks	1962	6.25	12.50	25.00
Liberty LRP-3334	M	Christmas with the Chipmunks, Vol. 2	1963	6.25	12.50	25.00
Liberty LST-7132	S	Let's All Sing with the Chipmunks	1959	20.00	40.00	80.00
— Same as 3132, but in stereo on red vinyl						
Liberty LST-7132	S	Let's All Sing with the Chipmunks	1959	10.00	20.00	40.00
— Same as 3132, but on black vinyl; original cover features "realistic" chipmunks and no reference to "The Alvin Show"						
Liberty LST-7132	S	Let's All Sing with the Chipmunks	1961	6.25	12.50	25.00
— Same as 3132, but with second cover featuring the "cartoon" Chipmunks and a reference to "The Alvin Show"						
Liberty LST-7170	S	Around the World with the Chipmunks	1960	12.50	25.00	50.00
— Same as 3170, but in stereo; original covers have "realistic" Chipmunks on and near a plane.						
Liberty LST-7170	S	Around the World with the Chipmunks	1960	6.25	12.50	25.00
— Same as 3170, but with second cover featuring the "cartoon" Chipmunks on and near a camel						
Liberty LST-7256	S	Christmas with the Chipmunks	1962	7.50	15.00	30.00
Liberty LST-7334	S	Christmas with the Chipmunks, Vol. 2	1963	7.50	15.00	30.00
Mistletoe MLP-1216		Christmas with the Chipmunks	197?	2.00	4.00	8.00
Mistletoe MLP-1217		Christmas with the Chipmunks, Vol. 2	197?	2.00	4.00	8.00
Sunset LST-7334	S	Christmas with the Chipmunks, Vol. 2	1968	5.00	10.00	20.00
United Artists UA-LA352-E2	(2)	Christmas with the Chipmunks	1974	5.00	10.00	20.00
— Entire contents of both original Liberty LPs; why hasn't this been reissued in this form on CD?						

On Various-Artists Collections

(All I Want for Christmas Is) My Two Front Teeth	Best of Christmas Vol. 2 (Mistletoe MLP-1221)	
Chipmunk Song, The	Best of Christmas Vol. 2 (Mistletoe MLP-1221)	
	Billboard Greatest Christmas Hits, 1955-Present (Rhino R1 70636)	
	12 Hits of Christmas (United Artists UA-LA669-R)	

CHIPPER

45s

Label, Number		Title (A Side/B Side)	Year	VG	VG+	NM
Malaco 2002	DJ	Groovy Christmas/Toy Soldier	197?	—	3.00	6.00

CHIPPS, JIMMY

45s

Label, Number		Title (A Side/B Side)	Year	VG	VG+	NM
Ovo 1928		On Santa Claus Island/Christmas Will Be Here	1964	2.50	5.00	10.00

CHOIR OF KING'S COLLEGE, CAMBRIDGE
On Various-Artists Collections

Coventry Carol	Time-Life Treasury of Christmas, The, Volume Two (Time-Life STL-108)
Shepherds in the Field Abiding	Time-Life Treasury of Christmas, The, Volume Two (Time-Life STL-108)

CHOIR OF LONDON, THE
Albums

Label, Number		Title (A Side/B Side)	Year	VG	VG+	NM
Acorn 693		Favorite Christmas Songs	196?	3.75	7.50	15.00

CHOIR OF THE BELLA VISTA CHILDREN'S HOME, THE
Albums

Label, Number		Title (A Side/B Side)	Year	VG	VG+	NM
Folkways FC 7714	M	Villancicos: Spanish Christmas Songs for Children	1967	3.75	7.50	15.00

CHRISTIAN HOLIDAY
45s

Label, Number		Title (A Side/B Side)	Year	VG	VG+	NM
North Side 103		A Cabbage Patch Doll on Christmas Eve/Jesus Loves Me	198?	—	3.00	6.00
— B-side by Maria & Elijah Sarge						

CHRISTIAN, BOBBY
45s

Label, Number		Title (A Side/B Side)	Year	VG	VG+	NM
Mal 1003		White Christmas/Let It Snow, Let It Snow, Let It Snow	196?	2.50	5.00	10.00

Label, Number		Title (A Side/B Side)	Year	VG	VG+	NM

CHRISTIAN, CHRIS
45s

Home Sweet Home 001		Christmas All Year 'Round/God Bless The Children	1981	—	2.00	4.00

CHRISTIAN, CHRIS, AND BOB BREUNIG
45s

Home Sweet Home 122586		Thinking Of You This Christmas/Living The American Dream	1986	2.00	4.00	8.00
— B-side by the Dallas Cowboys '86						

CHRISTIAN, ROGER
45s

Rendezvous 195		The Meaning of Merry Christmas/Little Mary Christmas	1962	6.25	12.50	25.00

CHRISTMAS CHARACTERS, THE
45s

Moebius 25825		Santa Claus Jr./Pee Wee The Pink Pine Tree	19??	—	2.00	4.00
Moebius 25825	PS	Santa Claus Jr./Pee Wee The Pink Pine Tree	19??	—	2.00	4.00

CHRISTMAS ON 45
45s

Rock Music Co SANTA 1		Christmas On 45/Have Mercy On The Child	1981	—	2.50	5.00
— B-side by Holly and the Ivys; U.K. import						
Rock Music Co SANTA 1	PS	Christmas On 45/Have Mercy On The Child	1981	—	2.50	5.00
— B-side by Holly and the Ivys; U.K. import						

CHRISTMAS REVELS, THE
Various spoken and musical bits by a collection of artists under one umbrella.

Albums

	Title	Year	VG	VG+	NM
Revels RC 1078	The Christmas Revels	1978	3.00	6.00	12.00
Revels RC 1082	Wassail! Wassail!	1982	3.00	6.00	12.00
Revels RC 1087	Christmas Day in the Morning: A Revels Celebration of the Winter Solstice	1987	3.00	6.00	12.00

CHRISTMAS SPIRIT, THE
Two different artists.

45s

	Title	Year	VG	VG+	NM
Duel 503	It's Christmas/A World to Grow Up In	1961	3.00	6.00	12.00
— William B. Williams, Narrator					
White Whale 290	Christmas Is My Time of Year/Will You Still Believe	1968	20.00	40.00	80.00
— Members of the Turtles with Linda Ronstadt					

CHRISTMAS STRINGS, THE
On Various-Artists Collections

Deck the Halls	20 Christmas Favorites (Yulesong SY-0220)
First Noel, The	20 Christmas Favorites (Yulesong SY-0220)
White Christmas	20 Christmas Favorites (Yulesong SY-0220)

CHRISTY, JUNE
Albums

		Title	Year	VG	VG+	NM
Capitol T 1605	M	That Time of Year	1961	10.00	20.00	40.00
Capitol ST 1605	S	That Time of Year	1961	12.50	25.00	50.00

CHRISTY, TOMMY
45s

	Title	Year	VG	VG+	NM
Scot 503	All Are Waiting For Christmas/Eight Tiny Reindeer	196?	2.50	5.00	10.00

CHUCK WAGON GANG, THE
45s

		Title	Year	VG	VG+	NM
Columbia 21286		Joy to the World/While Shepherds Watched Their Flock by Night	1954	3.00	6.00	12.00
Columbia 21287		It Came Upon a Midnight Clear/Silent Night	1954	3.00	6.00	12.00
Columbia 21288		The First Noel/It Came Upon a Midnight Clear	1954	3.00	6.00	12.00
Columbia 21289		Hark the Herald Angels Sing/O Little Town of Bethlehem	1954	3.00	6.00	12.00

Albums

		Title	Year	VG	VG+	NM
Harmony HL 7355		Christmas with the Chuck Wagon Gang	196?	3.00	6.00	12.00
Harmony HS 11155	R	Christmas with the Chuck Wagon Gang	196?	3.00	6.00	12.00

On Various-Artists Collections

First Noel, The	Joy of Christmas, The, Featuring Marty Robbins and His Friends (Columbia Special Products C 11087)

Label, Number	Title (A Side/B Side)	Year	VG	VG+	NM
Hark! The Herald Angels Sing	Country Christmas Favorites (Columbia Special Products C 10876)				
Joy to the World	Country Christmas (Columbia CS 9888)				
	Down-Home Country Christmas, A (Columbia Special Products P 14992)				

CIX BITS
45s
Enterprise 9087	Season's Greetings/New Year's Resolution	1973	—	3.00	6.00

CLANCY BROTHERS, THE
Albums
Columbia CS 9876	Christmas	1969	3.00	6.00	12.00

CLARK, BETTY
45s
MGM 11381	I Saw Mommy Kissing Santa Claus/You Can Fly	1952	5.00	10.00	20.00

CLARK, PETULA
45s
Coral 61077	Where Did My Snowman Go/Three Little Kittens	1953	6.25	12.50	25.00

On Various-Artists Collections
Happiest Christmas, The	Best of the Great Songs of Christmas (Album 10) (Columbia Special Products CSS 1478)				
	Great Songs of Christmas, Album Nine (Columbia Special Products CSS 1033)				
Silent Night, Holy Night	Great Songs of Christmas, Album Nine (Columbia Special Products CSS 1033)				

CLARK, RON, AND THE SWEETBRIAR TRIO
45s
Century 32396	A Season For Remembering/A Season For Remembering	19??	—	2.50	5.00
— B-side by the BYU Symphonic Band					

CLARK, ROY
45s
Churchill 94016	Christmas Wouldn't Be Christmas Without You/A Way Without Words	1982	—	2.00	4.00

On Various-Artists Collections
Mr. and Mrs. Snowman	Christmas America, Album Two (Capitol Special Markets SL-6950)				

CLASSICS, THE
45s
MV 1000	Christmas Is Here/(B-side unknown)	19??	2.50	5.00	10.00

CLASSICS IV, THE
45s
Algonquin 1650	Limbo Under The Christmas Tree/Early Christmas	19??	3.00	6.00	12.00

CLAW HAMMER
On Various-Artists Collections
Night Before Christmas, The	Happy Birthday, Baby Jesus (Sympathy For The Record Industry SFTRI 271)				

CLAY, CHRIS
45s
Veltone 111	Santa Under Analysis Part 1/Santa Under Analysis Part 2	1960	6.25	12.50	25.00

CLAYDERMAN, RICHARD
Albums
Columbia PC 40190	A Romantic Christmas	1985	2.50	5.00	10.00

CLEMENTS, ZEKE
45s
Gold Standard 271	Christmas Time Is Here Again/Christmas Star	19??	—	—	3.00
MGM 11872	Christmas Star/It's Christmas Time	1954	3.75	7.50	15.00

CLEMONS, T. L.
45s
HCT 105	Merry Christmas And A Happy New Year/It's Been A Long Time	19??	—	3.00	6.00

CLETRO, EDDIE
45s
Sage & Sand 214	Santa Claus Jr./Give Me An Old Fashioned Christmas	195?	3.00	6.00	12.00

Label, Number		Title (A Side/B Side)	Year	VG	VG+	NM

CLEVELAND ORCHESTRA (SZELL)
On Various-Artists Collections

Deck the Hall with Boughs of Holly		Great Songs of Christmas, The, Album Seven (Columbia Special Products CSS 547)				
Patapan		Great Songs of Christmas, The, Album Seven (Columbia Special Products CSS 547)				

CLEWER, JANEY
On Various-Artists Collections

Christmas in the Air		Starlight Christmas, A (MCA 10066)
Christmas Lullaby		Starlight Christmas, A (MCA 10066)
I'm All Lit Up Like a Christmas Tree		Starlight Christmas, A (MCA 10066)
Remember Christmas		Starlight Christmas, A (MCA 10066)
What a Christmas Feeling		Starlight Christmas, A (MCA 10066)

CLEWER, JANEY; GENE MOREFORD; AND DON SHELTON
On Various-Artists Collections

Ain't No Time for Diets		Starlight Christmas, A (MCA 10066)

CLINE, BOB
On Various-Artists Collections

Christmas Spirit, The		Merry Christmas (Rainbow Sound R-5032-LPS)

CLINTON, LARRY, AND HIS ORCHESTRA
On Various-Artists Collections

Parade of the Wooden Soldiers		Remembering Christmas with the Big Bands (RCA Special Products DPM1-0506)

CLODFELTER, AMY
45s

Label, Number		Title (A Side/B Side)	Year	VG	VG+	NM
Winston 1011		Christmas Time/Santa Claus	1957	3.75	7.50	15.00

CLOONEY, ROSEMARY
45s

Label, Number		Title (A Side/B Side)	Year	VG	VG+	NM
Columbia 4-123 (90137)		Suzy Snowflake/Little Red Riding Hood's Christmas	1951	3.75	7.50	15.00
— Yellow-label Children's Series record						
Columbia 4-123 (90137)	PS	Suzy Snowflake/Little Red Riding Hood's Christmas	1951	5.00	10.00	20.00
Columbia 4-149 (90170)		The Night Before Christmas Song/	1952	3.75	7.50	15.00
		Look Out The Window (The Winter Song)				
— With Gene Autry; yellow-label Children's Series record						
Columbia 4-149 (90170)	PS	The Night Before Christmas Song/	1952	5.00	10.00	20.00
		Look Out The Window (The Winter Song)				
Columbia 4-175		Winter Wonderland/Christmas Song	1954	3.75	7.50	15.00
— Yellow-label Children's Series record						
Columbia 4-175	PS	Winter Wonderland/Christmas Song	1954	5.00	10.00	20.00
Columbia 39612		Suzy Snowflake/Little Red Riding Hood's Christmas	1951	3.75	7.50	15.00
Columbia 39876		The Night Before Christmas Song/	1952	3.75	7.50	15.00
		Look Out the Window (The Winter Song)				
— With Gene Autry						
Columbia 40102		C-H-R-I-S-T-M-A-S/Happy Christmas, Little Friend	1953	3.75	7.50	15.00
Columbia 40317		(Let's Give) A Christmas Present to Santa Claus/	1954	3.75	7.50	15.00
		March of the Christmas Toys				
— With Jose Ferrer						
Columbia 40355		White Christmas/Count Your Blessings	1954	Unreleased?		
Columbia 40370		Count Your Blessings Instead of Sheep/White Christmas	1954	3.75	7.50	15.00
Columbia 40808		He'll Be Comin' Down the Chimney/Mommy Can I Keep the Kitten	1956	3.00	6.00	12.00
— With "Her Sister Gail"						

7-Inch Extended Plays

Label, Number		Title (A Side/B Side)	Year	VG	VG+	NM
Columbia B-1901		White Christmas/Mandy//Snow/Gee, I Wish I Was Back In The Army	195?	3.00	6.00	12.00
Columbia B-1901	PS	White Christmas Volume 2	195?	3.00	6.00	12.00

Albums

Label, Number		Title (A Side/B Side)	Year	VG	VG+	NM
Columbia CL 6338	10	White Christmas	1954	15.00	30.00	60.00
Holiday 1946		Christmas with Rosemary Clooney	1981	2.50	5.00	10.00

On Various-Artists Collections

C-H-R-I-S-T-M-A-S	First Christmas Record for Children (Harmony HS 14554)
Christmas Song, The	Bing Crosby and Rosemary Clooney: White Christmas (Holiday/Collector's Gold 598)
Count Your Blessings	Happy Holiday (Mistletoe 1243)
Have Yourself a Merry	Bing Crosby and Rosemary Clooney: White Christmas (Holiday/Collector's Gold 598)
Little Christmas	Happy Holiday (Mistletoe 1243)
It Came Upon a Midnight Clear	Bing Crosby and Rosemary Clooney: White Christmas (Holiday/Collector's Gold 598)
	Have Yourself a Merry Little Christmas (Reprise R 50001)
Jingle Bells	Bing Crosby and Rosemary Clooney: White Christmas (Holiday/Collector's Gold 598)
Little Drummer Boy	Bing Crosby and Rosemary Clooney: White Christmas (Holiday/Collector's Gold 598)
Night Before Christmas Song, The	Santa's Hit Parade (Columbia Record Club D-17)
	Spirit of Christmas, The (Columbia Special Products CSP 249)

Label, Number		Title (A Side/B Side)	Year	VG	VG+	NM
Suzy Snowflake		First Christmas Record for Children (Harmony HS 14554) Santa's Hit Parade (Columbia Record Club D-17)				

COASTAL CAROLINA
45s
| Target 0139 | | The Christmas Tree/Wanting You | 19?? | — | — | 3.00 |
| Target 0139 | PS | The Christmas Tree/Wanting You | 19?? | — | 2.00 | 4.00 |

COBINE, AL, SINGERS
45s
| Brite Star 482 | | Christmas City U.S.A./(B-side unknown) | 198? | — | — | 3.00 |
| Brite Star 482 | PS | Christmas City U.S.A./(B-side unknown) | 198? | — | 2.00 | 4.00 |

COCTAILS, THE
7-Inch Extended Plays
Hi Ball 1293		First Snowfall/Holiday In Paradise//Jingle Bells/Silent Night	1993	—	—	3.00
— Plays at 33 1/3 rpm						
Hi Ball 1293	PS	First Snowfall/Holiday In Paradise//Jingle Bells/Silent Night	1993	—	—	3.00

COCTEAU TWINS
45s
| Capitol S7-18208 | | Frosty the Snowman/Winter Wonderland | 1994 | — | 2.50 | 5.00 |
| — Red vinyl | | | | | | |

CODY, MICHELLE
45s
| Safari 601 | | Merry Christmas Elvis/All I Want For Christmas | 1978 | — | 2.50 | 5.00 |

COFFEE, RED
45s
| Warner Bros. 5128 | | Ducky Christmas/Jolly Jingle Bells | 1959 | 3.75 | 7.50 | 15.00 |

COLD CHILLIN' JUICE CREW (BIG DADDY KANE, MC SHAN, ROXANNE SHANTE)
On Various-Artists Collections
| Cold Chillin' Christmas | | Winter Warnerland (Warner Bros. PRO-A-3328) | | | | |

COLDCUT
45s
Ahead Of Time CCUT7		Coldcut's Christmas Break (Radio Version)/ Coldcut's Christmas Break (Club Mix)	1989	—	3.00	6.00
Ahead Of Time CCUT7	PS	Coldcut's Christmas Break (Radio Version)/ Coldcut's Christmas Break (Club Mix)	1989	—	3.00	6.00
— Record and sleeve are U.K. imports						

COLE, BUDDY
On Various-Artists Collections
| O Little Town of Bethlehem | | Spirit of Christmas, The (Columbia Special Products CSP 249) | | | | |

COLE, EDDIE
On Various-Artists Collections
| Santa Claus Is Coming to Town | | We Wish You a Merry Christmas (Warner Bros. W 1337) | | | | |

COLE, FREDDIE
45s
| Sue 775 | | It's Christmas Time/Right Now | 1962 | 3.75 | 7.50 | 15.00 |

COLE, GARDNER
On Various-Artists Collections
| Maybe This Could Be the Christmas | | Winter Warnerland (Warner Bros. PRO-A-3328) | | | | |

COLE, HOLLY, TRIO
45s
| Blue Note S7-18209 | | I'd Like to Hitch a Ride with Santa Claus/Christmas Blues | 1994 | — | 2.00 | 4.00 |
| — Green vinyl | | | | | | |

Label, Number		Title (A Side/B Side)	Year	VG	VG+	NM
COLE, JOHNNY						
Albums						
Crown CMX 100		Famous Christmas Carols	196?	3.00	6.00	12.00
Crown 165	S	Wishing You a Merry Christmas	196?	3.75	7.50	15.00
Crown CLP 5081	M	Famous Christmas Carols	196?	3.00	6.00	12.00
— Same as Crown CMX 100						
Crown CLP 5132	M	Wishing You a Merry Christmas	196?	3.00	6.00	12.00
— Same as Crown 165						
Custom CS 6	S	12 Days of Christmas	196?	3.00	6.00	12.00
— Reissue of Crown 165 with new title						
Yuletide Series YS-211		Famous Christmas Carols	197?	2.50	5.00	10.00
— Reissue of Crown LP of the same name						
Yuletide Series YS-213		Rudolph the Red-Nosed Reindeer	197?	2.50	5.00	10.00
Yuletide Series YS-216		12 Days of Christmas	197?	2.50	5.00	10.00
— Reissue of Custom album of the same name						
COLE, NAT KING						
45s						
American Pie 9067		The Christmas Song/Ramblin' Rose	198?	—	2.50	5.00
— Reissue; B-side not a Christmas song						
Capitol F1203		Frosty the Snow Man/A Little Christmas Tree	1950	7.50	15.00	30.00
Capitol F2616		Mrs. Santa Claus/The Little Boy That Santa Claus Forgot	1953	5.00	10.00	20.00
Capitol F2955		The Christmas Song (Merry Christmas to You)/ My Two Front Teeth (All I Want for Christmas)	1954	5.00	10.00	20.00
Capitol F3305		Take Me Back to Toyland/I'm Gonna Laugh You Right Out of My Life	1955	5.00	10.00	20.00
Capitol F3560		Mrs. Santa Claus/Take Me Back to Toyland	1956	3.75	7.50	15.00
Capitol F3561		The Christmas Song (Merry Christmas to You)/ The Little Boy That Santa Claus Forgot	1956	3.75	7.50	15.00
— Original with "F" prefix, Capitol logo on top						
Capitol 3561		The Christmas Song (Merry Christmas to You)/ The Little Boy That Santa Claus Forgot	1960	2.00	4.00	8.00
— Purple label, Capitol logo on side						
Capitol 3561		The Christmas Song (Merry Christmas to You)/ The Little Boy That Santa Claus Forgot	1962	—	3.00	6.00
— Orange and yellow swirl label						
Capitol 3561		The Christmas Song (Merry Christmas to You)/ The Little Boy That Santa Claus Forgot	1973	—	2.00	4.00
— Orange label with "Capitol" at bottom						
Capitol 4301		The Happiest Christmas Tree/Buon Natale	1959	3.00	6.00	12.00
Capitol S7-57887		The Christmas Song/O Holy Night	1992	—	2.00	4.00
— Originals on black vinyl						
Capitol S7-57887		The Christmas Song/O Holy Night	1993		2.00	4.00
— Second pressing on red vinyl						
Capitol F90036		(All I Want for Christmas Is) My Two Front Teeth/ The Christmas Song (Merry Christmas To You)	1949	5.00	10.00	20.00
— B-side is the original King Cole Trio version, possibly its only U.S. release on 45						
7-Inch Extended Plays						
Capitol EAP 1-9026		The Christmas Song/Mrs. Santa Claus// Frosty The Snowman/Little Christmas Tree	195?	3.00	6.00	12.00
Capitol EAP 1-9026	PS	The Christmas Song	195?	3.00	6.00	12.00
Albums						
Capitol WCL 1613	(3) M	The Nat King Cole Story	1961	6.25	12.50	25.00
Capitol SWCL 1613	(3) S	The Nat King Cole Story	1961	7.50	15.00	30.00
— Contains one Christmas song: Christmas Song, The (re-recorded)						
Capitol W 1926	M	The Nat King Cole Story, Volume 1	1962	3.00	6.00	12.00
Capitol SW 1926	S	The Nat King Cole Story, Volume 1	1962	3.75	7.50	15.00
— Contains one Christmas song: Christmas Song, The						
Capitol W 1967	M	The Christmas Song	1962	3.75	7.50	15.00
Capitol SW 1967	S	The Christmas Song	1962	3.75	7.50	15.00
— Black label with colorband						
Capitol SW 1967	S	The Christmas Song	1969	3.00	6.00	12.00
— Lime-green label						
Capitol SW 1967	S	The Christmas Song	1971	3.00	6.00	12.00
— Red label						
Capitol SW 1967	S	The Christmas Song	1973	2.50	5.00	10.00
— Orange label, "Capitol" at bottom						
Capitol SM-1967	S	The Christmas Song	197?	2.00	4.00	8.00
— Budget-line reissue						
On Various-Artists Collections						
Adeste Fideles		Merry Christmas with Nat King Cole/Fred Waring and the Pennsylvanians (Capitol Special Markets SL-6883)				

Label, Number	Title (A Side/B Side)	Year	VG	VG+	NM
Away in a Manger	Christmas Day (Pickwick SPC 1010)				
	Christmas to Remember, A (Capitol Creative Products SL-6573)				
	Merry Christmas with Nat King Cole/Fred Waring and the Pennsylvanians (Capitol Special Markets SL-6883)				
Caroling, Caroling	Best of Christmas, The, Vol. II (Capitol SM-11834)				
	Christmas Carousel (Capitol SQBE-94406)				
	Happy Holidays, Vol. 5 (Capitol Creative Products SL-6627)				
	Happy Holly Days (Capitol Creative Products SL-6761)				
	I'll Be Home for Christmas (Pickwick SPC-1009)				
	Magic of Christmas, The (Capitol SWBB-93810)				
	Merry Christmas with Nat King Cole/Fred Waring and the Pennsylvanians (Capitol Special Markets SL-6883)				
	Sound of Christmas, The (Capitol Creative Products SL-6515)				
Christmas Song, The	Best of Christmas, The, Vol. I (Capitol SM-11833)				
	Billboard Greatest Christmas Hits, 1935-1954 (Rhino R1 70637)				
	Celebrate the Season with Tupperware (RCA Special Products DPL1-0803)				
	Christmas America (Capitol Special Markets SL-6884)				
	Christmas Songs, The (Capitol SLB-57074)				
	Christmas Stocking (Capitol NP 90494)				
	Merry Christmas with Nat King Cole/Fred Waring and the Pennsylvanians (Capitol Special Markets SL-6883)				
	Popular Christmas Classics (Capitol Special Markets SL-8100)				
	Time-Life Treasury of Christmas, The, Volume Two (Time-Life STL-108)				
	12 Hits of Christmas (United Artists UA-LA669-R)				
	Very Merry Christmas, A, Volume VIII (Capitol Special Markets SL-6954)				
Cradle in Bethlehem, A	Happy Holidays, Album Seven (Capitol Creative Products SL-6730)				
	Merry Christmas with Nat King Cole/Fred Waring and the Pennsylvanians (Capitol Special Markets SL-6883)				
Deck the Hall	Sound of Christmas, The, Vol. 2 (Capitol Creative Products SL-6534)				
First Noel, The	Christmas America, Album Two (Capitol Special Markets SL-6950)				
	Christmas Treasury of Classics from Avon, A (RCA Special Products DPL1-0716)				
	Rocking Christmas Stocking, A (Capitol SPRO 9303/4/5/6)				
God Rest Ye Merry, Gentlemen	Happy Holidays, Vol. 21 (RCA Special Products DPL1-0739)				
	Merry Christmas with Nat King Cole/Fred Waring and the Pennsylvanians (Capitol Special Markets SL-6883)				
	Sound of Christmas, The, Vol. 2 (Capitol Creative Products SL-6534)				
Hark, the Herald Angels Sing	Time-Life Treasury of Christmas, The (Time-Life STL-107)				
Joy to the World	All-Time Christmas Favorites (Capitol Special Markets SL-6931)				
	Let's Celebrate Christmas (Capitol Special Markets SL-6923)				
	Merry Christmas with Nat King Cole/Fred Waring and the Pennsylvanians (Capitol Special Markets SL-6883)				
Mrs. Santa Claus	Little Drummer Boy, The (Capitol/Pickwick SPC-3462)				
O Holy Night	Happy Holidays, Volume 18 (RCA Special Products DPL1-0608)				
	Sound of Christmas, The (Capitol Creative Products SL-6515)				
O Little Town of Bethlehem	Christmas Songs, The (Capitol SLB-57074)				
	Merry Christmas with Nat King Cole/Fred Waring and the Pennsylvanians (Capitol Special Markets SL-6883)				
	Rocking Christmas Stocking, A (Capitol SPRO 9303/4/5/6)				
O Tannenbaum	Rocking Christmas Stocking, A (Capitol SPRO 9303/4/5/6)				
Silent Night	Christmas, A Gift of Music (Capitol Special Markets SL-6687)				
	Zenith Presents Christmas, A Gift of Music Vol. 4 (Capitol Creative Products SL-6687)				

COLE, NATALIE
45s
Elektra 64816	The Christmas Song (Chestnuts Roasting on an Open Fire)/ Nature Boy	1991	—	2.00	4.00

On Various-Artists Collections
Christmas Song, The	Scrooged (A&M SP-3921)				

COLE, SONNY
45s
Dee-Jay 5843	Santa To The Moon/Truck Driver's Hell	19??	2.50	5.00	10.00

COLEMAN, KING
45s
Karen 1008	Blue Grey Christmas/Holiday Season	1959	3.00	6.00	12.00

COLLETT, JIMMY
45s
Arcade 109	I Don't Want To Be Alone For Christmas/ What Do You Think My Heart Is Made Of	1952	10.00	20.00	40.00

COLLIER, DEBBIE
45s
Zip 4688	Oh The Man In The Moon Is Santa Claus/ I Know There Is A Santa Claus	19??	2.50	5.00	10.00

Label, Number		Title (A Side/B Side)	Year	VG	VG+	NM

COLLINGS, DAVID; RICHARD BEAUMONT; KAREN SCARGILL
On Various-Artists Collections
Christmas Children   Scrooge (Columbia Masterworks S 30258)

COLLINS, BERT
45s

| Sleet 1100 | | Ethelbert The Elf/Little Skidoo | 1980 | — | 2.00 | 4.00 |

COLLINS, DOROTHY
45s

| Coral 61539 | | Mister Santa/The Twelve Gifts of Christmas | 1955 | 3.00 | 6.00 | 12.00 |
| Coral 61736 | | Baby's First Christmas/Christmas Comes But Once a Year | 1956 | 3.00 | 6.00 | 12.00 |

COLLINS, JOHNNY
45s

| National 140 | | Spacey! Santa's Space Ship/ There's A Christmas Tree Up In Heaven | 19?? | 3.00 | 6.00 | 12.00 |

COLLINS, JUDY
On Various-Artists Collections
Beneath the Christmas Star   Stars of Christmas, The (RCA Special Products DPL1-0842)

COLLINS, SUE AND THE D.H.S. SWINGERS
45s

| Vandan 8156 | | Christmas Time Again/I Remember Christmas | 1966 | 2.50 | 5.00 | 10.00 |

COLMAN, RONALD
45s

Decca 40107		A Christmas Carol (Part 1)/A Christmas Carol (Part 6)	1950	3.75	7.50	15.00
— Sides 1 and 6 of "Album No. 9-71"						
Decca 40108		A Christmas Carol (Part 2)/A Christmas Carol (Part 5)	1950	3.75	7.50	15.00
— Sides 2 and 5 of "Album No. 9-71"						
Decca 40109		A Christmas Carol (Part 3)/A Christmas Carol (Part 4)	1950	3.75	7.50	15.00
— Sides 3 and 4 of "Album No. 9-71"						

7-Inch Extended Plays

| Decca 9-71 | (3) | A Christmas Carol | 1950 | 12.50 | 25.00 | 50.00 |
| — Includes records 40107, 40108 and 40109 (also priced separately) and box | | | | | | |

Albums

Decca DLP 8010	M	A Christmas Carol/Mr. Pickwick's Christmas	1955	5.00	10.00	20.00
— Side 2 read by Charles Laughton						
MCA 15010		A Christmas Carol/Mr. Pickwick's Christmas	1973	2.50	5.00	10.00
— Side 2 read by Charles Laughton; reissue of Decca LP						

COLONNA, JERRY
45s

| Decca 28884 | | Too Fat For the Chimney/Sleigh Bells In The Sky | 1953 | 3.00 | 6.00 | 12.00 |

COLT, BOBBY
45s

| Murbo 1051 | | The Crooked Little Christmas Tree/Scattered Toys | 19?? | — | 2.00 | 4.00 |

COLUMBIA CHOIR, THE
Also see ALBERT BURT CAROLS.
Albums

Columbia CL ????	10	The Christmas Mood	1954	12.50	25.00	50.00
— First appearance of the "Albert Burt Carols" on record						
Columbia CL 1051	M	The Christmas Mood	1957	7.50	15.00	30.00
— Expanded version of 10-inch LP with B-side instrumentals						

COLUMBUS BOYCHOIR
45s

Decca 34123		Deck The Halls/Jingle Bells/We Wish You a Merry Christmas// What Child Is This/Here We Come a-Wassailing/Joy to the World	1963	3.00	6.00	12.00
— 7-inch 33 1/3 rpm record						
Decca 34123	PS	Christmas Club Presents Yuletide Favorites Volume 2	1963	3.00	6.00	12.00

Label, Number		Title (A Side/B Side)	Year	VG	VG+	NM
Albums						
Decca DL 8920	M	Joy to the World	1959	3.75	7.50	15.00
Decca DL 78920	S	Joy to the World	1959	5.00	10.00	20.00
On Various-Artists Collections						
Angels We Have Heard on High		Decca 38170 (title unknown) (Decca DL 38170)				
Carol of the Bells		Firestone Presents Your Favorite Christmas Carols, Volume 2 (Firestone MLP 7006)				
Deck the Hall		Decca 38170 (title unknown) (Decca DL 38170)				
I Wish You a Merry Christmas		Family Christmas Favorites from Bing Crosby and the Columbus Boychoir (Decca DL 34487)				
Jingle Bells		Family Christmas Favorites from Bing Crosby and the Columbus Boychoir (Decca DL 34487)				
Medley: Hark! The Herald Angels Sing/ The First Noel		Firestone Presents Your Favorite Christmas Carols, Volume 2 (Firestone MLP 7006)				
O Come All Ye Faithful		Family Christmas Favorites from Bing Crosby and the Columbus Boychoir (Decca DL 34487)				
Silent Night		Family Christmas Favorites from Bing Crosby and the Columbus Boychoir (Decca DL 34487)				
We Wish You a Merry Christmas		Decca 38170 (title unknown) (Decca DL 38170)				

COLUMBUS BOYCHOIR AND FIRESTONE CHORUS
On Various-Artists Collections

Label, Number	Title (A Side/B Side)	Year	VG	VG+	NM
Little Drummer Boy, The	Firestone Presents Your Christmas Favorites, Volume 3 (Firestone MLP 7008)				
Medley: Hark! The Herald Angels Sing/It Came Upon a Midnight Clear/Joy to the World	Firestone Presents Your Christmas Favorites, Volume 3 (Firestone MLP 7008)				
Medley: Here We Come a-Wassailing/God Rest You Merry, Gentlemen/ Bring a Torch, Jeanette, Isabella/Good King Wenceslas	Firestone Presents Your Christmas Favorites, Volume 3 (Firestone MLP 7008)				
Medley: O Holy Night/ O Come All Ye Faithful	Firestone Presents Your Favorite Christmas Carols, Volume 2 (Firestone MLP 7006)				
Medley: Silent Night/O Little Town of Bethlehem/Jingle Bells	Firestone Presents Your Favorite Christmas Carols, Volume 2 (Firestone MLP 7006)				

COMMANDER CODY AND HIS LOST PLANET AIRMEN
45s

Label, Number	Title (A Side/B Side)	Year	VG	VG+	NM
Dot 17487	Daddy's Drinking Up Our Christmas/Honeysuckle Honey	1973	—	3.00	6.00

COMMANDER SHEA SCHOOL BOYS' CHOIR
45s

Label, Number	Title (A Side/B Side)	Year	VG	VG+	NM
Cadence 1375	Chree-See-Mus/White Christmas	1959	3.00	6.00	12.00

COMO, PERRY
45s

Label, Number		Title (A Side/B Side)	Year	VG	VG+	NM
RCA 9096-7-R	DJ	I May Never Pass This Way Again (same on both sides)	1989	—	2.50	5.00
— Promotional record for Christmas Seals						
RCA PB-10122		Christmas Dream/Christ Is Born	1976	—	—	3.00
— Reissue; black label, dog near top						
RCA PB-13307		I Wish It Could Be Christmas Forever/Toyland	1982	—	2.00	4.00
RCA Victor 47-2969		That Christmas Feeling/Winter Wonderland	1949	5.00	10.00	20.00
RCA Victor 47-2970		I'll Be Home for Christmas/Santa Claus Is Coming to Town	1949	5.00	10.00	20.00
RCA Victor 47-2971		Silent Night/White Christmas	1949	5.00	10.00	20.00
RCA Victor 47-2972		Jingle Bells/O Come All Ye Faithful	1949	5.00	10.00	20.00
RCA Victor 47-3850		Bless This House/The Rosary	1950	3.00	6.00	12.00
RCA Victor 47-3933		The Christmas Symphony/ There Is No Christmas Like a Home Christmas	1950	3.75	7.50	15.00
RCA Victor 47-4314		It's Beginning to Look Like Christmas/ There Is No Christmas Like a Home Christmas	1951	3.75	7.50	15.00
RCA Victor 47-5524		Silver Bells/Kissing Bridge	1953	3.00	6.00	12.00
— With the Fontane Sisters						
RCA Victor 47-5950		(There's No Place Like) Home for the Holidays/Silk Stockings	1954	3.00	6.00	12.00
RCA Victor 47-6321		Home for the Holidays/God Rest Ye Merry Gentlemen	1955	3.00	6.00	12.00
RCA Victor 47-7650		Ave Maria/The Lord's Prayer	1959	2.50	5.00	10.00
RCA Victor 47-9367		Christmas Bells/Love Is a Christmas Rose	1967	2.00	4.00	8.00
RCA Victor 47-9367	PS	Christmas Bells/Love Is A Christmas Rose	1967	2.50	5.00	10.00
RCA Victor 47-9683		There Is No Christmas Like a Home Christmas/Christmas Eve	1968	—	3.00	6.00
RCA Victor 52-0071		Ave Maria/The Lord's Prayer	1949	6.25	12.50	25.00
— Blue vinyl original						
RCA Victor 52-0071		Ave Maria/The Lord's Prayer	1949	3.00	6.00	12.00
— Black vinyl reissue						
RCA Victor 447-0110		Ave Maria/The Lord's Prayer	1955	3.00	6.00	12.00
RCA Victor 447-0810		Silent Night/O Come, All Ye Faithful	196?	—	2.50	5.00
RCA Victor 447-0811		That Christmas Feeling/I'll Be Home For Christmas	196?	—	2.50	5.00
RCA Victor 447-0812		Home for the Holidays/God Rest Ye Merry Gentlemen	196?	—	2.50	5.00
RCA Victor E3VW 1339/ F70W 9047	DJ	Rudolph The Red-Nosed Reindeer/ Rudolph The Red-Nosed Reindeer	1955	3.75	7.50	15.00
— B-side by the Three Suns						

Label, Number		Title (A Side/B Side)	Year	VG	VG+	NM
RCA Victor K2NW 6096/7	DJ	(Intro) I May Never Pass This Way Again/ (Alternate Intro) I May Never Pass This Way Again	1959	3.00	6.00	12.00
— Promotional record for Christmas Seals						
RCA Victor PB-10122		Christmas Dream/Christ Is Born	1974	—	2.00	4.00
— Gray label						
RCA Victor SP-45-119	DJ	(There's No Place Like) Home For The Holidays/ I'll Be Home For Christmas	1962	3.00	6.00	12.00
USAF 85/86	DJ	"Special Christmas Show" Home For The Holidays/ Merry Merry Christmas To You	195?	3.75	7.50	15.00
— B-side by Art Mooney						

7-Inch Extended Plays

Label, Number		Title (A Side/B Side)	Year	VG	VG+	NM
RCA Victor EPA 496		The Night Before Christmas/God Rest Ye Merry, Gentlemen//The 12 Days of Christmas/C-H-R-I-S-T-M-A-S	195?	3.00	6.00	12.00
RCA Victor EPA 496	PS	Around The Christmas Tree	195?	3.00	6.00	12.00
RCA Victor EPB-1243 (547-1049)		Joy to the World/White Christmas// God Rest Ye Merry, Gentlemen/The Christmas Song	1955	2.50	5.00	10.00
RCA Victor EPB-1243	PS	Merry Christmas Music	1955	5.00	10.00	20.00
— Cover for 2-EP set						

Albums

Label, Number		Title (A Side/B Side)	Year	VG	VG+	NM
Pickwick CAS-660	R	Perry Como Sings Merry Christmas Music	1977	2.00	4.00	8.00
— Reissue of RCA Camden CAS-660 with another new cover						
RCA Camden CAL-660	M	Perry Como Sings Merry Christmas Music	1961	3.00	6.00	12.00
— Reissue of RCA Victor LPM-1243 with new cover						
RCA Camden CAS-660(e)	R	Perry Como Sings Merry Christmas Music	1961	2.50	5.00	10.00
RCA Victor LPM-51	10	Merry Christmas	1951	10.00	20.00	40.00
RCA Victor LPM-1243	M	Perry Como Sings Merry Christmas Music	1956	7.50	15.00	30.00
RCA Victor ANL1-1929		The Perry Como Christmas Album	1976	2.00	4.00	8.00
— Budget-line reissue of LSP-4016						
RCA Victor LPM-2066	M	Season's Greetings from Perry Como	1959	6.25	12.50	25.00
— Original front covers have "LPM-2066" in lower left corner						
RCA Victor LPM-2066	M	Season's Greetings from Perry Como	1959	5.00	10.00	20.00
— Later front covers have "LPM-2066" in upper right, inside RCA Victor box						
RCA Victor LSP-2066	S	Season's Greetings from Perry Como	1959	6.25	12.50	25.00
RCA Victor LPM-3133	10	Around the Christmas Tree	1953	10.00	20.00	40.00
RCA Victor LSP-4016		The Perry Como Christmas Album	1968	3.00	6.00	12.00
RCA Victor AYL1-4526		I Wish It Could Be Christmas Forever	1982	2.50	5.00	10.00

On Various-Artists Collections

Ave Maria	Goodyear Presents The Great Songs of Christmas (RCA Special Products DPL1-0285)
Bless This House	Time-Life Treasury of Christmas, The, Volume Two (Time-Life STL-108)
Christ Is Born	Happy Holidays, Volume 16 (RCA Special Products DPL1-0501)
Christmas Is	Blue Christmas (Welk Music Group WM-3002)
Christmas Song, The	Christmas Through the Years (Reader's Digest RDA-143)
	Goodyear Presents The Great Songs of Christmas (RCA Special Products DPL1-0285)
	Happy Holidays, Volume 14 (RCA Special Products DPL1-0376)
	Joyous Noel (Reader's Digest RDA-57A)
Do You Hear What I Hear	Family Christmas Collection, The (Time-Life STL-131)
Frosty the Snowman	Family Christmas Collection, The (Time-Life STL-131)
God Rest Ye Merry Gentlemen	Family Christmas Collection, The (Time-Life STL-131)
	Gift from Your RCA Victor Record Dealer, A (RCA Victor SP-45-35)
Have Yourself a Merry Little Christmas	Christmas Through the Years (Reader's Digest RDA-143)
Home for the Holidays	Brightest Stars of Christmas, The (RCA Special Products DPL1-0086)
	Christmas Programming from RCA Victor (RCA Victor SP-33-66)
	Christmas Through the Years (Reader's Digest RDA-143)
	Christmas Treasury of Classics from Avon, A (RCA Special Products DPL1-0716)
	Goodyear Presents The Great Songs of Christmas (RCA Special Products DPL1-0285)
	Happy Holidays, Volume 13 (RCA Special Products DPL1-0319)
	Merry Christmas (RCA Victor PRM-168)
	October Christmas Sampler 59-40-41 (RCA Victor SPS-33-54)
	Time-Life Treasury of Christmas, The (Time-Life STL-107)
	Very Merry Christmas, A, Volume 5 (RCA Special Products PRS-343)
I Wish It Could Be Christmas Forever	Christmas Through the Years (Reader's Digest RDA-143)
	Happy Holidays, Volume 18 (RCA Special Products DPL1-0608)
I'll Be Home for Christmas	Joyous Noel (Reader's Digest RDA-57A)
	Time-Life Treasury of Christmas, The (Time-Life STL-107)
It's Beginning to Look Like Christmas	Christmas Through the Years (Reader's Digest RDA-143)
	Time-Life Treasury of Christmas, The (Time-Life STL-107)
Little Drummer Boy, The	Very Merry Christmas, A, Volume VI (RCA Special Products PRS-427)
Love Is a Christmas Rose	Happy Holidays, Volume 17 (RCA Special Products DPL1-0555)
Medley: Caroling, Caroling/	Celebrate the Season with Tupperware (RCA Special Products DPL1-0803)
The First Noel/Hark! The Herald Angels Sing/Silent Night	Goodyear Presents The Great Songs of Christmas (RCA Special Products DPL1-0285)
Medley: Here We Come a-Caroling/ We Wish You a Merry Christmas	Time-Life Treasury of Christmas, The, Volume Two (Time-Life STL-108) Very Merry Christmas, A, Volume 5 (RCA Special Products PRS-343)

Medley: Here We Come a-Caroling/
  We Wish You a Merry Christmas/
  God Rest Ye Merry, Gentlemen
	Happy Holidays, Vol. 22 (RCA Special Products DPL1-0777)

Label, Number	Title (A Side/B Side)	Year	VG	VG+	NM
O Holy Night	Goodyear Presents The Great Songs of Christmas (RCA Special Products DPL1-0285)				
	Time-Life Treasury of Christmas, The (Time-Life STL-107)				
Santa Claus Is Coming to Town	Time-Life Treasury of Christmas, The (Time-Life STL-107)				
	Very Merry Christmas, A, Volume VII (RCA Special Products DPL1-0049)				
Silent Night	Henry Mancini Selects Great Songs of Christmas (RCA Special Products DPL1-0148)				
Silver Bells	Christmas Through the Years (Reader's Digest RDA-143)				
There Is No Christmas Like a	Happy Holidays, Volume 15 (RCA Special Products DPL1-0453)				
Home Christmas	Time-Life Treasury of Christmas, The, Volume Two (Time-Life STL-108)				
	Very Merry Christmas, A, Volume VI (RCA Special Products PRS-427)				
Toyland	Family Christmas Collection, The (Time-Life STL-131)				
	Goodyear Presents The Great Songs of Christmas (RCA Special Products DPL1-0285)				
	Happy Holidays, Vol. 20 (RCA Special Products DPL1-0713)				
	Very Merry Christmas, A, Volume VII (RCA Special Products DPL1-0049)				
Twelve Days of Christmas, The	Family Christmas Collection, The (Time-Life STL-131)				
White Christmas	Old Fashioned Christmas, An (Reader's Digest RDA 216-A)				
	Time-Life Treasury of Christmas, The, Volume Two (Time-Life STL-108)				
Winter Wonderland	Christmas Through the Years (Reader's Digest RDA-143)				

COMPUTONES, THE
45s
Clifton 66	Rudolph, The Red-Nosed Reindeer/I'll Stay Home	19??	2.50	5.00	10.00

CONFORTI, DONNA
45s
Glenco 125	Rockin' Roly Poly Santa Claus/Merry Christmas Santa Claus	1962	2.50	5.00	10.00

CONLEE, JOHN
On Various-Artists Collections
Pretty Paper	Nashville Christmas Album, The (Epic PE 40418)				

CONLEY, EARL THOMAS
45s
RCA PB-13688	White Christmas/Home So Fine	1983	—	2.00	4.00
RCA PB-13905	Blue Christmas/White Christmas	1984	—	2.00	4.00

On Various-Artists Collections
Blue Christmas	Best of Christmas, The (RCA Victor CPL1-7013)				
	Country Christmas, A, Volume 3 (RCA CPL1-5178)				
	Family Christmas Collection, The (Time-Life STL-131)				
White Christmas	Country Christmas, A, Volume 2 (RCA AYL1-4809)				

CONNICK, HARRY, JR.
Albums
Columbia 474551-1	When My Heart Finds Christmas	1993	3.75	7.50	15.00

— *Vinyl version is European import only*

On Various-Artists Collections
Winter Wonderland	When Harry Met Sally... (Columbia SC 45319)				

CONNICK, HARRY, JR. AND BRANFORD MARSALIS
On Various-Artists Collections
This Christmas	Jazzy Wonderland, A (Columbia 1P 8120)				

CONNIFF, RAY
45s
Columbia 41484		Christmas Bride/Silver Bells	1959	3.00	6.00	12.00
Columbia 43448		The Real Meaning of Christmas/Go Tell It on the Mountain	1965	2.00	4.00	8.00
Columbia JZSP 111913/4	DJ	Frosty The Snowman/The Real Meaning Of Christmas	1965	2.50	5.00	10.00

Albums
Columbia CL 1390	M	Christmas with Conniff	1959	3.75	7.50	15.00
Columbia CL 1892	M	We Wish You a Merry Christmas	1962	3.75	7.50	15.00
Columbia CL 2406	M	Here We Come a-Caroling	1965	3.00	6.00	12.00
Columbia CS 8185	S	Christmas with Conniff	1959	3.00	6.00	12.00

— *Same as 1390, but in stereo*

Columbia CS 8692	S	We Wish You a Merry Christmas	1962	3.00	6.00	12.00

— *Same as 1892, but in stereo*

Columbia CS 9206	S	Here We Come a-Caroling	1965	2.50	5.00	10.00

— *Same as 2406, but in stereo*

Columbia GP 3	(2)	Here We Come a-Caroling	196?	3.75	7.50	15.00
Columbia PC 38300		Christmas Album	1982	2.50	5.00	10.00
Columbia PC 39470		Christmas Caroling	1984	2.50	5.00	10.00

On Various-Artists Collections
Adoramus Te	Have a Happy Holiday (Columbia Special Products CSS 1432)				

Label, Number	Title (A Side/B Side)	Year	VG	VG+	NM
Christmas Greetings From Ray Conniff & The Singers	Christmas Greetings From The Entire Columbia Record Family (Columbia JZSP 58623/4)				
Christmas Song, The	Zenith Presents Christmas, A Gift of Music Vol. 5 (Columbia Special Products C 10395)				
Deck the Hall with Boughs of Holly	Christmas Greetings (Columbia Special Products CSS 1499)				
	Sounds of Christmas (Columbia Special Products P 12474)				
Frosty the Snowman	Great Songs of Christmas, The, Album Six (Columbia Special Products CSM 388)				
Go Tell It on a Mountain	Silent Night... (Columbia Special Products P 14989)				
Hark! The Herald Angels Sing	Great Songs of Christmas, The, Album Six (Columbia Special Products CSM 388)				
Here Comes Santa Claus	Great Songs of Christmas, The, Album Eight (Columbia Special Products CSS 888)				
	Home for Christmas (Columbia Musical Treasury P3S 5608)				
	Home for Christmas (Realm 2V 8101)				
	Magic of Christmas, The (Columbia Musical Treasury P3S 5806)				
Here We Come a-Caroling	Magic of Christmas, The (Columbia Musical Treasury P3S 5806)				
	Merry Christmas from... (Reader's Digest RD4-83)				
	That Christmas Feeling (Columbia Special Products P 11853)				
Jingle Bells	Happy Holidays, Album 8 (Columbia Special Products C 11086)				
	Home for Christmas (Columbia Musical Treasury P3S 5608)				
	Home for Christmas (Realm 2V 8101)				
Joy to the World	Christmas Greetings (Columbia Special Products CSS 1433)				
	Gift of Christmas, The, Vol. 1 (Columbia Special Products CSS 706)				
	WHIO Radio Christmas Feelings (Sound Approach/CSP P 16366)				
Little Drummer Boy, The	Collection of Christmas Favorites, A (Columbia Special Products P 14988)				
	Ronco Presents A Christmas Gift (Columbia Special Products P 12430)				
	Sounds of Christmas (Columbia Special Products P 12474)				
	Very Merry Christmas, A (Columbia Special Products CSS 563)				
Medley: Jolly Old St. Nicholas/ The Little Drummer Boy	Christmas Greetings From The Entire Columbia Record Family (Columbia JZSP 58623/4)				
	60 Christmas Classics (Sessions DVL2-0723)				
Medley: Let It Snow! Let It Snow! Let It Snow!/Count Your Blessings/ We Wish You a Merry Christmas	60 Christmas Classics (Sessions DVL2-0723)				
Medley: The First Noel/Hark! The Herald Angels Sing/O Come, All Ye Faithful/We Wish You a Merry Christmas	Spirit of Christmas, The (Columbia Special Products CSP 249)				
Real Meaning of Christmas, The	Very Merry Christmas, A, Volume 3 (Columbia Special Products CSS 997)				
Ring Christmas Bells	Christmas Song, The, And Other Favorites (Columbia Special Products P 12446)				
Santa Claus Is Comin' to Town	Merry Christmas (Columbia Musical Treasury 3P 6306)				
Sleigh Ride	Merry Christmas from... (Reader's Digest RD4-83)				
Twelve Days of Christmas, The	60 Christmas Classics (Sessions DVL2-0723)				
We Three Kings of Orient Are	Spirit of Christmas, The, Volume III (Columbia Special Products CSS 563)				
We Wish You a Merry Christmas	Best of the Great Songs of Christmas (Album 10) (Columbia Special Products CSS 1478)				
	Great Songs of Christmas, The, Album Six (Columbia Special Products CSM 388)				
	It's Christmas Time! (Columbia Special Products P 14990)				
	Joyous Songs of Christmas, The (Columbia Special Products C 10400)				
You'd Be So Nice to Come Home To	Happy Holidays, Volume II (Columbia Special Products CSM 348)				

CONRAD, BOB
On Various-Artists Collections

White Christmas	We Wish You a Merry Christmas (Warner Bros. W 1337)				

CONRAD, JOAN
45s

Alley 1007	Christmas Day/Gee Golly, the Holly	1962	2.50	5.00	10.00

CONSOLERS, THE
45s

Nashboro 933	Let The Bells Ring/No Room In The Inn	1967	2.00	4.00	8.00
Nashboro 956	Merry Christmas/There Will Be Peace One of These Days	1970	—	3.00	6.00

CONTE, JOHN
45s

Conte 828	The Gift (Of Love)/Christmas Is Here Again	197?	—	3.00	6.00

CONTI, TOM
Albums

Caedmon TC 1657	Charles Dickens' "A Christmas Carol"	1980	3.00	6.00	12.00
— Spoken-word recording					

CONWAY, DAVE
45s

Teddy Bear (no #)	Jingle Bears (same on both sides)	197?	—	3.00	6.00

CONWAY, JAMES F.
On Various-Artists Collections

Greetings to St. Louis City	Christmas in Saint Louis ((no label) TS77-558/9)				

Label, Number	Title (A Side/B Side)	Year	VG	VG+	NM

COOK, BILL
45s

| Okeh 6849 | A Letter to Santa/Christmas in Heaven | 1951 | 12.50 | 25.00 | 50.00 |

COOKE, SAM
On Various-Artists Collections

| Christmas Greetings | Christmas Greetings From RCA Victor And Groove Recording Artists (RCA Victor SP-45-128) | | | | |
| New Year's Greetings | Christmas Greetings From RCA Victor And Groove Recording Artists (RCA Victor SP-45-128) | | | | |

COOLBREEZERS, THE
45s

| Bale 102/103 | Let Christmas Ring/Hello, Mister New Year | 1958 | 50.00 | 100.00 | 200.00 |

COOPER, DICK
45s

| DJ 8371 | I Saw Mommy Spanking Santa Claus/My Mother's Birthday | 198? | 3.00 | 6.00 | 12.00 |

COPAGE, MARC
45s

| Metromedia 154 | Santa, Bring My Daddy Home for Christmas/ | 1969 | 2.00 | 4.00 | 8.00 |
| | Santa, Please Repair My Toys for Christmas | | | | |

COPAS, COWBOY
45s

King 1003	O Little Town Of Bethlehem/It Came Upon the Midnight Clear	1951	5.00	10.00	20.00
King 1004	White Christmas/Jingle Bells	1951	5.00	10.00	20.00
King 1053	O Little Town Of Bethlehem/It Came Upon the Midnight Clear	1952	5.00	10.00	20.00

CORALAIRS, THE
45s

| NRC 016 | Buon Natale/One, Two, Three | 1958 | 3.75 | 7.50 | 15.00 |
| NRC 5009 | Buon Natale/Little Louie the Elf | 1959 | 3.75 | 7.50 | 15.00 |

CORDOVA E CORO, ALVARO
On Various-Artists Collections

| Notte Sacra | Christmas in Italy (Capitol T 10093) | | | | |

COREA, CHICK, ELEKTRIC BAND
On Various-Artists Collections

| God Rest Ye Merry, Gentlemen | GRP Christmas Collection, A (GRP 9574) | | | | |

CORELLI, FRANCO
On Various-Artists Collections

Ave Maria (Bach-Gounod)	Sound of Christmas, The, Vol. 2 (Capitol Creative Products SL-6534)				
	Zenith Presents Christmas, A Gift of Music (Capitol Creative Products SL-6544)				
O Holy Night	Firestone Presents Your Christmas Favorites, Volume 3 (Firestone MLP 7008)				
Panis Angelicus	Firestone Presents Your Christmas Favorites, Volume 3 (Firestone MLP 7008)				

CORNELIUS, HELEN
45s

| Elektra 47232 | DJ | Oh Holy Night/Silent Night | 1981 | — | 2.50 | 5.00 |
| — B-side by Joe Sun | | | | | | |

CORNELL, DON
45s

| Coral 60859 | Let's Have an Old Fashioned Christmas/I've Got the Christmas Spirit | 1952 | 3.75 | 7.50 | 15.00 |

7-Inch Extended Plays

Coral 83010	DJ	Let's Have an Old Fashioned Christmas/I've Got the Christmas Spirit//	195?	3.75	7.50	15.00
		Sing a Song Of Santa Claus/Winter's Here Again				
— B-side by the Ames Brothers						

CORO DI ALLUNE DELLA PICCOLA CASA SAN GIUSEPPE
On Various-Artists Collections

Buon Natale	Christmas in Italy (Capitol T 10093)				
Dolce Risveglio	Christmas in Italy (Capitol T 10093)				
E Nato Gesu	Christmas in Italy (Capitol T 10093)				
La Stella di Betlemme	Christmas in Italy (Capitol T 10093)				

Label, Number		Title (A Side/B Side)	Year	VG	VG+	NM
COSBY, BILL						
45s						
Capitol 4523		Merry Christmas Mama (Vocal)/(Instrumental)	1977	5.00	10.00	20.00
COSTER, JANET						
On Various-Artists Collections						
What Child Is This?		Old Fashioned Christmas, An (Reader's Digest RDA 216-A)				
COSTLEY, MIKE						
45s						
Sine Wave 1001		It's Christmas Time/Happy New Year My Friends	198?	—	2.00	4.00
Sine Wave 1001	PS	It's Christmas Time/Happy New Year My Friends	198?	—	2.00	4.00
COTE, EMILE, CHORALE						
45s						
Treasure Aisle 663		The Day That Santa Cried/The Day That Santa Cried	19??	—	2.00	4.00
— B-side by Paul McNamara						
COTTON, BILLY, ORCHESTRA						
45s						
London 1388		Where Did My Snowman Go/Snow, Snow, Beautiful Snow	1953	3.00	6.00	12.00
COTTON, GENE						
45s						
(No label) NR16361	DJ	Child Of Peace (same on both sides)	1981	2.00	4.00	8.00
Myrrh 123		Great American Noel/Mrs. Oliver	1973	—	2.50	5.00
COULTER, PHIL						
Albums						
Shanachie 53005		Phil Coulter's Christmas	1983	2.50	5.00	10.00
COUNTRY CAVALIERS, THE						
45s						
Country Showcase 158		Everett the Evergreen/A Sing Along Christmas Song	1976	—	2.00	4.00
COUNTRY JOE AND WALDO						
45s						
Fantasy Prod. 101		Christmas Eve/The Weird Toy	197?	—	3.00	6.00
COUNTRY SQUIRRELS, THE						
45s						
Metromedia Country 903		How I Love Those Christmas Song/Country Christmas	1972	—	3.00	6.00
Metromedia Country BMBO-0166		How I Love Those Christmas Song/Country Christmas	1973	—	2.50	5.00
COUNTRYMAN, LEE						
45s						
Roaring 20's 104		Rinky-Dink Christmas Medley/Sleigh Ride	19??	—	2.50	5.00
COUNTRYMEN, THE						
45s						
Hickory 1286		Carol of the Drum/Scarlet Ribbons	1964	2.00	4.00	8.00
La Belle 778		Indian Christmas Song/The Virgin Mary	196?	2.00	4.00	8.00
COUSIN DAN						
45s						
Royal American 55		Christmas At The White House (Dancer, Prancer and Nixon)/ (B-side unknown)	1971	—	3.00	6.00
COUTURE, CHARLELIE						
45s						
Ze WIP 6763		Christmas Fever/Christmas Wrapping	1981	5.00	10.00	20.00
— B-side by the Waitresses; U.K. import						
COWAN, JOEL, AND THORNEL SCHWARTZ						
45s						
Value 103		Bells Of Auld Lang Syne/Walkin' Bells	19??	2.00	4.00	8.00

Label, Number		Title (A Side/B Side)	Year	VG	VG+	NM
COWBOY WEAVER						
45s						
Freestate 81		Sandy, Son of Rudolph (The Cowboy Reindeer)/ Christmas to Me Is Just Another Day	19??	—	2.50	5.00
COWSILLS, THE						
45s						
Gasatanka/Rockville 6139 — Clear vinyl		Christmastime (Song For Marisa)/Some Good Years	1993	—	2.00	4.00
Gasatanka/Rockville 6139 — Green vinyl		Christmastime (Song for Marissa)/Some Good Years	1993	—	—	3.00
Gasatanka/Rockville 6139	PS	Christmastime (Song for Marissa)/Some Good Years	1993	—	—	3.00
COX, BETTY						
45s						
Hansen 105		Holly Boy/Hi! To You	19??	—	3.00	6.00
COX, DANNY						
45s						
Cowtown 002		Little Drummer Boy & Joy To The World/Red, White & Blue	19??	—	—	3.00
CRAFTY LADIES, THE						
7-Inch Extended Plays						
Harold 1		Rudolph.../Deck the Halls/O Christmas Tree/ Santa Claus Is Coming to Town//I Want a Hippopotamus for Christmas/ Silent Night/We Wish You a Merry Christmas	1996	—	—	2.00
Harold 1	PS	(title unknown)	1996	—	—	2.00
CRAIG AND HIS DADDY						
45s						
Amy 834		Bring My Daddy An Electric Train/All Around the Christmas Tree	1961	3.00	6.00	12.00
CRAIG, BOBBY						
45s						
Palladium RE-2		Ghost Of Christmas Past/Have You Got Any Pot, Nancy Reagan	198?	—	2.50	5.00
CRAMER, FLOYD						
45s						
Step One 454		Christmas Medley//We Wish You A Merry Christmas/ I'll Be Home For Christmas	1992	—	2.50	5.00
— Red vinyl						
On Various-Artists Collections						
Jingle Bell Rock		Old Fashioned Christmas, An (Reader's Digest RDA 216-A)				
Medley: Silver Bells/ Winter Wonderland		Happy Holidays, Volume IV (RCA Victor PRS-267)				
Medley: Up on the Housetop/ Jingle Bells		Christmas Eve with Colonel Sanders (RCA Victor PRS-256)				
Silver Bells		Joyous Noel (Reader's Digest RDA-57A)				
CRANE, LOR						
45s						
Boardwalk 1055		Christmas In The Country/Jingle Bell Rock	196?	2.50	5.00	10.00
CRASS						
45s						
Crass COLD TURKEY 1		Merry Crassmas (same on both sides)	1981	5.00	10.00	20.00
Crass COLD TURKEY 1	PS	Merry Crassmas (same on both sides)	1981	5.00	10.00	20.00
— Record and sleeve are U.K. imports						
CRAVER, SONNY						
45s						
Stanson 1118		Wrap The World In Christmas Paper/Make Someone Love You	196?	2.00	4.00	8.00
CRAWFORD, HANK						
45s						
Atlantic 5042		Merry Christmas Baby/Read 'Em and Weep	1964	2.50	5.00	10.00
Kudu 911		The Christmas Song/Winter Wonderland	1974	—	2.50	5.00

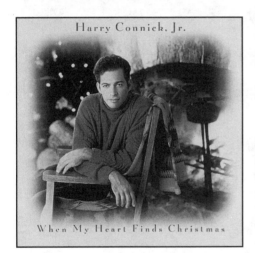

(Top left) The picture sleeve from the original release of "Merry Christmas Darling."
A little-known fact: The 45 has a different vocal take than the later LP releases.
(Top right) This album was reissued often with different covers, but this is the
original 12-inch LP jacket for *Perry Como Sings Merry Christmas Music.* (Bottom
left) The only vinyl pressing of Harry Connick Jr.'s LP *When My Heart Finds
Christmas* was this very limited edition from the UK. (Bottom right) Long after their
heyday, the Cowsills recorded a Christmas 45 in 1992 with two former members of
the Bangles (Vicki Peterson and Michael Steele) helping out.

Label, Number		Title (A Side/B Side)	Year	VG	VG+	NM
CRAWFORD, JESSE						
45s						
Decca 24143		Joy To The World/White Christmas	1950	3.00	6.00	12.00
— *78 rpm released in 1947*						
Albums						
Decca DL 8794	M	Christmas	1958	3.00	6.00	12.00
Decca DL 78794	S	Christmas	1958	3.75	7.50	15.00
Design DLPX-7	M	Organ and Chimes for Christmas	196?	3.00	6.00	12.00
— *Same recordings as Promenade LP, but in slightly different order*						
Design SDLPX-7	S	Organ and Chimes for Christmas	196?	3.75	7.50	15.00
Promenade CH-1000	M	Organ and Chimes for Christmas	196?	3.00	6.00	12.00
CRAWFORD, JOSEPH						
On Various-Artists Collections						
Rise Up Shephard		Merry Christmas from David Frost and Billy Taylor (Bell 6053)				
CRAYNE, LESLIE 'UGGAMS' – See LESLIE UGGAMS.						
CRAZY EMMA						
45s						
Scepter 12372		Let's Get It Together For Christmas/Christmas Song	1972	—	3.00	6.00
CRAZY OTTO						
45s						
Decca 31185		Medley: Sleigh Ride-Winter Wonderland-White Christmas/ Medley: Rudolph The Red-Nosed Reindeer- I Saw Mommy Kissing Santa Claus-Jingle Bells	1960	3.00	6.00	12.00
CREAMERS, THE						
45s						
Sympathy For The Record Industry 100		Bob Kringle/Father Christmas	198?	—	3.00	6.00
Sympathy For The Record Industry 100	PS	Bob Kringle/Father Christmas	198?	—	3.00	6.00
CREARY, BETTY						
45s						
United Sound 2876		Where Is Christ In Christmas?/ Welcome To Our Home At Christmas Time	19??	—	2.00	4.00
CREATORS, THE						
45s						
Philips 40083		I'll Stay Home (New Year's Eve)/Shoom Ba Boom	1962	75.00	150.00	300.00
CREEPER						
45s						
ABC 12147		Santa Claus Wants Some Lovin'/Politicking	1975	—	2.50	5.00
CREW CUTS, THE						
45s						
Mercury 70491		Dance, Mr. Snowman, Dance/Twinkle Toes	1954	3.75	7.50	15.00
CRICKET CHORAL GROUP, THE						
45s						
Cricket 7CX12		White Christmas/Joy To The World	195?	2.00	4.00	8.00
Cricket 7CX12	PS	White Christmas/Joy To The World	195?	2.00	4.00	8.00
CRICKET, JIMINY						
45s						
Disneyland F-42		'Twas The Night Before Christmas/Kris Kringle	195?	2.50	5.00	10.00
CRICKETONE CHORUS & ORCHESTRA						
45s						
Cricket CX-19		All I Want For Christmas Is My Two Front Teeth/The Snowflake Song	195?	2.00	4.00	8.00

Label, Number		Title (A Side/B Side)	Year	VG	VG+	NM

CRICKETONES, THE
45s

Cricket CX11		Santa Claus Is Coming To Town/Ding-A-Ling Dong	195?	2.00	4.00	8.00
Cricket CX11	PS	Santa Claus Is Coming To Town/Ding-A-Ling Dong	195?	2.00	4.00	8.00
Cricket CX13		The Night Before Christmas/Mixie Pixie	195?	2.00	4.00	8.00
— 7-inch 78 rpm record						
Cricket CX13	PS	The Night Before Christmas/Mixie Pixie	195?	2.00	4.00	8.00
Cricket CX16		Winter Wonderland/The Sound Of Christmas	195?	2.00	4.00	8.00
— 7-inch 78 rpm record						
Cricket CX16	PS	Winter Wonderland/The Sound Of Christmas	195?	2.00	4.00	8.00
Cricket CX-16B		Winter Wonderland/The Sound Of Christmas	195?	2.50	5.00	10.00

CRISTAL, LINDA
On Various-Artists Collections

Reminder Spot		For Christmas Seals. . .A Matter of Life and Breath (Decca Custom Style E)				

CRISTINA
12-Inch Singles

Ze IPR 2052	DJ	Things Fall Apart/It's A Holiday	1981	5.00	10.00	20.00
— B-side by Material with Nona Hendryx; U.K. import						

On Various-Artists Collections

Things Fall Apart		Christmas Record, A (Ze/Passport PB 6020)				

CROCE, JIM
45s

ABC 11346		One Less Set of Footsteps/It Doesn't Have to Be That Way	1973	—	2.00	4.00
ABC 11413		It Doesn't Have to Be That Way/Roller Derby Queen	1973	—	2.00	4.00
ABC 11413	PS	It Doesn't Have to Be That Way/Roller Derby Queen	1973	—	2.50	5.00
Lifesong 45018	DJ	It Doesn't Have to Be That Way (mono/stereo)	1976	—	2.50	5.00
— Promo-only release; Lifesong sleeve has custom sticker (add $4)						
21 Records 94970		It Doesn't Have to Be That Way/Time in a Bottle	1987	—	—	3.00

Albums

ABC ABCX-769		Life and Times	1973	5.00	10.00	20.00
— Contains one Christmas song: It Doesn't Have to Be That Way						
Lifesong LS 6007		Time in a Bottle — Jim Croce's Greatest Love Songs	1976	3.75	7.50	15.00
— Contains one Christmas song: It Doesn't Have to Be That Way						

CROFT, MONTE, AND TERENCE BLANCHARD
On Various-Artists Collections

O Come All Ye Faithful		Jazzy Wonderland, A (Columbia 1P 8120)				

CRONHAM, CHARLES R.
7-Inch Extended Plays

Mercury 3151		Stand Up, Stand Up For Jesus/Love Divine, All Loves Excelling// Lead On, O King Eternal/God Of Our Fathers	1956	2.50	5.00	10.00
Mercury 3151	PS	Sacred Hymns	1956	2.50	5.00	10.00

CROOKS, RICHARD
On Various-Artists Collections

Nazareth		Joyous Noel (Reader's Digest RDA-57A)				
O Little Town of Bethlehem		Joyous Noel (Reader's Digest RDA-57A)				

CROSBY, BING
45s

Bing Crosby (no #)	DJ	How Lovely Is Christmas/Never Be Afraid	195?	5.00	10.00	20.00
— Crowley's Milk promotional item						
Capitol 5088		Do You Hear What I Hear/Christmas Dinner Country Style	1963	2.00	4.00	8.00
Columbia 41496		The Secret of Christmas/Just What I Wanted for Christmas	1959	3.75	7.50	15.00
Daybreak 1001		A Time to Be Jolly/And the Bells Rang	1971	—	3.00	6.00
— Black label						
Daybreak 1001		A Time to Be Jolly/And the Bells Rang	1971	—	2.50	5.00
— Yellow label						
Decca 23281		Jingle Bells/Santa Claus Is Comin' to Town	1950	3.00	6.00	12.00
— With the Andrews Sisters; lines label; Sides 1 and 2 of "Album No. 9-65"						
Decca 23281 (1-256)	PS	Jingle Bells/Santa's Coming	19??	3.75	7.50	15.00
— With the Andrews Sisters						
Decca 23777		Silent Night/Adeste Fideles (O Come All Ye Faithful)	1950	3.00	6.00	12.00
— Lines label; Sides 3 and 4 of "Album No. 9-65"						

Label, Number		Title (A Side/B Side)	Year	VG	VG+	NM
Decca 23777		Silent Night/Adeste Fideles (O Come All Ye Faithful)	1955	2.50	5.00	10.00
— Star on label						
Decca 23777		Silent Night/Adeste Fideles (O Come All Ye Faithful)	1960	2.00	4.00	8.00
— Color bars on label						
Decca 23777	PS	Silent Night/Adeste Fideles (O Come All Ye Faithful)	1960	3.75	7.50	15.00
— Sleeve came with early 1960s pressings						
Decca 23778		White Christmas/God Rest Ye Merry Gentlemen	1950	3.00	6.00	12.00
— Lines label; Sides 5 and 6 of "Album No. 9-65"						
Decca 23778		White Christmas/God Rest Ye Merry Gentlemen	1955	2.50	5.00	10.00
— Star on label						
Decca 23778		White Christmas/God Rest Ye Merry Gentlemen	1960	2.00	4.00	8.00
— Color bars on label						
Decca 23778	PS	White Christmas/God Rest Ye Merry Gentlemen	1960	3.75	7.50	15.00
— Sleeve came with early 1960s pressings						
Decca 23779		I'll Be Home for Christmas (If Only in My Dreams)/ Faith of Our Fathers	1950	3.00	6.00	12.00
— Lines label; Sides 7 and 8 of "Album No. 9-65"						
Decca 27159		Rudolph, the Red-Nosed Reindeer/The Teddy Bear's Picnic	1950	3.00	6.00	12.00
Decca 27159/30126	DJ	Rudolph The Red-Nosed Reindeer/ I Heard The Bells On Christmas Day	1956	5.00	10.00	20.00
— Green label promo with two different numbers on the record!						
Decca 27228		Mele Kalikimaka/Poppa Santa Claus	1950	3.00	6.00	12.00
— With the Andrews Sisters						
Decca 27229		Silver Bells/That Christmas Feeling	1950	3.00	6.00	12.00
— A-side with Carol Richards						
Decca 27230		A Marshmallow World/Looks Like a Cold, Cold Winter	1950	3.00	6.00	12.00
Decca 27249		A Crosby Christmas (Part 1)/(Part 2)	1950	—	—	—
— As "Gary, Phillip, Dennis, Lindsay and Bing Crosby"; unreleased on this number?						
Decca 27831		Christmas in Killarney/It's Beginning to Look Like Christmas	1951	3.75	7.50	15.00
Decca 28463		Sleigh Ride/Little Jack Frost Get Lost	1952	3.75	7.50	15.00
Decca 28511		Sleigh Bell Serenade/Keep It a Secret	1952	3.75	7.50	15.00
Decca 29342		White Christmas/Snow	1954	3.75	7.50	15.00
— A-side with Danny Kaye; B-side by Peggy Lee and Trudi Stevens						
Decca 29790		Christmas Is A-Comin'/Is Christmas Only a Tree	1955	3.00	6.00	12.00
Decca 30126		I Heard the Bells on Christmas Day/Christmas Is a-Comin'	1956	3.00	6.00	12.00
Decca 30126	DJ	I Heard the Bells on Christmas Day/Christmas Is a-Comin'	1956	3.00	6.00	12.00
— Pink label, black type						
Decca 40181		A Crosby Christmas (Part 1)/A Crosby Christmas (Part 2)	1950	7.50	15.00	30.00
— As "Gary, Phillip, Dennis, Lindsay and Bing Crosby"						
Kapp 196		How Lovely Is Christmas/My Own Individual Star	1957	3.00	6.00	12.00
Kapp 196	PS	How Lovely Is Christmas/My Own Individual Star	1957	5.00	10.00	20.00
Little Golden EP407		Boy At A Window/How Lovely Is Christmas	195?	2.50	5.00	10.00
Little Golden EP407	PS	Boy At A Window/How Lovely Is Christmas	195?	3.00	6.00	12.00
MCA 38056		Rudolph The Red-Nosed Reindeer/ I Heard The Bells On Christmas Day	198?	—	2.00	4.00
MCA 40830		White Christmas/ When the Blue of the Night Meets the Gold of the Day	1977	—	2.50	5.00
MCA 40830	PS	White Christmas/ When the Blue of the Night Meets the Gold of the Day	1977	—	2.50	5.00
MCA 65019		Jingle Bells/Santa Claus Is Comin' to Town	1973	—	2.00	4.00
— With the Andrews Sisters; black label with rainbow						
MCA 65019		Jingle Bells/Santa Claus Is Comin' to Town	1980	—	—	3.00
— With the Andrews Sisters; blue label with rainbow						
MCA 65021		Silent Night/Adeste Fideles (O Come All Ye Faithful)	1973	—	2.00	4.00
— Black label with rainbow						
MCA 65021		Silent Night/Adeste Fideles (O Come All Ye Faithful)	1980	—	—	3.00
— Blue label with rainbow						
MCA 65022		White Christmas/God Rest Ye Merry Gentlemen	1973	—	2.00	4.00
— Black label with rainbow						
MCA 65022		White Christmas/God Rest Ye Merry Gentlemen	1980	—	—	3.00
— Blue label with rainbow						
Reprise 0315		It's Christmas Time Again/Christmas Candles	1964	3.00	6.00	12.00
— With Fred Waring and the Pennsylvanians						
Reprise 0315	PS	It's Christmas Time Again/Christmas Candles	1964	3.75	7.50	15.00
Reprise 0317		We Wish You the Merriest/Go Tell It on the Mountain	1964	10.00	20.00	40.00
— By Frank Sinatra/Bing Crosby/Fred Waring						
Reprise 0317	PS	We Wish You the Merriest/Go Tell It on the Mountain	1964	15.00	30.00	60.00
— By Frank Sinatra/Bing Crosby/Fred Waring						
Reprise 0424		The White World of Winter/The Secret of Christmas	1965	2.00	4.00	8.00
Warner Bros. PRO 146	DJ	I Wish You a Merry Christmas/Winter Wonderland//The Littlest Angel	1962	5.00	10.00	20.00

Label, Number		Title (A Side/B Side)	Year	VG	VG+	NM
7-Inch Extended Plays						
Decca 9-65	(4)	Merry Christmas	1950	12.50	25.00	50.00
— Includes records 23281, 23777, 23778 and 23779 (also priced separately) and box						
Decca 9-66	(4)	Christmas Greetings	1950	12.50	25.00	50.00
— Includes records and box						
Decca ED 547 (91123)		Silent Night/Adeste Fideles//White Christmas/	195?	3.00	6.00	12.00
		God Rest Ye Merry Gentlemen				
Decca ED 547 (91124)		I'll Be Home for Christmas/Faith of Our Fathers//	195?	3.00	6.00	12.00
		Jingle Bells/Santa Claus Is Comin' to Town				
Decca ED 547	PS	Merry Christmas	195?	6.25	12.50	25.00
— Cover for 2-EP set						
Decca ED 2547		(contents unknown)	195?	3.00	6.00	12.00
Decca ED 2547	PS	Christmas Time	195?	3.00	6.00	12.00
Decca ED 2659		Silver Bells/The Christmas Song//	195?	3.00	6.00	12.00
		Christmas Carols/God Rest Ye Merry Gentlemen				
Decca ED 2659	PS	Christmas Songs	195?	3.00	6.00	12.00
Decca 7-38274		The First Nowell/Medley: Deck The Hall-Away In A Manger-	196?	3.00	6.00	12.00
		I Saw Three Ships//God Rest Ye Merry, Gentlemen/Jingle Bells				
Decca 7-38274	PS	General Electric Wishes You a Merry Christmas	196?	3.00	6.00	12.00
Albums						
Capitol T 2176	M	Favorite Songs of Christmas	1964	3.75	7.50	15.00
Capitol ST 2176	S	Favorite Songs of Christmas	1964	5.00	10.00	20.00
Capitol SM-11732		Bing Crosby's Christmas Classics	1977	2.50	5.00	10.00
— "A Capitol Re-Issue"; same recordings as on Warner Bros. 1484						
Daybreak 2006		A Time to Be Jolly	1971	3.00	6.00	12.00
Decca DL 4283		Two Favorite Stories by Bing Crosby	1962	6.25	12.50	25.00
Decca DL 5019	10	Merry Christmas	1949	15.00	30.00	60.00
Decca DL 5020	10	Christmas Greetings	1949	15.00	30.00	60.00
Decca DL 8128	M	Merry Christmas	1955	10.00	20.00	40.00
— Expanded version of 10-inch LP; all-black label						
Decca DL 8128	M	Merry Christmas	1960	6.25	12.50	25.00
— Reissue on black label with color bars						
Decca DL 8419		A Christmas Sing with Bing Around the World	1957	10.00	20.00	40.00
— Soundtrack of radio program						
Decca DL 8781	M	That Christmas Feeling	1958	7.50	15.00	30.00
— Expanded version of DL 5020; all-black label						
Decca DL 8781	M	That Christmas Feeling	1960	5.00	10.00	20.00
— Reissue on black label with color bars						
Decca DL 34522		Favorite Songs of Christmas	1968	3.75	7.50	15.00
— Decca Records Custom Division pressing						
Decca DL 78128	R	Merry Christmas	196?	2.50	5.00	10.00
— Same as 8128, except in rechanneled stereo						
Decca DL 78419	R	A Christmas Sing with Bing Around the World	196?	2.50	5.00	10.00
— Same as 8419, except in rechanneled stereo						
Decca DL 78781	R	That Christmas Feeling	196?	2.50	5.00	10.00
— Rechanneled stereo version of DL 8781						
Fox American SMF 210		Bing Crosby Sings Christmas	1978	2.50	5.00	10.00
— Side 1 from radio show Dec. 19, 1951; Side 2 from radio show Dec. 14, 1949						
MCA 3031		Bing Crosby's Greatest Hits	1977	2.50	5.00	10.00
— Contains one Christmas song: White Christmas						
MCA 15017		Two Favorite Stories by Bing Crosby	197?	2.50	5.00	10.00
— Reissue of Decca DL 4283						
MCA 15018	R	A Christmas Sing with Bing Around the World	197?	2.00	4.00	8.00
— Reissue of Decca DL7-8419						
MCA 15019	R	That Christmas Feeling	1973	2.00	4.00	8.00
— Reissue of Decca DL7-8781						
MCA 15024	R	Merry Christmas	197?	2.00	4.00	8.00
— Reissue of Decca DL7-8128						
Reader's Digest RDA-175		Christmas with Bing	1980	2.50	5.00	10.00
— Repackage of Warner Bros. and Capitol recordings						
20th Century T-551		A Holiday Toast	1977	3.00	6.00	12.00
Warner Bros. W 1484	M	I Wish You a Merry Christmas	1962	3.75	7.50	15.00
Warner Bros. WS 1484	S	I Wish You a Merry Christmas	1962	5.00	10.00	20.00

On Various-Artists Collections

Adeste Fideles	Bing Crosby and Rosemary Clooney: White Christmas (Holiday/Collector's Gold 598)
	Christmas Through the Years (Reader's Digest RDA-143)
Angels We Have Heard on High	Family Christmas Favorites from Bing Crosby and the Columbus Boychoir (Decca DL 34487)
Away in a Manger	Bing Crosby and Rosemary Clooney: White Christmas (Holiday/Collector's Gold 598)
	Family Christmas Favorites from Bing Crosby and the Columbus Boychoir (Decca DL 34487)
Christmas Dinner, Country Style	Magic of Christmas, The (Capitol SWBB-93810)
Christmas Is	Many Moods of Christmas, The (Columbia Special Products P 12013)
Christmas Song, The	Family Christmas Favorites from Bing Crosby and the Columbus Boychoir (Decca DL 34487)

Label, Number	Title (A Side/B Side)	Year	VG	VG+	NM
Christmas Toast, A	Happy Holidays, Vol. 21 (RCA Special Products DPL1-0739)				
	Henry Mancini Selects Great Songs of Christmas (RCA Special Products DPL1-0148)				
Come Dear Children 'Round and 'Round the Christmas Tree	Christmas Treasury of Classics from Avon, A (RCA Special Products DPL1-0716)				
Deck the Halls	Family Christmas Favorites from Bing Crosby and the Columbus Boychoir (Decca DL 34487)				
Do You Hear What I Hear	Best of Christmas, The, Vol. II (Capitol SM-11834)				
	Christmas Songs, The (Capitol SLB-57074)				
	Christmas Through the Years (Reader's Digest RDA-143)				
	Happy Holidays, Volume 19 (RCA Special Products DPL1-0689)				
	Joys of Christmas (Capitol Creative Products SL-6610)				
	Popular Christmas Classics (Capitol Special Markets SL-8100)				
	Sound of Christmas, The (Capitol Creative Products SL-6515)				
	Time-Life Treasury of Christmas, The (Time-Life STL-107)				
	12 Hits of Christmas (United Artists UA-LA669-R)				
	Very Merry Christmas, A, Volume VIII (Capitol Special Markets SL-6954)				
Family Christmas, A	Christmas Through the Years (Reader's Digest RDA-143)				
God Rest You Merry Gentlemen	Collection of Christmas Favorites, A (Columbia Special Products P 14988)				
	Old Fashioned Christmas, An (Reader's Digest RDA 216-A)				
Happy Holiday	Holiday Inn (Decca DL 4256)				
	Magic of Christmas, The (Columbia Musical Treasury P3S 5806)				
Have Yourself a Merry Little Christmas	Christmas America (Capitol Special Markets SL-6884)				
Here Comes Santa Claus	Old Fashioned Christmas, An (Reader's Digest RDA 216-A)				
I Heard the Bells on Christmas Day	Family Christmas Collection, The (Time-Life STL-131)				
	Magic of Christmas, The (Columbia Musical Treasury P3S 5806)				
	Old-Fashioned Christmas, An (Longines Symphonette LS 214)				
I Saw Three Ships	Family Christmas Favorites from Bing Crosby and the Columbus Boychoir (Decca DL 34487)				
I Wish You a Merry Christmas	Best of Christmas, The, Vol. I (Capitol SM-11833)				
	Christmas Songs, The (Capitol SLB-57074)				
I'll Be Home for Christmas	Christmas Through the Years (Reader's Digest RDA-143)				
	Time-Life Treasury of Christmas, The, Volume Two (Time-Life STL-108)				
It's Beginning to Look Like Christmas	Christmas Is... (Columbia Special Products P 11417)				
	Home for the Holidays (MCA MSM-35007)				
Jingle Bells	Time-Life Treasury of Christmas, The, Volume Two (Time-Life STL-108)				
Just What I Wanted for Christmas	Joyous Christmas, Volume 6 (Columbia Special Products C 11083)				
Let's Start the New Year Right	Holiday Inn (Decca DL 4256)				
Little Drummer Boy, The	Happy Holidays, Vol. 20 (RCA Special Products DPL1-0713)				
	Rocking Christmas Stocking, A (Capitol SPRO 9303/4/5/6)				
Marshmallow World, A	Christmas Through the Years (Reader's Digest RDA-143)				
Medley: Hark the Herald Angels Sing/ It Came Upon a Midnight Clear	All-Time Christmas Favorites (Capitol Special Markets SL-6931)				
	American Christmas, An (Capitol Special Markets CP-68)				
	Christmas America, Album Two (Capitol Special Markets SL-6950)				
	Let's Celebrate Christmas (Capitol Special Markets SL-6923)				
Medley: Pat-a-Pan/While Shepherds Watched Their Flocks	Zenith Presents Christmas, A Gift of Music (Capitol Creative Products SL-6544)				
Medley: We Wish You a Merry Christmas/Silent Night	All-Time Christmas Favorites (Capitol Special Markets SL-6931)				
Medley: What Child Is This/ The Holly and the Ivy	Christmas Carousel (Capitol SQBE-94406)				
	Sound of Christmas, The, Vol. 2 (Capitol Creative Products SL-6534)				
	Very Merry Christmas, A, Volume Two (Columbia Special Products CSS 788)				
	Zenith Presents Christmas, A Gift of Music (Capitol Creative Products SL-6544)				
Mele Kalikimaka	Blue Christmas (Welk Music Group WM-3002)				
O Holy Night	Christmas Songs, The (Capitol SLB-57074)				
	Spirit of Christmas, The (Capitol Creative Products SL-6516)				
Rudolph, the Red-Nosed Reindeer	Bing Crosby and Rosemary Clooney: White Christmas (Holiday/Collector's Gold 598)				
	Christmas Through the Years (Reader's Digest RDA-143)				
	Family Christmas Favorites from Bing Crosby and the Columbus Boychoir (Decca DL 34487)				
	Happy Holiday (Mistletoe 1243)				
	Time-Life Treasury of Christmas, The, Volume Two (Time-Life STL-108)				
Secret of Christmas, The	Great Songs of Christmas, Album Nine (Columbia Special Products CSS 1033)				
	Joyous Christmas, Volume V (Columbia Special Products C 10398)				
	Say One for Me (Columbia CL 1337)				
	Seasons Greetings (A Christmas Festival of Stars) (Columbia CS 8189)				
	60 Christmas Classics (Sessions DVL2-0723)				
	Very Merry Christmas, A, Volume IV (Columbia Special Products CSS 1464)				
Silent Night	Billboard Greatest Christmas Hits, 1935-1954 (Rhino R1 70637)				
	Bing Crosby and Rosemary Clooney: White Christmas (Holiday/Collector's Gold 598)				
	Christmas Through the Years (Reader's Digest RDA-143)				
Time to Be Jolly, A	Happy Holidays, Volume 14 (RCA Special Products DPL1-0376)				
Twelve Days of Christmas, The	Family Christmas Favorites from Bing Crosby and the Columbus Boychoir (Decca DL 34487)				
We Three Kings of Orient Are	Family Christmas Favorites from Bing Crosby and the Columbus Boychoir (Decca DL 34487)				
White Christmas	Billboard Greatest Christmas Hits, 1935-1954 (Rhino R1 70637)				
	Bing Crosby and Rosemary Clooney: White Christmas (Holiday/Collector's Gold 598)				
	Happy Holiday (Mistletoe 1243)				
	Happy Holidays, Vol. 23 (MCA Special Products 15042)				
	Holiday Inn (Decca DL 4256)				
	Stars of Christmas, The (RCA Special Products DPL1-0842)				
	Time-Life Treasury of Christmas, The (Time-Life STL-107)				
White World of Winter, The	60 Christmas Classics (Sessions DVL2-0723)				
	Great Songs of Christmas, The, Album Six (Columbia Special Products CSM 388)				
	Ronco Presents A Christmas Gift (Columbia Special Products P 12430)				

Label, Number		Title (A Side/B Side)	Year	VG	VG+	NM

CROSBY, BING, AND FRANK SINATRA
On Various-Artists Collections

O Little Town of Bethlehem — Bing Crosby and Rosemary Clooney: White Christmas (Holiday/Collector's Gold 598)

CROSBY, BING, AND FRED WARING
On Various-Artists Collections

Christmas Candles — 12 Songs of Christmas (Reprise F-2022)
It's Christmas Time Again — 12 Songs of Christmas (Reprise F-2022)
Secret of Christmas, The — 12 Songs of Christmas (Reprise F-2022)

CROSBY, LINDSAY
45s

Label, Number		Title (A Side/B Side)	Year	VG	VG+	NM
Ariola America 7682		Christmas Won't Be the Same/Old Friends of Mine	1977	—	2.00	4.00
Ariola America 7682	PS	Christmas Won't Be the Same/Old Friends of Mine	1977	2.00	4.00	8.00
Decca 27812		That's What I Want for Christmas/Dear Mister Santa Claus	1951	5.00	10.00	20.00
Decca 88080	PS	That's What I Want for Christmas/Dear Mister Santa Claus	195?	5.00	10.00	20.00
Era 3170		Christmas Won't Be the Same/Old Friends of Mine	1966	2.50	5.00	10.00

CROSS, MILTON
45s

Label, Number		Title (A Side/B Side)	Year	VG	VG+	NM
RCA Victor WY 20 (47-0141)		The Night Before Christmas/Jingle Bells Fantasy	1949	3.00	6.00	12.00
— From the "Little Nipper" children's series						
RCA Victor WY 20 (47-0141)	PS	The Night Before Christmas/Jingle Bells Fantasy	1949	3.75	7.50	15.00
— From the "Little Nipper" children's series						

On Various-Artists Collections

'Twas the Night Before Christmas — Joyous Christmas, Volume 2 (Columbia Special Products CSS 808)

CROSSTONES, THE
7-Inch Extended Plays

Label, Number		Title (A Side/B Side)	Year	VG	VG+	NM
Clifton 511		Johnny (Missing Christmas Day)/Rockin' Around the Christmas Tree// Merry Christmas Darling/All I Want This Christmas	197?	—	2.50	5.00
Clifton 511	PS	Johnny (Missing Christmas Day)/Rockin' Around the Christmas Tree// Merry Christmas Darling/All I Want This Christmas	197?	—	3.50	7.00

CRUCIAL YOUTH
45s

Label, Number		Title (A Side/B Side)	Year	VG	VG+	NM
Faith 003		Christmas Time (For The Skins)// Santa Claus Is Coming (And You're On His List)/I'm Straight	19??	—	3.00	6.00
— Green vinyl						
Faith 003	PS	Christmas Time (For The Skins)// Santa Claus Is Coming (And You're On His List)/I'm Straight	19??	—	3.00	6.00

CRUSADERS, THE
45s

Label, Number		Title (A Side/B Side)	Year	VG	VG+	NM
Tower 286		The Little Drummer Boy/Battle Hymn of the Republic	1966	2.50	5.00	10.00

CRYSTAL, BILLY
45s

Label, Number		Title (A Side/B Side)	Year	VG	VG+	NM
A&M 2795		The Christmas Song/The Christmas Song (Long Version)	1985	—	2.00	4.00
A&M 2795	PS	The Christmas Song/The Christmas Song (Long Version)	1985	—	2.00	4.00

CRYSTALS, THE
45s

Label, Number		Title (A Side/B Side)	Year	VG	VG+	NM
Pavillion 03333		Rudolph the Red-Nosed Reindeer/ I Saw Mommy Kissing Santa Claus	1982	—	2.50	5.00
— B-side by The Ronettes						

On Various-Artists Collections

Parade of the Wooden Soldiers — Christmas Gift for You from Phil Spector, A (Philles PHLP-4005)
Phil Spector's Christmas Album (Apple SW 3400)
Phil Spector: Back to Mono 1958-1969 (Phil Spector/Abkco 7118-1)
Rudolph, the Red-Nosed Reindeer — Christmas Gift for You from Phil Spector, A (Philles PHLP-4005)
Phil Spector's Christmas Album (Apple SW 3400)
Phil Spector: Back to Mono 1958-1969 (Phil Spector/Abkco 7118-1)
Santa Claus Is Coming to Town — Christmas EP (Philles X-EP)
Christmas Gift for You from Phil Spector, A (Philles PHLP-4005)
Phil Spector's Christmas Album (Apple SW 3400)
Phil Spector: Back to Mono 1958-1969 (Phil Spector/Abkco 7118-1)

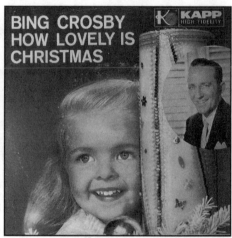

Bing Crosby is the unquestioned "King of Christmas Music." His "White Christmas" is generally considered the top-selling recording in music history. (Top left) One of the early versions of his perennial *Merry Christmas* album was released on two 7-inch EP records with this cover. Originally on three 78s in 1947, it also appeared on four regular 45s and a 10-inch LP before the final 12-song 12-inch LP was released in the mid-1950s. (Top right) A picture sleeve for one of Bing's lesser-known holiday hits, "How Lovely Is Christmas," from 1957. (Bottom left) *Favorite Songs Of Christmas* was a scarce Decca Custom release from the late 1960s. (Bottom right) The last Bing Crosby picture sleeve, from a rare 1977 reissue of "White Christmas." This pressing, on MCA 40830, was available only during that holiday season.

Label, Number		Title (A Side/B Side)	Year	VG	VG+	NM
CUMIN, JOE						
45s						
King 5406		Jingle Bells/Auld Lang Syne	1960	2.50	5.00	10.00
CUPID						
45s						
Brown Bag 90003		'Twas The Night Before Christmas (mono/stereo)	1971	—	2.50	5.00
CURTIS, KEN						
45s						
Pop Sacred 7106		Christmas Cowboy/Christmas Everyday	19??	—	2.00	4.00
CURTIS, SONNY						
45s						
Elektra 47231	DJ	The Christmas Song/Little Drummer Boy	1981	2.00	4.00	8.00
— B-side by Hank Williams, Jr.						
CURTIS, TONY						
On Various-Artists Collections						
Reminder Spot		For Christmas Seals...A Matter of Life and Breath (Decca Custom Style E)				
CURTOLA, BOBBY						
45s						
King 6136		My Christmas Tree/Jingle Bells	1967	2.00	4.00	8.00

D

Label, Number		Title (A Side/B Side)	Year	VG	VG+	NM
D'EGIDIO, MICHAEL						
45s						
Saxtone 100		Santa's Vacation/(Instrumental)	1986	—	—	3.00
Saxtone 100	PS	Santa's Vacation/(Instrumental)	1986	—	—	3.00
D'RIVERA, PASQUITO, AND JOHN MILLER						
On Various-Artists Collections						
God Rest Ye Merry, Gentlemen		God Rest Ye Merry, Jazzmen (Columbia FC 37551)				
DA YOOPERS						
45s						
You Guys 71245		Rusty Chevrolet/Smelting USA	198?	—	3.00	6.00
DAIGLE, PAUL						
45s						
Swallow 10294		Christmas In Cajunland/La Vaille De Noel (Christmas Eve)	199?	—	—	3.00
DAKIL, FLOYD						
45s						
Pompeii 66687		Merry Christmas, Baby/One Girl	1968	6.25	12.50	25.00
DALE, JIMMY						
45s						
Door Knob 018		Merry Christmas, Darling/Happy Anniversary, Darling	1976	—	2.00	4.00
DALGLISH, MALCOLM						
On Various-Artists Collections						
Come Life Shaker Life		Winter's Solstice II, A (Windham Hill WH-1077)				
Northumbrian Lullabye		Winter's Solstice, A (Windham Hill WH-1045)				
DALLAS COWBOYS '86, THE						
45s						
Home Sweet Home 122586		Living The American Dream/Thinking Of You This Christmas	1986	2.00	4.00	8.00
— B-side by Chris Christian and Bob Breunig						

Label, Number		Title (A Side/B Side)	Year	VG	VG+	NM
DALTON, LACY J.						
On Various-Artists Collections						
Away in a Manger		Christmas for the 90's, Volume 2 (Capitol Nashville 1P 8118)				
Silver Bells		Christmas for the 90's, Volume 1 (Capitol Nashville 1P 8117)				
DALY, WILLIAM						
Albums						
Yuletide Series YS 217		Silent Night	197?	2.50	5.00	10.00
DAMAGED PUDS						
45s						
Damgood 33 1/3		Happiest Time Of The Year/Where's Me Fuckin' Presents?	19??	—	3.00	6.00
— B-side by Helen Love; brown vinyl						
Damgood 33 1/3	PS	Happiest Time Of The Year/Where's Me Fuckin' Presents?	19??	—	3.00	6.00
— B-side by Helen Love						
DAMIAN, MICHAEL						
45s						
Cypress 1465		Christmas Time Without You/What Are You Looking For	1989	—	2.00	4.00
— May be cassette only						
Weir Brothers 413		Christmas Time Without You/What Are You Looking For	1987	—	2.00	4.00
Weir Brothers 413	PS	Christmas Time Without You/What Are You Looking For	1987	—	2.00	4.00
DAMNED, THE						
45s						
Big Beat NS 92		There Ain't No Sanity Clause (Remix)/Looking At You (Live)	1982	—	3.00	6.00
Big Beat NS 92	PS	There Ain't No Sanity Clause (Remix)/Looking At You (Live)	1982	—	3.00	6.00
— Record and sleeve are U.K. imports; reissue of Chiswick 139						
Chiswick 139	PS	There Ain't No Sanity Clause//Hit Or Miss/Looking At You (Live)	1981	3.00	6.00	12.00
Chiswick 139		There Ain't No Sanity Clause//Hit Or Miss/Looking At You (Live)	1981	—	3.00	6.00
— Record and sleeve are U.K. imports						
DAMONE, VIC						
45s						
Mercury 5496		A Marshmallow World/When the Lights Are Low	1950	3.75	7.50	15.00
Mercury 5515		Silent Night/White Christmas	1950	3.75	7.50	15.00
Rebecca 714		The Christmas Song/Silver Bells	1977	—	2.00	4.00
Rebecca 715		Christmas In San Francisco/(B-side unknown)	1977	—	2.00	4.00
Albums						
Mercury MG-25092	10	Christmas Favorites	1951	10.00	20.00	40.00
Rebecca 1213		Inspiration	19??	2.50	5.00	10.00
On Various-Artists Collections						
Deck the Halls		Christmas in California (RCA Victor PRS-276)				
		Christmas in New York Volume 2 (RCA Victor PRS-270)				
		Christmas in the Air (RCA Special Products DPL1-0133)				
		Christmastime in Carol and Song (RCA PRM-271)				
		Family Christmas Collection, The (Time-Life STL-131)				
		Music to Trim Your Tree By (RCA Victor PRM 225)				
		Old Fashioned Christmas, An (Reader's Digest RDA 216-A)				
Have Yourself a Merry		Firestone Presents Your Favorite Christmas Music, Volume 4 (Firestone MLP 7011)				
Little Christmas						
It Came Upon a Midnight Clear		Firestone Presents Your Favorite Christmas Music, Volume 4 (Firestone MLP 7011)				
		Old Fashioned Christmas, An (Reader's Digest RDA 216-A)				
		We Wish You a Merry Christmas (RCA Victor PRS-277)				
Joy to the World		Christmas Eve with Colonel Sanders (RCA Victor PRS-256)				
Santa Claus Is Coming to Town		Christmas in New York (RCA Victor PRM-257)				
		Family Christmas Collection, The (Time-Life STL-131)				
		Happy Holidays, Volume IV (RCA Victor PRS-267)				
DAMONE, VIC, AND LIZA MINNELLI						
On Various-Artists Collections						
Woodsman's Serenade/		Dangerous Christmas of Red Riding Hood, The (ABC-Paramount 536)				
Granny's Gulch/Along the Way						
DAMONE, VIC; LIZA MINNELLI; CYRIL RITCHARD						
On Various-Artists Collections						
Granny/Along the Way (reprise)		Dangerous Christmas of Red Riding Hood, The (ABC-Paramount 536)				
We Wish the World a Happy Yule		Dangerous Christmas of Red Riding Hood, The (ABC-Paramount 536)				
(reprise)						

Label, Number		Title (A Side/B Side)	Year	VG	VG+	NM

DAMONE, VIC; PATRICE MUNSEL
On Various-Artists Collections

Golden Dreams		Stingiest Man in Town, The (Columbia CL 950)				
It Might Have Been		Stingiest Man in Town, The (Columbia CL 950)				

DANA, BILL – See JOSE JIMENEZ.

DANCER, PRANCER, AND NERVOUS
45s

Capitol 4300		The Happy Reindeer/Dancer's Waltz	1959	3.00	6.00	12.00
Capitol 4300	PS	The Happy Reindeer/Dancer's Waltz	1959	6.25	12.50	25.00

DANDRIDGE, PUTNEY, SWING BAND
On Various-Artists Collections

Santa Claus Came in the Spring		Stash Christmas Album, The (Stash 125)				

DANDY WARHOLS, THE
45s

Tim/Kerr 947088		Little Drummer Boy/Dick	1994	—	2.50	5.00
— *Red vinyl*						
Tim/Kerr 947088	PS	Little Drummer Boy/Dick	1994	—	2.50	5.00

DANFORTH, WILLIAM H.
On Various-Artists Collections

Dedication		Christmas in Saint Louis (no label) TS77-558/9)				

DANIEL SINGERS, THE
45s

Timely 1041		Dancing Prancing Reindeer/Christmas Star	19??	2.00	4.00	8.00

DANIELS, BILLY
45s

World Wide 121		Season's Greetings/Holiday's	19??	2.00	4.00	8.00

DANIELS, DAN, AND THE SQUIRRELS
45s

Cameo 447		The First Christmas Carol/Grandma's House	1966	3.00	6.00	12.00

DANIELS, EDDIE
On Various-Artists Collections

Sleigh Ride		GRP Christmas Collection, A (GRP 9574)				

DANNY AND THE JUNIORS
45s

Swan 4064		Candy Cane. Sugary Plum/Oh Holy Night	1960	6.25	12.50	25.00
Swan 4064	PS	Candy Cane. Sugary Plum/Oh Holy Night	1960	50.00	100.00	200.00

DANNY BOY
On Various-Artists Collections

Christmas Song, The		Christmas on Death Row (Death Row/Interscope INT2-90108)				
Peaceful Christmas		Christmas on Death Row (Death Row/Interscope INT2-90108)				
This Christmas		Christmas on Death Row (Death Row/Interscope INT2-90108)				

DANTE AND THE EVERGREENS
45s

Madison 143		What Are You Doing New Year's Eve/Yeah Baby	1960	3.75	7.50	15.00

DANTON, RAY
On Various-Artists Collections

God Rest Ye Merry Gentlemen		We Wish You a Merry Christmas (Warner Bros. W 1337)				

DARIEN, FRED
45s

Jaf 2026		Story Of Christmas/Bells Of Laredo	196?	2.50	5.00	10.00

Label, Number		Title (A Side/B Side)	Year	VG	VG+	NM
DARIN, BOBBY						
45s						
Atco 6183		Christmas Auld Lang Syne/Child of God	1960	6.25	12.50	25.00
Atco 6183	PS	Christmas Auld Lang Syne/Child of God	1960	10.00	20.00	40.00
Atco 6211		Ave Maria/O Come All Ye Faithful	1961	3.00	6.00	12.00
Atco 6211	PS	Ave Maria/O Come All Ye Faithful	1961	40.00	80.00	160.00
Albums						
Atco 33-125	M	The 25th Day of December	1960	12.50	25.00	50.00
— First pressing: Yellow label with harp						
Atco SD 33-125	S	The 25th Day of December	1960	15.00	30.00	60.00
— First pressing: yellow label with harp						
Atco 33-125	M	The 25th Day of December	1962	5.00	10.00	20.00
— Second pressing, gold and gray label						
Atco SD 33-125	S	The 25th Day of December	1962	6.25	12.50	25.00
— Second pressing, gold and gray label						

DARLING, DAVID
On Various-Artists Collections
Away in a Manger   Narada: The Christmas Collection (Narada N-63902)

DARNELL, AUGUST
Also see KID CREOLE AND THE COCONUTS.
On Various-Artists Collections
Christmas on Riverside Drive   Christmas Record, A (Ze/Passport PB 6020)

DARNELL, BILL
45s

Label, Number		Title (A Side/B Side)	Year	VG	VG+	NM
"X" 0067		Too Fat to Be Santa/We Wanna See Santa Do the Mambo	1954	3.75	7.50	15.00

DARNELL, LARRY
45s

Label, Number		Title (A Side/B Side)	Year	VG	VG+	NM
Okeh 6926		Christmas Blues/I Am the Sparrow	1952	6.25	12.50	25.00

DASH RIP ROCK
45s

Label, Number		Title (A Side/B Side)	Year	VG	VG+	NM
Mammoth MR 0023		Christmas In El Paso/Little Girl Blue	1992	—	2.00	4.00
Mammoth MR 0023	PS	Christmas In El Paso/Little Girl Blue	1992	—	2.00	4.00

DAVID
On Various-Artists Collections
Night Before Christmas   Merry Christmas from Sesame Street (CRA CTW 25516)
  on Sesame Street, The

DAVIDSON, JOHN
On Various-Artists Collections
First Noel, The   Best of the Great Songs of Christmas (Album 10) (Columbia Special Products CSS 1478)
　　　Carols and Candlelight (Columbia Special Products P 12525)
　　　Great Songs of Christmas, The, Album Seven (Columbia Special Products CSS 547)
　　　Happy Holidays, Album Nine (Columbia Special Products P 11793)
　　　Joy of Christmas, The (Columbia Special Products P 12042)
　　　Merry Christmas (Columbia Musical Treasury 3P 6306)
Hark! The Herald Angels Sing   Great Songs of Christmas, The, Album Seven (Columbia Special Products CSS 547)
　　　Joyous Christmas, Volume 4 (Columbia Special Products CSS 1485)
O Holy Night   Joy to the World (30 Classic Christmas Melodies) (Columbia Special Products P3 14654)
Santa Claus Is Comin' to Town   Home for Christmas (Columbia Musical Treasury P3S 5608)
　　　Home for Christmas (Realm 2V 8101)
Silver Bells   Joy to the World (30 Classic Christmas Melodies) (Columbia Special Products P3 14654)
What Child Is This   Home for Christmas (Columbia Musical Treasury P3S 5608)
　　　Home for Christmas (Realm 2V 8101)
　　　Magic of Christmas, The (Columbia Musical Treasury P3S 5806)
　　　Silent Night... (Columbia Special Products P 14989)

DAVIES, WILLIAM
On Various-Artists Collections
Alleluia   Old Fashioned Christmas, An (Reader's Digest RDA 216-A)

DAVIS SISTERS, THE
45s

Label, Number		Title (A Side/B Side)	Year	VG	VG+	NM
RCA Victor 47-5906		The Christmas Boogie/Tomorrow I'll Cry	1954	3.75	7.50	15.00

Label, Number		Title (A Side/B Side)	Year	VG	VG+	NM

On Various-Artists Collections
Christmas Boogie   Country Christmas (Time-Life STL-109)

DAVIS SISTERS OF PHILADELPHIA, THE
45s

Gotham 676		The First Nowell/We Shall Walk In The Sunlight Of The Lord	195?	3.75	7.50	15.00

DAVIS, DANNY, AND THE NASHVILLE BRASS
45s

RCA 74-0858		White Christmas/Winter Wonderland	1972	—	2.50	5.00
RCA Victor 47-9936		Jingling Brass/Silent Night	1970	—	3.00	6.00
RCA Victor 47-9936	DJ	Silent Night/Jingling Brass	1970	—	3.00	6.00

— *Promos available on either yellow or green labels*

On Various-Artists Collections
Blue Christmas   Blue Christmas (Welk Music Group WM-3002)
Jingling Brass   Henry Mancini Selects Great Songs of Christmas (RCA Special Products DPL1-0148)
                                    Very Merry Christmas, A, Volume VII (RCA Special Products DPL1-0049)
Santa Claus Is Comin' to Town   Happy Holidays, Volume 13 (RCA Special Products DPL1-0319)
Winter Wonderland   60 Christmas Classics (Sessions DVL2-0723)
                                    Brightest Stars of Christmas, The (RCA Special Products DPL1-0086)

DAVIS, EDDIE "LOCKJAW"
45s

Prestige 186		Santa Claus Is Coming To Town/Christmas Song	1958	3.00	6.00	12.00

DAVIS, HONEY
45s

Life Death 2097		Blue Christmas/You Gotta Friend	19??	—	2.00	4.00
— *B-side by Hollyrock*						
Life Death 2097	PS	Blue Christmas/You Gotta Friend	19??	—	2.00	4.00
— *B-side by Hollyrock*						

DAVIS, JESSE ED
On Various-Artists Collections
Santa Claus Is Getting Down   Winter Warnerland (Warner Bros. PRO-A-3328)

DAVIS, JIMMIE
45s

Decca 28912		Christmas Choo Choo/I Love to Ride with Santa Claus	1953	3.75	7.50	15.00
Decca 31686		Go Tell It on the Mountain/It's Christmas Time Again	1964	2.50	5.00	10.00
Decca 32062		Forgive Me Santa/Take Me Back to Babylon	1966	2.00	4.00	8.00
Decca 32236		Going Home for Christmas/Sniffles (Santa's Pet)	1967	—	3.00	6.00

Albums

Decca DL 4587	M	It's Christmas Time Again	1964	3.00	6.00	12.00
Decca DL 4868	M	Going Home for Christmas	1967	3.00	6.00	12.00
Decca DL 74587	S	It's Christmas Time Again	1964	3.75	7.50	15.00
Decca DL 74868	S	Going Home for Christmas	1967	3.00	6.00	12.00

DAVIS, JO
45s

Cuca 1112		Christmas Vacation/Jamaican Holiday	1962	3.00	6.00	12.00

DAVIS, MILES
On Various-Artists Collections
Blue Xmas (To Whom It May Concern)   Jingle Bell Jazz (Columbia PC 36803)

DAVIS, MILES; LARRY CARLTON; DAVID SANBORN; AND PAUL SHAFFER
On Various-Artists Collections
We Three Kings of Orient Are   Scrooged (A&M SP-3921)

DAVIS, MONA
45s

Stop 100		Special Christmas, Special Mother/Within My Heart	196?	3.00	6.00	12.00

DAVIS, SAMMY, JR.
45s

Reprise (no #)	DJ	Here's A Kiss For Christmas (The Christmas Seal Song)/ What Kind Of Fool Am I	1963	3.75	7.50	15.00

Label, Number	Title (A Side/B Side)	Year	VG	VG+	NM

On Various-Artists Collections

It's Christmas Time All Over the World	Christmas Trimmings (Columbia Special Products P 12795)				
	Ronco Presents A Christmas Gift (Columbia Special Products P 12430)				
	That Christmas Feeling (Columbia Special Products P 11853)				
Jingle Bells	Have Yourself a Merry Little Christmas (Reprise R 50001)				
Medley: Jingle Bells/ It's Christmas	Great Songs of Christmas, The, Album Five (Columbia Special Products CSP 238M)				
Time All Over the World	Many Moods of Christmas, The (Columbia Special Products P 12013)				
Winter Wonderland	Columbia 40109 (title unknown) (Columbia 4-40109)				

DAVIS, SKEETER
On Various-Artists Collections

Christmas Greetings	Christmas Greetings From RCA Victor And Groove Recording Artists (RCA Victor SP-45-128)				
New Year's Greetings	Christmas Greetings From RCA Victor And Groove Recording Artists (RCA Victor SP-45-128)				
Santa Claus Is Comin' to Town	Country Style Christmas, A (Columbia Musical Treasury 3P 6316)				

DAWN, GINGER
45s

Lee 1001	Rocking With Santa/Madness	1959	3.00	6.00	12.00

DAWN, JANICE
45s

Brooke 108	Christmas Angel/Shine Every Day	1959	3.00	6.00	12.00

DAWSON, WILLIAM, CHORALE
7-Inch Extended Plays

Sesac 84	DJ	Here We Come A'Wassailing/In A Cave//	19??	—	2.50	5.00
		Silent Night/Merry Are The Bells				
Sesac 84	PS	Here We Come A'Wassailing/In A Cave//	19??	—	2.50	5.00
		Silent Night/Merry Are The Bells				

DAX, DANIELLE
On Various-Artists Collections

Blue Christmas	Winter Warnerland (Warner Bros. PRO-A-3328)				

DAY, DENNIS
45s

RCA Victor 47-3859		O Holy Night/Jesu Bambino	1950	3.75	7.50	15.00
RCA Victor 47-3860		Away in a Manger/God Rest Ye Merry, Gentlemen	1950	3.75	7.50	15.00
RCA Victor 47-3861		We Three Kings of Orient Are/Silent Night	1950	3.75	7.50	15.00
— Above three with the Mitchell Boy Choir						
RCA Victor 47-3970		Christmas in Killarney/I'm Praying to St. Christopher	1950	3.75	7.50	15.00
RCA Victor 47-4321		Christmas in Killarney/Corn Keeps a-Growin'	1951	3.75	7.50	15.00

Albums

Design DLPX-1	M	Dennis Day Sings "Christmas Is for the Family"	195?	5.00	10.00	20.00
— Cover features Jack Benny as Santa; he also appears briefly on the LP						
Design DLP-X-17	M	White Christmas	1965	3.00	6.00	12.00
Design SDLP-X-17	S	White Christmas	1965	3.75	7.50	15.00
Glendale 6029		Christmas Winterland	19??	2.50	5.00	10.00
Stereo Spectrum SDLPX-1	S	Dennis Day Sings "Christmas Is for the Family"	195?	7.50	15.00	30.00
— Same as Design 1, but in stereo						

On Various-Artists Collections

Christmas in Killarney	Christmas Through the Years (Reader's Digest RDA-143)				
	Joyous Noel (Reader's Digest RDA-57A)				

DAY, DORIS
45s

Columbia 39032		Christmas Story/Silver Bells	1950	3.00	6.00	12.00
Columbia 39453		Christmas Story/I'm Forever Blowing Bubbles	1951	3.00	6.00	12.00
— With Jack Smith						
Columbia 43174		Christmas Present/Be a Child at Christmas Time	1964	2.00	4.00	8.00
Columbia JZSP 55070/1	DJ	Let No Walls Divide/God Rest Ye Merry, Gentlemen	1961	3.00	6.00	12.00
— B-side by Andre Previn						
Columbia JZSP 79171/2	DJ	Silver Bells/Winter Wonderland	1963	2.50	5.00	10.00
— "Special Album Excerpt" promo						

Albums

Columbia CL 2226	M	Doris Day's Christmas Album	1964	3.00	6.00	12.00
Columbia CS 9026	S	Doris Day's Christmas Album	1964	3.75	7.50	15.00
Columbia Special Products P13346		Doris Day's Christmas Album	197?	2.50	5.00	10.00
— Reissue of CS 9026						

Label, Number		Title (A Side/B Side)	Year	VG	VG+	NM
On Various-Artists Collections						
Christmas Song, The		Gift of Christmas, The, Vol. 1 (Columbia Special Products CSS 706)				
Have Yourself a Merry Little Christmas		Merry Christmas from. . . (Reader's Digest RD4-83)				
Here Comes Santa Claus		Very Merry Christmas, A, Volume Two (Columbia Special Products CSS 788)				
I'll Be Home for Christmas		First Christmas Record for Children (Harmony HS 14554)				
		Carols and Candlelight (Columbia Special Products P 12525)				
		Christmas Is... (Columbia Special Products P 11417)				
		Joyous Christmas, Volume 2 (Columbia Special Products CSS 808)				
		Merry Christmas (Columbia Musical Treasury 3P 6306)				
Let It Snow! Let It Snow! Let It Snow!		Happy Holidays, Volume II (Columbia Special Products CSM 348)				
		Magic of Christmas, The (Columbia Musical Treasury P3S 5806)				
Silver Bells		Great Songs of Christmas, The, Album Five (Columbia Special Products CSP 238M)				
		Home for Christmas (Columbia Musical Treasury P3S 5608)				
		Home for Christmas (Realm 2V 8101)				
		Merry Christmas from... (Reader's Digest RD4-83)				
		Season's Greetings from Barbra Streisand...And Friends (Columbia Special Products CSS 1075)				
Toyland		Best of the Great Songs of Christmas (Album 10) (Columbia Special Products CSS 1478)				
		Christmas Greetings, Vol. 3 (Columbia Special Products P 11383)				
		Great Songs of Christmas, The, Album Four (Columbia Special Products CSP 155M)				
		Joyous Christmas, Volume 6 (Columbia Special Products C 11083)				
		Many Moods of Christmas, The (Columbia Special Products P 12013)				
		Merry Christmas from... (Reader's Digest RD4-83)				
		Season's Greetings from Barbra Streisand...And Friends (Columbia Special Products CSS 1075)				
		Zenith Presents Christmas, A Gift of Music Vol. 5 (Columbia Special Products C 10395)				
White Christmas		Joyous Christmas, Volume 4 (Columbia Special Products CSS 1485)				
DAY, JACK						
45s						
Coral 64058		An Old Christmas Card/Jolly Old St. Nicholas	1950	5.00	10.00	20.00
DAYMON, RUSTY						
45s						
Multimedia 1201		He Didn't Bring Daddy Home For Christmas/ That's The Way Kids Are	19??	—	2.00	4.00
Multimedia 1201	PS	He Didn't Bring Daddy Home For Christmas/ That's The Way Kids Are	19??	—	2.00	4.00
DAYSPRING						
45s						
Con Brio 143		Elfie, the Littlest Elf/Christmas, Christmas (Comes But Once a Year)	197?	—	2.00	4.00
Con Brio 143	PS	Elfie, the Littlest Elf/Christmas, Christmas (Comes But Once a Year)	197?	—	2.50	5.00
DE LA SOUL						
12-Inch Singles						
Tommy Boy 500		Millie Pulled a Pistol on Santa (2 versions)/ Keepin' the Faith (6 versions)	1991	2.00	4.00	8.00
DE VOL, FRANK						
On Various-Artists Collections						
Medley: Ring, Christmas Bells/ The First Noel/We Wish You a Merry Christmas		Great Songs of Christmas, The (Columbia Special Products XTV 69406/7)				
Medley: We Three Kings of Orient Are/ Good King Wenceslas/O Tannenbaum		Spirit of Christmas, The (Columbia Special Products CSP 249)				
DEACON, MICHAEL						
45s						
Mustard Seed 651		Christmas Comes To Dallas/It's Home	19??	—	2.50	5.00
DEAN, BILLY						
45s						
Capitol Nashville S7-19345 — B-side by the Oak Ridge Boys		I Still Believe in Christmas/Blue Christmas	1996	—	—	3.00
DEAN, EDDIE						
45s						
Sage and Sand 208		The First Christmas Bell/Somebody Great	1957	3.75	7.50	15.00

Label, Number		Title (A Side/B Side)	Year	VG	VG+	NM
DEAN, JIMMY						
45s						
Columbia 41025		Little Sandy Sleighfoot/When They Ring the Golden Bells	1957	3.75	7.50	15.00
Columbia 41025	PS	Little Sandy Sleighfoot/When They Ring the Golden Bells	1957	6.25	12.50	25.00
Columbia 43172		Yes, Patricia, There Is a Santa Claus/Little Sandy Sleighfoot	1964	2.50	5.00	10.00
Columbia 43457		Blue Christmas/Yes, Patricia, There Is a Santa Claus	1965	2.00	4.00	8.00
Columbia JZSP 111915/6	DJ	Blue Christmas/Yes, Patricia, There Is a Santa Claus	1965	5.00	10.00	20.00
— Promo only on green vinyl						
Albums						
Columbia CL 2404	M	Jimmy Dean's Christmas Card	1965	3.75	7.50	15.00
Columbia CS 9204	S	Jimmy Dean's Christmas Card	1965	3.00	6.00	12.00
On Various-Artists Collections						
Have Yourself a Merry		Country Style Christmas, A (Columbia Musical Treasury 3P 6316)				
Little Christmas		Down-Home Country Christmas, A (Columbia Special Products P 14992)				
It Came Upon the Midnight Clear		Country Christmas (Columbia CS 9888)				
		Country Style Christmas, A (Columbia Musical Treasury 3P 6316)				
		We Wish You a Country Christmas (Columbia Special Products P 14991)				
Jingle Bells		Very Merry Christmas, A (Columbia Special Products CSS 563)				
Medley: It Came Upon a Midnight Clear/		Wonderful World of Christmas, The, Album Two (Capitol Special Markets SL-8025)				
O Come, All Ye Faithful						
Reminder Spot		For Christmas Seals...A Matter of Life and Breath (Decca Custom Style E)				
Silent Night, Holy Night		Gift of Christmas, The, Vol. 1 (Columbia Special Products CSS 706)				
White Christmas		Philco Album of Holiday Music, The (Columbia Special Products CSM 431)				
DEANNA - DARLENE						
45s						
Rising Star 20		Rag Doll (For Christmas)/(B-side unknown)	1976	—	2.00	4.00
DEBBIE AND THE TEEN DREAMS						
45s						
Vernon 101		Santa, Teach Me How To Dance/The Time	1962	6.25	12.50	25.00
DEBOY, DAVID						
45s						
Outrageous 21217		Crabs For Christmas/(Instrumental)	19??	2.50	5.00	10.00
DeBURGH, CHRIS						
45s						
A&M 1891		A Spaceman Came Travelling/Poor Boy	1976	—	3.00	6.00
A&M 1998	DJ	A Spaceman Came Travelling (mono/stereo)	1977	—	3.00	6.00
— Stock copies do not exist						
A&M 7267		A Spaceman Came Travelling/Just a Poor Boy	1976	—	2.50	5.00
A&M 7267	PS	A Spaceman Came Travelling/Just a Poor Boy	1976	2.50	5.00	10.00
— Both sleeve and record are U.K. imports						
DeCASTRO SISTERS, THE						
45s						
Abbott 3012		Snowbound for Christmas/Christmas Is a-Comin'	1955	3.75	7.50	15.00
Boha 1001		Feliz Navidad/Santa Claus Is Coming To Town	197?	—	2.00	4.00
DECCA CONCERT ORCHESTRA						
On Various-Artists Collections						
Christmas Medley		Rudolph the Red-Nosed Reindeer (Decca DL 4815)				
Holly Jolly Christmas, A		Rudolph the Red-Nosed Reindeer (Decca DL 4815)				
I Heard the Bells on Christmas Day		Rudolph the Red-Nosed Reindeer (Decca DL 4815)				
Jingle, Jingle, Jingle		Rudolph the Red-Nosed Reindeer (Decca DL 4815)				
Most Wonderful Day of the Year, The		Rudolph the Red-Nosed Reindeer (Decca DL 4815)				
Rudolph the Red-Nosed Reindeer		Rudolph the Red-Nosed Reindeer (Decca DL 4815)				
Silver and Gold		Rudolph the Red-Nosed Reindeer (Decca DL 4815)				
There's Always Tomorrow		Rudolph the Red-Nosed Reindeer (Decca DL 4815)				
We Are Santa's Elves		Rudolph the Red-Nosed Reindeer (Decca DL 4815)				
We're a Couple of Misfits		Rudolph the Red-Nosed Reindeer (Decca DL 4815)				
DEE, LENNY						
45s						
Decca 31332		Mr. Santa/Auld Lang Syne	1961	2.50	5.00	10.00
DEE, PEGGIE						
45s						
Conex 500		Susie Snowflake/Christmas 76	1976	—	2.00	4.00

Label, Number	Title (A Side/B Side)	Year	VG	VG+	NM

DEE, TOMMY
45s
Crest 1067 — Merry Christmas, Mary/Angel of Love — 1959 — 6.25 — 12.50 — 25.00
— With Carol Kay

| Crest 1067 | Merry Christmas, Mary/Angel of Love | 1959 | 6.25 | 12.50 | 25.00 |

DEES, ASHLEY
45s
| Star-Win 7004 | Santa's Comin' in a Whirlybird/ Christmas Isn't Christmas (If Mama Isn't Here) | 196? | 2.00 | 4.00 | 8.00 |

DEES, RICK
45s
| Atlantic 89462 | We Are the Weird/Merry Christmas (Wherever You Are) | 1985 | — | 2.00 | 4.00 |
| No Budget 1680 | Merry Christmas (Wherever You Are)/ Hurt Me Baby, Make Me Write Bad Checks | 1984 | 2.50 | 5.00 | 10.00 |

DeFRANCESCO, JOE, AND DWIGHT SILLS
On Various-Artists Collections
Santa Claus Is Comin' to Town   Jazzy Wonderland, A (Columbia 1P 8120)

DeHAVEN, DOC, COMBO
45s
| Cuca 1435 | Santa Claus/Christmas Medley | 19?? | 2.00 | 4.00 | 8.00 |

DeJOHN SISTERS, THE
45s
| Epic 9133 | The Only Thing I Want for Christmas/ That's How Santa Claus Will Look This Year | 1955 | 3.75 | 7.50 | 15.00 |

DEL-VETTS, THE
45s
| End 1106 | I Want a Boy for Christmas/Repeat After Me | 1961 | 7.50 | 15.00 | 30.00 |

DEL-VUES, THE
45s
| U-Town 8008 | After New Year's/My Confession | 195? | 125.00 | 250.00 | 500.00 |

DELIMA, FRANK
45s
| Pocholinga 107 | Christmas In Honolulu/Island Christmas | 19?? | 2.50 | 5.00 | 10.00 |

DELLER, ALFRED
Albums
| Vanguard VRS-499 | M | The Holly and the Ivy – Christmas Songs of Old England | 1956 | 10.00 | 20.00 | 40.00 |

DeLUGG, MILTON
45s
Epic 9728	Hooray for Santa Claus/Ghost Meet Ghoul	1964	3.75	7.50	15.00
4 Corners Of The World 114	Hooray For Santa Claus/Lonely Beach	1963	3.75	7.50	15.00
MGM 11099	Shake Hands With Santa Claus/Thirty-Two Feet	1951	3.75	7.50	15.00

DeMARCO, ANN
45s
| Orchid 5001 | Santa Claus Rock/Time Didn't Change A Thing | 19?? | 3.00 | 6.00 | 12.00 |

DEMENSIONS, THE
45s
| Mohawk 121 | God's Christmas/Ave Maria | 1960 | 15.00 | 30.00 | 60.00 |

DeMOTTO, BEN
45s
| Highland 712 | 3rd Floor Santa/Twas The Night Before (The Morning After) | 19?? | — | 2.50 | 5.00 |

DEMPSEY, PAUL
45s
| Soundwaves 4782 | Willie Wrinkles (same on both sides) | 1986 | — | — | 3.00 |

Label, Number		Title (A Side/B Side)	Year	VG	VG+	NM
DENNIS, CLARK						
45s						
Capitol 54-90038		O Little Town of Bethlehem and Joy to the World/Cantique de Noel	1949	5.00	10.00	20.00
Decca 27849		Littlest Angel's Christmas/If It Doesn't Snow on Christmas	1951	3.75	7.50	15.00
— With Victor Young and His Singing Strings						
DENSON, LEE						
45s						
Enterprise 9086		A Mom and Dad for Christmas/The Miracle of the Rosary	1973	—	2.50	5.00
DENVER, JOHN						
45s						
RCA Victor APBO-0182		Please, Daddy (Don't Get Drunk This Christmas)/ Rocky Mountain High	1973	—	2.50	5.00
RCA Victor PB-10464		Christmas for Cowboys/Silent Night, Holy Night	1975	—	2.00	4.00
Albums						
RCA Victor APL1-1201		Rocky Mountain Christmas	1975	2.50	5.00	10.00
RCA Victor APL2-1263	(2)	The John Denver Gift Pak	1974	7.50	15.00	30.00
— Contains "Rocky Mountain Christmas" and "Windsong" in a special Christmas sleeve.						
DENVER, JOHN, AND THE MUPPETS						
45s						
RCA PB-11767		Have Yourself a Merry Little Christmas// We Wish You a Merry Christmas/A Baby Just Like You	1979	—	2.50	5.00
RCA PB-11767	PS	Have Yourself A Merry Little Christmas// We Wish You A Merry Christmas/A Baby Just Like You	1979	—	2.50	5.00
Albums						
RCA AFL1-3451		A Christmas Together	1979	3.00	6.00	12.00
On Various-Artists Collections						
Twelve Days of Christmas, The		Christmas Treasury of Classics from Avon, A (RCA Special Products DPL1-0716)				
DEPAUR CHORUS, THE						
45s						
Columbia B-9233	PS	Calypso Christmas	1956	3.75	7.50	15.00
DEPECHE MODE						
45s						
Sire 28697		A Question of Lust/Christmas Island	1986	—	—	3.00
— A-side not a Christmas song						
Sire 28697	PS	A Question of Lust/Christmas Island	1986	—	—	3.00
DER RUFO						
45s						
Rama 28		My Christmas Wish/Greetings	1954	6.25	12.50	25.00
DeSHANNON, JACKIE						
45s						
Imperial 66430		One Christmas/Do You Know How Christmas Trees Are Grown	1969	—	3.00	6.00
DESMOND, JOHNNY						
45s						
Coral 60862		Christmas in the Air/Christmas Is a Time	1952	3.75	7.50	15.00
Coral 61543		Santo Natale/Happy Holidays to You	1955	3.00	6.00	12.00
Coral 61747		Old Fashioned Christmas/Birthday Party of the King	1956	3.00	6.00	12.00
MGM 10827		Sleigh Ride/Marshmallow World	1950	3.75	7.50	15.00
7-Inch Extended Plays						
Coral 83011		Christmas In The Air/Christmas Is A Time// The Little Match Girl/The Night Before Christmas	195?	3.75	7.50	15.00
— B-side by Eileen Barton						
On Various-Artists Collections						
Birthday Party of the King		Stingiest Man in Town, The (Columbia CL 950)				
Old Fashioned Christmas, An		Stingiest Man in Town, The (Columbia CL 950)				
		Stingiest Man in Town, The (Columbia CL 950)				
DETROIT JR.						
45s						
Foxy 002		This Time Last Christmas/Christmas Day	1961	3.00	6.00	12.00

Label, Number		Title (A Side/B Side)	Year	VG	VG+	NM

DEVIL DOGS
On Various-Artists Collections
I Wish It Could Be Christmas Everyday Happy Birthday, Baby Jesus (Sympathy For The Record Industry SFTRI 271)

DeVITO, KARLA
45s

Epic 03404		Santa Claus Is Coming to My House/Cool World	1982	—	3.00	6.00

DeVOL, FRANK
Albums

Columbia CL 1543	M	The Old Sweet Songs of Christmas	1960	3.75	7.50	15.00
Columbia CS 8343	S	The Old Sweet Songs of Christmas	1960	3.75	7.50	15.00
Harmony HL 7356	M	The Old Sweet Songs of Christmas	196?	3.00	6.00	12.00
Harmony HS 11156	S	The Old Sweet Songs of Christmas	196?	3.75	7.50	15.00

On Various-Artists Collections
Skaters' Waltz Happy Holidays, Volume II (Columbia Special Products CSM 348)

DeWITT, DONNA
45s

Nomad 5077		It's Christmas Eve in Richmond Tonight/No Matter How You Say It	19??	—	3.00	6.00

DeWOLF, DEAN
45s

Argo 5457		The Little Drummer Boy/As Joseph Was a-Walkin'	1963	3.00	6.00	12.00

DIABLOS, THE
45s

Pyramid 159		White Christmas/Danny Boy	19??	5.00	10.00	20.00

DIAMOND, NEIL
45s

Columbia 04719		You Make It Feel Like Christmas/Crazy	1984	2.00	4.00	8.00

DIANA SISTERS, THE
45s

Celebrity 103		All I Can Give You (For Christmas)/Season's Greetings	19??	—	—	3.00

DIAZ AND MENDEZ
45s

Chartmaker 421		Feliz Navidad/Christmas Day Parade	19??	—	—	3.00

DICK AND RICHARD
45s

Capitol 5097		Santa Caught a Cold on Christmas Eve/Stinky, the Little Reindeer	1963	3.75	7.50	15.00

DICKENS, JIMMY
45s

Columbia 21167		No Place Like Home on Christmas/Barefooted Little Cowboy	1953	3.75	7.50	15.00

DICKIES, THE
45s

A&M 2092		Silent Night/Sounds of Silence	1978	2.50	5.00	10.00
— All copies on white vinyl						
A&M 2092	DJ	Silent Night/Sounds Of Silence	1978	2.00	4.00	8.00
— All copies on white vinyl						
A&M 2092	PS	Silent Night/Sounds of Silence	1978	2.50	5.00	10.00

DICKINSON, HAL
45s

Coral 61536		Merry Christmas Baby/Tenderly	1955	3.00	6.00	12.00

DIERDORF, DAN/JEFF SEVERSON/ST. LOUIS FOOTBALL CARDINALS
On Various-Artists Collections
We Wish You a Merry Christmas Christmas in Saint Louis ((no label) TS77-558/9)

Label, Number		Title (A Side/B Side)	Year	VG	VG+	NM
DIETRICH, MARLENE						
45s						
Decca 32076		Candles Glowing/This World Of Ours	1966	—	3.00	6.00
DIFFIE, JOE						
45s						
Epic 78201		Leroy the Redneck Reindeer/Wrap Me in Your Love	1995	—	—	3.00
DIMARA SISTERS, THE						
45s						
Pip 100		Santa's Italian Wife/My Very First Christmas	19??	—	2.50	5.00
Slicko 1001		Let's Turn On The Lights On The Christmas Tree/Mistletoe Waltz	19??	—	2.00	4.00
DINGO & THE FIVE LITTLE ELVES						
45s						
Alpha 639		"Santa's Little Helper" Dingo/(Know You Know) Lulabelle	19??	2.00	4.00	8.00
DINU, RICHARD						
45s						
Theme 122587		I'd Like To Be Your Santa Claus/(B-side unknown)	1987	—	2.00	4.00
DION						
45s						
The Right Stuff S7-17651		Christmas (Baby Please Come Home)/Jingle Bell Rock	1993	—	2.50	5.00
— Red vinyl						
DIRKSEN, SENATOR EVERETT MCKINLEY						
45s						
Capitol 2034		The First Time the Christmas Story Was Told/ I Heard the Bells on Christmas Day	1967	2.00	4.00	8.00
DIRTY DOGS						
On Various-Artists Collections						
White Christmas		Stuff This in Your Stocking! Elves in Action (Veebltronics/Skyclad 68)				
DIRTY OLD MEN, THE						
45s						
Trash 520		Hang Them High At Xmas/Decorations	19??	2.50	5.00	10.00
DISNEYLAND BOYS' CHOIR, THE						
45s						
Buena Vista 449		Silent Night/It's a Small World	1965	3.75	7.50	15.00
DISPOTA SISTERS, THE						
45s						
Verve 10188		Whistling 'Neath the Mistletoe/Willie Claus	1959	3.75	7.50	15.00
DITTMARS, IVAN						
Albums						
Crown CST 8	S	Joy to the World	196?	3.75	7.50	15.00
Crown 5049	M	Joy to the World	196?	3.00	6.00	12.00
— Same as Crown CST 8, but in mono						
Yuletide Series YS-218	S	Joy to the World	197?	2.50	5.00	10.00
— Same as Crown CST 8						
DIXON, REGINALD						
On Various-Artists Collections						
I Heard the Bells on Christmas Day		Old Fashioned Christmas, An (Reader's Digest RDA 216-A)				
Sleigh Ride		Old Fashioned Christmas, An (Reader's Digest RDA 216-A)				
DO-RE-MI CHILDREN'S CHORUS, THE						
45s						
Kapp 627	PS	Silver and Gold/Do You Hear What I Hear	1964	2.50	5.00	10.00
Kapp 627		Silver and Gold/Do You Hear What I Hear	1964	2.00	4.00	8.00
Kapp 2071		Do You Know How Christmas Trees Are Grown?/ The Wonderful Things (That He Can Do)	1969	—	3.00	6.00

Label, Number		Title (A Side/B Side)	Year	VG	VG+	NM
Albums						
Kapp KL-1368	M	More of the Christmas Songs Children Love to Sing	1964	3.00	6.00	12.00
Kapp KS-3368	S	More of the Christmas Songs Children Love to Sing	1964	3.75	7.50	15.00
MCA 15008		Do You Hear What I Hear?	1973	2.50	5.00	10.00
— Reissue of Kapp KS-3368						

DOAN, JOHN
On Various-Artists Collections

God Rest Ye Merry Gentlemen	Narada: The Christmas Collection (Narada N-63902)

DOBSON, ANITA
45s

Parlophone RS 6172		I Dream Of Christmas/Silly Christmas	1987	—	3.00	6.00
— U.K. import						
Parlophone RS 6172	PS	I Dream Of Christmas/Silly Christmas	1987	—	3.00	6.00
— U.K. import; cardboard stock sleeve						
Parlophone RS 6172	PS	I Dream Of Christmas/Silly Christmas	1987	—	3.00	6.00
— U.K. import; paper stock sleeve						

DOCKETT, JIMMY
45s

Hull 769	Merry Christmas Mother/Season's Greetings	1964	2.50	5.00	10.00

DOCTOR RON
45s

Mary Lou 23045	The Gift/I Got My Christmas When You Came To Me	19??	—	—	3.00

DODD, SUSAN
45s

Hereford 0032	Merry Christmas, I Love You/Sing Me A Love Song	19??	—	3.00	6.00

DODDS, MALCOLM
45s

Aurora 3250	Ich Bin Verry Happy (Merry, Merry Christmas)/Perfect Strangers	1962	2.50	5.00	10.00

DODGE, SUE
On Various-Artists Collections

Angels We Have Heard on High	Merry Christmas (Rainbow Sound R-5032-LPS)
Go Tell It on the Mountain	Merry Christmas (Rainbow Sound R-5032-LPS)

DODSON, HERB
45s

Stacy 954	A Disc Jockey's Christmas Eve/What Is a Disc Jockey	1962	3.75	7.50	15.00

DOGGETT, BILL
45s

King 4742		The Christmas Song/Winter Wonderland	1954	5.00	10.00	20.00
Albums						
King 295-89	10	All-Time Christmas Favorites	1955	50.00	100.00	200.00
King 395-600	M	A Bill Doggett Christmas	1959	10.00	20.00	40.00

DOLCE, JOE
45s

Montage 1208	DJ	The 12 Days Of Christmas/Jingle Bell Rock	1981	—	2.00	4.00

DOLENZ, JONES & TORK
45s

Christmas 700		Christmas Is My Time of Year/White Christmas	1976	5.00	10.00	20.00
Christmas 700	PS	Christmas Is My Time of Year/White Christmas	1976	10.00	20.00	40.00

DOLLAR, JOHNNY
45s

Gemini 1200	Do The Reindeer/Ringo	1964	3.00	6.00	12.00

Label, Number		Title (A Side/B Side)	Year	VG	VG+	NM
DOMINGO, PLACIDO						
45s						
CBS AE7 1789	DJ	It's Christmas Time This Year (same on both sides)	1981	—	2.50	5.00
Albums						
CBS FM 37245		Christmas with Placido Domingo	1981	3.00	6.00	12.00
On Various-Artists Collections						
Adeste Fideles		Family Christmas Collection, The (Time-Life STL-131)				
Ave Maria (Bach-Gounod)		Family Christmas Collection, The (Time-Life STL-131)				
		Happy Holidays, Volume 16 (RCA Special Products DPL1-0501)				
DOMINO, FATS						
45s						
The Right Stuff S7-18216		Christmas Is a Special Day/	1994	—	2.00	4.00
		Please Come Home for Christmas (Christmas Once Again)				
— Red vinyl						
DOMO, MAJOR & THE JOLLY GNOME BAND						
45s						
North Pole 404		Santa's Safety Songs	19??	—	3.00	6.00
North Pole 404	PS	Santa's Safety Songs	19??	3.00	6.00	12.00
DONALD, PETER						
45s						
Golden FF33		The Night Before Christmas Part 1/The Night Before Christmas Part 2	19??	2.00	4.00	8.00
DONLEY, JIMMY						
45s						
Chess 1843		Santa, Don't Pass Me By/Think It Over	1962	3.00	6.00	12.00
Crazy Cajun 9001		Santa, Don't Pass Me By/Think It Over	19??	—	2.50	5.00
Teardrop 3007		Santa, Don't Pass Me By/Forever Lillie Mae	1962	3.00	6.00	12.00
Teardrop 3021		Santa, Don't Pass Me By/Santa's Alley	1963	3.00	6.00	12.00
DONNA & DEES						
45s						
B.C.S. 101		I Know There Is A Santa Claus/Jingle Bells	196?	6.25	12.50	25.00
B.C.S. 102		Happy Holiday/Hunky Was Doing The Monkey	196?	6.25	12.50	25.00
DONNA Z						
45s						
TPF 001		For Those Who Need Homes This Christmas/	198?	—	—	3.00
		For Those Who Need Homes This Christmas (Instrumental)				
DONNER, RAL						
45s						
Reprise 20,135		(These Are the Things That Make Up) Christmas Day/	1962	10.00	20.00	40.00
		Second Miracle (Of Christmas)				
Starfire 103		(Things That Make Up) Christmas Day/Second Miracle (Of Christmas)	1978	2.50	5.00	10.00
— Green vinyl						
Starfire 103	PS	(Things That Make Up) Christmas Day/Second Miracle (Of Christmas)	1978	2.50	5.00	10.00
DONY L						
45s						
Epitome 102		Christmas In L.A./You're Why I Believe In Santa Claus	19??	—	2.50	5.00
DORAN, JEAN						
45s						
Dalton 102		Shepherds & Kings/My Christmas Star	19??	—	2.00	4.00
— B-side by Buell Thomas						
DORSEY, JIMMY						
45s						
Columbia 39578		Jiminy Christmas/Manhattan	1951	3.75	7.50	15.00
DORSEY, TOMMY						
On Various-Artists Collections						
Santa Claus Is Comin' to Town		Happy Holidays, Vol. 21 (RCA Special Products DPL1-0739)				

Label, Number		Title (A Side/B Side)	Year	VG	VG+	NM

DOUCET, CAMEY
45s

| Swallow 10259 | | What Christmas Meant To Me/Amen, Hallelujah | 198? | — | 2.00 | 4.00 |

DOUGLAS, MIKE
45s

Epic 10089		Touch Hands on Christmas Morning/	1966	3.00	6.00	12.00
		(The Story Of) The First Christmas Carol				
Epic JZSP 135100/1	DJ	Silver Bells (mono/stereo)	1967	2.50	5.00	10.00

Albums

Epic LN 24322	M	My Kind of Christmas	1967	3.00	6.00	12.00
Epic BN 26322	S	My Kind of Christmas	1967	3.00	6.00	12.00
Word 8815		Christmas Album	198?	2.50	5.00	10.00

On Various-Artists Collections

First Noel, The		Joy to the World (30 Classic Christmas Melodies) (Columbia Special Products P3 14654)				
Holy Night		Wondrous Winter: Songs of Winter, Songs of Christmas				
		(Columbia Special Products CSS 708/9)				
Touch Hands on Christmas Morning		Very Merry Christmas, A (Columbia Special Products CSS 563)				

DOUGLAS, STEVE
45s

| Texas Opry 588 | | Tyke (The Christmas Elf)/(Instrumental) | 19?? | — | 2.00 | 4.00 |

DOWELL, JOE
45s

| Smash 1728 | | (I Wonder) Who's Spending Christmas with You/A Kiss for Christmas | 1961 | 3.75 | 7.50 | 15.00 |

DOWLING, CHET, & BILL MINKIN
45s

Columbia ZLP 135464/5	DJ	Christmas Eve With The Senator//The Opening and the Gift List/	1967	3.00	6.00	12.00
		The Christmas Haircut/What to Get the Kids/The Christmas Cards				
— Small hole, 33 1/3 rpm; promo for "Senator Bobby's Christmas Party"						

Albums

| Columbia CL 2776 | M | Senator Bobby's Christmas Party | 1967 | 5.00 | 10.00 | 20.00 |
| Columbia CS 9576 | S | Senator Bobby's Christmas Party | 1967 | 5.00 | 10.00 | 20.00 |

DR. STRANGE & THE LOVERS
45s

| Jam 105 | | Santa's Brother/Doc's Resolution | 1962 | 3.00 | 6.00 | 12.00 |

DRAKE AND COMPANY
45s

| Samarah 10985 | | What Is Christmas Without A Toy/(Instrumental) | 1985 | — | — | 3.00 |
| Samarah 10985 | PS | What Is Christmas Without A Toy/(Instrumental) | 1985 | — | — | 3.00 |

DRAKE, JIMMY
45s

| As-Is 100 | | The Orphan's Christmas Song/That's Who | 19?? | 12.50 | 25.00 | 50.00 |

DREAD ZEPPELIN
45s

I.R.S. S7-19353		All I Want for Christmas Is My Two Front Teeth/	1996	—	—	3.00
		Happy Xmas (War Is Over)				
— B-side by the Alarm						

DREAD, JUDGE
45s

| Cactus 80 | | Christmas In Dreadland/Come Outside | 19?? | 2.50 | 5.00 | 10.00 |
| — U.K. import | | | | | | |

DREAMS SO REAL
45s

Arista 9784		Red Lights (Merry Christmas)/Bearing Witness (Lay Me Down)	1988	—	3.00	6.00
— Green vinyl						
Arista 9784	PS	Red Lights (Merry Christmas)/Bearing Witness (Lay Me Down)	1988	—	3.00	6.00

Label, Number		Title (A Side/B Side)	Year	VG	VG+	NM
DRIFTERS, THE						
45s						
Atlantic 1048		White Christmas/The Bells of St. Mary's	1954	10.00	20.00	40.00
— Yellow label, no spinner (original)						
Atlantic 1048		White Christmas/The Bells of St. Mary's	1956	6.25	12.50	25.00
— Red label, no spinner						
Atlantic 1048		White Christmas/The Bells of St. Mary's	1962	2.00	4.00	8.00
— Red label with spinner						
Atlantic 1048		White Christmas/The Bells of St. Mary's	197?	—	2.50	5.00
— Glossy yellow label with spinner						
Atlantic 1048	DJ	White Christmas/The Bells of St. Mary's	1956	6.25	12.50	25.00
— White label promo						
Atlantic 2261		The Christmas Song/I Remember Christmas	1964	3.00	6.00	12.00
Atlantic 2261	PS	The Christmas Song/I Remember Christmas	1964	6.25	12.50	25.00
EMI-Capitol Music S7-19351		Christmas Time Is Here/I'll Be Home for Christmas	1996	—	—	3.00
— As "The Drifters Featuring Rick Sheppard"						
On Various-Artists Collections						
White Christmas		Billboard Greatest Christmas Hits, 1955-Present (Rhino R1 70636)				
		Jingle Bell Rock (Time-Life SRNR-XM)				
DRUMS, DONALD						
45s						
Challenge 59099		Merry Christmas Window/	1960	3.00	6.00	12.00
		(There's Something About a) Home Town Band				
DUCK'S BREATH MYSTERY THEATRE						
45s						
Duck's Breath 4502		I'm Going Out Of My Mind (It's Christmas Time)/I Deliver Toys	19??	—	3.00	6.00
Duck's Breath 4502	PS	I'm Going Out Of My Mind (It's Christmas Time)/I Deliver Toys	19??	2.00	4.00	8.00
DUDES, THE						
45s						
Sue 723		Rudolph the Red-Nosed Reindeer/Jingle Bells	1959	3.75	7.50	15.00
DUDLEY DOGG JR.						
45s						
Holiday 1214		The Christmas Puppy/Theme For A Christmas Puppy	19??	—	3.00	6.00
Holiday 1214	PS	The Christmas Puppy/Theme For A Christmas Puppy	19??	2.00	4.00	8.00
DUDLEY, DAVE						
45s						
Mercury 73142		Old Time Merry Christmas/Six Tons of Toys	1970	2.00	4.00	8.00
DUFF, HOWARD						
On Various-Artists Collections						
Reminder Spot		For Christmas Seals...A Matter of Life and Breath (Decca Custom Style E)				
DUKE, DENVER, AND JEFFREY NULL						
45s						
Blue Hen 127		A Babe, A Star, A Manger/Christ, Who Came To Bethlehem	19??	3.00	6.00	12.00
DUKE, PATTI, WITH NORMAN VINCENT PEALE						
Albums						
Guideposts GP-101	M	Guideposts for Christmas	1963	20.00	40.00	80.00
DUMBELLS, THE						
45s						
Polydor EGO 3		A Christmas Dream/Giddy-Up	198?	2.50	5.00	10.00
— U.K. import						
DUMMAR, MELVIN						
45s						
ATC 85218		Souped-Up Santa's Sleigh/Souped-Up Santa's Sleigh (Instrumental)	19??	5.00	10.00	20.00
ATC 85218	PS	Souped-Up Santa's Sleigh/Souped-Up Santa's Sleigh (Instrumental)	19??	7.50	15.00	30.00

Label, Number		Title (A Side/B Side)	Year	VG	VG+	NM
DUNCAN SISTERS, THE						
45s						
Duncan-Disc 2021		Dear Santy/Jolly Ole Fellow	198?	—	2.50	5.00
7-Inch Extended Plays						
Duncan Sisters DS-1		Twimmin' De Cwis'mas Twee/Dear Santy//	198?	—	2.50	5.00
		Angel On Top Of The Xmas Tree/Jolly Ole Fella'				
DUNSTEDTER, EDDIE						
Albums						
Capitol T 1264	M	The Bells of Christmas	1959	3.00	6.00	12.00
Capitol ST 1264	S	The Bells of Christmas	1959	3.75	7.50	15.00
Capitol T 1968	M	The Bells of Christmas Chime Again	1963	3.00	6.00	12.00
Capitol ST 1968	S	The Bells of Christmas Chime Again	1963	3.75	7.50	15.00
Capitol T 2395	M	Christmas Candy	1965	3.00	6.00	12.00
Capitol ST 2395	S	Christmas Candy	1965	3.75	7.50	15.00
On Various-Artists Collections						
Deck the Halls		Christmas Stocking (Capitol NP 90494)				
DUPHINEY, CLIFF						
45s						
Decora 2003		Winter Wonderland/(B-side unknown)	196?	3.00	6.00	12.00
DURAND, AL						
45s						
Alfie 102		Christmas Makes Everything Alright/This Christmas	19??	3.00	6.00	12.00
DURANTE, JIMMY						
45s						
MGM 30257		Frosty The Snowman/Christmas Comes But Once A Year	1950	3.75	7.50	15.00
DURKIN, BILL						
45s						
In Victa 101		God's Christmas/'Till There Was You	19??	—	2.00	4.00
7-Inch Extended Plays						
In Victa 7112		God's Christmas/Silent Night//O Come All Ye Faithful/The First Noel	19??	—	2.50	5.00
In Victa 7112	PS	The Cardinal Cushing Christmas Record: God's Christmas	19??	2.50	5.00	10.00
DYESS, DAVID WAYNE						
45s						
Ace 578		Hi Ho Merry Christmas/Christmas Morn	1959	3.75	7.50	15.00
DYKE, MIKE						
45s						
Southern Tracks 1073	DJ	A Christmas Card (same on both sides)	1986	—	2.00	4.00
DYNAMICS, THE						
45s						
Dynamic 578/9		Christmas Plea/Dream Girl	1962	12.50	25.00	50.00

E

Label, Number		Title (A Side/B Side)	Year	VG	VG+	NM
EA 80						
7-Inch Extended Plays						
EA80 S-6/7		It's Christmas/Xmas Is Over//Know That You Know/Hallelujah	19??	—	2.50	5.00
EA80 S-6/7	PS	It's Christmas/Xmas Is Over//Know That You Know/Hallelujah	19??	—	3.00	6.00
— U.K. import						
EAGLES						
45s						
Asylum 45555		Please Come Home for Christmas/Funky New Year	1978	—	2.00	4.00
— Original with "clouds" label						
Asylum 45555		Please Come Home for Christmas/Funky New Year	1984	—	—	3.00
— Reissue with black and yellow label						

Label, Number		Title (A Side/B Side)	Year	VG	VG+	NM
Asylum 45555	PS	Please Come Home for Christmas/Funky New Year	1978	—	2.00	4.00
— *Sleeve was available with both issues*						

EANES, JIM
45s
| Starday 414 | | Christmas Doll/It Won't Seem Like Christmas | 1958 | 5.00 | 10.00 | 20.00 |

EAST, DOTTIE
45s
| Tiny Tike 1030 | | Christmas Dream/Christmas Tree | 19?? | — | 2.00 | 4.00 |

EASTON, SHEENA
On Various-Artists Collections
| It's Christmas All Over the World | | Santa Claus The Movie (EMI America SJ-17177) | | | | |

EBONYS, THE
45s
| Philadelphia Int'l. 3513 | DJ | (Christmas Ain't Christmas, New Year's Ain't New Year's) Without The One You Love (mono/stereo) | 1971 | 2.00 | 4.00 | 8.00 |

ECHELONS, THE
45s
BAB 129		A Christmas Long Ago (Jingle Jingle)/Mystery	19??	3.75	7.50	15.00
Collectables 3997		A Christmas Long Ago (Jingle Jingle)/ Have Yourself A Merry Little Christmas	199?	—	—	3.00
— *B-side by Johnny Maestro and the Brooklyn Bridge*						

ECKSTINE, BILLY
45s
MGM 10525		O Come, All Ye Faithful/O, Holy Night	1949	3.75	7.50	15.00
MGM 10796		Blue Christmas/The Lonely Shepherd	1950	3.75	7.50	15.00
MGM 11623		What Are You Doing New Year's Eve/Christmas Eve	1953	5.00	10.00	20.00

ECSTASIES, THE
45s
| Clifton 40 | | White Christmas/Silent Night | 19?? | 3.75 | 7.50 | 15.00 |

EDDIE AND THE DE HAVELONS
45s
| Peacock 1920 | | Christmas Party/Baby Dumplings | 1963 | 2.50 | 5.00 | 10.00 |

EDDY, NELSON
On Various-Artists Collections
First Noel, The		Great Songs of Christmas, The, Album Two (Columbia Special Products XTV 86100/1)				
		Joyous Christmas, Volume 4 (Columbia Special Products CSS 1485)				
		Merry Christmas from... (Reader's Digest RD4-83)				
Holy City, The		Merry Christmas from... (Reader's Digest RD4-83)				
Jingle Bells		Great Songs of Christmas, The, Album Two (Columbia Special Products XTV 86100/1)				

EDISON, HARRY "SWEETS"
45s
| Sue 117 | | Blues for Christmas/Green Dolphin Christmas | 1964 | 3.75 | 7.50 | 15.00 |

EDMUNDS, DAVE
45s
Columbia 03428		Run Rudolph Run/Deep in the Heart of Texas	1982	—	2.00	4.00
Columbia 03428	PS	Run Rudolph Run/Deep in the Heart of Texas	1982	2.00	4.00	8.00
Columbia 05487		Run Rudolph Run/From Small Things (Big Things One Day Come)	198?	—	—	3.00
— *"Golden Oldies" reissue*						
On Various-Artists Collections
| Run Rudolph Run | | Christmas Rock Album, The (Priority SL 9465) | | | | |

EDWARD BEAR
45s
| Capitol 3780 | | Coming Home Christmas/Does Your Mother Know | 1973 | 2.00 | 4.00 | 8.00 |

Label, Number	Title (A Side/B Side)	Year	VG	VG+	NM

EDWARDS, JOHN
45s

| Cotillion 44209 | The Christmas Song/White Christmas | 1976 | — | 2.00 | 4.00 |

EDWARDS, STONEY
45s

| Hill Country 901 | Our Little Christmas Tree/Silent Night - Holy Night | 198? | — | 2.00 | 4.00 |

EDWARDS, TOMMY
45s

| MGM 11097 | Christmas Is for Children/Kris Kringle | 1951 | 5.00 | 10.00 | 20.00 |
| MGM 11624 | Every Day Is Christmas/It's Christmas Once Again | 1953 | 5.00 | 10.00 | 20.00 |

EEK-A-MOUSE
On Various-Artists Collections

| Night Before Christmas, The | Reggae Christmas, A (Real Authentic Sound RAS 3101) | | | | |

EGAN, MARK
On Various-Artists Collections

| What Child Is This | GRP Christmas Collection, A (GRP 9574) | | | | |

EGR, BILLY
45s

| Pacific Avenue 1151 | What Would Santa Claus Think/Barbara Henri | 19?? | — | 2.00 | 4.00 |

816
On Various-Artists Collections

| On This Glorious Day | Christmas on Death Row (Death Row/Interscope INT2-90108) | | | | |

EIGHTH DAY, THE
45s

| Crib 101 | Let's Share The Miracle/It's Christmas Day | 19?? | — | 2.00 | 4.00 |

ELAINE AND DEREK
45s

| Vee Jay 415 | The Christmas Story/It's Christmas | 1961 | 3.75 | 7.50 | 15.00 |

ELECTRIC SHOES, THE
On Various-Artists Collections

| It's Christmas (And I Love You) | Stuff This in Your Stocking! Elves in Action (Veebltronics/Skyclad 68) | | | | |

ELIAS, ELAINE
On Various-Artists Collections

| Medley: I'll Be Home for Christmas/ Sleigh Ride | Yule Struttin' — A Blue Note Christmas (Blue Note 1P 8119) | | | | |

ELIGIBLES, THE
45s

| Capitol 4304 | My First Christmas with You/Little Engine | 1959 | 3.75 | 7.50 | 15.00 |

ELKINS, CURTIS
On Various-Artists Collections

| God Rest Ye Merry Gentlemen | Merry Christmas (Rainbow Sound R-5032-LPS) | | | | |

ELLEN, IVY, & FAMILY
45s

Felsted 8609	Go Tell Santa/(Instrumental)	1960	3.75	7.50	15.00
— B-side by the Reindeers					
Felsted 8609 PS	Go Tell Santa/(Instrumental)	1960	5.00	10.00	20.00

ELLINGTON, DUKE
On Various-Artists Collections

Jingle Bells	Jingle Bell Jazz (Columbia PC 36803)				
	Joy of Christmas, The (Columbia Special Products P 12042)				
	Ronco Presents A Christmas Gift (Columbia Special Products P 12430)				

Label, Number	Title (A Side/B Side)	Year	VG	VG+	NM

ELLIOTT, WALTER & BENNETT
45s

Paid DAL 1	The Twelve Days of a Dallas Cowboy Christmas/It	1980	2.00	4.00	8.00
Paid OAK 2	The Twelve Days of an Oakland Raider Christmas/It	1980	2.00	4.00	8.00
Paid ATL 3	The Twelve Days of a Atlanta Falcon Christmas/It	1980	2.00	4.00	8.00
— Label is ungrammatical as above					
Paid PIT 4	The Twelve Days of a Pittsburg Steelers Christmas/It	1980	2.00	4.00	8.00
— The label misspells "Pittsburgh"					
Paid NEP 5	The Twelve Days of a New England Patriot Christmas/It	1980	2.00	4.00	8.00
Paid BBS 6	The Twelve Days of a Buffalo Bill Christmas/It	1980	2.00	4.00	8.00
Paid PES 7	The Twelve Days of a Philadelphia Eagle Christmas/It	1980	2.00	4.00	8.00
Paid LAX 8	The Twelve Days of a Los Angeles Ram Christmas/It	1980	2.00	4.00	8.00
Paid COB 9	The Twelve Days of a Cleveland Brown Christmas/It	1980	2.00	4.00	8.00
Paid SDC 10	The Twelve Days of a San Diego Charger Christmas/It	1980	2.00	4.00	8.00

ELLIS, JONAH
45s

Total Experience 2410	Christmas Won't Be Christmas Without My Baby/(Instrumental)	1984	—	2.00	4.00

On Various-Artists Collections

Christmas Won't Be Christmas Without My Baby	Total Experience Christmas, A (Total Experience TEL8-5707)

ELLIS, LARRY
45s

Seasons Greetings FMK-7S-186	I Love That Feeling Of Christmas/Cold, Cold Christmas	19??	—	—	3.00
— Possibly a demo recording					
Seasons Greetings FMK-7S-186 PS	I Love That Feeling Of Christmas/Cold, Cold Christmas	19??	—	—	3.00

ELLIS, RAY & HIS ORCHESTRA
45s

Columbia 41056	Like Jingle Bells/Snow, Snow, Beautiful Snow	1957	3.00	6.00	12.00

ELLISON, HAROLD L.
45s

He 1001	Santa's Gone Away/Santa's Gone Away	19??	—	3.00	6.00

ELLWOOD, WILLIAM
On Various-Artists Collections

Return of the Magi	Narada: The Christmas Collection (Narada N-63902)

ELMO & PATSY
Also see PATSY.
45s

Elmo 'n' Patsy (# unknown)	Grandma Got Run Over by a Reindeer/Christmas	1979	5.00	10.00	20.00
— Original pressing of this Christmas classic					
Epic 04703	Grandma Got Run Over by a Reindeer/Percy, the Puny Poinsettia	1984	—	2.00	4.00
— New recording					
Epic 04703 PS	Grandma Got Run Over by a Reindeer/Percy, the Puny Poinsettia	1984	—	2.00	4.00
Epic 05479	Grandma Got Run Over by a Reindeer/Percy, the Puny Poinsettia	1985	—	—	3.00
— Gray label reissue (many have the above picture sleeve)					
Oink 2984	Grandma Got Run Over by a Reindeer/Christmas	1979	2.00	4.00	8.00
— Second issue of original recording					
Soundwaves 4658	Grandma Got Run Over by a Reindeer/Christmas	1979	—	3.00	6.00
— Third issue of original recording					

Albums

Epic PE 39931	Grandma Got Run Over by a Reindeer	1984	2.00	4.00	8.00

On Various-Artists Collections

Grandma Got Run Over by a Reindeer	Billboard Greatest Christmas Hits, 1955-Present (Rhino R1 70636)
	Dr. Demento Presents the Greatest Novelty Records of All Time Volume VI: Christmas (Rhino RNLP 825)

ELMORE, RUSS AND RUSSANNE
45s

Dolton 14	What Does Santa Claus Want for Christmas/Big Words	1959	3.75	7.50	15.00

ELVES CHORUS, THE
45s

Weber 170	Mrs. Santa Claus/Mrs. Santa Claus (With Toy Band)	19??	2.00	4.00	8.00

Label, Number	Title (A Side/B Side)	Year	VG	VG+	NM
EMERSON, KEITH					
Also see EMERSON, LAKE AND PALMER.					
Albums					
Emerson KEITH LP1	The Christmas Album	1993	5.00	10.00	20.00
— British import only (as far as we know)					
EMERSON, LAKE AND PALMER					
Also see KEITH EMERSON, GREG LAKE.					
Albums					
Atlantic SD 19147	Works Volume 2	1977	2.50	5.00	10.00
— Contains one Christmas song: I Believe in Father Christmas (has a different ending than the single version)					
EMERY, RALPH					
45s					
Liberty 55524	Christmas Dinner/Christmas Can't Be Far Away	1962	3.00	6.00	12.00
EMMONS, BOBBY & THE CROSSTONES					
45s					
Empo 1001	Why Should I Lie/Christmas Bell Rock	19??	—	2.50	5.00
EMMONS, BUDDY					
45s					
Columbia 40922	Silver Bells/Border Serenade	1957	3.00	6.00	12.00
Step One 380	Sleigh Ride/The Christmas Song	198?	—	2.00	4.00
EMMONS, WAYNE (COUSIN BUBBA)					
45s					
Brody 1989	Christmas Request	198?	—	—	3.00
EMOTIONS					
45s					
Stax 1056	What Do The Lonely Do At Christmas?/	197?	—	3.00	6.00
	Santa Claus Wants Some Lovin'				
— B-side by Albert King; reissue					
Stax 3215	What Do the Lonely Do at Christmas/(Instrumental)	1978	—	2.50	5.00
Volt 4053	Black Christmas//(Instrumental)	1970	2.00	4.00	8.00
Volt 4104	What Do the Lonely Do at Christmas/(Instrumental)	1973	—	3.50	7.00
EMULATIONS, THE					
45s					
Emulate 7121	The Christmas Tree/The Story Of Life	19??	2.50	5.00	10.00
ENCHANTERS, THE					
45s					
Coral 61916	Mambo Santa Mambo/Bottle Up and Go	1957	5.00	10.00	20.00
On Various-Artists Collections					
Mambo Santa Mambo	Rockin' Little Christmas (MCA 25084)				
ENGEL, LEHMAN, AND HIS ORCHESTRA					
On Various-Artists Collections					
March of the Toys	Old Fashioned Christmas, An (Reader's Digest RDA 216-A)				
Toyland	Old Fashioned Christmas, An (Reader's Digest RDA 216-A)				
ENGINE KID					
45s					
C/Z 073	Little Drummer Boy/In The Bleak Midwinter	1994	—	2.00	4.00
C/Z 073 PS	Little Drummer Boy/In The Bleak Midwinter	1994	—	2.00	4.00
ENGLISH CHAMBER ORCHESTRA/AMBROSIAN SINGERS					
On Various-Artists Collections					
For Unto Us a Child Is Born	Very Merry Christmas, A, Volume VIII (Capitol Special Markets SL-6954)				
ENSEMBLE FOR EARLY MUSIC					
Frederick Renz, director					
Albums					
Nonesuch H-71315	Christemas in Anglia: Early English Music for Christmastide	1979	3.00	6.00	12.00

Label, Number		Title (A Side/B Side)	Year	VG	VG+	NM
EPIC CHOIR, THE						
Albums						
Epic LC 3144		Story of Christmas, The	1954	6.25	12.50	25.00
EPISODES, THE						
45s						
Four Seasons 1014		The Christmas Tree/Where Is My Love	1965	15.00	30.00	60.00
ERASURE						
45s						
Sire PRO-S-3409	DJ	She Won't Be Home (Lonely Christmas)/ God Rest Ye Merry Gentlemen	1988	3.00	6.00	12.00
— Released with promo insert (add 50%), no picture sleeve						
ERVIN, FRANKIE						
45s						
Hollywood 1045		Christmas Eve Baby/Christmas Everyday	1955	10.00	20.00	40.00
— With Johnny Moore's Blazers						
Punchline 9923		It's Christmas Time/Decorate My Christmas Tree	1985	—	—	3.00
7-Inch Extended Plays						
Hollywood 1044		Christmas Everyday/Christmas Letter// Christmas Eve Baby/Christmas Dreams	1955	25.00	50.00	100.00
— With Johnny Moore's Blazers						
ESQUIVEL						
On Various-Artists Collections						
Blue Christmas		Christmas Programming from RCA Victor (RCA Victor SP-33-66) October Christmas Sampler 59-40-41 (RCA Victor SPS-33-54)				
ESSEX, DAVID						
45s						
Lamplight LAMP 11		Back In England For Christmas/ Back In England For Christmas (Re-Mix)	198?	2.50	5.00	10.00
Lamplight LAMP 11	PS	Back In England For Christmas/ Back In England For Christmas (Re-Mix)	198?	2.50	5.00	10.00
— U.K. import						
ESTHER AND MEL						
45s						
Savoy 1146		My Christmas Blues/Love for Christmas	1954	10.00	20.00	40.00
ETHERIDGE, DICK						
45s						
MarGil 8346		I Can't Come Home For Christmas/Lonesome River	198?	—	2.00	4.00
EUGENE						
45s						
Viscione 101		Christmas Feelings/Christmas Feelings (Instrumental)	1985	—	—	3.00
EURYTHMICS						
On Various-Artists Collections						
Winter Wonderland		Very Special Christmas, A (A&M SP-3911)				
EVANS QUARTET, THE						
Albums						
Decca DL 4162	M	Merry Christmas — Barbershop Style	1961	3.00	6.00	12.00
Decca DL 74162	S	Merry Christmas — Barbershop Style	1961	3.75	7.50	15.00
EVANS, DOTTIE						
45s						
Waldorf 219		When Christmas Comes To Our House/Jingle Bells	195?	3.00	6.00	12.00
— B-side by Knuckles O'Toole						
EVANS, FRANK & SANTA'S HELPERS						
45s						
Simlar 001		Nite Before A Hip Christmas/Like Auld Lang Syne, Dad	19??	10.00	20.00	40.00

Label, Number	Title (A Side/B Side)	Year	VG	VG+	NM

EVANS, MONSIEUR JEFFREY, WITH ROSS JOHNSON AND THE AMF
On Various-Artists Collections

Mr. Blue X-mas (Cut Your Head on Christmas)	Happy Birthday, Baby Jesus (Sympathy For The Record Industry SFTRI 271)				

EVANS, PAUL
45s

Kapp 499	The Bell That Couldn't Jingle/Gilding the Lily	1962	3.00	6.00	12.00

EVANS, REVEREND CLAY
45s

Jewel 283	Go Tell It On The Mountain/Angels Sing	1981	—	2.00	4.00

EVANS, ROBERT
Albums

Custom CS 2	O Come All Ye Faithful	196?	3.00	6.00	12.00
Yuletide Series YS-212	O Come All Ye Faithful	197?	2.50	5.00	10.00
— *Reissue of Custom LP*					

On Various-Artists Collections

12 Days of Chrsitmas	20 Christmas Favorites (Yulesong SY-0220)				
Jingle Bells	20 Christmas Favorites (Yulesong SY-0220)				
O Come All Ye Faithful	20 Christmas Favorites (Yulesong SY-0220)				
O Holy Night	20 Christmas Favorites (Yulesong SY-0220)				
O Little Town of Bethlehem	20 Christmas Favorites (Yulesong SY-0220)				
O Tannenbaum	20 Christmas Favorites (Yulesong SY-0220)				
Rudolph the Red-Nosed Reindeer	20 Christmas Favorites (Yulesong SY-0220)				
Silent Night	20 Christmas Favorites (Yulesong SY-0220)				
Twas the Night Before Christmas	20 Christmas Favorites (Yulesong SY-0220)				
We Three Kings	20 Christmas Favorites (Yulesong SY-0220)				

EVERETTE, LEON
On Various-Artists Collections

Every Time I Hear Blue Christmas (I Get the Christmas Blues)	Country Christmas, A (RCA CPL1-4396)				

EVERGREENS, THE
45s

Birthstone 1022	They Came A Long Way To Christmas (Part 1)/ They Came A Long Way To Christmas (Part 2)	19??	—	2.00	4.00

EVERLY BROTHERS, THE
Albums

Harmony HS 11350		Christmas with the Everly Brothers and the Boys Town Choir	1969	5.00	10.00	20.00
Warner Bros. W 1483	M	Christmas with the Everly Brothers and the Boys Town Choir	1962	10.00	20.00	40.00
Warner Bros. WS 1483	S	Christmas with the Everly Brothers and the Boys Town Choir	1962	12.50	25.00	50.00

On Various-Artists Collections

Silent Night	Christmas Tradition, A (Warner Bros. 25630)				

EVIE
45s

Evie 761	Come On, Ring Those Bells/A Thousand Candles	19??	—	2.00	4.00
Word 761	Come On, Ring Those Bells/A Thousand Candles	19??	—	2.00	4.00

Albums

Word 8297	Christmas, A Happy Time	198?	3.00	6.00	12.00
Word 8770	Come On, Ring Those Bells	198?	2.50	5.00	10.00

EXCALIBURS, THE
45s

Trent Town 1017	Christmas Dreaming/Peace On Earth	19??	2.50	5.00	10.00

EXECUTIVE COMMITTEE, ST. LOUIS CHRISTMAS CAROLS ASSOCIATION
On Various-Artists Collections

Christmas Caroling Song	Christmas in Saint Louis ((no label) TS77-558/9)				

(Top left) Dave Edmunds recorded one of the better remakes of Chuck Berry's "Run Rudolph Run" in 1982. This is its scarce picture sleeve. (Top right) In the holiday season of 1980, Elliott, Walter and Bennett recorded 10 targeted Christmas records for fans of top NFL football teams of the time, including the Philadelphia Eagles. (Bottom left) One of the earliest 45s, from 1979, of the recent Christmas classic, "Grandma Got Run Over by a Reindeer." In 1984, the song was re-recorded for release on Epic. (Bottom right) An intriguing Epic Records LP from the mid-1950s, complete with gatefold and bound-in booklet.

Label, Number		Title (A Side/B Side)	Year	VG	VG+	NM

F

FABIAN
On Various-Artists Collections
Reminder Spot		For Christmas Seals...A Matter of Life and Breath (Decca Custom Style E)				

FABULOUS THUNDERBIRDS, THE
45s
Epic ES7 2594	DJ	Merry Christmas Darling/(Rockin') Winter Wonderland	1983	—	2.50	5.00

FACE OF CONCERN, THE
45s
Press 1011		Christmas (Baby Please Come Home)/Christmas (Instrumental)	1986	—	2.00	4.00
Press 1011	PS	Christmas (Baby Please Come Home)/Christmas (Instrumental)	1986	—	2.00	4.00

FACENDA, JOHN (NARRATOR)
Albums
RCA Victor LOP-1504	M	The Nativity	1958	7.50	15.00	30.00
— Gatefold with 12-page booklet						

FACES, THE
45s
Iguana 601		Christmas/New Year's Resolution	1965	12.50	25.00	50.00

FAGAN, SCOTT
45s
Bournefield 800		Sandy The Blue-Nosed Reindeer/	19??	—	2.00	4.00
		The Story Of Sandy The Blue-Nosed Reindeer				

FAHEY, JOHN
Albums
Takoma 7020		New Possibility	197?	3.00	6.00	12.00
Takoma 7045		Christmas with John Fahey, Vol. 2	198?	3.00	6.00	12.00
Varrick VR-002		John Fahey Christmas Guitar, Volume 1	1982	3.75	7.50	15.00
Varrick VR-012		Popular Songs of Christmas and New Year's	1983	3.75	7.50	15.00

FAITH, ADAM
45s
EMI 2691		What Do You Want/Lonely Pup (In A Christmas Shop)//	1977	2.00	4.00	8.00
		How About That/Someone Else's Baby				
— U.K. import						

FAITH, PERCY
45s
Columbia 1-899		Christmas In Killarney/Norah	1950	4.50	9.00	18.00
— Microgroove 33 1/3 rpm 7-inch single						
Columbia 6-899		Christmas in Killarney/Norah	1950	3.75	7.50	15.00
Columbia 39559		Sleigh Ride/Christmas in Killarney	1951	3.75	7.50	15.00
Columbia 43846		Christmas Is.../Silver Bells	1966	—	3.00	6.00
Columbia JZSP 111903/4	DJ	Away In A Manger/We Three Kings Of Orient Are	1965	3.00	6.00	12.00
— Promo only on green vinyl						
Columbia JZSP 119961/2	DJ	Christmas Is.../Happy Holiday	1966	2.50	5.00	10.00
— Yellow label						
Columbia JZSP 119961/2	DJ	Christmas Is.../Happy Holiday	1967	2.50	5.00	10.00
— White label						
Columbia JZSP 119961/2	PS	Christmas Is.../Happy Holiday	1967	3.75	7.50	15.00
— Sleeve announces this as the 1967 Christmas Seals Record						
Albums
Columbia CL 1381	M	Music of Christmas	1959	5.00	10.00	20.00
Columbia CL 2405	M	Music of Christmas, Volume 2	1965	3.75	7.50	15.00
Columbia CL 2577	M	Christmas Is...	1966	3.00	6.00	12.00
Columbia CS 8176	S	Music of Christmas	1959	3.75	7.50	15.00
Columbia CS 9205	S	Music of Christmas, Volume 2	1965	3.00	6.00	12.00
Columbia CS 9377	S	Christmas Is...	1966	3.00	6.00	12.00
Columbia PC 38302		Music of Christmas	1983	2.50	5.00	10.00
Columbia PC 39471		Christmas Melodies	1984	2.50	5.00	10.00

Label, Number	Title (A Side/B Side)	Year	VG	VG+	NM

On Various-Artists Collections

Angels We Have Heard on High	Sounds of Christmas (Columbia Special Products P 12474)				
	Very Merry Christmas, A, Volume 3 (Columbia Special Products CSS 997)				
Brazilian Sleighride	Blue Christmas (Welk Music Group WM-3002)				
Carol of the Bells	Zenith Presents Christmas, A Gift of Music Vol. 5 (Columbia Special Products C 10395)				
Christmas Is	Carols and Candlelight (Columbia Special Products P 12525)				
Deck the Halls	Joy of Christmas, The (Columbia Special Products P 12042)				
	Ronco Presents A Christmas Gift (Columbia Special Products P 12430)				
	Spirit of Christmas, The (Columbia Special Products CSP 249)				
God Rest Ye Merry, Gentlemen	Christmas Greetings (Columbia Special Products CSS 1499)				
	Happy Holidays, Album Nine (Columbia Special Products P 11793)				
Good King Wenceslas	Christmas with Johnny Mathis and Percy Faith (Columbia Special Products P 11805)				
	Great Songs of Christmas, The, Album Four (Columbia Special Products CSP 155M)				
	Home for Christmas (Columbia Musical Treasury P3S 5608)				
	Home for Christmas (Realm 2V 8101)				
	Merry Christmas from... (Reader's Digest RD4-83)				
Hallelujah Chorus	Seasons Greetings (A Christmas Festival of Stars) (Columbia CS 8189)				
	Spirit of Christmas, The, Volume III (Columbia Special Products CSS 1463)				
Happy Holiday	Collection of Christmas Favorites, A (Columbia Special Products P 14988)				
	Have a Happy Holiday (Columbia Special Products CSS 1432)				
	Merry Christmas from... (Reader's Digest RD4-83)				
	60 Christmas Classics (Sessions DVL2-0723)				
	WHIO Radio Christmas Feelings (Sound Approach/CSP P 16366)				
Hark! The Herald Angels Sing	Great Songs of Christmas, The, Album Two (Columbia Special Products XTV 86100/1)				
	Magic of Christmas, The (Columbia Musical Treasury P3S 5806)				
	Merry Christmas (Columbia Musical Treasury 3P 6306)				
Have Yourself a Merry Little Christmas	Great Songs of Christmas, The, Album Eight (Columbia Special Products CSS 888)				
I Wonder As I Wander	Happy Holidays, Volume II (Columbia Special Products CSM 348)				
	Magnavox Album of Christmas Music (Columbia Special Products CSQ 11093)				
It Came Upon the Midnight Clear	Christmas with Johnny Mathis and Percy Faith (Columbia Special Products P 11805)				
Joy to the World	Christmas Album, A (Columbia PC 39466)				
	Christmas Greetings, Vol. 4 (Columbia Special Products P 11987)				
	Christmas with Johnny Mathis and Percy Faith (Columbia Special Products P 11805)				
	Great Songs of Christmas, The, Album Two (Columbia Special Products XTV 86100/1)				
	Home for Christmas (Columbia Musical Treasury P3S 5608)				
	Home for Christmas (Realm 2V 8101)				
Little Drummer Boy, The	Best of the Great Songs of Christmas (Album 10) (Columbia Special Products CSS 1478)				
	Christmas Song, The, And Other Favorites (Columbia Special Products P 12446)				
	Great Songs of Christmas, The, Album Eight (Columbia Special Products CSS 888)				
	WHIO Radio Christmas Feelings (Sound Approach/CSP P 16366)				
Medley: I Saw Three Ships/ Here We Come a-Caroling	Great Songs of Christmas, The, Album Three (Columbia Special Products CSP 117)				
O Come All Ye Faithful/ Jesu Bambino	Great Songs of Christmas, The (Columbia Special Products XTV 69406/7)				
O Come, All Ye Faithful	Christmas with Johnny Mathis and Percy Faith (Columbia Special Products P 11805)				
O Holy Night	Christmas with Johnny Mathis and Percy Faith (Columbia Special Products P 11805)				
O Tannenbaum	Great Songs of Christmas, The, Album Three (Columbia Special Products CSP 117)				
	Silent Night... (Columbia Special Products P 14989)				
Silent Night, Holy Night	Seasons Greetings (A Christmas Festival of Stars) (Columbia CS 8189)				
We Need a Little Christmas	60 Christmas Classics (Sessions DVL2-0723)				
	Joyous Songs of Christmas, The (Columbia Special Products C 10400)				
	That Christmas Feeling (Columbia Special Products P 11853)				
	Wondrous Winter: Songs of Winter, Songs of Christmas (Columbia Special Products CSS 708/9)				

FALCONS, THE

45s

Silhouette 522	Can This Be Christmas/Sent Up	1957	75.00	150.00	300.00

FANS, THE

45s

Dot 16688	I Want a Beatle for Christmas/ How Far Should I Let My Heart Go Tonight	1964	3.75	7.50	15.00

FARAGO, JOHNNY

45s

Concorde 23	Blue Christmas/(B-side unknown)	19??	2.00	4.00	8.00

FARDEN FAMILY, THE

45s

49th State 21	Santa's Gone Hawaiian (Part 1)/Santa's Gone Hawaiian (Part 2)	195?	5.00	10.00	20.00

FARGO, DONNA

45s

ABC/Dot 17586	What Will the New Year Bring/A Woman's Prayer	1975	—	2.50	5.00

Label, Number	Title (A Side/B Side)	Year	VG	VG+	NM

On Various-Artists Collections

Santa Claus Is Coming to Town	Wonderful World of Christmas, The, Album Two (Capitol Special Markets SL-8025)				
What Will the New Year Bring	Christmas America, Album Two (Capitol Special Markets SL-6950)				

FARR, LITTLE JOEY
45s

Band Box 286	Rock & Roll Santa/Big White Cadillac	196?	3.00	6.00	12.00

FARRELL, EILEEN
On Various-Artists Collections

Adeste Fideles	Merry Christmas from... (Reader's Digest RD4-83)				
Away in a Manger	Home for Christmas (Columbia Musical Treasury P3S 5608)				
	Joy to the World (30 Classic Christmas Melodies) (Columbia Special Products P3 14654)				
Coventry Carol	Great Songs of Christmas, The, Album Two (Columbia Special Products XTV 86100/1)				
First Noel, The	It's Christmastime! (Columbia Special Products CSM 429)				
	Philco Album of Holiday Music, The (Columbia Special Products CSM 431)				
It Came Upon the Midnight Clear	Great Songs of Christmas, The, Album Two (Columbia Special Products XTV 86100/1)				
O Little Town of Bethlehem	Great Songs of Christmas, The (Columbia Special Products XTV 69406/7)				
Sleep, Holy Babe	Great Songs of Christmas, The, Album Two (Columbia Special Products XTV 86100/1)				

FARROW, LARRY
45s

Capitol 4808	Let This Be a Merry Christmas/You Know It's Christmas	1979	—	2.00	4.00

FAULTLINE
45s

Faultline F500		Too Cool For Yule/Plymouth Rock	1986	—	2.00	4.00
Faultline F500	PS	Too Cool For Yule/Plymouth Rock	1986	—	2.00	4.00

FAYE, LITTLE RITA
45s

MGM 11625	The Miracle of Christmas/I Fell Out of a Christmas Tree	1953	5.00	10.00	20.00
MGM 11867	I Want Santa Claus for Christmas/There Really Is a Santa Claus	1954	4.00	8.00	16.00
MGM 12104	The Santa Claus Parade/Sleigh Bells, Reindeer and Snow	1955	3.75	7.50	15.00

FEAR
45s

Slash 900	Fuck Christmas/*Uck Christmas	1979	10.00	20.00	40.00

— Not issued with picture sleeve; add 20% for plain white sleeve rubber-stamped with Christmas tree

FELICIANO, JOSE
45s

EMI Latin S7-18214	Feliz Navidad/Blue Christmas	1994	—	2.00	4.00

— B-side on Liberty by Glen Campbell; red vinyl

RCA 447-0936	Feliz Navidad/The Little Drummer Boy	197?	—	—	3.00

— Black label, dog near top

RCA Victor 74-0404	Feliz Navidad/The Little Drummer Boy	1970	2.50	5.00	10.00
RCA Victor 447-0936	Feliz Navidad/The Little Drummer Boy	197?	—	2.00	4.00

— Red label reissue

Albums

RCA Victor LSP-4421	Jose Feliciano	1970	3.75	7.50	15.00

On Various-Artists Collections

Feliz Navidad	Celebrate the Season with Tupperware (RCA Special Products DPL1-0803)				
	Christmas Through the Years (Reader's Digest RDA-143)				
	Christmas Treasury of Classics from Avon, A (RCA Special Products DPL1-0716)				
	Happy Holidays, Vol. 22 (RCA Special Products DPL1-0777)				
	Time-Life Treasury of Christmas, The (Time-Life STL-107)				
Jingle Bells	Stars of Christmas, The (RCA Special Products DPL1-0842)				

FELL, TERRY, AND THE FELLOWS
45s

"X" 0069	We Wanna See Santa Do the Mambo/ Let's Stay Together Till After Christmas	1954	3.75	7.50	15.00

FENDER, FREDDY
45s

ABC/Dot 17734	Christmas Time in the Valley/Please Come Home for Christmas	1977	—	2.50	5.00

Albums

ABC/Dot (# unknown)	Merry Christmas	1977	3.00	6.00	12.00
MCA 15025	Merry Christmas	198?	2.00	4.00	8.00

Label, Number		Title (A Side/B Side)	Year	VG	VG+	NM
On Various-Artists Collections						
Christmas Time in the Valley		Country Christmas (Time-Life STL-109)				
Medley: Noche De Pas (Silent Night)/ Feliz Navidad a Todos (We Wish You a Merry Christmas)		Wonderful World of Christmas, The, Album Two (Capitol Special Markets SL-8025)				
Santa! Don't Pass Me By		Country Christmas (Time-Life STL-109)				

FENDER, HARRY
On Various-Artists Collections

Introduction		Christmas in Saint Louis ((no label) TS77-558/9)				
Jingle Bells		Christmas in Saint Louis ((no label) TS77-558/9)				

FENNELL, FREDERICK
45s

Mercury 71238		A Christmas Festival/Sleigh Ride	1957	3.00	6.00	12.00

FENSTERMAKER, JOHN
On Various-Artists Collections

Noel Etranger		Christmas in San Francisco (Embarcadero Center EC-101)				

FERGUSON, MAYNARD
45s

Roulette 4317		Christmas for Moderns (Part 1)/Christmas for Moderns (Part 2)	1960	3.00	6.00	12.00
On Various-Artists Collections						
O Come, All Ye Faithful		Philco Album of Holiday Music, The (Columbia Special Products CSM 431)				

FERGUSON, TOMMY, TRIO
45s

Arcade 119		Christmas Is On Its Way/Just an Old-Fashioned Christmas	1953	5.00	10.00	20.00

FERRA, ANNETTE
45s

Mipat 101		Can I Stay Up Late/Santa's Coming	19??	—	2.50	5.00
Mipat 101	PS	Can I Stay Up Late/Santa's Coming	19??	—	2.50	5.00

FERRANTE AND TEICHER
Albums

United Artists UAL 3536	M	We Wish You a Merry Christmas	1966	3.75	7.50	15.00
United Artists UAS 6536	S	We Wish You a Merry Christmas	1966	3.00	6.00	12.00
— Same as above, but in stereo						
United Artists UAS 6536	S	We Wish You a Merry Christmas	1972	2.00	4.00	8.00
— Tan label (may also exist on late-1960s UA labels)						
On Various-Artists Collections						
I've Got My Love to Keep Me Warm		Christmas Songs, The, Volume II (Capitol SL-57065)				
Santa Claus Is Coming to Town		Best of Christmas Vol. 2 (Mistletoe MLP-1221)				
Silent Night Medley		Best of Christmas Vol. 2 (Mistletoe MLP-1221)				
Sleigh Ride		Christmas Songs, The (Capitol SLB-57074)				

FERRARA, DEBRA
45s

Deblyn 718		Christmas Time/(B-side unknown)	19??	2.50	5.00	10.00

FERRARI, LARRY
Albums

Sure SM 701	M	Merry Christmas Carols	196?	2.50	5.00	10.00
Sure SS 701	S	Merry Christmas Carols	196?	3.00	6.00	12.00

FERRER, JOSE
45s

RCA Victor 47-7823		Yes, Virginia, There Is a Santa Claus/Santa's Marching Song	1960	3.75	7.50	15.00
RCA Victor 47-7823	PS	Yes, Virginia, There Is A Santa Claus/Santa's Marching Song	1960	5.00	10.00	20.00
On Various-Artists Collections						
March of the Christmas Toys		Child's Christmas, A (Harmony HS 14563)				

FERRIER, GARRY
45s

Academy 112		Ringo-Deer/Just My Luck	1964	5.00	10.00	20.00

Label, Number		Title (A Side/B Side)	Year	VG	VG+	NM

FIEDLER, ARTHUR
Also see BOSTON POPS ORCHESTRA (FIEDLER).
On Various-Artists Collections

Carol of the Bells	Christmastime in Carol and Song (RCA PRS-289)
Little Drummer Boy, The	Christmastime in Carol and Song (RCA PRS-289)
	Old Fashioned Christmas, An (Reader's Digest RDA 216-A)
Medley: Here We Come a-Caroling/	Christmastime in Carol and Song (RCA PRS-289)
O Christmas Tree/I Saw Three Ships	
	Old Fashioned Christmas, An (Reader's Digest RDA 216-A)
Medley: Joy to the World/	Christmastime in Carol and Song (RCA PRS-289)
Jingle Bells/Away in a Manger/	
We Wish You a Merry Christmas	
Nutcracker Suite Excerpts:	Christmastime in Carol and Song (RCA PRS-289)
Overture/Russian Dance/Dance of the	
Sugar-Plum Fairy/Dance of the Reed Flutes	
Silent Night	Christmastime in Carol and Song (RCA PRS-289)

FIELD, SALLY
On Various-Artists Collections

Reminder Spot	For Christmas Seals...A Matter of Life and Breath (Decca Custom Style E)

FIELDS, LILY
45s

			Year	VG	VG+	NM
Spectrum 138		Disco Santa/(B-side unknown)	197?	—	2.00	4.00

FIELDS, SHEP
45s

			Year	VG	VG+	NM
MGM 10841		Silver Bells/Christmas Symphony	1950	3.75	7.50	15.00

FIFTH ESTATE, THE
45s

			Year	VG	VG+	NM
Jubilee 5683	DJ	Parade of the Wooden Soldiers (mono/stereo)	1969	2.50	5.00	10.00

— *Stock copies may not exist ("I Knew You Before I Met You" was listed as B-side)*

50 GUITARS, THE
Albums

			Year	VG	VG+	NM
Mistletoe MLP-1229		Christmas with the 50 Guitars	1977	2.50	5.00	10.00

54-40
On Various-Artists Collections

2000 Years of Love	Winter Warnerland (Warner Bros. PRO-A-3328)

FINLAY, KATHERINE
45s

			Year	VG	VG+	NM
Recards (# unknown)		December 25th - Poems of Christmas/(B-side unknown)	19??	2.00	4.00	8.00

FINLEY, MILO, COMBO
45s

			Year	VG	VG+	NM
Milo 12902		Under The Christmas Tree/Mr. Santa Claus	19??	—	—	3.00

FINNEY, ALBERT
On Various-Artists Collections

Christmas Carol, A	Scrooge (Columbia Masterworks S 30258)
I Hate People	Scrooge (Columbia Masterworks S 30258)
I Like Life (Reprise)	Scrooge (Columbia Masterworks S 30258)
I'll Begin Again	Scrooge (Columbia Masterworks S 30258)
Medley: Father Christmas/	Scrooge (Columbia Masterworks S 30258)
Thank You Very Much	
You...You	Scrooge (Columbia Masterworks S 30258)

FINOIA, AL
45s

			Year	VG	VG+	NM
Rainbow 1271		All I Want Is You For Christmas/ So I Won't Be Alone Christmas Night	1983	—	2.00	4.00

FIREFALL
45s

			Year	VG	VG+	NM
Atlantic PR 473	DJ	Christmas in Love (same on both sides)	1982	—	2.50	5.00
Atlantic PR 473	DJ	Christmas in Love/Always	1982	—	3.00	6.00
Eva-Tone 928213XS		Christmas in Love	198?	—	3.00	6.00

— *Flexidisc*

Label, Number	Title (A Side/B Side)	Year	VG	VG+	NM

FIREHOUSE FIVE PLUS TWO
45s
Good Time Jazz 45030	Jingle Bells/Tavern In The Town	195?	2.50	5.00	10.00

FIRESIDE SINGERS, THE
On Various-Artists Collections
Carol of the Bells	Old Fashioned Christmas, An (Reader's Digest RDA 216-A)
Children, Go Where I Send Thee	Old Fashioned Christmas, An (Reader's Digest RDA 216-A)
Christmas Is	Christmas Through the Years (Reader's Digest RDA-143)
First Noel, The	Old Fashioned Christmas, An (Reader's Digest RDA 216-A)
Go Tell It on the Mountain	Old Fashioned Christmas, An (Reader's Digest RDA 216-A)
Good King Wenceslas	Old Fashioned Christmas, An (Reader's Digest RDA 216-A)
Hark! The Herald Angels Sing	Old Fashioned Christmas, An (Reader's Digest RDA 216-A)
I'll Be Home for Christmas	Old Fashioned Christmas, An (Reader's Digest RDA 216-A)
Jingle Bells	Old Fashioned Christmas, An (Reader's Digest RDA 216-A)
Joy to the World	Old Fashioned Christmas, An (Reader's Digest RDA 216-A)
Let It Snow! Let It Snow! Let It Snow!	Old Fashioned Christmas, An (Reader's Digest RDA 216-A)
O Come, All Ye Faithful	Old Fashioned Christmas, An (Reader's Digest RDA 216-A)
O Holy Night	Old Fashioned Christmas, An (Reader's Digest RDA 216-A)
Silent Night	Old Fashioned Christmas, An (Reader's Digest RDA 216-A)
Silver Bells	Old Fashioned Christmas, An (Reader's Digest RDA 216-A)
Twelve Days of Christmas, The	Old Fashioned Christmas, An (Reader's Digest RDA 216-A)
We Three Kings of Orient Are	Old Fashioned Christmas, An (Reader's Digest RDA 216-A)
We Wish You a Merry Christmas	Old Fashioned Christmas, An (Reader's Digest RDA 216-A)
Winter Wonderland	Old Fashioned Christmas, An (Reader's Digest RDA 216-A)

FIRESTONE CHORUS
On Various-Artists Collections
And the Glory of the Lord	Firestone Presents Your Favorite Christmas Music, Volume 6 (Firestone MLP 7014)
Hallelujah Chorus	Firestone Presents Your Favorite Christmas Carols, Volume 2 (Firestone MLP 7006)
I Heard the Bells on Christmas Day	Firestone Presents Your Favorite Christmas Music, Volume 6 (Firestone MLP 7014)
Medley: A Virgin Unspotted/God Rest You Merry, Gentlemen/Deck the Hall	Favorite Christmas Carols from the Voice of Firestone (Firestone MLP 7005)
Medley: Here We Come a-Wassailing/ Good King Wenceslas/O Christmas Tree	Favorite Christmas Carols from the Voice of Firestone (Firestone MLP 7005)
Medley: Jingle Bells/Up on the House-Top/Jolly Old St. Nicholas/ We Wish You a Merry Christmas	Favorite Christmas Carols from the Voice of Firestone (Firestone MLP 7005)
Medley: Joy to the World/Away in a Manger/We Three Kings of Orient Are/Hark! The Herald Angels Sing	Favorite Christmas Carols from the Voice of Firestone (Firestone MLP 7005)

FISCHER, TERRY
45s
Bal Records 100	Christmas Is Coming/Yule Time	1985	—	—	3.00

FISCHER, WILD MAN (WITH DR. DEMENTO)
On Various-Artists Collections
I'm a Christmas Tree	Dr. Demento Presents the Greatest Novelty Records of All Time Volume VI: Christmas (Rhino RNLP 825)

FISCHOFF, GEORGE
45s
Lisa 17315	Starry Night/(B-side unknown)	198?	—	—	3.00

FISHER, EDDIE
45s
Label, Number	Title		Year	VG	VG+	NM
Dot 16792		White Christmas/Mary Christmas	1965	5.00	10.00	20.00
RCA Victor 47-4910		Silent Night/White Christmas	1952	3.75	7.50	15.00
RCA Victor 47-4911		Christmas Baby/You're All I Want for Christmas	1952	3.75	7.50	15.00
RCA Victor 47-4912		Here Comes Santa/Christmas Means	1952	3.75	7.50	15.00
RCA Victor 47-4913		Jingle Bells/O Come All Ye Faithful	1952	3.75	7.50	15.00
RCA Victor 47-5038		Christmas Day/That's What Christmas Means to Me	1952	3.75	7.50	15.00
RCA Victor 47-5871		Count Your Blessings (Instead of Sheep)/Fanny	1954	3.75	7.50	15.00
Albums						
Dot DLP 3658	M	Mary Christmas	1965	3.75	7.50	15.00
Dot DLP 25658	S	Mary Christmas	1965	5.00	10.00	20.00
RCA Victor LPM-3065	10	Christmas with Fisher	1952	12.50	25.00	50.00

On Various-Artists Collections
Do You Hear What I Hear	12 Days of Christmas, The (Pickwick SPC-1021)
Here Comes Santa Claus	Christmas Through the Years (Reader's Digest RDA-143)
	Family Christmas Collection, The (Time-Life STL-131)
	60 Christmas Classics (Sessions DVL2-0723)
Silent Night	For a Musical Merry Christmas (RCA Victor PR-149A)

Label, Number		Title (A Side/B Side)	Year	VG	VG+	NM

FITZGERALD, ELLA
45s

Label, Number		Title (A Side/B Side)	Year	VG	VG+	NM
Decca 27255		Santa Claus Got Stuck (In My Chimney)/ Molasses, Molasses (It's Icky Sticky Goo)	1950	5.00	10.00	20.00
Verve 10186		The Christmas Song/The Secret of Christmas	1959	3.75	7.50	15.00
Verve 10224		Jingle Bells/Good Morning Blues	1960	3.75	7.50	15.00

Albums

Label, Number		Title	Year	VG	VG+	NM
Capitol T 2805	M	Ella Fitzgerald's Christmas	1967	5.00	10.00	20.00
Capitol ST 2805	S	Ella Fitzgerald's Christmas	1967	3.00	6.00	12.00
Verve MGV 4042	M	Ella Wishes You a Swingin' Christmas	1960	12.50	25.00	50.00
Verve MGVS 4042	S	Ella Wishes You a Swingin' Christmas	1960	15.00	30.00	60.00
Verve V 4042	M	Ella Wishes You a Swingin' Christmas	1961	10.00	20.00	40.00
Verve V6 4042	S	Ella Wishes You a Swingin' Christmas	1961	12.50	25.00	50.00
Verve VE-1-2539		Ella Wishes You a Swingin' Christmas	197?	3.00	6.00	12.00
— 1970s reissue						

On Various-Artists Collections

Angels We Have Heard on High	Christmas Songs, The (Capitol SLB-57074)
Away in a Manger	Happy Holly Days (Capitol Creative Products SL-6761)
First Noel, The	All-Time Christmas Favorites (Capitol Special Markets SL-6931)
	Christmas — The Season of Music (Capitol Creative Products SL-6679)
	Christmas Songs, The, Volume II (Capitol SL-57065)
	Zenith Presents Christmas, A Gift of Music Vol. 3 (Capitol Creative Products SL-6659)
Hark! The Herald Angels Sing	Christmas America (Capitol Special Markets SL-6884)
	Christmas Songs, The (Capitol SLB-57074)
It Came Upon a Midnight Clear	Christmas, A Gift of Music (Capitol Special Markets SL-6687)
	Little Drummer Boy, The (Capitol/Pickwick SPC-3462)
	Zenith Presents Christmas, A Gift of Music Vol. 4 (Capitol Creative Products SL-6687)
O Come All Ye Faithful	Christmas to Remember, A, Vol. 3 (Capitol Creative Products SL-6681)
	Happy Holidays, Album Seven (Capitol Creative Products SL-6730)
O Little Town of Bethlehem	Christmas Carousel (Capitol SQBE-94406)
	Christmas Sounds of Music, The (Capitol Creative Products SL-6643)
	Happy Holidays, Vol. 5 (Capitol Creative Products SL-6627)
	Magic of Christmas, The (Capitol SWBB-93810)
Santa Claus Got Stuck in My Chimney	Stash Christmas Album, The (Stash 125)
Silent Night	Best of Christmas, The, Vol. II (Capitol SM-11834)
	Christmas Day (Pickwick SPC 1010)
	Happy Holidays, Vol. 22 (RCA Special Products DPL1-0777)
	Sound of Christmas, The, Vol. 3 (Capitol Creative Products SL-6680)
Sleigh Ride	Happy Holidays, Volume 16 (RCA Special Products DPL1-0501)
	Henry Mancini Selects Great Songs of Christmas (RCA Special Products DPL1-0148)
What Are You Doing New Year's Eve	Many Moods of Christmas, The (Columbia Special Products P 12013)
White Christmas	Many Moods of Christmas, The (Columbia Special Products P 12013)

FIVE BOROUGHS, THE
45s

Label, Number	Title (A Side/B Side)	Year	VG	VG+	NM
Classic Artists 135	Like A Kid At Christmas/Only At Christmas	1990	—	2.50	5.00

FIVE KEYS, THE
45s

Label, Number	Title (A Side/B Side)	Year	VG	VG+	NM
Aladdin 3113	It's Christmas Time/Old Mac Donald	1951	200.00	400.00	800.00
Classic Artists 115	I Want You For Christmas/Express Yourself Back Home	1989	—	2.50	5.00
— As "Rudy West and the Five Keys"					
Liberty 1394	It's Christmas Time/It's Christmas	1980	2.00	4.00	8.00
— B-side by Marvin and Johnny					

FLACK, ROBERTA
45s

Label, Number	Title (A Side/B Side)	Year	VG	VG+	NM
Atlantic 3441	The 25th of Last December/Move In with Me	1977	—	2.00	4.00

FLAMING LIPS, THE
Albums

Label, Number	Title	Year	VG	VG+	NM
Warner Bros. 45911	Clouds Taste Metallic	1995	2.50	5.00	10.00
— Contains one Christmas song: Christmas at the Zoo					

FLAMINGO, JOHNNY
45s

Label, Number	Title (A Side/B Side)	Year	VG	VG+	NM
Whirlybird 2001	Drive Slow/This Was Really Love	19??	2.50	5.00	10.00

FLANAGAN, RALPH
45s

Label, Number	Title (A Side/B Side)	Year	VG	VG+	NM
RCA Victor 54-0004	White Christmas/She Wore A Yellow Ribbon	1949	3.75	7.50	15.00

Label, Number		Title (A Side/B Side)	Year	VG	VG+	NM
On Various-Artists Collections						
Winter Wonderland		Remembering Christmas with the Big Bands (RCA Special Products DPM1-0506)				

FLAT DUO JETS
45s

Label, Number		Title (A Side/B Side)	Year	VG	VG+	NM
Norton 031		I'll Have A Merry Christmas Without You/Caravan	199?	—	2.50	5.00
— *Green vinyl*						
Norton 031	PS	I'll Have A Merry Christmas Without You/Caravan	199?	—	2.50	5.00

FLAX, FOGWELL, AND THE ANKLE BITERS FROM FREEHOLD JUNIOR SCHOOL
45s

Label, Number	Title (A Side/B Side)	Year	VG	VG+	NM
EMI 5255	One-Nine For Santa/Cheers To You At Christmas	1981	—	3.00	6.00
— *U.K. import*					

FLIRTATIONS, THE
45s

Label, Number	Title (A Side/B Side)	Year	VG	VG+	NM
Deram 85036	Christmas Time Is Here Again/Nothing But a Heartache	1968	2.00	4.00	8.00
— *B-side was a chart hit on Deram 85038 with a different flip*					

FLORES, ROSIE
On Various-Artists Collections

Label, Number	Title (A Side/B Side)	Year	VG	VG+	NM
Rockin' Around the Christmas Tree	Christmas Tradition, A, Volume II (Warner Bros. 25762)				

FLOYD, EDDIE
45s

Label, Number	Title (A Side/B Side)	Year	VG	VG+	NM
Malaco 1039	Special Christmas Day/Mother, My Dear Mother	1976	—	2.50	5.00
Safice 336	Can This Be Christmas/I'll Be Home For Christmas	1964	3.00	6.00	12.00

FODERA, BAMBI
45s

Label, Number	Title (A Side/B Side)	Year	VG	VG+	NM
Colors 1001	The Christmas Tree That Cried/Christmas Moments	198?	—	—	3.00

FOGELBERG, DAN
45s

Label, Number		Title (A Side/B Side)	Year	VG	VG+	NM
Full Moon/Epic 03087		Same Old Lang Syne/Hard to Say	1982	—	—	3.00
— *Reissue*						
Full Moon/Epic 50961		Same Old Lang Syne/Hearts and Crafts	1980	—	2.00	4.00
Full Moon/Epic 50961	PS	Same Old Lang Syne/Hearts and Crafts	1980	—	3.00	6.00
Albums						
Full Moon/Epic KE2 37393	(2)	The Innocent Age	1981	3.75	7.50	15.00
— *Contains one Christmas song:* Same Old Lang Syne						
Full Moon/Epic QE 28208		Greatest Hits	1982	2.50	5.00	10.00
— *Contains one Christmas song* Same Old Lang Syne						

FOGHAT
45s

Label, Number		Title (A Side/B Side)	Year	VG	VG+	NM
Bearsville PRO-S-780	DJ	Run, Run, Rudolph (same on both sides)	1978	2.50	5.00	10.00
Bearsville PRO-S-1002	DJ	All I Want For Christmas Is You (same on both sides)	1981	2.50	5.00	10.00
Foghat 1069		Goin' Home For Christmas/Santa Claus Is Back In Town	1986	—	3.00	6.00
Foghat 1069	PS	Goin' Home For Christmas/Santa Claus Is Back In Town	1986	—	3.00	6.00
On Various-Artists Collections						
All I Want for Christmas Is You		Christmas Rock Album, The (Priority SL 9465)				

FOLDY, PETE
45s

Label, Number	Title (A Side/B Side)	Year	VG	VG+	NM
Nightflite 108	My Christmas Wish For You (vocal)/(Instrumental)	1981	—	2.50	5.00

FOLEY, RED
45s

Label, Number	Title (A Side/B Side)	Year	VG	VG+	NM
Decca 28147	I'm Bound For Christmas/I'd Rather Have Jesus	1951	3.75	7.50	15.00
Decca 28940	Put Christ Back in Christmas/The Gentle Carpenter of Bethlehem	1953	3.75	7.50	15.00
Decca 32063	Is There Really a Santa Claus?/From Our House to Your House	1966	2.00	4.00	8.00
Decca 46185	Our Christmas Waltz/Here Comes Santa Claus	1949	3.75	7.50	15.00
— *With Judy Martin; 78 released in 1949*					
Decca 46267	Frosty the Snowman/Rudolph the Red-Nosed Reindeer	1950	5.00	10.00	20.00
Decca 88060	Frosty the Snowman/Rudolph the Red-Nosed Reindeer	1950	5.00	10.00	20.00
— *Yellow label "Chidren's Series" issue*					
7-Inch Extended Plays					
Decca ED 2090	(contents unknown)	195?	3.75	7.50	15.00
Decca ED 2090 PS	Sing a Song of Christmas	195?	3.75	7.50	15.00

Label, Number		Title (A Side/B Side)	Year	VG	VG+	NM
On Various-Artists Collections						
Frosty the Snowman		Time-Life Treasury of Christmas, The, Volume Two (Time-Life STL-108)				

FOLEY, WEBB
45s

M Records 666		Littletown Christmas/Extra Christmas	19??	—	2.00	4.00

FONTANE SISTERS, THE
Also see PERRY COMO.
45s

Dot 15434		Nuttin' for Christmas/Silver Bells	1955	3.00	6.00	12.00
RCA Victor 47-3940		Sleigh Bells/Jing-a-Ling, Jing-a-Ling	1950	3.00	6.00	12.00
— With Dick Contino						
RCA Victor 47-4322		A Howdy Doody Christmas/The Popcorn Song	1951	5.00	10.00	20.00
— With Howdy Doody						
RCA Victor 47-4449		Snowflakes/River in Moonlight	1952	3.00	6.00	12.00
— With Merv Griffin and Freddie Martin						
On Various-Artists Collections						
Silver Bells		Remembering Christmas with the Big Bands (RCA Special Products DPM1-0506)				

FONTENOT, HARRY
45s

Swallow 10228		Jingle Bells/Silent Night	19??	—	2.00	4.00

FORD, CAROL
45s

King 6188		Christmas Letters/Please Come Home For Christmas	1968	3.00	6.00	12.00

FORD, GLENN
On Various-Artists Collections

Reminder Spot		For Christmas Seals...A Matter of Life and Breath (Decca Custom Style E)				

FORD, JOY, AND JOHN KRONDES
45s

Country Int'l. 176		Christmas Card/(B-side unknown)	1982	—	2.00	4.00

FORD, MARILYN
45s

Tower LO8W 2629/30		Please, Dear God, Help Santa Claus/I'm A Little Elf	1960	3.00	6.00	12.00

FORD, PENNYE, AND OLIVER SCOTT
On Various-Artists Collections

Silent Night		Total Experience Christmas, A (Total Experience TEL8-5707)				

FORD, RITA
Albums

Columbia CL 1698	M	A Music Box Christmas	1961	5.00	10.00	20.00
Columbia CS 8498	R	A Music Box Christmas	1961	3.75	7.50	15.00
Epic LN 24022	M	Music Box Wonderland Christmas with Rita Ford's Music Boxes	1962	5.00	10.00	20.00
Epic BN 26022	R	Music Box Wonderland Christmas with Rita Ford's Music Boxes	1962	3.75	7.50	15.00
Harmony KH 31577		Christmas with Rita Ford's Music Boxes	1972	3.00	6.00	12.00
— Reissue of Epic BN 26022						
On Various-Artists Collections						
Holy City, The		Home for Christmas (Columbia Musical Treasury P3S 5608)				
		Home for Christmas (Realm 2V 8101)				
O Tannenbaum		Zenith Presents Christmas, A Gift of Music Vol. 5 (Columbia Special Products C 10395)				
Silent Night, Holy Night		Zenith Presents Christmas, A Gift of Music Vol. 5 (Columbia Special Products C 10395)				

FORD, TENNESSEE ERNIE
45s

Canada Dry 72-6596	DJ	The Real Story Of Christmas from St. Luke, Chapter 2	1972	—	2.50	5.00
— Special promo for his 1972 Christmas TV special						
Canada Dry 72-6596	PS	The Real Story Of Christmas from St. Luke, Chapter 2	1972	—	2.50	5.00
Capitol F1830		A Rootin' Tootin' Santa Claus/Christmas Dinner	1951	3.75	7.50	15.00
Capitol 2334		The Little Boy King/Bring a Torch, Jeanette, Isabella	1968	—	3.00	6.00
Capitol 4446		Little Klinker/Jingle-O-The-Brownie	1960	3.00	6.00	12.00
Capitol 4446	PS	Little Klinker/Jingle-O-The-Brownie	1960	5.00	10.00	20.00
Capitol 5534		Sing We Now of Christmas/The Little Drummer Boy	1965	2.00	4.00	8.00

Label, Number		Title (A Side/B Side)	Year	VG	VG+	NM
Albums						
Capitol T 1071	M	The Star Carol	1958	7.50	15.00	30.00
— Originals have black labels with colorband and "Capitol" logo on left						
Capitol T 1071	M	The Star Carol	1962	5.00	10.00	20.00
— Later pressings have black label with colorband, "Capitol" logo on top						
Capitol ST 1071	S	The Star Carol	1958	10.00	20.00	40.00
— Originals have black labels with colorband and "Capitol" logo on left						
Capitol ST 1071	S	The Star Carol	1962	7.50	15.00	30.00
— Black label with colorband, "Capitol" logo on top. This was also likely reissued on later Capitol labels into the 1970s with values no more than half the above.						
Capitol T 1994	M	The Story of Christmas	1963	5.00	10.00	20.00
— With the Roger Wagner Chorale						
Capitol ST 1994	S	The Story of Christmas	1963	7.50	15.00	30.00
Capitol T 2394	M	Sing We Now of Christmas	1965	3.00	6.00	12.00
Capitol ST 2394	S	Sing We Now of Christmas	1965	3.75	7.50	15.00
Capitol ST 2968		O Come All Ye Faithful	1968	3.00	6.00	12.00
Capitol SN-16289		The Star Carol	1982	2.00	4.00	8.00
— Budget-line reissue						

On Various-Artists Collections

Born a Child in Bethlehem	On This Christmas Night (Songbird MCA-3184)
First Noel, The	Christmas to Remember, A (Capitol Creative Products SL-6573)
	Sound of Christmas, The (Capitol Creative Products SL-6515)
God Rest Ye Merry Gentlemen	Christmas Day (Pickwick SPC 1010)
	Christmas Songs, The (Capitol SLB-57074)
It Came Upon a Midnight Clear	Very Merry Christmas, A, Volume VIII (Capitol Special Markets SL-6954)
Joy to the World	Christmas to Remember, A, Vol. 3 (Capitol Creative Products SL-6681)
My Favorite Things	All-Time Christmas Favorites (Capitol Special Markets SL-6931)
	Christmas America (Capitol Special Markets SL-6884)
	Holiday Magic (Capitol Creative Products SL-6728)
	Magic of Christmas, The (Capitol SWBB-93810)
	Zenith Presents Christmas, A Gift of Music Vol. 3 (Capitol Creative Products SL-6659)
O Come All Ye Faithful	Happy Holidays, Vol. 5 (Capitol Creative Products SL-6627)
O Harken Ye	Christmas Carousel (Capitol SQBE-94406)
Sing We Now of Christmas	Christmas — The Season of Music (Capitol Creative Products SL-6679)
	Happy Holidays, Album Seven (Capitol Creative Products SL-6730)
Star Carol, The	Best of Christmas, The, Vol. II (Capitol SM-11834)
	Christmas Songs, The, Volume II (Capitol SL-57065)
	Popular Christmas Classics (Capitol Special Markets SL-8100)
Twelve Days of Christmas, The	Christmas Songs, The (Capitol SLB-57074)
	I'll Be Home for Christmas (Pickwick SPC-1009)
Virgin's Slumber Song, The	Sound of Christmas, The, Vol. 2 (Capitol Creative Products SL-6534)

FORESTER SISTERS, THE
45s

Warner Bros 28207		The First Noel/This Old White Doorway	1987	—	—	3.00
Albums						
Warner Bros. 25623		A Christmas Card	1987	2.50	5.00	10.00

On Various-Artists Collections

Carpenter, A Mother and a King, A	Christmas Tradition, A (Warner Bros. 25630)
I'll Be Home for Christmas	Christmas Tradition, A, Volume II (Warner Bros. 25762)
Rockin' Around the Christmas Tree	Stars of Christmas, The (RCA Special Products DPL1-0842)

FORTUNE
45s

Songuild 926		Christmas Without You/For One Moment In Time You Were Mine	198?	—	2.00	4.00

FOSTER, DAVID
45s

Atlantic 87788		Grown-Up Christmas List/Freedom	1990	—	2.50	5.00
— A-side lead vocal: Natalie Cole						

FOSTER, LARRY
45s

20th Century Fox 325		My Christmas Message to the World/My Son, the Folk Monster	1962	3.75	7.50	15.00

FOSTER, MICHAEL
45s

Amer Romance 29		Mistletoe Time/When You Give It Away	19??	—	—	3.00
— B-side by Jimbeau Hinson; red vinyl						
Amer Romance 29	PS	Mistletoe Time/When You Give It Away	19??	—	—	3.00
— B-side by Jimbeau Hinson						

Label, Number		Title (A Side/B Side)	Year	VG	VG+	NM
FOTINE, LARRY						
45s						
Decca 27331		Christmas In Killarney/Jumpin' Jiminey	1950	3.75	7.50	15.00
FOUNTAIN, PETE						
45s						
Coral 65605		The Christmas Song (Merry Christmas To You)/Santa Claus Medley	196?	2.00	4.00	8.00
On Various-Artists Collections						
I'll Be Home for Christmas		Home for the Holidays (MCA MSM-35007)				
Jingle Bell Rock		Many Moods of Christmas, The (Columbia Special Products P 12013)				
FOUR ACES						
45s						
Decca 29702		The Christmas Song (Merry Christmas to You)/Jingle Bells	1955	3.00	6.00	12.00
Decca 29712		O Holy Night/Silent Night	1955	3.00	6.00	12.00
Decca 30775		Ol' Fatso/Christmas Tree	1958	3.00	6.00	12.00
Victoria 102		There's a Christmas Tree in Heaven/There's a Small Hotel	1951	7.50	15.00	30.00
7-Inch Extended Plays						
Decca ED 2309		White Christmas/The Christmas Song//Silent Night/	1956	3.00	6.00	12.00
		O Little Town of Bethlehem/Joy to the World				
Decca ED 2309	PS	A Merry Christmas with the Four Aces, Part 1	1956	3.00	6.00	12.00
Decca ED 2310		(contents unknown)	1956	3.00	6.00	12.00
Decca ED 2310	PS	A Merry Christmas with the Four Aces, Part 2	1956	3.00	6.00	12.00
Decca ED 2311		(contents unknown)	1956	3.00	6.00	12.00
Decca ED 2311	PS	A Merry Christmas with the Four Aces, Part 3	1956	3.00	6.00	12.00
Albums						
Decca DL 8191	M	Merry Christmas	1956	12.50	25.00	50.00
On Various-Artists Collections						
Hark! The Herald Angels Sing		Decca 38170 (title unknown) (Decca DL 38170)				
Jingle Bells		Decca 38170 (title unknown) (Decca DL 38170)				
		Thank You for Opening Your Christmas Club with Us (Decca 34211)				
Rudolph, the Red-Nosed Reindeer		Old-Fashioned Christmas, An (Longines Symphonette LS 214)				
Silent Night		Decca 38170 (title unknown) (Decca DL 38170)				
FOUR IMPERIALS, THE						
45s						
Twirl 2005		Santa's Got a Coupe de Ville/Seven Lonely Days	1960	6.25	12.50	25.00
4 JACKS AND A JILL						
45s						
Heart Song 103		It's Christmas Time Again/(B-side unknown)	19??	2.50	5.00	10.00
FOUR KNIGHTS, THE						
7-Inch Extended Plays						
Monogram 2		Speaking Of Angels/What Are You Doing New Year's Eve// + 2	19??	2.50	5.00	10.00
FOUR LADS, THE						
45s						
Columbia 40788		Mary's Little Boy Child/The Stingiest Man in Town	1956	3.00	6.00	12.00
On Various-Artists Collections						
Christmas Carol, A		Stingiest Man in Town, The (Columbia CL 950)				
Christmas Carol, A/		Stingiest Man in Town, The (Columbia CL 950)				
The Christmas Spirit						
Stingiest Man in Town, The		Stingiest Man in Town, The (Columbia CL 950)				
FOUR SEASONS, THE						
45s						
Four Seasons 0019		I Saw Mommy Kissing Santa Claus/	198?	—	2.00	4.00
		Santa Claus Is Coming To Town				
Vee Jay 478		Santa Claus Is Coming to Town/Christmas Tears	1962	6.25	12.50	25.00
Vee Jay 626		I Saw Mommy Kissing Santa Claus/Christmas Tears	1964	5.00	10.00	20.00
Vee Jay 626	PS	I Saw Mommy Kissing Santa Claus/Christmas Tears	1964	12.50	25.00	50.00
Albums						
Philips PHM 200-223	M	The Four Seasons' Christmas Album	1966	6.25	12.50	25.00
— Reissue of Vee Jay album with new cover						
Philips PHS 600-223	S	The Four Seasons' Christmas Album	1966	7.50	15.00	30.00
Rhino RNLP 70234		The Four Seasons' Christmas Album	1987	3.00	6.00	12.00
— Reissue of Philips album						
Vee Jay LP 1055	M	The Four Seasons Greetings	1962	7.50	15.00	30.00
Vee Jay SR 1055	S	The Four Seasons Greetings	1962	10.00	20.00	40.00

Label, Number		Title (A Side/B Side)	Year	VG	VG+	NM
FOUR SEVILLES, THE						
45s						
Starlight 30		What Are You Doing New Year's Eve/Heart And Soul	19??	5.00	10.00	20.00
FOX, HENRY						
45s						
Maestro 2103		Santa Claus Speaks/Christmas Bells	19??	—	2.50	5.00
FOX, TONY						
45s						
El Apache 803		I Saw Santa's Reindeer/Rollin' All Through The Night	19??	—	3.00	6.00
FOX, VIRGIL						
7-Inch Extended Plays						
RCA Victor ERA-1-1845		Hark the Herald Angels Sing/We Three Kings/It Came Upon a	1958	3.00	6.00	12.00
		Midnight Clear//Joy to the World/Gesu Bambino/God Rest Ye Merry Gentlemen				
RCA Victor ERA-1-1845	PS	Christmas Carols on the Organ	1958	3.00	6.00	12.00
On Various-Artists Collections						
Angels We Have Heard on High		Christmas in the Air (RCA Special Products DPL1-0133)				
		Old Fashioned Christmas, An (Reader's Digest RDA 216-A)				
Joy to the World		Old Fashioned Christmas, An (Reader's Digest RDA 216-A)				
O Come, O Come, Emmanuel		Time-Life Treasury of Christmas, The, Volume Two (Time-Life STL-108)				
FOXWORTHY, JEFF						
45s						
Warner Bros. 17526		Redneck 12 Days of Christmas/'Twas the Night After Christmas	1996	—	2.00	4.00
— Green vinyl						
FOXX, REDD						
45s						
Dooto 464		Christmas Hard Times/Jaw Resting	1961	3.00	6.00	12.00
7-Inch Extended Plays						
Authentic 218		Christmas Time/Dragnet//The Preachers/The Two Oars	195?	3.75	7.50	15.00
FRANCHI, SERGIO						
Albums						
4 Corners of the World	M	Buon Natale	196?	3.00	6.00	12.00
FCL 4223						
4 Corners of the World	S	Buon Natale	196?	3.75	7.50	15.00
FCS 4223						
RCA Victor LPM-3437	M	The Heart of Christmas (Cuor' di Natale)	1965	3.00	6.00	12.00
RCA Victor LSP-3437	S	The Heart of Christmas (Cuor' di Natale)	1965	3.75	7.50	15.00
On Various-Artists Collections						
Ave Maria (Bach-Gounod)		Happy Holidays, Vol. 20 (RCA Special Products DPL1-0713)				
Away in a Manger		Christmas in the Air (RCA Special Products DPL1-0133)				
Buon Natale (Christmastime		Joyous Noel (Reader's Digest RDA-57A)				
in Rome)						
First Noel, The		Christmas with Colonel Sanders (RCA Victor PRS-291)				
		Time-Life Treasury of Christmas, The (Time-Life STL-107)				
Medley: Tu Scendi Dalle Stelle/		Old Fashioned Christmas, An (Reader's Digest RDA 216-A)				
O Bambino						
O Little Town of Bethlehem		Family Christmas Collection, The (Time-Life STL-131)				
		Happy Holidays, Vol. III (RCA Victor PRS-255)				
		Old Fashioned Christmas, An (Reader's Digest RDA 216-A)				
Panis Angelicus		Old Fashioned Christmas, An (Reader's Digest RDA 216-A)				
Silent Night		Brightest Stars of Christmas, The (RCA Special Products DPL1-0086)				
		Time-Life Treasury of Christmas, The, Volume Two (Time-Life STL-108)				
FRANCIS, CONNIE						
45s						
MGM 13051		When the Boy in Your Arms (Is the Boy in Your Heart)/	1961	3.75	7.50	15.00
		Baby's First Christmas				
MGM 13051	PS	When the Boy in Your Arms (Is the Boy in Your Heart)/	1961	5.00	10.00	20.00
		Baby's First Christmas				
Albums						
MGM E-3792	M	Christmas in My Heart	1959	7.50	15.00	30.00
MGM SE-3792	S	Christmas in My Heart	1959	10.00	20.00	40.00
MGM E-4399	M	Connie's Christmas	1966	6.25	12.50	25.00
MGM SE-4399	S	Connie's Christmas	1966	7.50	15.00	30.00
On Various-Artists Collections						
First Noel, The		Great Songs of Christmas, Album Nine (Columbia Special Products CSS 1033)				
O Little Town of Bethlehem		Great Songs of Christmas, Album Nine (Columbia Special Products CSS 1033)				

Label, Number		Title (A Side/B Side)	Year	VG	VG+	NM
FRANCIS, DAYTON						
45s						
Pepper 2		Xmas in Your Heart/Tiny Ballerina	196?	2.50	5.00	10.00
FRANCIS, JOEY						
45s						
Clinton 24		Christmas Nite/Seeing You There	19??	—	2.50	5.00
FRANCIS, MISS						
45s						
RCA Victor WBY 28		'Twas The Night Before Christmas Part 1/	195?	3.00	6.00	12.00
		'Twas The Night Before Christmas Part 2				
— "Little Nipper" children's series						
FRANCIS, STAN						
On Various-Artists Collections						
Jingle, Jingle, Jingle		Rudolph the Red-Nosed Reindeer (Decca DL 4815)				
FRANK AND JACK						
45s						
Bergen 100		'Twas The Night Before Christmas/Jingle Bells	1957	5.00	10.00	20.00
Josie 827		Twas the Night Before Christmas (Breaking Thru the Sound Barrier)/	1957	3.75	7.50	15.00
		Jingle Bells (From the Sound Track)				
FRANKLIN, ARETHA						
45s						
Columbia 42933		Johnny/Kissin' by the Mistletoe	1963	2.50	5.00	10.00
— A-side is not a Christmas song						
Columbia 43177		Winter Wonderland/	1964	2.50	5.00	10.00
		The Christmas Song (Chestnuts Roasting on an Open Fire)				
On Various-Artists Collections						
Kissin' by the Mistletoe		Joy of Christmas, The (Columbia Special Products P 12042)				
Winter Wonderland		Jingle Bell Rock (Time-Life SRNR-XM)				
		Very Merry Christmas, A, Volume IV (Columbia Special Products CSS 1464)				
FRANKLIN, JIM						
45s						
Jed 0017		Is It Christmas Time In Vietnam/You Took The Wind Out Of My Sails	196?	2.00	4.00	8.00
FRANKO, TED						
45s						
Nawpost NTF 2		Santa Baby (If You Kiss My Wife You'll Lose Your Life)/	19??	—	2.50	5.00
		Santa Beer Reindeer				
Nawpost NTF 2	PS	Santa Baby (If You Kiss My Wife You'll Lose Your Life)/	19??	—	2.50	5.00
		Santa Beer Reindeer				
FREBERG, STAN						
45s						
Capitol F2671		Christmas Dragnet Part 1/Christmas Dragnet Part 2	1953	7.50	15.00	30.00
Capitol F2986		Yulenet (Part 1)/Yulenet (Part 2)	1954	6.25	12.50	25.00
— Same recording as "Christmas Dragnet" (Capitol 2671)						
Capitol F3280		Nuttin' for Christmas/The Night Before Christmas	1955	6.25	12.50	25.00
Capitol 3503		Green Chritma (Part 1)/Green Chritma (Part 2)	1972	2.50	5.00	10.00
Capitol F4097		Green Chritma/The Meaning of Christmas	1958	5.00	10.00	20.00
Capitol F4097	PS	Green Chritma/The Meaning of Christmas	1958	7.50	15.00	30.00
Capitol S7-57891		Nuttin' for Christmas/I Yust Go Nuts at Christmas	1992	—	2.00	4.00
— B-side by Yogi Yorgesson						
On Various-Artists Collections						
Green Chritma		Dr. Demento Presents the Greatest Novelty Records of All Time Volume VI: Christmas (Rhino RNLP 825)				
Nuttin' for Christmas		Christmas Through the Years (Reader's Digest RDA-143)				
		Dr. Demento Presents the Greatest Novelty Records of All Time Volume VI: Christmas (Rhino RNLP 825)				
FREDRICK, MARK						
45s						
GP 586		Christmas Tree Angel (Vocal)/(Instrumental)	19??	2.50	5.00	10.00

Label, Number		Title (A Side/B Side)	Year	VG	VG+	NM
FREE DESIGN, THE						
45s						
Project 3 1347	DJ	Close Your Mouth (It's Christmas)/Christmas Is The Day	1968	2.50	5.00	10.00
— Stock copy may not exist						
FREE SPEECH CAROLS						
45s						
FSM 1		Oski Dolls/We Three Deans/UC Administration/Hail to IBM/ It Belongs to the University//Silent Night/Call Out the Deans/ Masters of Sproul Hall/God Rest Ye Free Speech/ Come All Ye Mindless/Joy to UC	1964	5.00	10.00	20.00
FSM 1	PS	Oski Dolls/We Three Deans/UC Administration/Hail to IBM/ It Belongs to the University//Silent Night/Call Out the Deans/Masters of Sproul Hall/God Rest Ye Free Speech/ Come All Ye Mindless/Joy to UC	1964	10.00	20.00	40.00
FREEMAN, PAUL						
45s						
Columbia 06576		Carol of the Birds/Adeste Fideles	1985	—	—	3.00
FREITAS, PAUL & RICHARD						
45s						
Pab 915		Christmas Fever/What Gift (Shall We Give Him)	198?	—	—	3.00
FRENCH LEMON SANTAS						
On Various-Artists Collections						
Merry Xmas Everybody!		Stuff This in Your Stocking! Elves in Action (Veebltronics/Skyclad 68)				
FREY, CINDY						
45s						
York Lynn 447		Grandmother's Lullaby/The Christmas Tree	19??	—	2.50	5.00
— B-side by Little Piney						
FRICKIE, JANIE						
On Various-Artists Collections						
What Child Is This		Nashville Christmas Album, The (Epic PE 40418)				
FRIEDEMANN						
On Various-Artists Collections						
Man from Ceasaria, The		Narada: The Christmas Collection (Narada N-63902)				
FROGS, THE (1970S GROUP)						
45s						
Mums 6025		Alfie, the Christmas Tree/Tweedlee Dee	1973	—	2.50	5.00
FROGS, THE (1990S GROUP)						
45s						
Matador ELO 069-7		Here Comes Santa's Pussy//Have a Merry X-Mas/Snow Kisses	1995	—	—	2.50
— Green vinyl, small hole						
Matador ELO 069-7	PS	Here Comes Santa's Pussy//Have a Merry X-Mas/Snow Kisses	1995	—	—	2.50
FRONTIERSMEN, THE						
45s						
Crystal 270		Toyland Polka/It's Christmas Time Again	19??	—	3.00	6.00
— B-side by Lee Nash						
Sage and Sand 380		Green Christmas/Mrs. Santa Claus	196?	2.50	5.00	10.00
FROST, DAVID, AND BILLY TAYLOR						
45s						
Bell 950		The House of Christmas/Away in a Manger	1970	—	3.00	6.00
On Various-Artists Collections						
House of Christmas, The		Merry Christmas from David Frost and Billy Taylor (Bell 6053)				
FRY, DICK						
45s						
Rodeo 264		The Night Before Christmas/Jingle Bells	19??	2.00	4.00	8.00

Label, Number	Title (A Side/B Side)	Year	VG	VG+	NM

FUDGE LIPS
45s

Osiris 005	Please Come Home For Christmas/Satan's Triangle	19??	—	2.00	4.00

FULSON, LOWELL
45s

Hollywood 1022	The Original Lonesome Christmas Part 1/ The Original Lonesome Christmas Part 2	1955	5.00	10.00	20.00
Hollywood 567-242	The Original Lonesome Christmas Part 1/ The Original Lonesome Christmas Part 2	196?	2.50	5.00	10.00
Jewel 813	Lonesome Christmas (Part 1)/Lonesome Christmas (Part 2)	1970	—	3.00	6.00
Kent 477	I Wanna Spend Christmas with You Part 1/ I Wanna Spend Christmas with You Part 2	1967	3.00	6.00	12.00

On Various-Artists Collections

Lonesome Christmas Part 1	Merry Christmas Baby (Christmas Music for Young Lovers) (Hollywood HLP 501) Merry Christmas Baby (Gusto/Hollywood K-5018-X)				
Lonesome Christmas Part 2	Merry Christmas Baby (Christmas Music for Young Lovers) (Hollywood HLP 501) Merry Christmas Baby (Gusto/Hollywood K-5018-X)				

FUMBLERS, THE
45s

Pongo-Britt 45	Jangle Bells/Santa Is A Dirty Old Man	198?	—	3.00	6.00
— B-side by the Wardettes					

FURTHER AND THE SUMMER HITS
45s

Christmas 111		Christmas Has Been Cancelled Due to Lack of Interest/ Have Yourself a Merry Little Christmas	198?	—	2.50	5.00
— B-side by O and Judy						
Christmas 111	PS	Christmas Has Been Cancelled Due to Lack of Interest/ Have Yourself a Merry Little Christmas	198?	—	2.50	5.00
— B-side by O and Judy						

FUSEK, GEORGE
45s

Winterland 9383	Icy, The Icicle Song/Christmas Fairy Tale About Icy the Icicle	198?	—	—	3.00

G

GABEL, NORMAN
45s

Stem 22-2	It's Christmas Time/I've Seen	19??	—	2.00	4.00

GABRIEL
45s

ABC Dunhill 4172	Christmas Is Love/Chocolate on a Sunday	1968	2.50	5.00	10.00
Dunhill 4058	Christmas Is Love/Chocolate on a Sunday	1966	3.00	6.00	12.00

GABRIEL AND GRANDPA
45s

Billijan 1225	Christmas Is/What's The Secret?	19??	—	2.00	4.00

GAITHER, BILL, TRIO
Albums

Word 8825	Christmas...Back Home in Indiana	198?	3.00	6.00	12.00
Word 8886	He Started the Whole World Singing	198?	3.00	6.00	12.00

GALANLADS, THE
45s

PIV 1005	The Mistletoe Polka/Seein's Believin'	19??	—	2.00	4.00

GALLAGHER, FRANK
45s

Dana 2026	You're All I Want For Christmas/Merry Christmas	19??	2.00	4.00	8.00

Label, Number	Title (A Side/B Side)	Year	VG	VG+	NM
GALLI SISTERS, THE					
45s					
National 9133	Santa, Send Someone To Me/Because He's Santa Claus	1950	5.00	10.00	20.00
GALWAY, JAMES					
Albums					
RCA Red Seal HRC1-5888	James Galway's Christmas Carol	1986	2.50	5.00	10.00
On Various-Artists Collections					
Fantasia on "I Saw Three Ships"	Family Christmas Collection, The (Time-Life STL-131)				
Have Yourself a Merry Little Christmas	Happy Holidays, Vol. 21 (RCA Special Products DPL1-0739)				
I Saw Three Ships	Stars of Christmas, The (RCA Special Products DPL1-0842)				
GANT, CECIL					
45s					
Decca 48185	It's Christmas Time Again/Hello Santa Claus	1950	10.00	20.00	40.00
GAP BAND, THE					
45s					
Total Experience 2435	The Christmas Song (Chestnuts Roasting on an Open Fire)/ Joy to the World	1985	—	2.00	4.00
— B-side by Oliver Scott					
On Various-Artists Collections					
Christmas Song, The	Total Experience Christmas, A (Total Experience TEL8-5707)				
I Miss You Most of All at Christmas	Total Experience Christmas, A (Total Experience TEL8-5707)				
This Christmas	Total Experience Christmas, A (Total Experience TEL8-5707)				
GARBER, JAN					
45s					
Capitol F1257	Blue Christmas/Whatcha Gonna Get	1950	3.75	7.50	15.00
Albums					
Decca DL 78932 S	Christmas Dance Party	1959	6.25	12.50	25.00
Decca DL 8932 M	Christmas Dance Party	1959	5.00	10.00	20.00
GARCED, JORGE					
Albums					
Caytronics CYZ 6011	Recuerdos	1981	3.00	6.00	12.00
GARDINER, BORIS					
12-Inch Singles					
Revue REV 40	The Meaning Of Christmas/Version	1986	2.00	4.00	8.00
GARFUNKEL, ART, AND AMY GRANT					
Also see AMY GRANT, SIMON AND GARFUNKEL.					
45s					
Columbia 06590	Carol of the Birds/The Decree	1986	—	—	3.00
Columbia 06590 PS	Carol of the Birds/The Decree	1986	—	—	3.00
Albums					
Columbia FC 40212	The Animals' Christmas By Jimmy Webb	1986	2.50	5.00	10.00
GARLAND, JUDY					
45s					
Decca 23658	The Birthday of a King/The Star of the East	195?	3.75	7.50	15.00
Decca 29295	Have Yourself a Merry Little Christmas/You'll Never Walk Alone	1954	3.75	7.50	15.00
Albums					
Decca DXB 172 (2) M	The Best of Judy Garland	1963	5.00	10.00	20.00
— Contains one Christmas song: Have Yourself a Merry Little Christmas					
Decca DXSB 7172 (2) R	The Best of Judy Garland	1963	5.00	10.00	20.00
— Same as above, but in rechanneled stereo					
Decca DL 75150 R	Judy Garland's Greatest Hits	1969	3.00	6.00	12.00
— Contains one Christmas song : Have Yourself a Merry Little Christmas					
On Various-Artists Collections					
Have Yourself a Merry Little Christmas	Christmas Is... (Columbia Special Products P 11417)				
	Meet Me in St.Louis (Decca DL 8498)				
	Old Fashioned Christmas, An (Reader's Digest RDA 216-A)				
	Time-Life Treasury of Christmas, The (Time-Life STL-107)				

Label, Number		Title (A Side/B Side)	Year	VG	VG+	NM

GARVER, KATHY
45s

| Aquarius 381 | | Lem, The Orphan Reindeer/(B-side unknown) | 19?? | — | 3.00 | 6.00 |
| Aquarius 381 | PS | Lem, The Orphan Reindeer | 19?? | — | 3.00 | 6.00 |

GARY, JOHN
45s

| RCA Victor 47-8475 | | Do You Hear What I Hear/Little Snow Girl | 1964 | 3.00 | 6.00 | 12.00 |

Albums

| RCA Victor LPM-2940 | M | The John Gary Christmas Album | 1964 | 3.75 | 7.50 | 15.00 |
| RCA Victor LSP-2940 | S | The John Gary Christmas Album | 1964 | 5.00 | 10.00 | 20.00 |

On Various-Artists Collections

Christmas Song, The	Family Christmas Collection, The (Time-Life STL-131)
	For a Musical Merry Christmas, Volume 3 (RCA Victor PRM-221)
	Henry Mancini Selects Great Songs of Christmas (RCA Special Products DPL1-0148)
	RCA Victor Presents Music for the Twelve Days of Christmas (RCA Victor PRS-188)
	60 Christmas Classics (Sessions DVL2-0723)
Do You Hear What I Hear	Happy Holidays, Volume 15 (RCA Special Products DPL1-0453)
	Very Merry Christmas, A, Volume VI (RCA Special Products PRS-427)
Hark! The Herald Angels Sing	Family Christmas Collection, The (Time-Life STL-131)
Have Yourself a Merry Little Christmas	Christmas with Colonel Sanders (RCA Victor PRS-291)
	Family Christmas Collection, The (Time-Life STL-131)
If Came Upon the Midnight Clear	Firestone Presents Your Christmas Favorites, Volume 7 (Firestone CSLP 7015)
Medley: Hark! The Herald Angels Sing/	Christmas Festival of Songs and Carols, Volume 2 (RCA Victor PRM-195)
O Little Town of Bethlehem/Silent Night
	Happy Holidays, Volume 13 (RCA Special Products DPL1-0319)
Medley: The First Noel/O Come, All Ye	Christmas in the Air (RCA Special Products DPL1-0133)
Faithful/O Holy Night	60 Christmas Classics (Sessions DVL2-0723)
Rise Up, Shepherd, and Follow	Firestone Presents Your Christmas Favorites, Volume 7 (Firestone CSLP 7015)
Sweet Little Jesus Boy	Very Merry Christmas, A, Volume 5 (RCA Special Products PRS-343)
White Christmas	Happy Holidays, Volume 14 (RCA Special Products DPL1-0376)
	Joyous Noel (Reader's Digest RDA-57A)
	Music to Trim Your Tree By (RCA Victor PRM 225)
Winter Wonderland	Joyous Noel (Reader's Digest RDA-57A)
Wintertime and Christmastime	Family Christmas Collection, The (Time-Life STL-131)

GARZA, IRMA
45s

| Falcon 950 | | Donde Este Santa Claus/Ya Viene Santa Claus | 19?? | 2.50 | 5.00 | 10.00 |

GATEMEN, THE
45s

| Colpix 671 | | Silent Night/White Christmas | 1962 | 5.00 | 10.00 | 20.00 |

GATES, DAVID
45s

| Arista 0653 | | Come Home for Christmas/Lady Valentine | 1981 | 2.00 | 4.00 | 8.00 |

GATLIN, LARRY, AND THE GATLIN BROTHERS (GATLIN BROTHERS, THE)
Albums

| Columbia FC 38183 | | A Gatlin Family Christmas | 1982 | 3.00 | 6.00 | 12.00 |
| Columbia PC 38183 | | A Gatlin Family Christmas | 198? | 2.00 | 4.00 | 8.00 |
| — Budget-line reissue |

On Various-Artists Collections

Do You Hear What I Hear	Christmas for the 90's, Volume 2 (Capitol Nashville 1P 8118)
Hallelujah Chorus	Nashville's Greatest Christmas Hits, Volume II (Columbia PC 44413)
Little Drummer Boy, The	Christmas for the 90's, Volume 1 (Capitol Nashville 1P 8117)
O Holy Night	Christmas Greetings from Nashville (Columbia PC 39467)
Sweet Baby Jesus	Nashville's Greatest Christmas Hits (Columbia PC 44412)

GAUDET, JOHN, AND THE LAURELS
45s

| Mary Glen 1001/2 | | Christmas Will Soon Be Here/
Your Name Shall Be Remembered | 1961 | 6.25 | 12.50 | 25.00 |

GAY SPORTSCASTERS
45s

| Only Boy 9402 | | St. Nick's Farm/Writin' Yer Name In The Snow | 1994 | — | 2.00 | 4.00 |
| Only Boy 9402 | PS | St. Nick's Farm/Writin' Yer Name In The Snow | 1994 | — | 2.00 | 4.00 |

Label, Number	Title (A Side/B Side)	Year	VG	VG+	NM
GAYE, MARVIN					
45s					
Tamla 54229	Christmas in the City/I Want to Come Home for Christmas	1972		*Unreleased*	
GAYLE, CRYSTAL					
45s					
Warner Bros. 28210	Oh Holy Night/I'll Be Home for Christmas	1987	—	2.00	4.00
Warner Bros. 28555	Have Yourself a Merry Little Christmas/Silver Bells	1986	—	2.00	4.00
Albums					
Warner Bros. 25508	A Crystal Christmas	1986	2.50	5.00	10.00
On Various-Artists Collections					
Have Yourself a Merry Little Christmas	Christmas Tradition, A (Warner Bros. 25630)				
Little Drummer Boy, The	Happy Holidays, Vol. 22 (RCA Special Products DPL1-0777)				
GAYLORD, RONNIE					
45s					
Mercury 70504	Santo Natale/My Vow	1954	3.75	7.50	15.00
GEDDA, NICOLAI					
On Various-Artists Collections					
Ave Maria	Firestone Presents Your Christmas Favorites, Volume 7 (Firestone CSLP 7015)				
GEDDA, NICOLAI, AND FIRESTONE CHORUS					
On Various-Artists Collections					
Good Christian Men, Rejoice	Firestone Presents Your Christmas Favorites, Volume 7 (Firestone CSLP 7015)				
GEER, WILL, AND THE HOLIDAY SINGERS					
On Various-Artists Collections					
Grandpa's Christmas Wish	Waltons' Christmas Album, The (Columbia KC 33193)				
GEEZINSLAWS, THE					
45s					
Step One 453	Lighten Up It's Christmas/Merry Christmas Baby	1992	—	2.00	4.00
GELLER, HERB, QUARTET					
45s					
EmArcy 16016	Sleigh Ride/Silver Rain	195?	5.00	10.00	20.00
GEMS, THE					
45s					
Chess 1917	Love For Christmas/All Of It	1964	3.00	6.00	12.00
On Various-Artists Collections					
Love for Christmas	Have a Merry Chess Christmas (Chess/MCA CH-25210)				
	Rockin' Little Christmas (MCA 25084)				
GENE AND JERRY					
45s					
Roulette 4537	Hootenanny Christmas/Carousel	1963	3.00	6.00	12.00
GENTRY, BOBBIE					
On Various-Artists Collections					
Away in a Manger	Christmas Songs, The (Capitol SLB-57074)				
	Christmas Sounds of Music, The (Capitol Creative Products SL-6643)				
	Holiday Magic (Capitol Creative Products SL-6728)				
	Magic of Christmas, The (Capitol SWBB-93810)				
Scarlet Ribbons	Christmas Sounds of Music, The (Capitol Creative Products SL-6643)				
	Let's Celebrate Christmas (Capitol Special Markets SL-6923)				
GEORGE AND GARY					
45s					
Play 101	It Must Be Christmas/I Remember Christmas	19??	2.50	5.00	10.00
GEORGE, CASSIETTA					
45s					
Audio Arts! 60004	Silent Night/The Greatest Gift	196?	5.00	10.00	20.00

Label, Number	Title (A Side/B Side)	Year	VG	VG+	NM

GERHARD, RAMONA
45s

Soma 1049	White Christmas/Sleigh Ride	195?	3.00	6.00	12.00

GERRARD, JIMMY, AND WALKS OF LIFE
45s

Walks of Life 6990	Spirit of Christmas/(Instrumental)	198?	—	—	3.00

GETSET V.O.P.
12-Inch Singles

Polydor PRO 1085-1	DJ	Timberlands for Xmas (House of the Seven Do's)/ Timberlands for Christmas (Alternate Mix)//Timberlands for Xmas (Instrumental)	1993	2.00	4.00	8.00

GETZ, STAN
On Various-Artists Collections

Moonlight in Vermont	Carols and Candlelight (Columbia Special Products P 12525)

GIBSON, GERALD, AND HIS SING-A-LONGERS
Albums

International Award Series AK-X7	Christmas Sing-a-Long	196?	3.00	6.00	12.00

GIBSON, RICK
45s

HA 715	Christmas Spirit/Christmas Eve	19??	—	2.50	5.00
— B-side by Julie Koblish					

GIGI
45s

Colpix 668	Peace for Christmas/The Sound of Angels	1962	3.00	6.00	12.00

GILLEY, MICKEY
45s

Epic AE7 1774	Home to Texas for Christmas/I'm Spending Christmas with You	1982	—	2.50	5.00
Epic 03332	Blue Christmas/Jingle Bell Rock	1982	—	2.00	4.00
Playboy 6095	Pretty Paper/Lonely Christmas Call	1976	—	2.50	5.00

Albums

Epic FE 37595	Christmas at Gilley's	1981	2.50	5.00	10.00

On Various-Artists Collections

Blue Christmas	Blue Christmas (Welk Music Group WM-3002)
I'll Be Home for Christmas	Nashville's Greatest Christmas Hits, Volume II (Columbia PC 44413)
Lonely Christmas Call	Country Christmas (Time-Life STL-109)
White Christmas	Christmas Greetings from Nashville (Columbia PC 39467)

GILLEY, MICKEY, AND LIBBY HURLEY
On Various-Artists Collections

Rockin' Around the Christmas Tree	Nashville Christmas Album, The (Epic PE 40418)

GILLIS, RICHARD
45s

20th Century 2316	C. B. Santa Claus/Come Love Me Long	1976	—	2.00	4.00

GIRL TROUBLE
45s

Regal Select 007		Blue Christmas//Sleigh Ride/Christmas With The Kings	198?	2.00	4.00	8.00
— B-side by Kings of Rock; blue vinyl						
Regal Select 007	PS	Blue Christmas//Sleigh Ride/Christmas With The Kings	198?	2.00	4.00	8.00
— B-side by Kings of Rock						

GIRLS OF THE GOLDEN WEST, THE
45s

Manco 1059	Christmas Secret/Christmas	1964	2.50	5.00	10.00

GIVENS, VAN
45s

Paula 1291	Droopy Christmas Tree/Daddy's Baby Boy	198?	—	2.00	4.00
Paula 286	Droopy Christmas Tree/Daddy's Baby Boy	1967	2.50	5.00	10.00

Label, Number	Title (A Side/B Side)	Year	VG	VG+	NM

GLAD SINGERS, THE
45s

Columbia JZSP 111919/20 DJ	Deck The Halls/Happy New Year	1965	3.00	6.00	12.00

— *Promo only on green vinyl*

On Various-Artists Collections

Deck the Halls	Gift of Christmas, The, Vol. 1 (Columbia Special Products CSS 706)				

GLADWELL, GARY
45s

Big Sound 100	Merry Christmas Little Fellow/Are You Santa?	19??	—	—	3.00

GLEASON, JACKIE
7-Inch Extended Plays

Capitol EAP 1-758	(contents unknown)	1956	2.50	5.00	10.00
Capitol EAP 1-758 PS	Merry Christmas	1956	3.00	6.00	12.00

Albums

Capitol STBB-346 (2)	All I Want for Christmas	1969	3.75	7.50	15.00
Capitol W 758 M	Merry Christmas	1956	6.25	12.50	25.00
Capitol DW 758 R	Merry Christmas	196?	2.50	5.00	10.00
Capitol T 2791 M	'Tis the Season	1967	5.00	10.00	20.00
Capitol ST 2791 S	'Tis the Season	1967	3.75	7.50	15.00
Pickwick SPC-1008	White Christmas	197?	2.50	5.00	10.00

— *Abridged version of Capitol ST 2791*

On Various-Artists Collections

Blue Christmas	Blue Christmas (Welk Music Group WM-3002)
Christmas Song, The	Zenith Presents Christmas, A Gift of Music (Capitol Creative Products SL-6544)
I Saw Mommy Kissing Santa Claus	Best of Christmas, The, Vol. II (Capitol SM-11834)
I'll Be Home for Christmas	Zenith Presents Christmas, A Gift of Music (Capitol Creative Products SL-6544)
White Christmas	Best of Christmas, The, Vol. I (Capitol SM-11833)

GLENN, DARRELL
45s

Valley 119	Christmas Is Just Around The Corner/(B-side unknown)	195?	5.00	10.00	20.00

GLENN, LLOYD, TRIO
On Various-Artists Collections

Sleigh Ride	Merry Christmas Baby (Christmas Music for Young Lovers) (Hollywood HLP 501)
	Merry Christmas Baby (Gusto/Hollywood K-5018-X)

GLITTER, GARY
45s

Arista 592	Another Rock and Roll Christmas/(Instrumental Re-Mix)	1984	—	2.50	5.00
Arista 592 PS	Another Rock and Roll Christmas/(Instrumental Re-Mix)	1984	—	2.50	5.00

— *Record and sleeve are U.K. imports*

Arista ARISD 592	Another Rock and Roll Christmas/(Instrumental Re-Mix)	1984	3.00	6.00	12.00

— *U.K. import; shaped picture disc with plinth*

EMI 256	Through The Years/Another Rock And Roll Christmas	1992	—	2.00	4.00
EMI 256 PS	Through The Years/Another Rock And Roll Christmas	1992	—	2.00	4.00

— *U.K. import; reissue*

GO GO JOES, THE
45s

Josie 770	Cool Yule/No Dough Blues	1954	5.00	10.00	20.00

GOBEL, GEORGE
On Various-Artists Collections

Give Your Heart a Try	'Twas the Night Before Christmas (Disneyland 1367)

GODFREY, ARTHUR
45s

Contempo 905	Every Christmas Morning/Pine Cones & Holly Berries	1963	2.00	4.00	8.00
Listen 2 752	Christmas Is Christmas All Over The World/(Instrumental)	19??	2.00	4.00	8.00

On Various-Artists Collections

Jingle Bells	First Christmas Record for Children (Harmony HS 14554)
White Christmas	Columbia 40109 (title unknown) (Columbia 4-40109)

GOING THING, THE
45s

Chatham 3002	My Christmas Tree/Have Yourself A Merry Little Christmas	198?	—	2.00	4.00

Label, Number	Title (A Side/B Side)	Year	VG	VG+	NM

GOLD, MARTY
On Various-Artists Collections

Rags	Old Fashioned Christmas, An (Reader's Digest RDA 216-A)				

GOLDDIGGERS, THE
45s

Metromedia 156	We Need A Little Christmas/I Just Want You For Christmas	1969	—	3.00	6.00
Albums					
Metromedia MD 1012	We Need a Little Christmas	1969	3.75	7.50	15.00

GOLDEN TRUMPETS
45s

Nashboro 835	So Called Christmas/Sweeter Life	1964	2.50	5.00	10.00

GOLDEN WEST COLLEGE COMMERCIAL MUSIC PROGRAM, THE
7-Inch Extended Plays

(no label) GWC-79-102 DJ	Christmas with You/The Joy of Christmas// Christmas/Time for the Holly	1979	—	3.00	6.00

GOLDSBORO, BOBBY
45s

United Artists 50470	A Christmas Wish/Look Around You (It's Christmas Time)	1968	2.50	5.00	10.00

GONNEAU, PIERRE
45s

Laurie 3280	The Little Boy That Santa Forgot/Chanson du Soir	1964	3.00	6.00	12.00

GONZALES, BABS
45s

Atlas 1206	Teenage Santa Claus/Pay Dem Dues	1959	3.00	6.00	12.00
Bruce 122	The Be-Bop Santa Claus/Manhattan Fable	1955	5.00	10.00	20.00
End 1008	Rock and Roll Santa Claus/Me — Spelled M-E-M-E	1957	5.00	10.00	20.00
Essex 377	The Be-Bop Santa Claus/Manhattan Fable	1954	5.00	10.00	20.00
King 4836 DJ	Be-Bop Santa Claus/Watch Them Resolutions	1955	3.75	7.50	15.00

GONZALES, NITOY
Albums

Capitol T 10305 M	Christmas in the Philippines	196?	3.00	6.00	12.00
Capitol ST 10305 S	Christmas in the Philippines	196?	3.75	7.50	15.00

GONZALES-GONZALES, JOSE
45s

Liberty 55770	Pancho Claus/Tacos for Two	1964	3.00	6.00	12.00

GOOD QUESTION
On Various-Artists Collections

Winter Wonderland	Winter Warnerland (Warner Bros. PRO-A-3328)				

GOODIE
On Various-Artists Collections

Please Come Home for Christmas	Total Experience Christmas, A (Total Experience TEL8-5707)				

GOODLEY, GERRI
45s

Dootone 316	Santa Claus Walks Just Like Daddy/You're My Christmas	1953	7.50	15.00	30.00
— B-side by Buell Thomas					

GOODMAN, AL
45s

RCA Victor 47-3833	Adeste Fideles/Because You're You	1950	3.75	7.50	15.00

GOODMAN, BENNY
45s

RCA Victor 47-2973	Jingle Bells/Santa Claus Is Coming to Town	1949	5.00	10.00	20.00

On Various-Artists Collections

Jingle Bells	Stash Christmas Album, The (Stash 125)				

Label, Number		Title (A Side/B Side)	Year	VG	VG+	NM
GOODMAN, DICKIE						
Also see BUCHANAN AND GOODMAN.						
45s						
Rori 701		Santa and the Touchables/North Pole Rock	1961	6.25	12.50	25.00
Albums						
Cash CR 6000		Mr. Jaws and Other Fables	1975	6.25	12.50	25.00
— *Contains two Christmas tracks:* Santa and the Satellite (Part 1); Santa and the Satellite (Part 2)						
GOODRICH, ALEXANDER						
Albums						
Diplomat X-1711	M	Organ and Chimes at Christmas	1965	3.00	6.00	12.00
Diplomat SX-1711	S	Organ and Chimes at Christmas	1965	3.00	6.00	12.00
GOODTIME WASHBOARD THREE, THE						
45s						
Fantasy 609		Santa Charges Through Your Bank Account/(B-side unknown)	1966	2.50	5.00	10.00
GOODWIN, BOBBY						
45s						
Open 2600		Christmas Song/Stranger In A Manger	19??	2.00	4.00	8.00
GOONS, THE						
45s						
Decca F 10756		I'm Walking Backwards for Christmas/Bluebottle Blues	1956	5.00	10.00	20.00
— *U.K. import (original)*						
Decca F 13414		I'm Walking Backwards for Christmas/Ying Tong Song	1973	3.75	7.50	15.00
— *U.K. import (reissue)*						
London 1684		I'm Walking Backwards for Christmas/Bluebottle Blues	1956	6.25	12.50	25.00
GORDON, BARRY						
45s						
MGM 12092		Nuttin' for Christmas/Santa Claus Looks Like Daddy	1955	5.00	10.00	20.00
— *With Art Mooney and His Orchestra*						
MGM 12367		Zoomah, the Santa Claus from Mars/ I Like Christmas (I Like It, I Like It)	1956	5.00	10.00	20.00
MGM 12367	PS	Zoomah, the Santa Claus from Mars/ I Like Christmas (I Like It, I Like It)	1956	6.25	12.50	25.00
On Various-Artists Collections						
Nuttin' for Christmas		Billboard Greatest Christmas Hits, 1955-Present (Rhino R1 70636)				
GORDON, DEXTER						
On Various-Artists Collections						
Have Yourself a Merry Little Christmas		God Rest Ye Merry, Jazzmen (Columbia FC 37551)				
		Yule Struttin' — A Blue Note Christmas (Blue Note 1P 8119)				
GORDON, ROBERT						
45s						
RCA JH-11452	DJ	Blue Christmas (mono/stereo)	1978	—	3.00	6.00
RCA PB-11452		Blue Christmas/Fire	1978	—	2.50	5.00
— *With Link Wray*						
GORDY, POPPA JOHN						
45s						
RCA Victor 47-5902		Santa Plays the Trombone (In the North Pole Band)/ Oh Didn't He Ramble	1954	3.75	7.50	15.00
GORMAN SISTERS, THE						
45s						
Arrow 721		Jesus Is My Santa Claus/Silent Night	1957	3.75	7.50	15.00
Joy 224		Daddy Is My Santa Claus/Chickery Check	1958	3.75	7.50	15.00
GORME, EYDIE						
45s						
Columbia JZSP 116419/20	DJ	Alegre Navidad/Blanca Navidad	1966	2.50	5.00	10.00
— *With Trio Los Panchos*						
United Artists 283		Let Me Be the First to Wish You a Merry Christmas/ I Love to Dance (But Never on Sunday)	1960	3.00	6.00	12.00

Label, Number		Title (A Side/B Side)	Year	VG	VG+	NM

On Various-Artists Collections

It Came Upon a Midnight Clear		Christmastime in Carol and Song (RCA PRS-289)				
My Favorite Things		Wondrous Winter: Songs of Winter, Songs of Christmas (Columbia Special Products CSS 708/9)				
Silent Night		Merry Christmas from... (Reader's Digest RD4-83)				
White Christmas		Very Merry Christmas, A, Volume Two (Columbia Special Products CSS 788)				

GOSPEL CLEFS, THE
On Various-Artists Collections

Mary's Boy Child		Mahalia (Jackson) and Friends at Christmastime (Columbia Special Products P 11804)				

GOSPEL HILITES, THE
45s

Checker 1251		Joy And A Christmas Way/One More Time	197?	—	2.50	5.00

GOULD, MORTON
Albums

Columbia Masterworks ML 2065 10		Christmas Music for Orchestra	1949	7.50	15.00	30.00

On Various-Artists Collections

Good King Wenceslas		60 Christmas Classics (Sessions DVL2-0723)
		Christmas in California (RCA Victor PRS-276)
		Christmas in New York Volume 2 (RCA Victor PRS-270)
		Christmas with Colonel Sanders (RCA Victor PRS-291)
		Christmastime in Carol and Song (RCA PRM-271)
		Very Merry Christmas, A, Volume VII (RCA Special Products DPL1-0049)
		Time-Life Treasury of Christmas, The (Time-Life STL-107)
Home for Christmas		Time-Life Treasury of Christmas, The, Volume Two (Time-Life STL-108)
Jingle Bells		Happy Holidays, Volume IV (RCA Victor PRS-267)
Little Drummer Boy, The		Christmas in New York (RCA Victor PRM-257)

GOULET, ROBERT
45s

Columbia 44710		Hurry Home for Christmas/Wonderful World of Christmas	1968	2.00	4.00	8.00
Columbia JZSP 76415/6	DJ	December Time/Silver Bells	1963	2.50	5.00	10.00
Columbia JZSP 111805/6	DJ	This Christmas I Spend With You/White Christmas	1965	2.50	5.00	10.00
— Promotional record for Christmas Seals						
Columbia JZSP 111805/6	PS	This Christmas I Spend With You/White Christmas	1965	3.00	6.00	12.00

Albums

Columbia CL 2076	M	This Christmas I Spend with You	1963	3.00	6.00	12.00
Columbia CS 8876	S	This Christmas I Spend with You	1963	3.75	7.50	15.00
Columbia CS 9734		Robert Goulet's Wonderful World of Christmas	1968	3.00	6.00	12.00
Columbia Special Products P13345		Robert Goulet's Wonderful World of Christmas	1976	3.00	6.00	12.00
— Same as CS 9734, but "Exclusively distributed by Sutton Distributors, Inc."						

On Various-Artists Collections

Christmas Song, The		Home for Christmas (Columbia Musical Treasury P3S 5608)
		Home for Christmas (Realm 2V 8101)
Do You Hear What I Hear		Very Merry Christmas, A, Volume 3 (Columbia Special Products CSS 997)
		WHIO Radio Christmas Feelings (Sound Approach/CSP P 16366)
God Rest Ye Merry Gentlemen		Christmas Trimmings (Columbia Special Products P 12795)
		Joy of Christmas, The (Columbia Special Products P 12042)
		Joy to the World (30 Classic Christmas Melodies) (Columbia Special Products P3 14654)
		Merry Christmas from... (Reader's Digest RD4-83)
Have Yourself a Merry Little Christmas		Christmas Album, A (Columbia PC 39466)
Home for the Holidays		Spirit of Christmas, The, Volume III (Columbia Special Products CSS 1463)
		That Christmas Feeling (Columbia Special Products P 11853)
O Come All Ye Faithful		Christmas Greetings (Columbia Special Products CSS 1433)
		Christmas Greetings (Columbia Special Products CSS 1499)
		Great Songs of Christmas, The, Album Four (Columbia Special Products CSP 155M)
		Magic of Christmas, The (Columbia Musical Treasury P3S 5806)
		Sounds of Christmas (Columbia Special Products P 12474)
O Holy Night		Joyous Christmas, Volume 2 (Columbia Special Products CSS 808)
		Very Merry Christmas, A, Volume Two (Columbia Special Products CSS 788)
Panis Angelicus		Great Songs of Christmas, The, Album Three (Columbia Special Products CSP 117)
		Joy to the World (30 Classic Christmas Melodies) (Columbia Special Products P3 14654)
Reminder Spot		For Christmas Seals...A Matter of Life and Breath (Decca Custom Style E)
Silver Bells		Happy Holidays, Album Nine (Columbia Special Products P 11793)
		Merry Christmas (Columbia Musical Treasury 3P 6306)
This Christmas I Spend with You		Great Songs of Christmas, The, Album Seven (Columbia Special Products CSS 547)
White Christmas		Joy to the World (30 Classic Christmas Melodies) (Columbia Special Products P3 14654)
		Merry Christmas from... (Reader's Digest RD4-83)

GOULET, ROBERT, AND CAROL LAWRENCE
On Various-Artists Collections

Angels We Have Heard on High		Collection of Christmas Favorites, A (Columbia Special Products P 14988)
		Joyous Christmas, Volume V (Columbia Special Products C 10398)
Christmas Waltz, The		Great Songs of Christmas, The, Album Eight (Columbia Special Products CSS 888)

Label, Number	Title (A Side/B Side)	Year	VG	VG+	NM
GRAB THIS					
12-Inch Singles					
Oops OOPS3	Get Your Tits Out for Christmas (7" Mix)/Get Your Tits Out for Christmas (Hard, Funky & Long Mix)//Wet 'n' Wild (7" Mix)/ Wet 'n' Wild (12" Remix)/Wet 'n' Wild (Techno Mix)	1995	2.00	4.00	8.00
— B-side by the U.K. Centerfolds					
GRABEAU, BOBBY					
45s					
Class 805 DJ	Souvenirs Of Christmas/Once A Fool	19??	—	2.50	5.00
— B-side by Ann Young					
GRACE CATHEDRAL BOYS' AND MEN'S CHOIR					
On Various-Artists Collections					
Silent Night	Christmas in San Francisco (Embarcadero Center EC-101)				
GRACE CATHEDRAL MEN'S CHOIR					
On Various-Artists Collections					
O Come Emmanuel	Christmas in San Francisco (Embarcadero Center EC-101)				
GRACE, EARL					
45s					
United Southern 111	Christmas Is Just Around The Corner/Santa Town	19??	3.00	6.00	12.00
GRADY, LEIGH					
45s					
Appaloosa 112	Blue Christmas Without Elvis/(B-side unknown)	1977	—	2.50	5.00
Appaloosa 115	Let's Put Christ Back In Christmas/The Joy Of Christmas Day	1977	—	2.00	4.00
GRAHAM, DON					
45s					
Warner Bros. 5131	I Saw Mommy Kissing Santa Claus/And It Ain't Paid For Yet	1959	3.75	7.50	15.00
GRAHAM, ROSE					
45s					
Klondike 2224	Black Christmas/What Soul Is	19??	2.00	4.00	8.00
GRAMERCY (NYC) BOYS' CLUB CHOIR					
On Various-Artists Collections					
We Wish You a Merry Christmas	Joyous Christmas, Volume 2 (Columbia Special Products CSS 808)				
GRANGER, GERRI					
On Various-Artists Collections					
Christmas Song	Merry Christmas from David Frost and Billy Taylor (Bell 6053)				
Wexford Carol	Merry Christmas from David Frost and Billy Taylor (Bell 6053)				
GRANNY					
45s					
Obscurity 300	Granny's Holiday Fruitcake/(B-side unknown)	19??	3.00	6.00	12.00
GRANT, AMY					
45s					
A&M 2777	Tennessee Christmas/Little Town	1985	—	2.00	4.00
A&M 2777 PS	Tennessee Christmas/Little Town	1985	—	2.50	5.00
A&M 31458 0104 7	Grown-Up Christmas List/Have Yourself a Merry Little Christmas	1992	—	2.00	4.00
Albums					
A&M SP-5057	A Christmas Album	1984	2.50	5.00	10.00
— Mass-market edition, a year after original issue; same contents as Myrrh 6768					
Myrrh MSB-6768	A Christmas Album	1983	3.00	6.00	12.00
— Original issue of this album; available primarily at Christian bookstores					
On Various-Artists Collections					
Santa's Reindeer Ride	On This Christmas Night (Songbird MCA-3184)				
GRANT, CARY					
45s					
Columbia 44377	Christmas Lullaby/Here's to You	1967	5.00	10.00	20.00

Label, Number		Title (A Side/B Side)	Year	VG	VG+	NM

On Various-Artists Collections

Christmas Lullaby		Joyous Christmas, Volume 6 (Columbia Special Products C 11083)				
		Very Merry Christmas, A, Volume 3 (Columbia Special Products CSS 997)				
Here's to You		Christmas Greetings, Vol. 3 (Columbia Special Products P 11383)				

GRANT, EARL
45s

Decca 25683		Rudolph the Red-Nosed Reindeer/Santa Claus Is Comin' to Town	1965	2.00	4.00	8.00
Decca 25703		Jingle Bells/Silver Bells	1966	—	3.00	6.00
Decca 31022		Christmas Card/Swingin' Christmas	1959	2.50	5.00	10.00
MCA 65023		Silver Bells/Jingle Bells	1973	—	2.00	4.00
— Black label with rainbow						
MCA 65023		Silver Bells/Jingle Bells	1980	—	—	3.00
— Blue label with rainbow						

Albums

| Decca DL 4677 | M | Winter Wonderland | 1965 | 3.00 | 6.00 | 12.00 |
| Decca DL 74677 | S | Winter Wonderland | 1965 | 3.75 | 7.50 | 15.00 |

GRANT, GEORGE, AND THE CASTELLES – See THE CASTELLES.

GRAY, MARK
On Various-Artists Collections

| O Little Town of Bethlehem | | Nashville Christmas Album, The (Epic PE 40418) | | | | |

GREAT WHYTE LYIN' SNAKE
45s

Highly Collectable 01		Jolly Old St. Nicholas/Last Christmas	199?	—	2.00	4.00
— Red vinyl						
Highly Collectable 01		Jolly Old St. Nicholas/Last Christmas	199?	—	2.00	4.00
— Green vinyl						
Highly Collectable 01	PS	Jolly Old St. Nicholas/Last Christmas	199?	—	2.00	4.00

GREEDIES, THE
45s

Vertigo GREED 1		A Merry Jingle/A Merry Jangle	198?	2.00	4.00	8.00
Vertigo GREED 1	PS	A Merry Jingle/A Merry Jangle	198?	2.00	4.00	8.00
— Record and sleeve are U.K. imports						

GREELEY, GEORGE
Albums

| Warner Bros. W 1560 | M | Best Loved Christmas Piano Concertos | 1965 | 3.00 | 6.00 | 12.00 |
| Warner Bros. WS 1560 | S | Best Loved Christmas Piano Concertos | 1965 | 3.75 | 7.50 | 15.00 |

GREEN, AL
45s

| The Right Stuff S7-18217 | | I'll Be Home for Christmas/It Feels Like Christmas | 1994 | — | 2.50 | 5.00 |

Albums

| Word WR-8117 | | White Christmas | 198? | 3.00 | 6.00 | 12.00 |

GREEN, BENNY
On Various-Artists Collections

| Merrier Christmas, A | | Yule Struttin' — A Blue Note Christmas (Blue Note 1P 8119) | | | | |
| Silent Night | | Yule Struttin' — A Blue Note Christmas (Blue Note 1P 8119) | | | | |

GREEN, BYRDIE
45s

| Penda Mungu 100 | | We Need Christmas Now, More Than Any Other/(Instrumental) | 19?? | 2.00 | 4.00 | 8.00 |

GREEN, GRIZ
45s

| Scott 102875 | | Yuletide Song/Toyland Jamboree | 1975 | — | 2.50 | 5.00 |

GREEN, JERRY K.
45s

| Penguin 1289 | | Peter The Penguin/Tripod The Three Legged Dog | 19?? | — | 3.00 | 6.00 |

Label, Number		Title (A Side/B Side)	Year	VG	VG+	NM
GREEN, JOHN						
45s						
Sausalito Sound 009		I Want A Girl For Christmas/Live Wire	19??	2.00	4.00	8.00
GREEN, LARRY						
45s						
RCA Victor 47-3074		Our Christmas Waltz/Follow The Swallow To Hide-A-Way Hollow	1949	3.75	7.50	15.00
GREEN, MARTYN; BASIL RATHBONE						
On Various-Artists Collections						
One Little Boy		Stingiest Man in Town, The (Columbia CL 950)				
GREENE, JACK						
45s						
EMH 0015		I'd Be Home On Christmas Day/(B-side unknown)	1982	—	2.50	5.00
EMH 0019		From Cotton to Satin/I'd Be Home on Christmas Day	1983	—	2.00	4.00
— A-side not a Christmas song						
GREENE, LORNE						
45s						
RCA Victor 47-9037		Must Be Santa/One Solitary Life	1966	2.50	5.00	10.00
Albums						
RCA Victor LPM-3410	M	Have a Happy Holiday	1965	3.00	6.00	12.00
RCA Victor LSP-3410	S	Have a Happy Holiday	1965	3.75	7.50	15.00
On Various-Artists Collections						
'Twas the Night Before Christmas		Happy Holidays, Volume 16 (RCA Special Products DPL1-0501)				
We Wish You a Merry Christmas		Joyous Noel (Reader's Digest RDA-57A)				
GREENE, LORNE; MICHAEL LANDON; DAN BLOCKER						
Albums						
RCA Victor LPM-2757	M	Christmas on the Ponderosa	1963	5.00	10.00	20.00
RCA Victor LSP-2757	S	Christmas on the Ponderosa	1963	7.50	15.00	30.00
On Various-Artists Collections						
Merry Christmas Neighbor		Christmas with Colonel Sanders (RCA Victor PRS-291)				
		RCA Victor Presents Music for the Twelve Days of Christmas (RCA Victor PRS-188)				
GREENWOOD, LEE						
45s						
MCA S45-17739	DJ	Christmas to Christmas (Loving You) (same on both sides)	1987	—	2.50	5.00
MCA 52733		Christmas to Christmas (Loving You)/Lone Star Christmas	1987	—	—	3.00
Albums						
MCA 5623		Christmas to Christmas	1985	2.50	5.00	10.00
On Various-Artists Collections						
Greatest Gift of All, The		Family Christmas Collection, The (Time-Life STL-131)				
GREER, BIG JOHN						
45s						
Groove 0038		We Wanna See Santa Do the Mambo/Wait Till After Christmas	1954	10.00	20.00	40.00
GREGG, RICKY LYNN						
45s						
Capitol Nashville S7-18911		Santa Claus Is Coming to Town/What Child Is This	1995	—	—	3.00
GREGORY, CLINTON						
45s						
Step One 443		Christmas in Virginia/Blue Christmas	1992	—	2.50	5.00
GREGORY, DAVE						
45s						
Sagittar 111		Theodore (Santa's Helper)/Here Comes Ole Santa Claus	19??	—	2.50	5.00
GREGORY, EDDY						
45s						
Aztec 001		Underneath the Christmas Tree/Merry Christmas, Everybody	19??	—	2.50	5.00

Label, Number		Title (A Side/B Side)	Year	VG	VG+	NM
GREY, BILLY						
45s						
Tin Pan Alley 459		Christmas in the Army/Lover's Lane	19??	—	2.00	4.00
GREY, JOEL						
On Various-Artists Collections						
Even a Miracle Needs a Hand		'Twas the Night Before Christmas (Disneyland 1367)				
Joel Grey Reminder Show, The		For Christmas Seals...A Matter of Life and Breath (Decca Custom Style E)				
GRIFFIN, KEN						
45s						
Columbia 38908		Joy to the World/The First Nowell	1951	3.00	6.00	12.00
Columbia 38909		Silent Night/Adeste Fideles	1951	3.00	6.00	12.00
Columbia 38910		Away In A Manger/O, Little Town Of Bethlehem	1951	3.00	6.00	12.00
Columbia 38911		I'll Be Home For Christmas/White Christmas	1951	3.00	6.00	12.00
7-Inch Extended Plays						
Columbia 6923		White Christmas/I'll Be Home For Christmas// + 2	195?	3.75	7.50	15.00
Royale 711	PS	Christmas Music	195?	3.00	6.00	12.00
Royale 711		(contents unknown)	195?	3.00	6.00	12.00
Albums						
Columbia CL 692	M	The Organ Plays at Christmas	1955	6.25	12.50	25.00
Columbia CS 8760	S	The Organ Plays at Christmas	1963	3.00	6.00	12.00
On Various-Artists Collections						
Away in a Manger		Christmas Greetings (Columbia Special Products CSS 1433)				
GRIFFITH, ANDY						
On Various-Artists Collections						
Frosty the Snowman		Frosty's Winter Wonderland (Disneyland 1368)				
GRIMES, SCOTT						
45s						
Jamex 017		We Believe In Christmas/I Saw Christmas	1984	—	3.00	6.00
Jamex 017	PS	We Believe In Christmas/I Saw Christmas	1984	2.50	5.00	10.00
GRIMES, TAMMY						
On Various-Artists Collections						
Even a Miracle Needs a Hand (Reprise)		'Twas the Night Before Christmas (Disneyland 1367)				
GRISMAN, DAVID						
Albums						
Rounder 0190		Acoustic Christmas	198?	3.00	6.00	12.00
GROCE, LARRY						
On Various-Artists Collections						
Away in a Manger		Disney's Christmas All-Time Favorites (Disneyland 1V 8150)				
Deck the Halls		Disney's Christmas All-Time Favorites (Disneyland 1V 8150)				
		Disney's Christmas Favorites (Disneyland 2506)				
Frosty the Snowman		Disney's Christmas All-Time Favorites (Disneyland 1V 8150)				
		Disney's Christmas Favorites (Disneyland 2506)				
		Frosty the Snowman (Disneyland 253)				
Have Yourself a Merry Little Christmas		Disney's Christmas All-Time Favorites (Disneyland 1V 8150)				
Here We Come a-Caroling		Disney's Christmas All-Time Favorites (Disneyland 1V 8150)				
Joy to the World		Disney's Christmas All-Time Favorites (Disneyland 1V 8150)				
O Christmas Tree		Disney's Christmas All-Time Favorites (Disneyland 1V 8150)				
		Disney's Christmas Favorites (Disneyland 2506)				
Santa Claus Is Coming to Town		Disney's Christmas All-Time Favorites (Disneyland 1V 8150)				
		Disney's Christmas Favorites (Disneyland 2506)				
Silent Night		Disney's Christmas All-Time Favorites (Disneyland 1V 8150)				
		Disney's Christmas Favorites (Disneyland 2506)				
Silver Bells		Disney's Christmas All-Time Favorites (Disneyland 1V 8150)				
White Christmas		Disney's Christmas All-Time Favorites (Disneyland 1V 8150)				
		Disney's Christmas Favorites (Disneyland 2506)				
Winter Wonderland		Disney's Christmas All-Time Favorites (Disneyland 1V 8150)				
		Disney's Christmas Favorites (Disneyland 2506)				
GROOM, SUZANNE						
On Various-Artists Collections						
Silver Bells		Christmas in Saint Louis ((no label) TS77-558/9)				

Label, Number		Title (A Side/B Side)	Year	VG	VG+	NM
GROOVIE GHOULIES						
45s						
Crimson Corpse 2004		Christmas On Mars/My Christmas Card To You	19??	2.00	4.00	8.00
— Red vinyl						
Crimson Corpse 2004	PS	Christmas On Mars/My Christmas Card To You	19??	2.00	4.00	8.00
GRUSIN, DAVE						
On Various-Artists Collections						
Some Children See Him		GRP Christmas Collection, A (GRP 9574)				
GUARALDI, VINCE						
45s						
Fantasy 608		Christmas Time Is Here/What Child Is This	1966	5.00	10.00	20.00
Albums						
Fantasy 8431		A Charlie Brown Christmas	1971	6.25	12.50	25.00
— Original soundtrack from the cartoon and more (the LP is longer than the show!). Dark blue label.						
Fantasy 8431		A Charlie Brown Christmas	1988	3.75	7.50	15.00
— Remastered version of above with "1988" on back cover. Lighter blue label.						
GUARINO, GIAN MARIO, ORCHESTRA DIRETTA DA						
On Various-Artists Collections						
Pastorale		Christmas in Italy (Capitol T 10093)				
Presepe		Christmas in Italy (Capitol T 10093)				
GUERRERO, JUAN						
On Various-Artists Collections						
Posida-s		Christmas in San Francisco (Embarcadero Center EC-101)				
GUERRERO, LALO						
45s						
Capitol Latino 6887		Pancho Claus/The Burrito	19??	—	3.00	6.00
L&M 1000		Pancho Claus/Pound Dog (Hound Dog)	1956	10.00	20.00	40.00
L&M 1004		Pancho Claus/Christmas In Mexico	1956	5.00	10.00	20.00
GUESS						
On Various-Artists Collections						
Christmas Everyday		Christmas on Death Row (Death Row/Interscope INT2-90108)				
White Christmas		Christmas on Death Row (Death Row/Interscope INT2-90108)				
GUEST, CORNELIA						
45s						
Epic 04744		It's Christmas in New York/Right Time	1984	—	2.00	4.00
GUINNESS, ALEC						
On Various-Artists Collections						
See the Phantoms		Scrooge (Columbia Masterworks S 30258)				
GUITAR, BONNIE						
45s						
Dot 16968		I'll Be Missing You (Under the Mistletoe)/Blue Christmas	1966	5.00	10.00	20.00
Albums						
Dot DLP-3746	M	Merry Christmas from Bonnie Guitar	1966	5.00	10.00	20.00
Dot DLP-25746	S	Merry Christmas from Bonnie Guitar	1966	6.25	12.50	25.00
On Various-Artists Collections						
It Came Upon a Midnight Clear		12 Days of Christmas, The (Pickwick SPC-1021)				
GUTHRIE, ARLO						
Albums						
Reprise RS 6299		Arlo	1968	3.75	7.50	15.00
— With two-tone orange ":r" and "W7" label. Contains one Christmas song: Pause of Mr. Claus, The						
GYPSIES, THE						
45s						
Groove 0129		Rock Around the Christmas Tree/You've Been Away Too Long	1955	5.00	10.00	20.00

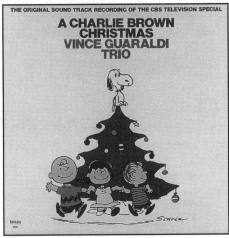

(Top left) Not technically a holiday song, Dan Fogelberg's "Same Old Lang Syne" is closely associated with the end of the year. This is not an easy sleeve to find. (Top right) *The 4 Seasons Greetings* was their second album, originally released in the late fall of 1962. This was later reissued on Philips and Rhino. (Bottom left) Amy Grant's *A Christmas Album* was available on the Christian label Myrrh a full year before its release to the secular market on A&M. (Bottom right) The jazz soundtrack to one of the best-loved Christmas TV shows ever, *A Charlie Brown Christmas,* is almost 15 minutes longer than the show!

Label, Number		Title (A Side/B Side)	Year	VG	VG+	NM

H

HABAT, EDDIE
45s
Decca 45158		Santa Claus Polka/Ting-A-Ling-A-Jingle Waltz	195?	3.00	6.00	12.00

HACKETT, BUDDY
45s
Coral 61921		Dear Santa Claus/Funny Li'l Duck (That Just Says Moo)	1957	3.75	7.50	15.00

HADAWAY, HENRY, ORCHESTRA AND CHORUS
45s
RCA JH-13378	DJ	Turned On Winter Medley (same on both sides)	1982	—	2.00	4.00

HAGGARD, MERLE
45s
Capitol 3746		If We Make It Through December/	1973	—	2.50	5.00
		Bobby Wants a Puppy Dog for Christmas				
Capitol 3989		Santa Claus and Popcorn/If We Make It Through December	1974	—	2.00	4.00
Capitol Nashville S7-19346		White Christmas/Silver Bells	1996	—	—	3.00
Epic AE7 1777	DJ	Santa Claus and Popcorn/Grandma's Homemade Christmas Card	1982	—	2.50	5.00
Epic 03406		Goin' Home for Christmas/If We Make It Through December	1982	—	2.00	4.00

Albums
Capitol ST 11230		Merle Haggard's Christmas Present (Something Old, Something New)	1973	3.00	6.00	12.00
Capitol ST 11276		If We Make It Through December	1974	3.00	6.00	12.00
— Contains one Christmas song: If We Make It Through December						
Epic PE 38307		Goin' Home for Christmas	1983	2.50	5.00	10.00
MCA 2314		My Farewell to Elvis	1977	3.00	6.00	12.00
— Contains one Christmas song: Blue Christmas						

On Various-Artists Collections
Blue Christmas	Blue Christmas (Welk Music Group WM-3002)
Goin' Home for Christmas	Country Christmas (Time-Life STL-109)
If We Make It Through December	Country Christmas (Time-Life STL-109)
Jingle Bells	Wonderful World of Christmas, The, Album Two (Capitol Special Markets SL-8025)
Santa Claus and Popcorn	Christmas America, Album Two (Capitol Special Markets SL-6950)
Santa Claus Is Coming to Town	Christmas Greetings from Nashville (Columbia PC 39467)
Silver Bells	Christmas Songs, The (Capitol SLB-57074)
White Christmas	Nashville Christmas Album, The (Epic PE 40418)
	Nashville's Greatest Christmas Hits (Columbia PC 44412)
	Wonderful World of Christmas, The, Album Two (Capitol Special Markets SL-8025)

HALE, CORKY
45s
Columbia 44713	DJ	Christmas Day/Twinky (The Star That Couldn't Shine)	1968	2.50	5.00	10.00
— Stock copy may not exist						

HALL, DARYL, AND JOHN OATES
12-Inch Singles
RCA JM-13705	DJ	Jingle Bell Rock from Daryl/Jingle Bell Rock from John	1983	6.25	12.50	25.00
— Promo-only picture disc in plastic sleeve						
RCA JD-13983	DJ	Jingle Bell Rock (same on both sides)	1984	3.00	6.00	12.00

45s
RCA JR-14259	DJ	Jingle Bell Rock from Daryl/Jingle Bell Rock from John	1985	2.50	5.00	10.00
— Promo only on red vinyl						
RCA JR-14259	DJ	Jingle Bell Rock from Daryl/Jingle Bell Rock from John	1985	2.50	5.00	10.00
— Promo only on green vinyl						
RCA JR-14259	PS	Jingle Bell Rock from Daryl/Jingle Bell Rock from John	1985	2.50	5.00	10.00

HALL, DORA
45s
Calamo 1024		Blue Christmas/Rockin' Around the Christmas Tree	196?	2.00	4.00	8.00
Calamo 1024	PS	Blue Christmas/Rockin' Around the Christmas Tree	196?	2.00	4.00	8.00
Premore 1002		Give Me Your Heart for Christmas/Kissing by the Mistletoe	19??	—	2.00	4.00
Premore 1002	PS	Give Me Your Heart for Christmas/Kissing by the Mistletoe	19??	—	2.50	5.00
Premore 1024	PS	Rockin' Around the Christmas Tree/Blue Christmas	19??	—	2.50	5.00
Premore 1024		Rockin' Around the Christmas Tree/Blue Christmas	19??	—	2.00	4.00
— White label						
Premore 1024		Rockin' Around the Christmas Tree/Blue Christmas	19??	—	2.50	5.00
— Photo label						

Label, Number		Title (A Side/B Side)	Year	VG	VG+	NM
Premore 1280		Ole Tex Kringle/Great Big Friendly Town, Chicago	19??	—	2.00	4.00
Premore 1280	PS	Ole Tex Kringle/Great Big Friendly Town, Chicago	19??	—	2.00	4.00

HALL, FRANCES
45s
| Surf 5031 | | Christmas Lullaby/Jack in the Box | 1958 | 5.00 | 10.00 | 20.00 |

HALL, JIMMY
45s
| Cimarron 2767 | | Cowboy's Christmas/Steel Guitar Chimes | 198? | — | 2.00 | 4.00 |

HALL, SANDI
45s
| K-Tel KS-077 | DJ | A Christmas-y Day (same on both sides) | 1982 | — | 2.00 | 4.00 |

On Various-Artists Collections
| Christmas-y Day, A | | Heidi's Song (K-Tel NU 5310) | | | | |

HALL, TOM T.
45s
| Mercury 872 180-7 | | Let's Spend Christmas at My House/Let's Go Shopping Today | 1988 | — | — | 3.00 |
| RCA PB-11765 | | Christmas Is/Thanksgiving Is | 1979 | — | 2.00 | 4.00 |

HALLMAN, VICKI
45s
| Briar 123 | | Merry Christmas Time/Send My Daddy Home | 1961 | 2.50 | 5.00 | 10.00 |

HALLORAN, JACK, SINGERS
45s
Dot 16275		Mary's Little Boy Chile/Little Girl and Boy	1961	2.50	5.00	10.00
Dot 16410		The Little Drummer Boy/Mary's Little Boy Chile	1962	2.50	5.00	10.00
Reprise 245		The Christmas Star/What Can I Give Him	1963	2.50	5.00	10.00

HALSEY, JOHN, AND FRIEND
45s
| Warner Bros K 16867 | | Without Santa/The Wind Is Blowing | 1976 | 2.00 | 4.00 | 8.00 |

— B-side by Woolpit Carollers; U.K. import

HAMILTON, CHICO
On Various-Artists Collections
| Winter Wonderland | | Jingle Bell Jazz (Columbia PC 36803) | | | | |

HAMILTON, GEORGE, IV
45s
| RCA Victor 47-9775 | | Natividad (The Nativity)/The Little Grave | 1969 | 2.00 | 4.00 | 8.00 |
| RCA Victor 47-9937 | | Natividad (The Nativity)/The Little Grave | 1970 | — | 3.00 | 6.00 |

On Various-Artists Collections
| George Hamilton IV Show, The | | For Christmas Seals...A Matter of Life and Breath (Decca Custom Style F) | | | | |
| New Year's Greetings | | Christmas Greetings From RCA Victor And Groove Recording Artists (RCA Victor SP-45-128) | | | | |

HAMPTON STRING QUARTET
Albums
| RCA 5621-1-R | | What If Mozart Wrote | 1986 | 2.50 | 5.00 | 10.00 |
| | | "Have Yourself a Merry Little Christmas" | | | | |

HAMPTON, LIONEL
45s
| Decca 27325 | | Boogie Woogie Santa Claus/Merry Christmas | 1950 | 5.00 | 10.00 | 20.00 |

On Various-Artists Collections
| Merry Christmas Baby | | Stash Christmas Album, The (Stash 125) | | | | |
| White Christmas | | Jingle Bell Jazz (Columbia PC 36803) | | | | |

HANCOCK, HERBIE
On Various-Artists Collections
| Deck the Halls | | Jingle Bell Jazz (Columbia PC 36803) | | | | |

Label, Number		Title (A Side/B Side)	Year	VG	VG+	NM
HANEY, RAY						
45s						
MGM 12106	DJ	The Picture On The Christmas Card/Story Of A Christmas Tree	1955	3.00	6.00	12.00
HANK THE HOBO						
45s						
Lewis 9336		The Dutchman's Xmas Eve/The Night Before Xmas	19??	6.25	12.50	25.00
— Artist not identified on label; this is what he calls himself on the record						
HANNON, BOB						
On Various-Artists Collections						
Santa Claus Is Comin' to Town		First Christmas Record for Children (Harmony HS 14554)				
HANSEN BROTHERS, THE						
45s						
Crystal Ball 146		Doo Wop Jingle Bells/Christmas Peace	1981	—	2.00	4.00
HANSEN SISTERS, THE						
45s						
Rita 111		I Dreamt That Daddy Was Santa Claus/Cactus Pete	19??	—	2.00	4.00
HAPPENINGS, THE						
45s						
B.T. Puppy 181	DJ	Have Yourself a Merry Little Christmas (same on both sides)	1966	7.50	15.00	30.00
— Stock copies do not exist						
HAPPY CONTINENTALS, THE						
45s						
MGM 13402		Sleigh Ride Kisses/Hello Mr. Strauss	1965	2.00	4.00	8.00
HAPPY CRICKETS, THE						
Albums						
Grand Prix KX-9		Christmas with the Happy Crickets	1959	3.75	7.50	15.00
HAPPY ELVES, THE						
45s						
Garlin 101		Santa Got Stuck In The Chimney/(B-side unknown)	1960	3.00	6.00	12.00
HAPPY HARTS, THE						
45s						
Kapp 314		Let's All Sing a Song for Christmas/ I Want the South to Win the War for Christmas	1959	5.00	10.00	20.00
— B-side by Spike Jones and the City Slickers						
HAPPY JOE TORTILLA BAND						
45s						
World Enterprises 101		Just Because Polka/Senor Santa Claus	19??	—	2.50	5.00
HARDIN, TY						
On Various-Artists Collections						
It Came Upon a Midnight Clear		We Wish You a Merry Christmas (Warner Bros. W 1337)				
HARIAN, KENT, ORCHESTRA AND CHORUS						
45s						
Caravan 15502		Christmas Cha-Cha Choo Choo Train/Christmas Kiddie Polka	19??	3.00	6.00	12.00
HARLEM CHILDREN'S CHOIR, THE						
45s						
Commonwealth United 3003		Black Christmas/Do You Hear What I Hear	1969	2.50	5.00	10.00
Commonwealth United 3003	PS	Black Christmas/Do You Hear What I Hear	1969	3.75	7.50	15.00
HARLOW, JAN						
45s						
Popularity 701		Christmas/Indiana, Indiana	19??	2.00	4.00	8.00

Label, Number		Title (A Side/B Side)	Year	VG	VG+	NM
HARMONAIRES, THE						
45s						
Athena 6512/13		If I Had One Wish For Christmas/Impact	19??	2.00	4.00	8.00
HARMONIZING FOUR, THE						
45s						
Gotham 677		Silent Night/Sweet Little Jesus Boy	195?	3.00	6.00	12.00
HARMONY GRITS, THE						
45s						
End 1063		Gee/Santa Claus Is Coming to Town	1959	10.00	20.00	40.00
HARPER, HERMAN H., II						
45s						
Loadstone 3960		Waiting Up For Santa Claus/Headed For The Streets	1967	3.00	6.00	12.00
HARPER, TONI						
45s						
Columbia 39571		That's All I Want for Christmas/Mom and Dad's Waltz	1951	3.75	7.50	15.00
HARPO						
45s						
DJM 10723		Beautiful Christmas/Smile	1975	2.00	4.00	8.00
HARRINGTON, AL						
45s						
So. Pacific Man 100		I Want a Daddy for Christmas/Dream Away	19??	—	2.00	4.00
HARRIS, EMMYLOU						
45s						
Reprise 1341		Light of the Stable/Bluebird Wine	1975	2.50	5.00	10.00
— A-side is a longer version than later releases						
Reprise 1341	PS	Light of the Stable/Bluebird Wine	1975	3.00	6.00	12.00
Reprise 1379		Light of the Stable/Boulder to Birmingham	1976	—	2.50	5.00
Warner Bros. PRO-S-2872	DJ	Light of the Stable/It Came Upon a Midnight Clear	1987	2.50	5.00	10.00
— B-side by Highway 101						
Warner Bros. 29138		Someone Like You/Light of the Stable	1984	—	2.00	4.00
Warner Bros. 49633		Beautiful Star of Bethlehem/The Little Drummer Boy	1980	—	2.00	4.00
Warner Bros. 49645		Light of the Stable/The Little Drummer Boy	1980	—	2.00	4.00
Albums						
Warner Bros. BSK 3484		Light of the Stable: The Christmas Album	1979	2.50	5.00	10.00
On Various-Artists Collections						
Light of the Stable		Christmas Tradition, A (Warner Bros. 25630)				
HARRIS, GEORGIA, AND THE LYRICS						
45s						
Hy-Tone 111		Let's Exchange Hearts for Christmas/It's Time to Rock	1958	125.00	250.00	500.00
Hy-Tone 117		Let's Exchange Hearts for Christmas/Kiss, Kiss, Kiss	1958	125.00	250.00	500.00
HARRISON, GEORGE						
Also see THE BEATLES, TRAVELING WILBURYS.						
45s						
Apple 1879		Ding Dong, Ding Dong/Hari's on Tour (Express)	1974	5.00	10.00	20.00
— Black and white custom photo label						
Apple 1879		Ding Dong, Ding Dong/Hari's on Tour (Express)	1974	62.50	125.00	250.00
— Blue and white custon photo label						
Apple 1879	PS	Ding Dong, Ding Dong/Hari's on Tour (Express)	1974	5.00	10.00	20.00
Apple P-1879	DJ	Ding Dong, Ding Dong (remixed mono/edited stereo)	1974	10.00	20.00	40.00
Capitol 1879		Ding Dong, Ding Dong/Hari's on Tour (Express)	1978	2.00	4.00	8.00
— Purple late-1970s label						
HARRISON, HARRY						
45s						
Amy 944		Auld Lang Syne/May You Always	1965	2.50	5.00	10.00

Label, Number	Title (A Side/B Side)	Year	VG	VG+	NM
HART, FREDDIE					
45s					
Capitol 3789	Blue Christmas/I Believe in Santa Claus	1973	—	2.00	4.00
HART, JOHN					
On Various-Artists Collections					
O Tannenbaum	Yule Struttin' — A Blue Note Christmas (Blue Note 1P 8119)				
HARVEY, ALEX					
45s					
Capitol 3493	Good Time Christmas/Someone Who Cares	1972	—	2.00	4.00
— With Son Lex					
HARVIE JUNE VAN					
45s					
Kapp 875	Natividad (Nativity)/Dasher	1967	2.00	4.00	8.00
Kapp 2066	Natividad (Nativity)/Dasher	1969	—	3.00	6.00
HATHAWAY, DONNIE					
45s					
Atco 6799	This Christmas/Be There	1970	2.00	4.00	8.00
Atco 7066	This Christmas/Be There	1975	—	2.50	5.00
Atco 7320	This Christmas/Be There	1980	—	2.00	4.00
Atco 99956	This Christmas/Be There	1982	—	2.00	4.00
On Various-Artists Collections					
This Christmas	Jingle Bell Rock (Time-Life SRNR-XM)				
HATTON SISTERS, THE					
45s					
Skyway 115	Seasons Greetings/On Catalina	19??	2.00	4.00	8.00
HAURAKI GOOD GUYS WITH SALTY DOGG, THE					
45s					
Family 1113	Please Daddy Don't Get Drunk This Christmas/ I Saw Mama Kissin' Santa Claus	19??	2.00	4.00	8.00
— U.K. import					
HAWK, EDDIE					
45s					
Skokie 11034	Poor Little Christmas Tree/Cast	19??	—	2.50	5.00
HAWKINS, BOYCE					
7-Inch Extended Plays					
Hawk 321	Deck the Halls/Rudolph the Red-Nosed Reindeer// Santa Claus Is Coming to Town/Jingle Bells/White Christmas	19??	—	2.00	4.00
HAWKS, EDDIE					
45s					
Mercury 6367	Santa Claus Is Coming To Town/Jingle Bells	1951	3.75	7.50	15.00
HAWN, KATHY					
45s					
Accent 1163	I Want a Lotta Love for Christmas/I Wanna Play House with You	196?	2.00	4.00	8.00
HAYES, ISAAC					
45s					
Enterprise 9006	The Mistletoe and Me/Winter Snow	1969	—	3.00	6.00
HAYES, RICHARD, AND KITTY KALLEN					
45s					
Mercury 5501	Silver Bells/A Bushel and a Peck	1950	3.75	7.50	15.00
Mercury 5532	Silver Bells/Jing-a-Ling	1950	3.75	7.50	15.00
HAYES, ROLAND					
Albums					
Vanguard VRS-7016	10 Christmas Carols of the Nations	195?	12.50	25.00	50.00

Label, Number		Title (A Side/B Side)	Year	VG	VG+	NM
HAYMAN, RICHARD						
45s						
Mercury 70514		Winter Wonderland/Vera Cruz	1954	3.00	6.00	12.00
HAYMES, DICK						
45s						
Decca 24120		Oh, Little Town Of Bethlehem/Joy To The World	1950	3.00	6.00	12.00
— Sides 1 and 2 of "Album No. 9-70"						
Decca 24121		Ave Maria/It Came Upon a Midnight Clear	1950	3.00	6.00	12.00
7-Inch Extended Plays						
Decca 9-70	(3)	Christmas Songs	1950	10.00	20.00	40.00
— Includes records (24120 and two others) and box						
Albums						
Decca DL-5022	10	Christmas Songs	1949	12.50	25.00	50.00
On Various-Artists Collections						
Christmas Dreaming (A Little Early This Year)		Christmas Through the Years (Reader's Digest RDA-143)				
First Noel, The		Decca 38170 (title unknown) (Decca DL 38170)				
It Came Upon a Midnight Clear		Decca 38170 (title unknown) (Decca DL 38170)				
O Little Town of Bethlehem		Christmas Through the Years (Reader's Digest RDA-143)				
Oh, Little Town of Bethlehem		Decca 38170 (title unknown) (Decca DL 38170)				
HAZA, OFRA						
On Various-Artists Collections						
Holiday I.D.		Winter Warnerland (Warner Bros. PRO-A-3328)				
HAZELWOOD, EDDIE						
45s						
Intro 6031		Blue Shadows on a White Christmas/Don't Baby Your Baby	195?	3.75	7.50	15.00
HEADROOM, MAX						
45s						
Chrysalis 44000		Merry Christmas Santa Claus (You're a Lovely Guy)/Gimme Shades	1985	2.00	4.00	8.00
Chrysalis 44000	DJ	Merry Christmas Santa Claus (You're a Lovely Guy) (same on both sides)	1985	—	2.00	4.00
Chrysalis 44000	PS	Merry Christmas Santa Claus (You're a Lovely Guy)/Gimme Shades	1985	2.50	5.00	10.00

HEART – See ANN AND NANCY WILSON.

Label, Number		Title (A Side/B Side)	Year	VG	VG+	NM
HEARTBEATS, THE						
45s						
Gee 1047		500 Miles to Go/After New Year's Eve	1958	10.00	20.00	40.00
— Red label						
Gee 1047		500 Miles to Go/After New Year's Eve	1958	5.00	10.00	20.00
— Gray label						
HEATH BROTHERS, THE						
On Various-Artists Collections						
Our Little Town		God Rest Ye Merry, Jazzmen (Columbia FC 37551)				
HEATHERTON, RAY						
45s						
Playtime 380		Rudolph the Red-Nosed Reindeer/Jolly Old Saint Nicholas	195?	—	3.00	6.00
— 7-inch 78 rpm						
Playtime 380	PS	Rudolph the Red-Nosed Reindeer/Jolly Old Saint Nicholas	195?		3.00	6.00
Playtime 381		Frosty the Snowman/Punkinhead (The Little Bear)	195?		3.00	6.00
— 7-inch 78 rpm						
Playtime 381	PS	Frosty the Snowman/Punkinhead (The Little Bear)	195?	—	3.00	6.00
On Various-Artists Collections						
'Twas the Night Before Christmas, Part One/Part Two		First Christmas Record for Children (Harmony HS 14554)				
Parade of the Wooden Soldiers		Child's Christmas, A (Harmony HS 14563)				
HEAVEN AND EARTH						
45s						
Ovation 1038		Home for Christmas/Country Women	1972	—	2.50	5.00
Ovation 1038	PS	Home for Christmas/Country Women	1972	—	3.00	6.00

Label, Number	Title (A Side/B Side)	Year	VG	VG+	NM

HEAVY DUCK
45s

Derrick 113	This Christmas I Wanna	19??	—	2.50	5.00

HEBERT, ADAM
45s

Swallow 10116	Christmas Blues/Donnez Moi Colinda	19??	—	2.50	5.00

HEDGES, MICHAEL
On Various-Artists Collections

Prelude to Cello Suite #1 in G Major	Winter's Solstice II, A (Windham Hill WH-1077)

HELLO DISASTER
On Various-Artists Collections

I'll Be Home for Christmas	Stuff This in Your Stocking! Elves in Action (Veebltronics/Skyclad 68)

HELMS, BOBBY
45s

Certron 10021	Jingle Bell Rock/The Old Year Is Gone	1970	—	2.50	5.00
Decca 30513	Jingle Bell Rock/Captain Santa Claus	1957	6.25	12.50	25.00
— Black label with star					
Decca 30513 PS	Jingle Bell Rock/Captain Santa Claus	1957	12.50	25.00	50.00
Decca 30513	Jingle Bell Rock/Captain Santa Claus	1960	3.00	6.00	12.00
— Black label with color bars					
Kapp 719	Jingle Bell Rock/The Bell That Couldn't Jingle	1965	2.00	4.00	8.00
Little Darlin' 0038	Jingle Bell Rock/I Wanta Go to Santa Claus Land	1967	2.50	5.00	10.00
Little Darlin' 7809	Jingle Bell Rock/I Wanta Go to Santa Claus Land	1978	—	2.00	4.00
MCA 65026	Jingle Bell Rock/Captain Santa Claus	1973	—	2.00	4.00
— Black label with rainbow					
MCA 65026	Jingle Bell Rock/Captain Santa Claus	1980	—	—	3.00
— Blue label with rainbow					
MCA 65029	Jingle Bell Rock/The Bell That Couldn't Jingle	1973	—	2.00	4.00
— Black label with rainbow; this contains the 1965 Kapp re-recording of the A-side					
MCA 65029	Jingle Bell Rock/The Bell That Couldn't Jingle	1980	—	—	3.00
— Blue label with rainbow					
Mistletoe 802	Jingle Bell Rock/Jingle Bells	19??	—	2.50	5.00

On Various-Artists Collections

Jingle Bell Rock	Best of Christmas (Mistletoe MLP-1209)
	Billboard Greatest Christmas Hits, 1955-Present (Rhino R1 70636)
	Christmas Through the Years (Reader's Digest RDA-143)
	Jingle Bell Rock (Time-Life SRNR-XM)
	Rockin' Christmas — The '50s (Rhino RNLP-066)
	Rockin' Little Christmas (MCA 25084)
	Time-Life Treasury of Christmas, The (Time-Life STL-107)
	12 Hits of Christmas (United Artists UA-LA669-R)
Jingle Bells	Best of Christmas (Mistletoe MLP-1209)

HENDERSON, FLORENCE
On Various-Artists Collections

My Favorite Things	Happy Holidays, Vol. III (RCA Victor PRS-255)

HENDERSON, SKITCH
On Various-Artists Collections

Medley: Hark! The Herald Angels Sing/	For a Musical Merry Christmas, Vol. Two (RCA Victor PRM 189)
God Rest Ye Merry, Gentlemen	Happy Holidays, Vol. III (RCA Victor PRS-255)
	Merry Christmas (RCA Victor PRM-168)
Merry Bells, The	Merriest Time!, The (Sesac 35)
We Need a Little Christmas	Very Merry Christmas, A, Volume Two (Columbia Special Products CSS 788)

HENDRICKS, BELFORD
45s

Mercury 71556	This Time of the Year/Ask Any Fool	1959	3.00	6.00	12.00

HENDRIX SINGERS, THE
45s

Excello 2001	Away in the Manger/O Come All Ye Faithful	1952	5.00	10.00	20.00

Label, Number		Title (A Side/B Side)	Year	VG	VG+	NM
HENDRIX, BILL						
45s						
Film City 1077		Sharing Christmas with You/I Wish I Was Santa Claus	19??	3.00	6.00	12.00
HENDRIX, JIMI						
45s						
Reprise PRO 595	DJ	Medley: The Little Drummer Boy-Silent Night/Auld Lang Syne	1974	45.00	90.00	180.00
Reprise PRO 595	PS	...And a Happy New Year	1974	30.00	60.00	120.00
HENRY, JIM						
45s						
Unique 0003		Daddy Used To Tell Me/Christmas Cheer	198?	—	2.00	4.00
HEPSTERS, THE						
45s						
Ronel 107		Rockin' N' Rollin' with Santa Claus/I Had To Let You Go	1955	100.00	200.00	400.00
Xmas 3711		Rockin' & Rollin' With Santa/Sleigh Bell Rock	19??	2.00	4.00	8.00

— B-side by Three Aces and a Joker; reissue of rare R&B sides

HERMAN, PEE-WEE
On Various-Artists Collections

Christmas Medley	Winter Warnerland (Warner Bros. PRO-A-3328)
Don't Drink and Drive, Duh	Winter Warnerland (Warner Bros. PRO-A-3328)
Pee-wee Wilbury I.D.	Winter Warnerland (Warner Bros. PRO-A-3328)

Label, Number		Title (A Side/B Side)	Year	VG	VG+	NM
HESS, TROY						
45s						
Janalyn 1970		Christmas on the Moon/I Dreamed About Christmas	1970	2.50	5.00	10.00
HESTER, BILL, CARAVAN						
45s						
Musicor 1452		Little Drummer Boy/(B-side unknown)	1971	—	3.00	6.00
HESTON, CHARLTON						
45s						
Vanguard 35011		The Virgin Mary Had One Son/The Baptism of Christ	1961	3.00	6.00	12.00
HEWITT, DOLPH						
45s						
Janie 460		If You Are Present at Christmas/Look Into Your Heart	195?	3.00	6.00	12.00
HI FI						
45s						
SP&S 600		It's Almost Christmas/(B-side unknown)	19??	—	2.00	4.00
SP&S 600	PS	It's Almost Christmas	19??	—	2.00	4.00

HI-LO'S, THE
On Various-Artists Collections

Deck the Halls	Have Yourself a Merry Little Christmas (Reprise R 50001)
Star Carol, The	Seasons Greetings (A Christmas Festival of Stars) (Columbia CS 8189)
	Spirit of Christmas, The (Columbia Special Products CSP 249)

Label, Number		Title (A Side/B Side)	Year	VG	VG+	NM
HIBBLER, AL						
45s						
Decca 30127		White Christmas/Silent Night	1956	3.75	7.50	15.00
HICKOIDS, THE						
45s						
Toxic Shock 014		We Got The Eggnog If You Got The Whiskey/Frosty Blue Christmas	1989	—	2.00	4.00
— Green vinyl						
Toxic Shock 014	PS	We Got The Eggnog If You Got The Whiskey/Frosty Blue Christmas	1989	—	3.00	6.00

HIGBIE, BARBARA, AND EMILY KLION
On Various-Artists Collections
Flute Sonata in E minor, 3rd Movement Winter's Solstice II, A (Windham Hill WH-1077)

Label, Number	Title (A Side/B Side)	Year	VG	VG+	NM

HIGH HOPES, THE
45s

Jazy Bea 1975	Jingle Bell Time Ring Ding/Winter Champagne	1975	—	3.00	6.00

HIGH ON "POPS" ORCHESTRA, THE
45s

Parade 111	Up On Holidays/Holiday Medley	198?	—	—	3.00

HIGH, RAY "WEATHER MAN"
On Various-Artists Collections

Ahameric Ismas	Ital Christmas (Top Ranking (no #))
Bionic Christmas	Ital Christmas (Top Ranking (no #))
Ismas Drew	Ital Christmas (Top Ranking (no #))
Rock This Christmas Rocker	Ital Christmas (Top Ranking (no #))
Twelve Days at G.P.	Ital Christmas (Top Ranking (no #))

HIGHWAY 101
45s

Warner Bros. PRO-S-2872 DJ	It Came Upon a Midnight Clear/Light of the Stable	1987	2.50	5.00	10.00
— B-side by Emmylou Harris					

On Various-Artists Collections

Blue Christmas	Christmas Tradition, A, Volume II (Warner Bros. 25762)
It Came Upon a Midnight Clear	Christmas Tradition, A (Warner Bros. 25630)

HILDEGARDE
45s

Yuletide 752	Christmas Is Christmas All Over the World/(Instrumental)	19??	—	2.00	4.00

HILL, DAVID
45s

RCA Victor 47-7430	Christmas in Your Heart/Christmas Bride	1958	3.00	6.00	12.00

HILLSIDE SINGERS, THE
On Various-Artists Collections

Christmas Is...	Christmas Is... (Columbia Special Products P 11417)
Christmas Is... (Reprise)	Christmas Is... (Columbia Special Products P 11417)

HINES, JEROME
On Various-Artists Collections

Holy City, The	Joyous Noel (Reader's Digest RDA-57A)

HINES, MIMI
45s

RCA Victor 47-7646	Santa Baby/I Saw Mommy Kissing Santa Claus	1959	3.00	6.00	12.00

On Various-Artists Collections

I Saw Mommy Kissing Santa Claus	Joyous Noel (Reader's Digest RDA-57A)
Rudolph, the Red-Nosed Reindeer	For a Musical Merry Christmas, Volume 3 (RCA Victor PRM-221)

HINSON, JIMBEAU
45s

American Romance 29	Mistletoe Time/When You Give It Away	19??	—	—	3.00
— B-side by Michael Foster; red vinyl					
American Romance 29 PS	Mistletoe Time/When You Give It Away	19??	—	—	3.00
— B-side by Michael Foster					

HIPSCO MYSTERY BAND, THE
45s

Shadow 3351	Disco Christmas/Native West Banker	1978	2.00	4.00	8.00
Shadow 3351 PS	Disco Christmas/Native West Banker	1978	2.00	4.00	8.00

HIPSTERS, THE
On Various-Artists Collections

Rockin' and Rollin' with Santa Claus	Rockin' Christmas — The '50s (Rhino RNLP-066)

HIRT, AL
45s

RCA Victor 47-8478	Hooray for Santa Claus/White Christmas	1964	3.00	6.00	12.00
RCA Victor 47-8478 PS	Hooray for Santa Claus/White Christmas	1964	3.75	7.50	15.00

Label, Number		Title (A Side/B Side)	Year	VG	VG+	NM
RCA Victor 47-8706		Nutty Jingle Bells/Santa Claus Is Comin' to Town	1965	2.50	5.00	10.00
RCA Victor 47-8706	PS	Nutty Jingle Bells/Santa Claus Is Comin' to Town	1965	3.00	6.00	12.00
Albums						
RCA Victor LPM-3417	M	The Sound of Christmas	1965	2.50	5.00	10.00
RCA Victor LSP-3417	S	The Sound of Christmas	1965	3.00	6.00	12.00
On Various-Artists Collections						
Christmas Greetings		Christmas Greetings From RCA Victor And Groove Recording Artists (RCA Victor SP-45-128)				
Here Comes Santa Claus		Christmas in California (RCA Victor PRS-276)				
		Christmas in New York Volume 2 (RCA Victor PRS-270)				
		Christmastime in Carol and Song (RCA PRM-271)				
New Year's Greetings		Christmas Greetings From RCA Victor And Groove Recording Artists (RCA Victor SP-45-128)				
Silver Bells		Music to Trim Your Tree By (RCA Victor PRM 225)				

HITCH, MICHAEL
45s

Label, Number		Title (A Side/B Side)	Year	VG	VG+	NM
NSD 212		Alone At Christmas/	1984	—	2.00	4.00
		There Was Always Something Special At Christmas				

HIX, LENA
45s

Label, Number		Title (A Side/B Side)	Year	VG	VG+	NM
Cap Tone 0012		Christmas Memories/I Want My Daddy For Christmas	19??	—	2.00	4.00

HO, DON
45s

Label, Number		Title (A Side/B Side)	Year	VG	VG+	NM
Hel 149		Christmas Is for Everyone/Christmas Is You and Me	1977	—	2.00	4.00
Hel 149	PS	Christmas Is for Everyone/Christmas Is You and Me	1977	—	2.00	4.00

HODGES, JESSE
45s

Label, Number		Title (A Side/B Side)	Year	VG	VG+	NM
Fable 603		I Think It's Almost Christmas Time/My Christmas Prayer	19??	—	3.00	6.00
— B-side by Donna Zuker						

HOGG, SMOKEY
45s

Label, Number		Title (A Side/B Side)	Year	VG	VG+	NM
Specialty 753		I Want My Baby for Christmas/I Want My Baby for Christmas	197?	2.50	5.00	10.00
— B-side by Jimmy Liggins						

HOLBROOK, TINA MARIA
45s

Label, Number		Title (A Side/B Side)	Year	VG	VG+	NM
Holiday 0001		If Santa Retires/(B-side unknown)	198?	—	2.00	4.00

HOLDEN, RON
45s

Label, Number		Title (A Side/B Side)	Year	VG	VG+	NM
Donna 1331		Who Says There Ain't No Santa Claus/Your Line Is Busy	1960	6.25	12.50	25.00
On Various-Artists Collections						
Who Says There Ain't No Santa Claus		Rockin' Christmas — The '50s (Rhino RNLP-066)				

HOLIDAY BELLS, THE
Albums

Label, Number		Title (A Side/B Side)	Year	VG	VG+	NM
Kapp KL-1155	M	Ring the Bells on Christmas Day	1959	3.75	7.50	15.00

HOLIDAY SINGERS, THE
On Various-Artists Collections

First Noel, The	Waltons' Christmas Album, The (Columbia KC 33193)
God Rest Ye Merry, Gentlemen	Waltons' Christmas Album, The (Columbia KC 33193)
Hark the Herald Angels Sing	Waltons' Christmas Album, The (Columbia KC 33193)
It Came Upon a Midnight Clear	Waltons' Christmas Album, The (Columbia KC 33193)
Joy to the World	Waltons' Christmas Album, The (Columbia KC 33193)
O Come All Ye Faithful	Waltons' Christmas Album, The (Columbia KC 33193)
O Little Town of Bethlehem	Waltons' Christmas Album, The (Columbia KC 33193)
Silent Night	Waltons' Christmas Album, The (Columbia KC 33193)

HOLIDAY STRINGS, THE
Albums

Label, Number		Title (A Side/B Side)	Year	VG	VG+	NM
Diplomat X 1717	M	Silent Night	196?	3.00	6.00	12.00
Diplomat SX 1717	S	Silent Night	196?	3.75	7.50	15.00

Label, Number	Title (A Side/B Side)	Year	VG	VG+	NM
HOLIDAY, GEORGIE					
45s					
Date 1541	Have a Gluey Christmas/Clarence the Cross-Eyed Bear	1966	3.00	6.00	12.00
— As " 'Little' Georgie Holiday"					
Map City 302	Have a Gluey Christmas/A Little Boy's Christmas Prayer	1969	2.50	5.00	10.00
HOLIDAYS, THE					
45s					
Monument 431	Merry Christmas Song/A Very Merry Christmas	1960	3.75	7.50	15.00
HOLLARAN SINGERS					
On Various-Artists Collections					
We Wish You a Merry Christmas	12 Days of Christmas, The (Pickwick SPC-1021)				
HOLLOWAY, BOBBY					
45s					
Smash 2137	Funky Little Drummer Boy/Cornbread, Hog Maw, and Chitterlin's	1967	2.50	5.00	10.00
HOLLOWAY, STERLING					
45s					
Disneyland 127	Mouse Square Dance/Jingle Bells	19??	2.50	5.00	10.00
HOLLY TWINS, THE					
45s					
Liberty 55048	I Want Elvis for Christmas/The Tender Age	1956	12.50	25.00	50.00
HOLLYHILL SINGERS, THE					
45s					
Valiant 6061	The Virgin Mary Had a Little Baby/Hanukkah	1964	4.00	8.00	16.00
Valiant 734	The Virgin Mary Had a Little Baby/Hanukkah	1965	3.75	7.50	15.00
HOLLYRIDGE STRINGS, THE					
45s					
Capitol 5533	Santa's Got a Brand New Bag/Have Yourself a Merry Little Christmas	1965	2.50	5.00	10.00
Albums					
Capitol T 2404 M	Christmas Favorites	1965	3.00	6.00	12.00
Capitol ST 2404 S	Christmas Favorites	1965	3.75	7.50	15.00
On Various-Artists Collections					
Christmas Song, The	Happy Holidays, Album 6 (Capitol Creative Products SL-6669)				
	Sound of Christmas, The (Capitol Creative Products SL-6515)				
Have Yourself a Merry Little Christmas	Spirit of Christmas, The (Capitol Creative Products SL-6516)				
Jingle Bells	Christmas Carousel (Capitol SQBE-94406)				
	Little Drummer Boy, The (Capitol/Pickwick SPC-3462)				
Santa Claus Is Coming to Town	Christmas to Remember, A, Vol. 3 (Capitol Creative Products SL-6681)				
White Christmas	Spirit of Christmas, The (Capitol Creative Products SL-6516)				
HOLLYTONES, THE					
45s					
Eaglestone 1601	Gridlock Christmas/	1988	—	—	3.00
	How's Santa Gonna Find Us (In The Fallout Shelter)				
Eaglestone 1601 PS	Gridlock Christmas/	1988	—	—	3.00
	How's Santa Gonna Find Us (In The Fallout Shelter)				
HOLLYWOOD BOWL SYMPHONY ORCHESTRA					
On Various-Artists Collections					
Deck the Hall	Christmas Songs, The (Capitol SLB-57074)				
	Christmas to Remember, A (Capitol Creative Products SL-6573)				
	Zenith Presents Christmas, A Gift of Music (Capitol Creative Products SL-6544)				
Hark, the Herald Angels Sing	Christmas, A Gift of Music (Capitol Special Markets SL-6687)				
	Christmas to Remember, A (Capitol Creative Products SL-6573)				
	Happy Holidays, Vol. 5 (Capitol Creative Products SL-6627)				
	Happy Holly Days (Capitol Creative Products SL-6761)				
	Sound of Christmas, The, Vol. 3 (Capitol Creative Products SL-6680)				
	Zenith Presents Christmas, A Gift of Music Vol. 4 (Capitol Creative Products SL-6687)				
Joy to the World	Christmas Songs, The (Capitol SLB-57074)				
	Sound of Christmas, The (Capitol Creative Products SL-6515)				
O Tannenbaum	Christmas — The Season of Music (Capitol Creative Products SL-6679)				
	Christmas Stocking (Capitol NP 90494)				
	Zenith Presents Christmas, A Gift of Music Vol. 3 (Capitol Creative Products SL-6659)				
Silent Night	Zenith Presents Christmas, A Gift of Music (Capitol Creative Products SL-6544)				
We Three Kings	Sound of Christmas, The (Capitol Creative Products SL-6515)				

Label, Number		Title (A Side/B Side)	Year	VG	VG+	NM
HOLLYWOOD JOE						
45s						
Nania 10122		White Christmas/Hello December	19??	—	2.50	5.00
— *White vinyl*						
Nania 10122		White Christmas/Hello December	19??	—	2.00	4.00
— *Black vinyl*						
Nania 10122	PS	White Christmas/Hello December	19??	—	2.50	5.00

HOLLYWOOD POPS ORCHESTRA
On Various-Artists Collections

Adeste Fideles	Christmas with Glen Campbell and the Hollywood Pops Orchestra (Capitol Creative Products SL-6699)
	Let's Celebrate Christmas (Capitol Special Markets SL-6923)
Caroling, Caroling	Sound of Christmas, The, Vol. 2 (Capitol Creative Products SL-6534)
Christmas America - Suite No. 1	Christmas America, Album Two (Capitol Special Markets SL-6950)
Christmas America - Suite No. 2	Christmas America, Album Two (Capitol Special Markets SL-6950)
Christmas America — Part One	Christmas America (Capitol Special Markets SL-6884)
Christmas America — Part Two	Christmas America (Capitol Special Markets SL-6884)
Christmas Colors (Medley)	Sound of Christmas, The, Vol. 2 (Capitol Creative Products SL-6534)
Christmas Medley for Children, A	Very Merry Christmas, A, Volume VIII (Capitol Special Markets SL-6954)
Christmas Song, The	Happy Holidays, Album Seven (Capitol Creative Products SL-6730)
Dream of Toyland, A	Sound of Christmas, The, Vol. 2 (Capitol Creative Products SL-6534)
Holly and the Ivy, The	Christmas — The Season of Music (Capitol Creative Products SL-6679)
	Christmas with Glen Campbell and the Hollywood Pops Orchestra (Capitol Creative Products SL-6699)
	Zenith Presents Christmas, A Gift of Music Vol. 3 (Capitol Creative Products SL-6659)
Hymn to Christmas, A	American Christmas, An (Capitol Special Markets CP-68)
Jesu, Joy of Man's Desiring	Christmas America, Album Two (Capitol Special Markets SL-6950)
	Christmas — The Season of Music (Capitol Creative Products SL-6679)
	Zenith Presents Christmas, A Gift of Music Vol. 3 (Capitol Creative Products SL-6659)
Medley: Away in a Manger/ Silent Night/Caroling, Caroling	Christmas to Remember, A, Vol. 3 (Capitol Creative Products SL-6681)
Medley: Jingle Bells/Up on the House Top/Jolly Old St. Nicholas	Christmas with Glen Campbell and the Hollywood Pops Orchestra (Capitol Creative Products SL-6699)
	Happy Holidays, Album 6 (Capitol Creative Products SL-6669)
Medley: Toyland/March of the Toys	Joys of Christmas (Capitol Creative Products SL-6610)
Medley: Toyland/March of the Toys/ We Wish You a Merry Christmas	Happy Holidays, Album 6 (Capitol Creative Products SL-6669)
Medley: We Three Kings/We Wish You a Merry Christmas	Joys of Christmas (Capitol Creative Products SL-6610)
Over the River and Through the Woods	Christmas America (Capitol Special Markets SL-6884)
We Wish You a Merry Christmas	Sound of Christmas, The, Vol. 2 (Capitol Creative Products SL-6534)
Yule Medley	Sound of Christmas, The, Vol. 3 (Capitol Creative Products SL-6680)

Label, Number		Title (A Side/B Side)	Year	VG	VG+	NM
HOLLYWOOD, KENNY						
45s						
Billy K 211983		Sleigh Ride//The Christmas Song/Let It Snow	1983	—	2.00	4.00
HOLY COWS, THE						
45s						
Picnic Horn 8665		Winter Wonderland/Get Along	1991	—	2.50	5.00
Picnic Horn 8665	PS	Winter Wonderland/Get Along	1991	—	2.50	5.00
HOMEMADE THEATER						
45s						
A&M 1776		Santa Jaws (Part 1)/Santa Jaws (Part 2)	1975	3.75	7.50	15.00
A&M 1887		C.B. Santa/Soup of the Day	1976	3.75	7.50	15.00
HOMER AND JETHRO						
45s						
RCA Victor 47-5456		I Saw Mommy Smoochin' Santa Claus/ (All I Want for Christmas Is) My Upper Plate	1953	5.00	10.00	20.00
RCA Victor 47-5456	PS	I Saw Mommy Smoochin' Santa Claus/ (All I Want for Christmas Is) My Upper Plate	1953	7.50	15.00	30.00
RCA Victor 47-5903		The Night After Christmas/Santy Baby	1954	5.00	10.00	20.00
RCA Victor 47-6322		Nuttin' for Christmas/Santy's Movin' On	1955	5.00	10.00	20.00
7-Inch Extended Plays						
RCA Victor EPA 534		Randolph the Flat-Nosed Reindeer/ (All I Want for Christmas Is) My Upper Plate//I Saw Mommy Smoochin' Santa Claus/Frosty the De-Frosted Snow Man	195?	3.00	6.00	12.00
RCA Victor EPA 534	PS	Seasoned Greetings	195?	3.00	6.00	12.00
Albums						
RCA Victor LSP-4001		Cool, Crazy Christmas	1968	3.75	7.50	15.00

Label, Number	Title (A Side/B Side)	Year	VG	VG+	NM

On Various-Artists Collections

Night After Christmas, The	Merry Christmas And A Happy New Year (Modern Radio 102)				
Nuttin' for Christmas	Country Christmas (Time-Life STL-109)				

HONEY AND THE BEES
45s

Chess 2088	Jing Jing A Ling/Auld Lang Syne	1970	2.50	5.00	10.00
North Bay 303	Jing Jing A Ling/Auld Lang Syne	1970	3.00	6.00	12.00

HONEY DREAMERS, THE
45s

Columbia 40564	The Little Bell (That Just Went Ding)/ Rootie Tootie Tootie (The Kewtee Bear Song)	1955	2.50	5.00	10.00
Decca 31183	Jillfingle Bell Fells/Show Me The Way To Go Home	1960	2.00	4.00	8.00

On Various-Artists Collections

Wild Bells	Merriest Time!, The (Sesac 35)				

HONEYMOON SUITE
On Various-Artists Collections

I Believe in Father Christmas	Winter Warnerland (Warner Bros. PRO-A-3328)				

HONEYTREE
Albums

Birdwing BWR 2029	Merry Christmas	1981	3.00	6.00	12.00

HOOKER, JOHN LEE
45s

Elmor 303	Blues for Christmas/Big Fine Woman	1959	5.00	10.00	20.00
Hi-Q 5018	Blues for Christmas/Big Fine Woman	1960	5.00	10.00	20.00

HOPEFUL, THE
45s

Mercury 72637	7 O'Clock News (Silent Night)/ 6 O'Clock News (America The Beautiful)	1966	3.00	6.00	12.00

HOPKINS, HERNANDO
45s

ABC-Paramount 9973	Rudolph the Red Nose Reindeer Cha Cha/ Notre Dame Victory March Cha Cha	1958	3.00	6.00	12.00

HOPKINS, LIGHTNIN'
45s

Decca 48306	Merry Christmas/Happy New Year	1953	6.25	12.50	25.00
Sphere Sound 710	Santa/Black Mare Trot	196?	2.50	5.00	10.00

On Various-Artists Collections

Merry Christmas	Stash Christmas Album, The (Stash 125)				

HOPPER BROTHERS AND CONNIE
7-Inch Extended Plays

Trail 1884	God Rest Ye Merry, Gentlemen/Star of the East// C H R I S T M A S/Christmas Time's a-Comin'	19??	—	2.00	4.00

HOPPER, EVELYN
45s

Country Star 1009	It's Christmas/Watch Bird	19??	—	2.50	5.00

HORN, JIM
On Various-Artists Collections

Silver Bells	Christmas Tradition, A, Volume II (Warner Bros. 25762) Winter Warnerland (Warner Bros. PRO-A-3328)				

HORN, PAUL
On Various-Artists Collections

We Three Kings of Orient Are	Jingle Bell Jazz (Columbia PC 36803)				

Label, Number	Title (A Side/B Side)	Year	VG	VG+	NM

HORNE, LENA
45s

Label, Number	Title (A Side/B Side)	Year	VG	VG+	NM
Capitol S7-57888	Let It Snow! Let It Snow! Let It Snow!/Jingle Bells	1992	—	2.00	4.00
— B-side by Count Basie					
United Artists 1661	Let It Snow! Let It Snow! Let It Snow!/ What Are You Doing New Year's Eve	1966	2.50	5.00	10.00
— Silver Spotlight Series					
United Artists 1661 DJ	Let It Snow! Let It Snow! Let It Snow! (same on both sides)	1966	2.00	4.00	8.00
— Silver Spotlight Series promo					

On Various-Artists Collections

Jingle Bells	Great Songs of Christmas, Album Nine (Columbia Special Products CSS 1033)
Let It Snow! Let It Snow! Let It Snow!	Christmas Songs, The (Capitol SLB-57074)
	Joyous Songs of Christmas, The (Columbia Special Products C 10400)
	Time-Life Treasury of Christmas, The (Time-Life STL-107)
Winter Wonderland	Christmas Songs, The (Capitol SLB-57074)
	Great Songs of Christmas, Album Nine (Columbia Special Products CSS 1033)

HORNE, MARILYN
Albums

Label, Number	Title (A Side/B Side)	Year	VG	VG+	NM
CBS Masterworks IM 37836	Christmas with Marilyn Horne and the Mormon Tabernacle Choir	1983	2.50	5.00	10.00

HOROWITZ, VLADIMIR
On Various-Artists Collections

Christmas Tale for Children, A	Great Songs of Christmas, Album Nine (Columbia Special Products CSS 1033)

HORSE FEATHERS
7-Inch Extended Plays

Label, Number	Title (A Side/B Side)	Year	VG	VG+	NM
Rowena 1287	Get Your Reindeer Off My Roof/How Ya Do That, Santa Claus?// Do You Remember Me, Santa?/Me, My Dog 'N My Cat 'N My Bird	1987	—	2.00	4.00
— 7-inch 33 1/3 rpm					
Rowena 1287 PS	Get Your Reindeer Off My Roof/How Ya Do That, Santa Claus?// Do You Remember Me, Santa?/Me, My Dog 'N My Cat 'N My Bird	1987	—	2.00	4.00

HORSLIPS
Albums

Label, Number	Title (A Side/B Side)	Year	VG	VG+	NM
Horslips M 009	Drive the Cold Winter Away	1975	5.00	10.00	20.00
— U.K./Ireland import					

HORTON, JOHNNY
45s

Label, Number	Title (A Side/B Side)	Year	VG	VG+	NM
Columbia 41522	They Shined Up Rudolph's Nose/The Electrified Donkey	1959	3.75	7.50	15.00

HOUSER, WESLEY
45s

Label, Number	Title (A Side/B Side)	Year	VG	VG+	NM
Eubank ER 3	Christmas This Year/Turn Around	19??	—	2.00	4.00

HOUSTON, WHITNEY
On Various-Artists Collections

Do You Hear What I Hear	Very Special Christmas, A (A&M SP-3911)

HOVDE, RIEBER
45s

Label, Number	Title (A Side/B Side)	Year	VG	VG+	NM
Repeat 190	Jingle Bells/Norwegian Mode	19??	—	2.00	4.00

HOWARD, EDDY
45s

Label, Number	Title (A Side/B Side)	Year	VG	VG+	NM
Mercury 5516	I'll Be Home for Christmas/Dearest Santa	1950	3.75	7.50	15.00
Mercury 5722	Uncle Mistletoe/When Christmas Rolls Around	1951	3.75	7.50	15.00
Mercury 5752	There's a Christmas Tree/Auld Lang Syne	1951	3.75	7.50	15.00
Mercury 70272	Ebenezer Scrooge/Bimbo	1953	3.75	7.50	15.00
Mercury 70763	Round, Round the Christmas Tree/Silver Bells	1955	3.00	6.00	12.00
Mercury 71002	Uncle Mistletoe/Silver Bells	1956	3.00	6.00	12.00

HOWARD, MICHAEL
45s

Label, Number	Title (A Side/B Side)	Year	VG	VG+	NM
Keepsake 500	Home For Christmas/God's Little Angel	19??	—	2.00	4.00

Label, Number		Title (A Side/B Side)	Year	VG	VG+	NM
HOWARD, RONNIE						
45s						
Big Top 3093		If Santa Fell/Give My Toy to the Boy Next Door	1961	3.75	7.50	15.00
HOWARD, STEVE						
45s						
Pal 1101		If You Knew How Long I've Been So Good For Christmas/	1969	2.00	4.00	8.00
		If You Knew How Long I've Been So Good For Christmas				
— B-side by Howie Stevie						
HOWES, SALLY ANN						
On Various-Artists Collections						
It Came Upon a Midnight Clear		Great Songs of Christmas, The, Album Eight (Columbia Special Products CSS 888)				
O Little Town of Bethlehem		Great Songs of Christmas, The, Album Seven (Columbia Special Products CSS 547)				
Toyland		Great Songs of Christmas, The, Album Seven (Columbia Special Products CSS 547)				
HUDSON AND LANDRY						
45s						
Dore 880		Frontier Christmas (Harlowe and The Mrs.)/The Soul Bowl	1972	2.50	5.00	10.00
HUGHES, LINDA						
45s						
Great Northwest 714		Elvis Won't Be Here For Christmas/Here Comes That Hurt Again	1977	2.00	4.00	8.00
HUGO AND LUIGI CHILDREN'S CHORUS						
45s						
RCA Victor SP-45-101	DJ	RCA Victor Special DJ Spots	1959	2.50	5.00	10.00
Albums						
RCA Victor LPM-2254	M	The Sound of Children at Christmas	1960	3.75	7.50	15.00
RCA Victor LSP-2254	S	The Sound of Children at Christmas	1960	5.00	10.00	20.00
On Various-Artists Collections						
Little Drummer Boy, The		For a Musical Merry Christmas (RCA Victor PR-149A)				
		For a Musical Merry Christmas, Vol. Two (RCA Victor PRM 189)				
		Happy Holidays, Volume IV (RCA Victor PRS-267)				
		October 1960 Popular Stereo Sampler (RCA Victor SPS-33-96)				
Medley: Hark! The Herald Angels Sing/Good King Wenceslas/God Rest Ye Merry, Gentlemen		Christmas Eve with Colonel Sanders (RCA Victor PRS-256)				
Medley: Silent Night/Jingle Bells		Music to Trim Your Tree By (RCA Victor PRM 225)				
Medley: We Wish You a Merry Christmas/Jingle Bells		Christmas Festival of Songs and Carols, Volume 2 (RCA Victor PRM-195)				
We Wish You a Merry Christmas		Happy Holidays, Vol. III (RCA Victor PRS-255)				
HUGO LARGO						
On Various-Artists Collections						
Medley: Angels We Have Heard on High/Gloria		Winter Warnerland (Warner Bros. PRO-A-3328)				
HUMAN DRAMA						
On Various-Artists Collections						
I Believe in Father Christmas		Stuff This in Your Stocking! Elves in Action (Veebltronics/Skyclad 68)				
HUMMINGBIRD						
45s						
Instant 3336		Hot Dog, You Must Be Santa Claus/(B-side unknown)	1972	—	3.00	6.00
HUMPERDINCK, ENGELBERT						
45s						
Epic AE7 1170	DJ	Christmas Song/Silent Night	1978	—	2.00	4.00
Epic AE7 1170	PS	Christmas Song/Silent Night	1978	—	2.00	4.00
Epic 50488		A Night to Remember/Silent Night	1977	—	2.00	4.00
Albums						
Epic PE 35031		Christmas Tyme	1977	3.00	6.00	12.00
Epic PE 36765		A Merry Christmas with Engelbert Humperdinck	1980	2.50	5.00	10.00
— Some copies of the record have a "JE" prefix						
Epic PE 39469		White Christmas	1984	2.50	5.00	10.00

Label, Number		Title (A Side/B Side)	Year	VG	VG+	NM
HUMPERS						
On Various-Artists Collections						
Run, Run, Rudolph		Happy Birthday, Baby Jesus (Sympathy For The Record Industry SFTRI 271)				
HUNGRY DUTCHMEN, THE						
12-Inch Singles						
Black Tulip BT0001		Lookin' For Santa/Caught Unprepared	1988	—	3.00	6.00
45s						
Flying A 19763		Lookin' For Santa/(I'll Be Glad When) Christmas Is Over	1988	—	2.50	5.00
— B-side by Bite the Wax Godhead; red vinyl						
Flying A 19763	PS	Lookin' For Santa/(I'll Be Glad When) Christmas Is Over	1988	—	2.50	5.00
— B-side by Bite the Wax Godhead						
HUNT SISTERS, THE						
45s						
Samson 415		Christmas Piggy (With the Apple in His Mouth)/Silent Night	1961	2.50	5.00	10.00
HUNT, GEORGE & ARLENE						
45s						
(no label) 2468		Silver Bells//White Christmas/Silent Night	19??	—	2.00	4.00
HUNTER, CHRISTINE						
45s						
Roulette 4589		Santa Bring Me Ringo/Where Were You Daddy	1964	3.75	7.50	15.00
HUNTER, RALPH, CHOIR						
On Various-Artists Collections						
Here We Come a-Wassailing		Family Christmas Collection, The (Time-Life STL-131)				
Santa Claus Is Comin' to Town		Christmas Programming from RCA Victor (RCA Victor SP-33-66)				
		October Christmas Sampler 59-40-41 (RCA Victor SPS-33-54)				
Twelve Days of Christmas, The		For a Musical Merry Christmas (RCA Victor PR-149A)				
		RCA Victor Presents Music for the Twelve Days of Christmas (RCA Victor PRS-188)				
Wassail Song		60 Christmas Classics (Sessions DVL2-0723)				
HUNTINGTON, KAY						
45s						
Metrobeat 4454		Christmas Stands for Love/Once More	1965	2.50	5.00	10.00
HURST, LARRY						
45s						
American Voice 7		Snowball and Mistletoe/The First Christmas Day	19??	—	2.00	4.00
HUSHTONES, THE						
45s						
20th Century Fox 559		Christmas Is Over/Christmas Is Over	1964	2.00	4.00	8.00
— B-side by Bernie Wayne						
HUSKY, FERLIN						
45s						
Capitol 2023		Christmas Dream/Christmas Is Holy	1967	2.00	4.00	8.00
Albums						
Capitol T 2793	M	Christmas All Year Long	1967	3.75	7.50	15.00
Capitol ST 2793	S	Christmas All Year Long	1967	3.75	7.50	15.00
HUSTON AND FRIENDS						
45s						
Ticfaw 11		Santa's a Bionic Man/Baby's Name	197?	2.00	4.00	8.00
HUTTON, JUNE						
45s						
Capitol F2318		Song of Sleigh Bells/I Had a Little Too Much to Dream	1952	3.75	7.50	15.00
HYLAND, BRIAN						
45s						
Dot 17061		It's Christmas Time Once Again/Words on Paper	1967	3.00	6.00	12.00

Label, Number		Title (A Side/B Side)	Year	VG	VG+	NM

I

IDLES, THE
45s
| Jayrem 715 | | No, No, No/Xmas Day | 19?? | 3.00 | 6.00 | 12.00 |

ILFORD GIRL'S CHOIR, THE
45s
| London 30155 | | Hark! The Herald Angels Sing/Jerusalem | 19?? | 2.00 | 4.00 | 8.00 |

IMPERIALS, THE
Albums
| Word 8237 | | Christmas with the Imperials | 198? | 2.50 | 5.00 | 10.00 |

IMPRESSIONS, THE
45s
| Cotillion 44211 | | Silent Night/I Saw Mommy Kissing Santa Claus | 1976 | — | 3.00 | 6.00 |
| Curtom SP-3 | DJ | Merry Christmas Happy New Year | 197? | 3.00 | 6.00 | 12.00 |

INCREDIBLE PENGUINS
12-Inch Singles
Mushroom 13232		Happy Xmas (War Is Over) (Extended Version)//	1985	3.75	7.50	15.00
		Happy Xmas (War Is Over) (Radio Mix)/				
		Happy Xmas (War Is Over) (Penguin Instrumental Mix)				

— U.K. import

INGRAM, JAMES
On Various-Artists Collections
| Holiday I.D. | | Winter Warnerland (Warner Bros. PRO-A-3328) | | | | |

INSIGHT, THE
45s
| Cascade 364 | | Please Come Home For Christmas/Out Of Sight | 1964 | 7.50 | 15.00 | 30.00 |

INTVELD, JAMES
45s
| Penny Ellen 2001 | | What's A Christmas Without An Angel/ | 198? | — | — | 3.00 |
| | | Christmas Just Ain't Christmas Without You | | | | |

— B-side by Dale Watson; green vinyl
| Penny Ellen 2001 | PS | What's A Christmas Without An Angel/ | 198? | — | — | 3.00 |
| | | Christmas Just Ain't Christmas Without You | | | | |

— B-side by Dale Watson

IRISH ROVERS, THE
45s
| Decca 32775 | | The Marvelous Toy/Marika's Lullaby | 1970 | — | 3.00 | 6.00 |

IRONSTRINGS, IRA
45s
| Warner Bros. 5117 | | Christmas Is for the Birds/Deck Them Halls | 1959 | 3.75 | 7.50 | 15.00 |

IRWIN, BIG DEE
45s
Dimension 1021		The Christmas Song/I Wish You a Merry Christmas	1963	3.75	7.50	15.00
— With Little Eva						
Imperial 66334		All I Want for Christmas Is Your Love//	1968	3.00	6.00	12.00
		By the Time I Get to Phoenix/I Say a Little Prayer				

— With Mamie Galore

ISABEL, DAVE
45s
| Sarg 109 | | Make Believe It's Christmas/Let's Down It Up Brown | 1957 | 3.75 | 7.50 | 15.00 |

(Top left) Never released to the general public, Daryl Hall and John Oates' remake of "Jingle Bell Rock" remains a popular radio staple. Any copy of the record (on red or green vinyl) or sleeve is rare. (Top right) Emmylou Harris' Christmas album from 1979 was named after "Light of the Stable," a song she made into a holiday perennial in 1975. (Bottom left) This Jimi Hendrix holiday promo from the 1970s is one of the most sought-after items in his catalog. (Bottom right) Burl Ives is best-known to Christmas fans for his narrator's role in the TV special "Rudolph the Red-Nosed Reindeer." Long before that, he recorded this holiday record for Columbia.

Label, Number		Title (A Side/B Side)	Year	VG	VG+	NM
ISHAM, MARK						
On Various-Artists Collections						
Tale of Two Cities, A		Winter's Solstice, A (Windham Hill WH-1045)				
ISLER. ELMER, SINGERS						
45s						
MMG 4		Hallelujah Chorus/All We Like Sheep	19??	—	2.00	4.00
IVES, BURL						
45s						
Columbia 4-124 (90138)		Grandfather Kringle/The 12 Days Of Christmas	1951	3.00	6.00	12.00
— Yellow-label "Chidren's Series" record						
Columbia 4-124 (90138)	PS	Grandfather Kringle/The 12 Days Of Christmas	1951	3.75	7.50	15.00
Columbia 44711	PS	Santa Mouse/Oh What a Lucky Boy Am I	1968	2.50	5.00	10.00
Columbia 44711		Santa Mouse/Oh What a Lucky Boy Am I	1968	—	3.00	6.00
Decca 25585		Twelve Days of Christmas/The Indian Christmas Carol	1962	2.50	5.00	10.00
Decca 28347		The Friendly Beasts/There Were Three Ships	1952	3.00	6.00	12.00
Decca 28348		Jesous Anatonia/What Child Is This	1952	3.00	6.00	12.00
Decca 28349		The Seven Joys of Mary (Part 1)/The Seven Joys of Mary (Part 2)	1952	3.00	6.00	12.00
Decca 28350		King Herod and the Clock/Down in Yon Forest	1952	3.00	6.00	12.00
Decca 31695		A Holly Jolly Christmas/Snow for Johnny	1964	2.50	5.00	10.00
MCA 31695		A Holly Jolly Christmas/Snow For Johnny	1989	—	2.50	5.00
— Double the NM value if insert is enclosed						
Monkey Joe MJ-1	DJ	The Christmas Legend of Monkey Joe/	19??	2.50	5.00	10.00
		It's Gonna Be A Mixed Up Xmas				
Albums						
Columbia CS 9728		Burl Ives Christmas Album	1968	3.00	6.00	12.00
Decca DL 4689	M	Have a Holly Jolly Christmas	1965	3.00	6.00	12.00
Decca DL-5428	10	Christmas Day in the Morning	1952	12.50	25.00	50.00
Decca DL 8391	M	Christmas Eve	1957	6.25	12.50	25.00
Decca DL 74689	S	Have a Holly Jolly Christmas	1965	3.75	7.50	15.00
Decca DL 78391	R	Christmas Eve	196?	2.50	5.00	10.00
MCA 15002		Have a Holly Jolly Christmas	1973	3.00	6.00	12.00
— Reissue of Decca 74689; black label with rainbow						
MCA 15002		Have a Holly Jolly Christmas	1980	2.00	4.00	8.00
— Blue label with rainbow						
On Various-Artists Collections						
Christmas Story, The		Merry Christmas from... (Reader's Digest RD4-83)				
		Very Merry Christmas, A, Volume 3 (Columbia Special Products CSS 997)				
Happy Birthday, Jesus		Spirit of Christmas, The, Volume III (Columbia Special Products CSS 1463)				
Holly Jolly Christmas, A		Popular Christmas Classics (Capitol Special Markets SL-8100)				
		Rudolph the Red-Nosed Reindeer (Decca DL 4815)				
		Time-Life Treasury of Christmas, The (Time-Life STL-107)				
Jingle Bells		Christmas Greetings (Columbia Special Products CSS 1433)				
O Holy Night		Country Christmas (Columbia CS 9888)				
O Little Town of Bethlehem		Country Style Christmas, A (Columbia Musical Treasury 3P 6316)				
		Home for the Holidays (MCA MSM-35007)				
Rudolph the Red-Nosed Reindeer		Rudolph the Red-Nosed Reindeer (Decca DL 4815)				
Santa Claus Is Coming to Town		Magic of Christmas, The (Columbia Musical Treasury P3S 5806)				
Silver and Gold		Rudolph the Red-Nosed Reindeer (Decca DL 4815)				
Twelve Days of Christmas, The		Child's Christmas, A (Harmony HS 14563)				
		Great Songs of Christmas, The (Columbia Special Products XTV 69406/7)				
		Happy Holidays, Album 8 (Columbia Special Products C 11086)				
		Home for Christmas (Columbia Musical Treasury P3S 5608)				
		Home for Christmas (Realm 2V 8101)				
		Very Merry Christmas, A (Columbia Special Products CSS 563)				

J

Label, Number		Title (A Side/B Side)	Year	VG	VG+	NM
JABLONSKI, SIR						
45s						
Ducan 1500		Jingle On Christmas Day/Merry Christmas Day	19??	5.00	10.00	20.00
JACK AND JONIE						
45s						
Jet 105		Bells Of Christmastime/Keep A Cozy Corner (In Your Heart For Me)	19??	—	2.50	5.00

Label, Number	Title (A Side/B Side)	Year	VG	VG+	NM
JACKIE AND JILL					
45s					
U.S.A. 791	I Want a Beatle for Christmas/Jingle Bells	1964	5.00	10.00	20.00
JACKKNIFE					
On Various-Artists Collections					
Santa Claus Never Forgets	Happy Birthday, Baby Jesus (Sympathy For The Record Industry SFTRI 271)				
JACKSON FIVE, THE					
Also see MICHAEL JACKSON.					
45s					
Motown 1174	Santa Claus Is Coming to Town/	1970	3.00	6.00	12.00
	Christmas Won't Be the Same This Year				
Albums					
Motown MS 713	Christmas Album	1970	6.25	12.50	25.00
Motown 5250ML	Christmas Album	1982	2.00	4.00	8.00
— Reissue of Motown 713					
On Various-Artists Collections					
Christmas Song, The	Motown Christmas, A (Motown 795V2)				
Frosty the Snowman	Motown Christmas, A (Motown 795V2)				
Give Love on Christmas Day	Motown Christmas, A (Motown 795V2)				
Have Yourself a Merry Little Christmas	Motown Christmas, A (Motown 795V2)				
I Saw Mommy Kissing Santa Claus	Jingle Bell Rock (Time-Life SRNR-XM)				
	Motown Christmas, A (Motown 795V2)				
Santa Claus Is Coming to Town	Motown Christmas, A (Motown 795V2)				
Someday at Christmas	Jingle Bell Rock (Time-Life SRNR-XM)				
JACKSON SOUTHERNAIRES, THE					
45s					
Malaco 1038	It's Christmas Time Again/Prayer For Christmas	1975	—	2.50	5.00
JACKSON TRIO, THE					
45s					
Hollywood 1046	Jingle Bell Hop/Love For Christmas	1955	6.25	12.50	25.00
On Various-Artists Collections					
Jingle Bell Hop	Merry Christmas Baby (Christmas Music for Young Lovers) (Hollywood HLP 501)				
	Merry Christmas Baby (Gusto/Hollywood K-5018-X)				
Love for Christmas	Merry Christmas Baby (Christmas Music for Young Lovers) (Hollywood HLP 501)				
	Merry Christmas Baby (Gusto/Hollywood K-5018-X)				
JACKSON, ALAN					
45s					
Arista 12372	I Only Want You for Christmas/Merry Christmas to Me	1991	—	2.00	4.00
Arista 12611	Honky Tonk Christmas/The Angels Cried	1993	—	—	3.00
Arista Nashville 13060	Rudolph the Red-Nosed Reindeer/We Three Kings (Star of Wonder)	1996	—	—	3.00
— B-side by Blackhawk					
Arista/Fox 10001	A Holly Jolly Christmas/I Only Want You for Christmas	1992	—	2.00	4.00
JACKSON, BILLY & THE CITIZEN BAND					
45s					
Party Time 05	Have A Happy Christmas ('Twas The Night Before Christmas)/	19??	—	2.00	4.00
	Have A Happy, Happy, Happy Christmas				
JACKSON, BULL MOOSE					
45s					
King 4493	I'll Be Home for Christmas/I Never Loved Anyone But You	1951	15.00	30.00	60.00
On Various-Artists Collections					
I'll Be Home for Christmas	Merry Christmas Baby (Gusto/Hollywood K-5018-X)				
JACKSON, FREDDIE					
45s					
EMI S7-19350	Christmas Forever/Lovin' Little Christmas	1996	—	—	3.00
— B-side on Charisma by Danny Tate					
RCA 64230	The Christmas Song/O Holy Night	1994	—	—	3.00
RCA 64231	One Wish/This Christmas	1994	—	—	3.00

Label, Number		Title (A Side/B Side)	Year	VG	VG+	NM

JACKSON, LEE, AND THE CADILLAC BABY SPECIALS
45s

Bea & Baby 119		The Christmas Song/The Christmas Song	1960	7.50	15.00	30.00
— B-side by Clyde Lasley						
Bea & Baby 121		Christmas Song/Santa Came Home Drunk	1960	7.50	15.00	30.00
— B-side by Clyde Lasley						

JACKSON, MAHALIA
45s

Apollo 235		Silent Night, Holy Night/Go Tell It On The Mountain	1951	5.00	10.00	20.00
Apollo 539		Silent Night/The Lord's Prayer	1959	3.75	7.50	15.00
Apollo 750		Silent Night/The Lord's Prayer	1962	3.00	6.00	12.00
Columbia 40777		Silent Night, Holy Night/Mary's Little Boy Chile	1956	3.75	7.50	15.00
Columbia 41055		Sweet Little Jesus Boy/A Star Stood Still	1957	3.00	6.00	12.00
Columbia 42633		Joy To The World!/Go Tell It On The Mountain	1962	2.50	5.00	10.00
Columbia JZSP 137705/6	DJ	Happy Birthday To You, Our Lord/Silver Bells	1968	—	2.50	5.00
Kenwood 750		Silent Night/The Lord's Prayer	1964	2.50	5.00	10.00
Nashboro 750	DJ	The Lord's Prayer/Silent Night	197?	—	2.00	4.00
— Reissue of Kenwood 750						

Albums

Columbia CL 702		Sweet Little Jesus Boy	1955	10.00	20.00	40.00
Columbia CL 1903	M	Silent Night	1962	3.75	7.50	15.00
Columbia CS 8703	S	Silent Night	1962	5.00	10.00	20.00
Columbia CS 9727		Christmas with Mahalia	1969	3.00	6.00	12.00
Columbia 3C 38304		Silent Night	1982	2.00	4.00	8.00
— Reissue						

On Various-Artists Collections

Abide with Me	Great Songs of Christmas, The, Album Four (Columbia Special Products CSP 155M)
Away in a Manger	Best of the Great Songs of Christmas (Album 10) (Columbia Special Products CSS 1478)
	Great Songs of Christmas, The, Album Six (Columbia Special Products CSM 388)
	Mahalia (Jackson) and Friends at Christmastime (Columbia Special Products P 11804)
Christmas Comes to Us All Once a Year	Merry Christmas (Columbia Musical Treasury 3P 6306)
Go Tell It on the Mountain	Carols and Candlelight (Columbia Special Products P 12525)
	Home for Christmas (Columbia Musical Treasury P3S 5608)
	Home for Christmas (Realm 2V 8101)
	Joy of Christmas, The (Columbia Special Products P 12042)
	Merry Christmas from... (Reader's Digest RD4-83)
	Ronco Presents A Christmas Gift (Columbia Special Products P 12430)
Hark! The Herald Angels Sing	Christmas Greetings (Columbia Special Products CSS 1499)
	Mahalia (Jackson) and Friends at Christmastime (Columbia Special Products P 11804)
Holy, Holy, Holy	Great Songs of Christmas, The, Album Four (Columbia Special Products CSP 155M)
It Came Upon a Midnight Clear	Joy to the World (30 Classic Christmas Melodies) (Columbia Special Products P3 14654)
Joy to the World	Joyous Christmas, Volume 6 (Columbia Special Products C 11083)
	Spirit of Christmas, The, Volume III (Columbia Special Products CSS 1463)
Mary's Little Boy Child	Silent Night... (Columbia Special Products P 14989)
O Come, All Ye Faithful	Wondrous Winter: Songs of Winter, Songs of Christmas
	(Columbia Special Products CSS 708/9)
O Holy Night	Collection of Christmas Favorites, A (Columbia Special Products P 14988)
O Little Town of Bethlehem	Mahalia (Jackson) and Friends at Christmastime (Columbia Special Products P 11804)
	Very Merry Christmas, A, Volume Two (Columbia Special Products CSS 788)
Silent Night	Joy to the World (30 Classic Christmas Melodies) (Columbia Special Products P3 14654)
	Mahalia (Jackson) and Friends at Christmastime (Columbia Special Products P 11804)
Silver Bells	Very Merry Christmas, A, Volume 3 (Columbia Special Products CSS 997)
Sweet Little Jesus Boy	Magic of Christmas, The (Columbia Musical Treasury P3S 5806)
What Child Is This	Mahalia (Jackson) and Friends at Christmastime (Columbia Special Products P 11804)

JACKSON, MICHAEL
Also see THE JACKSON FIVE.
On Various-Artists Collections

Little Christmas Tree	Motown Christmas, A (Motown 795V2)

JACKSON, STONEWALL
45s

Columbia 43917		Mommy Look, Santa Is Crying/Blue Christmas	1966	2.50	5.00	10.00

On Various-Artists Collections

Blue Christmas	Country Christmas (Columbia CS 9888)
	Country Style Christmas, A (Columbia Musical Treasury 3P 6316)

JACOBY, DON
45s

Constellation 1101		The Christmas Party/The Holy City	19??	—	2.00	4.00

Label, Number		Title (A Side/B Side)	Year	VG	VG+	NM
JAGUARS, THE						
45s						
Classic Artists 117		Happy Holiday/More Than Enough for Me	1989	—	2.50	5.00
— B-side by Johnny Staton and the Feathers						
Classic Artists 136		Merry Christmas, Darling/Lost and Found	1990	—	2.50	5.00
JAKUS, JEAN						
Albums						
London SW 99018		German Christmas Singalong	195?	3.75	7.50	15.00
JAMAL, AHMAD & LARRY GOSHORN						
45s						
Atlantic 89476	DJ	It's That Time Of Year Again (same on both sides)	1985	—	2.50	5.00
— May be promo only						
JAMES, ANDY						
45s						
Amjam 6623		Chester The Chubby Elf/Cool Yule	19??	—	2.00	4.00
JAMES, DENNIS, AND HIS BOYS AND GIRLS						
45s						
Kapp 126		Let's All Sing a Song for Christmas/Jingle Bells	1955	3.75	7.50	15.00
JAMES, JIMMY						
45s						
LMH 124		This Christmas Feeling/The Christmas Hustle	19??	—	—	3.00
LMH 124	PS	This Christmas Feeling/The Christmas Hustle	19??	—	—	3.00
JAMES, JONI						
45s						
MGM 11637		Christmas and You/Nina-Non	1953	5.00	10.00	20.00
MGM 12091		The Christmas Song/Have Yourself a Merry Little Christmas	1955	6.25	12.50	25.00
MGM 12368		White Christmas/I'll Be Home for Christmas	1956	5.00	10.00	20.00
Albums						
MGM E-3468	M	Merry Christmas from Joni	1956	30.00	60.00	120.00
— Yellow label original						
MGM E-3468	M	Merry Christmas from Joni	1960	15.00	30.00	60.00
— Black label reissue						
JAMES, SONNY						
45s						
Capitol F2958		Christmas in My Home Town/I Forgot to Remember Santa Claus	1954	5.00	10.00	20.00
Capitol 5733		My Christmas Dream/Barefoot Santa Claus	1966	2.00	4.00	8.00
Capitol 5733	PS	My Christmas Dream/Barefoot Santa Claus	1966	3.00	6.00	12.00
Albums						
Capitol ST 2589	S	My Christmas Dream	1966	6.25	12.50	25.00
Capitol T 2589	M	My Christmas Dream	1966	5.00	10.00	20.00
On Various-Artists Collections						
Medley: Silent Night/The First Noel		Happy Holidays, Album 6 (Capitol Creative Products SL-6669)				
O Little Town of Bethlehem		RFD Christmas (Columbia Special Products P 15427)				
JAN AND DEAN						
45s						
Liberty 55522		Frosty (The Snow Man)/(She's Still Talking) Baby Talk	1962	37.50	75.00	150.00
— Promos worth about half this value						
On Various-Artists Collections						
Frosty the Snowman		Christmas Songs, The, Volume II (Capitol SL-57065)				
		Jingle Bell Rock (Time-Life SRNR-XM)				
JANSE, DON, CHORALE						
Albums						
Design SDLP-X-13	S	The Little Drummer Boy	196?	3.00	6.00	12.00
Design SDLPX-25		Hark! The Herald Angels Sing	196?	3.00	6.00	12.00
— Reissue of International Award Series LP with same contents						
International Award Series AX-X5		Christmas Chorale	196?	3.75	7.50	15.00

Label, Number			Title (A Side/B Side)	Year	VG	VG+	NM
JANSEN, GUSS							
45s							
Arvee 5085			Mr. Snowman Goes To Town/Rudolph, The Red-Nose Reindeer	1963	3.00	6.00	12.00
JANSSEN, DANNY							
45s							
Stepheny 1843			Christmas All Alone/Winter Wonderland	1960	3.75	7.50	15.00
JARREAU, AL							
45s							
Warner Bros. 29446			The Christmas Song/Our Love	1983	—	2.00	4.00
Warner Bros. 29446	PS		The Christmas Song/Our Love	1983	—	2.50	5.00
Warner Bros. PRA	DJ		The Christmas Song//Al's Greeting/The Christmas Song	1983	—	2.50	5.00
Warner Bros. PRA	PS		The Christmas Song//Al's Greeting/The Christmas Song	1983	—	3.00	6.00
— Promo sleeve has blank green back							
JAY, ERIC							
45s							
Bullseye 1021			Little Drummer Boy/Silent Night	1959	3.00	6.00	12.00
JAY, JERRY							
California DJ, better known as Jerry Osborne.							
45s							
Quality 201			The King's Country/Merry Christmas To You	1966	25.00	50.00	100.00
JAY, PETER & COMPANY							
45s							
Kevane 4-4-44			Upside Down on the Christmas Tree/Little Angel	198?	—	2.00	4.00
Kevane 4-4-44	PS		Upside Down on the Christmas Tree/Little Angel	198?	—	2.00	4.00
JAYNELLS, THE							
45s							
Cameo 286			I'll Stay Home New Year's Eve/Down Home	1963	5.00	10.00	20.00
JAYNETTS, THE							
45s							
Tuff 374			Snowman, Snowman, Sweet Potato Nose/(Instrumental)	1963	3.75	7.50	15.00
JEANETTE, JOAN & KAY							
45s							
Teen-Ed 5			Christmas Time (Part 1)/Christmas Time (Part 2)	19??	3.00	6.00	12.00
JELVING, AKE							
Albums							
Capitol T 10079	M		Christmas in Sweden	195?	5.00	10.00	20.00
— Black label with colorband, logo on left							
Capitol T 10079	M		Christmas in Sweden	196?	3.75	7.50	15.00
— Black label with colorband, logo on top							
Capitol SP-10079	R		Christmas in Sweden	1969	2.50	5.00	10.00
— Reissue with new label and prefix							
Capitol SM-10079	R		Christmas in Sweden	197?	2.00	4.00	8.00
— Reissue with new label and prefix							
JENKINS, GORDON							
45s							
Capitol F1263			White Christmas/I'm Always Chasing Rainbows	1950	3.75	7.50	15.00
JENKINS, GUS							
45s							
Flash 116			Remember Last Xmas/Spark Plug	1956	5.00	10.00	20.00
JENNINGS, WAYLON, AND JESSI COLTER							
45s							
RCA PB-13903			Silent Night, Holy Night/Precious Memories	1984	—	2.00	4.00

Label, Number		Title (A Side/B Side)	Year	VG	VG+	NM
On Various-Artists Collections						
Silent Night, Holy Night		Best of Christmas, The (RCA Victor CPL1-7013)				
		Country Christmas, A, Volume 3 (RCA CPL1-5178)				

JENSEN, WENDY
45s

Label, Number		Title (A Side/B Side)	Year	VG	VG+	NM
Bumble-B 1004		There's A Beautiful Star On Our Christmas Tree/Tom, Dick And Harry	19??	—	2.00	4.00

JENSON, JIMMY
45s

Label, Number		Title (A Side/B Side)	Year	VG	VG+	NM
Bangar 0650		Walkin' in My Vinter Underwear/Copenhagen	1964	3.75	7.50	15.00
Bangar 0651		I Yust Go Nuts At Christmas/Yingle Bells	1964	3.75	7.50	15.00

JERRY AND THE LANDSLIDERS
45s

Label, Number		Title (A Side/B Side)	Year	VG	VG+	NM
Holiday 1026	DJ	Get Off My Roof/White Christmas	197?	3.00	6.00	12.00
— B-side by the Statues						

JESUS AND MARY CHORAL GROUP, THE
On Various-Artists Collections

Label, Number		Title (A Side/B Side)	Year	VG	VG+	NM
O Holy Night		It's Christmastime! (Columbia Special Products CSM 429)				
Twelve Days of Christmas, The		It's Christmastime! (Columbia Special Products CSM 429)				

JETER, REVEREND CLAUDE
45s

Label, Number		Title (A Side/B Side)	Year	VG	VG+	NM
HOB 1331		Christmas In Heaven/Only Believe	197?	—	2.50	5.00

JETHRO TULL
12-Inch Singles

Label, Number		Title (A Side/B Side)	Year	VG	VG+	NM
Chrysalis CHS 3 PDJ	DJ	Ring Out, Solstice Bells/March, The Mad Scientist//	1976	6.25	12.50	25.00
		Christmas Song/Pan Dance				

45s

Label, Number		Title (A Side/B Side)	Year	VG	VG+	NM
Chrysalis TULL 5		Another Christmas Song/Intro - A Christmas Song	1989	2.00	4.00	8.00
Chrysalis TULL 5	PS	Another Christmas Song/Intro - A Christmas Song	1989	2.00	4.00	8.00
— Record and sleeve are U.K. imports						
Chrysalis 2006		Living in the Past/Christmas Song	1972	—	3.00	6.00
— A-side is not a Christmas song						
Chrysalis S7-18211		Christmas Song/Skating Away on the Thin Ice of a New Day	1994	—	2.50	5.00
— Green vinyl						

7-Inch Extended Plays

Label, Number		Title (A Side/B Side)	Year	VG	VG+	NM
Chrysalis CXP 2		Ring Out Solstice Bells/March, The Mad Scientist//	1976	—	3.00	6.00
		Christmas Song/Pan Dance				
Chrysalis CXP 2	PS	Ring Out Solstice Bells/March, The Mad Scientist//	1976	—	3.00	6.00
		Christmas Song/Pan Dance				
— Above record and sleeve are U.K. imports						
Chrysalis CHS 2443		Ring Out Solstice Bells/March, The Mad Scientist//	1979	—	2.50	5.00
		Christmas Song/Pan Dance				
Chrysalis CHS 2443		Ring Out Solstice Bells/March, The Mad Scientist//	1979	—	2.50	5.00
		Christmas Song/Pan Dance				
— Record and sleeve are U.K. imports; reissue of CXP 2						

Albums

Label, Number		Title (A Side/B Side)	Year	VG	VG+	NM
Chrysalis 2CH 1035	(2)	Living in the Past	1972	5.00	10.00	20.00
— Two-record set with booklet; difficult to find intact. Contains one Christmas song: Christmas Song						

JETS, THE
45s

Label, Number		Title (A Side/B Side)	Year	VG	VG+	NM
MCA 53446		Anytime/Christmas in My Heart	1988	—	—	3.00
— A-side is not a Christmas song						

Albums

Label, Number		Title (A Side/B Side)	Year	VG	VG+	NM
MCA 5856		Christmas with the Jets	1986	2.50	5.00	10.00

On Various-Artists Collections

Label, Number		Title (A Side/B Side)	Year	VG	VG+	NM
I Cannot Forget		Starlight Christmas, A (MCA 10066)				
This Christmas		Happy Holidays, Vol. 23 (MCA Special Products 15042)				

JETT, JOAN, AND THE BLACKHEARTS
12-Inch Singles

Label, Number		Title (A Side/B Side)	Year	VG	VG+	NM
Boardwalk 005	DJ	Little Drummer Boy/Victim of Circumstance	1981	5.00	10.00	20.00
MCA L33-1247	DJ	I Love You Love/New Orleans/Little Drummer Boy	1984	3.75	7.50	15.00

Label, Number		Title (A Side/B Side)	Year	VG	VG+	NM
45s						
Boardwalk NBS-7-006	DJ	Little Drummer Boy (same on both sides)	1981	3.75	7.50	15.00
Albums						
Boardwalk NB1-33243		I Love Rock-n-Roll	1982	2.50	5.00	10.00
— First pressing contains one Christmas song, which was replaced on second pressings: Little Drummer Boy						

JIGGLES AND THE ZANIES
45s

Dore 692		Hello Santa/Case No. 9851	1963	3.00	6.00	12.00

JIGSAW SEEN, THE
45s

Skyclad 51		God Rest Ye Merry, Gentlemen/Jesus of Hollywood	19??	2.50	5.00	10.00
— Red vinyl						
Skyclad 51	PS	God Rest Ye Merry, Gentlemen/Jesus of Hollywood	19??	2.50	5.00	10.00
On Various-Artists Collections						
God Rest Ye Merry, Gentlemen		Stuff This in Your Stocking! Elves in Action (Veebltronics/Skyclad 68)				

JIM AND CATHY
45s

Cadet 5524		Santa's Got A Brand New Bag/People, Stand Back	1965	2.50	5.00	10.00

JIMENEZ, JOSE
45s

Kapp 434		Christmas Sing Along with Jose: Jingle Bells/ Sing Along with Jose: Shine On Harvest Moon	1961	3.75	7.50	15.00
Albums						
Kapp KL-1257	M	Jose Jimenez in Orbit — Bill Dana on Earth	1961	5.00	10.00	20.00
— Contains one Christmas song: Christmas Sing Along with Jose: Jingle Bells						

JIMMY
45s

Fatima FTM-82		White Christmas/Spin the Bottle	1982	—	2.00	4.00
Fatima FTM-82	PS	White Christmas/Spin the Bottle	1982	—	2.00	4.00

JINGLE BELLS
45s

Disneyland 731		Jingle Bells/From All of Us to All of You	19??	—	3.00	6.00
Disneyland 731	PS	Jingle Bells/From All of Us to All of You	19??	—	3.00	6.00

JINGOLEERS, THE
45s

Brunswick 55108		Christmas Morn/Jingle Bell Rock	1958	3.75	7.50	15.00

JODI
45s

Great 124		Beneath Our Christmas Tree (same on both sides)	19??	—	2.00	4.00

JOEL, BILLY
45s

Columbia 04681		Keeping the Faith (Special Mix)/She's Right On Time	1984	—	—	3.00
— A-side is not a Christmas song						
Columbia 04681	PS	Keeping the Faith (Special Mix)/She's Right On Time	1984	—	2.00	4.00
Albums						
Columbia QC 38200		The Nylon Curtain	1982	2.50	5.00	10.00
— Contains one Christmas song: She's Right on Time						

JOERGER, RODDY
45s

Cima 101		I Gotta Bone To Pick With Santa/(B-side unknown)	198?	—	2.00	4.00

JOEY AND DANNY
45s

Swan 4276		Santa's Got a Brand New Bag/Rats in My Room	1967	5.00	10.00	20.00

Label, Number		Title (A Side/B Side)	Year	VG	VG+	NM
JOHN, ELTON						
12-Inch Singles						
Rocket EJS 312		Cold As Christmas (In the Middle of the Year)/ Crystal/J'Veux De La Tendresse	1983	3.00	6.00	12.00
— U.K. import						
45s						
Geffen 29402		Cold As Christmas (In the Middle of the Year)/(B-side unassigned)	1983		*Unreleased*	
MCA 65018		Step Into Christmas/Ho! Ho! Ho! (Who'd Be a Turkey at Christmas)	1973	—	2.50	5.00
— Originals have black labels with rainbow						
MCA 65018		Step Into Christmas/Ho! Ho! Ho! (Who'd Be a Turkey at Christmas)	1978	—	2.00	4.00
— Second edition: Tan label						
MCA 65018		Step Into Christmas/Ho! Ho! Ho! (Who'd Be a Turkey at Christmas)	1980	—	—	3.00
— Third edition: Blue label with rainbow						
Rocket EJS 3		Cold As Christmas (In the Middle of the Year)/Crystal	1983	—	2.50	5.00
— U.K. import						
Rocket EJS 3	PS	Cold As Christmas (In the Middle of the Year)/Crystal	1983	—	2.50	5.00
— U.K. import; also came in a "double pack" with the Elton John/Kiki Dee single Don't Go Breakin' My Heart/Snow Queen (add $5 NM)						
7-Inch Extended Plays						
Rocket EJSX 25		Step Into Christmas/Cold As Christmas// Easier to Walk Away/I Swear I Heard the Night Talking	1990	—	2.00	4.00
Rocket EJSX 25	PS	The Xmas E.P.	1990	—	2.00	4.00
— Record and sleeve are U.K. imports						
Albums						
Geffen GHS 4006		Too Low for Zero	1983	2.50	5.00	10.00
— Contains one Christmas song: Cold As Christmas (In the Middle of the Year)						
On Various-Artists Collections						
Step Into Christmas		Christmas Rock Album, The (Priority SL 9465) Jingle Bell Rock (Time-Life SRNR-XM)				
JOHN, LEVI						
45s						
Ngsk 007		Season's Greetings/Christmas In The City	19??	—	2.00	4.00
JOHNNY AND JON						
45s						
Jewel 776		Christmas in Viet Nam/Why Did You Leave Me Crawl	1966	7.50	15.00	30.00
JOHNNY AND THE DWELLERS						
45s						
EMI SPRO 19949	DJ	Depression/Rudolf The Red-Nosed Reindeer	1994	—	2.50	5.00
— B-side by the Ventures						
EMI SPRO 19949	PS	Depression/Rudolf The Red-Nosed Reindeer	1994	—	2.50	5.00
JOHNNY AND THE HIGH KEYS						
45s						
Jamie 1383		The Christmas Game/Do You Believe	1969	2.00	4.00	8.00
JOHNS, SYLVIA						
45s						
Duchess 701		The Miracle of Christmas/Christmas on the Bayou	19??	—	2.00	4.00
Duchess 701	PS	The Miracle of Christmas/Christmas on the Bayou	19??	—	2.00	4.00
JOHNSON FAMILY, THE						
On Various-Artists Collections						
What a Friend We Have in Jesus		October Christmas Sampler 59-40-41 (RCA Victor SPS-33-54)				
JOHNSON, BAYN						
45s						
RPI 105		Christmas Teddy Bear/Santa's Letter	1976	—	2.50	5.00
JOHNSON, BETTY						
45s						
New-Disc 10013		I Want Eddie Fisher For Christmas/Show Me	1954	6.25	12.50	25.00
JOHNSON, BRUCE						
45s						
MacGregor 2046		Jingle Bells/(Instrumental)	19??	—	2.00	4.00

Label, Number	Title (A Side/B Side)	Year	VG	VG+	NM

JOHNSON, BUBBER
45s

King 4855	It's Christmas Time/Let's Make Everyday a Christmas Day	1955	5.00	10.00	20.00

JOHNSON, DEREK,'S VOCAL ORCHESTRA
Albums

Impact R 3427	The ReGeneration: Christmas in Velvet	197?	3.75	7.50	15.00
— With velvet-like cover					

JOHNSON, GENERAL
With the Chairmen of the Board.
45s

Surfside 911119	Christmas Time Is Here/(B-side unknown)	1980	—	3.00	6.00

JOHNSON, JOE
45s

Abet 9417	Santa, Bring My Baby Back/Dirty Woman Blues	1966	2.50	5.00	10.00

JOHNSON, LONNIE
45s

King 4492	Happy New Year, Darling/Christmas Blues	1951	12.50	25.00	50.00
— B-side by Gatemouth Moore					

JOHNSON, MICHAEL
45s

RCA 5355-7-R		This Time of Year/There's a New Kid in Town	1987	—	—	3.00
RCA JK-14239	DJ	There's a New Kid In Town (same on both sides)	1985	—	—	3.00
RCA PB-14239		There's a New Kid in Town/Blue Colorado	1985	—	2.00	4.00

On Various-Artists Collections

This Time of Year	Mistletoe and Memories (RCA 8372-1-R)

JOHNSON, RAY
45s

Goad 4000	Merry Christmas Baby/God Bless The Funky People	196?	—	3.00	6.00

JOHNSON, RED
45s

Hep 2934	Christmas In Heaven/Memories Of A Christmas Tree	19??	—	2.00	4.00
— B-side by Bud O.J.					

JOLLY JESTERS, THE
45s

Crystalette 735	On This Silent Night/A Hundred Dollars Worth of Mistletoe	1959	3.00	6.00	12.00

JOLLY, PETE
On Various-Artists Collections

It's the Most Wonderful Time	Something Festive! (A&M SP-19003)

JONES, ALED
On Various-Artists Collections

Main Title: Every Christmas Eve & Santa's Theme	Santa Claus The Movie (EMI America SJ-17177)

JONES, GEORGE
45s

D 1226	New Baby for Christmas/Maybe Next Christmas	1961	3.00	6.00	12.00
Mercury 71225	New Baby for Christmas/Maybe Next Christmas	1957	5.00	10.00	20.00
Musicor 1339	Lonely Christmas Call/My Mom and Santa Claus	1968	2.00	4.00	8.00
United Artists 530	Lonely Christmas Call/My Mom and Santa Claus	1962	3.75	7.50	15.00

On Various-Artists Collections

Jingle Bells	Christmas Greetings from Nashville (Columbia PC 39467)
Joy to the World	RFD Christmas (Columbia Special Products P 15427)
My Mom and Santa Claus	Country Christmas (Time-Life STL-109)
O Come All Ye Faithful	RFD Christmas (Columbia Special Products P 15427)

Label, Number		Title (A Side/B Side)	Year	VG	VG+	NM

JONES, GEORGE, AND GENE WATSON
On Various-Artists Collections

Silver Bells		Nashville Christmas Album, The (Epic PE 40418)				
		Nashville's Greatest Christmas Hits (Columbia PC 44412)				

JONES, GEORGE, AND TAMMY WYNETTE
45s

Epic 11077		Mr. and Mrs. Santa Claus/The Greatest Christmas Gift	1973	—	2.50	5.00

On Various-Artists Collections

Mr. and Mrs. Santa Claus		Country Christmas (Time-Life STL-109)				

JONES, GRANDPA
45s

Monument 1179		Christmas Guest/Christmas Roses	1969	2.00	4.00	8.00
Monument 1939		Christmas Guest/Christmas Roses	1976	—	—	3.00
— "Golden Series" reissue						
Monument 8556		Christmas Guest/Christmas Roses	1972	—	3.00	6.00
Monument 8677		Christmas Guest/Christmas Roses	1975	—	2.50	5.00

JONES, JACK
45s

Kapp 629		Lullaby for Christmas Eve/The Village of St. Bernadette	1964	2.00	4.00	8.00

Albums

Kapp KL 1399	M	Jack Jones' Christmas Album	1964	3.00	6.00	12.00
Kapp KS 3399	S	Jack Jones' Christmas Album	1964	3.75	7.50	15.00
MCA 15014		Jack Jones' Christmas Album	197?	2.50	5.00	10.00
— Reissue						

On Various-Artists Collections

Christmas Is...		Happy Holidays, Volume 18 (RCA Special Products DPL1-0608)				
		Old Fashioned Christmas, An (Reader's Digest RDA 216-A)				
Joy to the World		We Wish You a Merry Christmas (RCA Victor PRS-277)				
Medley: God Rest Ye Merry Gentlemen/		Home for the Holidays (MCA MSM-35007)				
It Came Upon a Midnight Clear/						
The First Noel						
O Little Town of Bethlehem		Firestone Presents Your Favorite Christmas Music, Volume 6 (Firestone MLP 7014)				
Silver Bells		Happy Holidays, Volume 15 (RCA Special Products DPL1-0453)				
This Is That Time of the Year		Firestone Presents Your Favorite Christmas Music, Volume 6 (Firestone MLP 7014)				

JONES, LITTLE ANTHONY
45s

Ember 1090		Dear Gesu Bambino (Part 1)/Dear Gesu Bambino (Part 2)	1962	3.75	7.50	15.00

JONES, SPIKE, AND THE CITY SLICKERS
45s

Kapp 314		I Want the South to Win the War for Christmas/	1959	10.00	20.00	40.00
		Let's All Sing a Song for Christmas				
— B-side by the Happy Harts						
Kapp 314	PS	I Want the South to Win the War for Christmas/	1959	15.00	30.00	60.00
		Let's All Sing a Song for Christmas				
RCA Victor WY-461		Barnyard Christmas/Socko the Smallest Snowball	1952	5.00	10.00	20.00
— With the Bell Sisters; "Little Nipper" children's series						
RCA Victor 47-2795		Nutcracker Suite — 1 (The Little Girl's Dream)/	1949	5.00	10.00	20.00
		Nutcracker Suite — 6 (End of the Little Girl's Dream)				
— Originals with aqua labels and gold print						
RCA Victor 47-2795		Nutcracker Suite — 1 (The Little Girl's Dream)/	1951	3.75	7.50	15.00
		Nutcracker Suite — 6 (End of the Little Girl's Dream)				
— Reissue on black label with white print, outline of dog on right						
RCA Victor 47-2796		Nutcracker Suite — 2 (Land of the Sugar Plum Fairy)/	1949	5.00	10.00	20.00
		Nutcracker Suite — 5 (Back to the Fairy Ball)				
— Originals with aqua labels and gold print						
RCA Victor 47-2796		Nutcracker Suite — 2 (Land of the Sugar Plum Fairy)/	1951	3.75	7.50	15.00
		Nutcracker Suite — 5 (Back to the Fairy Ball)				
— Reissue on black label with white print, outline of dog on right						
RCA Victor 47-2797		Nutcracker Suite — 3 (The Fairy Ball)/	1949	5.00	10.00	20.00
		Nutcracker Suite — 4 (The Mysterious Room)				
— Originals with aqua labels and gold print						
RCA Victor 47-2797		Nutcracker Suite — 3 (The Fairy Ball)/	1951	3.75	7.50	15.00
		Nutcracker Suite — 4 (The Mysterious Room)				
— Reissue on black label with white print, outline of dog on right						
RCA Victor 47-2963		(All I Want for Christmas Is) My Two Front Teeth/Happy New Year	1949	7.50	15.00	30.00

Label, Number		Title (A Side/B Side)	Year	VG	VG+	NM
RCA Victor 47-3934		Rudolph the Red-Nosed Reindeer/	1950	5.00	10.00	20.00
		Mommy, Won't You Buy a Baby Brother				
RCA Victor 47-4315		Rudolph the Red-Nosed Reindeer/	1951	5.00	10.00	20.00
		(All I Want for Christmas Is) My Two Front Teeth				
RCA Victor 47-5015		Barnyard Christmas/Socko the Smallest Snowball	1952	5.00	10.00	20.00
— With the Bell Sisters						
RCA Victor 47-5067		I Saw Mommy Kissing Santa Claus/Winter	1952	5.00	10.00	20.00
RCA Victor 47-5067	PS	I Saw Mommy Kissing Santa Claus/Winter	1952	10.00	20.00	40.00
RCA Victor 47-5497		Where Did My Snowman Go/Santa Brought Me Choo Choo Trains	1953	5.00	10.00	20.00
RCA Victor 47-5920		I Want Eddie Fisher for Christmas/Japanese Skokiaan	1954	5.00	10.00	20.00
RCA Victor 447-0172		(All I Want for Christmas Is) My Two Front Teeth/	195?	3.75	7.50	15.00
		Rudolph the Red-Nosed Reindeer				
— Reissue (Gold Standard Series); black label, dog on top						
Verve 2026		My Birthday Comes on Christmas/Wouldn't It Be Fun	1956	3.75	7.50	15.00
7-Inch Extended Plays						
RCA Victor WP 143	(3)	The Nutcracker Suite	1949	20.00	40.00	80.00
— Includes aqua label records 47-2795, 47-2796 and 47-2797 plus box						
RCA Victor WP 143	(3)	The Nutcracker Suite	1951	15.00	30.00	60.00
— Includes black label records 47-2795, 47-2796 and 47-2797 plus box						
Albums						
Rhino R1 70196		It's a Spike Jones Christmas	1988	3.00	6.00	12.00
Verve MGV-2021	M	Let's Sing a Song for Christmas	1956	12.50	25.00	50.00
Verve V-2021	M	Let's Sing a Song for Christmas	1961	7.50	15.00	30.00
On Various-Artists Collections						
(All I Want for Christmas Is) My Two Front Teeth		Billboard Greatest Christmas Hits, 1935-1954 (Rhino R1 70637)				
		Christmas Through the Years (Reader's Digest RDA-143)				
		Dr. Demento Presents the Greatest Novelty Records of All Time Volume VI: Christmas (Rhino RNLP 825)				
		Joyous Noel (Reader's Digest RDA-57A)				
		12 Hits of Christmas (United Artists UA-LA669-R)				
I Saw Mommy Kissing Santa Claus		Christmas Through the Years (Reader's Digest RDA-143)				

JORDAN
45s

Sunrize 144	Tennessee Christmas/That's Not Love	198?	—	2.00	4.00

JORDAN, LOUIS
45s

Decca 27806	May Every Day Be Christmas/Bone Dry	1951	5.00	10.00	20.00
Pzazz 015	Santa Claus, Santa Claus/Sakatumi	1968	2.00	4.00	8.00

JORDAN, MARLON, AND DELFEAYO MARSALIS
On Various-Artists Collections

Little Drummer Boy, The	Jazzy Wonderland, A (Columbia 1P 8120)

JORDAN, STANLEY
On Various-Artists Collections

Silent Night	Yule Struttin' — A Blue Note Christmas (Blue Note 1P 8119)

JORDAN, VIC
45s

Gusto 123	Little Drummer Boy/Blue Christmas	197?	—	2.50	5.00
— B-side by Roy Wiggins					

JORDANAIRES, THE
Albums

Classic CCR 1935	Christmas to Elvis from the Jordanaires	1978	3.00	6.00	12.00

JORGENSON, DR. DWAYNE
45s

Knollwood 26937	Silver Spurs; A Christmas Story/Silver Spurs; A Christmas Song	1975	—	2.00	4.00

JOY GEMS, THE
45s

Strange ODD 4	I've Never Seen Snow (At Christmas)/Boiling Mud	19??	3.00	6.00	12.00
— B-side by Girvin O'Strange; U.K. import					

Label, Number	Title (A Side/B Side)	Year	VG	VG+	NM
JOY STRINGS, THE					
45s					
Epic 10259	O Little Town of Bethlehem/We Three Kings	1967	2.00	4.00	8.00
JUDDS, THE					
45s					
RCA 5048-7-R	Who Is This Babe/Light of the Stable	1986	—	—	3.00
RCA 5350-7-R	Silver Bells/Away in a Manger	1987	—	—	3.00
RCA 9069-7-R	Silver Bells/Oh Holy Night	1989	—	2.00	4.00
RCA PB-13906	Light of the Stable/Change of Heart	1984	—	2.00	4.00
RCA PB-14240	Who Is This Babe/Change of Heart	1985	—	2.00	4.00
Albums					
RCA Victor 6422-1-R	Christmas Time with the Judds	1987	2.50	5.00	10.00
On Various-Artists Collections					
Light of the Stable	Best of Christmas, The (RCA Victor CPL1-7013)				
	Country Christmas, A, Volume 3 (RCA CPL1-5178)				
Silver Bells	Mistletoe and Memories (RCA 8372-1-R)				
Who Is This Babe	Country Christmas, A, Volume 4 (RCA CPL1-7012)				
JUDGE DREAD					
45s					
Cactus 80	Christmas In Dreadland/Come Outside	19??	2.50	5.00	10.00
— U.K. import					
JUDY AND THE DUETS					
45s					
Ware 6000	Christmas With The Beatles/The Blind Boy	1964	5.00	10.00	20.00
JULIAN, DON, AND THE MEADOWLARKS					
45s					
Classic Artists 105	White Christmas/Marry Christmas, Baby	1988	—	3.00	6.00
JUNKYARD DOGS					
On Various-Artists Collections					
Brand New Bike	Happy Birthday, Baby Jesus (Sympathy For The Record Industry SFTRI 271)				

K

Label, Number	Title (A Side/B Side)	Year	VG	VG+	NM
KAEMPFERT, BERT					
45s					
Decca 31560	Little Drummer Boy/Jingo Jango	1963	2.50	5.00	10.00
Decca 31873	Holiday for Bells/Jumpin' Jiminy Christmas	1965	2.00	4.00	8.00
Albums					
Decca DL 4441	M	Christmas Wonderland	1963	3.75	7.50	15.00
Decca DL 74441	S	Christmas Wonderland	1963	4.00	8.00	16.00
On Various-Artists Collections					
Jingo Jango	Magic of Christmas, The (Columbia Musical Treasury P3S 5806)				
KAINAPAU, GEORGE					
45s					
Decca 27220	Silent Night/Mele Kalikimaka	1950	3.75	7.50	15.00
KAJA					
On Various-Artists Collections					
Shouldn't Do That	Santa Claus The Movie (EMI America SJ-17177)				
KALEIKINI, DANNY					
45s					
Kolapa 10	Christmas Means Aloha/Kanaka Waiwai	19??	3.00	6.00	12.00
KALLEN, KITTY					
45s					
Decca 29315	The Spirit of Christmas/ Baby Brother (Santa Claus, Dear Santa Claus)	1954	3.00	6.00	12.00

Label, Number		Title (A Side/B Side)	Year	VG	VG+	NM
Decca 88181		The Spirit of Christmas/ Baby Brother (Santa Claus, Dear Santa Claus)	1954	3.00	6.00	12.00
— *Children's Series issue*						
Decca 88181	PS	The Spirit of Christmas/ Baby Brother (Santa Claus, Dear Santa Claus)	1954	5.00	10.00	20.00

KALLMANN, GUNTER
On Various-Artists Collections
Medley: Little Donkey/Do You Hear What I Hear?		Magic of Christmas, The (Columbia Musical Treasury P3S 5806)				

KAMES, BOB
45s
King 5531		The Night Before Christmas (Part 1)/ The Night Before Christmas (Part 2)	1961	2.50	5.00	10.00
King 5566		The Night Before Christmas (Part 1)/ The Night Before Christmas (Part 2)	1961	2.00	4.00	8.00
King 5725		Don't Wait 'Till the Night Before Christmas/ Dance with Me the Christmas Tree 'Round	1962	2.00	4.00	8.00
King 6189		Jingle Bells/Please Come Home For Christmas	1968	—	3.00	6.00

KANE, KANDY
45s
Kef 4450		Christmas Prayer/Oh, The Jolly Green Giant	196?	2.50	5.00	10.00

KANTER, HILLARY
On Various-Artists Collections
California Christmas		Country Christmas, A, Volume 4 (RCA CPL1-7012)				

KARLOFF, BORIS (NARRATOR)
On Various-Artists Collections
How the Grinch Stole Christmas		How the Grinch Stole Christmas (Mercury Nashville 528 439-1)				
Reminder Spot		For Christmas Seals...A Matter of Life and Breath (Decca Custom Style E)				

KAY, JOHNNY
Albums
Promenade 2122		Johnny Kay Sings Season's Greeetings	196?	3.00	6.00	12.00
Spinorama 4009		White Christmas	196?	3.00	6.00	12.00

KAYE, BARRY
45s
Paid 114		Randolph The Redneck Reindeer/The Season to Be Lonely	1980	—	3.00	6.00

KAYE, DANNY
45s
Decca 27829		Santa Claus Looks Like My Daddy/Eat, Eat, Eat!	1951	3.75	7.50	15.00

On Various-Artists Collections
Deck the Hall with Boughs of Holly		Joyous Christmas, Volume 6 (Columbia Special Products C 11083)				
		Joyous Songs of Christmas, The (Columbia Special Products C 10400)				
Jingle Bells		Joyous Christmas, Volume 6 (Columbia Special Products C 11083)				
Medley: O Come, All Ye Faithful/ The First Noel		Great Songs of Christmas, The, Album Five (Columbia Special Products CSP 238M)				

KAYE, JOHNNY
45s
Legend 127		A Christmas Love/Christmas In Paree	19??	—	2.50	5.00

KAYE, MARY, TRIO
45s
Columbia 1-33?		All I Want For Christmas/Down Christmas Tree Lane	1949	5.00	10.00	20.00
— *Microgroove 33 1/3 rpm 7-inch single*						

KAYE, ROBERT R.
45s
Hawkeye 1001		This Christmas/Fav'rite Memories	19??	—	—	3.00
Hawkeye 1001	PS	This Christmas/Fav'rite Memories	19??	—	—	3.00

Label, Number		Title (A Side/B Side)	Year	VG	VG+	NM
KAYE, SAMMY						
45s						
Columbia 39572		Silent Night-O Little Town Of Bethlehem/Joy To The World-Hark the Herald Angels Sing-O Come All Ye Faithful	1951	3.00	6.00	12.00
Columbia 39573		White Christmas/Jingle Bells	1951	3.00	6.00	12.00
Columbia 39574		Winter Wonderland/Rudolph the Red-Nosed Reindeer	1951	3.00	6.00	12.00
Columbia 39575		Frosty the Snow Man/Santa Claus Is Coming to Town	1951	3.00	6.00	12.00
Columbia 39894		All Around the Christmas Tree/Santa, Santa, Santa Claus	1952	3.75	7.50	15.00
Decca 27829		Santa Claus Looks Like My Daddy/Eat, Eat, Eat	1951	3.75	7.50	15.00
Decca 31174		Merry Merry Christmas (To You)/Silver Bells	1960	2.50	5.00	10.00
Decca 31175		Christmas Child (Loo, Loo, Loo)/Let It Snow, Let It Snow, Let It Snow	1960	2.50	5.00	10.00
RCA Victor 47-2864		White Christmas/Winter Wonderland	1949	3.75	7.50	15.00
RCA Victor 47-3071		Here Comes Santa Claus/I Want to Wish You a Merry Christmas	1949	3.75	7.50	15.00
Albums						
Decca DL 4070	M	Christmas Day with Sammy Kaye	1960	3.00	6.00	12.00
Decca DL 74070	S	Christmas Day with Sammy Kaye	1960	3.75	7.50	15.00
On Various-Artists Collections						
It's Beginning to Look Like Christmas		Old-Fashioned Christmas, An (Longines Symphonette LS 214)				
O Come All Ye Faithful		Thank You for Opening Your Christmas Club with Us (Decca 34211)				
White Christmas		Remembering Christmas with the Big Bands (RCA Special Products DPM1-0506)				
KEESHAN, BOB (CAPTAIN KANGAROO)						
45s						
Columbia 4-291		'Twas the Night Before Christmas/The Littlest Snowman	195?	5.00	10.00	20.00
On Various-Artists Collections						
Littlest Snowman, The		First Christmas Record for Children (Harmony HS 14554)				
KEITH, TOBY						
45s						
Polydor 577 416-7		Santa, I'm Right Here/Blame It on the Mistletoe	1995	—	—	3.00
KELLAWAY, ROGER						
On Various-Artists Collections						
Spirit of Christmas		Waltons' Christmas Album, The (Columbia KC 33193)				
Waltons Theme, The		Waltons' Christmas Album, The (Columbia KC 33193)				
KELLY, AL						
45s						
RCA Thesaurus HO7H-0934	DJ	An Exclusive Interview with Santa Claus//O Come, All Ye Faithful/Lo! How A Rose E'er Blooming/Silent Night	1957	3.75	7.50	15.00
— B-side by Domenico Savino and His Orchestra						
KELLY, JERI						
45s						
MPI 1002		Poor Ole Santa Claus/Hide 'n' Seek	19??	2.00	4.00	8.00
KEMP, WAYNE						
45s						
Door Knob 206		Merry Christmas, Darling/Happy Birthday, Darling	1983	—	2.00	4.00
KENDALL, CHARLES S.						
Albums						
Dot DLP 3083	M	Christmas Chimes	1958	3.75	7.50	15.00
KENIA						
45s						
LGM 467		Merry Christmas To Daddy & Mom/Little Love	19??	2.50	5.00	10.00
KENNEDY, ED						
45s						
Columbia 41856		Numba One Day Of Christmas/Kaalalea	1960	2.50	5.00	10.00
On Various-Artists Collections						
Number One Day of Christmas		Seasons Greetings (A Christmas Festival of Stars) (Columbia CS 8189)				
KENNY AND CORKY						
45s						
Big Top 3031		Nuttin' for Christmas/Suzy Snowflake	1959	5.00	10.00	20.00
Big Top 3031	PS	Nuttin' for Christmas/Suzy Snowflake	1959	10.00	20.00	40.00

Label, Number		Title (A Side/B Side)	Year	VG	VG+	NM
KENT, DICK						
45s						
M.S.R. Records 703		Santa Claus Sweetheart/Is Santa the Man in the Moon?	19??	—	2.50	5.00
KENT, JAMES						
45s						
Boyd 124		Christmas Without You/Empty House	196?	2.00	4.00	8.00
KENTON, STAN						
45s						
Capitol 5085		O Tannenbaum/What Is a Santa Claus	1963	2.50	5.00	10.00
Creative World 1001	DJ	The Twelve Days of Christmas// O Tannenbaum/We Three Kings Of Orient Are	197?	—	2.00	4.00
Albums						
Creative World 1001		Kenton's Christmas	197?	2.50	5.00	10.00
On Various-Artists Collections						
O Tannenbaum		Christmas Songs, The (Capitol SLB-57074)				
KERR, ANITA, SINGERS						
45s						
Ampex 11050		Shine, Shine//Medley: O Come All Ye Faithful-Noel	1970	—	3.00	6.00
Ampex 11051		Oh Holy Night/Medley: Angels We Have Heard on High-What Child Is This?-Joy to the World	1970	—	3.00	6.00
Sesac AD-49	DJ	On This Holy Night/Bring a Torch, Jeanette, Isabella//Sleep, Sweet Jesus, Sleep/The 12 Days Of Christmas	197?	—	3.00	6.00
Sesac AD-56	DJ	Deck the Halls/All Through The Night// Rise Up Shepherd and Foller/Christmas Is the Day	197?	—	3.00	6.00
Sesac AD-56	PS	Deck the Halls/All Through The Night// Rise Up Shepherd and Foller/Christmas Is the Day	197?	—	3.00	6.00
Albums						
Ampex A10142		A Christmas Story	1971	3.00	6.00	12.00
— With the Royal Philharmonic Orchestra						
On Various-Artists Collections						
God Rest Ye Merry, Gentlemen		Joyous Noel (Reader's Digest RDA-57A)				
O Little Town of Bethlehem		Christmas Eve with Colonel Sanders (RCA Victor PRS-256)				
KERSHAW, SAMMY						
45s						
Mercury 856 408-7		Christmas Time's a-Comin'/Up on the Housetop	1994	—	2.00	4.00
KEYE, JIM						
45s						
IW 8501		Letter to Mom/Silent Night	19??	—	2.00	4.00
— B-side by St. John's University Men's Chorus						
KID CREOLE AND THE COCONUTS						
Also see AUGUST DARNELL.						
45s						
Ze/Island PWIP 6840	PD	Dear Addy//No Fish TodayXmas on Riverside Drive	1982	2.50	5.00	10.00
— U.K. import picture disc						
KIESELL, HELEN						
45s						
Kiesell 5308		It's Christmas Time Again/Search Your Heart	1974	—	2.50	5.00
KILEY, RICHARD						
On Various-Artists Collections						
Medley: O Come All Ye Faithful/ God Rest Ye Merry, Gentlemen		Great Songs of Christmas, Album Nine (Columbia Special Products CSS 1033)				
Panis Angelicus		Great Songs of Christmas, Album Nine (Columbia Special Products CSS 1033) Magnavox Album of Christmas Music (Columbia Special Products CSQ 11093)				
KING COLEMAN						
45s						
Karen 1008		Blue Grey Christmas/Holiday Season	19??	3.00	6.00	12.00

Label, Number	Title (A Side/B Side)	Year	VG	VG+	NM

KING CURTIS
45s

Atco 6630	The Christmas Song/What Are You Doing New Year's Eve?	1968	3.00	6.00	12.00

On Various-Artists Collections

Christmas Song, The	Jingle Bell Rock (Time-Life SRNR-XM)				

KING DIAMOND
12-Inch Singles

Roadracer RR 125485	No Presents For Christmas/Charon	1985	2.00	4.00	8.00

KING FAMILY, THE
45s

Warner Bros. PRO 216	DJ	Go Tell It on the Mountain/Here the Sledges with the Bells	1965	2.50	5.00	10.00

Albums

Fanny Farmer/Fleetwood FCLP 3039		Fanny Farmer Presents The King Family Christmas Album	196?	3.00	6.00	12.00
Warner Bros. W 1627	M	Christmas with the King Family	1965	3.00	6.00	12.00
Warner Bros. WS 1627	S	Christmas with the King Family	1965	3.75	7.50	15.00

On Various-Artists Collections

Medley: Holiday of Love/Caroling, Caroling	Great Songs of Christmas, The, Album Six (Columbia Special Products CSM 388)
Medley: O Little Town of Bethlehem/ It Came Upon the Midnight Clear	Great Songs of Christmas, The, Album Six (Columbia Special Products CSM 388)

KING KAROLEERS, THE
45s

King 15140	Silent Night/Rejoice	19??	3.00	6.00	12.00
King 15141	O, Little Town Of Bethlehem/Hark, The Herald Angels Sing	19??	3.00	6.00	12.00
King 15143	It Came Upon A Midnight Clear/God Rest Ye Merry Gentlemen	19??	3.00	6.00	12.00
King 15144	Good King Wenceslas/Away In A Manger	19??	3.00	6.00	12.00

KING SISTERS, THE
45s

Capitol 4099	DJ	Holiday of Love/Over The River	1958	3.00	6.00	12.00
Capitol 4310		Chree-See-Mus/Girls and Boys	1959	3.00	6.00	12.00

KING'S SINGERS, THE
Albums

MMG 1108	Deck the Hall — Songs for Christmas	1973	3.00	6.00	12.00
MMG 1126	Christmas With the King's Singers	197?	3.00	6.00	12.00

KING, AL
45s

Sahara 115	Christmas Is Gone/Peace And Understanding	1966	2.50	5.00	10.00

KING, ALBERT
45s

Stax 0234	Santa Claus Wants Some Lovin'/Don't Burn Down the Bridges	1974	—	3.50	7.00
Stax 1056	What Do The Lonely Do At Christmas?/ Santa Claus Wants Some Lovin'	197?	—	3.00	6.00
— B-side by Emotions; reissue					
Stax 1073	Christmas Comes Once A Year/I'll Be Your Santa Claus	197?	—	2.50	5.00
— B-side by Rufus Thomas; reissue					
Stax 3225	Santa Claus Wants Some Lovin'/Don't Burn Down the Bridges	1979	—	3.00	6.00

KING, B.B.
45s

Kent 387	Christmas Celebration/Easy Listening	1962	3.00	6.00	12.00
Kent 412	Christmas Celebration/Easy Listening	1964	3.00	6.00	12.00

KING, CHUCK
45s

Live Productions 9419	Merry Christmas To You (same on both sides)	19??	—	3.00	6.00

KING, DAVE
45s

London 1702	Christmas and You/You Make Nice	1956	2.50	5.00	10.00

Label, Number		Title (A Side/B Side)	Year	VG	VG+	NM
KING, FREDDY						
45s						
Federal 12439		Christmas Tears/I Hear Jingle Bells	1961	3.00	6.00	12.00
On Various-Artists Collections						
Christmas Tears		Merry Christmas Baby (Gusto/Hollywood K-5018-X)				
I Hear Jingle Bells		Merry Christmas Baby (Gusto/Hollywood K-5018-X)				
KING, KATHRYN						
45s						
Prevue 111		I Want A Puppy In My Stocking For Christmas/(B-side unknown)	19??	2.00	4.00	8.00
KING, MIKE						
45s						
Tone-King 001		The Night Time Christmas Candle/A Christmas Lul-A-Bye	19??	—	—	3.00
Tone-King 001	PS	The Night Time Christmas Candle/A Christmas Lul-A-Bye	19??	—	—	3.00
KING, PEGGY						
45s						
Columbia 40362		I'm Gonna Put Some Glue 'Round The Christmas Tree/ Counting Sheep	1954	3.75	7.50	15.00
KING, PETE, CHORALE						
45s						
Kapp 360		Little Shepherd Boy/My Favorite Things	1960	2.50	5.00	10.00
Kapp AS-918X	DJ	White Christmas (same on both sides)	196?	2.00	4.00	8.00
Albums						
Kapp KL 1214	M	Christmas Time	1960	3.75	7.50	15.00
KING, RANDY						
45s						
Bandbox 340		Legend Of Little Orphan Joe/Merry Christmas	1963	3.00	6.00	12.00
KING, RAY						
45s						
Santa's Land 103		Christmas Dreaming/Old Time Christmas	19??	—	2.00	4.00
KING, WAYNE						
45s						
Decca 25616		Winter Wonderland/Jing-a-Ling-a-Ling	1963	2.50	5.00	10.00
Albums						
Decca DL 4438	M	Have Yourself a Merry Little Christmas	1963	3.75	7.50	15.00
Decca DL 74438	S	Have Yourself a Merry Little Christmas	1963	4.00	8.00	16.00
On Various-Artists Collections						
Silver Bells		Old-Fashioned Christmas, An (Longines Symphonette LS 214)				
KINGS OF ROCK						
45s						
Regal Select 007		Blue Christmas//Sleigh Ride/Christmas With The Kings	198?	2.00	4.00	8.00
— B-side by Girl Trouble; blue vinyl						
Regal Select 007	PS	Blue Christmas//Sleigh Ride/Christmas With The Kings	198?	2.00	4.00	8.00
— B-side by Girl Trouble						
KINGSLEY, BETTY, AND THE DEADBEATS						
45s						
Dondee 1938		Christy The Christmas Angel/The Wonder Of Christmas	19??	—	2.00	4.00
KINGSTON TRIO, THE						
45s						
Capitol 4475		Somerset Gloucestershire Wassail/Goodnight My Baby	1960	3.75	7.50	15.00
Capitol 4475	PS	Somerset Gloucestershire Wassail/Goodnight My Baby	1960	15.00	30.00	60.00
7-Inch Extended Plays						
Capitol XE1-1446		We Wish You A Merry Christmas/A Round About Christmas// The Last Month Of The Year	1960	· 3.00	6.00	12.00
— 33 1/3 rpm, small hole jukebox pressing						
Albums						
Capitol T 1446	M	The Last Month of the Year	1960	7.50	15.00	30.00
Capitol ST 1446	S	The Last Month of the Year	1960	10.00	20.00	40.00

Label, Number		Title (A Side/B Side)	Year	VG	VG+	NM
On Various-Artists Collections						
Sing We Noel		Christmas Songs, The, Volume II (Capitol SL-57065)				
We Wish You a Merry Christmas		Christmas Stocking (Capitol NP 90494)				

KINKS, THE
45s

Label, Number		Title (A Side/B Side)	Year	VG	VG+	NM
Arista 0296		Father Christmas/Prince of the Punks	1977	—	2.50	5.00
Arista 0296	PS	Father Christmas/Prince of the Punks	1977	—	2.50	5.00
Albums						
Arista AL11 8428	(2)	Come Dancing with the Kinks	1986	3.00	6.00	12.00
— Contains one Christmas song: Father Christmas						
On Various-Artists Collections						
Father Christmas		Christmas Rock Album, The (Priority SL 9465)				

KINNAMON, LARRY
45s

Label, Number		Title (A Side/B Side)	Year	VG	VG+	NM
Audan 110		The Miracle of Christmas/Ho-Ho	19??	—	2.00	4.00

KIRBY, FRED
Albums

Label, Number		Title (A Side/B Side)	Year	VG	VG+	NM
Crown 5196	M	Christmas Favorites	196?	3.00	6.00	12.00
Custom CS 4	S	Christmas Favorites	196?	3.00	6.00	12.00
— Same as Crown LP, but in stereo						
Yuletide Series YS-214	S	Christmas Favorites	197?	2.50	5.00	10.00
— Reissue of Custom LP						

KIRBY, ROGER
45s

Label, Number		Title (A Side/B Side)	Year	VG	VG+	NM
Ace 20618		Rockin Reindeer/The Ugliest Little Christmas Tree	19??	—	—	3.00
— B-side by Doc Wallace						

KIRSTEN, DOROTHY
On Various-Artists Collections

Label, Number	Title (A Side/B Side)
I Wonder As I Wander	Firestone Presents Your Favorite Christmas Music, Volume 4 (Firestone MLP 7011)
Joy to the World	Firestone Presents Your Favorite Christmas Music, Volume 4 (Firestone MLP 7011)

KITT THE AMAZING CAR OF TOMORROW
45s

Label, Number	Title (A Side/B Side)	Year	VG	VG+	NM
MCA 52330	A Knight Rider Christmas/(Instrumental)	1983	2.00	4.00	8.00

KITT, EARTHA
45s

Label, Number		Title (A Side/B Side)	Year	VG	VG+	NM
RCA Victor 47-5502		Santa Baby/Under the Bridges of Paris	1953	6.25	12.50	25.00
RCA Victor 47-5502	PS	Santa Baby/Under The Bridges Of Paris	1953	10.00	20.00	40.00
RCA Victor 47-5914		(This Year's) Santa Baby/Hey Jacque	1954	5.00	10.00	20.00
RCA Victor 47-6319		Nothin' for Christmas/Je Cherche Un Homme (I Want a Man)	1955	3.75	7.50	15.00
On Various-Artists Collections						
Santa Baby		Billboard Greatest Christmas Hits, 1935-1954 (Rhino R1 70637)				
		Merry Christmas And A Happy New Year (Modern Radio 102)				
		12 Hits of Christmas (United Artists UA-LA669-R)				

KLEIN, JOHN
Albums

Label, Number		Title (A Side/B Side)	Year	VG	VG+	NM
Columbia PC 44387	M	Caroling on the Carillon	1987	2.50	5.00	10.00
RCA Victor LPM-2914	M	Let's Ring the Bells All Around the Christmas Tree	1964	3.00	6.00	12.00
RCA Victor LSP-2914	S	Let's Ring the Bells All Around the Christmas Tree	1964	3.75	7.50	15.00
On Various-Artists Collections						
Frosty the Snow Man		Joyful Sound of Christmas, The (RCA Record Club CSP-0601)				
Let It Snow! Let It Snow! Let It Snow!		Joyful Sound of Christmas, The (RCA Record Club CSP-0601)				
Medley: Away in a Manger/The First Noel/It Came Upon a Midnight Clear		Merry Christmas (RCA Victor PRM-168)				
White Christmas		Christmas Programming from RCA Victor (RCA Victor SP-33-66)				
		October Christmas Sampler 59-40-41 (RCA Victor SPS-33-54)				

KNEE, BERNIE
45s

Label, Number	Title (A Side/B Side)	Year	VG	VG+	NM
Pat 106	Take Off Those Whiskers Daddy/The Holiday Hop	19??	2.00	4.00	8.00

Label, Number		Title (A Side/B Side)	Year	VG	VG+	NM

KNIGHT, GLADYS, AND THE PIPS
45s

Label, Number		Title (A Side/B Side)	Year	VG	VG+	NM
Buddah 1974	DJ	Do You Hear What I Hear/Silent Night	1974	—	3.00	6.00
Columbia 03418		That Special Time of Year/Santa Claus Is Comin' to Town	1982	—	2.00	4.00
Columbia 11409		When a Child Is Born/The Lord's Prayer	1980	—	2.00	4.00
— With Johnny Mathis						
MCA 53002		Send It to Me/When You Love Somebody (It's Christmas Every Day)	1987	—	—	3.00

Albums

Label, Number		Title (A Side/B Side)	Year	VG	VG+	NM
Columbia FC 38114		That Special Time of Year	1982	2.50	5.00	10.00
Columbia PC 38114		That Special Time of Year	1983	2.00	4.00	8.00
— Same as above with new prefix						

On Various-Artists Collections

That Special Time of Year	Time-Life Treasury of Christmas, The, Volume Two (Time-Life STL-108)	

KNIGHT, MARIE
45s

Label, Number	Title (A Side/B Side)	Year	VG	VG+	NM
Decca 48262	Adeste Fideles/It Came Upon A Midnight Clear	1951	5.00	10.00	20.00

KOBLISH, JULIE
45s

Label, Number	Title (A Side/B Side)	Year	VG	VG+	NM
HA 715	Christmas Spirit/Christmas Eve	19??	—	2.50	5.00
— B-side by Rick Gibson					

KOLE, RONNIE, TRIO
45s

Label, Number	Title (A Side/B Side)	Year	VG	VG+	NM
Paula 317	Silent Night, Holy Night/Winter Wonderland	1969	—	2.50	5.00

KOONSE, JOHNNY
45s

Label, Number	Title (A Side/B Side)	Year	VG	VG+	NM
JIN 328	Old Fashioned Christmas/Nosey	197?	—	2.00	4.00

KOREAN ORPHAN CHOIR
On Various-Artists Collections

First Noel, The	Joys of Christmas (Capitol Creative Products SL-6610)
Hark! The Herald Angels Sing	Happy Holidays, Album 6 (Capitol Creative Products SL-6669)
	Zenith Presents Christmas, A Gift of Music (Capitol Creative Products SL-6544)
Little Drummer Boy, The	Christmas — The Season of Music (Capitol Creative Products SL-6679)
	Sound of Christmas, The (Capitol Creative Products SL-6515)
	Sound of Christmas, The, Vol. 3 (Capitol Creative Products SL-6680)
	Zenith Presents Christmas, A Gift of Music Vol. 3 (Capitol Creative Products SL-6659)
O Little Town of Bethlehem	Joys of Christmas (Capitol Creative Products SL-6610)

KOSTELANETZ, ANDRE
45s

Label, Number		Title (A Side/B Side)	Year	VG	VG+	NM
Columbia JZSP 76389/90	DJ	Medley: Santa Claus Is Coming To Town & Have Yourself A Merry Little Christmas/Christmas Chopsticks	1963	2.50	5.00	10.00
Columbia JZSP 111905/6	DJ	O Come All Ye Faithful/Oh Tannenbaum	1965	3.00	6.00	12.00
— Green vinyl						
Columbia JZSP 111905/6	DJ	O Come All Ye Faithful/Oh Tannenbaum	1965	2.00	4.00	8.00
— Black vinyl						

Albums

Label, Number		Title (A Side/B Side)	Year	VG	VG+	NM
Columbia CL 1528	M	Joy to the World: Music for Christmas	1959	3.75	7.50	15.00
Columbia CL 2068	M	Wonderland of Christmas	1963	3.00	6.00	12.00
Columbia CS 8328	S	Joy to the World: Music for Christmas	1959	5.00	10.00	20.00
— Same as CL 1528, but in stereo						
Columbia CS 8868	S	Wonderland of Christmas	1963	3.75	7.50	15.00
— Same as CL 2068, but in stereo						
Columbia LE 10083		Joy to the World: Music for Christmas	197?	2.50	5.00	10.00
— Reissue of CS 8328						
Columbia LE 10086		Wonderland of Christmas	197?	2.50	5.00	10.00
— Reissue of CS 8868						
Columbia Masterworks ML 6179	M	Wishing You a Merry Christmas	1960	3.00	6.00	12.00
Columbia Masterworks MS 6779	S	Wishing You a Merry Christmas	1960	3.75	7.50	15.00

On Various-Artists Collections

Angels We Have Heard on High	Merry Christmas from... (Reader's Digest RD4-83)
Away in a Manger	Great Songs of Christmas, The, Album Two (Columbia Special Products XTV 86100/1)
Christmas Chimes	Very Merry Christmas, A, Volume 3 (Columbia Special Products CSS 997)
It Came Upon the Midnight Clear	Great Songs of Christmas, The, Album Five (Columbia Special Products CSP 238M)
It's Beginning to Look a Lot Like Christmas	Magnavox Album of Christmas Music (Columbia Special Products CSQ 11093)

Label, Number	Title (A Side/B Side)	Year	VG	VG+	NM
Joy to the World	Carols and Candlelight (Columbia Special Products P 12525)				
	It's Christmastime! (Columbia Special Products CSM 429)				
Medley: Hark! The Herald Angels	Great Songs of Christmas, The, Album Five (Columbia Special Products CSP 238M)				
Sing/Angels We Have Heard on High	Season's Greetings from Barbra Streisand...And Friends				
	(Columbia Special Products CSS 1075)				
Medley: March of the Toys/Toyland	Christmas Greetings (Columbia Special Products CSS 1433)				
	Great Songs of Christmas, The, Album Two (Columbia Special Products XTV 86100/1)				
	60 Christmas Classics (Sessions DVL2-0723)				
Medley: The First Noel/It Came Upon a	Very Merry Christmas, A (Columbia Special Products CSS 563)				
Midnight Clear/O Come All Ye Faithful	Season's Greetings from Barbra Streisand...And Friends				
	(Columbia Special Products CSS 1075)				
O Holy Night	Home for Christmas (Columbia Musical Treasury P3S 5608)				
O Little Town of Bethlehem	Merry Christmas (Columbia Musical Treasury 3P 6306)				
Skater's Waltz	Christmas Greetings, Vol. 3 (Columbia Special Products P 11383)				
Sleigh Ride	Christmas Greetings (Columbia Special Products CSS 1499)				
	Christmas Song, The, And Other Favorites (Columbia Special Products P 12446)				
	Collection of Christmas Favorites, A (Columbia Special Products P 14988)				
	Great Songs of Christmas, The (Columbia Special Products XTV 69406/7)				
	Happy Holidays, Volume II (Columbia Special Products CSM 348)				
	Very Merry Christmas, A, Volume Two (Columbia Special Products CSS 788)				
Toyland	Spirit of Christmas, The, Volume III (Columbia Special Products CSS 1463)				
We Wish You a Merry Christmas	Christmas Album, A (Columbia PC 39466)				
	Have a Happy Holiday (Columbia Special Products CSS 1432)				
	Home for Christmas (Columbia Musical Treasury P3S 5608)				
	Home for Christmas (Realm 2V 8101)				
	Joy to the World (30 Classic Christmas Melodies) (Columbia Special Products P3 14654)				
	Magic of Christmas, The (Columbia Musical Treasury P3S 5806)				
	WHIO Radio Christmas Feelings (Sound Approach/CSP P 16366)				

KRAMER, PAT
45s

Centaur 754	Letter To Santa/Christmas Carousel	1975	—	2.00	4.00
— B-side with Peter London					

KRAYOLAS, THE
45s

Krayolas 1018/9	Christmas Time/Cry, Cry, Laugh, Laugh	19??	—	2.00	4.00

KREMPANSKY, JOHN
45s

Cuca 1439	Christmas Bright/Christmas Swirl	19??	2.00	4.00	8.00

KRISS, DON
45s

Carrot 911031	It's Christmas/Jingle Bell Rock	1991	—	2.00	4.00

KRISTA
45s

NWNC 120	Mama Loves Santa Man/(Instrumental)	19??	—	2.00	4.00

KRISTI
45s

Jads 1031	I Wanna Take a Peek at Santa/	19??	2.00	4.00	8.00
	Mommy's Getting a New Baby for Christmas				

KRISTIN
45s

Sutra 128	Cabbage Patch Christmas/Love You	1983	—	2.50	5.00
— B-side by 57th Street Players					

L

L-STATUS
On Various-Artists Collections

Holiday Cheer	Stuff This in Your Stocking! Elves in Action (Veebltronics/Skyclad 68)				

Label, Number		Title (A Side/B Side)	Year	VG	VG+	NM
LaBAMBA						
45s						
Front Row 1185		There's Still Christmas/(Instrumental)	1985	—	2.50	5.00
LaBELLE, PATTI						
On Various-Artists Collections						
I'm Christmasing with You		Starlight Christmas, A (MCA 10066)				
LaBELLE, PATTI, AND THE BLUE BELLES						
Albums						
Newtown 632	M	Sleigh Bells, Jingle Bells and Blue Bells	1963	75.00	150.00	300.00
LACKOWSKI, BIG DADDY						
45s						
S Sound 222		Jingle Bell Polka/Christmas Medley	19??	2.00	4.00	8.00
S Sound 222		Jingle Bell Polka/Christmas Medley	19??	—	3.00	6.00
— As "Marshall Lackowski with Andy Desso"; same recordings as above						
LAFEVRE, JERRY, AND FRIENDS						
45s						
Wilby 913		Wilby The Christmas Tree/A Christmas Waltz	1988	—	2.00	4.00
LAFITS AND KITTY						
45s						
Apollo 520		Christmas Letters/Can Can Rock and Roll	1957	3.75	7.50	15.00
LAGUNA, KENNY						
45s						
Sire 4030		Home for Christmas/Carianne and Meryl's Song	1979	2.50	5.00	10.00
Sire 4030	PS	Home for Christmas/Carianne and Meryl's Song	1979	—	3.00	6.00
— Above record and sleeve are U.K. imports						
Sire 49142		Home for Christmas/Carianne and Meryl's Song	1979	—	2.50	5.00
LAI, FRANCIS						
45s						
Paramount 0086		Holiday For Jenny (The Christmas Tree)/Snow Frolic	1971	—	3.00	6.00
LAINE, FRANKIE						
45s						
Columbia 39893		Christmas Roses/Chow Willy	1952	3.75	7.50	15.00
— With Jo Stafford						
Mercury 5553		Merry Christmas Everywhere/What Am I Gonna Do This Christmas	1950	5.00	10.00	20.00
Albums						
Mercury MG-25082	10	Christmas Favorites	1951	12.50	25.00	50.00
On Various-Artists Collections						
You're All I Want for Christmas		Have a Happy Holiday (Columbia Special Products CSS 1432)				
		Merry Christmas from... (Reader's Digest RD4-83)				
LAKE, ARTHUR "DAGWOOD"						
45s						
Ensign 2012		Rudolph the Red-Nosed Reindeer/Katie the Kangaroo	1958	3.75	7.50	15.00
LAKE, GREG						
Also see EMERSON, LAKE AND PALMER.						
45s						
Atlantic 3305		I Believe in Father Christmas/Humbug	1975	—	3.00	6.00
Atlantic 3305	PS	I Believe in Father Christmas/Humbug	1975	2.50	5.00	10.00
LAMB, BECKY						
45s						
Warner Bros. 7154		Little Becky's Christmas Wish/Go to Sleep, Little Lambs	1967	3.00	6.00	12.00
— B-side by Bill Lamb						
LAMB, REGGIE						
45s						
Starville 711		Christmas Confession (Vocal)/Christmas Confession (Rap)	198?	—	2.00	4.00

Label, Number	Title (A Side/B Side)	Year	VG	VG+	NM

LAMBERT, HENDRICKS AND ROSS
On Various-Artists Collections

Deck Us All with Boston Charlie	Jingle Bell Jazz (Columbia PC 36803)				

LANCERS, THE
45s

Coral 61314	'Twas the Night Before Christmas/ I Wanna Do More Than Whistle (Under the Mistletoe)	1954	3.00	6.00	12.00

LANDERS, RICK
45s

Door Knob 044	A Christmas Request/Santa's Helping Hand	1977	—	2.00	4.00

LANDS, LIZ
45s

T&L 201	Silent Night (Part 1)/Silent Night (Part 2)	19??	2.00	4.00	8.00

LANE, CRISTY
45s

LS 148	Shake Me I Rattle/Pretty Paper	1977	—	2.50	5.00

— A-side not a Christmas song; this record was also released with an alternate B-side, "I Can't Tell You" (not a Christmas song)

LS 9146	Man From Galilee/Shake Me I Rattle (Squeeze Me I Cry)	1984	—	—	3.00

Albums

Liberty LN-10226	Christmas with Cristy	198?	2.50	5.00	10.00
LS SLL-8358	Christmas Is the Man from Galilee	1983	2.50	5.00	10.00

LANE, ROCKI, AND THE GROSS GROUP
45s

Epic 10556	Happy Hairy Hippy Harry Claus/Santa Soul	1969	6.25	12.50	25.00

LANIN, LESTER
45s

Epic 9349		Winter Wonderland/Dance of the Sugar-Plum Fairies	1959	3.00	6.00	12.00
Epic 9350		Sleigh Ride/Christmas Carol Medley	1959	3.00	6.00	12.00
Epic JZSP 123255/6	DJ	Winter Wonderland/Sleigh Ride	1967	2.00	4.00	8.00
Epic JZSP 123257/8	DJ	Dance of the Sugar-Plum Fairies/Ring In the New	1967	2.00	4.00	8.00
Epic JZSP 123259/60	DJ	Christmas Medley/Jingle Bells	1967	2.00	4.00	8.00

On Various-Artists Collections

Auld Lang Syne	Merry Christmas (Columbia Musical Treasury 3P 6306)				
Medley: Deck the Halls/Good King Wenceslas	It's Christmastime! (Columbia Special Products CSM 429)				
Winter Wonderland	Spirit of Christmas, The (Columbia Special Products CSP 249)				

LANOIS, DANIEL
On Various-Artists Collections

Fais Do-Do	Winter Warnerland (Warner Bros. PRO-A-3328)				

LANSBURY, ANGELA; FRANKIE MICHAELS; JANE CONNELL; AND SAB SHIMONO
On Various-Artists Collections

We Need a Little Christmas	Mame (Columbia Masterworks KOS 3000)				

LANZ, DAVID, AND PAUL SPEER
On Various-Artists Collections

O Holy Night	Narada: The Christmas Collection (Narada N-63902)				

LANZA, MARIO
45s

RCA Victor 47-6334	Ave Maria/I'll Walk with God	1955	3.75	7.50	15.00
RCA Victor 49-3639	The Lord's Prayer/Guardian Angels	195?	3.00	6.00	12.00

— Side 1 and Side 8 of WDM-1649; red vinyl

RCA Victor 49-3639	The Lord's Prayer/Guardian Angels	195?	2.00	4.00	8.00

— Side 1 and Side 8 of WDM-1649; black vinyl

RCA Victor 49-3640	The First Noel/Silent Night	195?	3.00	6.00	12.00

— Side 2 and Side 7 of WDM-1649; red vinyl

RCA Victor 49-3640	The First Noel/Silent Night	195?	2.00	4.00	8.00

— Side 2 and Side 7 of WDM-1649; black vinyl

RCA Victor 49-3641	O Come, All Ye Faithful/Oh Little Town Of Bethlehem	195?	3.00	6.00	12.00

— Side 3 and Side 6 of WDM-1649; red vinyl

Label, Number		Title (A Side/B Side)	Year	VG	VG+	NM
RCA Victor 49-3641		O Come, All Ye Faithful/Oh Little Town Of Bethlehem	195?	2.00	4.00	8.00
— Side 3 and Side 6 of WDM-1649; black vinyl						
RCA Victor 49-3642		Away in a Manger/We Three Kings of Orient Are	195?	3.00	6.00	12.00
— Side 4 and Side 5 of WDM-1649; red vinyl						
RCA Victor 49-3642		Away in a Manger/We Three Kings of Orient Are	195?	2.00	4.00	8.00
— Side 4 and Side 5 of WDM-1649; black vinyl						
RCA Victor 447-0774		Ave Maria/The Lord's Prayer	196?	2.00	4.00	8.00
— Reissue; black label, dog on top						
RCA Victor 447-0777		Oh, Holy Night/I'll Walk With God	196?	2.00	4.00	8.00
— Reissue; black label, dog on top						

7-Inch Extended Plays

Label, Number		Title (A Side/B Side)	Year	VG	VG+	NM
RCA Victor ERA 115		O Come All Ye Faithful/Silent Night//	195?	3.00	6.00	12.00
		We Three Kings Of Orient Are/The First Noel				
RCA Victor ERA 115	PS	Four Favorite Christmas Carols	195?	3.00	6.00	12.00
— Ornament-shaped sleeve						
RCA Victor WDM-1649	(4)	Sings Christmas Songs	195?	12.50	25.00	50.00
— 4 records, all red vinyl, plus box						
RCA Victor WDM-1649	(4)	Sings Christmas Songs	195?	10.00	20.00	40.00
— 4 records, all black vinyl, plus box						

Albums

Label, Number		Title (A Side/B Side)	Year	VG	VG+	NM
Pickwick CAS-777(e)	R	Christmas Hymns and Carols	1977	2.00	4.00	8.00
— Same contents as RCA Camden CAS-777(e)						
RCA Camden CAL-777	M	Christmas Hymns and Carols	196?	3.75	7.50	15.00
RCA Camden CAS-777(e)	R	Christmas Hymns and Carols	196?	3.00	6.00	12.00
— Same as above, but in electronically rechanneled stereo						
RCA Red Seal LM-2333	M	Lanza Sings Christmas Carols	1959	3.00	6.00	12.00
RCA Red Seal LSC-2333	S	Lanza Sings Christmas Carols	1959	3.75	7.50	15.00
— Original copies have "shaded dog" on labels						

On Various-Artists Collections

Ave Maria (Schubert)	For the First Time (RCA Red Seal LM-2338)
Away in a Manger	Joyous Noel (Reader's Digest RDA-57A)
First Noel, The	Christmas in New York (RCA Victor PRM-257)
I Saw Three Ships	Joyous Noel (Reader's Digest RDA-57A)
O Christmas Tree	Christmas Programming from RCA Victor (RCA Victor SP-33-66)
	Joyous Noel (Reader's Digest RDA-57A)
	October Christmas Sampler 59-40-41 (RCA Victor SPS-33-54)
O Come, All Ye Faithful	RCA Victor Presents Music for the Twelve Days of Christmas (RCA Victor PRS-188)
O Holy Night	Christmas Festival of Songs and Carols, Volume 2 (RCA Victor PRM-195)
	Family Christmas Collection, The (Time-Life STL-131)
	For a Musical Merry Christmas, Volume 3 (RCA Victor PRM-221)
	Happy Holidays, Vol. 20 (RCA Special Products DPL1-0713)
	Very Merry Christmas, A, Volume 5 (RCA Special Products PRS-343)
O Little Town of Bethlehem	For a Musical Merry Christmas (RCA Victor PR-149A)

LaPLANTE, NANCY
45s

Label, Number	Title (A Side/B Side)	Year	VG	VG+	NM
Laurie 3516	Debbie's Last Christmas/(Theme From) Debbie's Last Christmas	1969	2.00	4.00	8.00

LARCHMONT SINGERS, THE
45s

Label, Number	Title (A Side/B Side)	Year	VG	VG+	NM
Crusader 112	A Christmas Wish/Welcome, Little Stranger	1964	2.50	5.00	10.00

LaROSA, JULIUS
45s

Label, Number		Title (A Side/B Side)	Year	VG	VG+	NM
Cadence 1252		Campanelle (Jingle Bells)/I Hope You'll Be Very Happy	1954	3.00	6.00	12.00
Cadence 1253		Jingle Dingle/Campanelle (Jingle Bells)	1954	3.00	6.00	12.00
GP 592		A Christmas Gift/To Find Our Children	1981	—	3.00	6.00
MGM 13651		We Need A Little Christmas/Our Venetian Affair	1966	2.00	4.00	8.00

7-Inch Extended Plays

Label, Number		Title (A Side/B Side)	Year	VG	VG+	NM
Cadence EP 1234		Ave Maria/Adeste Fideles//Silent Night/Oh Holy Night	1953	3.75	7.50	15.00
Cadence EP 1234	PS	Julius LaRosa Sings...	1953	3.75	7.50	15.00

On Various-Artists Collections

Christmas Song, The	Columbia 40109 (title unknown) (Columbia 4-40109)

LARSON, NICOLETTE
On Various-Artists Collections

One Bright Star	Tennessee Christmas (MCA 5620)
	Tennessee Christmas (MCA S45-17046)

Label, Number		Title (A Side/B Side)	Year	VG	VG+	NM

LARSON, TONY RODELLE
45s

| Band Box 237 | | Cool Yule/Bear Rug | 196? | 2.00 | 4.00 | 8.00 |
| Band Box 237 | PS | Cool Yule/Bear Rug | 196? | 3.75 | 7.50 | 15.00 |

LARY, HOWELL
45s

| GWS 2680 | | Red, White and Blue Christmas/Proud Mary | 19?? | — | 2.00 | 4.00 |

LaSALLE, DENISE
45s

| Malaco 2124 | | Santa Claus Got the Blues/Love Is a Five Letter Word | 1985 | — | 2.50 | 5.00 |

LaSPINA, FRANK
45s

| Holly 6010 | | Christmas Dreams/One Solitary Life | 19?? | — | 2.50 | 5.00 |

LAST GENERATION, THE
45s

| Rapture 101 | | It's Christmas Time/The Bells Are Ringing Out | 19?? | — | 2.00 | 4.00 |

LAST, JAMES
On Various-Artists Collections

Medley: O Tannenbaum/Jingle Bells   Magic of Christmas, The (Columbia Musical Treasury P3S 5806)

LAUGHTON, CHARLES
45s

| Decca 23365 | | The Oldest Christmas Story/The Story of the Three Wise Men | 1950 | 3.75 | 7.50 | 15.00 |

Albums

Decca DLP 8010	M	A Christmas Carol/Mr. Pickwick's Christmas	1955	5.00	10.00	20.00
— A-side read by Ronald Colman						
MCA 15010		A Christmas Carol/Mr. Pickwick's Christmas	1955	5.00	10.00	20.00
— A-side read by Ronald Colman; reissue of Decca LP						

LAVOIE, KATHY
45s

| Anahwac 1146 | | Christmas Time Is Coming/(B-side unknown) | 19?? | — | 2.00 | 4.00 |

LAWRENCE, CAROL
On Various-Artists Collections

Reminder Spot   For Christmas Seals...A Matter of Life and Breath (Decca Custom Style E)

LAWRENCE, CAROL, AND ROBERT GOULET
Also see ROBERT GOULET AND CAROL LAWRENCE.
On Various-Artists Collections

Angels We Have Heard on High   Ronco Presents A Christmas Gift (Columbia Special Products P 12430)

LAWRENCE, EDDIE
45s

| Coral 61915 | | The Merry Old Philosopher/That Holiday Spirit | 1957 | 5.00 | 10.00 | 20.00 |

LAWRENCE, LINDA
45s

| Serena 105 | | Have A Happy Ho! Ho! Ho!/The Christmas Lady | 19?? | — | — | 3.00 |

LAWRENCE, MARK
45s

| GNP Crescendo 419 | | Is There A Santa Claus?/The Heavenly Forest | 1968 | — | 3.00 | 6.00 |
| Jerden 110 | | Is There A Santa Claus/Santa Claus Square Dance | 196? | 2.00 | 4.00 | 8.00 |

LAWRENCE, STEVE
On Various-Artists Collections

'Twas the Night Before Christmas   Great Songs of Christmas, The, Album Seven (Columbia Special Products CSS 547)
Christmas Song, The   Very Merry Christmas, A, Volume Two (Columbia Special Products CSS 788)
Go Tell It on the Mountain   Christmastime in Carol and Song (RCA PRS-289)

Label, Number	Title (A Side/B Side)	Year	VG	VG+	NM
Let Me Be the First (To Wish You a Merry Christmas)	Great Songs of Christmas, The, Album Seven (Columbia Special Products CSS 547)				
Night Before Christmas, The	Best of the Great Songs of Christmas (Album 10) (Columbia Special Products CSS 1478)				
That Old Christmas Spirit	Gift of Christmas, The, Vol. 1 (Columbia Special Products CSS 706)				

LAWRENCE, STEVE, AND EYDIE GORME
45s

Label, Number		Title (A Side/B Side)	Year	VG	VG+	NM
Columbia 43179		Happy Holiday/That Holiday Feeling	1964	2.50	5.00	10.00
RCA Victor 47-9694		Hurry Home for Christmas/Dedicated to Love	1968	2.00	4.00	8.00

Albums

Columbia CL 2262	M	That Holiday Feeling	1964	3.00	6.00	12.00
Columbia CS 9062	S	That Holiday Feeling	1964	3.75	7.50	15.00

On Various-Artists Collections

Happy Holiday	Christmas Greetings (Columbia Special Products CSS 1499)
	Ronco Presents A Christmas Gift (Columbia Special Products P 12430)
Hurry Home for Christmas	Christmastime in Carol and Song (RCA PRS-289)
	Happy Holidays, Vol. 21 (RCA Special Products DPL1-0739)
Let It Snow! Let It Snow! Let It Snow!	Great Songs of Christmas, The, Album Six (Columbia Special Products CSM 388)
	Have a Happy Holiday (Columbia Special Products CSS 1432)
	Merry Christmas from... (Reader's Digest RD4-83)
	WHIO Radio Christmas Feelings (Sound Approach/CSP P 16366)
	Zenith Presents Christmas, A Gift of Music Vol. 5 (Columbia Special Products C 10395)
Santa Claus Is Coming to Town	Christmas Song, The, And Other Favorites (Columbia Special Products P 12446)
	Merry Christmas from... (Reader's Digest RD4-83)
Sleigh Ride	Great Songs of Christmas, The, Album Five (Columbia Special Products CSP 238M)
That Holiday Feeling	Merry Christmas (Columbia Musical Treasury 3P 6306)
	Very Merry Christmas, A, Volume IV (Columbia Special Products CSS 1464)
Winter Wonderland	Happy Holidays, Album Nine (Columbia Special Products P 11793)
	Joyous Christmas, Volume 2 (Columbia Special Products CSS 808)

LAWSON, JANET
45s

Big Apple 404	Yes My Darling There's a Santa Claus/ Dear Santa (I've Been a Teensy Weensy Bad)	19??	—	2.50	5.00

LAWSON, YANK, AND BOB HAGGART
On Various-Artists Collections

Christmas Song	Carols and Candlelight (Columbia Special Products P 12525)

LAYNA, MARIA
45s

Pulse 1007	The Christmas Child (Bambino)/The Christmas Child (Bambino)	19??	—	2.00	4.00
— B-side by Craig Brown					

LAYTON, EDDIE
Albums

Epic LN 24118	M	Organ Music for Christmas	1964	3.00	6.00	12.00
Epic BN 26118	S	Organ Music for Christmas	1964	3.75	7.50	15.00

On Various-Artists Collections

Hark! The Herald Angels Sing	Christmas Greetings (Columbia Special Products CSS 1433)

LAZY COWGIRLS
45s

Bomp! 137		Sock It To Me Santa/Goddamn Bottle	1986	2.50	5.00	10.00
Bomp! 137	PS	Sock It To Me Santa/Goddamn Bottle	1986	2.50	5.00	10.00

LE CHOEUR DE NOTRE DAME DES VICTOIRES
On Various-Artists Collections

Il est ne le Divin Enfant	Christmas in San Francisco (Embarcadero Center EC-101)

LE ROUX
7-Inch Extended Plays

RCA Victor JF-13012	DJ	Seasons Greetings/You Know How Those Boys Are// Addicted/Last Safe Place on Earth	1981	—	3.00	6.00
— Promo only on green vinyl						

LEA, MELVA
On Various-Artists Collections

What Child Is This?	Merry Christmas (Rainbow Sound R-5032-LPS)

Label, Number		Title (A Side/B Side)	Year	VG	VG+	NM
LEAPPO (THE FROG)						
45s						
Del-Ray 213		Christmas In Frogville/Look Before You Leap	19??	2.50	5.00	10.00
LEAR, JO ANN						
45s						
Vanity 583		Let's All Have A Happy New Year/Leave My Toys Alone	19??	—	2.50	5.00
LEDOUX, CHRIS						
45s						
Capitol Nashville S7-19348		Santa Claus Is Comin' to Town/'Twas the Night Before Christmas	1996	—	—	3.00
LEE, BRENDA						
45s						
Decca 30107		Christy Christmas/I'm Gonna Lasso Santa Claus	1956	6.25	12.50	25.00
Decca 30776		Rockin' Around the Christmas Tree/Papa Noel	1958	6.25	12.50	25.00
— Originals have black labels with star under "Decca"						
Decca 30776		Rockin' Around the Christmas Tree/Papa Noel	1960	3.75	7.50	15.00
— Reissues have black labels with color bars						
Decca 30776	PS	Rockin' Around the Christmas Tree/Papa Noel	1960	7.50	15.00	30.00
Decca 31687		Jingle Bell Rock/Winter Wonderland	1964	3.00	6.00	12.00
Decca 31687	PS	Jingle Bell Rock/Winter Wonderland	1964	4.00	8.00	16.00
Decca 31688		This Time of the Year/Christmas Will Be Just Another Lonely Day	1964	3.00	6.00	12.00
Decca 31688	PS	This Time of the Year/Christmas Will Be Just Another Lonely Day	1964	4.00	8.00	16.00
Decca 88215		Christy Christmas/I'm Gonna Lasso Santa Claus	1956	12.50	25.00	50.00
— As "Little Brenda Lee" on Decca's Children's Series						
Decca 88215	PS	Christy Christmas/I'm Gonna Lasso Santa Claus	1956	15.00	30.00	60.00
MCA 65027		Rockin' Around the Christmas Tree/Papa Noel	1973	—	2.00	4.00
— Black label with rainbow						
MCA 65027		Rockin' Around the Christmas Tree/Papa Noel	1980	—	—	3.00
— Blue label with rainbow						
MCA 65028		Jingle Bell Rock/Winter Wonderland	1973	—	2.00	4.00
— Black label with rainbow						
MCA 65028		Jingle Bell Rock/Winter Wonderland	1980	—	—	3.00
— Blue label with rainbow						
7-Inch Extended Plays						
Decca 34254		This Time of the Year/Blue Christmas/Jingle Bell Rock//Rockin' Around the Christmas Tree/Marshmallow World/Winter Wonderland	1964	3.75	7.50	15.00
— Stereo 7-inch 33 1/3 rpm (small hole) jukebox pressing						
Decca 34254	PS	Merry Christmas	1964	6.25	12.50	25.00
— Sleeve says this is "DL 74583"; price includes title strips						
Albums						
Decca DL 4583	M	Merry Christmas from Brenda Lee	1964	3.75	7.50	15.00
Decca DL 74583	S	Merry Christmas from Brenda Lee	1964	5.00	10.00	20.00
— Same as above, but in stereo						
Decca R 103619	S	Merry Christmas from Brenda Lee	1971	5.00	10.00	20.00
— Same as above, but RCA Music Service edition						
MCA 232	S	Merry Christmas from Brenda Lee	1973	3.00	6.00	12.00
— Reissue of above						
MCA 15021	S	Merry Christmas from Brenda Lee	197?	2.50	5.00	10.00
— Reissue of above						

On Various-Artists Collections

Christmas Song, The	Tennessee Christmas (MCA 5620)
Frosty the Snowman	Old-Fashioned Christmas, An (Longines Symphonette LS 214)
I'm Gonna Lasso Santa Claus	Rockin' Little Christmas (MCA 25084)
Jingle Bell Rock	Happy Holidays, Vol. 23 (MCA Special Products 15042)
Rockin' Around the Christmas Tree	Billboard Greatest Christmas Hits, 1955-Present (Rhino R1 70636)
	Christmas Through the Years (Reader's Digest RDA-143)
	Jingle Bell Rock (Time-Life SRNR-XM)
	Old Fashioned Christmas, An (Reader's Digest RDA 216-A)
	Rockin' Little Christmas (MCA 25084)
	Time-Life Treasury of Christmas, The (Time-Life STL-107)
	12 Hits of Christmas (United Artists UA-LA669-R)

Label, Number		Title (A Side/B Side)	Year	VG	VG+	NM
LEE, BYRON, AND THE DRAGONAIRES						
45s						
Jad 210		Everyday Will Be Like A Holiday/Show Rain	1968	2.00	4.00	8.00

Label, Number		Title (A Side/B Side)	Year	VG	VG+	NM
LEE, DEANNA						
45s						
Sundance 2205		I Want a Snake for Christmas/Remember; Suite Christmas	19??	2.00	4.00	8.00
Sundance 2205	PS	I Want a Snake for Christmas/Remember; Suite Christmas	19??	2.00	4.00	8.00
LEE, DENA						
45s						
Santa's Land 105		How Santa Got His Name/What If Mama?	19??	—	3.00	6.00
LEE, FREDDIE FINGERS						
45s						
Charly 1059		White Christmas/My Mother	19??	—	2.00	4.00
Charly 1059	PS	White Christmas/My Mother	19??	—	2.00	4.00
LEE, JOHNNY						
45s						
Elektra 47230	DJ	Please Come Home for Christmas/Silver Bells	1981	—	2.50	5.00
— B-side by Tompall and the Glaser Brothers						
LEE, PAUL						
45s						
M.S.R. 714		Jesus And Nice Old Santa Claus/When The Roll Is Called Up Yonder	19??	—	2.50	5.00
— B-side by Dick Kent						
LEE, PEGGY						
45s						
Capitol 4311		The Tree/The Christmas List	1959	3.75	7.50	15.00
Capitol 4311	PS	The Tree/The Christmas List	1959	5.00	10.00	20.00
Capitol 4474		I Like a Sleighride (Jingle Bells)/Christmas Carousel	1960	3.00	6.00	12.00
Capitol 4474	PS	I Like A Sleighride (Jingle Bells)/Christmas Carousel	1960	10.00	20.00	40.00
Decca 28939		Ring Those Christmas Bells/It's Christmas Time Again	1953	3.75	7.50	15.00
Decca 29342		God Rest Ye Merry Gentlemen/White Christmas	1954	3.75	7.50	15.00
— A-side with Trudi Stevens; B-side by Bing Crosby and Danny Kaye						
Albums						
Capitol T 1423	M	Christmas Carousel	1960	5.00	10.00	20.00
Capitol ST 1423	S	Christmas Carousel	1960	6.25	12.50	25.00
Capitol T 2390	M	Happy Holiday	1965	3.00	6.00	12.00
Capitol ST 2390	S	Happy Holiday	1965	3.75	7.50	15.00

On Various-Artists Collections

Christmas Carousel	Happy Holidays, Album Seven (Capitol Creative Products SL-6730)
	Holiday Magic (Capitol Creative Products SL-6728)
	Zenith Presents Christmas, A Gift of Music (Capitol Creative Products SL-6544)
Christmas Song, The	Happy Holidays, Volume 19 (RCA Special Products DPL1-0689)
	I'll Be Home for Christmas (Pickwick SPC-1009)
	Sound of Christmas, The, Vol. 2 (Capitol Creative Products SL-6534)
Christmas Waltz, The	All-Time Christmas Favorites (Capitol Special Markets SL-6931)
	Christmas America (Capitol Special Markets SL-6884)
	Happy Holly Days (Capitol Creative Products SL-6761)
	Very Merry Christmas, A, Volume VIII (Capitol Special Markets SL-6954)
	Zenith Presents Christmas, A Gift of Music (Capitol Creative Products SL-6544)
Deck the Halls	Christmas Day (Pickwick SPC 1010)
Don't Forget to Feed the Reindeer	Spirit of Christmas, The (Capitol Creative Products SL-6516)
Happy Holiday	Christmas Songs, The (Capitol SLB-57074)
	Christmas to Remember, A (Capitol Creative Products SL-6573)
	Magic of Christmas, The (Capitol SWBB-93810)
I Like a Sleighride	Best of Christmas, The, Vol. I (Capitol SM-11833)
	Happy Holidays, Album 6 (Capitol Creative Products SL-6669)
	Holiday Magic (Capitol Creative Products SL-6728)
Little Drummer Boy	Christmas Carousel (Capitol SQBE-94406)
	Christmas to Remember, A, Vol. 3 (Capitol Creative Products SL-6681)
Santa Claus Is Comin' to Town	Christmas Stocking (Capitol NP 90494)
Star Carol, The	Christmas Carousel (Capitol SQBE-94406)
	Spirit of Christmas, The (Capitol Creative Products SL-6516)
White Christmas	Christmas Day (Pickwick SPC 1010)
	Christmas, A Gift of Music (Capitol Special Markets SL-6687)
	Zenith Presents Christmas, A Gift of Music Vol. 4 (Capitol Creative Products SL-6687)

Label, Number		Title (A Side/B Side)	Year	VG	VG+	NM
LEE, ROBBIE						
45s						
Autumn Gold 1001		A Christmas Love Song/(Instrumental)	19??	—	2.00	4.00

Label, Number		Title (A Side/B Side)	Year	VG	VG+	NM

LEFEVRE, RAYMOND & HIS ORCHESTRA
45s
| Kapp AS-949 | DJ | Silver Bells (mono/stereo) | 196? | 2.00 | 4.00 | 8.00 |

LEGACY, DOUG, AND THE LEGENDS OF THE WEST
45s
| Some Pun'kins 2121 | | Christmas On The Range/Christmas In Prison | 19?? | 2.00 | 4.00 | 8.00 |
| Some Pun'kins 2121 | PS | Christmas On The Range/Christmas In Prison | 19?? | 2.00 | 4.00 | 8.00 |

LEHRER, TOM
Albums
| Lehrer TL 202 | M | An Evening Wasted with Tom Lehrer | 1959 | 6.25 | 12.50 | 25.00 |
| Lehrer TL 202S | S | An Evening Wasted with Tom Lehrer | 1959 | 10.00 | 20.00 | 40.00 |

— *Contains one Christmas song:* Christmas Carol

| Reprise R 6199 | M | An Evening Wasted with Tom Lehrer | 1966 | 5.00 | 10.00 | 20.00 |

— *Reissue of Lehrer 202*

| Reprise RS 6199 | S | An Evening Wasted with Tom Lehrer | 1966 | 7.50 | 15.00 | 30.00 |

On Various-Artists Collections
| Christmas Carol, A | | Dr. Demento Presents the Greatest Novelty Records of All Time Volume VI: Christmas (Rhino RNLP 825) | | | | |

LEIBERT, DICK
45s
RCA Victor 47-2965		It Came Upon A Midnight Clear// Joy To The World/Away In A Manger	1949	3.00	6.00	12.00
RCA Victor 47-2966		Hark The Herald Angels Sing/The First Noel/ As With Gladness Men of Old	1949	3.00	6.00	12.00
RCA Victor 47-2967		O Come All Ye Faithful/Angels From The Realms	1949	3.00	6.00	12.00
RCA Victor 47-2968		Deck The Halls/God Rest Ye Merry Gentlemen// We Three Kings / Good King Wenceslaus	1949	3.00	6.00	12.00

Albums
RCA Camden ADL2-0243	(2)	Christmas at Radio City Music Hall	1973	3.75	7.50	15.00
RCA Victor LPM-2558	M	The Sound of Christmas on the Radio City Music Hall Organ	1962	3.00	6.00	12.00
RCA Victor LSP-2558	S	The Sound of Christmas on the Radio City Music Hall Organ	1962	3.75	7.50	15.00
Westminster WST 15020	S	A Merry Wurlitzer Christmas	195?	5.00	10.00	20.00

On Various-Artists Collections
Ding Dong! Merrily on High		Old Fashioned Christmas, An (Reader's Digest RDA 216-A)				
Holly and the Ivy, The		Old Fashioned Christmas, An (Reader's Digest RDA 216-A)				
Medley: Deck the Halls/Good King Wenceslas/It Came Upon the Midnight Clear/Under the Christmas Mistletoe		Music to Trim Your Tree By (RCA Victor PRM 225)				
Rudolph the Red-Nosed Reindeer		Joyful Sound of Christmas, The (RCA Record Club CSP-0601)				
We Three Kings		Family Christmas Collection, The (Time-Life STL-131)				

LEIGH, BARBARA E.
45s
| Everlov'in 109 | | Greenie The Christmas Tree/I Saw Mama Kissing Santa Claus | 19?? | — | — | 3.00 |

LEIGHTON, BERNIE
On Various-Artists Collections
| Dance of the Christmas Doll | | Firestone Presents Your Favorite Christmas Music, Volume 6 (Firestone MLP 7014) | | | | |

LENNON SISTERS, THE
Also see LAWRENCE WELK.
45s
| Brunswick 55044 | | Let's Light the Christmas Tree/Merry, Merry Christmas | 1957 | 3.00 | 6.00 | 12.00 |
| Mercury 72883 | | The Christmas Waltz/Lullaby for Christmas | 1968 | — | 3.00 | 6.00 |

Albums
| Dot DLP 3343 | M | Christmas with the Lennon Sisters | 1961 | 3.75 | 7.50 | 15.00 |
| Dot DLP 25343 | S | Christmas with the Lennon Sisters | 1961 | 5.00 | 10.00 | 20.00 |

On Various-Artists Collections
| Christmas Waltz, The | | Joyous Songs of Christmas, The (Columbia Special Products C 10400) | | | | |
| Little Drummer Boy, The | | Magic of Christmas, The (Columbia Musical Treasury P3S 5806) 12 Days of Christmas, The (Pickwick SPC-1021) | | | | |

LENNON, JOHN
(JOHN & YOKO/PLASTIC ONO BAND WITH THE HARLEM COMMUNITY CHOIR)
45s
| Apple 1842 | | Happy Xmas (War Is Over)/Listen, the Snow Is Falling | 1971 | 3.75 | 7.50 | 15.00 |

— *Green vinyl, faces label*

Label, Number		Title (A Side/B Side)	Year	VG	VG+	NM
Apple 1842		Happy Xmas (War Is Over)/Listen, the Snow Is Falling	1971	2.50	5.00	10.00
— Green vinyl, Apple label						
Apple 1842	PS	Happy Xmas (War Is Over)/Listen, the Snow Is Falling	1971	5.00	10.00	20.00
Apple S45X-47663/4	DJ	Happy Xmas (War Is Over)/Listen, the Snow Is Falling	1971	187.50	375.00	750.00
— White label on styrene						
Capitol 1842		Happy Xmas (War Is Over)/Listen, the Snow Is Falling	1976	12.50	25.00	50.00
— Orange label						
Capitol 1842		Happy Xmas (War Is Over)/Listen, the Snow Is Falling	1978	—	3.00	6.00
— Purple late-1970s label						
Capitol 1842		Happy Xmas (War Is Over)/Listen, the Snow Is Falling	1983	—	3.00	6.00
— Black colorband label						
Capitol 1842		Happy Xmas (War Is Over)/Listen, the Snow Is Falling	1988	5.00	10.00	20.00
— Purple late-1980s label (wider)						
Capitol S7-17644		Happy Xmas (War Is Over)/Listen, the Snow Is Falling	1993	—	2.00	4.00
— John & Yoko/The Plastic Ono Band; green vinyl						
Geffen 29855		Happy Xmas (War Is Over)/Beautiful Boy (Darling Boy)	1982	—	2.50	5.00
Geffen 29855	PS	Happy Xmas (War Is Over)/Beautiful Boy (Darling Boy)	1982	—	2.50	5.00
Albums						
Apple SW-3421		Shaved Fish	1975	5.00	10.00	20.00
— Contains one Christmas song: Medley: Happy Xmas (War Is Over)/Give Peace a Chance						
Capitol SW-3421		Shaved Fish	1978	3.00	6.00	12.00
— Reissue of above on purple Capitol label with Apple logo on cover						
Capitol SW-3421		Shaved Fish	1978	10.00	20.00	40.00
— Reissue of above on purple Capitol label with Capitol logo on cover						
Capitol SW-3421		Shaved Fish	1983	5.00	10.00	20.00
— Reissue of above on black Capitol label with Apple logo on cover						
Capitol SW-3421		Shaved Fish	1983	10.00	20.00	40.00
— Reissue of above on black Capitol label with Capitol logo on cover						
Capitol SW-3421		Shaved Fish	1989	10.00	20.00	40.00
— Reissue of above on purple Capitol label (small logo) with Capitol logo on cover						

LENNOX, ANNIE, AND AL GREEN
Also see AL GREEN.

12-Inch Singles

A&M 12288		Put a Little Love in Your Heart (3 versions)	1988	2.00	4.00	8.00

45s

A&M 1255		Put a Little Love in Your Heart/A Great Big Piece of Love	1988	—	—	3.00
— B-side by Spheres of Celestial Influence						
A&M 1255	PS	Put a Little Love in Your Heart/A Great Big Piece of Love	1988	—	—	3.00
— "Scrooged" sleeve with large hole in center						

LENOX AVENUE
45s

Chess 2101	Little Drummer Boy/Sunshine	1970	2.00	4.00	8.00

LEONARD AT THE THOMAS ORGAN
45s

I.R.C. 2088	Cross Eyed Little Santa Claus/Jingle Jam	19??	2.50	5.00	10.00

LEONARD, GLORIA
45s

High Society (no #)	Opens Her Holiday Gift Box And Talks To You	197?	20.00	40.00	80.00
— Flexidisc					

LEONARDS, THE
On Various-Artists Collections

Father Christmas   Stuff This in Your Stocking! Elves in Action (Veebltronics/Skyclad 68)

LEONETTI, TOMMY
45s

RCA Victor 74-0403	I Remember (Christmas Time) White Christmas/ Handful of Happy New Years	1970	—	3.00	6.00

On Various-Artists Collections

New Year's Greetings   Christmas Greetings From RCA Victor And Groove Recording Artists (RCA Victor SP-45-128)

Label, Number		Title (A Side/B Side)	Year	VG	VG+	NM
LES DJINNS SINGERS						
45s						
ABC Paramount 10281		Pour Noel (For Christmas)/Minuit, Chretriens (O, Holy Night)	1961	2.50	5.00	10.00
Albums						
ABC-Paramount ABC-397	M	Joyeaux Noel	1961	3.75	7.50	15.00
ABC-Paramount ABCS-397	S	Joyeaux Noel	1961	5.00	10.00	20.00
On Various-Artists Collections						
He Is Born a Divine Child		O. Henry's The Gift of the Magi (E.F. MacDonald EFMX-62)				
O Holy Night		O. Henry's The Gift of the Magi (E.F. MacDonald EFMX-62)				
LESTER FAMILY, THE						
On Various-Artists Collections						
Santa Claus Is Coming to Town		Christmas in Saint Louis ((no label) TS77-558/9)				
LESTER, MARIE						
45s						
Mosrite 504		Mommie's Playing Santa Claus/(B-side unknown)	1987	—	—	3.00
— Red vinyl with insert						
LETTERMEN, THE						
45s						
Alpha Omega 078501		It Feels Like Christmas/I Believe	1985	—	2.00	4.00
Alpha Omega 078501	PS	It Feels Like Christmas/I Believe	1985	—	2.00	4.00
Albums						
Capitol T 2587	M	For Christmas This Year	1966	3.00	6.00	12.00
Capitol ST 2587	S	For Christmas This Year	1966	3.75	7.50	15.00
Capitol ST-8-2587	S	For Christmas This Year	1966	5.00	10.00	20.00
— Capitol Record Club edition						

On Various-Artists Collections

Christmas Song, The	Christmas to Remember, A, Vol. 3 (Capitol Creative Products SL-6681)
	Holiday Magic (Capitol Creative Products SL-6728)
	Spirit of Christmas, The (Capitol Creative Products SL-6516)
Christmas Waltz	Christmas Through the Years (Reader's Digest RDA-143)
	Spirit of Christmas, The (Capitol Creative Products SL-6516)
Have Yourself a Merry Little Christmas	Best of Christmas, The, Vol. II (Capitol SM-11834)
Little Drummer Boy, The	Christmas Songs, The (Capitol SLB-57074)
	Christmas to Remember, A (Capitol Creative Products SL-6573)
	Happy Holly Days (Capitol Creative Products SL-6761)
Mary's Little Boy Child	Sound of Christmas, The, Vol. 3 (Capitol Creative Products SL-6680)
O Holy Night	Christmas America, Album Two (Capitol Special Markets SL-6950)
	Christmas Sounds of Music, The (Capitol Creative Products SL-6643)
	Christmas Through the Years (Reader's Digest RDA-143)
	Happy Holidays, Vol. 22 (RCA Special Products DPL1-0777)
	Happy Holidays, Vol. 5 (Capitol Creative Products SL-6627)
Silent Night	Happy Holidays, Album Seven (Capitol Creative Products SL-6730)
	Sound of Christmas, The, Vol. 2 (Capitol Creative Products SL-6534)
What Child Is This	Christmas — The Season of Music (Capitol Creative Products SL-6679)
	Magic of Christmas, The (Capitol SWBB-93810)
	Zenith Presents Christmas, A Gift of Music Vol. 3 (Capitol Creative Products SL-6659)
White Christmas	Christmas Sounds of Music, The (Capitol Creative Products SL-6643)

Label, Number		Title (A Side/B Side)	Year	VG	VG+	NM
LEVANT, LOUIE						
45s						
Dyna 7325		Merry Christmas, My Love/Silver Bells	19??	—	2.00	4.00
LEWIS, DEBRA LEE						
45s						
Door Knob 225		Mrs. Santa/Please Santa	19??	—	2.00	4.00
LEWIS, JERRY						
45s						
Capitol F2317		I've Had a Very Merry Christmas/Strictly for the Birds	1952	5.00	10.00	20.00
LEWIS, JERRY LEE						
45s						
Mercury 73155		I Can't Have a Merry Christmas, Mary (Without You)/ In Loving Memories	1970	—	3.00	6.00

On Various-Artists Collections

I Can't Have a Merry Christmas, Mary (Without You)	Country Christmas (Time-Life STL-109)

Label, Number		Title (A Side/B Side)	Year	VG	VG+	NM
LEWIS, L. PRESLEY						
45s						
Southwest 402-S-55/403-S-55		Jimminy Christmas/Be Wise, Be Humble and Worship	19??	3.00	6.00	12.00
LEWIS, MONICA – See RAY BLOCH.						
LEWIS, RAMSEY, TRIO						
45s						
Argo 5377		Santa Claus Is Coming to Town/Winter Wonderland	1960	3.00	6.00	12.00
Argo 5407		Sound of Christmas/Merry Christmas Baby	1961	3.00	6.00	12.00
Argo 5488		Jingle Bells/Egg Nog	1964	2.50	5.00	10.00
Cadet 5377		Santa Claus Is Coming To Town/Winter Wonderland	196?	2.00	4.00	8.00
— Reissue of Argo 5377						
Cadet 5553		Rudolph the Red-Nosed Reindeer/Day Tripper	1966	2.00	4.00	8.00
Cadet 5629		Mary's Boy Child/	1968	—	3.00	6.00
		Have Yourself a Merry Little Christmas				
Cadet 5662		Mary's Boy Child/My Cherie Amour	1969	—	3.00	6.00
7-Inch Extended Plays						
Argo EP-1084		Sleigh Ride/Christmas Blues//Sound of Christmas/	1961	2.50	5.00	10.00
		The Christmas Song				
Argo EP-1084	PS	Sound of Christmas	1961	3.00	6.00	12.00
Albums						
Argo 687	M	The Sound of Christmas	1961	6.25	12.50	25.00
Argo 687-S	S	The Sound of Christmas	1961	5.00	10.00	20.00
Argo 745	M	More Sounds of Christmas	1964	6.25	12.50	25.00
Argo 745-S	S	More Sounds of Christmas	1964	5.00	10.00	20.00
Chess CH 9716		Sound of Christmas	1984	2.50	5.00	10.00
— Reissue of Argo 687-S						
On Various-Artists Collections						
Santa Claus Is Coming to Town		Have a Merry Chess Christmas (Chess/MCA CH-25210)				
LEWIS, ROBERT Q.						
45s						
MGM 12740		Santa Claus Jr./(I Love That) Little Green Girl	1958	2.50	5.00	10.00
LEWIS, SHARI, AND LAMB CHOP						
45s						
Musicor 1140		Some Things For Xmas/Mr. Santa	1965	3.75	7.50	15.00
Musicor 1140	PS	Some Things For Xmas/Mr. Santa	1965	5.00	10.00	20.00
LI'L WALLY						
45s						
Drum Boy 115		Christmas In Your Heart/Hawaiian Christmas	1965	2.00	4.00	8.00
Jay Jay 150		Sleigh Bells Waltz/Jingle Bells Polka	1966	2.00	4.00	8.00
Jay Jay 209		Happy New Year/Jesus Was Born	1967	2.00	4.00	8.00
Jay Jay 228		Santa Claus Is Coming To Town/How Lovely Is Christmas	1968	—	3.00	6.00
— Yellow vinyl						
Jay Jay 229		Auld Lang Syne/Dance Around The Christmas Tree	1968	—	3.00	6.00
— Yellow vinyl						
Jay Jay 230		Merry Christmas Mom & Dad/Oh Lovely Christmas Tree	1968	—	3.00	6.00
— Yellow vinyl						
Jay Jay 253		White Christmas/Winter Wonderland	1969	—	3.00	6.00
Albums						
Jay Jay 1023	M	Polish Christmas Carols	196?	3.75	7.50	15.00
Jay Jay 5011		Polish Christmas Carols, Vol. 2	19??	3.00	6.00	12.00
Jay Jay 5012		Dance Around the Christmas Tree	19??	3.00	6.00	12.00
Jay Jay 5026		Christmas Time	19??	3.00	6.00	12.00
Jay Jay 5080		Polka Christmas	19??	3.00	6.00	12.00
Jay Jay 8003		Christmas from Poland	19??	3.00	6.00	12.00
LIBERACE						
45s						
Columbia 40379		The Spirit of Christmas/O Holy Night	1954	3.00	6.00	12.00
Columbia 40380		The Christmas Song/The Toy Piano//	1954	3.00	6.00	12.00
		The Beauty of Holiness/Santa Claus Medley				
Columbia 40381		Gesu Bambino/Sleigh Ride//Star Bright/Ave Maria	1954	3.00	6.00	12.00
Columbia 40382		Twas the Night Before Christmas/Christmas Medley	1954	3.00	6.00	12.00
Columbia 48001		Ave Maria/Christmas Medley (White Christmas/Jingle	1954	3.75	7.50	15.00
		Bells/O Come All Ye Faithful/Silent Night)				
Columbia 48001	PS	Ave Maria/Christmas Medley (White Christmas/Jingle	1954	5.00	10.00	20.00
		Bells/O Come All Ye Faithful/Silent Night)				

Label, Number		Title (A Side/B Side)	Year	VG	VG+	NM
7-Inch Extended Plays						
Columbia 5-2050		The Spirit of Christmas/Christmas Medley// Star Bright/The Beauty of Holiness	1954	3.00	6.00	12.00
Columbia 5-2050	PS	(title unknown)	1954	3.75	7.50	15.00
Columbia 5-2051		O Holy Night/The Toy Piano//Sleigh Ride/The Christmas Song	1954	3.00	6.00	12.00
Columbia 5-2051	PS	(title unknown)	1954	3.75	7.50	15.00
Albums						
Columbia CL 589	M	Christmas at Liberace's	1954	12.50	25.00	50.00
Mistletoe MLP-1208		Twas the Night Before Christmas	1974	2.50	5.00	10.00
On Various-Artists Collections						
'Twas the Night Before Christmas		Best of Christmas (Mistletoe MLP-1209)				
Ave Maria		Best of Christmas Vol. 2 (Mistletoe MLP-1221)				
Christmas Song, The		Best of Christmas (Mistletoe MLP-1209)				
Jesu Bambino		Home for the Holidays (MCA MSM-35007)				
O Holy Night		Best of Christmas Vol. 2 (Mistletoe MLP-1221)				
Oh Little Town of Bethlehem		12 Days of Christmas, The (Pickwick SPC-1021)				

LIGGINS, JIMMY
45s

Specialty 753	I Want My Baby For Christmas/I Want My Baby For Christmas	197?	2.50	5.00	10.00
— B-side by Smokey Hogg					

LIGHT, BEN, AND HIS SURF CLUB BOYS
45s

Hollywood Hot 338	Christmas Balls/(B-side unknown)	19??	2.50	5.00	10.00

LIGHT, ENOCH
On Various-Artists Collections

Snowfall	Carols and Candlelight (Columbia Special Products P 12525)

LILE, FORD
45s

Jan-ell 101		Who Said It's Christmas (In San Francisco)/ Have Yourself A Merry Little Christmas	19??	2.00	4.00	8.00
Pennant 106	DJ	Who Said It's Christmas In San Francisco/(Bridges) To Christmasland	19??	—	3.00	6.00

LILII, NIFO
45s

Rae-Ann 100	Hello, Merry Christmas/Neath A Blanket Of White	19??	—	2.00	4.00

LINDENWOOD COLLEGES MADRIGAL SINGERS
On Various-Artists Collections

How Far Is It to Bethlehem?	Christmas in Saint Louis ((no label) TS77-558/9)

LINDSAY, MARK
On Various-Artists Collections

Greensleeves	Christmas Greetings, Vol. 3 (Columbia Special Products P 11383)
What Child Is This	Very Merry Christmas, A, Volume IV (Columbia Special Products CSS 1464)

LINE MATERIAL
Note: All of these are identified by the A-side matrix number. The B-side matrix number is the same as earlier releases of the same title.

45s

McGraw-Edison HO8W-0439	Santa's North Pole Band	1957	5.00	10.00	20.00
— Blank B-side					
McGraw-Edison JO8W-1438	The Sounds of Christmas/Santa's North Pole Band	1958	3.75	7.50	15.00
McGraw-Edison KO9H-2065	The Kinds of Christmas/Santa's North Pole Band	1959	3.75	7.50	15.00
McGraw-Edison LO9H-3092	Santa's Factoree/The Kinds of Christmas	1960	3.75	7.50	15.00
McGraw-Edison NO9W-1867	Let's Trim the Christmas Tree/The Sounds of Christmas	1962	3.00	6.00	12.00

LINN AND LINDA WITH THE JORDANAIRES AND MILLIE
45s

Dusi 800	Christmas Orphan/Happy Christmas Time	197?	2.00	4.00	8.00

LINN, ROBERTA
45s

Keen 2013	Merry Christmas Darling/Katie the Kangaroo	1958	3.75	7.50	15.00

Label, Number		Title (A Side/B Side)	Year	VG	VG+	NM
LINTON, SHERWIN						
45s						
Breaker 3902		Santa Got a DWI/An Old Christmas Card	198?	—	2.00	4.00
Breaker 3902	PS	Santa Got a DWI/An Old Christmas Card	198?	—	3.00	6.00
LIPPARINI, R., TENOR						
On Various-Artists Collections						
La Ninna Nanna a Gesu		Christmas in Italy (Capitol T 10093)				
LIPTON, CELIA						
45s						
Independent 2359		Child/Puppet On A String	198?	—	—	3.00
Independent 2359	PS	Child/Puppet On A String	198?	—	—	3.00
LISA AND THE LOLLIPOPS						
45s						
Sing Me 18		Don'tcha Try to Tell Me There Ain't No Santa Claus/Stumpy	1977	—	2.00	4.00
LITTLE ALFRED AND THE LINDEN BLACK YOUTH CHOIR						
45s						
Wizdom 1983		I'm Dreaming Of A Black Christmas/For The Money	19??	—	2.00	4.00
LITTLE ANGELS, THE						
45s						
Riverdale 1960		(I'll Be a) Little Angel/The Santa Claus Parade	1960	5.00	10.00	20.00
Warwick 672		(I'll Be a) Little Angel/The Santa Claus Parade	1961	3.75	7.50	15.00
LITTLE CHORUS AND ORCHESTRA, THE						
45s						
ABC 10883		Little Christmas Sleigh Ride/Petit Noel	1966	2.00	4.00	8.00
LITTLE CINDY						
45s						
Columbia 41320		Happy Birthday Jesus/Blue Christmas	1958	2.50	5.00	10.00
— B-side by the Willis Sisters; red label						
Columbia 41320		Happy Birthday Jesus/Blue Christmas	1958	3.00	6.00	12.00
— B-side by the Willis Sisters; yellow label						
Columbia 41320	PS	Happy Birthday Jesus/Blue Christmas	1958	5.00	10.00	20.00
— B-side by the Willis Sisters						
Salem 2515		Happy Birthday Jesus/He's Around When Everybody Turns You Down	19??	2.00	4.00	8.00
LITTLE DUBLIN SINGERS, THE						
45s						
Coral 62470		Silent Night/The Lord's Prayer	1965	2.00	4.00	8.00
LITTLE EVA						
45s						
Dimension 1021		The Christmas Song/I Wish You a Merry Christmas	1963	3.75	7.50	15.00
— With Big Dee Irwin						
LITTLE FOLK OF MT. ROSKILL, THE						
45s						
RCA Victor HR 383		Hooray for Santa Claus/Come Go with Me	1969	2.50	5.00	10.00
— New Zealand import						
LITTLE JINGLE SINGERS, THE						
45s						
Thimble 010		Merry Christmas (To All the Children)/Winter Waltz	19??	—	2.50	5.00
LITTLE JO						
45s						
Santa's Land 102		Dear Santa/I Can Hardly Wait for Christmas	19??	—	2.00	4.00
— B-side by Ruff, Buff, Elmo & Stuffy (Santa's Gnomes)						

Label, Number		Title (A Side/B Side)	Year	VG	VG+	NM
LITTLE JOEY						
45s						
Fidelity 3014		Comin' Down The Chimney #2/Comin' Down The Chimney #1	1959	3.00	6.00	12.00
— B-side by Little Tootsie						
Variety 1011		Jingle Bells/Silent Night//Ave Maria	19??	2.00	4.00	8.00
LITTLE JOSEPH						
45s						
Blue Cat 103		The Story Of Christmas/Christmas Jingle	1964	2.50	5.00	10.00
LITTLE KID LEX AND ELIAS						
45s						
Capitol 3989		New Year Rock/Tom Hark	1958	3.75	7.50	15.00
LITTLE KIDS, THE						
45s						
Tower 298		Santa Claus Is Stuck in the Chimney/Tambourine Jingle	1966	3.75	7.50	15.00
LITTLE LANCE						
45s						
Silver Slipper 1006		Daddy's Christmas Train/Santa's Coming in a Whirlybird	19??	—	2.00	4.00
Silver Slipper 1006	PS	Daddy's Christmas Train/Santa's Coming in a Whirlybird	19??	—	3.00	6.00
LITTLE MILTON						
45s						
Malaco 2123		Lonesome Christmas/Come To Me	1985	—	2.00	4.00
LITTLE PINEY						
45s						
York Lynn 447		The Christmas Tree/Grandmother's Lullaby	19??	—	2.50	5.00
— B-side by Cindy Frey						
LITTLE ROGER AND THE GOOSEBUMPS						
45s						
Ambition 102		Xmas In The Hot Tub/ (What's So Funny 'Bout) Peace, Love, & Understanding	1980	3.00	6.00	12.00
— B-side by Dick Bright Youth Chorale						
LITTLE SISTERS, THE						
45s						
Liberty 55220		Are My Ears On Straight/A Little Star Came Down	1959	3.00	6.00	12.00
LITTLE SUSIE						
45s						
MGM 12396		Who Put the Gum in Santa's Whiskers/Christmas Season	1956	3.75	7.50	15.00
LITTLE TOMMY						
45s						
Laurie 3077		(All I Want for Christmas Is) My Two Front Teeth/Cuddly Wuddly	1960	3.75	7.50	15.00
— Also released as "Little Tommy Tucker"						
Wan-Dell 1715		I Played a Trick on Santa Claus/Away in the Manger	196?	3.00	6.00	12.00
LITTLE TOODLES						
45s						
Chris 711		Happy Christmas/Auld Lang Syne	19??	3.00	6.00	12.00
LITTLE TOOTSIE						
45s						
Fidelity 3014		Comin' Down The Chimney #1/Comin' Down The Chimney #2	1959	3.00	6.00	12.00
— B-side by Little Joey						
LITTLE TOY BAND, THE						
45s						
Christmas 373		Little Lost Sax/(B-side unknown)	19??	—	2.00	4.00

Label, Number		Title (A Side/B Side)	Year	VG	VG+	NM
LITTLE, "BIG" TINY						
45s						
Coral 62294		Tiny's Christmas Medley/Silver Bells	1961	2.50	5.00	10.00
Albums						
Coral CRL 57391	M	Christmas with Big Tiny Little	1961	3.75	7.50	15.00
Coral CRL 757391	S	Christmas with Big Tiny Little	1961	5.00	10.00	20.00
LITTLE, PEGGY						
45s						
Dot 17364		My Santa in Tennis Shoes/Ho Ho Ho	1970	—	3.00	6.00
LIVING STRINGS						
45s						
RCA PB-11155		Christmas Eve in My Home Town/Flying Home for Christmas	1977	—	2.00	4.00
— B-side by Living Voices						
Albums						
Pickwick ACL-9006		The Sound of Christmas	197?	2.00	4.00	8.00
— Reissue of RCA Camden CAS-2426						
RCA Camden CAL-783	M	The Spirit of Christmas	196?	2.50	5.00	10.00
RCA Camden CAS-783	S	The Spirit of Christmas	196?	3.00	6.00	12.00
RCA Camden CAS-2426		The Sound of Christmas	1970	3.00	6.00	12.00
On Various-Artists Collections						
Christmas Eve in My Home Town		60 Christmas Classics (Sessions DVL2-0723)				
Christmas Song, The		Happy Holidays, Volume IV (RCA Victor PRS-267)				
Have Yourself a Merry Little Christmas		Joyful Sound of Christmas, The (RCA Record Club CSP-0601)				
Mary's Boy Child		Joyful Sound of Christmas, The (RCA Record Club CSP-0601)				
Medley: Deck the Halls/It's Beginning to Look Like Christmas		60 Christmas Classics (Sessions DVL2-0723)				
(There's No Place Like) Home for the Holidays		Joyful Sound of Christmas, The (RCA Record Club CSP-0601) 60 Christmas Classics (Sessions DVL2-0723)				
LIVING STRINGS AND LIVING VOICES						
Albums						
RCA Camden CAS 2258		White Christmas	1968	3.00	6.00	12.00
On Various-Artists Collections						
Happy Holiday		Joyful Sound of Christmas, The (RCA Record Club CSP-0601)				
Medley: Ring Christmas Bells/We Wish You a Merry Christmas		60 Christmas Classics (Sessions DVL2-0723)				
White Christmas		Joyful Sound of Christmas, The (RCA Record Club CSP-0601)				
LIVING VOICES						
45s						
RCA JPC6-5314/5292	DJ	Christmas Is Christmas (All Over The World)/Long Long Kiss	197?	2.00	4.00	8.00
— A-side with the Living Strings; white label promo with no RCA logo						
RCA JH-11155	DJ	Flying Home for Christmas (mono/stereo)	1977	—	2.50	5.00
RCA PB-11155		Flying Home For Christmas/Christmas Eve In My Home Town	1977	—	2.00	4.00
— B-side by Living Strings						
Albums						
RCA Camden CAL-725	M	Sing Christmas Music	1962	2.50	5.00	10.00
RCA Camden CAS-725	S	Sing Christmas Music	1962	3.00	6.00	12.00
RCA Camden CAL-911	M	The Little Drummer Boy	1965	2.50	5.00	10.00
RCA Camden CAS-911	S	The Little Drummer Boy	1965	3.00	6.00	12.00
On Various-Artists Collections						
Blue Christmas		Blue Christmas (Welk Music Group WM-3002)				
Christmas Song, The		Joyful Sound of Christmas, The (RCA Record Club CSP-0601)				
Flying Home for Christmas		Happy Holidays, Vol. 22 (RCA Special Products DPL1-0777)				
Medley: Wassail Song/The First Noel/ O Christmas Tree/Green Needles		60 Christmas Classics (Sessions DVL2-0723)				
Santa Claus Is Coming to Town		Joyful Sound of Christmas, The (RCA Record Club CSP-0601)				
Silent Night		For a Musical Merry Christmas, Volume 3 (RCA Victor PRM-221)				
Winter Wonderland		Joyful Sound of Christmas, The (RCA Record Club CSP-0601)				
LLOYD SINGERS, THE						
45s						
Rivola 301		Christmas (Comes To Us All)/When You're Lonely Again	19??	—	2.00	4.00
LLOYD, BOBBY, AND THE SKELETONS						
45s						
Borrowed 1225		Do You Hear What I Hear/Jingle Bell Rock (Live)	198?	2.00	4.00	8.00

Label, Number		Title (A Side/B Side)	Year	VG	VG+	NM
LLOYD, TOMMY						
45s						
Blue Hen 205		Christmas Day/Christmas Time	19??	—	2.00	4.00
LOCAL H						
45s						
Island PR7 6902-7	DJ	Disgruntled Christmas/White Christmas	1994	2.00	4.00	8.00
— B-side by Sybil Vane; green vinyl						
LOCKLIN, HANK						
On Various-Artists Collections						
Rudolph the Red-Nosed Reindeer		Joyous Noel (Reader's Digest RDA-57A)				
LOCO, JOE, QUINTET						
45s						
Columbia 40599		White Christmas/Rudolph the Red-Nosed Reindeer	1955	3.00	6.00	12.00
LODGE, JUNE						
On Various-Artists Collections						
Joy to the World		Reggae Christmas, A (Real Authentic Sound RAS 3101)				
LOGAN, BUD						
45s						
RCA Victor 47-9678		Sock It To Me Santa/(Old Mr. Winter) Here You Come Again	1968	2.00	4.00	8.00
LOLA THE LADYBUG AND MYRON THE MOOSE						
On Various-Artists Collections						
Let's Build a Snowman		Starlight Christmas, A (MCA 10066)				
LOLLIPOPS, THE						
45s						
Warner Bros. 5122		Mister Santa/Little Donkey (Carry Mary Safely on Her Way)	1959	3.00	6.00	12.00
LOMBARDO, GUY						
Also see THE ANDREWS SISTERS.						
45s						
Decca 27257		Frosty the Snowman/If I Were Santa Claus	1950	3.00	6.00	12.00
Decca 27802		He'll Be Coming Down the Chimney/Christmas Chopsticks	1951	3.00	6.00	12.00
Decca 27803		Rudolph the Red-Nosed Reindeer/Christmas Tree at Home	1951	3.00	6.00	12.00
Decca 28408		Santa Claus Is Coming to Town/Jingle Bells	1952	3.00	6.00	12.00
Decca 28409		White Christmas/Merry Christmas Waltz	1952	3.00	6.00	12.00
Decca 28410		Rudolph, the Red-Nosed Reindeer/Frosty the Snowman	1952	3.00	6.00	12.00
— Lines label						
Decca 28410		Rudolph, the Red-Nosed Reindeer/Frosty the Snowman	1952	2.50	5.00	10.00
— Star label						
Decca 28905		Auld Lang Syne/Hot Time in the Old Town Tonight	1953	3.75	7.50	15.00
— Lines label						
Decca 28905		Auld Lang Syne/Hot Time in the Old Town Tonight	1955	3.00	6.00	12.00
— Star label						
Decca 28905		Auld Lang Syne/Hot Time in the Old Town Tonight	1960	2.50	5.00	10.00
— Color bars label						
Decca 28942		I Saw Mommy Kissing Santa Claus/ Please Bring My Daddy a Train, Santa	1953	3.75	7.50	15.00
7-Inch Extended Plays						
Decca ED 550 (91131)		Jingle Bells/Santa Claus Is Coming to Town// White Christmas/Merry Christmas Waltz	195?	3.00	6.00	12.00
Decca ED 550 (91132)		Rudolph the Red-Nosed Reindeer/Frosty the Snowman//He'll Be Coming Down the Chimney/Christmas Chopsticks	195?	3.00	6.00	12.00
Decca ED 550	PS	Christmas Songs	195?	3.00	6.00	12.00
— Cover for 2-EP set						
Decca ED 2657		(contents unknown)	195?	3.00	6.00	12.00
Decca ED 2657	PS	Christmas Songs	195?	3.00	6.00	12.00
Albums						
Capitol TAO 1443	M	Sing the Songs of Christmas	1960	3.75	7.50	15.00
Capitol STAO 1443	S	Sing the Songs of Christmas	1960	5.00	10.00	20.00
Decca DL 8354	M	Jingle Bells	1956	5.00	10.00	20.00
Decca DL 78354	R	Jingle Bells	196?	2.50	5.00	10.00
MCA 15012		Jingle Bells	197?	2.50	5.00	10.00
— Reissue						

Label, Number	Title (A Side/B Side)	Year	VG	VG+	NM
Pickwick SPC 1011	Deck the Halls	196?	2.50	5.00	10.00
— Silver label					
Pickwick SPC 1011	Deck the Halls	197?	2.00	4.00	8.00
— Reissue on black label					

On Various-Artists Collections

Auld Lang Syne	Christmas Greetings, Vol. 4 (Columbia Special Products P 11987)
Frosty the Snow Man	Christmas Through the Years (Reader's Digest RDA-143)
	Magic of Christmas, The (Columbia Musical Treasury P3S 5806)
	Old Fashioned Christmas, An (Reader's Digest RDA 216-A)
Here Comes Santa Claus	Christmas Songs, The (Capitol SLB-57074)
I Saw Mommy Kissing Santa Claus	Old-Fashioned Christmas, An (Longines Symphonette LS 214)
Jingle Bells	Christmas Stocking (Capitol NP 90494)
	I'll Be Home for Christmas (Pickwick SPC-1009)
O Little Town of Bethlehem	Christmas Day (Pickwick SPC 1010)
Rudolph, the Red-Nosed Reindeer	Christmas to Remember, A (Capitol Creative Products SL-6573)
Silent Night	Little Drummer Boy, The (Capitol/Pickwick SPC-3462)

LONDON PHILHARMONIC ORCHESTRA
On Various-Artists Collections

And He Shall Purify	Joyous Music for Christmas Time (Reader's Digest RD 45-M)
And the Glory of the Lord Shall Be Revealed	Joyous Music for Christmas Time (Reader's Digest RD 45-M)
Behold the Lamb of God	Joyous Music for Christmas Time (Reader's Digest RD 45-M)
Comfort Ye My People; Every Valley Shall Be Exalted	Joyous Music for Christmas Time (Reader's Digest RD 45-M)
For Unto Us a Child Is Born	Joyous Music for Christmas Time (Reader's Digest RD 45-M)
	Old Fashioned Christmas, An (Reader's Digest RDA 216-A)
Hallelujah	Joyous Music for Christmas Time (Reader's Digest RD 45-M)
	Old Fashioned Christmas, An (Reader's Digest RDA 216-A)
He Shall Feed His Flock; Come Unto Him	Joyous Music for Christmas Time (Reader's Digest RD 45-M)
	Old Fashioned Christmas, An (Reader's Digest RDA 216-A)
He Was Despised and Rejected of Men	Joyous Music for Christmas Time (Reader's Digest RD 45-M)
I Know That My Redeemer Liveth	Joyous Music for Christmas Time (Reader's Digest RD 45-M)
	Old Fashioned Christmas, An (Reader's Digest RDA 216-A)
Pastoral Symphony	Joyous Music for Christmas Time (Reader's Digest RD 45-M)
The Trumpet Shall Sound	Joyous Music for Christmas Time (Reader's Digest RD 45-M)

LONDON POPS ORCHESTRA
On Various-Artists Collections

Glory to God in the Highest	Home for Christmas (Columbia Musical Treasury P3S 5608)
Joseph Dearest, Joseph Mine	Home for Christmas (Columbia Musical Treasury P3S 5608)
We Three Kings of Orient Are	Home for Christmas (Columbia Musical Treasury P3S 5608)

LONDON SYMPHONY ORCHESTRA
Albums

Hallmark 625 XPR	Hallmark Presents: The Best Loved Christmas Carols	1985	3.00	6.00	12.00

— *Sold only at Hallmark Cards dealers. Also see other "Hallmark Presents:" LPs in the various artists section.*

On Various-Artists Collections

While Shepherds Watched	60 Christmas Classics (Sessions DVL2-0723)

LONDON SYMPHONY ORCHESTRA/ROGER WAGNER CHORALE
On Various-Artists Collections

In Dulci Jubilo	Great Songs of Christmas, Album Nine (Columbia Special Products CSS 1033)
O Sanctissima	Great Songs of Christmas, Album Nine (Columbia Special Products CSS 1033)

LONDON, JULIE
45s

Liberty 55108	I'd Like You for Christmas/Saddle the Wind	1957	3.00	6.00	12.00

LONG, JOHNNY
45s

Coral 60866	Jingle Bells/Winter Wonderland	1952	3.75	7.50	15.00

LONGET, CLAUDINE
45s

A&M 895	Snow/Don't Intend to Spend My Christmas Without You	1967	2.00	4.00	8.00

On Various-Artists Collections

Snow	Something Festive! (A&M SP-19003)

Label, Number		Title (A Side/B Side)	Year	VG	VG+	NM
LONGINES SYMPHONETTE SOCIETY						
Albums						
Longines Symphonette LW 155	M	The Sweet Voices of Christmas	196?	2.50	5.00	10.00
— With the children's voices from the choirs of Westminster Abbey and St. Paul's Cathedral						
Longines Symphonette LWS 155	S	The Sweet Voices of Christmas	196?	3.00	6.00	12.00
Longines Symphonette LWS 192		Home for Christmas	196?	3.00	6.00	12.00
LONNIE AND THE CRISIS						
45s						
Relic 532		Bells in the Chapel/Santa Town USA	196?	—	3.00	6.00
— Reissue of Universal 103						
Times Square 25		Bells in the Chapel/Santa Town USA	196?	2.00	4.00	8.00
— Reissue of Universal 103						
Universal 103		Bells in the Chapel/Santa Town USA	1961	50.00	100.00	200.00
LONZO AND OSCAR						
45s						
Decca 28961		Frosty the De-Frosted Snowman/Jangle Bells	1953	5.00	10.00	20.00
LOPER, EDDIE						
45s						
Sing Me 38		Don't Hang the Mistletoe/Ease My Mind on You	198?	—	—	3.00
Sing Me 38	PS	Don't Hang the Mistletoe/Ease My Mind on You	198?	—	—	3.00
LOPEZ, TRINI						
45s						
Reprise 0801	DJ	El Nino Del Tambor/Nocho De Paz (Let There Be Peace)	1968	2.00	4.00	8.00
— Stock copy may not exist						
LOPEZ, VINCENT						
45s						
Coral 61902		Silver Bells/Whistlin' Otto	1957	2.50	5.00	10.00
On Various-Artists Collections						
Cantique de Noel		Decca 38170 (title unknown) (Decca DL 38170)				
LORBER, JEFF						
On Various-Artists Collections						
God Rest the House		Winter Warnerland (Warner Bros. PRO-A-3328)				
LORD INVINCIBLE AND THE TROPICAL SPADES						
45s						
Charmur 1001		Sleigh Ride/The Twelve Days Of Christmas	19??	—	2.00	4.00
Charmur 1001	PS	Sleigh Ride/The Twelve Days Of Christmas	19??	—	2.00	4.00
LORENZ, MIKE						
45s						
Hottrax 15007		The Rap Before Christmas/Auld Lang Syne (Go-Go)	198?	—	2.00	4.00
Hottrax 15007	PS	The Rap Before Christmas/Auld Lang Syne (Go-Go)	198?	—	2.00	4.00
LOS LOBOS						
On Various-Artists Collections						
Rudolph the Manic Reindeer		Winter Warnerland (Warner Bros. PRO-A-3328)				
LOS NINOS DE MEXICO						
45s						
Fantasy 577		La PiÒata/It's Christmas Eve And We're Alone	196?	3.00	6.00	12.00
— B-side by Little Cathy Tippins						
LOS STRAITJACKETS						
45s						
Spinout 45-013		A Marshmallow World/Sleigh Ride	1996	—	2.00	4.00
— Red vinyl, no picture sleeve						
LOUD MOUSE						
45s						
Nashville American 029		Merry Christmas From The Loud Mouse/I Like Christmas Time	19??	—	3.00	6.00
Nashville American 029	PS	Merry Christmas From The Loud Mouse/I Like Christmas Time	19??	—	3.00	6.00

Label, Number		Title (A Side/B Side)	Year	VG	VG+	NM
LOUIS, LOUISE						
45s						
Skyway 139		Merry Christmas, Dear Jesus (Happy Birthday)/ The Greatest Shepherd	196?	3.00	6.00	12.00
LOUVIN BROTHERS, THE						
45s						
Capitol 4473		Santa Claus Parade/It's Christmas Time	1960	3.00	6.00	12.00
Albums						
Capitol T 1616	M	Country Christmas	1961	12.50	25.00	50.00
— Black rainbow label with "Capitol" at left						
Capitol ST 1616	S	Country Christmas	1961	20.00	40.00	80.00
— Black rainbow label with "Capitol" at left						
Capitol T 1616	M	Country Christmas	1962	5.00	10.00	20.00
— Black rainbow label with "Capitol" at top						
Capitol ST 1616	S	Country Christmas	1962	6.25	12.50	25.00
— Black rainbow label with "Capitol" at top						

On Various-Artists Collections

Friendly Beasts, The		Country Christmas (Time-Life STL-109)				
It Came Upon the Midnight Clear		Country Christmas (Time-Life STL-109)				

LOVE, DARLENE						
45s						
Arista 74621 124767		All Alone on Christmas/(Instrumental)	1992	—	2.50	5.00
Arista 74621 124767	PS	All Alone on Christmas/(Instrumental)	1992	—	2.50	5.00
— 45 and sleeve released only in Europe						
Passport 7926		Christmas (Baby Please Come Home)/Playing for Keeps	1983	3.00	6.00	12.00
Philles 119		Christmas (Baby Please Come Home)/Harry and Milt Meet Hal B.	1963	10.00	20.00	40.00
Philles 125		Christmas (Baby Please Come Home)/X-Mas Blues	1964	100.00	200.00	400.00
Philles 125X		Christmas (Baby Please Come Home)/Winter Wonderland	1965	6.25	12.50	25.00
Warner/Spector 0401		Christmas (Baby Please Come Home)/Winter Wonderland	1974	2.50	5.00	10.00

On Various-Artists Collections

Christmas (Baby Please Come Home)		Christmas EP (Philles X-EP)
		Christmas Gift for You from Phil Spector, A (Philles PHLP-4005)
		Phil Spector's Christmas Album (Apple SW 3400)
		Phil Spector: Back to Mono 1958-1969 (Phil Spector/Abkco 7118-1)
Marshmallow World, A		Christmas Gift for You from Phil Spector, A (Philles PHLP-4005)
		Phil Spector's Christmas Album (Apple SW 3400)
		Phil Spector: Back to Mono 1958-1969 (Phil Spector/Abkco 7118-1)
White Christmas		Christmas Gift for You from Phil Spector, A (Philles PHLP-4005)
		Phil Spector's Christmas Album (Apple SW 3400)
		Phil Spector: Back to Mono 1958-1969 (Phil Spector/Abkco 7118-1)
Winter Wonderland		Christmas Gift for You from Phil Spector, A (Philles PHLP-4005)
		Phil Spector's Christmas Album (Apple SW 3400)
		Phil Spector: Back to Mono 1958-1969 (Phil Spector/Abkco 7118-1)

LOVE, HELEN						
45s						
Damgood 33 1/3		Happiest Time of the Year/Where's Me Fuckin' Presents?	19??	—	3.00	6.00
— B-side by Damaged Puds; brown vinyl						
Damgood 33 1/3	PS	Happiest Time of the Year/Where's Me Fuckin' Presents?	19??	—	3.00	6.00
— B-side by Damaged Puds						

LOVE, MIKE, AND DEAN TORRENCE
Also see THE BEACH BOYS, JAN AND DEAN.

45s						
Hitbound X-2		Jingle Bell Rock/Jingle Bells	1983	3.00	6.00	12.00
— B-side by Paul Revere and the Raiders						
Hitbound X-2	PS	Jingle Bell Rock/Jingle Bells	1983	5.00	10.00	20.00
— B-side by Paul Revere and the Raiders						

LOVE, SHIRLEY
On Various-Artists Collections

Coventry Carol		Life Treasury of Christmas Music, The (Project/Capitol TL 100)

LOVE, TRUDY						
45s						
Christmas '70 111070		That Day Of The Year/Turkey Lurkey Time	1970	—	3.00	6.00
— B-side by the Today Generation						

Label, Number	Title (A Side/B Side)	Year	VG	VG+	NM

LOVETONES, THE
45s
Love-Tone 101	You Can Tell Me That This Is Christmas/When I Asked My Love	1961	5.00	10.00	20.00

LOWE, JIM
45s
Mercury 70265	Santa Claus Rides a Strawberry Roan/Love in Both Directions	1953	5.00	10.00	20.00
Mercury 71016	Prince of Peace/Santa Claus Rides a Strawberry Roan	1956	3.75	7.50	15.00

LUBOFF, NORMAN, CHOIR
45s
Columbia 40785		What Child Is This/The Twelve Days of Christmas	1956	2.50	5.00	10.00
Columbia 41065		Let's Make It Christmas All Year 'Round/Mary Had a Baby (Amen!)	1957	2.50	5.00	10.00

Albums
Columbia CL 926	M	Songs of Christmas	1957	3.75	7.50	15.00
Columbia CS 8846	R	Songs of Christmas	1963	3.00	6.00	12.00
RCA Victor LPM-2941	M	Christmas with the Norman Luboff Choir	1964	3.00	6.00	12.00
RCA Victor LSP-2941	S	Christmas with the Norman Luboff Choir	1964	3.75	7.50	15.00

On Various-Artists Collections
Angels We Have Heard on High	60 Christmas Classics (Sessions DVL2-0723)
Do You Hear What I Hear?	Joyous Noel (Reader's Digest RDA-57A)
	Music to Trim Your Tree By (RCA Victor PRM 225)
Hark! The Herald Angels Sing	Joy to the World (30 Classic Christmas Melodies) (Columbia Special Products P3 14654)
	Merry Christmas from... (Reader's Digest RD4-83)
Holly and the Ivy, The	Great Songs of Christmas, The, Album Two (Columbia Special Products XTV 86100/1)
	Happy Holidays, Volume II (Columbia Special Products CSM 348)
Jesu, Joy of Man's Desiring	Family Christmas Collection, The (Time-Life STL-131)
Let There Be Peace on Earth	For a Musical Merry Christmas, Vol. Two (RCA Victor PRM 189)
	Merry Christmas (RCA Victor PRM-168)
Little Drummer Boy, The	Christmas Eve with Colonel Sanders (RCA Victor PRS-256)
	Family Christmas Collection, The (Time-Life STL-131)
	Happy Holidays, Volume 14 (RCA Special Products DPL1-0376)
	RCA Victor Presents Music for the Twelve Days of Christmas (RCA Victor PRS-188)
Medley: God Rest Ye Merry Gentlemen/	Wondrous Winter: Songs of Winter, Songs of Christmas
Hark! The Herald Angels Sing	(Columbia Special Products CSS 708/9)
Medley: God Rest Ye Merry,	Great Songs of Christmas, The (Columbia Special Products XTV 69406/7)
Gentlemen/We Three Kings/Deck the Halls	
Medley: Hark the Herald Angels Sing/	Great Songs of Christmas, The, Album Three (Columbia Special Products CSP 117)
A La Nanita Nana	
Medley: Hark the Herald Angels Sing/	Christmas in California (RCA Victor PRS-276)
God Rest Ye Merry Gentlemen/The First Noel	
	Christmas in New York Volume 2 (RCA Victor PRS-270)
	Christmastime in Carol and Song (RCA PRM-271)
Medley: Joy to the World/	Zenith Presents Christmas, A Gift of Music Vol. 5 (Columbia Special Products C 10395)
I Saw Three Ships	
Medley: Joy to the World/Oh Little	60 Christmas Classics (Sessions DVL2-0723)
Town of Bethlehem/Hark! The Herald Angels Sing	
Medley: O Little Town of Bethlehem/	Philco Album of Holiday Music, The (Columbia Special Products CSM 431)
Deck the Hall with Boughs of Holly	
Medley: O Tannenbaum/	Great Songs of Christmas, The, Album Two (Columbia Special Products XTV 86100/1)
Here We Come a-Caroling	
Medley: The First Noel/Wassail,	Seasons Greetings (A Christmas Festival of Stars) (Columbia CS 8189)
Wassail,All Over the Town/Hark! The	
Herald Angels Sing/God Rest	
Ye Merry Gentlemen	
Medley: The Little Drummer Boy/	Very Merry Christmas, A, Volume 5 (RCA Special Products PRS-343)
Hark the Herald Angels Sing	
Medley: What Child Is This/The Twelve	Spirit of Christmas, The (Columbia Special Products CSP 249)
Days of Christmas/Baloo Lammy	
O Little Town of Bethlehem	Merry Christmas from... (Reader's Digest RD4-83)
	That Christmas Feeling (Columbia Special Products P 11853)
O Tannenbaum	Merry Christmas from... (Reader's Digest RD4-83)
Silent Night	Very Merry Christmas, A, Volume VI (RCA Special Products PRS-427)
Silver Bells	Happy Holidays, Volume 19 (RCA Special Products DPL1-0689)
Twelve Days of Christmas, The	Gift of Christmas, The, Vol. 1 (Columbia Special Products CSS 706)
White Christmas	Christmas Festival of Songs and Carols, Volume 2 (RCA Victor PRM-195)
	Christmas in New York (RCA Victor PRM-257)

LUCK, LUCKY
45s
Mahalo 1000	Twelve Days of Christmas/Kanaka Christmas	19??	—	2.00	4.00

LUMAN, BOB
45s
Polydor 14444	A Christmas Tribute/	1977	—	2.00	4.00
	Give Someone You Love (A Little Bit of Love This Year)				

Label, Number		Title (A Side/B Side)	Year	VG	VG+	NM
LUNA						
45s						
Elektra 64679	DJ	Time/Egg Nog	1992	2.00	4.00	8.00
— Promo only on green vinyl						
LUND, ART						
45s						
MGM 10780		(Sweet Angie) The Christmas Tree Angel/Little Toy Town Parade	1950	3.75	7.50	15.00
On Various-Artists Collections						
I'll Be Home for Christmas		Original Amateur Hour 25th Anniversary Album (United Artists UXL 2)				
LUNDBERG, KARL, AND FULL CIRCLE						
On Various-Artists Collections						
Little Drummer Boy, The		Jazzy Wonderland, A (Columbia 1P 8120)				
LUTHER – See LUTHER VANDROSS.						
LUTHER & THE B.B.B.'S						
45s						
Jargon 211		Are You Ready for Christmas/What'd You Get?	19??	—	2.50	5.00
Jargon 211	PS	Are You Ready for Christmas/What'd You Get?	19??	—	2.50	5.00
LUTHER, FRANK						
45s						
Decca 27897		Ting-a-Ling Jingle/Santa Claus Is Coming to Town	1951	3.75	7.50	15.00
Decca 88078		Ting-a-Ling Jingle/Santa Claus Is Coming to Town	1951	3.00	6.00	12.00
— Children's Series release						
Decca 88078	PS	Ting-a-Ling Jingle/Santa Claus Is Coming to Town	1951	5.00	10.00	20.00
LYMAN, ARTHUR						
45s						
Hifi 5058		We Three Kings/Little Drummer Boy	1962	3.00	6.00	12.00
Hifi 5081		Winter Wonderland/Rudolph, the Red-Nosed Reindeer	1963	3.00	6.00	12.00
Hifi 5083		We Three Kings/Little Drummer Boy	1963	3.00	6.00	12.00
Albums						
Hifi L 1018	M	Mele Kalikimaka (Merry Christmas)	1963	5.00	10.00	20.00
Hifi SL 1018	S	Mele Kalikimaka (Merry Christmas)	1963	6.25	12.50	25.00
LYMON, FRANKIE						
45s						
Roulette 4035		It's Christmas Once Again/Little Girl	1957	6.25	12.50	25.00
LYNDON, FRANK						
45s						
Laurie 3322		Santa's Jet/Sing Along with Santa's Jet	1965	5.00	10.00	20.00
LYNETTE, SHANA						
7-Inch Extended Plays						
Antique 009		Mr. Russian (Please Don't Shoot Down Santa's Sleigh)/ Angel In The Snow//Getting Ready For Christmas/ Hey Mister Santa Claus	1986	—	2.00	4.00
Antique 009	PS	Merry Christmas 1983-1984-1985-1986 From The Sensational Little Shana Lynette	1986	—	2.00	4.00
LYNN, JENNY						
45s						
Beta 1000		Gee! It's Christmas Day/Jingle Bells	19??	—	2.50	5.00
LYNN, JOYCE						
45s						
Wrimus 712		Christmas Time Is Here Again/Christmas Candles	1961	2.00	4.00	8.00
LYNN, LORETTA						
45s						
Decca 32043		It Won't Seem Like Christmas/To Heck with Santa Claus	1966	2.50	5.00	10.00
Decca 32043	PS	It Won't Seem Like Christmas/To Heck with Santa Claus	1966	3.75	7.50	15.00
MCA 65034		Shadrack, the Black Reindeer/Let's Put Christ Back in Christmas	1974	—	2.00	4.00
— Black label with rainbow						
MCA 65034		Shadrack, the Black Reindeer/Let's Put Christ Back in Christmas	1980	—	—	3.00
— Blue label with rainbow						

(Top left) Jethro Tull's "Christmas Song" isn't too hard to find on a single, but this one, "Ring Out, Solstice Bells," is a different story. This is a rare 12-inch US promo from 1977. (Top right) Tough to find on its original US pressing with its sleeve is the Kinks' "Father Christmas," from 1977. (Bottom left) One of the sultriest holiday recordings of all time is Eartha Kitt's "Santa Baby." The 1953 holiday hit had been largely lost to time until Madonna revived it in 1987. (Bottom right) "Rockin' Around the Christmas Tree" by Brenda Lee was first released in 1958, but didn't become a hit until the holiday season of 1960.

Label, Number		Title (A Side/B Side)	Year	VG	VG+	NM
Albums						
Decca DL 4817	M	A Country Christmas	1966	6.25	12.50	25.00
Decca DL 74817	S	A Country Christmas	1966	7.50	15.00	30.00
MCA 15022		A Country Christmas	197?	3.00	6.00	12.00
— Reissue of Decca LP						
On Various-Artists Collections						
Away in a Manger		Wonderful World of Christmas, The, Album Two (Capitol Special Markets SL-8025)				
Country Christmas		Country Christmas (Time-Life STL-109)				
First Noel, The		Tennessee Christmas (MCA 5620)				
It Won't Seem Like Christmas		Country Christmas (Time-Life STL-109)				
Santa Claus Is Coming to Town		Happy Holidays, Vol. 23 (MCA Special Products 15042)				
		Home for the Holidays (MCA MSM-35007)				

LYNNE, GLORIA
45s

Everest 2051		On Christmas Day/Wouldn't It Be Loverly	1964	2.00	4.00	8.00

LYONS, RUTH
45s

Candee 502		Christmas Marching Song/This Is Christmas	196?	3.00	6.00	12.00
— B-side by Ruby Wright						
Candee EP-50-50		Have A Merry Merry Merry Merry Christmas/	196?	2.00	4.00	8.00
		The Happy Time//Christmas Is A Birthday Time				
— B-side by Ruby Wright						
Columbia 41810		All Because It's Christmas/Everywhere the Bells Are Ringing	1960	3.00	6.00	12.00
— B-side by Ruby Wright						
Columbia 41810	PS	All Because It's Christmas/Everywhere the Bells Are Ringing	1960	5.00	10.00	20.00
— B-side by Ruby Wright						

LYONS, RUTH, AND THE DELLO-LARKS
On Various-Artists Collections

Hey Nonnie Nonnie	Ten Tunes of Christmas (Candee 50-50)

M

M.A.C. APOLLOS AND ORCHESTRA
On Various-Artists Collections

I Hear America Singing	Christmas in Saint Louis ((no label) TS77-558/9)

M.C. MIKER "G" & DEEJAY SVEN
12-Inch Singles

JDC 0097		Holiday Rap/Holiday Rap (Accapella)//	198?	—	3.00	6.00
		Whimsical Touch/Holiday Hip Hop				

MacGOWAN, SHANE, AND THE POPES
45s

Zit ZANG88		A Christmas Lullaby/Paddy Rolling Stone//	1996	—	2.00	4.00
		Hippy Hippy Shake/Danny Boy				
Zit ZANG88	PS	A Christmas Lullaby/Paddy Rolling Stone//	1996	—	2.00	4.00
		Hippy Hippy Shake/Danny Boy				
— Record and sleeve are U.K. imports						

MACIAS, ENRICO
45s

Mercury 72884		Noel In Jerusalem/Noel A' Jerusalem	1968	—	3.00	6.00

MACK, WARNER
45s

Lost Gold 4		Dasher With The Light Upon His Tail (same on both sides)	1993	—	—	3.00
— Green vinyl						

MacKENZIE, GISELE
45s

Vik 0300		Too Fat for the Chimney/Jingle Bells	1957	3.00	6.00	12.00
Vik 0300	PS	Too Fat for the Chimney/Jingle Bells	1957	5.00	10.00	20.00

Label, Number		Title (A Side/B Side)	Year	VG	VG+	NM
Albums						
RCA Victor LPM-2006	M	Christmas with Gisele	1959	7.50	15.00	30.00
RCA Victor LSP-2006	S	Christmas with Gisele	1959	10.00	20.00	40.00
"X" LX-1099	M	Christmas with Gisele	1957	10.00	20.00	40.00
On Various-Artists Collections						
Have Yourself a Merry Little Christmas		Joyous Noel (Reader's Digest RDA-57A)				
		October Christmas Sampler 59-40-41 (RCA Victor SPS-33-54)				
He's Too Fat for the Chimney		Family Christmas Collection, The (Time-Life STL-131)				
Medley: We Three Kings/		Christmas in the Air (RCA Special Products DPL1-0133)				
Good King Wenceslas						
We Three Kings of Orient Are		For a Musical Merry Christmas, Vol. Two (RCA Victor PRM 189)				

MacRAE, GORDON
45s

Label, Number		Title (A Side/B Side)	Year	VG	VG+	NM
Capitol F2927		Count Your Blessings Instead of Sheep/Cara Mia	1954	3.75	7.50	15.00
Capitol F3284		(Here's to) A Wonderful Christmas/A Woman in Love	1955	3.75	7.50	15.00
On Various-Artists Collections						
Go Tell It on the Mountain		Firestone Presents Your Christmas Favorites, Volume 3 (Firestone MLP 7008)				
Reminder Spot		For Christmas Seals...A Matter of Life and Breath (Decca Custom Style E)				
Sleigh Ride		Firestone Presents Your Christmas Favorites, Volume 3 (Firestone MLP 7008)				

MacRAE, GORDON, AND MARTHA WRIGHT
On Various-Artists Collections

	Title (A Side/B Side)
White Christmas	Firestone Presents Your Christmas Favorites, Volume 3 (Firestone MLP 7008)

MAD MILO
45s

Label, Number	Title (A Side/B Side)	Year	VG	VG+	NM
Million 20018	Elvis for Christmas/New Year	1957	12.50	25.00	50.00
— B-side by Ron Tan and Combo					

MADDOCK, JOHN
45s

Label, Number	Title (A Side/B Side)	Year	VG	VG+	NM
Glitter 43872	Sally Claus/Sally Claus	1984	—	—	3.00

MADDOX BROTHERS AND ROSE
45s

Label, Number	Title (A Side/B Side)	Year	VG	VG+	NM
Decca 28478	Jingle Bells/Silent Night	1952	3.75	7.50	15.00

MADDOX, JOHNNY
45s

Label, Number	Title (A Side/B Side)	Year	VG	VG+	NM
Dot 15120	I Saw Mommy Kissing Santa Claus/Rudolph the Red-Nosed Reindeer	1953	3.75	7.50	15.00

MADIGAN, BETTY
45s

Label, Number	Title (A Side/B Side)	Year	VG	VG+	NM
MGM 12093	We're All Kids At Christmas/The Story Of Christmas	1955	2.50	5.00	10.00
On Various-Artists Collections					
Story of Christmas, The	Merry Christmas And A Happy New Year (Modern Radio 102)				
Yes, There Is a Santa Claus	Stingiest Man in Town, The (Columbia CL 950)				

MADONNA
On Various-Artists Collections

	Title (A Side/B Side)
Santa Baby	Very Special Christmas, A (A&M SP-3911)

MADRID CONCERT ORCHESTRA AND CHORUS
Albums

Label, Number		Title (A Side/B Side)	Year	VG	VG+	NM
United Artists UAL 3059	M	Christmas in Spain	1959	3.75	7.50	15.00

MAESTRO, JOHNNY, AND THE BROOKLYN BRIDGE
45s

Label, Number	Title (A Side/B Side)	Year	VG	VG+	NM
Collectables 3997	Have Yourself A Merry Little Christmas/	199?	—	—	3.00
	A Christmas Long Ago (Jingle Jingle)				
— B-side by the Echelons					

MAGGARD, JOHNNY
45s

Label, Number		Title (A Side/B Side)	Year	VG	VG+	NM
Award 9201		Sparky/The Christmas Bunny	19??	—	2.50	5.00
Award 9201	PS	Sparky/The Christmas Bunny	19??	2.50	5.00	10.00

Label, Number		Title (A Side/B Side)	Year	VG	VG+	NM

MAGIC MOSE AND HIS ROYAL ROCKERS FEATURING 'BLIND SAM'
45s

Jingle Jungle 002		I'm Dreaming Of A Noir X-mas/	1984	—	2.50	5.00
		Have Yourselves A Groovy Little Solstice				
Jingle Jungle 002	PS	I'm Dreaming Of A Noir X-mas/	1984	—	2.50	5.00
		Have Yourselves A Groovy Little Solstice				

MALCHAK AND RUCKER
45s

Revolver 006		All I Want for Christmas Is Your Love/Christmas Is for Kids	1986	—	—	3.00
— Red vinyl						
Revolver 006	PS	All I Want for Christmas Is Your Love/Christmas Is for Kids	1986	—	—	3.00

MALCHAK, TIM (WITH DWIGHT RUCKER)
45s

Alpine 005		Christmas Is For Kids/All I Want For Christmas Is Your Love	1984	—	—	3.00
Alpine 005	PS	Christmas Is For Kids/All I Want For Christmas Is Your Love	1984	—	—	3.00

MALCOLM, CARLOS
45s

H&M 2003		Santa Claus Is Coming to Town/Mary's Little Boy Child	19??	—	—	3.00
— B-side by Eddie Parkin						

MALON, CRAIG
45s

Duck Milk 22-01		Kristy for Christmas/Laura	19??	5.00	10.00	20.00

MALONE, ANNIE
45s

Spin It 105		Keep Christmas in Your Heart/The Christmas Song	19??	—	—	3.00

MALTBY, RICHARD
On Various-Artists Collections

Jangle Waltz		Merriest Time!, The (Sesac 35)
Skater's Holiday		Merriest Time!, The (Sesac 35)

MANCE, JUNIOR
45s

Atlantic 2588		Silent Night/I Wish I Knew (How It Would Feel to Be Free)	1968	2.50	5.00	10.00

MANCHE, TOM
45s

(no label) 8701		Santa Used to Be a Baker/Snowflake Lullaby	198?	—	2.50	5.00
(no label) 8702		There's a Reindeer at My Window/Oh, What a Feeling	198?	—	2.00	4.00

MANCINI, HENRY
Albums

RCA Victor ANL1-1928	S	A Merry Mancini Christmas	1976	2.00	4.00	8.00
— Reissue with new number and new front cover						
RCA Victor LPM-3612	M	A Merry Mancini Christmas	1966	2.50	5.00	10.00
— Original front cover has a photo of Henry Mancini and family						
RCA Victor LSP-3612	S	A Merry Mancini Christmas	1966	3.00	6.00	12.00

On Various-Artists Collections

Arrival of the Elves		Santa Claus The Movie (EMI America SJ-17177)
Carol for Another Christmas		Christmas with Colonel Sanders (RCA Victor PRS-291)
		Happy Holidays, Volume 17 (RCA Special Products DPL1-0555)
Christmas Greetings		Christmas Greetings From RCA Victor And Groove Recording Artists (RCA Victor SP-45-128)
Christmas Rhapsody		Santa Claus The Movie (EMI America SJ-17177)
Christmas Song, The		Christmas in New York (RCA Victor PRM-257)
		Christmas with Eddy Arnold/Christmas with Henry Mancini
		(RCA Special Products DPL1-0079)
		Happy Holidays, Volume 13 (RCA Special Products DPL1-0319)
		Old Fashioned Christmas, An (Reader's Digest RDA 216-A)
Have Yourself a Merry Little Christmas		Henry Mancini Selects Great Songs of Christmas (RCA Special Products DPL1-0148)
Little Drummer Boy, The		Christmas with Eddy Arnold/Christmas with Henry Mancini
		(RCA Special Products DPL1-0079)
		Joyous Noel (Reader's Digest RDA-57A)
March of the Elves		Santa Claus The Movie (EMI America SJ-17177)
Medley: Frosty the Snowman/Rudolph,		Very Merry Christmas, A, Volume 5 (RCA Special Products PRS-343)
the Red-Nosed Reindeer		

Label, Number		Title (A Side/B Side)	Year	VG	VG+	NM
Medley: God Rest Ye Merry, Gentlemen/Deck the Halls/Hark! The Herald Angels Sing		Christmas with Eddy Arnold/Christmas with Henry Mancini (RCA Special Products DPL1-0079) Very Merry Christmas, A, Volume VI (RCA Special Products PRS-427)				
Medley: It Came Upon a Midnight Clear/Away in a Manger/The First Noel		Brightest Stars of Christmas, The (RCA Special Products DPL1-0086) Happy Holidays, Volume 16 (RCA Special Products DPL1-0501) 60 Christmas Classics (Sessions DVL2-0723)				
Medley: We Three Kings of Orient Are/O Come All Ye Faithful/Joy to the World		Christmas with Eddy Arnold/Christmas with Henry Mancini (RCA Special Products DPL1-0079) Happy Holidays, Volume 15 (RCA Special Products DPL1-0453)				
Medley: What Are You Doing New Year's Eve/Auld Lang Syne		Celebrate the Season with Tupperware (RCA Special Products DPL1-0803) Henry Mancini Selects Great Songs of Christmas (RCA Special Products DPL1-0148) Remembering Christmas with the Big Bands (RCA Special Products DPM1-0506)				
Medley: Winter Wonderland/Silver Bells		Christmas Eve with Colonel Sanders (RCA Victor PRS-256)				
New Year's Greetings		Christmas Greetings From RCA Victor And Groove Recording Artists (RCA Victor SP-45-128)				
O Little Town of Bethlehem		Christmas in California (RCA Victor PRS-276) Christmas in New York Volume 2 (RCA Victor PRS-270) Christmastime in Carol and Song (RCA PRM-271)				
Patch Versus Santa		Santa Claus The Movie (EMI America SJ-17177)				
Sad Patch		Santa Claus The Movie (EMI America SJ-17177)				
Sleigh Ride Over Manhattan		Santa Claus The Movie (EMI America SJ-17177)				
White Christmas		Happy Holidays, Vol. III (RCA Victor PRS-255) Henry Mancini Selects Great Songs of Christmas (RCA Special Products DPL1-0148)				

MANDRELL, BARBARA
45s

Label, Number		Title (A Side/B Side)	Year	VG	VG+	NM
MCA S45-1241	DJ	Santa, Bring My Baby Back Home// It Must Have Been the Mistletoe/From Our House to Yours	1984	2.50	5.00	10.00

Albums

Label, Number	Title (A Side/B Side)	Year	VG	VG+	NM
MCA 5519	Christmas at Our House	1984	3.00	6.00	12.00

On Various-Artists Collections

Winter Wonderland	Tennessee Christmas (MCA 5620)

MANDRELL, LOUISE
On Various-Artists Collections

I've Got What You Want for Christmas	Country Christmas, A, Volume 2 (RCA AYL1-4809)

MANDRELL, LOUISE, AND R.C. BANNON
45s

Label, Number	Title (A Side/B Side)	Year	VG	VG+	NM
RCA PB-13358	Christmas Is Just a Song for Us This Year/Christmas in Dixie	1982	—	2.50	5.00
— B-side by Alabama					

On Various-Artists Collections

Christmas Is Just a Song for Us This Year	Country Christmas, A (RCA CPL1-4396)

MANHATTAN JAZZ ALL-STARS, THE
On Various-Artists Collections

If I Were a Bell	Jingle Bell Jazz (Columbia PC 36803)

MANHATTAN TRANSFER, THE
45s

Label, Number		Title (A Side/B Side)	Year	VG	VG+	NM
(no label) 1984	DJ	The Christmas Song (same on both sides)	1984	7.50	15.00	30.00
(no label) 1984	PS	The Christmas Song (same on both sides)	1984	7.50	15.00	30.00
— Above sleeve and record are a private pressing for friends and associates of the group						

MANHATTANS, THE
45s

Label, Number	Title (A Side/B Side)	Year	VG	VG+	NM
Carnival 524	It's That Time of the Year/Alone on New Year's Eve	1966	3.75	7.50	15.00
Starfire 121	Alone On New Year's Eve/It's That Time Of The Year	1979	—	2.00	4.00

MANIFEST DESTINY, THE
45s

Label, Number	Title (A Side/B Side)	Year	VG	VG+	NM
Champ 3405	Christmas Toy Shop/I Hear Bells	19??	—	3.00	6.00

MANILOW, BARRY
45s

Label, Number	Title (A Side/B Side)	Year	VG	VG+	NM
Arista 2094	Jingle Bells/Because It's Christmas (For All the Children)	1990	—	—	3.00
— A-side: With Expose					

Albums

Label, Number	Title (A Side/B Side)	Year	VG	VG+	NM
Arista AL-8644	Because It's Christmas	1990	3.00	6.00	12.00

Label, Number		Title (A Side/B Side)	Year	VG	VG+	NM
MANN, BARBARA						
45s						
Buzz 106		All I Want for Christmas Is a Steady/I'll Never Forget You	1960	2.50	5.00	10.00
MANN, JOHNNY, SINGERS						
45s						
Liberty 55653		African Noel/Children, Board That Train	1963	2.00	4.00	8.00
— By "The Johnny Mann Children's Choir"						
Albums						
Liberty LRP-3522	M	We Wish You a Merry Christmas	1967	3.75	7.50	15.00
Liberty LST-7522	S	We Wish You a Merry Christmas	1967	3.75	7.50	15.00
On Various-Artists Collections						
Deck the Hall with Boughs of Holly		Christmas Greetings, Vol. 4 (Columbia Special Products P 11987)				
		Christmas Song, The, And Other Favorites (Columbia Special Products P 12446)				
		Christmas Trimmings (Columbia Special Products P 12795)				
Jingle Bells		Christmas Songs, The (Capitol SLB-57074)				
We Wish You a Merry Christmas		Sounds of Christmas (Columbia Special Products P 12474)				
MANN, LINDA						
45s						
Pace 1500		It's Our Baby's First Christmas/It's Christmas Time in Fairyland	196?	2.00	4.00	8.00
MANN, LORENE						
45s						
RCA Victor 47-9776		Indian Santa Claus/I Know My Man Too Well	1969	2.00	4.00	8.00
MANNHEIM STEAMROLLER						
45s						
American Gramaphone AGS 1984		Deck the Halls/Silent Night	1984	—	2.50	5.00
American Gramaphone AGS 1984	PS	Deck the Halls/Silent Night	1984	—	2.50	5.00
Albums						
American Gramaphone AG-1984		Mannheim Steamroller Christmas	1984	3.75	7.50	15.00
American Gramaphone AG-1988		A Fresh Aire Christmas	1988	3.75	7.50	15.00
On Various-Artists Collections						
Good King Wenceslas		Sampler III (American Gramaphone AG-366)				
MANRING, MICHAEL						
On Various-Artists Collections						
Sung to Sleep		Winter's Solstice II, A (Windham Hill WH-1077)				
MANTOVANI						
45s						
London 1253		Teddy Bear's Christmas/The Whistling Boy	1952	3.00	6.00	12.00
London 1280		White Christmas/Adeste Fideles	1952	3.00	6.00	12.00
Albums						
Holiday HDY 1928		Holy Night	1981	2.50	5.00	10.00
London PS 142	S	Christmas Carols	1959	3.75	7.50	15.00
London PS 338	S	Christmas Greetings from Mantovani	1963	3.75	7.50	15.00
London BP 720	(2)	Christmas Favorites	19??	3.75	7.50	15.00
London LL 913	M	Christmas Carols	1953	3.75	7.50	15.00
— Original recordings in mono						
London LL 913	M	Christmas Carols	1959	3.00	6.00	12.00
— Mono versions of stereo re-recordings						
London LL 3338	M	Christmas Greetings from Mantovani	1963	3.00	6.00	12.00
On Various-Artists Collections						
I Saw Three Ships		Magic of Christmas, The (Columbia Musical Treasury P3S 5806)				
O Holy Night		Great Songs of Christmas, Album Nine (Columbia Special Products CSS 1033)				
		Henry Mancini Selects Great Songs of Christmas (RCA Special Products DPL1-0148)				
Silent Night		Happy Holidays, Volume 16 (RCA Special Products DPL1-0501)				
Skater's Waltz		Great Songs of Christmas, Album Nine (Columbia Special Products CSS 1033)				
The Great Songs of Christmas (Medley)		Happy Holidays, Vol. 20 (RCA Special Products DPL1-0713)				
Twelve Days of Christmas, The		Magic of Christmas, The (Columbia Musical Treasury P3S 5806)				
MARAIS, JOSEPH AND MIRANDA						
Albums						
Decca DL 9030	M	Christmas with Joseph and Miranda	1955	7.50	15.00	30.00

Label, Number		Title (A Side/B Side)	Year	VG	VG+	NM
MARCELS, THE						
45s						
Colpix 617		Merry Twist-Mas/Don't Cry for Me This Christmas	1961	6.25	12.50	25.00
Colpix 617	PS	Merry Twist-Mas/Don't Cry for Me This Christmas	1961	15.00	30.00	60.00
MARCH, APRIL						
45s						
Keystone 666		Christmas In Killarney/When Christmas Rolls Around	19??	3.00	6.00	12.00
MARCH, JO						
45s						
Kapp 247		The Virgin Mary Had One Son/I, Said the Donkey	1958	3.00	6.00	12.00
MARCH, PEGGY						
On Various-Artists Collections						
Christmas Greetings		Christmas Greetings From RCA Victor And Groove Recording Artists (RCA Victor SP-45-128)				
New Year's Greetings		Christmas Greetings From RCA Victor And Groove Recording Artists (RCA Victor SP-45-128)				
MARGITZA, RICK						
On Various-Artists Collections						
Little Drummer Boy		Yule Struttin' — A Blue Note Christmas (Blue Note 1P 8119)				
MARI-AN						
12-Inch Singles						
Optimist ORC 5000		Santa's Holiday (Dance Mix)/Santa's Holiday (Radio Mix)// Santa's Holiday (Radio Mix II)/Santa's Holiday (Instrumental)	1988	—	3.00	6.00
MARIA AND LUIS						
On Various-Artists Collections						
Arrurrru		Merry Christmas from Sesame Street (CRA CTW 25516)				
Saludo (aguinaldo)		Merry Christmas from Sesame Street (CRA CTW 25516)				
MARKEY, GRACE						
45s						
Paramount 0137		Merry Xmas/Times Have Changed	1971	—	3.00	6.00
MARKO						
45s						
K&R 1010		Here's a Kiss for Christmas/Think Happy, Think Summer, Think Love	19??	—	2.00	4.00
MAROTTA, JOE						
45s						
Respect Life 411013X		Silent Night/O Holy Night	198?	—	2.00	4.00
MARQUEES, THE						
45s						
Warner Bros. 5127		Christmas in the Crowd/Sunset to Sunrise	1959	10.00	20.00	40.00

MARSALIS, BRANFORD, AND HARRY CONNICK, JR.
Also see HARRY CONNICK, JR.
On Various-Artists Collections

Some Children See Him	Jazzy Wonderland, A (Columbia 1P 8120)	

MARSALIS, ELLIS
On Various-Artists Collections

This Is Christmas	Jazzy Wonderland, A (Columbia 1P 8120)	

MARSALIS, WYNTON
Albums

Label, Number	Title (A Side/B Side)	Year	VG	VG+	NM
Columbia FC 45287	Crescent City Christmas Card	1989	2.50	5.00	10.00

On Various-Artists Collections

We Three Kings of Orient Are	God Rest Ye Merry, Jazzmen (Columbia FC 37551)
Winter Wonderland	Jazzy Wonderland, A (Columbia 1P 8120)

Label, Number		Title (A Side/B Side)	Year	VG	VG+	NM
MARSHALL BROTHERS, THE						
45s						
Savoy 825		Mr. Santa's Boogie/Who'll Be the Fool from Now On	1951	125.00	250.00	500.00
MARSHALL, SAMMY						
45s						
Roxie 324		It's Christmas Time Again/Maybe We'll Have Snow for Christmas	1961	3.75	7.50	15.00
Silver 108		Manger of Bethlehem/Holy Day	1958	5.00	10.00	20.00
MARSHANS, THE						
45s						
Johnson 736		My Letter To Santa/Main Man	1966	5.00	10.00	20.00
MARSHON, CHRIS						
45s						
Phono 2658		The Bluest Christmas Ever/Elvis, God's Ready For A Song	1977	—	3.00	6.00
MARTELS, THE						
45s						
Bella 20		Rockin' Santa Claus/Carol Lee	1959	10.00	20.00	40.00
— B-side by Eulis Mason						
MARTERIE, RALPH						
45s						
Mercury 5734		Christmas in Killarney/When Your Lover Has Gone	1951	3.75	7.50	15.00
Mercury 70493		Dig That Crazy Santa Claus/Rock, Rock	1954	3.75	7.50	15.00
MARTIN, BET E.						
45s						
Ford 107		Mrs. Santa Claus/Toys	1961	2.50	5.00	10.00
MARTIN, CLIFF & THE NEIGHBOR'S KIDS						
45s						
Pic 0018		Santa Claus Is On His Way/Three Little Dwarfs and Santa Claus	19??	—	2.00	4.00
MARTIN, DEAN						
45s						
Capitol F2640		The Christmas Blues/If I Should Love Again	1953	3.00	6.00	12.00
Capitol S7-57889		Rudolph, the Red-Nosed Reindeer/White Christmas	1992	—	2.50	5.00
Reprise PRO 248	DJ	White Christmas (same on both sides)	1966	2.50	5.00	10.00
Reprise 0542		Blue Christmas/A Marshmallow World	1966	—	3.00	6.00
Albums						
Capitol T 1285	M	A Winter Romance	1959	5.00	10.00	20.00
Capitol ST 1285	S	A Winter Romance	1959	7.50	15.00	30.00
— Same as above, but in stereo						
Capitol TT 2343	M	Holiday Cheer	1965	3.00	6.00	12.00
— Reissue of 1285 with one fewer track						
Capitol STT 2343	S	Holiday Cheer	1965	3.75	7.50	15.00
— Some copies of this LP have labels that state the title as "Baby, It's Cold Outside."						
Reprise R 6222	M	The Dean Martin Christmas Album	1966	3.75	7.50	15.00
Reprise RS 6222	S	The Dean Martin Christmas Album	1966	5.00	10.00	20.00

On Various-Artists Collections

Baby, It's Cold Outside	Christmas Songs, The, Volume II (Capitol SL-57065)
God Rest Ye Merry, Gentlemen	Christmas Stocking (Capitol NP 90494)
Let It Snow! Let It Snow! Let It Snow!	Best of Christmas, The, Vol. I (Capitol SM-11833)
	Christmas Carousel (Capitol SQBE-94406)
	Merry Christmas (Columbia Musical Treasury 3P 6306)
	Zenith Presents Christmas, A Gift of Music Vol. 3 (Capitol Creative Products SL-6659)
Peace on Earth and Silent Night	Have Yourself a Merry Little Christmas (Reprise R 50001)
Rudolph, the Red-Nosed Reindeer	Best of Christmas, The, Vol. II (Capitol SM-11834)
	Christmas Songs, The (Capitol SLB-57074)
	Christmas Stocking (Capitol NP 90494)
	I'll Be Home for Christmas (Pickwick SPC-1009)
White Christmas	Christmas Songs, The (Capitol SLB-57074)
	Let's Celebrate Christmas (Capitol Special Markets SL-6923)
	Little Drummer Boy, The (Capitol/Pickwick SPC-3462)
	Magic of Christmas, The (Capitol SWBB-93810)
	Popular Christmas Classics (Capitol Special Markets SL-8100)
Winter Wonderland	Christmas — The Season of Music (Capitol Creative Products SL-6679)
	Christmas America (Capitol Special Markets SL-6884)
	Family Christmas Collection, The (Time-Life STL-131)

Label, Number	Title (A Side/B Side)	Year	VG	VG+	NM

MARTIN, DORIS STATLER
45s

Kimbo 131	I've Got the Chicken Pox for Christmas/(Instrumental)	19??	—	3.00	6.00

MARTIN, FREDDY
45s

RCA Victor 47-3072	Merry Christmas Polka/Your Kiss	1949	3.75	7.50	15.00
RCA Victor 47-3935	Sleigh Ride/Christmas Time	1950	3.75	7.50	15.00
RCA Victor 47-4300	The Night Before Christmas/Toy Piano Boogie	1951	3.75	7.50	15.00

On Various-Artists Collections

Merry Christmas Polka, The	Christmas Through the Years (Reader's Digest RDA-143)
Parade of the Wooden Soldiers	Joyous Noel (Reader's Digest RDA-57A)
Sleigh Ride	Remembering Christmas with the Big Bands (RCA Special Products DPM1-0506)
White Christmas	Christmas Through the Years (Reader's Digest RDA-143)

MARTIN, JESSE
45s

Impala 101	Love Can't Be Bad/Xmas Thief	1963	2.50	5.00	10.00

MARTIN, JIMMY
45s

Decca 31176	An Old-Fashioned Christmas/Hold to God's Unchanging Hand	1960	3.00	6.00	12.00

MARTIN, MARTY
45s

Anvil 1001	All I Got for Christmas Was a Broken Heart/Hootenanny Santa	1963	2.50	5.00	10.00

MARTIN, MARY
45s

Buena Vista 332	Making Believe It's Christmas Eve/Motherless Child	1958	3.75	7.50	15.00

On Various-Artists Collections

My Favorite Things	60 Christmas Classics (Sessions DVL2-0723)
Silent Night	Great Songs of Christmas, The, Album Four (Columbia Special Products CSP 155M)

MARTIN, TONY
45s

Decca 25235	Christmas Candle/Nazareth	195?	2.50	5.00	10.00
— Reissue of a release from the early 1940s					
RCA Victor 47-6317	Christmas in America/Christmas in Rio	1955	3.75	7.50	15.00

On Various-Artists Collections

Silent Night	Christmas in the Air (RCA Special Products DPL1-0133)
	60 Christmas Classics (Sessions DVL2-0723)

MARTINELLI, GIOVANNI
On Various-Artists Collections

Gesu Bambino (The Infant Jesus)	Joyous Noel (Reader's Digest RDA-57A)

MARTINO, AL
45s

Capitol 5311	Silver Bells/You're All I Want for Christmas	1964	2.00	4.00	8.00

Albums

Capitol T 2165	M	A Merry Christmas from Al Martino	1964	3.00	6.00	12.00
Capitol ST 2165	S	A Merry Christmas from Al Martino	1964	3.75	7.50	15.00
— Same as above, but in stereo						

On Various-Artists Collections

I'll Be Home for Christmas	Best of Christmas, The, Vol. I (Capitol SM-11833)
	Christmas to Remember, A (Capitol Creative Products SL-6573)
	Happy Holidays, Vol. 5 (Capitol Creative Products SL-6627)
Medley: We Wish You a Merry	Happy Holly Days (Capitol Creative Products SL-6761)
Christmas/Silver Bells	Sound of Christmas, The (Capitol Creative Products SL-6515)
O Come All Ye Faithful	Christmas Carousel (Capitol SQBE-94406)
	Christmas Day (Pickwick SPC 1010)
	Christmas Songs, The (Capitol SLB-57074)
	Christmas to Remember, A (Capitol Creative Products SL-6573)
	Christmas, A Gift of Music (Capitol Special Markets SL-6687)
	Holiday Magic (Capitol Creative Products SL-6728)
	Merry Christmas (Columbia Musical Treasury 3P 6306)
	Spirit of Christmas, The (Capitol Creative Products SL-6516)
	Zenith Presents Christmas, A Gift of Music Vol. 4 (Capitol Creative Products SL-6687)
O Holy Night	Magic of Christmas, The (Capitol SWBB-93810)

Label, Number	Title (A Side/B Side)	Year	VG	VG+	NM
Rudolph the Red-Nosed Reindeer	Family Christmas Collection, The (Time-Life STL-131)				
Silver Bells	I'll Be Home for Christmas (Pickwick SPC-1009)				
We Wish You a Merry Christmas/ You're All I Want for Christmas	Happy Holidays, Album Seven (Capitol Creative Products SL-6730)				
What Child Is This	Little Drummer Boy, The (Capitol/Pickwick SPC-3462)				
	Spirit of Christmas, The (Capitol Creative Products SL-6516)				
White Christmas	Christmas Stocking (Capitol NP 90494)				
	Christmas to Remember, A, Vol. 3 (Capitol Creative Products SL-6681)				

MARTINSON, KEN
45s
Label, Number	Title (A Side/B Side)	Year	VG	VG+	NM
Caloma 7851 — Red and black label	Jingle, Jangle & Joe/Jingle, Jangle & Joe (Sing-Along Version)	1984	—	2.00	4.00
Caloma 7851 — Gold label	Jingle, Jangle & Joe/Jingle, Jangle & Joe (Sing-Along Version)	1985	—	—	3.00

MARTY, ELLEN
45s
Label, Number	Title (A Side/B Side)	Year	VG	VG+	NM
Marty 102	Xmas Gift/I Wanna	1964	2.00	4.00	8.00
Rain Coat 107	Xmas Gift/I Will Come To You Some Night	196?	—	3.00	6.00

MARVIN AND JOHNNY
45s
Label, Number	Title (A Side/B Side)	Year	VG	VG+	NM
Aladdin 3439	It's Christmas/The Valley of Love	1958	7.50	15.00	30.00
Liberty 1394 — B-side by the Five Keys	It's Christmas/It's Christmas Time	1980	—	2.50	5.00

On Various-Artists Collections
Label, Number	Title (A Side/B Side)	Year	VG	VG+	NM
It's Christmas	Jingle Bell Rock (Time-Life SRNR-XM)				
	Rockin' Christmas — The '50s (Rhino RNLP-066)				

MARVIN AND THE CHIRPS
45s
Label, Number	Title (A Side/B Side)	Year	VG	VG+	NM
Tip Top 202	I'll Miss You This Christmas/Sixteen Tons	1958	50.00	100.00	200.00

MARX, RICHARD
45s
Label, Number	Title (A Side/B Side)	Year	VG	VG+	NM
Capitol S7-18907	You'll Never Be Alone/One More Try	1995	—	—	3.00

MARY B & THE DALLAS PLAYBOYS
45s
Label, Number	Title (A Side/B Side)	Year	VG	VG+	NM
Town & Country 86-85	A Letter To Santa Claus/My Music Man	19??	2.00	4.00	8.00

MASON DIXON
45s
Label, Number	Title (A Side/B Side)	Year	VG	VG+	NM
Texas 5511	Silent Night/O Come All Ye Faithful	1985	—	2.00	4.00

MASON, EULIS
45s
Label, Number	Title (A Side/B Side)	Year	VG	VG+	NM
Bella 20 — B-side by the Martels	Carol Lee/Rockin' Santa Claus	1959	10.00	20.00	40.00

MASTERS, SAMMY
45s
Label, Number	Title (A Side/B Side)	Year	VG	VG+	NM
Galahad 602	Sammy the Little Square Snowball/Blue Christmas	196?	—	3.00	6.00

MATERIAL WITH NONA HENDRYX
12-Inch Singles
Label, Number		Title (A Side/B Side)	Year	VG	VG+	NM
Ze IPR 2052 — B-side by Cristina; U.K. import	DJ	It's A Holiday/Things Fall Apart	1981	5.00	10.00	20.00

On Various-Artists Collections
Label, Number	Title (A Side/B Side)	Year	VG	VG+	NM
It's a Holiday	Christmas Record, A (Ze/Passport PB 6020)				

MATHEWS, JIM, M.D.
45s
Label, Number	Title (A Side/B Side)	Year	VG	VG+	NM
Music Emporium 7029	A Blue Christmas Elvis/(B-side unknown)	1977	—	3.00	6.00

Label, Number		Title (A Side/B Side)	Year	VG	VG+	NM

MATHIEU, WILLIAM ALLAUDIN
On Various-Artists Collections
By the Fireside		Winter's Solstice II, A (Windham Hill WH-1077)				

MATHIS, JOHNNY
45s

Label, Number		Title (A Side/B Side)	Year	VG	VG+	NM
Columbia 06561		Where Can I Find Christmas?/	1986	—	2.00	4.00
		It's Beginning to Look a Lot Like Christmas				
Columbia 10447		When a Child Is Born/Turn the Lights Down	1976	—	2.50	5.00
Columbia 10640		When a Child Is Born/Everytime You Touch Me	1977	—	2.50	5.00
Columbia 11158		The Very First Christmas Day/Christmas in the City of the Angels	1979	—	2.50	5.00
Columbia 11409		When a Child Is Born/The Lord's Prayer	1980	—	2.00	4.00
— With Gladys Knight and the Pips						
Columbia 3-42238		My Kind of Christmas/Christmas Eve	1961	5.00	10.00	20.00
— "Columbia Single 33"; small hole						
Columbia 42238		My Kind of Christmas/Christmas Eve	1961	3.00	6.00	12.00
Columbia 45035		Give Me Your Love for Christmas/Calypso Noel	1969	—	3.00	6.00
Columbia 45035	PS	Give Me Your Love for Christmas/Calypso Noel	1969	2.00	4.00	8.00
Columbia 45100	DJ	Give Me Your Love for Christmas/Calypso Noel	1969	2.00	4.00	8.00
Columbia 45100	PS	Give Me Your Love for Christmas/Calypso Noel	1969	2.50	5.00	10.00
— The above sleeve and record were the 1969 Christmas Seals promo						
Columbia 45281		Christmas Is/Sign of the Dove	1970	—	2.50	5.00
Columbia 45513		Christmas Is/Sign of the Dove	1971	—	2.50	5.00
Mercury 72217		The Little Drummer Boy/Have Reindeer, Will Travel	1963	2.50	5.00	10.00
Mercury 72217	PS	The Little Drummer Boy/Have Reindeer, Will Travel	1963	5.00	10.00	20.00

Albums

Label, Number		Title (A Side/B Side)	Year	VG	VG+	NM
Columbia CL 1195	M	Merry Christmas	1958	10.00	20.00	40.00
— Original cover has Johnny standing, holding skis and poles						
Columbia CL 1195	M	Merry Christmas	196?	7.50	15.00	30.00
— Second cover has Johnny sitting, with skis and poles in snow						
Columbia CS 8021	S	Merry Christmas	1959	6.25	12.50	25.00
— Same as CL 1195; cover 1						
Columbia CS 8021	S	Merry Christmas	196?	5.00	10.00	20.00
— Same as CL 1195; cover 2						
Columbia CS 9923		Give Me Your Love for Christmas	1969	3.00	6.00	12.00
Columbia LE 10196		Christmas with Johnny Mathis	1976	2.50	5.00	10.00
— Reissue of Harmony KH 30684 with same contents						
Columbia 3C 38306		Christmas with Johnny Mathis	1982	2.00	4.00	8.00
Columbia PC 39468		For Christmas	1984	2.00	4.00	8.00
Columbia FC 40447		Christmas Eve with Johnny Mathis	1986	2.50	5.00	10.00
Columbia Special Products C 10896		Merry Christmas	1972	2.50	5.00	10.00
— Reissue						
Harmony KH 30684		Christmas with Johnny Mathis	1971	3.00	6.00	12.00
Mercury MG 20837	M	Sounds of Christmas	1963	3.00	6.00	12.00
Mercury SR 60837	S	Sounds of Christmas	1963	3.75	7.50	15.00

On Various-Artists Collections

Blue Christmas	Blue Christmas (Welk Music Group WM-3002)
	Merry Christmas from... (Reader's Digest RD4-83)
Christmas Song, The	Great Songs of Christmas, The, Album Six (Columbia Special Products CSM 388)
	Ronco Presents A Christmas Gift (Columbia Special Products P 12430)
	Seasons Greetings (A Christmas Festival of Stars) (Columbia CS 8189)
Do You Hear What I Hear	Silent Night... (Columbia Special Products P 14989)
First Noel, The	Magic of Christmas, The (Columbia Musical Treasury P3S 5806)
God Rest Ye Merry, Gentlemen	That Christmas Feeling (Columbia Special Products P 11853)
I'll Be Home for Christmas	Home for Christmas (Columbia Musical Treasury P3S 5608)
	Home for Christmas (Realm 2V 8101)
	Very Merry Christmas, A, Volume 3 (Columbia Special Products CSS 997)
It Came Upon a Midnight Clear	Merry Christmas from... (Reader's Digest RD4-83)
Jingle Bell Rock	Christmas with Johnny Mathis and Percy Faith (Columbia Special Products P 11805)
Let It Snow! Let It Snow! Let It Snow!	Celebrate the Season with Tupperware (RCA Special Products DPL1-0803)
	Stars of Christmas, The (RCA Special Products DPL1-0842)
Marshmallow World, A	Great Songs of Christmas, The, Album Eight (Columbia Special Products CSS 888)
O Holy Night	Christmas Greetings, Vol. 3 (Columbia Special Products P 11383)
	Christmas Trimmings (Columbia Special Products P 12795)
	Happy Holidays, Album 8 (Columbia Special Products C 11086)
	Merry Christmas (Columbia Musical Treasury 3P 6306)
	Very Merry Christmas, A (Columbia Special Products CSS 563)
Silent Night	Christmas with Johnny Mathis and Percy Faith (Columbia Special Products P 11805)
Silver Bells	Christmas Song, The, And Other Favorites (Columbia Special Products P 12446)
	Christmas with Johnny Mathis and Percy Faith (Columbia Special Products P 11805)
	Joyous Christmas, Volume 2 (Columbia Special Products CSS 808)
	Joyous Songs of Christmas, The (Columbia Special Products C 10400)
	Sounds of Christmas (Columbia Special Products P 12474)
	Very Merry Christmas, A, Volume Two (Columbia Special Products CSS 788)

Label, Number	Title (A Side/B Side)	Year	VG	VG+	NM
Sleigh Ride	Christmas Album, A (Columbia PC 39466)				
	Christmas with Johnny Mathis and Percy Faith (Columbia Special Products P 11805)				
	Joyous Christmas, Volume 4 (Columbia Special Products CSS 1485)				
What Child Is This	Christmas with Johnny Mathis and Percy Faith (Columbia Special Products P 11805)				
	It's Christmas Time! (Columbia Special Products P 14990)				
	Seasons Greetings (A Christmas Festival of Stars) (Columbia CS 8189)				
	Spirit of Christmas, The, Volume III (Columbia Special Products CSS 1463)				
White Christmas	Christmas Greetings (Columbia Special Products CSS 1499)				

MATTERO, RICKY
45s

| Hillside 502 | Merry, Merry Christmas/Don't Ever Leave Me | 19?? | — | 2.50 | 5.00 |

MATTINA, TONY
45s

| Lanor 512 | My Baby Won't Be Home For Christmas/Don't Ever Break My Heart | 196? | 2.50 | 5.00 | 10.00 |

MATTY, JAY
45s

| Lute 6021 | Merry Twist Mas/Teenage Monster | 1961 | 5.00 | 10.00 | 20.00 |

MAXWELL, LEN
45s

| 20th Fox 551 | A Merry Monster Christmas/The Sounds of Christmas | 1964 | 5.00 | 10.00 | 20.00 |

MAY, BILLY
45s

| Capitol F2948 | Rudolph the Red-Nosed Reindeer/Loop De Loop Mambo | 1954 | 3.75 | 7.50 | 15.00 |

On Various-Artists Collections

| Vision of Sugar Plums, A | Have Yourself a Merry Little Christmas (Reprise R 50001) | | | | |

MAY, BROTHER JOE
45s

| Nashboro 908 | Silent Night/Sweet Little Jesus Boy | 1966 | 2.00 | 4.00 | 8.00 |

MAY, PATRICIA
45s

| Parkway 858 | What Christmas Means to Me/Angel of Love | 1962 | 3.75 | 7.50 | 15.00 |

MAYE, MARILYN
On Various-Artists Collections

| Christmas Song, The | Christmas in the Air (RCA Special Products DPL1-0133) | | | | |

MAYER, NATHANIEL
45s

| Fortune 550 | Mr. Santa Claus/(B-side unknown) | 1962 | 7.50 | 15.00 | 30.00 |

MAYNOR, DOROTHY
On Various-Artists Collections

| Rise Up, Shepherd, an' Foller | Joyous Noel (Reader's Digest RDA-57A) | | | | |

MAYS, REV. ORIS
45s

| Jewel 155 | Another Christmas Without My Son/Stand Still | 1970 | 2.00 | 4.00 | 8.00 |

McARDLE, ANDREA; REID SHELTON; SANDY FAISON; RAYMOND THORNE
On Various-Artists Collections

| New Deal for Christmas, A | Annie (Columbia Masterworks JS 34712) | | | | |

McCALL, C.W.
45s

| Polydor 14445 | Sing Silent Night/Old Glory | 1977 | — | 2.50 | 5.00 |

On Various-Artists Collections

| Sing Silent Night | Wonderful World of Christmas, The, Album Two (Capitol Special Markets SL-8025) | | | | |

Label, Number		Title (A Side/B Side)	Year	VG	VG+	NM

McCANDLESS, PAUL; JAMES MATHESON; ROBIN MAY
On Various-Artists Collections

17th Century Canon		Winter's Solstice II, A (Windham Hill WH-1077)				

McCARTERS, THE
On Various-Artists Collections

O Little Town of Bethlehem		Christmas Tradition, A, Volume II (Warner Bros. 25762)				

McCARTHY, JOHN, CHORALE
On Various-Artists Collections

Angels from the Realms		60 Christmas Classics (Sessions DVL2-0723)				
Angels from the Realms of Glory		Christmas Through the Years (Reader's Digest RDA-143)				
Gather Around the Christmas Tree		Old Fashioned Christmas, An (Reader's Digest RDA 216-A)				
Here We Come a-Caroling		Christmas Through the Years (Reader's Digest RDA-143)				
Holly and the Ivy, The		Christmas Through the Years (Reader's Digest RDA-143)				
I Saw Three Ships		Christmas Through the Years (Reader's Digest RDA-143)				
O Christmas Tree		Christmas Through the Years (Reader's Digest RDA-143)				
O Sanctissima		Christmas Through the Years (Reader's Digest RDA-143)				
We Three Kings of Orient Are		60 Christmas Classics (Sessions DVL2-0723)				
We Wish You a Merry Christmas		Christmas Through the Years (Reader's Digest RDA-143)				
What Child Is This?		Christmas Through the Years (Reader's Digest RDA-143)				

McCARTNEY, PAUL
Also see THE BEATLES.

45s

Capitol S7-17643		Wonderful Christmastime/Rudolph, the Red-Nosed Reggae	1993	—	3.00	6.00
— Paul McCartney & Wings; red vinyl						
Columbia 04127		Wonderful Christmastime/Rudolph, the Red-Nosed Reggae	1983	7.50	15.00	30.00
— Scarce reissue with B-side in stereo						
Columbia 11162		Wonderful Christmastime/Rudolph, the Red-Nosed Reggae	1979	2.50	5.00	10.00
Columbia 11162	PS	Wonderful Christmastime/Rudolph, the Red-Nosed Reggae	1979	3.75	7.50	15.00

McCARTY, JACKI
45s

Paisano 101		Pancho Claus/Paisano In A Pinon Tree	19??	—	2.00	4.00
Paisano 101	PS	Pancho Claus/Paisano In A Pinon Tree	19??	—	2.00	4.00

McCLAIN, CHARLY, AND WAYNE MASSEY
On Various-Artists Collections

Winter Wonderland		Nashville Christmas Album, The (Epic PE 40418)				

McCLAIN, PAT
45s

Country Fare 701		I Don't Want To Ride With Santa Claus/Who Shot Cock Robin	19??	—	2.00	4.00

McCLINTOCK, DON
45s

37 Records 3		Christmas Needs Love to Be Christmas/ Christmas Needs Love to Be Christmas (Sing Along Version)	19??	—	2.00	4.00
— Red vinyl						
37 Records 3	PS	Christmas Needs Love to Be Christmas/ Christmas Needs Love to Be Christmas (Sing Along Version)	19??	—	2.00	4.00

McCORMACK, JOHN
On Various-Artists Collections

Adeste Fideles		Joyous Noel (Reader's Digest RDA-57A)				
Panis Angelicus		Joyous Noel (Reader's Digest RDA-57A)				

McCORMACK, JOHN, AND FRITZ KREISLER
On Various-Artists Collections

Ave Maria (Bach-Gounod)		Joyous Noel (Reader's Digest RDA-57A)				

McCOY, CHARLIE
45s

Monument 1938		Christmas Cheer/Blue Christmas	1976	—	—	3.00
— "Golden Series" reissue						
Monument 8633		Blue Christmas/Christmas Cheer	1974	—	2.50	5.00

Label, Number	Title (A Side/B Side)	Year	VG	VG+	NM

On Various-Artists Collections

| Christmas Cheer | Country Style Christmas, A (Columbia Musical Treasury 3P 6316) | | | | |
| Christmas Song, The | Country Style Christmas, A (Columbia Musical Treasury 3P 6316) | | | | |

McCRACKEN, JAMES
On Various-Artists Collections

| Angels We Have Heard on High | Firestone Presents Your Favorite Christmas Music, Volume 4 (Firestone MLP 7011) | | | | |
| Ave Maria | Firestone Presents Your Favorite Christmas Music, Volume 4 (Firestone MLP 7011) | | | | |

McCRACKLIN, JIMMY
45s

| Art-Tone 826 | Christmas Time (Part 1)/Christmas Time (Part 2) | 1961 | 3.00 | 6.00 | 12.00 |

McDONALD, DAVID
45s

| DRC 156 | Christmas Spirit/Winter Song | 1981 | — | 2.00 | 4.00 |

McDONALD, RONALD
45s

| McDonald's 1820 | The Night Before Christmas (Part 1)/ The Night Before Christmas (Part 2) | 197? | 3.00 | 6.00 | 12.00 |

McDUFF, EDDIE
45s

| Giant 1105 | Santa Claus Is Comin But He Ain't Gonna Come See You/Merry Christmas Mr. Heartache | 198? | — | — | 3.00 |

McENTIRE, PAKE
45s

| RCA 5050-7-R | Santa Are You Coming to Atlanta/A Christmas Letter | 1986 | — | — | 3.00 |
| *— B-side by Keith Whitley* | | | | | |

On Various-Artists Collections

| Santa Are You Coming to Atlanta | Country Christmas, A, Volume 4 (RCA CPL1-7012) | | | | |

McENTIRE, REBA
45s

| MCA S45-17446 | DJ | The Christmas Song (Chestnuts Roasting on an Open Fire)/ O Holy Night | 1987 | 2.50 | 5.00 | 10.00 |
| MCA S45-17725 | DJ | I'll Be Home for Christmas/The Christmas Guest | 1987 | 2.50 | 5.00 | 10.00 |

Albums

MCA 42031	Merry Christmas to You	1987	2.50	5.00	10.00
MCA R 164184	Merry Christmas to You	1987	3.75	7.50	15.00
— Same as above, except BMG Direct Marketing edition					

On Various-Artists Collections

Away in a Manger	Country Christmas (Time-Life STL-109)				
	Tennessee Christmas (MCA 5620)				
Silent Night	Country Christmas (Time-Life STL-109)				

McGEHEAN, HALLY
45s

| Eighties 606 | Let Me Be Annie for Christmas/(Instrumental) | 1980 | — | 3.00 | 6.00 |

McGILLIS, KELLY, AND MICHAEL HEDGES
Albums

| Windham Hill WH-0700 | Santabear's First Christmas | 1986 | 3.00 | 6.00 | 12.00 |
| *— McGillis narrates Side 1; Hedges plays music on both sides* | | | | | |

McGINNIS, DON
45s

| Rena 1036 | I'll Be Home For Christmas/When Santa Comes | 19?? | 2.00 | 4.00 | 8.00 |

McGOWAN, SYNG
45s

| Hope 2052 | Loneliness Is A Pleasure/Dear Santa | 19?? | — | 3.00 | 6.00 |

Label, Number		Title (A Side/B Side)	Year	VG	VG+	NM
McGREGOR, FREDDIE						
On Various-Artists Collections						
Come All Ye Faithful		Reggae Christmas, A (Real Authentic Sound RAS 3101)				
Feliz Navidad		Reggae Christmas, A (Real Authentic Sound RAS 3101)				
McGRIFF, JIMMY						
45s						
Jell 503		Soul Song Of Christmas (Silent Nite)/Chip! Chip!	1965	2.00	4.00	8.00
Sue 804		Christmas with McGriff Part 1/Christmas with McGriff Part 2	1963	3.00	6.00	12.00
Sue 804		Winter with McGriff Pt. 1/Winter with McGriff Pt. 2	1963	2.50	5.00	10.00
McGUIRE SISTERS, THE						
45s						
Coral 61303		Christmas Alphabet/Give Me Your Heart for Christmas	1954	3.00	6.00	12.00
Coral 61531		The Littlest Angel/I'd Like to Trim a Tree with You	1955	3.00	6.00	12.00
Coral 61911		Santa Claus Is Comin' to Town/Honorable Congratulations	1957	2.50	5.00	10.00
Albums						
Coral CRL 57097	M	Children's Holiday	1956	10.00	20.00	40.00
On Various-Artists Collections						
Ave Maria		Thank You for Opening Your Christmas Club with Us (Decca 34211)				
What Child Is This		Have Yourself a Merry Little Christmas (Reprise R 50001)				
McKAY, FAY						
45s						
Pax 7002		The 12 Daze Of Christmas/Those Swingin' Bells	19??	—	2.00	4.00
Pax 7002	PS	The 12 Daze Of Christmas/Those Swingin' Bells	19??	—	2.00	4.00
McKAY, JOHN						
45s						
Rooster 61009		Miracle On Christmas Eve/(B-side unknown)	1985	—	—	3.00
Rooster 61009	PS	Miracle On Christmas Eve/(B-side unknown)	1985	—	—	3.00
McKENZIE, BOB AND DOUG						
45s						
Mercury 76133	DJ	Twelve Days of Christmas (same on both sides)	1981	2.50	5.00	10.00
— May be promo only						
Mercury 810 323-7		Twelve Days Of Christmas/Take Off	1983	—	3.00	6.00
Albums						
Mercury SRM-1-4034		Great White North	1981	3.00	6.00	12.00
— Contains one Christmas song: Twelve Days of Christmas						
McKUEN, ROD						
45s						
Stanyan 34		Simple Christmas/A Hand To Hold At Christmas	1974	—	2.50	5.00
— B-side by Glenn Yarbrough						
Warner Bros. 7542		The Carols of Christmas/So My Sheep May Safely Graze	1971	—	2.50	5.00
Warner Bros. 7542	PS	The Carols of Christmas/So My Sheep May Safely Graze	1971	—	3.00	6.00
McLEAN, JAMES, AND THE BETHLEHEM GOSPEL SINGERS						
45s						
HSE 467		Silent Night/The Lord Is My Shepherd	19??	—	2.50	5.00
McLOLLIE, OSCAR						
45s						
Modern 943		God Gave Us Christmas/Dig That Crazy Santa Claus	1954	10.00	20.00	40.00
Modern 976		God Gave Us Christmas/(B-side unknown)	1955	7.50	15.00	30.00
On Various-Artists Collections						
Dig That Crazy Santa Claus		Rockin' Christmas — The '50s (Rhino RNLP-066)				
McNABB, KENNY						
45s						
MacGregor 2023		Santa Claus Is Coming To Town/(Instrumental)	19??	—	2.00	4.00
McNAMARA, PAUL						
45s						
Treasure Aisle 663		The Day That Santa Cried/The Day That Santa Cried	19??	—	2.00	4.00
— B-side by Emile Cote Chorale						

Label, Number		Title (A Side/B Side)	Year	VG	VG+	NM
McNARY, GENE						
On Various-Artists Collections						
Greetings to St. Louis County		Christmas in Saint Louis ((no label) TS77-558/9)				
McRAE, CARMEN						
On Various-Artists Collections						
Christmas Song, The		Jingle Bell Jazz (Columbia PC 36803)				
McSPADDEN, GARY						
On Various-Artists Collections						
Christmas Time Is the Best Time of the Year		Merry Christmas (Rainbow Sound R-5032-LPS)				
MEADER, VAUGHN						
45s						
Verve 10309		St. Nick Visits the White House/'Twas the Night Before Christmas	1963	5.00	10.00	20.00
MEADOWLARKS, THE – See DON JULIAN AND THE MEADOWLARKS.						
MEATH, ED						
45s						
Rainbow 228		Cosmic Christmas/Jimminy Christmas	19??	—	2.50	5.00
— Red vinyl						
MEAUX, HUEY						
45s						
Crazy Cajun 531		Christmas, A Day I Can't Forget/Sundown Playboy Special	197?	—	3.00	6.00
MECO						
45s						
RSO 1058		What Can You Get a Wookiee for Christmas (When He Already Owns a Comb)/We Wish You a Merry Christmas	1980	—	2.00	4.00
— By "The Star Wars Intergalactic Droid Choir and Chorale"; silver label						
RSO 1058		What Can You Get a Wookiee for Christmas (When He Already Owns a Comb)/We Wish You a Merry Christmas	1980	2.00	4.00	8.00
— By "The Star Wars Intergalactic Droid Choir and Chorale"; tan label						
RSO 1058	PS	What Can You Get a Wookiee for Christmas (When He Already Owns a Comb)/We Wish You a Merry Christmas	1980	2.50	5.00	10.00
RSO 815 718-7		Sleigh Ride/Christmas in the Stars	1983	2.00	4.00	8.00
— With R2-D2 and C-3PO						
RSO 815 718-7	PS	Sleigh Ride/Christmas In The Stars	1983	2.50	5.00	10.00
MEDEIROS, GLENN, AND JANEY CLEWER						
On Various-Artists Collections						
Love Will Keep Us Warm This Year for Christmas		Starlight Christmas, A (MCA 10066)				
MEDITATION SINGERS, THE						
On Various-Artists Collections						
Blue Christmas		Have a Merry Chess Christmas (Chess/MCA CH-25210)				
MEDLEY, BILL						
On Various-Artists Collections						
Santa, Please		Country Christmas, A, Volume 3 (RCA CPL1-5178)				
MEECE, DAVID						
On Various-Artists Collections						
Almost Christmastime		On This Christmas Night (Songbird MCA-3184)				
MEEK, LARRY						
45s						
Caprice 2043		The Night Before Christmas/(B-side unknown)	19??	2.00	4.00	8.00
MEISNER, VERNE						
45s						
Cuca 1195		Winter Wonderland/Caroling	1963	2.50	5.00	10.00

Label, Number		Title (A Side/B Side)	Year	VG	VG+	NM

MELACHRINO STRINGS, THE
On Various-Artists Collections

Sleigh Ride		Christmas Festival of Songs and Carols, Volume 2 (RCA Victor PRM-195)				
		Joyous Noel (Reader's Digest RDA-57A)				
		RCA Victor Presents Music for the Twelve Days of Christmas (RCA Victor PRS-188)				
White Christmas		For a Musical Merry Christmas, Vol. Two (RCA Victor PRM 189)				

MELACHRINO, GEORGE, ORCHESTRA
Albums

RCA Victor LPM-1045	M	Christmas in High Fidelity	1954	6.25	12.50	25.00

On Various-Artists Collections

Winter Wonderland		Christmas Programming from RCA Victor (RCA Victor SP-33-66)				
		October Christmas Sampler 59-40-41 (RCA Victor SPS-33-54)				

MELANIE
45s

Buddah 202		Ruby Tuesday/Merry Christmas	1970	—	2.50	5.00
— A-side is not a Christmas song						

7-Inch Extended Plays

Buddah SP 2	DJ	Merry Christmas/Christopher Robin//	1971	2.50	5.00	10.00
		I'm Back In Town/I Really Loved Harold				
Buddah SP 2	PS	I'm Back in Town	1971	2.50	5.00	10.00

MELIS, JOSE
45s

Seeco 6015		The Story Of Christmas/Sleigh Ride	1958	3.00	6.00	12.00

Albums

Seeco CELP 423	M	Christmas with Melis	196?	3.00	6.00	12.00

MELLENCAMP, JOHN COUGAR
On Various-Artists Collections

I Saw Mommy Kissing Santa Claus		Very Special Christmas, A (A&M SP-3911)				

MELLOW MOODS, THE
45s

Ronnie 202		The Christmas Song/Love Me	19??	2.50	5.00	10.00
— B-side by the Rainbows						

MELLOWMEN, THE
45s

Greeting 2001		Christmas Ride/Christmas Angel	19??	2.50	5.00	10.00
— B-side by Gloria Wood						

MELODEERS, THE
45s

Studio 9908		Rudolph the Red-Nosed Reindeer/Wishing Is for Fools	1959	5.00	10.00	20.00

MELTON, JAMES
45s

RCA Victor 49-0485		Silent Night/Oh Come, All Ye Faithful	1949	3.75	7.50	15.00
— Red vinyl						

On Various-Artists Collections

Silent Night		Joyous Noel (Reader's Digest RDA-57A)				

MEMPHIS SOUND ORCHESTRA
45s

RSO 865		Sleigh Ride/Winter Wonderland	1976	—	2.50	5.00

MENARD, D.L.
45s

Swallow 10258		You're All I Want For Christmas/Heartbroken Waltz	19??	—	2.00	4.00

MENDELL, JOHNNY
45s

Jamie 1208		Jingle Bell Twist U.S.A./A Real Old-Fashioned Christmas	1961	3.00	6.00	12.00

Label, Number	Title (A Side/B Side)	Year	VG	VG+	NM
MENDELSOHN, DANNY, SINGERS					
45s					
X 0068	Auld Lang Syne/When Good Fellows Get Together	1954	3.00	6.00	12.00
MENDES, SERGIO, AND BRASIL '66					
On Various-Artists Collections					
Christmas Song, The	Something Festive! (A&M SP-19003)				
MERCER, JOHNNY					
45s					
Capitol F1261	Jingle Bells/Santa Claus Is Comin' to Town	1950	3.75	7.50	15.00
Capitol F1285	Winter Wonderland/Goofus	1950	3.75	7.50	15.00
MERCER, TOMMY					
45s					
Plantation 213	Jingle Bell Night/(B-side unknown)	1983	—	2.00	4.00
MERCEY BROTHERS, THE					
45s					
RCA Victor PB-50307	Day Of Love (same on both sides)	1976	—	2.00	4.00
— Canadian import					
MERCHANT, MARTY					
45s					
Fresville 1040	E.T.'s Helping Santa/(B-side unknown)	1982	2.00	4.00	8.00
— Red vinyl					
MERCOURI, MELINA					
On Various-Artists Collections					
Christmas Eve on Skid Row	Gaily, Gaily (United Artists UAS 5202)				
MEREDITH, MARY, ORCHESTRA					
45s					
Strand 25010	Swingin' Sleighbells/Teen Sleighride	1959	3.75	7.50	15.00
MERLIN, LINDA					
45s					
Celebrity 103/4	All I Can Give You (For Christmas)/Season's Greetings	19??	—	2.00	4.00
MERRILL, HELEN					
45s					
Pumpkin 1001	A Christmas Gift/A Christmas Gift	1984	—	—	3.00
— B-side by Chuck Wayne					
MERRILL, RAY					
45s					
Vita 147	Oooh! What Santa Said/Peppy, the Peppermint Bear	1956	3.75	7.50	15.00
MERRILL, ROBERT					
On Various-Artists Collections					
Medley: March of the Kings/Hark! The Herald Angels Sing	Great Songs of Christmas, The, Album Eight (Columbia Special Products CSS 888)				
	Ronco Presents A Christmas Gift (Columbia Special Products P 12430)				
O Come, All Ye Faithful	Christmas Greetings, Vol. 4 (Columbia Special Products P 11987)				
MERRIWETHER, ROY, TRIO					
45s					
Columbia 43941	Jingle Bells (Part 1)/Jingle Bells (Part 2)	1966	2.00	4.00	8.00
MERRY ELVES, THE					
45s					
Argus 250	Rock & Roll Around the Christmas Tree/I Love Christmas	1964	2.50	5.00	10.00
MERRY MACS, THE					
45s					
Portrait 102	The Christmas Cha-Cha/Close Your Eyes	19??	—	2.00	4.00

Label, Number		Title (A Side/B Side)	Year	VG	VG+	NM
MESSINA, TONY						
45s						
December 138		Christmas Prayer/Old Days - Old Times - Old Friends	19??	—	2.00	4.00
METAL GURUS, THE						
45s						
Mercury GURU 1		Merry Xmas Everybody/Metal Guru	198?	—	3.00	6.00
Mercury GURU 1	PS	Merry Xmas Everybody/Metal Guru	198?	—	3.00	6.00
— Both record and sleeve are U.K. imports						
METAL MIKE, ALISON AND JULIA						
45s						
Triple X 51115		Deck the Halls/S&M Party//Slave to My Dick	199?	2.50	5.00	10.00
Triple X 51115	PS	Deck the Halls/S&M Party//Slave to My Dick	199?	2.50	5.00	10.00
METAMORA						
On Various-Artists Collections						
This Rush of Wings		Winter's Solstice II, A (Windham Hill WH-1077)				
METROPOLITAN OPERA MADRIGAL SINGERS, THE						
Albums						
Met 202		Welcome, Welcome Every Guest	1980	3.00	6.00	12.00
MEXICALI BRASS, THE						
Albums						
Custom CS 10	S	Jingle Bells	196?	3.00	6.00	12.00
MEYERSON, BESS						
On Various-Artists Collections						
Reminder Spot		For Christmas Seals...A Matter of Life and Breath (Decca Custom Style E)				
MICHAELS, DANNY						
45s						
Redwood 157		Christmas Shopping/Happy New Year	19??	—	2.50	5.00
MICHEL'LE						
On Various-Artists Collections						
Silver Bells		Christmas on Death Row (Death Row/Interscope INT2-90108)				
MICHELLE AND THE VALANETTES						
45s						
Santa 1129		Po-Ee, The Polar Bear/At Christmas Time	19??	—	2.50	5.00
MICHIGAN AND SMILEY						
On Various-Artists Collections						
Drummer Boy		Reggae Christmas, A (Real Authentic Sound RAS 3101)				
MICKELSON, PAUL						
Albums						
RCA Victor LPM-1115	M	Christmas Bells	1955	5.00	10.00	20.00
MICKEY MOUSE/ DONALD DUCK/ GOOFY/ LARRY GROCE						
On Various-Artists Collections						
Here Comes Santa Claus		Disney's Christmas All-Time Favorites (Disneyland 1V 8150)				
Sleigh Ride		Disney's Christmas All-Time Favorites (Disneyland 1V 8150)				
MICKEY MOUSE/ DONALD DUCK/ GOOFY/ MINNIE MOUSE/CHIP 'N' DALE/ CLARABELLE COW/ LARRY						
On Various-Artists Collections						
Twelve Days of Christmas, The		Disney's Christmas All-Time Favorites (Disneyland 1V 8150)				
MIDNIGHT STRING QUARTET						
45s						
Viva 622		The Little Drummer Boy/Silent Night	1967	—	3.00	6.00
Albums						
Viva V-36010	S	Christmas Rhapsodies for Young Lovers	1968	3.75	7.50	15.00

Label, Number	Title (A Side/B Side)	Year	VG	VG+	NM

MIGHTY BLASTERS
45s

Lanor 611	Old Time White Christmas/A Change Is Gonna Come	19??	—	2.00	4.00
— B-side by Lula Bolden					

MILAN
45s

Migon 1962	Santa's Doing The Twist/(B-side unknown)	1962	3.75	7.50	15.00

MILBURN, AMOS
45s

King 5405	Christmas (Comes But Once a Year)/Please Come Home for Christmas	1960	3.00	6.00	12.00
— B-side by Charles Brown					

MILBURN, BILL
45s

Bonnie 527	(I Took a Little Ride on) Santa's Sleigh/Santa Comes on Christmas Eve	19??	—	2.50	5.00

MILDRED AND C. P.
45s

Mac Gregor (no #)	Season's Greetings From (Side 1)/Season's Greetings From (Side 2)	1958	3.00	6.00	12.00
— Yellow vinyl					

MILLARD AND NELS
45s

Chris 2008	Christmas Without Daddy/Just Let Me Go	19??	—	3.00	6.00

MILLER BROTHERS, THE
45s

4 Star 1686	Rudolph Junior/Happy Birthday, Dear Jesus	1955	3.00	6.00	12.00

MILLER, ASHLEY
Albums

Command COM-K1	M	Christmas Carols with Organ and Chimes	1963	3.00	6.00	12.00
— Sold only at Korvettes department stores						
Command COM-K1 SD	S	Christmas Carols with Organ and Chimes	1963	3.75	7.50	15.00
— Sold only at Korvettes department stores						

MILLER, DREW, AND THE BEL-AIRES
45s

MGM 11627	When Christmas Angels Sing/Mystery Trail	1953	5.00	10.00	20.00

MILLER, GLENN, AND HIS ORCHESTRA
On Various-Artists Collections

Jingle Bells	Christmas Through the Years (Reader's Digest RDA-143)
	Happy Holidays, Vol. 21 (RCA Special Products DPL1-0739)
	Joyous Noel (Reader's Digest RDA-57A)
	Remembering Christmas with the Big Bands (RCA Special Products DPM1-0506)

MILLER, JACOB "KILLER"
On Various-Artists Collections

All I Want for Ismas	Ital Christmas (Top Ranking (no #))
Broke Pocket Christmas	Ital Christmas (Top Ranking (no #))
Deck the Halls	Ital Christmas (Top Ranking (no #))
Silver Bells	Ital Christmas (Top Ranking (no #))
Twelve Days of Ismas	Ital Christmas (Top Ranking (no #))

MILLER, JODY
45s

Epic 11076	Silent Night, Lonely Night/(B-side unknown)	1973	—	3.00	6.00

On Various-Artists Collections

First Noel, The	RFD Christmas (Columbia Special Products P 15427)
What Child Is This	Down-Home Country Christmas, A (Columbia Special Products P 14992)
	RFD Christmas (Columbia Special Products P 15427)

Label, Number		Title (A Side/B Side)	Year	VG	VG+	NM

MILLER, LISE
45s
Canterbury 519		The Loneliest Christmas Tree/Love	1967	2.50	5.00	10.00

MILLER, MITCH
45s
Columbia 41814		Must Be Santa/Christmas Spirit	1960	2.50	5.00	10.00
Columbia 42210		Sleigh Ride/The Christmas Song	1961	2.00	4.00	8.00
Columbia 42211		Rudolph the Red-Nosed Reindeer/The Twelve Days of Christmas	1961	2.00	4.00	8.00
Columbia 42212		Jingle Bells/White Christmas	1961	2.00	4.00	8.00
Columbia 42213		Silent Night, Holy Night/Deck The Halls With Boughs Of Holly	1961	2.00	4.00	8.00
Columbia 42214		God Rest Ye Merry Gentlemen/O Come, All Ye Faithful	1961	2.00	4.00	8.00
Columbia 3-42240		Must Be Santa/Be a Santa	1961	3.00	6.00	12.00

— "Columbia Single 33"; small hole

Columbia 42240		Must Be Santa/Be a Santa	1961	2.00	4.00	8.00
Columbia 42914		Pine Cones and Holly Berries/Whispering Hope	1963	2.00	4.00	8.00
Columbia 42914	PS	Pine Cones and Holly Berries/Whispering Hope	1963	2.50	5.00	10.00

7-Inch Extended Plays
Columbia C 7791		The Blizzard Song/Frosty The Snow Man//Let It Snow/Sleigh Ride	1966	—	3.00	6.00
Columbia C 7791	PS	Singin' Up a Blizzard	1966	2.00	4.00	8.00

— Free with a 6-pack of Fresca (sleeve is designed to slip over the neck of a bottle)

Albums
Columbia CL 1205	M	Christmas Sing Along with Mitch	1958	3.75	7.50	15.00

— Originals have gatefold cover with eight detachable lyric sheets inside

Columbia CL 1701	M	Holiday Sing Along with Mitch	1961	3.75	7.50	15.00
Columbia CS 8027	S	Christmas Sing Along with Mitch	1959	5.00	10.00	20.00

— Originals have gatefold cover with eight detachable lyric sheets inside

Columbia CS 8501	S	Holiday Sing Along with Mitch	1961	5.00	10.00	20.00
Columbia 3C 39297		Holiday Sing Along with Mitch	1984	2.00	4.00	8.00
Columbia PC 39298		Christmas Sing Along with Mitch	1984	2.00	4.00	8.00

On Various-Artists Collections
Auld Lang Syne	Seasons Greetings (A Christmas Festival of Stars) (Columbia CS 8189)
Coventry Carol	Great Songs of Christmas, The, Album Four (Columbia Special Products CSP 155M)
	60 Christmas Classics (Sessions DVL2-0723)
Deck the Hall with Boughs of Holly	Have a Happy Holiday (Columbia Special Products CSS 1432)
First Noel, The	Great Songs of Christmas, The, Album Four (Columbia Special Products CSP 155M)
	Wondrous Winter: Songs of Winter, Songs of Christmas
	(Columbia Special Products CSS 708/9)
Frosty the Snowman	Merry Christmas from... (Reader's Digest RD4-83)
God Rest Ye Merry Gentlemen	Gift of Christmas, The, Vol. 1 (Columbia Special Products CSS 706)
Jingle Bells	Merry Christmas from... (Reader's Digest RD4-83)
Joy to the World	Joyous Christmas, Volume 2 (Columbia Special Products CSS 808)
	Very Merry Christmas, A, Volume Two (Columbia Special Products CSS 788)
Medley: It Came Upon the Midnight Clear/Away in the Manger	Great Songs of Christmas, The, Album Three (Columbia Special Products CSP 117)
O Come All Ye Faithful	Seasons Greetings (A Christmas Festival of Stars) (Columbia CS 8189)
Santa Claus Is Comin' to Town	Christmas Greetings (Columbia Special Products CSS 1499)
	Sounds of Christmas (Columbia Special Products CSS 708/9)
Seasons Greetings	Seasons Greetings (A Christmas Festival of Stars) (Columbia CS 8189)
Silent Night, Holy Night	Happy Holidays, Album Nine (Columbia Special Products P 11793)
Twelve Days of Christmas, The	Merry Christmas from... (Reader's Digest RD4-83)
We Three Kings of Orient Are	It's Christmas Time! (Columbia Special Products P 14990)
	Merry Christmas from... (Reader's Digest RD4-83)
What Child Is This	Great Songs of Christmas, The (Columbia Special Products XTV 69406/7)
	Merry Christmas from... (Reader's Digest RD4-83)
	Very Merry Christmas, A, Volume 3 (Columbia Special Products CSS 997)
Winter Wonderland	Christmas Album, A (Columbia PC 39466)
	Merry Christmas (Columbia Musical Treasury 3P 6306)

MILLER, OLIVETTE
45s
Protone 117		Real Cool Yule/The Money Man	1959	3.00	6.00	12.00

MILLER, PAT
45s
Holiday 101		I Saw Mommy Kissing Santa Claus/You're All I Want For Christmas	19??	—	2.50	5.00

MILLER, ROGER
45s
Smash 2130		Old Toy Trains/Silent Night	1967	2.50	5.00	10.00
Smash 2130	PS	Old Toy Trains/Silent Night	1967	3.00	6.00	12.00

On Various-Artists Collections
Old Toy Trains	Country Christmas (Time-Life STL-109)
	Time-Life Treasury of Christmas, The, Volume Two (Time-Life STL-108)

Label, Number		Title (A Side/B Side)	Year	VG	VG+	NM
MILLER, TAD						
45s						
Somewhat Off 310065		Santa, I Hope You'll Understand (same on both sides)	19??	—	3.00	6.00
MILLISON, BRAD						
45s						
Fifth Street 1103		Christmas In Kansas City/The Christmas Song	19??	—	—	3.00
— Red vinyl						
Fifth Street 1103	PS	Christmas In Kansas City/The Christmas Song	19??	—	—	3.00
MILLS BROTHERS, THE						
45s						
Decca 29754		I Believe in Santa Claus/You Don't Have to Be a Santa Claus	1955	3.00	6.00	12.00
Albums						
Dot DLP-3232	M	Merry Christmas	1959	5.00	10.00	20.00
Dot DLP-25232	S	Merry Christmas	1959	7.50	15.00	30.00
— With cursive "Dot" logo						
Dot DLP-25232	S	Merry Christmas	1968	3.00	6.00	12.00
— With "Dot"/"Paramount" logo						
Pickwick SPC-1025		Merry Christmas	1979	2.50	5.00	10.00
— Reissue of Dot album with one fewer track and rearranged contents						
On Various-Artists Collections						
Jingle Bells		Christmas Is... (Columbia Special Products P 11417)				
Silent Night		12 Days of Christmas, The (Pickwick SPC-1021)				
MILLS, ALAN						
Albums						
Folkways FC-7750	M	Christmas Songs from Many Lands	1956	7.50	15.00	30.00
Scholastic FC-7750	M	Christmas Songs from Many Lands	196?	3.75	7.50	15.00
— Reissue of Folkways album						
On Various-Artists Collections						
Bagpipers' Carol		How the Grinch Stole Christmas (Random House/Scholastic 0-394-05008-8)				
Bring a Torch		How the Grinch Stole Christmas (Random House/Scholastic 0-394-05008-8)				
Come and Sing		How the Grinch Stole Christmas (Random House/Scholastic 0-394-05008-8)				
Friendly Beasts, The		How the Grinch Stole Christmas (Random House/Scholastic 0-394-05008-8)				
Fum-Fum-Fum		How the Grinch Stole Christmas (Random House/Scholastic 0-394-05008-8)				
Gently, the Maiden		How the Grinch Stole Christmas (Random House/Scholastic 0-394-05008-8)				
Haidom-Haidom		How the Grinch Stole Christmas (Random House/Scholastic 0-394-05008-8)				
Little Bitty Baby		How the Grinch Stole Christmas (Random House/Scholastic 0-394-05008-8)				
Mary Had a Baby		How the Grinch Stole Christmas (Random House/Scholastic 0-394-05008-8)				
O Christmas Tree		How the Grinch Stole Christmas (Random House/Scholastic 0-394-05008-8)				
Saint Basil		How the Grinch Stole Christmas (Random House/Scholastic 0-394-05008-8)				
Simple Birth, The		How the Grinch Stole Christmas (Random House/Scholastic 0-394-05008-8)				
Twelve Days of Christmas		How the Grinch Stole Christmas (Random House/Scholastic 0-394-05008-8)				
MILLS, FRANK						
On Various-Artists Collections						
Cathedral Bells Are Ringing		60 Christmas Classics (Sessions DVL2-0723)				
Fanfare/Joy to the World		60 Christmas Classics (Sessions DVL2-0723)				
MILLY & SILLY						
45s						
Right-On 113		I'm A Xmas Tree/Gettin' Down For Xmas	19??	—	2.50	5.00
MILMAN, ALAN, SECT						
45s						
Britz 1		Punk Rock Christmas/Stitches In My Head//	1977	2.00	4.00	8.00
		I Wanna Kill Somebody/Teen Tour				
Britz 1	PS	Punk Rock Christmas/Stitches In My Head//	1977	2.00	4.00	8.00
		I Wanna Kill Somebody/Teen Tour				
MILSAP, RONNIE						
45s						
Capitol Nashville S7-18909		The Christmas Song/Till the Season Comes 'Round Again	1995	—	—	3.00
RCA 5049-7-R		Only One Night of the Year/	1986	—	—	3.00
		It's Just Not Christmas (If I Can't Spend It With You)				
RCA 5351-7-R		Christmas Medley: Carol of the Bells/O Come, Come Emmanuel/	1987	—	—	3.00
		Silent Night/Joy to the World//I'll Be Home for Christmas				
RCA 9071-7-R		I'll Be Home for Chrirtmas/We're Here to Love	1989	—	—	3.00
RCA PB-13665		It's Christmas/We're Here to Love	1983	—	2.00	4.00

Label, Number		Title (A Side/B Side)	Year	VG	VG+	NM
Albums						
RCA Victor 5624-1-R		Christmas with Ronnie Milsap	1986	2.50	5.00	10.00
On Various-Artists Collections						
It's Christmas		Best of Christmas, The (RCA Victor CPL1-7013)				
		Country Christmas (Time-Life STL-109)				
		Country Christmas, A, Volume 3 (RCA CPL1-5178)				
		Family Christmas Collection, The (Time-Life STL-131)				
		Happy Holidays, Vol. 20 (RCA Special Products DPL1-0713)				
It's Not Christmas		Mistletoe and Memories (RCA 8372-1-R)				
Silver Bells		Happy Holidays, Vol. 22 (RCA Special Products DPL1-0777)				

MINNELLI, LIZA
On Various-Artists Collections

I'm Naïve		Dangerous Christmas of Red Riding Hood, The (ABC-Paramount 536)				
My Red Riding Hood		Dangerous Christmas of Red Riding Hood, The (ABC-Paramount 536)				
Raggedy Ann and Raggedy Andy		Something Festive! (A&M SP-19003)				

MINNELLI, LIZA, AND CYRIL RITCHARD
On Various-Artists Collections

Ding-a-Ling, Ding-a-Ling		Dangerous Christmas of Red Riding Hood, The (ABC-Paramount 536)				

MIRACLE LEGION
45s

Incas ML2		Little Drummer Boy/Blue Christmas	19??	2.00	4.00	8.00
Incas ML2	PS	Little Drummer Boy/Blue Christmas	19??	2.00	4.00	8.00

MIRACLES, THE
Also see SMOKEY ROBINSON AND THE MIRACLES.
45s

Tamla EX-009	DJ	The Christmas Song/Christmas Everyday	1963	50.00	100.00	200.00
Albums						
Motown 5253ML		The Season for Miracles	1982	2.00	4.00	8.00
Motown 5254ML		Christmas with the Miracles	1982	2.00	4.00	8.00
Tamla T 236		Christmas with the Miracles	1963	75.00	150.00	300.00
— Originals have two globes on the top of the label						
Tamla T 307		The Season for Miracles	1970	3.75	7.50	15.00

MIRROR IMAGE
Albums

Pickwick SPC-1027		Yuletide Disco	1979	2.50	5.00	10.00

MISS LL AND THE THREE MICE, BLIMP, WHIMP & SKIMP,
45s

Skyway 138		No Cheese (On The Christmas Tree)/Wedding Ring For Christmas	1963	3.00	6.00	12.00

MR. BO AND HIS BLUES BOY'S
45s

Big D 3025		Santa's On His Way/Let's Go To The Party	19??	3.75	7.50	15.00

MR. HOOPER, ERNIE AND BERT
On Various-Artists Collections

Christmas Story, A		Merry Christmas from Sesame Street (CRA CTW 25516)				

MISTLETOE DISCO BAND
45s

Mistletoe 806		Sleigh Ride (Disco)/Little Drummer Boy (Disco)	197?	—	2.50	5.00
Albums						
Holiday HDY-1019		More Christmas Disco	1980	2.50	5.00	10.00

MISTLETOE SINGERS, THE
Albums

Mistletoe MLX-1211	(2)	Happy Holidays	197?	3.75	7.50	15.00

MITCHELL BOY CHOIR, THE
45s

Jimmy McHugh 401		Let's Have An Old Fashioned Christmas/Ol' Kris Kringle	198?	—	—	3.00
— B-side by Don Robertson and Lou Dinning						

Label, Number		Title (A Side/B Side)	Year	VG	VG+	NM
RCA Victor 47-3862		Oh Come All Ye Faithful/It Came Upon a Midnight Clear// Silent Night/Oh Little Town of Bethlehem	1950	3.75	7.50	15.00
RCA Victor 47-3863		Angels We Have Heard on High/Good King Wenceslas// The First Noel/Joy to the World	1950	3.75	7.50	15.00
RCA Victor 47-3864		Hark! The Herald Angels Sing/The Wassail Song// Jingle Bells/Deck the Halls	1950	3.75	7.50	15.00

MITCHELL, BRUCE
On Various-Artists Collections
Joy to the World   Narada: The Christmas Collection (Narada N-63902)

MITCHELL, CHAD, TRIO
45s

Mercury 72197		The Marvelous Toy/Bonny Streets of Fyve-10	1963	2.50	5.00	10.00
Mercury 72197	PS	The Marvelous Toy/Bonny Streets of Fyve-10	1963	3.75	7.50	15.00

MITCHELL, DUKE, FAMILY
45s

Verve 10229	Buzzy the Christmas Bee/My New Year's Resolution	1960	3.75	7.50	15.00

MITCHELL, ELLA
On Various-Artists Collections
Away in a Manger   Merry Christmas from David Frost and Billy Taylor (Bell 6053)

MITCHELL, ELLA, AND BILLY TAYLOR
On Various-Artists Collections
Stable Down the Road   Merry Christmas from David Frost and Billy Taylor (Bell 6053)

MITCHELL, ELLA, AND MILT GRAYSON
On Various-Artists Collections
Go Tell It on the Mountain   Merry Christmas from David Frost and Billy Taylor (Bell 6053)

MITT AND THE MERRYMAKERS
45s

XL 350	Elmer The Elf/Mr. Santa Claus	19??	2.00	4.00	8.00

MITZELFELT CHORALE
45s

Fiamma 101	Hear The Bells Ring/White Christmas	19??	—	2.00	4.00
Fiamma 102	Christmas Eve/The Christmas Song	19??	—	2.00	4.00

MIXED CHORUS AND ORCHESTRA – See WERNER MULLER.

MODERN JAZZ QUARTET, THE
45s

Atlantic 2085	England's Carol (Part 1)/England's Carol (Part 2)	1960	5.00	10.00	20.00

MODERN MANDOLIN QUARTET
On Various-Artists Collections
Medley: E'en So, Lord Jesus Quickly   Winter's Solstice II, A (Windham Hill WH-1077)
Come/Dadme Albricias Hijos D'Eva
(Sons of Eve Reward My Tidings)

MODERNAIRES, THE
45s

Coral 61547	Santa's Little Sleigh Bells/Sleepy Little Space Cadet	1955	3.75	7.50	15.00

MOFFO, ANNA
On Various-Artists Collections
Ave Maria   Christmas Greetings, Vol. 3 (Columbia Special Products P 11383)
                Great Songs of Christmas, The, Album Eight (Columbia Special Products CSS 888)
Ave Maria (Schubert)   Joyous Christmas, Volume V (Columbia Special Products C 10398)
Joy to the World   Best of the Great Songs of Christmas (Album 10) (Columbia Special Products CSS 1478)
                Great Songs of Christmas, The, Album Eight (Columbia Special Products CSS 888)

MOM AND DADS, THE
45s

GNP Crescendo 460	Jingle Bell Rock/Auld Lang Syne	1972	—	2.50	5.00
GNP Crescendo 803	Silver Bells/Bill Bailey	1975	—	2.00	4.00

Label, Number		Title (A Side/B Side)	Year	VG	VG+	NM
MONAHAN, LEN FRANCIS						
45s						
World Airwave 594S15		Being Alone for Christmas/Christmas Lullaby	1975	—	2.50	5.00
World Airwave 594S15	PS	Being Alone for Christmas/Christmas Lullaby	1975	—	3.00	6.00
MONDAY MORNING QUARTERBACK, THE						
45s						
Warner Bros. 7664		The 12 Days of Christmas (The Game Plan to Beat Miami)/ Santa Claus Medley	1972	2.50	5.00	10.00
Warner Bros 7664	PS	The 12 Days of Christmas (The Game Plan to Beat Miami)/ Santa Claus Medley	1972	3.75	7.50	15.00
MONETTES, THE						
45s						
Monava 1006		Christmas Is Coming/Indiana Rose	19??	—	2.50	5.00
MONROE, BILL						
45s						
Decca 46386		Christmas Time's A-Comin'/The First Whip-Poor-Wills	1951	7.50	15.00	30.00
On Various-Artists Collections						
Christmas Time's a-Comin'		Country Christmas (Time-Life STL-109)				
MONROE, VAUGHN						
45s						
RCA Victor 47-3070		The Jolly Old Man in the Bright Red Suit/Auld Lang Syne	1949	3.75	7.50	15.00
RCA Victor 47-3915		Frosty the Snowman/Could Be	1950	3.75	7.50	15.00
RCA Victor 47-3942		A Marshmallow World/Snowy White Snow and Jingle Bells	1950	3.75	7.50	15.00
RCA Victor 47-4299		Frosty the Snowman/The Jolly Old Man in the Bright Red Suit	1951	3.75	7.50	15.00
On Various-Artists Collections						
Frosty the Snowman		Joyous Noel (Reader's Digest RDA-57A)				
Let It Snow! Let It Snow! Let It Snow!		Billboard Greatest Christmas Hits, 1935-1954 (Rhino R1 70637)				
		Christmas Through the Years (Reader's Digest RDA-143)				
MONTAGUE						
45s						
Class 218		Thanks for Christmas (Narration)/Thanks for Christmas	1957	5.00	10.00	20.00
— B-side by Judy Lynn Phelps						
MONTANA ORCHESTRA						
45s						
MJS 4502		Montana Christmas Medley/Get Down New Years Eve	1981	—	3.00	6.00
Albums						
MJS 3302		Merry Christmas/Happy New Year's	1981	2.50	5.00	10.00
MONTANA SLIM						
45s						
RCA Victor 47-4303		The Night Before Christmas/Punkinhead	1951	5.00	10.00	20.00
— As "Wilf Carter"						
RCA Victor 48-0392		Jolly Old St. Nicholas/Rudolph the Red-Nosed Reindeer	1950	10.00	20.00	40.00
— Originals on green vinyl						
MONTE, LOU						
45s						
RCA Victor 47-6320		Santo Natale/Italian Jingle Bells	1955	3.00	6.00	12.00
RCA Victor 47-7641		Santa Nicola/All Because It's Christmas	1959	3.00	6.00	12.00
Roulette 4308		Christmas at Our House/Dominick the Donkey	1960	3.00	6.00	12.00
On Various-Artists Collections						
Adeste Fideles		Have Yourself a Merry Little Christmas (Reprise R 50001)				
Silent Night		Happy Holiday (Mistletoe 1243)				
Silver Bells		Happy Holiday (Mistletoe 1243)				
MONTGOMERY, RITA						
45s						
Liberty 55049		I Believe in Santa Claus/Many, Many Christmases Ago	1956	3.75	7.50	15.00
MONYAKA						
12-Inch Singles						
A&M SP-12156	DJ	Got the Beat for Christmas// Got the Beat for Christmas (Dub Version)/Got the Beat for Christmas (Single Version)	1985	2.00	4.00	8.00

Label, Number		Title (A Side/B Side)	Year	VG	VG+	NM
MOODS, THE						
45s						
Sarg 184		Rockin' Santa Claus/Teenager's Past	1959	10.00	20.00	40.00
On Various-Artists Collections						
Rockin' Santa Claus		Rockin' Christmas — The '50s (Rhino RNLP-066)				
MOODY, CARLTON						
45s						
Lamon 10059		Last Christmas Eve/It Don't Seem Like Christmas Anymore	197?	—	2.00	4.00
MOOG, EBENEEZER						
45s						
Rocket ROKN 503		God Rest Ye Merry Gentlemen/Silent Night	1975	—	3.00	6.00
Rocket ROKN 503	PS	God Rest Ye Merry Gentlemen/Silent Night	1975	2.50	5.00	10.00
MOOLAH CHANTERS EL KORAN						
On Various-Artists Collections						
Do You Hear What I Hear?		Christmas in Saint Louis ((no label) TS77-558/9)				
MOON, JACK						
45s						
Aardell 0005		Jolly Santa Claus/Ha Ha Ha, Ho Ho Ho	19??	—	3.00	6.00
MOONEY, ART						
45s						
MGM 10522		Jingle Bells/The Mistletoe Kiss	1949	3.75	7.50	15.00
MGM 10851		Christmas Choo Choo/Candyland Parade	1950	3.00	6.00	12.00
MGM 12092		Nuttin' for Christmas/Santa Claus Looks Like Daddy	1955	5.00	10.00	20.00
— Vocal by Barry Gordon						
MGM 12847		A Merry Merry Christmas to You/Sunset to Sunrise	1959	2.50	5.00	10.00
MGM 12847	PS	A Merry Merry Christmas to You/Sunset to Sunrise	1959	3.00	6.00	12.00
MOONGLOWS, THE						
45s						
Chance 1150		Just a Lonely Christmas/Hey, Santa Claus	1953	375.00	750.00	1,500.
— Red vinyl (this may not exist legitimately on black vinyl)						
Lost Nite 275		Just a Lonely Christmas/Baby Please	196?	3.00	6.00	12.00
— Reissue						
Mello 69		Just a Lonely Christmas/Hey, Santa Claus	19??	2.00	4.00	8.00
— Reissue						
On Various-Artists Collections						
Hey Santa Claus		Have a Merry Chess Christmas (Chess/MCA CH-25210)				
		Rockin' Christmas — The '50s (Rhino RNLP-066)				
		Rockin' Little Christmas (MCA 25084)				
Just a Lonely Christmas		Rockin' Christmas — The '50s (Rhino RNLP-066)				
		Rockin' Little Christmas (MCA 25084)				
MOONLION						
45s						
P.I.P. 6513		The Little Drummer Boy/Laid Back	1975	—	2.50	5.00
P.I.P. 6513	DJ	The Little Drummer Boy (Airplay Version)/	1975	—	2.00	4.00
		The Little Drummer Boy (Disco Version)				
MOORE, GATEMOUTH						
45s						
King 4492		Christmas Blues/Happy New Year, Darling	1951	12.50	25.00	50.00
— B-side by Lonnie Johnson						
MOORE, JOHNNY'S, BLAZERS						
Also see CHARLES BROWN, FRANKIE ERVIN.						
45s						
Hollywood 1045		Christmas Everyday/Christmas Eve, Baby	1955	10.00	20.00	40.00
— With Frankie Ervin						
On Various-Artists Collections						
Christmas Dreams		Merry Christmas Baby (Christmas Music for Young Lovers) (Hollywood HLP 501)				
		Merry Christmas Baby (Gusto/Hollywood K-5018-X)				
Christmas Eve Baby		Merry Christmas Baby (Christmas Music for Young Lovers) (Hollywood HLP 501)				
		Merry Christmas Baby (Gusto/Hollywood K-5018-X)				

Label, Number		Title (A Side/B Side)	Year	VG	VG+	NM
Christmas Every Day		Merry Christmas Baby (Christmas Music for Young Lovers) (Hollywood HLP 501)				
		Merry Christmas Baby (Gusto/Hollywood K-5018-X)				
Christmas Letter		Merry Christmas Baby (Christmas Music for Young Lovers) (Hollywood HLP 501)				
		Merry Christmas Baby (Gusto/Hollywood K-5018-X)				

MOORE, MEL, AND IMAGE
45s
| Sterling 924 | | Merry Christmas Angel/Here's To A Sad And Lonely New Year's | 19?? | — | — | 3.00 |

MOORE, PHIL, AND THE PHIL MOORE FOUR
45s
| RCA Victor 47-5538 | | Blink Before Christmas/Chincy Old Scrooge | 1953 | 5.00 | 10.00 | 20.00 |

MOORE, ROGER
On Various-Artists Collections
| Once in Royal David's City | | We Wish You a Merry Christmas (Warner Bros. W 1337) | | | | |

MORALES, NORO & HIS ORCHESTRA
45s
| RCA Victor 47-5674 | | Santa/Me And My Shadow | 1954 | 3.00 | 6.00 | 12.00 |

MORANDI, CHRISTIAN
45s
| Decca 31343 | | Dear Gesu Bambino/Caro Gesu Bambino | 1961 | 3.00 | 6.00 | 12.00 |
| — B-side by Bruno Pallesi | | | | | | |

MORE, KENNETH; ALBERT FINNEY
On Various-Artists Collections
| I Like Life | | Scrooge (Columbia Masterworks S 30258) | | | | |

MORGAN, GEORGE
On Various-Artists Collections
Blue Snowfall		Country Christmas (Columbia CS 9888)				
		Country Christmas Favorites (Columbia Special Products C 10876)				
		Country Style Christmas, A (Columbia Musical Treasury 3P 6316)				
		We Wish You a Country Christmas (Columbia Special Products P 14991)				

MORGAN, LORRIE
45s
| BNA 64406 | | Up on Santa Claus Mountain/My Favorite Things | 1995 | — | 2.00 | 4.00 |

MORGAN, RUSS
45s
Decca 24766		Blue Christmas/The Mistletoe Kiss	1950	3.75	7.50	15.00
Decca 28493		The Night Before Christmas Song/Willy Claus	1952	3.75	7.50	15.00
Decca 30147		The Santa Claus March/I Will Always Believe in Santa Claus	1956	3.00	6.00	12.00

On Various-Artists Collections
| Blue Christmas | | Christmas Through the Years (Reader's Digest RDA-143) | | | | |

MORMON TABERNACLE CHOIR
45s
Columbia 41515		Hallelujah Chorus/Jesu, Joy of Man's Desiring	1959	3.00	6.00	12.00
Columbia JZSP 111909/10	DJ	Joy to the World/I Heard the Bells	1965	2.50	5.00	10.00
— Green vinyl						
Columbia JZSP 111909/10	DJ	Joy to the World/I Heard the Bells	1965	—	3.00	6.00
— Black vinyl, yellow label						
Columbia JZSP 111909/10	DJ	Joy to the World/I Heard the Bells	1965	—	3.00	6.00
— Black vinyl, white label						

Albums
Book-of-the-Month 71-6406	(3)	Christmas Celebration	1980	5.00	10.00	20.00
CBS Masterworks IM 37206		Silent Night — The Greatest Hits of Christmas	1981	3.00	6.00	12.00
CBS Masterworks MG 37853	(2)	The Greatest Hits of Christmas	1981	3.75	7.50	15.00
CBS Masterworks XM 38299		Christmas Carols Around the World	1982	2.00	4.00	8.00
Columbia LE 10091		Christmas Carols Around the World	1976	2.50	5.00	10.00
— A Columbia "Limited Edition" reissue (see title under Columbia Masterworks for contents)						
Columbia House 1P 6075		Christmas with the Mormon Tabernacle Choir	1973	2.50	5.00	10.00
Columbia Masterworks M 32935		The Great Messiah Choruses	1974	2.50	5.00	10.00
Columbia Masterworks M 34546		White Christmas	1976	3.00	6.00	12.00
Columbia Masterworks ML 5222	M	Sings Christmas Carols	1957	5.00	10.00	20.00

Label, Number	Title (A Side/B Side)	Year	VG	VG+	NM
Columbia Masterworks ML 5500 M	The Spirit of Christmas	1959	3.00	6.00	12.00
Columbia Masterworks ML 5592 M	The Holly and the Ivy	1960	3.00	6.00	12.00
Columbia Masterworks ML 56?? M	Christmas Carols Around the World	1961	3.00	6.00	12.00
Columbia Masterworks ML 5899 M	The Joy of Christmas	1963	2.50	5.00	10.00
— With the New York Philharmonic conducted by Leonard Bernstein					
Columbia Masterworks MS 6100 S	The Spirit of Christmas	1959	3.75	7.50	15.00
— Same as ML 5500					
Columbia Masterworks ML 6177 M	Sings Christmas Carols	1965	3.00	6.00	12.00
— A new recording of ML 5222					
Columbia Masterworks MS 6192 S	The Holly and the Ivy	1960	3.75	7.50	15.00
— Same as ML 5592					
Columbia Masterworks MS 62?? S	Christmas Carols Around the World	1961	3.75	7.50	15.00
— Same as ML 56??					
Columbia Masterworks ML 6351 M	The Mormon Tabernacle Choir's Greatest Hits	1966	2.50	5.00	10.00
— Contains one Christmas song: Hallelujah Chorus					
Columbia Masterworks MS 6499 S	The Joy of Christmas	1963	3.00	6.00	12.00
— Same as ML 5899					
Columbia Masterworks MS 6777 S	Sings Christmas Carols	1965	3.75	7.50	15.00
— Same as ML 6177					
Columbia Masterworks MS 6951 S	The Mormon Tabernacle Choir's Greatest Hits	1966	3.00	6.00	12.00
— Same as ML 6351					
Columbia Masterworks M 30077	Joy to the World	1970	3.00	6.00	12.00
Columbia Masterworks XM 30077	Joy to the World	197?	2.50	5.00	10.00
— Reissue of M 30077					

On Various-Artists Collections

Angels We Have Heard on High	Great Songs of Christmas, The, Album Two (Columbia Special Products XTV 86100/1)
	Magic of Christmas, The (Columbia Musical Treasury P3S 5806)
Away in the Manger	That Christmas Feeling (Columbia Special Products P 11853)
Break Forth, O Beauteous, Heavenly Light	Merry Christmas from... (Reader's Digest RD4-83)
Carol of the Bells	Great Songs of Christmas, The (Columbia Special Products XTV 69406/7)
Deck the Halls with Boughs of Holly	Christmas Album, A (Columbia PC 39466)
	Great Songs of Christmas, The, Album Four (Columbia Special Products CSP 155M)
	Great Songs of Christmas, The, Album Six (Columbia Special Products CSM 388)
Good King Wenceslas	Great Songs of Christmas, The, Album Two (Columbia Special Products XTV 86100/1)
Hallelujah Chorus	Christmas Greetings (Columbia Special Products CSS 1433)
	Home for Christmas (Columbia Musical Treasury P3S 5608)
	Very Merry Christmas, A (Columbia Special Products CSS 563)
I Heard the Bells	Happy Holidays, Album 8 (Columbia Special Products C 11086)
Joy to the World	Great Songs of Christmas, The, Album Three (Columbia Special Products CSP 117)
	Joyous Christmas, Volume 4 (Columbia Special Products CSS 1485)
	Joyous Songs of Christmas, The (Columbia Special Products C 10400)
	Merry Christmas (Columbia Musical Treasury 3P 6306)
	Ronco Presents A Christmas Gift (Columbia Special Products P 12430)
March of the Kings	Great Songs of Christmas, The, Album Six (Columbia Special Products CSM 388)
O Come All Ye Faithful	Great Songs of Christmas, The, Album Three (Columbia Special Products CSP 117)
O Come, O Come, Emmanuel	Merry Christmas from... (Reader's Digest RD4-83)
	WHIO Radio Christmas Feelings (Sound Approach/CSP P 16366)
O Little Town of Bethlehem	Great Songs of Christmas, The, Album Two (Columbia Special Products XTV 86100/1)
	Great Songs of Christmas, The, Album Four (Columbia Special Products CSP 155M)
Once in Royal David's City	Merry Christmas from... (Reader's Digest RD4-83)
Silent Night	Great Songs of Christmas, The (Columbia Special Products XTV 69406/7)
	Joyous Christmas, Volume 2 (Columbia Special Products CSS 808)
	Very Merry Christmas, A, Volume Two (Columbia Special Products CSS 788)
Silent Night, Holy Night	Sounds of Christmas (Columbia Special Products P 12474)
Still, Still, Still	Great Songs of Christmas, The, Album Six (Columbia Special Products CSM 388)
Twelve Days of Christmas, The	Christmas Greetings (Columbia Special Products CSS 1499)
	Christmas Greetings, Vol. 4 (Columbia Special Products P 11987)
	Christmas Song, The, And Other Favorites (Columbia Special Products P 12446)
	Christmas Trimmings (Columbia Special Products P 12795)
	Have a Happy Holiday (Columbia Special Products CSS 1432)
	Spirit of Christmas, The, Volume III (Columbia Special Products CSS 1463)
We Three Kings of Orient Are	Great Songs of Christmas, The, Album Three (Columbia Special Products CSP 117)
While Shepherds Watched Their Flocks	Merry Christmas from... (Reader's Digest RD4-83)

MORMON TABERNACLE ORGAN AND CHIMES
Albums

Label, Number	Title	Year	VG	VG+	NM
Columbia Masterworks ML 6037 M	Christmas with the Mormon Tabernacle Organ and Chimes	1964	3.00	6.00	12.00
Columbia Masterworks MS 6637 S	Christmas with the Mormon Tabernacle Organ and Chimes	1964	3.75	7.50	15.00
— Same as above, but in stereo					

On Various-Artists Collections

I Heard the Bells on Christmas Day	Zenith Presents Christmas, A Gift of Music Vol. 5 (Columbia Special Products C 10395)
It Came Upon a Midnight Clear	Zenith Presents Christmas, A Gift of Music Vol. 5 (Columbia Special Products C 10395)
Oh Little Town of Bethlehem	Zenith Presents Christmas, A Gift of Music Vol. 5 (Columbia Special Products C 10395)

Label, Number		Title (A Side/B Side)	Year	VG	VG+	NM
MORPHINE						
45s						
Singles Only 356		Sexy Christmas Baby Mine/Cure For Pain	199?	2.00	4.00	8.00
— Green vinyl						
MORRIS, GARY						
45s						
Warner Bros 27706		Every Christmas/Silver Bells	1988	—	—	3.00
Warner Bros 27706	PS	Every Christmas/Silver Bells	1988	—	—	3.00
Albums						
Universal 76010		Every Christmas	1989	2.50	5.00	10.00
— Same as Warner Bros. 25760 with one track deleted and one added						
Warner Bros. 25760		Every Christmas	1988	3.00	6.00	12.00
MORRIS, HOWARD						
45s						
Roulette 4309		Department Store Santa Claus (Before Christmas)/ Department Store Santa Claus (After Christmas)	1960	3.75	7.50	15.00
MORRIS, MARLOWE						
On Various-Artists Collections						
Rockin' Around the Christmas Tree		Jingle Bell Jazz (Columbia PC 36803)				
MORRIS, PAUL T.						
45s						
Triumph 942		The Day They Busted Santa/Everybody Loves a Cowboy	19??	—	2.00	4.00
MORRIS, SUE						
On Various-Artists Collections						
I Heard the Bells on Christmas Day		Merry Christmas (Rainbow Sound R-5032-LPS)				
MORRISON, BOB						
45s						
Columbia 43786		Santa Mouse/It's Christmas	1966	2.50	5.00	10.00
MORSE, ROBERT, AND CHARLES NELSON REILLY						
Albums						
Capitol T 1862	M	A Jolly Theatrical Christmas	1963	5.00	10.00	20.00
Capitol ST 1862	S	A Jolly Theatrical Christmas	1963	6.25	12.50	25.00
MOSS, RITA						
45s						
Arvee 5084		Jingle Bells/I'm Shooting High	1963	2.50	5.00	10.00
MOSSBURG, TOMMY						
45s						
Mlay 328		Santa's On His Way/Santa's Letter	19??	2.00	4.00	8.00
— B-side by Maria Sacco						
MOSTEL, ZERO						
On Various-Artists Collections						
How the Grinch Stole Christmas		How the Grinch Stole Christmas (Random House/Scholastic 0-394-05008-8)				
MOTHER AND THE LITTLE TOTS						
45s						
Little Tots 113		Christmas Morning/The Coming Of Santa Claus	195?	2.50	5.00	10.00
— B-side by Santa Claus & His Band; 78 rpm 7-inch record						
MOTIVATIONS, THE						
45s						
Lonely 1001		Christmas Spirit/So Long	19??	2.00	4.00	8.00
MOULE, BOB'S, DIXIELAND EXPRESS						
45s						
MSK 709		Santa Claus Is Comin' to Town/Let It Snow	1975	—	2.00	4.00

Label, Number		Title (A Side/B Side)	Year	VG	VG+	NM

MOUNT ALVERNIA SEMINARY CHOIR
Albums

ABC-Paramount 211	M	Christmas in a Monastery: The Sons of St. Francis Sing	1957	5.00	10.00	20.00

MOUSE, KRIS
45s

Fraternity 3543		Santa Clause Is Full Of You Know What/The Little Fat Man	1988	—	2.00	4.00

MOYE, EUGENE, JR. (CELLO SOLO)
On Various-Artists Collections

Ave Maria (Gounod)		Joyous Christmas, Volume 2 (Columbia Special Products CSS 808)

MOYET, ALISON
On Various-Artists Collections

Coventry Carol		Very Special Christmas, A (A&M SP-3911)

MRS. SANTA CLAUS
45s

Weber 170		Elve's Christmas Party (part 1)/Elve's Christmas Party (part 2)	19??	2.00	4.00	8.00

MUCUS AND THE BLOODY PHLEGM
45s

Christabelle 43147		I Hate Christmas Morning/Let's Give Thanks To Santa	198?	2.00	4.00	8.00

MUD
45s

Rak 187		Lonely This Christmas/I Can't Stand It	1973	3.00	6.00	12.00
Rak 187	PS	Lonely This Christmas/I Can't Stand It	1973	3.75	7.50	15.00

— *Record and sleeve are U.K. imports*

MULCAYS, THE
45s

Cardinal 1005		Mother's Christmas Tree/Winter Wonderland	195?	3.00	6.00	12.00

— *As "Fran McKenna and the Mulcays"*

Cardinal 1024		White Christmas/Silent Night	195?	3.00	6.00	12.00
Cardinal 1025		Jingle Bells/Rudolph, The Red-Nosed Reindeer	195?	3.00	6.00	12.00

MULL, MARTIN
45s

Capricorn 0037		Santafly/Santa Doesn't Cop Out On Dope	1973	3.00	6.00	12.00
Capricorn 0282		Santafly/Santa Doesn't Cop Out On Dope	1977	2.50	5.00	10.00

MULLER, WERNER
Albums

Decca DL 8388	M	O, Tannenbaum (Christmas on the Rhine)	1956	5.00	10.00	20.00

— *Original version with all-black labels with silver print*

Decca DL 8388	M	O, Tannenbaum (Christmas on the Rhine)	1960	3.00	6.00	12.00

— *Black label with color bars; album by "Mixed Chorus and Orchestra" (Muller's name is on the jacket spine only); two fewer tracks*

Decca DL 78388	S	O, Tannenbaum (Christmas on the Rhine)	1960	3.75	7.50	15.00

— *Same as above, but in stereo*

MCA 15023		O, Tannenbaum (Christmas on the Rhine)	197?	2.00	4.00	8.00

— *Reissue still credited to "Mixed Chorus and Orchestra"*

MULLIGAN, GERRY, QUARTET
45s

Pacific Jazz 614		Winter Wonderland/I Fall in Love Too Easily	1953	5.00	10.00	20.00

MULLINS, DEE
45s

Plantation 68	DJ	Remember Bethlehem (same on both sides)	1970	—	2.50	5.00

— *Green vinyl*

Plantation 68		Remember Bethlehem/California, the Promised Land	1970	—	2.50	5.00

MULLOY, BOB
Albums

Classic Christmas CCR-1932		The Musical Magic of Christmas Organ and Chimes	1977	2.50	5.00	10.00

Label, Number		Title (A Side/B Side)	Year	VG	VG+	NM
MUNSON, ESTELLA						
Albums						
Mel-So'Nance SLP-33-100		Christmas Is In the Air	1968	3.00	6.00	12.00
MURAD, JERRY'S, HARMONICATS						
On Various-Artists Collections						
Winter Wonderland		Merry Christmas from... (Reader's Digest RD4-83)				
MURPHEY, MICHAEL MARTIN						
45s						
Warner Bros PRO-S-2869	DJ	Colorado Christmas/The Cowboy's Christmas Ball	1987	—	3.00	6.00
— B-side by Nitty Gritty Dirt Band						
On Various-Artists Collections						
Cowboys' Christmas Ball, The		Christmas Tradition, A (Warner Bros. 25630)				
Santa Claus Is Coming to Town		Christmas Tradition, A, Volume II (Warner Bros. 25762)				
MURPHY BROTHERS, THE						
45s						
Ocean 88		Peace On Earth/Christmastime	1988	—	—	3.00
Ocean 88	PS	Peace On Earth/Christmastime	1988	—	—	3.00
MURPHY, CHUCK						
45s						
Columbia 21322		Santa Plays the Trombone (In the North Pole Band)/	1954	3.75	7.50	15.00
		Let's Have an Old-Fashioned Christmas				
MURPHY, DAN & THE MERRY ELVES						
45s						
Road Apple 1012821		Santa Claus Ain't A' Gonna Come to Town This Year	198?	2.00	4.00	8.00
— One-sided flexidisc						
Road Apple 1012821	PS	Santa Claus Ain't A' Gonna Come to Town This Year	198?	2.00	4.00	8.00
MURPHY, RON						
45s						
Suite 16 S109		Christmas Time/This Year	19??	—	2.50	5.00
MURPHY, WALTER ORCHESTRA						
45s						
Major (no #)		Disco Bells/Deck The Halls	1975	—	3.00	6.00
MURRAY, ANNE						
45s						
Capitol B-5536		Go Tell It On the Mountain/O Holy Night	1985	—	2.00	4.00
Capitol B-5536	PS	Go Tell It On the Mountain/O Holy Night	1985	—	2.50	5.00
Capitol SPRO-9723	DJ	Christmas Medley: Silver Bells/I'll Be Home for Christmas/	1981	2.00	4.00	8.00
		Winter Wonderland (same on both sides)				
SBK S7-18912		Winter Wonderland/The Little Drummer Boy	1995	—	—	3.00
Albums						
Capitol SN-16232		Christmas Wishes	1981	2.50	5.00	10.00
Capitol C1-90886		Christmas	1987	2.00	4.00	8.00
On Various-Artists Collections						
Away in a Manger		Rocking Christmas Stocking, A (Capitol SPRO 9303/4/5/6)				
Christmas Wishes		Christmas America, Album Two (Capitol Special Markets SL-6950)				
Joy to the World		Christmas Songs, The, Volume II (Capitol SL-57065)				
		Christmas Treasury of Classics from Avon, A (RCA Special Products DPL1-0716)				
Silver Bells		Happy Holidays, Volume 17 (RCA Special Products DPL1-0555)				
Snowbird		Christmas Carousel (Capitol SQBE-94406)				
Winter Wonderland		Celebrate the Season with Tupperware (RCA Special Products DPL1-0803)				
		Happy Holidays, Volume 18 (RCA Special Products DPL1-0608)				
MURRAY, ELZY						
45s						
Timestar 2226		Christmas In Prison/(B -side unknown)	19??	2.00	4.00	8.00
MUSAD AND WARM EXPRESSIONS						
45s						
Narobi 1006		Black Christmas/Getting' Down Ghetto Style	197?	—	2.50	5.00

(Top left) The original 1966 pressing of *A Merry Mancini Christmas*, with Henry and his clan around the piano. This cover was later changed. (Top right) Johnny Mathis' tenure at Mercury Records from 1963-66 is all but forgotten today. But while he was there, he recorded a holiday album, *Sounds of Christmas,* from which this single and accompanying scarce sleeve was taken. (Bottom left) "Wonderful Christmastime" was Paul McCartney's 1979 attempt to write a holiday classic the way his old partner, John Lennon, had. Though not in the same league as "Happy Xmas (War Is Over)," it does have merit. (Bottom right) This 1985 single was taken from Anne Murray's *Christmas Wishes* LP.

Label, Number		Title (A Side/B Side)	Year	VG	VG+	NM

MUSIC CITY SINGERS, THE
Albums

| Halo 1003 | | Christmas Favorites | 196? | 3.75 | 7.50 | 15.00 |

— *Includes Bobby Russell, Bill Pursell, Boots Randolph, Willie Ackerman, The Jordanaires and the Anita Kerr Singers, among others*

MUSICAL CAST OF TOYS, THE
45s

| Geffen 19146 | | The Closing of the Year/(instrumental) | 1992 | — | — | 3.00 |

— *Featuring Wendy and Lisa, with guest vocal by Seal*

MUSICAL LINN TWINS, THE
45s

| Blue Feather 1307 | | Christmas Candlelight/Christmas Fun | 198? | — | — | 3.00 |

N

NABBIE, JIM
45s

| Toy 104 | | Inside Santa's Town/Inside Santa's Town (Add Your Own Voice) | 19?? | 2.00 | 4.00 | 8.00 |

NABORS, JIM
45s

| Columbia 44359 | | White Christmas/In A Humble Place | 1967 | — | 3.00 | 6.00 |
| Columbia 45053 | | O Holy Night/I Was a King at Jesus' Birth | 1969 | — | 3.00 | 6.00 |

Albums

| Columbia CL 2731 | M | Jim Nabors' Christmas Album | 1967 | 3.00 | 6.00 | 12.00 |
| Columbia CS 9531 | S | Jim Nabors' Christmas Album | 1967 | 3.00 | 6.00 | 12.00 |

— *Originals with "360 Sound" label*

| Columbia CS 9531 | | Jim Nabors' Christmas Album | 1970 | 2.50 | 5.00 | 10.00 |

— *Later editions with orange label*

| Columbia KC 31630 | | Merry Christmas | 1972 | 2.50 | 5.00 | 10.00 |

On Various-Artists Collections

Christmas Song, The	Merry Christmas (Columbia Musical Treasury 3P 6306)
Do You Hear What I Hear?	Home for Christmas (Columbia Musical Treasury P3S 5608)
	Home for Christmas (Realm 2V 8101)
Go Tell It on the Mountain	Country Christmas Favorites (Columbia Special Products C 10876)
	Joy to the World (30 Classic Christmas Melodies) (Columbia Special Products P3 14654)
	Joyous Songs of Christmas, The (Columbia Special Products C 10400)
	We Wish You a Country Christmas (Columbia Special Products P 14991)
Home for the Holidays	Country Style Christmas, A (Columbia Musical Treasury 3P 6316)
I'll Be Home for Christmas	Magic of Christmas, The (Columbia Musical Treasury P3S 5806)
Jingle Bells	Season's Greetings from Barbra Streisand...And Friends (Columbia Special Products CSS 1075)
	Very Merry Christmas, A, Volume Two (Columbia Special Products CSS 788)
Joy to the World	Collection of Christmas Favorites, A (Columbia Special Products P 14988)
	Joy to the World (30 Classic Christmas Melodies) (Columbia Special Products P3 14654)
O Come, All Ye Faithful	Christmas Album, A (Columbia PC 39466)
	Down-Home Country Christmas, A (Columbia Special Products P 14992)
	Happy Holidays, Album 8 (Columbia Special Products C 11086)
	Joy to the World (30 Classic Christmas Melodies) (Columbia Special Products P3 14654)
O Holy Night	Season's Greetings from Barbra Streisand...And Friends (Columbia Special Products CSS 1075)
	We Wish You a Country Christmas (Columbia Special Products P 14991)
Three Wise Men, Wise Men Three	Very Merry Christmas, A, Volume 3 (Columbia Special Products CSS 997)

NAISMITH, LAURENCE
On Various-Artists Collections

December the 25th	Scrooge (Columbia Masterworks S 30258)

NALLE, BILLY
On Various-Artists Collections

Parade of the Wooden Soldiers, The	Old Fashioned Christmas, An (Reader's Digest RDA 216-A)

NALUAI BROTHERS, THE
45s

| Chaale 101 | | Christmas In Hawaii/Santa's Holiday | 19?? | — | 2.50 | 5.00 |
| Chaale 101 | PS | Christmas In Hawaii/Santa's Holiday | 19?? | — | 2.50 | 5.00 |

Label, Number		Title (A Side/B Side)	Year	VG	VG+	NM
NANNAC, GARREL						
45s						
CBM 999		I Believe In Santa Claus/Wide-Awake Dream	19??	2.00	3.00	8.00
NARCISSE, KING LOUIS H.						
45s						
Smith-Som 1495		Silent Night (Part 1)/Silent Night (Part 2)	19??	2.50	5.00	10.00
NASH, LEE						
45s						
Crystal 270		It's Christmas Time Again/Toyland Polka	19??	—	3.00	6.00
— B-side by the Frontiersmen						
NATE DOGG						
On Various-Artists Collections						
Be Thankful		Christmas on Death Row (Death Row/Interscope INT2-90108)				
NEIGHBORHOOD KIDS, THE						
45s						
Brunswick 55466		The Christmas Party of the Eighth Reindeer/Christmas Is for Everyone	1971	2.00	4.00	8.00
NEIL, JIMMY						
45s						
Martin 101		My Letter To Santa/I Overlooked An Orchid	19??	—	2.00	4.00
NELSON, KATHY						
45s						
Liberty 55115		Santa Dear/Gimmie a Little Kiss, Will Ya Huh?	1957	5.00	10.00	20.00
NELSON, WILLIE						
45s						
Columbia AE7 1182	DJ	White Christmas/Blue Christmas	1979	6.25	12.50	25.00
— Green vinyl						
Columbia AE7 1183	DJ	Pretty Paper/Rudolph the Red-Nosed Reindeer	1979	6.25	12.50	25.00
— Red vinyl						
Columbia AE7 1775	DJ	Pretty Paper/White Christmas	1982	—	3.00	6.00
Columbia 03476		Pretty Paper/White Christmas	1982	—	2.50	5.00
RCA Victor 47-8484		Pretty Paper/What a Merry Christmas This Could Be	1964	3.75	7.50	15.00
RCA Victor 47-9029		Pretty Paper/What a Merry Christmas This Could Be	1966	3.00	6.00	12.00
RCA Victor 47-9778		Pretty Paper/What a Merry Christmas This Could Be	1969		*Unreleased*	
RCA Victor 47-9931		Pretty Paper/What a Merry Christmas This Could Be	1970	2.00	4.00	8.00
RCA Victor PB-10461		Pretty Paper/What a Merry Christmas This Could Be	1975	2.00	4.00	8.00
Albums						
Columbia JC 36189		Pretty Paper	1979	2.50	5.00	10.00
On Various-Artists Collections						
Blue Christmas		Blue Christmas (Welk Music Group WM-3002)				
Jingle Bells		Country Christmas (Time-Life STL-109)				
Pretty Paper		Best of Christmas, The (RCA Victor CPL1-7013)				
		Country Christmas, A (RCA CPL1-4396)				
		Happy Holidays, Volume 17 (RCA Special Products DPL1-0555)				
		Nashville's Greatest Christmas Hits, Volume II (Columbia PC 44413)				
		60 Christmas Classics (Sessions DVL2-0723)				
		Time-Life Treasury of Christmas, The, Volume Two (Time-Life STL-108)				
Silent Night, Holy Night		Nashville's Greatest Christmas Hits (Columbia PC 44412)				
What a Merry Christmas This Could Be		Country Christmas (Time-Life STL-109)				
		Family Christmas Collection, The (Time-Life STL-131)				
		Happy Holidays, Volume 19 (RCA Special Products DPL1-0689)				
Winter Wonderland		Christmas Greetings from Nashville (Columbia PC 39467)				
NEPHI AND IVA						
45s						
El Leon 102		Christmas Time Again, Aloha/Santa Claus Is Coming To Town	19??	—	3.00	6.00
NERO, PETER						
On Various-Artists Collections						
Christmas Greetings		Christmas Greetings From RCA Victor And Groove Recording Artists (RCA Victor SP-45-128)				
Christmas Medley (Hallelujah/Hark the Herald Angels Sing/Deck the Halls/Joy to the World)		Very Merry Christmas, A, Volume IV (Columbia Special Products CSS 1464)				
Deck the Hall		Happy Holidays, Album 8 (Columbia Special Products C 11086)				

Label, Number		Title (A Side/B Side)	Year	VG	VG+	NM
Medley: Jingle Bells/Winter Wonderland		Christmas in California (RCA Victor PRS-276)				
		Christmas in New York Volume 2 (RCA Victor PRS-270)				
		Christmastime in Carol and Song (RCA PRM-271)				
My Favorite Things		Christmas with Colonel Sanders (RCA Victor PRS-291)				
New Year's Greetings		Christmas Greetings From RCA Victor And Groove Recording Artists (RCA Victor SP-45-128)				
O Holy Night		Magnavox Album of Christmas Music (Columbia Special Products CSQ 11093)				
Trepak (from Nutcracker Suite)		Magnavox Album of Christmas Music (Columbia Special Products CSQ 11093)				
		Silent Night... (Columbia Special Products P 14989)				

NESSER, JACK
45s
| Briar 125 | | The Christmas Day Song/Still In Love | 1961 | 2.50 | 5.00 | 10.00 |

NEVE, SUZANNE
On Various-Artists Collections
| Happiness | | Scrooge (Columbia Masterworks S 30258) | | | | |

NEVE, SUZANNE; ALBERT FINNEY
On Various-Artists Collections
| Happiness (Reprise) | | Scrooge (Columbia Masterworks S 30258) | | | | |

NEVILLE
45s
| V & N 3755 | | Christmas J.A./J.A. Anday | 19?? | — | 3.00 | 6.00 |

NEVILLE, AARON
45s
| A&M 31458 0442 7 | | Please Come Home for Christmas/Louisiana Christmas Day | 1993 | — | 2.50 | 5.00 |

NEW BOMB TURKS
On Various-Artists Collections
| Christmas (Baby Please Come Home) | | Happy Birthday, Baby Jesus (Sympathy For The Record Industry SFTRI 271) | | | | |

NEW CHRISTY MINSTRELS, THE
45s
Columbia 43940		We Need a Little Christmas/Oh Holy Night	1966	2.50	5.00	10.00
Columbia JZSP 116417/8	DJ	We Need a Little Christmas/Sleigh Ride	1966	3.00	6.00	12.00
— Yellow label						
Columbia JZSP 116417/8	DJ	We Need a Little Christmas/Sleigh Ride	1966	3.00	6.00	12.00
— White label						

Albums
Columbia CL 2096	M	Merry Christmas	1963	3.00	6.00	12.00
Columbia CL 2556	M	Christmas with the Christies	1966	3.00	6.00	12.00
Columbia CS 8896	S	Merry Christmas	1963	3.75	7.50	15.00
Columbia CS 9356	S	Christmas with the Christies	1966	3.75	7.50	15.00

On Various-Artists Collections
Go Tell It on the Mountain		Happy Holidays, Volume II (Columbia Special Products CSM 348)				
Here We Come a-Caroling		Christmas Greetings (Columbia Special Products CSS 1433)				
		Great Songs of Christmas, The, Album Seven (Columbia Special Products CSS 547)				
		Very Merry Christmas, A, Volume Two (Columbia Special Products CSS 788)				
Il Est Ne		Great Songs of Christmas, The, Album Six (Columbia Special Products CSM 388)				
Little Drummer Boy, The		Merry Christmas from... (Reader's Digest RD4-83)				
Medley: Snow in the Street/Joseph Dearest, Joseph Mine		Great Songs of Christmas, The, Album Three (Columbia Special Products CSP 117)				
O Bambino (One Cold and Blessed Winter)		That Christmas Feeling (Columbia Special Products P 11853)				
Shepherd Boy, The		Great Songs of Christmas, The, Album Four (Columbia Special Products CSP 155M)				
Silent Night		Great Songs of Christmas, The, Album Seven (Columbia Special Products CSS 547)				
Sing Hosanna, Hallelujah		Great Songs of Christmas, The, Album Four (Columbia Special Products CSP 155M)				
Sleigh Ride		Great Songs of Christmas, The, Album Eight (Columbia Special Products CSS 888)				
		Happy Holidays, Album Nine (Columbia Special Products P 11793)				
		Joy of Christmas, The (Columbia Special Products P 12042)				
Wassail, Wassail		Great Songs of Christmas, The, Album Three (Columbia Special Products CSP 117)				
We Need a Little Christmas		Great Songs of Christmas, The, Album Six (Columbia Special Products CSM 388)				

NEW EDITION
45s
MCA 52745		It's Christmas (All Over the World)/All I Want for Christmas Is My Girl	1985	—	2.00	4.00
— Red vinyl stock copy						
MCA 52745	DJ	It's Christmas (All Over the World) (same on both sides)	1985	—	3.00	6.00
— Promo on red vinyl						
MCA 52745	PS	It's Christmas (All Over the World)/All I Want for Christmas Is My Girl	1985	—	2.00	4.00

Label, Number		Title (A Side/B Side)	Year	VG	VG+	NM
Albums						
MCA 39040	EP	Christmas All Over the World	1985	2.00	4.00	8.00

NEW ENGLAND CHRISTMASTIDE
45s

North Star 8096		Carol of the Bells//The First Noel/Deck the Halls	198?	—	—	3.00
North Star 8096	PS	Carol of the Bells//The First Noel/Deck the Halls	198?	—	—	3.00

NEW GLENN MILLER ORCHESTRA (MCKINLEY)
On Various-Artists Collections

Greensleeves (What Child Is This)   Remembering Christmas with the Big Bands (RCA Special Products DPM1-0506)

NEW KIDS ON THE BLOCK
45s

Columbia 69088		Cover Girl/Merry, Merry Christmas	1989	—	—	3.00
Columbia 73064		This One's for the Children/Funky, Funky Christmas	1989	—	—	3.00
Columbia 73939		This One's for the Children/Funky, Funky Christmas	1991	—	—	3.00
— Reissue						
Columbia 73940		Cover Girl/Merry, Merry Christmas	1991	—	—	3.00
— Reissue						
Albums						
Columbia FC 45280		Merry Merry Christmas	1989	2.50	5.00	10.00

NEW LONDON CHORALE, THE
Albums

Myrrh 6658		The Young Messiah	1981	3.00	6.00	12.00

NEW SOUNDS OF CHRISTMAS, THE
On Various-Artists Collections

Child's Christmas Medley, A   Happy Holidays, Album Seven (Capitol Creative Products SL-6730)
Twelve Days of Christmas, The   Happy Holly Days (Capitol Creative Products SL-6761)
We Three Kings   Happy Holidays, Album Seven (Capitol Creative Products SL-6730)
Let's Celebrate Christmas (Capitol Special Markets SL-6923)

NEW SYMPHONY ORCHESTRA OF LONDON
On Various-Artists Collections

Dance of the Sugar Plum Fairy/   Old Fashioned Christmas, An (Reader's Digest RDA 216-A)
  Trepak/Waltz of the Flowers

NEW YORK BRASS QUINTET
45s

New York Brass 537		Little Drummer Boy/Jesu Bambino (The Christ Child)	19??	—	2.00	4.00

NEW YORK CITY GAY MEN'S CHORUS
Albums

Pro Arte 159		A Festival of Song	198?	3.00	6.00	12.00

NEW YORK PHILHARMONIC (BERNSTEIN)
On Various-Artists Collections

Carol of the Bells   Best of the Great Songs of Christmas (Album 10) (Columbia Special Products CSS 1478)
  Great Songs of Christmas, The, Album Three (Columbia Special Products CSP 117)
  Home for Christmas (Columbia Musical Treasury P3S 5608)
  Magic of Christmas, The (Columbia Musical Treasury P3S 5806)
  That Christmas Feeling (Columbia Special Products P 11853)
Dance of the Sugar-Plum Fairy   Wondrous Winter: Songs of Winter, Songs of Christmas
  (Columbia Special Products CSS 708/9)
Medley: Dance of the Sugar Plum Fairy/   Great Songs of Christmas, The, Album Two (Columbia Special Products XTV 86100/1)
  Waltz of the Flowers
Overture to "The Nutcracker Suite"   Wondrous Winter: Songs of Winter, Songs of Christmas (Columbia Special Products CSS 708/9)
Twelve Days of Christmas, The   Silent Night... (Columbia Special Products P 14989)
Unto Us a Child Is Born   Great Songs of Christmas, The (Columbia Special Products XTV 69406/7)

NEWLEY, ANTHONY
On Various-Artists Collections

Coventry Carol   It's Christmas Time! (Columbia Special Products P 14990)
Little Jesus, Sweetly Sleep   Great Songs of Christmas, The, Album Eight (Columbia Special Products CSS 888)
On Christmas Night All Christians Sing   Great Songs of Christmas, The, Album Eight (Columbia Special Products CSS 888)

Label, Number		Title (A Side/B Side)	Year	VG	VG+	NM
NEWPORTS, THE						
45s						
Crystal Ball 129		Jingle Bells/My Juanita	1979	2.00	4.00	8.00
NEWTON, WAYNE						
45s						
Chelsea 3058		It Could Have Been a Wonderful Christmas/Jingle Bell Hustle	1976	—	2.50	5.00
Curb 10520		Cowboy's Christmas/(B-side unknown)	1988	—	—	3.00
MGM 14019		Christmas Prayer/Santa Claus Is Comin' to Town	1968	—	2.50	5.00
7-Inch Extended Plays						
Aries II 102		White Christmas/It's the Season// I'll Be Home for Christmas/Blue Snow at Christmas	1979	—	2.00	4.00
Albums						
Aries II WY 201		Wayne Newton Christmas	1979	2.50	5.00	10.00
Capitol T 2588	M	Songs for a Merry Christmas	1966	3.00	6.00	12.00
Capitol ST 2588	S	Songs for a Merry Christmas	1966	3.75	7.50	15.00
— Same as above, but in stereo						
MGM SE-4593		Christmas Isn't Christmas Without You	1968	3.00	6.00	12.00
On Various-Artists Collections						
Blue Christmas		Merry Christmas (Columbia Musical Treasury 3P 6306)				
Little Drummer Boy, The		Little Drummer Boy, The (Capitol/Pickwick SPC-3462)				
Remember Me at Christmas		Holiday Magic (Capitol Creative Products SL-6728)				
Rudolph, the Red-Nosed Reindeer		Magic of Christmas, The (Capitol SWBB-93810)				
Silent Night		Christmas America, Album Two (Capitol Special Markets SL-6950)				
		Christmas Songs, The (Capitol SLB-57074)				
Silver Bells		Christmas Carousel (Capitol SQBE-94406)				
Winter Wonderland		Best of Christmas, The, Vol. I (Capitol SM-11833)				
NEWTON-JOHN, OLIVIA						
45s						
MCA 40600		Don't Stop Believin'/Greensleeves	1976	—	2.00	4.00
— A-side not a Christmas song						
MCA 40600	PS	Don't Stop Believin'/Greensleeves	1976	—	2.50	5.00
NEXT GENERATION, THE						
45s						
United Artists SP67		Rudolph/Don't Play This Side (blank groove)	1971	3.00	6.00	12.00
— Private pressing done by Terry, Andy and Eben Rose, Ages 8, 5 and 3, for UA executive Biff Rose						
NEXT OF KIN, THE						
45s						
Decca 732605		Merry Christmas/Sunday Children, Sunday Morning	1969	—	3.00	6.00
NIC NACS, THE						
45s						
RPM 342		Gonna Have a Merry Christmas/Found Me a Sugar Daddy	1951	50.00	100.00	200.00
NICHOLS, BOBBY						
45s						
Peter Pan X-6		Santa Claus Is Coming to Town/Silent Night	196?	2.00	4.00	8.00
Peter Pan X-6	PS	Santa Claus Is Coming to Town/Silent Night	196?	2.00	4.00	8.00
NICHOLS, LINDA LEE						
45s						
Gardena 113		A Roly Poly (Rockin' Rollin' Santa Claus)/We (You and Me)	1960	3.00	6.00	12.00
NICKS, STEVIE						
On Various-Artists Collections						
Silent Night		Very Special Christmas, A (A&M SP-3911)				
NIGHTNOISE						
On Various-Artists Collections						
Bring Me Back a Song		Winter's Solstice II, A (Windham Hill WH-1077)				
NILSSON						
45s						
RCA Victor 74-0855		Remember (Christmas)/The Lottery Song	1972	—	2.50	5.00
RCA Victor PB-10130		Remember (Christmas)/The Lottery Song	1974	—	2.00	4.00

Label, Number		Title (A Side/B Side)	Year	VG	VG+	NM
Albums						
RCA Victor LSP-4717		Son of Schmilsson	1972	3.00	6.00	12.00
— With custom black "Victor" label. Contains one Christmas song: Remember (Christmas)						

NILSSON, BIRGIT
On Various-Artists Collections

O Holy Night		Ronco Presents A Christmas Gift (Columbia Special Products P 12430)				

NINA AND FREDERIK
45s

Laurie 3079		Mary's Boy Child/Little Donkey	1960	3.00	6.00	12.00

NINO AND THE EBB TIDES
45s

Recorte 408		The Real Meaning of Christmas/Two Purple Shadows in the Snow	1958	75.00	150.00	300.00

NITTY GRITTY DIRT BAND
45s

Liberty 1513		Colorado Christmas/Mr. Bojangles	1983	—	3.00	6.00
Warner Bros PRO-S-2869	DJ	Colorado Christmas/The Cowboy's Christmas Ball	1987	—	3.00	6.00
— B-side by Michael Martin Murphey						

On Various-Artists Collections

Colorado Christmas		Christmas Tradition, A (Warner Bros. 25630)				

NIXON, MOJO, AND SKID ROPER
Albums

Restless 72185	EP	Get Out of My Way	1986	2.50	5.00	10.00
— Clear vinyl						

NOCTURNES, THE
45s

Carlson Int'l 4105		My Christmas Star/(B-side unknown)	1964	15.00	30.00	60.00

NOLTE, NANCY
45s

Le Cam 704		Christmas Night/Christmas Tree in Heaven	1960	3.00	6.00	12.00

NORAD
45s

Norad (no #)		Norad Tracks Santa Claus Christmas 1968	1968	2.50	5.00	10.00
Norad (no #)	PS	Norad Tracks Santa Claus Christmas 1968	1968	2.50	5.00	10.00

NORMAN, LARRY
45s

MGM 14676		Christmas Time/The Same Old Story	1973	—	2.50	5.00
Solid Rock 202		Christmas Time/The Christmas Song	1976	—	2.00	4.00

NORMETTES, THE
45s

Empala 125		Yuletime/His Birthday Is Here	19??	—	2.00	4.00

NORTH, JAY
45s

KEM 2756		The Cat And The Christmas Tree/Christmas For Tommy	1960	3.75	7.50	15.00

NORWOOD, DARON
45s

Giant 18005		The Working Elf Blues/Rockin' Little Christmas	1994	—	2.00	4.00
— B-side by Carlene Carter						

NOTREK, RAINY
45s

Pebble 010		Christmas Family/Come See Little One	19??	—	2.50	5.00

Label, Number		Title (A Side/B Side)	Year	VG	VG+	NM
NOVA, MARLENE						
45s						
Sonday 6004		Have Yourself a Merry Little Christmas/Holidays Are Happy Days	19??	—	2.50	5.00
NOW SINGERS, THE						
45s						
GP 552		Our Castle on the Moon/The Spirit of Christmas	19??	—	—	3.00
NRBQ						
45s						
Red Rooster 1006		Christmas Wish/Jolly Old St. Nicholas	1978	2.50	5.00	10.00
Red Rooster 1006	PS	Christmas Wish/Jolly Old St. Nicholas	1978	2.50	5.00	10.00
Rounder 4525		Christmas Wish/Jolly Old St. Nicholas	1979	—	2.50	5.00
Rounder 4525	PS	Christmas Wish/Jolly Old St. Nicholas	1979	—	3.00	6.00
7-Inch Extended Plays						
Red Rooster EP-1		Christmas Wish/Here Comes Santa Claus// God Rest Ye Merry Gentlemen/Message from the North Pole	1979	3.75	7.50	15.00
— Called "Merry Christmas from NRBQ"; not issued with cover						
Albums						
Rounder EP2501		EPA Christmas Wish	197?	3.00	6.00	12.00
NUPTOWN KEYS, THE						
45s						
EMI 5248		The Best Of Christmas/Superstar	1981	—	2.00	4.00
EMI 5248	PS	The Best Of Christmas/Superstar	1981	—	3.00	6.00
— Both record and sleeve are U.K. imports						
NUTT, DON						
45s						
Gold Rose 23332		Rudolph the Red-Nosed Reindeer/The Apple of My Eye	19??	—	—	3.00
NUTTY SQUIRRELS, THE						
45s						
Columbia 41818		Please Don't Take Our Tree for Christmas/Nutty Noel	1960	5.00	10.00	20.00
Columbia 41818	PS	Please Don't Take Our Tree for Christmas/Nutty Noel	1960	10.00	20.00	40.00
NYRO, LAURA						
Albums						
Columbia KC 30259		Christmas and the Beads of Sweat	1970	3.75	7.50	15.00
— Contains one Christmas song: Christmas in My Soul						

O

Label, Number		Title (A Side/B Side)	Year	VG	VG+	NM
O AND JUDY						
45s						
Christmas 111		Have Yourself a Merry Little Christmas/ Christmas Has Been Cancelled Due to Lack of Interest	198?	—	2.50	5.00
— B-side by Further and the Summer Hits						
Christmas 111	PS	Have Yourself a Merry Little Christmas/ Christmas Has Been Cancelled Due to Lack of Interest	198?	—	2.50	5.00
O'BRIEN, BENNY AND JOE						
45s						
United Artists 680		Rudolph the Red-Nosed Reindeer/Santa Claus Is Coming to Town	1963	3.00	6.00	12.00
O'BRIEN, LOUISE						
45s						
E-Z Records 685		Spend Christmas With Your Mother/Sweeter as the Years Go By	19??	—	2.00	4.00
O'BRIEN, RHYS						
45s						
MGM 13862		The Word Called Love/Christmas Morning	1967	2.00	4.00	8.00

Label, Number		Title (A Side/B Side)	Year	VG	VG+	NM
O'BRIEN, TIMMY						
45s						
Rason 1001		Just In Time For Christmas/I Been A Good Boy	1959	3.00	6.00	12.00
O'CONNELL, HELEN						
Albums						
Mark 56 #711		Christmas with Helen O'Connell	19??	3.00	6.00	12.00
O'CONNOR, MARK						
45s						
Warner Bros PRO-S-2842	DJ	Sleigh Ride/White Christmas Makes Me Blue	1987	—	2.00	4.00
— B-side by Randy Travis						
On Various-Artists Collections						
Sleigh Ride		Christmas Tradition, A (Warner Bros. 25630)				
What Child Is This		Christmas Tradition, A, Volume II (Warner Bros. 25762)				
		Winter Warnerland (Warner Bros. PRO-A-3328)				
O'DELL, DOYE						
45s						
Berdie 1009		I'm Picking Fights For Christmas//(B-side unknown)	19??	3.75	7.50	15.00
O'DELL, DOYLE						
45s						
Intro 6032		Ol' Tex Kringle/My Little Red Wagon	195?	3.75	7.50	15.00
O'DELL, KENNY						
45s						
Capricorn 0247		Together This Christmas/I Can't Think When You're Doing That to Me	1975	—	2.00	4.00
O'JAYS, THE						
45s						
EMI S7-18914		Have Yourself a Merry Little Christmas/ I Can Hardly Wait 'Til Christmas	1995	—	—	3.00
Neptune 20		Christmas Ain't Christmas New Year's Ain't New Year's Without the One You Love/There's Someone Waiting	1969	2.50	5.00	10.00
Neptune 33		Christmas Ain't Christmas New Year's Ain't New Year's Without the One You Love/Just Can't Get Enough	1970	2.00	4.00	8.00
Philadelphia Int'l. 3537		Christmas Ain't Christmas New Year's Ain't New Year's Without the One You Love/Just Can't Get Enough	1973	—	3.00	6.00
Philadelphia Int'l. 3581		Christmas Ain't Christmas New Year's Ain't New Year's Without the One You Love/Just Can't Get Enough	1975	—	2.50	5.00
TSOP 3771		Christmas Ain't Christmas New Year's Ain't New Year's Without the One You Love/Just Can't Get Enough	1980	—	2.00	4.00
Albums						
EMI E1-96420		Home for Christmas	1991	3.75	7.50	15.00
On Various-Artists Collections						
Christmas Ain't Christmas, New Year's Ain't New Year's Without the One You Love		Have a Merry Chess Christmas (Chess/MCA CH-25210) Jingle Bell Rock (Time-Life SRNR-XM)				
O'KEEFE, PAUL						
45s						
Everest 19322		(Santa Claus) What Would You Like for Christmas?/ A Baby in a Basket	1959	3.00	6.00	12.00
Everest 19322	PS	(Santa Claus) What Would You Like for Christmas?/ A Baby in a Basket	1959	3.75	7.50	15.00
O'LEARY, DICK						
45s						
Country Showcase 110		Christmas Flower/(B-side unknown)	197?	—	2.50	5.00
O'NEAL, ALEXANDER						
45s						
Tabu 08501		Our First Christmas/My Gift To You	1988	—	2.00	4.00
Albums						
Tabu OZ 45016		My Gift to You	1988	2.50	5.00	10.00

Label, Number		Title (A Side/B Side)	Year	VG	VG+	NM
O'STRANGE, GIRVIN						
45s						
Strange ODD 4		Boiling Mud/I've Never Seen Snow (At Christmas)	198?	3.00	6.00	12.00
— B-side by the Joy Gems; U.K. import						
O'SULLIVAN, GILBERT						
45s						
MAM 3645		Christmas Song/Just As You Are	1975	—	2.50	5.00
O'TOOLE, KNUCKLES						
45s						
Waldorf 219		Jingle Bells/When Christmas Comes To Our House	195?	3.00	6.00	12.00
— B-side by Dottie Evans						
O.F.T.B.						
On Various-Artists Collections						
Christmas in the Ghetto		Christmas on Death Row (Death Row/Interscope INT2-90108)				
OAK RIDGE BOYS, THE						
45s						
Capitol Nashville S7-19345		Blue Christmas/I Still Believe in Christmas	1996	—	—	3.00
— B-side by Billy Dean						
MCA S45-1154	DJ	Santa's Song/Happy Christmas Eve	1982	3.00	6.00	12.00
MCA S45-1250	DJ	Thank God for Kids/Jesus Is Born Today	1982	3.00	6.00	12.00
MCA S45-17233	DJ	When You Give It Away/The Voices Of Rejoicing Love	1986	3.75	7.50	15.00
— Promo only on green vinyl						
MCA S45-17450	DJ	There's A New Kid In Town/From a Distance	1986	2.50	5.00	10.00
— B-side by Nanci Griffith						
MCA 52145		Thank God for Kids/Christmas Is Paintin' the Town	1982	—	2.00	4.00
Albums						
MCA 5365		Christmas	1982	2.50	5.00	10.00
MCA 5799		Christmas Again	1986	2.50	5.00	10.00
On Various-Artists Collections						
Christmas Is Paintin' the Town		Tennessee Christmas (MCA 5620)				
It's Christmas Time		Happy Holidays, Vol. 23 (MCA Special Products 15042)				
OBERKIRCHEN CHILDREN'S CHOIR						
Conducted by Edite Moeller.						
Albums						
Angel 35914	M	Christmas Songs	196?	3.00	6.00	12.00
Angel S-35914	S	Christmas Songs	196?	3.75	7.50	15.00
OCEANS, THE						
45s						
Connelly 25		Christmas In Agana/Caretan Carabao	19??	—	—	3.00
ODDIS, RAY						
45s						
V.I.P. 25012		Happy Ghoul Tide/Ray the Newspaper Boy	1964	5.00	10.00	20.00
ODETTA						
Albums						
Vanguard VRS-9079	M	Christmas Spirituals	1961	5.00	10.00	20.00
Vanguard VSD-2079	S	Christmas Spirituals	1961	6.25	12.50	25.00
ODOM, RAY						
45s						
Rodeo 762		Cowboy's Christmas Prayer/Dear Daddy Uncle Sam	19??	—	2.00	4.00
ODUNCE CHORALE, THE						
45s						
Curlytail 520824		Tropical Christmas/(Instrumental)	19??	—	3.00	6.00
Curlytail 520824	PS	Tropical Christmas/(Instrumental)	19??	—	3.00	6.00
OHIO PLAYERS						
45s						
Mercury 73753		Happy Holidays (Part 1)/Happy Holidays (Part 2)	1975	—	3.00	6.00

Label, Number	Title (A Side/B Side)	Year	VG	VG+	NM
OKLAHOMA WRANGLERS, THE					
45s					
RCA Victor 47-4376	Unhappy New Year/Savannah River Rag	1951	3.75	7.50	15.00
OL' 55 AND THE O.K. CHORALE					
45s					
Mushroom 6587	(I Want A) Rockin' Christmas/Little Saint Nick	1976	3.00	6.00	12.00
— U.K. import					
OLDHAM, DOUG					
45s					
Impact 5174	Mary's Boy Child/Christmas Medley	19??	2.50	5.00	10.00
OLSEN, DOROTHY					
45s					
RCA Victor 47-7654	The Christmas Spirit/Little Donkey	1959	3.75	7.50	15.00
OLYMPICS, THE					
45s					
Tri Disc 107	Dancin' Holiday/Do the Slauson Shuffle	1963	3.75	7.50	15.00
100 VOICES OF CHRISTMAS, THE					
Albums					
Design DLP-X-15 M	Silent Night	196?	3.00	6.00	12.00
Design SDLP-X-15 S	Silent Night	196?	3.75	7.50	15.00

101 STRINGS

Label, Number	Title (A Side/B Side)	Year	VG	VG+	NM
Albums					
Alshire S-7100	The Glory of Christmas	1966	3.00	6.00	12.00

On Various-Artists Collections

Adeste Fideles	O. Henry's The Gift of the Magi (E.F. MacDonald EFMX-62)
Hark the Herald Angels Sing	O. Henry's The Gift of the Magi (E.F. MacDonald EFMX-62)
Medley: God Rest Ye Merry	Happy Holly Days (Capitol Creative Products SL-6761)
Gentlemen/Jingle Bells/Good King	
Wenceslas	
Noel	O. Henry's The Gift of the Magi (E.F. MacDonald EFMX-62)
Silent Night	O. Henry's The Gift of the Magi (E.F. MacDonald EFMX-62)

ORBISON, ROY

Label, Number	Title (A Side/B Side)	Year	VG	VG+	NM
45s					
Eric 7101	Pretty Paper/Oh Pretty Woman	197?	—	2.00	4.00
Monument 1936	Pretty Paper/Beautiful Dreamer	1976	—	2.00	4.00
Monument 830	Pretty Paper/Beautiful Dreamer	1963	3.75	7.50	15.00
Albums					
Monument MLP-8024 M	More of Roy Orbison's Greatest Hits	1964	7.50	15.00	30.00
— Contains one Chrsitmas song: Pretty Paper					
Monument MP-8600 (2)	The All-Time Greatest Hits of Roy Orbison	1977	4.00	8.00	16.00
Monument SLP-18024 S	More of Roy Orbison's Greatest Hits	1964	10.00	20.00	40.00
— Same as 8024, but in stereo					
Monument KZG 31484 (2)	The All-Time Greatest Hits of Roy Orbison	1972	6.25	12.50	25.00
— Contains one Christmas song: Pretty Paper					
Monument KWG 38389 (2)	The All-Time Greatest Hits of Roy Orbison	1982	2.00	4.00	8.00
Rhino R1 71493 (2)	For the Lonely: A Roy Orbison Anthology	1988	3.00	6.00	12.00
— Contains one Christmas song: Pretty Paper					

On Various-Artists Collections

Pretty Paper	Christmas Through the Years (Reader's Digest RDA-143)
	Country Christmas (Time-Life STL-109)

ORCHESTRA DE LA SOCIETE DES CONCERTS, SYMPHONIQUE DE PARIS
On Various-Artists Collections

March of the Little Lead Soldiers	Old Fashioned Christmas, An (Reader's Digest RDA 216-A)

ORCHIDS, THE

Label, Number	Title (A Side/B Side)	Year	VG	VG+	NM
45s					
Columbia 43175	Christmas Is the Time to Be With Your Baby/It Doesn't Matter	1964	5.00	10.00	20.00

Label, Number		Title (A Side/B Side)	Year	VG	VG+	NM
ORENSTEIN, JANET						
On Various-Artists Collections						
There's Always Tomorrow		Rudolph the Red-Nosed Reindeer (Decca DL 4815)				
ORIGINAL FIVE BLIND BOYS, THE						
On Various-Artists Collections						
White Christmas		Mahalia (Jackson) and Friends at Christmastime (Columbia Special Products P 11804)				
ORIOLES, THE						
Also see SONNY TIL.						
45s						
Charlie Parker 213		Back to the Chapel Again/(It's Gonna Be a) Lonely Christmas	1962	5.00	10.00	20.00
Charlie Parker 214		What Are You Doing New Year's Eve/	1962	5.00	10.00	20.00
		Don't Mess Around with My Love				
Harlem Sound 1001		Lonely Christmas/What Are You Doing New Year's Eve	19??		2.50	5.00
Jubilee 5017		What Are You Doing New Year's Eve/Lonely Christmas	1951	250.00	500.00	1,000.
Jubilee 5017	PS	What Are You Doing New Year's Eve/Lonely Christmas	1954	250.00	500.00	1,000.
Jubilee 5045		Oh Holy Night/The Lord's Prayer	1951	150.00	300.00	600.00
— Original on blue label						
Jubilee 5045	PS	Oh Holy Night/The Lord's Prayer	1954	200.00	400.00	800.00
Jubilee 5045		Oh Holy Night/The Lord's Prayer	196?	6.25	12.50	25.00
— Reissue on black label						
Lana 109		What Are You Doing New Year's Eve/Crying in the Chapel	196?	—	3.00	6.00
Virgo 6017		What Are You Doing New Year's Eve/Crying in the Chapel	1972	—	2.00	4.00
ORION						
45s						
Sun 1148		Remember Bethlehem/Silent Night	1979	—	2.00	4.00
Sun 1148	DJ	Remember Bethlehem (same on both sides)	1979	2.50	5.00	10.00
— Yellow vinyl promo						
ORR, CHERYL						
45s						
Summit 107		What I Saw on Christmas Night/Why Does My Daddy Come Here	1958	12.50	25.00	50.00
ORTEGO, HASA						
45s						
Swallow 10229		Christmas Eve on the Bayou/Christmas Eve on the Bayou (French)	19??	—	2.00	4.00
OSCAR						
On Various-Artists Collections						
I Hate Christmas		Merry Christmas from Sesame Street (CRA CTW 25516)				
OSKAY, BILLY, AND MICHEAL O DOMHNAILL						
On Various-Artists Collections						
Nollaig		Winter's Solstice, A (Windham Hill WH-1045)				
OSLIN, K.T.						
On Various-Artists Collections						
Blue Christmas		Mistletoe and Memories (RCA 8372-1-R)				
OSMOND BOYS, THE						
Younger generation of Osmonds.						
45s						
ARO 1987		Santa Claus Is Coming To Town/Kay Thompson's Jingle Bells	1987	—	2.00	4.00
OSMOND, JIMMY						
45s						
MGM 14199		Santa, No Chimney/I Hope You Have a Merry Christmas	1970	—	3.00	6.00
MGM 14328		If Santa Were My Daddy/Silent Night	1971	—	3.00	6.00
— As "Little Jimmy Osmond"						
MGM 14328	PS	If Santa Were My Daddy/Silent Night	1971	2.00	4.00	8.00
MGM 14770		Yes Virginia, There Is a Santa Claus/If Santa Were My Daddy	1974	—	3.00	6.00
OSMONDS, THE						
Albums						
Metro M 543	M	We Sing You a Merry Christmas	1965	3.75	7.50	15.00
— Reissue of 4187 with one track missing and rearranged contents						

Label, Number		Title (A Side/B Side)	Year	VG	VG+	NM
Metro MS 543	S	We Sing You a Merry Christmas	1965	5.00	10.00	20.00
MGM E-4187	M	We Sing You a Merry Christmas	1963	6.25	12.50	25.00
— As "The Osmond Brothers"						
MGM SE-4187	S	We Sing You a Merry Christmas	1963	7.50	15.00	30.00
Polydor PD-2-8001	(2)	The Osmond Christmas Album	1976	3.75	7.50	15.00
— Includes group, solo and duet recordings						

OTIS AND CARLA
Also see OTIS REDDING, CARLA THOMAS.
45s

Stax 244		Lovey Dovey/New Year's Resolution	1968	2.50	5.00	10.00
— A-side not a Christmas song						

OTIS, JOHNNY
45s

Savoy 764		Wedding Blues/Far Away Blues (Xmas Blues)	1950	15.00	30.00	60.00

OUANO, ROD
45s

People Tree 101		Sound Of Christmas/Hello There Christmas Day	1986	—	—	3.00
People Tree 101	PS	Sound Of Christmas/Hello There Christmas Day	1986	—	—	3.00

OWENS, BUCK
45s

Capitol 2328		Christmas Shopping/One of Everything You Got	1968	2.00	4.00	8.00
Capitol 3225		Santa's Gonna Come in a Stagecoach/One of Everything You Got	1971	2.00	4.00	8.00
— With Susan Raye						
Capitol 5537		Santa Looked a Lot Like Daddy/All I Want for Christmas Dear Is You	1965	2.50	5.00	10.00
Capitol 5537	PS	Santa Looked a Lot Like Daddy/All I Want for Christmas Dear Is You	1965	3.75	7.50	15.00
Capitol 5537		Santa Looked A Lot Like Daddy/All I Want For Christmas Dear Is You	1973	—	2.00	4.00
— Orange label, "Capitol" at bottom						

Albums

Capitol STBB-486	(2)	A Merry "Hee Haw" Christmas	1970	6.25	12.50	25.00
Capitol T 2396	M	Christmas with Buck Owens and His Buckaroos	1965	3.75	7.50	15.00
Capitol ST 2396	S	Christmas with Buck Owens and His Buckaroos	1965	5.00	10.00	20.00
— Same as above, but in stereo						
Capitol ST 2977		Christmas Shopping	1968	3.75	7.50	15.00

On Various-Artists Collections

Blue Christmas Lights	Country Christmas (Time-Life STL-109)
Santa Looked a Lot Like Daddy	Country Christmas (Time-Life STL-109)
Santa's Gonna Come in a Stagecoach	Christmas Stocking (Capitol NP 90494)
	Country Christmas (Time-Life STL-109)

OWENS, BUCK, AND SUSAN RAYE
Albums

Capitol ST-837		Merry Christmas from Buck Owens and Susan Raye	1971	3.75	7.50	15.00

P

PAC-MAN
Albums

Kid Stuff KSS-5029		Christmas Album	1982	3.75	7.50	15.00
— Written and produced by Patrick McBride and Dana Walden						

PAGE BOYS, THE
45s

Big B 1017		Santa's Snowdeer/White Wonderland	19??	2.00	4.00	8.00

PAGE, CHARLES
45s

Goldband 1151		Merry Christmas Tonight/Christmas In My Heart	196?	2.50	5.00	10.00
Goldband 1242		Merry Christmas Tonight/Coming For Christmas	197?	—	2.50	5.00
— B-side by Jo-El Sonnier						

Label, Number		Title (A Side/B Side)	Year	VG	VG+	NM

PAGE, GREG
45s

Lyra 1001		Christmas Is For You/The World Needs Love	19??	—	—	3.00

PAGE, MILTON
Albums

Diplomat X-1016		Pipe Organ	196?	2.50	5.00	10.00
— Reissue of Promenade album with same contents in same order						
Promenade CH-1006		Pipe Organ	196?	3.75	7.50	15.00

PAGE, PATTI
45s

Columbia 43447		Happy Birthday, Jesus (A Child's Prayer)/Christmas Bells	1965	2.00	4.00	8.00
Columbia 43447	PS	Happy Birthday, Jesus (A Child's Prayer)/Christmas Bells	1965	2.50	5.00	10.00
Columbia JZSP 111907/8	DJ	Happy Birthday, Jesus (A Child's Prayer)/Christmas Bells	1965	2.50	5.00	10.00
— Green vinyl						
Columbia JZSP 111907/8	DJ	Happy Birthday, Jesus (A Child's Prayer)/Christmas Bells	1965	2.00	4.00	8.00
— Black vinyl						
Mercury 5534		The Tennessee Waltz/Boogie Woogie Santa Claus	1950	5.00	10.00	20.00
— A-side is not a Christmas song; B-side was replaced on later pressings						
Mercury 5729		Boogie Woogie Santa Claus/Christmas Bells	1951	3.75	7.50	15.00
Mercury 5730		Jingle Bells/Christmas Choir	1951	3.75	7.50	15.00
Mercury 5731		Santa Claus Is Coming to Town/Silent Night	1951	3.75	7.50	15.00
Mercury 5732		White Christmas/The Christmas Song	1951	3.75	7.50	15.00
Mercury 70260		Where Did My Snowman Go/Changing Partners	1953	3.75	7.50	15.00
Mercury 70506		Pretty Snowflakes/I Wanna Go Dancing with Willie	1954	3.75	7.50	15.00

7-Inch Extended Plays

Mercury EP-1-3038		The Christmas Song/The First Noel//Christmas Choir/Christmas Bells	1956	3.00	6.00	12.00
Mercury EP-1-3038	PS	Christmas with Patti Page	1956	3.00	6.00	12.00

Albums

Columbia CL 2414	M	Christmas with Patti Page	1965	3.00	6.00	12.00
Columbia CS 9214	S	Christmas with Patti Page	1965	3.75	7.50	15.00
Mercury MG 20093	M	Christmas with Patti Page	1956	7.50	15.00	30.00
Mercury MG-25109	10	Christmas	1951	10.00	20.00	40.00
Wing MGW 12174	M	Christmas with Patti Page	196?	5.00	10.00	20.00
— Reissue of Mercury 20093						

On Various-Artists Collections

Christmas Bells	Merry Christmas (Columbia Musical Treasury 3P 6306)
Jingle Bells	60 Christmas Classics (Sessions DVL2-0723)
	Joy to the World (30 Classic Christmas Melodies) (Columbia Special Products P3 14654)
	Magnavox Album of Christmas Music (Columbia Special Products CSQ 11093)
Little Drummer Boy, The	Home for Christmas (Columbia Musical Treasury P3S 5608)
	Home for Christmas (Realm 2V 8101)
Pretty Snowflakes	Happy Holidays, Volume II (Columbia Special Products CSM 348)
Santo Natale	Gift of Christmas, The, Vol. 1 (Columbia Special Products CSS 706)
	It's Christmas Time! (Columbia Special Products P 14990)
	Very Merry Christmas, A (Columbia Special Products CSS 563)
Silver Bells	Christmas Is... (Columbia Special Products P 11417)
	Country Christmas Favorites (Columbia Special Products C 10876)
	Magic of Christmas, The (Columbia Musical Treasury P3S 5806)

PAGE, TOMMY
45s

Sire 27645		A Shoulder to Cry On/Christmas Without You	1988	—	—	3.00
— A-side is not a Christmas song						
Sire 27645	PS	A Shoulder to Cry On/Christmas Without You	1988	—	—	3.00

On Various-Artists Collections

Christmas Without You	Winter Warnerland (Warner Bros. PRO-A-3328)

PALLESI, BRUNO
45s

Decca 31343		Caro Gesu Bambino/Dear Gesu Bambino	1961	3.00	6.00	12.00
— B-side by Christian Morandi						

PALMER, BETSY
On Various-Artists Collections

Reminder Spot	For Christmas Seals...A Matter of Life and Breath (Decca Custom Style E)

PANDIT, KORLA
45s

Vita V-1		White Christmas/Merry Christmas	19??	—	2.00	4.00

Label, Number		Title (A Side/B Side)	Year	VG	VG+	NM
Vita V-2		Ava Maria/Bist Du Bi Mir	19??	—	2.00	4.00
Vita V-3		Adeste Fideles//Jesu Bambino/Silent Night	19??	—	2.00	4.00
Vita V-4		Joy to the World/Hark! The Herald Angels Sing	19??	—	2.00	4.00

PANE
45s
GSP 002		Christmas and You/Wishing You a Merry Christmas	19??	—	—	3.00

PANSY DIVISION
45s
Lookout 69		Fem In A Black Leather Jacket/Homo Christmas// Smells Like Queer Spirit	1992	2.00	4.00	8.00
Lookout 69	PS	Fem In A Black Leather Jacket/Homo Christmas// Smells Like Queer Spirit	1992	2.00	4.00	8.00

PAPPA HOP
45s
Ivory 134		Merry Christmas, Darling/Be Careful With The Blues	196?	2.50	5.00	10.00

PARADISE ISLANDERS, THE
Albums
Decca DL 4122	M	Christmas in Hawaii	1961	3.00	6.00	12.00
Decca DL 74122	S	Christmas in Hawaii	1961	3.75	7.50	15.00

PARIS SISTERS, THE
45s
Cavalier 828		Christmas in My Home Town/Man with the Mistletoe Moustache	197?	—	3.00	6.00

PARK, THE
45s
Paramount 0188		Hail, Raise Your Hands (A Brand-New Savior Has Been Born)/(B-side unknown)	1972	—	2.50	5.00

PARKER, RAY, JR.
45s
Arista 1035		Christmas Time Is Here/(Instrumental)	1982	—	2.50	5.00
Arista 1035	PS	Christmas Time Is Here/(Instrumental)	1982	—	3.00	6.00
Arista 9293		Jamie/Christmas Time Is Here	1984	—	—	3.00
— A-side not a Christmas song						
Flashback 9288		Christmas Time Is Here/(Instrumental)	1984	—	—	3.00
— Reissue						

PARKER, ROBERT
45s
Nola 730		A Letter To Santa/C.C. Rider	1966	2.50	5.00	10.00

PARKIN, EDDIE
45s
H&M 2003		Santa Claus Is Coming to Town/Mary's Little Boy Child	19??	—	—	3.00
— B-side by Carlos Malcolm						

PARTON, DOLLY
Also see KENNY ROGERS AND DOLLY PARTON.
45s
RCA GB-14070		Tennessee Homesick Blues/Hard Candy Christmas	1985	—	—	3.00
— Gold Standard Series						
RCA PB-13361		Hard Candy Christmas/Me and Little Andy	1982	—	2.00	4.00
RCA JK-13944	DJ	Medley: Winter Wonderland/Sleigh Ride (same on both sides)	1984	—	2.00	4.00
RCA PB-13944		Medley: Winter Wonderland-Sleigh Ride/The Christmas Song	1984	—	—	3.00
— B-side by Kenny Rogers						

Albums
RCA Victor AHL1-4422		Greatest Hits	1982	2.50	5.00	10.00
— Contains one Christmas song: Hard Candy Christmas						

On Various-Artists Collections
Hard Candy Christmas	Best Little Whorehouse in Texas, The (MCA 6112)
	Best of Christmas, The (RCA Victor CPL1-7013)
	Country Christmas (Time-Life STL-109)
	Country Christmas, A, Volume 2 (RCA AYL1-4809)

Label, Number		Title (A Side/B Side)	Year	VG	VG+	NM
Medley: Winter Wonderland/Sleigh Ride		Christmas Treasury of Classics from Avon, A (RCA Special Products DPL1-0716)				
		Country Christmas, A, Volume 4 (RCA CPL1-7012)				
		Time-Life Treasury of Christmas, The (Time-Life STL-107)				
White Christmas		Celebrate the Season with Tupperware (RCA Special Products DPL1-0803)				
		Happy Holidays, Vol. 22 (RCA Special Products DPL1-0777)				
		Mistletoe and Memories (RCA 8372-1-R)				

PARTRIDGE FAMILY, THE
Albums

Label, Number		Title (A Side/B Side)	Year	VG	VG+	NM
Bell 6066		A Partridge Family Christmas Card	1971	6.25	12.50	25.00
— With attached Christmas card						
Bell 6066		A Partridge Family Christmas Card	1971	3.75	7.50	15.00
— Same as above, but without Christmas card						
Bell 6066		A Partridge Family Christmas Card	1971	10.00	20.00	40.00
— Same as above, but with Christmas card printed on the cover (later pressing)						

PARTRIDGE, JUDY
On Various-Artists Collections

Label, Number		Title (A Side/B Side)	Year	VG	VG+	NM
O Holy Night		Merry Christmas (Rainbow Sound R-5032-LPS)				

PATRICK, MILT
45s

Label, Number		Title (A Side/B Side)	Year	VG	VG+	NM
Terri-Ann 101		Merry Twistmas/Just A Doggone Dream	1962	2.50	5.00	10.00

PATSY
Also see ELMO AND PATSY.
45s

Label, Number		Title (A Side/B Side)	Year	VG	VG+	NM
Roperry 2255		"Kid" Santa Claus (same on both sides)	198?	—	2.00	4.00
Roperry 2255	PS	"Kid" Santa Claus (same on both sides)	198?	—	2.00	4.00
Silly Goose 1088		Grandma Got Run Over by a Reindeer (Rap Version)/	1988	—	—	3.00
		Grandma Got Run Over by a Reindeer				

PATTERSON, DON
Albums

Label, Number		Title (A Side/B Side)	Year	VG	VG+	NM
Prestige PR 7415	M	Holiday Soul	1965	7.50	15.00	30.00
Prestige PRST 7415	S	Holiday Soul	1965	6.25	12.50	25.00

PATTI, SANDI
Albums

Label, Number		Title (A Side/B Side)	Year	VG	VG+	NM
Impact RO 3874		The Gift Goes On	1983	3.00	6.00	12.00

PATTY AND THE STREET TONES
45s

Label, Number		Title (A Side/B Side)	Year	VG	VG+	NM
Clifton 66		Rudolph the Red-Nosed Reindeer/I'll Stay Home	19??	—	3.00	6.00

PAUL AND PAULA
45s

Label, Number		Title (A Side/B Side)	Year	VG	VG+	NM
Philips 40158		Holiday for Teens/Holiday Hootenanny	1963	3.00	6.00	12.00

Albums

Label, Number		Title (A Side/B Side)	Year	VG	VG+	NM
Philips PHM 200-101	M	Holiday for Teens	1963	7.50	15.00	30.00
Philips PHS 600-101	S	Holiday for Teens	1963	10.00	20.00	40.00

PAUL, LES, AND MARY FORD
45s

Label, Number		Title (A Side/B Side)	Year	VG	VG+	NM
Capitol F1881		Jingle Bells/Silent Night	1951	3.75	7.50	15.00
Capitol F2617		Jungle Bells (Dingo-Dango-Day)/White Christmas	1953	3.00	6.00	12.00
Capitol F3302		Rudolph the Red-Nosed Reindeer/Santa Claus Is Comin' to Town	1955	3.00	6.00	12.00

PAUL, LOUIS
45s

Label, Number		Title (A Side/B Side)	Year	VG	VG+	NM
Enterprise 9060		It's Christmas Time/Santa Claus Is on His Way Again	1972	—	3.00	6.00

PAULA, MARLENA
45s

Label, Number		Title (A Side/B Side)	Year	VG	VG+	NM
Regent 7506		I Wanna Spend Christmas with Elvis/Once More It's Christmas	1956	12.50	25.00	50.00

Label, Number	Title (A Side/B Side)	Year	VG	VG+	NM

PAVAROTTI, LUCIANO
45s

| London 20102 | Ave Maria (Schubert)/Ave Maria (Bach-Gounod) | 1978 | — | 2.50 | 5.00 |

Albums

| London OS 26473 | O Holy Night | 1976 | 3.75 | 7.50 | 15.00 |

— Original U.S.-distributed version has "London" without "ffrr" on upper right front cover and a white back cover

| London OS 26473 | O Holy Night | 198? | 3.00 | 6.00 | 12.00 |

— Later pressings have "London/ffrr" on upper right front cover and have a yellow back cover

On Various-Artists Collections

Adeste Fideles	Time-Life Treasury of Christmas, The (Time-Life STL-107)
Ave Maria (Schubert)	Yes, Georgio (London PDV 9001)
Gesu Bambino	Time-Life Treasury of Christmas, The, Volume Two (Time-Life STL-108)
O Holy Night	Time-Life Treasury of Christmas, The, Volume Two (Time-Life STL-108)

PAYCHECK, JOHNNY
45s

| Little Darlin 0055 | Jingle Bells/The Old Year Is Gone | 1968 | 2.00 | 4.00 | 8.00 |

PAYNE, LEON
45s

| Starday 215 | Christmas Everyday/Christmas Love Song | 1955 | 5.00 | 10.00 | 20.00 |

PAYOLA$
45s

| A&M 2589 | Christmas Is Coming/I'll Find Another | 1983 | — | 3.00 | 6.00 |

PEACE, LYNDA
45s

| Reena 2090 | Twinkletoes (The Dancing Reindeer)/Jingles | 19?? | — | 2.00 | 4.00 |

PEARL JAM
45s

| Epic Associated ZS7 4354 | DJ | Let Me Sleep (Christmas Time)/Ramblings | 1991 | 5.00 | 10.00 | 20.00 |

— Small hole, plays at 33 1-3 RPM

| Epic Associated ZS7 4354 | PS | Let Me Sleep (Christmas Time)/Ramblings | 1991 | 5.00 | 10.00 | 20.00 |

7-Inch Extended Plays

| Jeremy CIPE10 | | Christmas Time/Ramblings//Sonic Reducer/Ramblings Continued | 199? | — | 2.50 | 5.00 |
| Jeremy CIPE10 | PS | Christmas Time/Ramblings//Sonic Reducer/Ramblings Continued | 199? | — | 2.50 | 5.00 |

— Bootleg EP of Pearl Jam's first two fan-club singles

PEARSON, LESLIE/JOHN PAICE/LONDON BELL RINGERS/ WESTMINSTER BRASS ENSEMBLE
On Various-Artists Collections

Ave Maria	Joyous Music for Christmas Time (Reader's Digest RD 45-M)
Carol of the Bells	Joyous Music for Christmas Time (Reader's Digest RD 45-M)
Christmas Is Coming	Joyous Music for Christmas Time (Reader's Digest RD 45-M)
First Noel, The	Joyous Music for Christmas Time (Reader's Digest RD 45-M)
Good King Wenceslas	Joyous Music for Christmas Time (Reader's Digest RD 45-M)
O Come, O Come, Emmanuel	Joyous Music for Christmas Time (Reader's Digest RD 45-M)

PEBBLES AND BAMM BAMM
7-Inch Extended Plays

| Hanna-Barbera CS 7044 | | Little Drummer Boy/We Three Kings// Silent Night/It Came Upon a Midnight Clear | 1965 | 12.50 | 25.00 | 50.00 |
| Hanna-Barbera CS 7044 | PS | We Wish You a Merry Christmas | 1965 | 25.00 | 50.00 | 100.00 |

PECK, GREGORY
45s

| Decca 24731 | Lullaby of Christmas (Part 1)/Lullaby of Christmas (Part 6) | 1950 | 2.50 | 5.00 | 10.00 |

— Side 1 and Side 6 of "Album No. 6-70"

| Decca 24732 | Lullaby of Christmas (Part 2)/Lullaby of Christmas (Part 5) | 1950 | 2.50 | 5.00 | 10.00 |

— Side 2 and Side 5 of "Album No. 6-70"

| Decca 24733 | Lullaby of Christmas (Part 3)/Lullaby of Christmas (Part 4) | 1950 | 2.50 | 5.00 | 10.00 |

— Side 3 and Side 4 of "Album No. 6-70"

7-Inch Extended Plays

| Decca 9-69 | (3) | Lullaby of Christmas | 1950 | 10.00 | 20.00 | 40.00 |

— Contains three 45s (24731, 24732 and 24733) and box

Label, Number		Title (A Side/B Side)	Year	VG	VG+	NM
Albums						
Decca DL 8009	M	Lullaby of Christmas	1966	5.00	10.00	20.00
Decca DL 78009	S	Lullaby of Christmas	1966	6.25	12.50	25.00

PEE WEE CHILDREN'S CHORUS, THE
45s

CCP 1002		Pee Wee The Pink Pine Tree/Santa Claus Junior	1976	—	2.00	4.00
— B-side by Reta, Alita & Marilyn						

PEEK, DAN
On Various-Artists Collections

Star, The	On This Christmas Night (Songbird MCA-3184)	

PEER, LEE
45s

Entas 63001	The Ad Man's Christmas/The Christmas Elves	19??	2.50	5.00	10.00

PEERCE, JAN
45s

RCA Victor 47-7109		A Child's First Christmas/Faith	1957	3.00	6.00	12.00
7-Inch Extended Plays						
RCA Victor ERA 132		Jesu Bambino/Oh, Holy Night//Maria On The Mountain/Behold A Branch Is Growing/O Sanctissima	195?	3.00	6.00	12.00
RCA Victor ERA 132	PS	Five Christmas Songs	195?	3.75	7.50	15.00
— Ornament-shaped sleeve						

On Various-Artists Collections

Gesu Bambino	For a Musical Merry Christmas (RCA Victor PR-149A)
Noel Nouvelet	Great Songs of Christmas, The, Album Six (Columbia Special Products CSM 388)
O Come, All Ye Faithful	Great Songs of Christmas, The, Album Six (Columbia Special Products CSM 388)
O Holy Night	Christmas in New York (RCA Victor PRM-257)
	Happy Holidays, Volume 14 (RCA Special Products DPL1-0376)

PEEVEY, GAYLA
45s

Columbia 4-186	I Want A Hippopotamus For Christmas/Are My Ears On Straight?	1953	3.75	7.50	15.00
— Yellow-label "Children's Series" record					
Columbia 4-224	Got A Cold In The Node For Christmas/ The Angel In The Christmas Play	1954	3.75	7.50	15.00
— Yellow-label "Children's Series" record					
Columbia 40106	I Want a Hippopotamus for Christmas/Are My Ears On Straight?	1953	5.00	10.00	20.00
Columbia 40364	Got A Cold In The Node For Christmas/ The Angel In The Christmas Play	1954	3.75	7.50	15.00
Columbia 40602	77 Santas/Rubberlegs (The Knock-Kneed Monkey)	1955	3.75	7.50	15.00

On Various-Artists Collections

I Want a Hippopotamus for Christmas	Dr. Demento Presents the Greatest Novelty Records of All Time Volume VI: Christmas (Rhino RNLP 825)

PEGGY SUE
45s

Door Knob 043	Mama's Country Christmas/Donkey Without A Name	1977	—	2.50	5.00

PEIL, DANNY, AND THE APOLLOS
45s

Reynard 602	Jingle Jump/Flip Side	1964	3.75	7.50	15.00

PELLETIER, CINDY
45s

Arundel Tree 4325	Christmas Candle/(Instrumental)	19??	—	2.00	4.00

PENA, PEPE
45s

Eureka 1203	Story Of Christmas/The Greatest Gift	19??	—	2.50	5.00

PENGUINS, THE
45s

Mercury 70762	A Christmas Prayer/Jingle Jangle	1955	20.00	40.00	80.00

On Various-Artists Collections

Jingle Jangle	Rockin' Christmas — The '50s (Rhino RNLP-066)

Label, Number		Title (A Side/B Side)	Year	VG	VG+	NM
PENN, LITTLE "LAMBSIE"						
45s						
Atco 6082		I Wanna Spend Christmas With Elvis/Painted Lips and Pigtails	1956	12.50	25.00	50.00
PENN, MICHAEL						
45s						
AGM 1135		Christmas Song/It's Gonna Take A Long Time	198?	—	2.00	4.00
PENN, PRESTON						
45s						
Accent 1173		Little Pee Wee (Christmas Tree)/Santa's Beard	196?	2.00	4.00	8.00
PENN, WILLIAM, AND THE QUAKERS						
45s						
Melron 5024		Santa Needs Ear Muffs on His Nose/Philly	1966	15.00	30.00	60.00
Melron 5024		Santa Needs Ear Muffs on His Nose/Sweet Caroline	1966	15.00	30.00	60.00
PENNING, RICK						
45s						
Alpha A7-4		Old Jolly It's Santa By Golly/No Holds Christmas	19??	—	2.00	4.00
PENNINGTON, RAY						
45s						
Dimension 1039		For Christmas/Don't Let Me Lie Again	1982	—	2.00	4.00
EMH 0027		For Christmas/Dark Haired Woman	198?	—	2.00	4.00
PENNINO, JOHNNY						
45s						
AMI 1904		White Christmas/Country Goose	198?	—	2.00	4.00
PENNY, ED						
45s						
Decca 29727		What Is Christmas?/Lonely Old Shepherd	1955	3.00	6.00	12.00
Essex 376		What Is Christmas?/Lonely Old Shepherd	1954	3.75	7.50	15.00
— As "Edward Penny and Larry Forbes"						
PEOPLES, RICK						
45s						
Omnisound 1025		Christmas In A Small Town/The Man With A Hundred Names	198?	—	2.50	5.00
— B-side by Mike Whorf						
PERLE, ADAM, AND WESLEY CROW						
45s						
Atco 6916	DJ	A Silent Night/Happiness Is a Sad, Sad Song	1972	—	2.50	5.00
PERRY, FRANK						
45s						
Belle 251		Santa's Caught On The Freeway/Young & Innocent	1959	3.00	6.00	12.00
PETER PAN PLAYERS, THE						
45s						
Peter Pan X36		Snoopy's Christmas/A Ride On Santa's Sleigh	196?	—	2.50	5.00
Peter Pan X36	PS	Snoopy's Christmas/A Ride On Santa's Sleigh	196?	—	3.00	6.00
Peter Pan 1037		Rudolph the Red-Nosed Reindeer/I Heard the Bells on Christmas Day	196?	—	3.00	6.00
PETER, PAUL AND MARY						
Also see NOEL PAUL STOOKEY.						
45s						
Warner Bros. (no #)		A-Soalin' (mono/stereo)	196?	3.00	6.00	12.00
— Green custom label						
Warner Bros. (no #)	PS	A-Soalin' (mono/stereo)	196?	5.00	10.00	20.00
— Illustrated book with lyrics						
Warner Bros. 5402		A-Soalin'/High-A-Bye	1963	3.00	6.00	12.00
Warner Bros. 5402	PS	A-Soalin'/High-A-Bye	1963	5.00	10.00	20.00
Warner Bros. 7359		Christmas Dinner/The Marvelous Toy	1969	2.50	5.00	10.00
Albums						
Gold Castle D1-71316		A Holiday Celebration	1988	2.50	5.00	10.00

Label, Number	Title (A Side/B Side)	Year	VG	VG+	NM
Gold Castle R 164086	A Holiday Celebration	1988	3.00	6.00	12.00
— Same as above, except BMG Direct Marketing edition					
Warner Bros. W 1473 M	(Moving)	1963	5.00	10.00	20.00
— Contains one Christmas song: A-Soalin'					
Warner Bros. WS 1473 S	(Moving)	1963	6.25	12.50	25.00
— Originals on gold label					
Warner Bros. WS 1473 S	(Moving)	1968	2.50	5.00	10.00
— Any later stereo edition (green "W7", green "WB", palm trees, white label)					

PETERS, ROBERTA
On Various-Artists Collections

Alleluia (Mozart)	Firestone Presents Your Favorite Christmas Music, Volume 6 (Firestone MLP 7014)
Ave Maria	Firestone Presents Your Christmas Favorites, Volume 3 (Firestone MLP 7008)
First Noel, The	Firestone Presents Your Favorite Christmas Music, Volume 6 (Firestone MLP 7014)
Gesu Bambino	Firestone Presents Your Christmas Favorites, Volume 3 (Firestone MLP 7008)

PETERS, ROBERTA, AND JACK JONES
On Various-Artists Collections

Hark the Herald Angels Sing	Firestone Presents Your Favorite Christmas Music, Volume 6 (Firestone MLP 7014)

PETERS, ROBERTA, AND JACK JONES WITH THE VIENNA CHOIR BOYS
On Various-Artists Collections

Medley: Christmas Is Coming/We Wish You a Merry Christmas	Firestone Presents Your Favorite Christmas Music, Volume 6 (Firestone MLP 7014)

PETERSON, LUCKY
45s

Today 1517	A Christmas Song/Daddy, Come Home For Christmas	1972	—	3.00	6.00

PETTIS, RAY
45s

Drexel 911	Does It Have To Be Christmas/Christmas Here, Christmas There	1956	12.50	25.00	50.00

PETTY, FRANK, TRIO
45s

MGM 11629	Italian Christmas Bells/Let It Snow, Let It Snow, Let It Snow	1953	3.75	7.50	15.00
MGM 11870	Rudolph the Red-Nosed Reindeer/Jingle Bells	1954	3.75	7.50	15.00

PHELPS, JUDY LYNN
45s

Class 218	Thanks for Christmas/Thanks for Christmas (Narration)	1957	5.00	10.00	20.00
— B-side by Montague					

PHELPS, MARTHA DELL
45s

Holly 2855	A Jolly Fellow (Is Santa Claus)/A Merry Christmas To You	19??	—	2.00	4.00

PHILADELPHIA BRASS ENSEMBLE
45s

Columbia JZSP 135463/7 DJ	We Wish You a Merry Christmas/Deck The Halls with Boughs of Holly	1967	—	3.00	6.00

Albums

Columbia Masterworks XMS 7033 S	A Festival of Carols in Brass	1967	3.00	6.00	12.00

On Various-Artists Collections

Dack the Hall with Boughs of Holly	Joy to the World (30 Classic Christmas Melodies) (Columbia Special Products P3 14654)
Medley: Good Christian Men Rejoice/O Holy Night	Christmas Greetings (Columbia Special Products CSS 1433)
O Tannenbaum	Gift of Christmas, The, Vol. 1 (Columbia Special Products CSS 706)
	Happy Holidays, Album Nine (Columbia Special Products P 11793)
	Home for Christmas (Columbia Musical Treasury P3S 5608)
Twelve Days of Christmas, The	Joy to the World (30 Classic Christmas Melodies) (Columbia Special Products P3 14654)

PHILADELPHIA MINSTRELS, THE
45s

Cameo 284	The Girl That I'll Adore/Grandma's House	1963	2.50	5.00	10.00
— B-side by the Squirrels					

Label, Number	Title (A Side/B Side)	Year	VG	VG+	NM

PHILADELPHIA ORCHESTRA (ORMANDY)
Some are with the Temple University Choir. Also see MORMON TABERNACLE CHOIR.

45s

Columbia 42621	Adeste Fideles/O Come, Little Children	1962	2.50	5.00	10.00
Columbia 43155	We Wish You a Merry Christmas/Little Drummer Boy	1964	2.50	5.00	10.00

— With the Temple University Choir (side A) and the De Sales Boys Choir (side B)

Albums

Columbia ML 5769	M	The Glorious Sound of Christmas	1962	3.00	6.00	12.00
Columbia MS 6369	S	The Glorious Sound of Christmas	1962	3.75	7.50	15.00
RCA Red Seal ARL1-0257		The Greatest Hits of Christmas, Volume 2	1973	2.50	5.00	10.00
RCA Red Seal LSC-3326		The Greatest Hits of Christmas	1972	2.50	5.00	10.00

On Various-Artists Collections

Angels We Have Heard on High	Happy Holidays, Volume 16 (RCA Special Products DPL1-0501)
Ave Maria	60 Christmas Classics (Sessions DVL2-0723)
Ave Maria (Schubert)	Home for Christmas (Columbia Musical Treasury P3S 5608)
Carol of the Bells	Family Christmas Collection, The (Time-Life STL-131)
Deck the Hall with Boughs of Holly	Great Songs of Christmas, The, Album Two (Columbia Special Products XTV 86100/1)
For Unto Us a Child Is Born	Joy to the World (30 Classic Christmas Melodies) (Columbia Special Products P3 14654)
	Merry Christmas from... (Reader's Digest RD4-83)
	Very Merry Christmas, A, Volume 3 (Columbia Special Products CSS 997)
Good King Wenceslas	Family Christmas Collection, The (Time-Life STL-131)
Hallelujah Chorus	Gift of Christmas, The, Vol. 1 (Columbia Special Products CSS 706)
	Joy to the World (30 Classic Christmas Melodies) (Columbia Special Products P3 14654)
	Merry Christmas from... (Reader's Digest RD4-83)
	Wondrous Winter: Songs of Winter, Songs of Christmas
	(Columbia Special Products CSS 708/9)
Hark! The Herald Angels Sing	Happy Holidays, Album 8 (Columbia Special Products C 11086)
	Happy Holidays, Volume 15 (RCA Special Products DPL1-0453)
	Home for Christmas (Columbia Musical Treasury P3S 5608)
	Joyous Songs of Christmas, The (Columbia Special Products C 10400)
Here We Go A-Caroling	Joy to the World (30 Classic Christmas Melodies) (Columbia Special Products P3 14654)
It Came Upon a Midnight Clear	Happy Holidays, Volume 13 (RCA Special Products DPL1-0319)
	Home for Christmas (Columbia Musical Treasury P3S 5608)
	Merry Christmas (Columbia Musical Treasury 3P 6306)
Joy to the World	Christmas Greetings, Vol. 3 (Columbia Special Products P 11383)
	Christmas Trimmings (Columbia Special Products P 12795)
	Goodyear Presents The Great Songs of Christmas (RCA Special Products DPL1-0285)
	Great Songs of Christmas, The, Album Four (Columbia Special Products CSP 155M)
	Happy Holidays, Volume 14 (RCA Special Products DPL1-0376)
	Joy of Christmas, The (Columbia Special Products P 12042)
	Merry Christmas from... (Reader's Digest RD4-83)
Little Drummer Boy	Great Songs of Christmas, The, Album Five (Columbia Special Products CSP 238M)
Medley: Hark! The Herald Angels Sing/	That Christmas Feeling (Columbia Special Products P 11853)
We Three Kings of Orient Are	
O Come Little Children	Great Songs of Christmas, The, Album Four (Columbia Special Products CSP 155M)
O Come, O Come Emmanuel	60 Christmas Classics (Sessions DVL2-0723)
O Little Town of Bethlehem	Great Songs of Christmas, The, Album Three (Columbia Special Products CSP 117)
O Sanctissima	60 Christmas Classics (Sessions DVL2-0723)
	Merry Christmas from... (Reader's Digest RD4-83)
O Tannenbaum	Joy to the World (30 Classic Christmas Melodies) (Columbia Special Products P3 14654)
Silent Night	Family Christmas Collection, The (Time-Life STL-131)
	Magic of Christmas, The (Columbia Musical Treasury P3S 5806)
Sleigh Ride	Family Christmas Collection, The (Time-Life STL-131)
	Goodyear Presents The Great Songs of Christmas (RCA Special Products DPL1-0285)
	Great Songs of Christmas, The, Album Five (Columbia Special Products CSP 238M)
We Three Kings of Orient Are	Brightest Stars of Christmas, The (RCA Special Products DPL1-0086)
We Wish You a Merry Christmas	Goodyear Presents The Great Songs of Christmas (RCA Special Products DPL1-0285)
	Time-Life Treasury of Christmas, The (Time-Life STL-107)

PHILADELPHIA ORCHESTRA (PAGE)
On Various-Artists Collections

It Came Upon a Midnight Clear	Goodyear Presents The Great Songs of Christmas (RCA Special Products DPL1-0285)
	Time-Life Treasury of Christmas, The (Time-Life STL-107)

PHILADELPHIA ORCHESTRA (SMITH)
On Various-Artists Collections

Go Tell It on the Mountain	Family Christmas Collection, The (Time-Life STL-131)
	Goodyear Presents The Great Songs of Christmas (RCA Special Products DPL1-0285)
Santa Claus Is Comin' to Town	Goodyear Presents The Great Songs of Christmas (RCA Special Products DPL1-0285)
White Christmas	Goodyear Presents The Great Songs of Christmas (RCA Special Products DPL1-0285)

PHILADELPHIA SINGERS AND CONCERTO SOLOISTS
CHAMBER ORCHESTRA OF PHILADELPHIA
On Various-Artists Collections

Medley: In Dulci Jubilo/Angels We Have Heard on High	Family Christmas Collection, The (Time-Life STL-131)

Label, Number		Title (A Side/B Side)	Year	VG	VG+	NM

PHILHARMONIC POPS ORCHESTRA
On Various-Artists Collections

Skater's Waltz		Old Fashioned Christmas, An (Reader's Digest RDA 216-A)				

PHILLIPS, SHAWN
45s

| A&M 1238 | | A Christmas Song/Lovely Lady | 1970 | 2.50 | 5.00 | 10.00 |
| A&M 1238 | PS | A Christmas Song/Lovely Lady | 1970 | 2.50 | 5.00 | 10.00 |

PHILLIPS, TEDDY, ORCHESTRA
45s

| Hallmark 11480 | | Ole Tex Kringle/When Santa Claus Invented Toys | 1980 | — | 2.00 | 4.00 |

PHILLIPSON, LARRY LEE
45s

| Phillipson 2004 | | Give Me Your Love For Christmas/Baby Sister's Christmas | 19?? | — | 2.00 | 4.00 |

PHROOMF
45s

| Phroomf 10405 | | Phroomf (same on both sides) | 19?? | — | 2.50 | 5.00 |
| Phroomf 10405 | PS | Phroomf (same on both sides) | 19?? | — | 2.50 | 5.00 |

PIAZZA, MARGURITE
7-Inch Extended Plays

| MCW 7304 | | Jingle Bells/Silent Night// It Came Upon a Midnight Clear/We Wish You a Merry Christmas | 19?? | — | 2.00 | 4.00 |

PICKENS, SLIM
45s

| Midsong 72021 | | Christmas In November/Sing a Song for Burdell | 1980 | — | 2.50 | 5.00 |

PICKETT, BOBBY "BORIS"
45s

Garpax 44171		Monster's Holiday/Monster's Motion	1962	6.25	12.50	25.00
Garpax 44171	PS	Monster's Holiday/Monster's Motion	1962	10.00	20.00	40.00
Parrot 366		Monster's Holiday/Monster Minuet	1971	2.50	5.00	10.00

PICKWICK CHILDREN'S CHORUS, THE
45s

| Showcase 9905 | | Thank God For Christmas//(B-side unknown) | 19?? | — | 2.00 | 4.00 |

PIERCE, WEBB
45s

| Decca 31867 | | Christmas at Home/Sweet Memories | 1965 | 2.00 | 4.00 | 8.00 |
| Plantation 145 | | Christmas Time's a Coming/The Family Christmas Tree | 1976 | — | 2.50 | 5.00 |

PIKE, PETE
45s

| Coral 61522 | | Old Fashioned Christmas/Happy Birthday, Dear Jesus | 1955 | 3.00 | 6.00 | 12.00 |
| Rebel 229 | | Would You Like To Ride With Santa/I Can See An Angel | 19?? | 3.00 | 6.00 | 12.00 |

PILGRIM TRAVELERS, THE
45s

Specialty 837		I'll Be Home for Christmas/Move Up to Heaven	1952	12.50	25.00	50.00
Specialty 856		Silent Night/I'll Be Home for Christmas	1953	10.00	20.00	40.00
Specialty 934		Silent Night/I'll Be Home for Christmas	197?	3.00	6.00	12.00

PINECONE, PRETTY POLLY
45s

| Tinsel 8 | | I Stole Away On Christmas Day/Santa's New Bag | 19?? | 2.00 | 4.00 | 8.00 |
| — B-side by Rudi and the Rain Dearz | | | | | | |

PINETOPPERS, THE
45s

| Coral 64106 | | Jolly Old Saint Nicholas/Ting-a-Ling-a-Jingle | 1951 | 3.75 | 7.50 | 15.00 |
| — With the Marlin Sisters | | | | | | |

Label, Number		Title (A Side/B Side)	Year	VG	VG+	NM
PINK SLIP DADDY						
On Various-Artists Collections						
Santa Claus		Stuff This in Your Stocking! Elves in Action (Veebltronics/Skyclad 68)				
PINKARD AND BOWDEN						
45s						
Warner Bros. 28837		A Christmas Gift/Noel Bon Temps Roullee	1985	—	2.00	4.00
PINKY & PERKY						
7-Inch Extended Plays						
Columbia SEG 8122		(contents unconfirmed)	1963	2.50	5.00	10.00
Columbia SEG 8122	PS	Christmas with Pinky and Perky	1963	2.50	5.00	10.00
— U.K. import						
EMI 170		Give Us A Kiss For Christmas//	1990	—	3.00	6.00
		I Saw Mommy Kissing Santa Claus/Nursery Romp				
EMI 170	PS	Give Us A Kiss For Christmas//	1990	—	3.00	6.00
		I Saw Mommy Kissing Santa Claus/Nursery Romp				
— U.K. import; reissue of older material						
PIPSQUEEKS, THE						
45s						
Warner Bros. 5878		Santa's Little Helpers/Santa's Magic Flute	1966	2.50	5.00	10.00
PIROUETTE ORCHESTRA AND CHORUS, THE						
Albums						
Pirouette XFM-58		Christmas Sing Along	195?	3.75	7.50	15.00
PITTSBURGH POPS ORCHESTRA						
45s						
United Artists 785		Holiday for Trumpet/Hello Dolly	1964	2.50	5.00	10.00
PIXIES, THE						
45s						
Balboa 007		Santa's Too Fat for the Hula Hoop/Kitty Kats on Parade	1958	5.00	10.00	20.00
PLAN 9						
45s						
Midnight 4508		Merry Christmas/White Christmas	198?	—	3.00	6.00
Midnight 4508	PS	Merry Christmas/White Christmas	198?	—	3.00	6.00
PLATTERS, THE						
Albums						
Columbia Special Products P 11834	S	Christmas with the Platters	1973	3.75	7.50	15.00
— Reissue of Mercury SR-60841 with fewer tracks						
Mercury MG-20841	M	Christmas with the Platters	1963	7.50	15.00	30.00
Mercury SR-60841	S	Christmas with the Platters	1963	10.00	20.00	40.00
PLAYBOYS, THE						
45s						
Legato 101		Mope De Mope/The Night Before Christmas	1963	7.50	15.00	30.00
PLUMLEY, JOHN						
45s						
Pinnacle Road 3000		The Miracle Of Christmas Eve/The Child Has Arrived	19??	—	2.00	4.00
— B-side by Polk						
PLUMMER, DAVE						
45s						
Cypress 105		Santa's Little Messenger Boy/It's Christmas Everywhere	196?	2.00	4.00	8.00
PLYMOUTH FESTIVAL CHORUS AND ORCHESTRA						
Albums						
Pro Arte PAD 152		Ralph Vaughan Williams: Carols (et al.)	1983	3.00	6.00	12.00

Label, Number	Title (A Side/B Side)	Year	VG	VG+	NM
PM					
On Various-Artists Collections					
Once in a Blue Moon	Winter Warnerland (Warner Bros. PRO-A-3328)				
POETS, THE					
45s					
Red Bird 10-046	Merry Christmas Baby/I'm Stuck on You	1965	3.00	6.00	12.00
POINDEXTER, BUSTER					
45s					
RCA 6893-7 DJ	Zat You Santa Claus/Hot Hot Hot	1987	3.75	7.50	15.00
POINDEXTER, PONY					
On Various-Artists Collections					
Rudolph, the Red-Nosed Reindeer	Jingle Bell Jazz (Columbia PC 36803)				
POINTER SISTERS, THE					
On Various-Artists Collections					
Santa Claus Is Comin' to Town	Stars of Christmas, The (RCA Special Products DPL1-0842) Very Special Christmas, A (A&M SP-3911)				
POISON IDEA					
45s					
Tim/Kerr 9370	Santa Claus Is Back In Town/I'm Mad At The Fat Man	1993	2.00	4.00	8.00
— B-side by Ray and Clover; picture disc					
POLK					
45s					
Pinnacle Road 3000	The Miracle Of Christmas Eve/The Child Has Arrived	19??	—	2.00	4.00
— B-side by John Plumley					
POLKATONES, THE					
45s					
Cuca 1443	White Christmas/Silver Bells	19??	—	2.50	5.00
PONCE, PONCIE					
On Various-Artists Collections					
Mele Kalikimaka	We Wish You a Merry Christmas (Warner Bros. W 1337)				
PONTRELLI, PETE					
45s					
Skyway 101	Season's Greetings/There's Room In My Heart	1960	2.50	5.00	10.00
Skyway 103	Season's Greetings (A Cheerful Hello)/ Season's Greetings (A Cheerful Hello)	1960	2.00	4.00	8.00
— B-side by Gaylord Carter					
POOLE, CHERYL					
45s					
Paula 1205	How About Your Love for Christmas/ It's Christmas Every Day of the Year	1968	—	3.00	6.00
POPCORN REBELLION, THE					
45s					
Date 1632	The Christmas Game/Dance to the Music of the Christmas Game	1968	2.50	5.00	10.00
POPE JOHN PAUL II					
Albums					
Infinity INF 9899	Pope John Paul II Sings at the Festival of Sacrosong	1979	3.00	6.00	12.00
— Contains two Christmas songs (in Polish): Do Not Be Afraid, Mary, You Lily; On a December Night					
POPE, SISTER LUCILLE					
45s					
Nashboro 1016	Merry Christmas/Silent Night	1974	—	2.50	5.00

(Top left) *Christmas With Patti Page,* released in 1956, was not her first Christmas album; Page had done a 10-inch LP in the 1951 holiday season. (Top right) The scarce 1972 reissue of *A Partridge Family Christmas Card* has the formerly detached Christmas card as part of the front cover artwork. The 1971 version, with an all-green front cover, is more common. (Bottom left) A 1980s reissue of Pavarotti's *O Holy Night*, which was first released in 1976. The original has wider lettering and no box around the London logo at top right. (Bottom right) A promo-only release, this 1987 Buster Poindexter release, with "Hot Hot Hot" on the B-side, is quite scarce.

Label, Number		Title (A Side/B Side)	Year	VG	VG+	NM
PORTER TWIN DISC MUSIC BOX, THE						
Albums						
Porter 103		Music Box Nutcracker Suite and More Christmas Favorites	1984	3.00	6.00	12.00
POSITIVE FORCE						
45s						
SGM 1102		Reindeer Rock/'Twas A Night Long Ago	1986	—	2.50	5.00
POWELL, GARY						
45s						
PSP 3981		Christmas Again/On Christmas Day	19??	—	2.00	4.00
POWELL, JANE						
On Various-Artists Collections						
Reminder Spot		For Christmas Seals...A Matter of Life and Breath (Decca Custom Style E)				
POWELL, TINY						
45s						
TCB 400		Christmas Time Again/(B-side unknown)	19??	2.00	4.00	8.00
PRAISE SINGERS, THE						
Albums						
Maranatha MM 0071		Emmanuel — A Christmas Praise Album	1980	2.50	5.00	10.00
PRANCERS, THE						
45s						
Guaranteed 204		Rudolph the Red-Nosed Reindeer/Short Short'nin'	1959	3.75	7.50	15.00
PRATT, DAVE, AND THE SEX MACHINE BAND						
45s						
Dave Pratt 6210		Red Christmas/Anti-Jackson Rap	1984	—	3.00	6.00
PRECISIONS, THE						
45s						
Rayna 1001		White Christmas/Silent Night	19??	2.00	4.00	8.00
PRELUDE						
45s						
Island IXPI 1	DJ	Christmas Message (same on both sides)	197?	2.50	5.00	10.00
PREMICE, JOSEPHINE						
45s						
GNP Crescendo 117		Mommy, Give Me What You Give To Santa/The Little Christmas Tree	1956	3.00	6.00	12.00
PRESLEY, ELVIS						
45s						
RCA 447-0647		Blue Christmas/Santa Claus Is Back in Town	1977	—	2.00	4.00
RCA 447-0647	PS	Blue Christmas/Santa Claus Is Back in Town	1977	2.50	5.00	10.00
— *Does not mention "Gold Standard Series" on sleeve*						
RCA 447-0681		If Every Day Was Like Christmas/How Would You Like to Be	1977	—	2.00	4.00
RCA PB-14237		Merry Christmas Baby/Santa Claus Is Back in Town	1985	3.75	7.50	15.00
— *"Elvis 50th Anniversary" label*						
RCA PB-14237		Merry Christmas Baby/Santa Claus Is Back in Town	1985	3.75	7.50	15.00
— *Green vinyl*						
RCA PB-14237		Merry Christmas Baby/Santa Claus Is Back in Town	1985	—	2.50	5.00
— *Normal black RCA label*						
RCA PB-14237	PS	Merry Christmas Baby/Santa Claus Is Back in Town	1985	3.00	6.00	12.00
RCA 62403		Blue Christmas/Love Me Tender	1992	—	2.50	5.00
RCA 62403	PS	Blue Christmas/Love Me Tender	1992	—	2.50	5.00
— *Generic white sleeve with "Elvis — The King of Rock 'n' Roll" sticker*						
RCA 62411		Silver Bells (Unreleased Version)/Silver Bells	1993	—	2.50	5.00
RCA Victor 47-8950		If Every Day Was Like Christmas/How Would You Like to Be	1966	5.00	10.00	20.00
RCA Victor 47-8950	PS	If Every Day Was Like Christmas/How Would You Like to Be	1966	10.00	20.00	40.00
RCA Victor 74-0572		Merry Christmas Baby/O Come All Ye Faithful	1971	3.75	7.50	15.00
RCA Victor 74-0572	PS	Merry Christmas Baby/O Come All Ye Faithful	1971	10.00	20.00	40.00
RCA Victor 447-0647		Blue Christmas/Santa Claus Is Back in Town	1965	3.00	6.00	12.00
— *Black label, dog on side*						

Label, Number		Title (A Side/B Side)	Year	VG	VG+	NM
RCA Victor 447-0647	PS	Blue Christmas/Santa Claus Is Back in Town	1965	7.50	15.00	30.00
— Has "Gold Standard Series" on sleeve						
RCA Victor 447-0647		Blue Christmas/Santa Claus Is Back in Town	1969	6.25	12.50	25.00
— Orange label						
RCA Victor 447-0647		Blue Christmas/Santa Claus Is Back in Town	1970	2.00	4.00	8.00
— Red label						
RCA Victor 447-0681		If Every Day Was Like Christmas/How Would You Like to Be	1972	2.00	4.00	8.00
RCA Victor 447-0720		Blue Christmas/Wooden Heart	1964	3.75	7.50	15.00
RCA Victor 447-0720	PS	Blue Christmas/Wooden Heart	1964	15.00	30.00	60.00
RCA Victor HO7W-0808	DJ	Blue Christmas (same on both sides)	1957	375.00	750.00	1,500.

7-Inch Extended Plays

Label, Number		Title (A Side/B Side)	Year	VG	VG+	NM
RCA Victor EPA-4108		Santa Bring My Baby Back (To Me)/Blue Christmas// Santa Claus Is Back in Town/I'll Be Home for Christmas	1957	10.00	20.00	40.00
— Black label, dog on top						
RCA Victor EPA-4108		Santa Bring My Baby Back (To Me)/Blue Christmas// Santa Claus Is Back in Town/I'll Be Home for Christmas	1965	7.50	15.00	30.00
— Black label, dog on left						
RCA Victor EPA-4108		Santa Bring My Baby Back (To Me)/Blue Christmas// Santa Claus Is Back in Town/I'll Be Home for Christmas	1969	20.00	40.00	80.00
— Orange label						
RCA Victor EPA-4108	PS	Elvis Sings Christmas Songs	1957	10.00	20.00	40.00
RCA Victor EPA-4340		White Christmas/Here Comes Santa Claus// Oh Little Town of Bethlehem/Silent Night	1958	17.50	35.00	70.00
— Black label, dog on top						
RCA Victor EPA-4340		White Christmas/Here Comes Santa Claus// Oh Little Town of Bethlehem/Silent Night	1965	10.00	20.00	40.00
— Black label, dog on left						
RCA Victor EPA-4340		White Christmas/Here Comes Santa Claus// Oh Little Town of Bethlehem/Silent Night	1969	10.00	40.00	80.00
— Orange label						
RCA Victor EPA-4340	PS	Christmas with Elvis	1958	20.00	40.00	80.00
— With copyright notice and "Printed in U.S.A." at lower right						
RCA Victor EPA-4340	PS	Christmas with Elvis	1965	10.00	20.00	40.00
— Without copyright notice and "Printed in U.S.A." at lower right						

Albums

Label, Number		Title (A Side/B Side)	Year	VG	VG+	NM
Pickwick CAL-2428	M	Elvis' Christmas Album	1975	3.00	6.00	12.00
— Same contents as RCA Camden LP; no Christmas trim on border						
Pickwick CAL-2428	M	Elvis' Christmas Album	1976	2.50	5.00	10.00
— Same as above, but with Christmas trim on cover border						
RCA Camden CAL-2428	M	Elvis' Christmas Album	1970	6.25	12.50	25.00
— Blue label, non-flexible vinyl						
RCA Camden CAL-2428	M	Elvis' Christmas Album	1971	3.00	6.00	12.00
— Blue label, flexible vinyl						
RCA Special Products DML5-0263 (5)		The Elvis Story	1977	15.00	30.00	60.00
— Available via mail order from Candelite Music. Contains one Christmas song: Blue Christmas						
RCA Special Products DPL5-0347 (5)		Memories of Elvis (A Lasting Tribute to the King of Rock 'n' Roll)	1978	18.75	37.50	75.00
— Available via mail-order from Candelite Music. Contains one Christmas song: If Everyday Was Like Christmas						
RCA Special Products	P DVM1-0704	Elvis (One Night with You)	1984	10.00	20.00	40.00
— Available only through the HBO cable channel. Contains one Christmas song: Blue Christmas						
RCA Special Products CAL-2428	M	Elvis' Christmas Album	1986	3.75	7.50	15.00
— Same contents as Pickwick LP; reissue for The Special Music Company						
RCA Victor LOC-1035	M	Elvis' Christmas Album	1957	150.00	300.00	600.00
— Gatefold cover; title printed in gold on LP spine; includes bound-in booklet but not sticker						
RCA Victor LOC-1035	M	Elvis' Christmas Album	1957	175.00	350.00	700.00
— Gatefold cover; title printed in silver on LP spine; includes bound-in booklet but not sticker						
RCA Victor LOC-1035	M	Elvis' Christmas Album	1957	7,500.	11,250.	15,000.
— Red vinyl; unique						
RCA Victor LOC-1035	M	Elvis' Christmas Album Sticker	1957	37.50	75.00	150.00
— Gold sticker with "To_____" and "From_____" blanks						
RCA Victor CPL1-1349	P	A Legendary Performer, Volume 2	1976	5.00	10.00	20.00
— With custom black and gold label, special innersleeve and booklet. Contains one Christmas song: Blue Christmas						
RCA Victor ANL1-1936		Elvis Sings the Wonderful World of Christmas	1975	3.75	7.50	15.00
— New number; same contents as LSP-4579. Orange label.						
RCA Victor ANL1-1936		Elvis Sings the Wonderful World of Christmas	1976	3.00	6.00	12.00
— Tan label						
RCA Victor ANL1-1936		Elvis Sings the Wonderful World of Christmas	1977	2.50	5.00	10.00
— Black label, dog near top						
RCA Victor LPM-1951	M	Elvis' Christmas Album	1958	25.00	50.00	100.00
— Same contents as LOC-1035, but with non-gatefold blue cover; "Long Play" at bottom of label						

Label, Number		Title (A Side/B Side)	Year	VG	VG+	NM
RCA Victor LPM-1951	M	Elvis' Christmas Album	1963	12.50	25.00	50.00
— Same as above; "Mono" at bottom of label: "RE" on lower left front cover (photos on back were altered)						
RCA Victor LPM-1951	M	Elvis' Christmas Album	1964	10.00	20.00	40.00
— Same as above; "Monaural" at bottom of label; "RE" on lower left front cover						
RCA Victor LSP-1951(e)	R	Elvis' Christmas Album	1964	12.50	25.00	50.00
— Black label, dog on top; "Stereo Electronically Reprocessed" at bottom of label						
RCA Victor LSP-1951(e)	R	Elvis' Christmas Album	1968	7.50	15.00	30.00
— Orange label, non-flexible vinyl						
RCA Victor CPL8-3699	(8)	Elvis Aron Presley	1980	25.00	50.00	100.00
— Box set; contains one Christmas song: Blue Christmas						
RCA Victor AYM1-3894	P	Elvis (NBC-TV Special)	1981	2.00	4.00	8.00
— "Best Buy" series; new prefix and number						
RCA Victor LPM-4088	P	Elvis (NBC-TV Special)	1968	6.25	12.50	25.00
— Orange label, non-flexible vinyl. Contains one Christmas song: Blue Christmas						
RCA Victor LPM-4088	P	Elvis (NBC-TV Special)	1971	3.75	7.50	15.00
— Same as above, except orange label, flexible vinyl						
RCA Victor LPM-4088	P	Elvis (NBC-TV Special)	1975	7.50	15.00	30.00
— Same as above, except tan label						
RCA Victor LPM-4088	P	Elvis (NBC-TV Special)	1976	3.00	6.00	12.00
— Same as above, except black label, dog near top						
RCA Victor AFM1-4088	P	Elvis (NBC-TV Special)	1977	2.50	5.00	10.00
— Reissue with new prefix						
RCA Victor CPL1-4395		Memories of Christmas	1982	3.75	7.50	15.00
— With 1982-83 calendar (deduct 1/3 if missing)						
RCA Victor LSP-4579		Elvis Sings the Wonderful World of Christmas	1971	7.50	15.00	30.00
— Orange label. Bonus postcard is priced separately						
RCA Victor LSP-4579		Elvis Sings the Wonderful World of Christmas Postcard	1971	5.00	10.00	20.00
RCA Victor CPM6-5172	(6)	A Golden Celebration	1984	20.00	40.00	80.00
— Contains one Christmas song: Blue Christmas						
RCA Victor AFL1-5418		Reconsider Baby	1985	3.00	6.00	12.00
— All copies on blue vinyl. Contains one Christmas song: Merry Christmas Baby						
RCA Victor AFM1-5486	M	Elvis' Christmas Album	1985	3.00	6.00	12.00
— Same as LOC-1035; green vinyl with booklet						
RCA Victor AFM1-5486	M	Elvis' Christmas Album	1985	3.75	7.50	15.00
— Same as LOC-1035; black vinyl with booklet						
RCA Victor UNRM-5697/8	DJ	Special Christmas Programming	1967	200.00	400.00	800.00
— White label promo. Add 25% for script.						
Reader's Digest 010/A	(7)	His Greatest Hits	1983	20.00	40.00	80.00
— White box. Contains one Christmas song: Blue Christmas						
Reader's Digest 010/A	(7)	His Greatest Hits	1990	10.00	20.00	40.00
— Same as above, but with yellow box						
Reader's Digest RD10/A	(8)	His Greatest Hits	1979	100.00	200.00	400.00
— Contains one Christmas song: Blue Christmas						

On Various-Artists Collections

Blue Christmas	Billboard Greatest Christmas Hits, 1955-Present (Rhino R1 70636)
	Blue Christmas (Welk Music Group WM-3002)
	Country Christmas (Time-Life STL-109)
	Happy Holidays, Vol. 20 (RCA Special Products DPL1-0713)
	October Christmas Sampler 59-40-41 (RCA Victor SPS-33-54)
	Time-Life Treasury of Christmas, The, Volume Two (Time-Life STL-108)
Here Comes Santa Claus	Brightest Stars of Christmas, The (RCA Special Products DPL1-0086)
	Time-Life Treasury of Christmas, The (Time-Life STL-108)
I'll Be Home for Christmas	Celebrate the Season with Tupperware (RCA Special Products DPL1-0803)
	Christmas Programming from RCA Victor (RCA Victor SP-33-66)
	Country Christmas (Time-Life STL-109)
	Family Christmas Collection, The (Time-Life STL-131)
If Every Day Was Like Christmas	Country Christmas (Time-Life STL-109)
	Family Christmas Collection, The (Time-Life STL-131)
	Happy Holidays, Volume 18 (RCA Special Products DPL1-0608)
	Stars of Christmas, The (RCA Special Products DPL1-0842)
	Time-Life Treasury of Christmas, The (Time-Life STL-107)
O Come All Ye Faithful	Mistletoe and Memories (RCA 8372-1-R)
Silver Bells	Best of Christmas, The (RCA Victor CPL1-7013)
	Christmas Treasury of Classics from Avon, A (RCA Special Products DPL1-0716)
	Country Christmas, A, Volume 2 (RCA AYL1-4809)
	Happy Holidays, Vol. 21 (RCA Special Products DPL1-0739)
White Christmas	Family Christmas Collection, The (Time-Life STL-131)

PRESTON, JOHNNY
45s

Label, Number	Title (A Side/B Side)	Year	VG	VG+	NM
Mercury 71728	New Baby for Christmas/(I Want a) Rock and Roll Guitar	1960	5.00	10.00	20.00

Label, Number		Title (A Side/B Side)	Year	VG	VG+	NM
PRETENDERS						
45s						
Sire 29444		Middle of the Road/2000 Miles	1983	—	—	3.00
— A-side is not a Christmas song						
Sire 29444	PS	Middle of the Road/2000 Miles	1983	—	—	3.00
WEA/Real ARE 20		2000 Miles/Fast Or Slow (The Law's The Law)	1983	—	2.50	5.00
WEA/Real ARE 20	PS	2000 Miles/Fast Or Slow (The Law's The Law)	1983	—	2.50	5.00
— Above record and sleeve are U.K. imports						
Albums						
Sire 23980		Learning to Crawl	1983	2.50	5.00	10.00
— Contains one Christmas song: 2000 Miles						
Sire 23980	DJ	Learning to Crawl	1983	3.00	6.00	12.00
— Promo-only Quiex II pressing; otherwise, same as above						
Sire 25664		The Singles	1987	2.50	5.00	10.00
— Contains one Christmas song: 2000 Miles						
Sire R 133248		The Singles	1987	3.00	6.00	12.00
— BMG Direct Marketing edition; otherwise, same as 25664						
On Various-Artists Collections						
Have Yourself a Merry Little Christmas		Very Special Christmas, A (A&M SP-3911)				

PREVIN, ANDRE
45s

Label, Number		Title (A Side/B Side)	Year	VG	VG+	NM
Columbia JZSP 55071/0	DJ	God Rest Ye Merry, Gentlemen/Let No Walls Divide	1961	3.00	6.00	12.00
— B-side by Doris Day						

On Various-Artists Collections

God Rest Ye Merry, Gentlemen	Great Songs of Christmas, The, Album Two (Columbia Special Products XTV 86100/1)
	Very Merry Christmas, A (Columbia Special Products CSS 563)
Hark! The Herald Angels Sing	Great Songs of Christmas, The, Album Four (Columbia Special Products CSP 155M)
Medley: The Holly and the Ivy/We Wish	Great Songs of Christmas, The, Album Three (Columbia Special Products CSP 117)
You a Merry Christmas	
O Little Town of Bethlehem	Firestone Presents Your Favorite Christmas Music, Volume 5 (Firestone MLP 7012)
	Time-Life Treasury of Christmas, The (Time-Life STL-107)
What Child Is This	Time-Life Treasury of Christmas, The (Time-Life STL-107)

PRICE, DOROTHY
45s

Label, Number	Title (A Side/B Side)	Year	VG	VG+	NM
Forever 1863	The Night Before Christmas/Favorite Christmas Carols	19??	—	2.50	5.00

PRICE, LEONTYNE
Albums

Label, Number	Title (A Side/B Side)	Year	VG	VG+	NM
London 410 198-1	Noel! Noel!	1983	2.50	5.00	10.00
London OS 25280	A Christmas Offering	1961	6.25	12.50	25.00

On Various-Artists Collections

Ave Maria	Christmas in California (RCA Victor PRS-276)
	Christmas in New York Volume 2 (RCA Victor PRS-270)
	Old Fashioned Christmas, An (Reader's Digest RDA 216-A)
Ave Maria (Bach-Gounod)	Christmastime in Carol and Song (RCA PRS-289)
Ave Maria (Schubert)	Christmastime in Carol and Song (RCA PRM-271)
	Happy Holidays, Volume 13 (RCA Special Products DPL1-0319)
	Henry Mancini Selects Great Songs of Christmas (RCA Special Products DPL1-0148)
	Time-Life Treasury of Christmas, The (Time-Life STL-107)
	Very Merry Christmas, A, Volume VI (RCA Special Products PRS-427)
He Shall Feed His Flock	Firestone Presents Your Christmas Favorites, Volume 7 (Firestone CSLP 7015)
I Wonder As I Wander	Christmastime in Carol and Song (RCA PRS-289)
	Happy Holidays, Vol. 20 (RCA Special Products DPL1-0713)
O Holy Night	Firestone Presents Your Christmas Favorites, Volume 7 (Firestone CSLP 7015)

PRICE, LEONTYNE; NICOLAI GEDDA; VIENNA CHOIR BOYS; FIRESTONE CHORUS
On Various-Artists Collections

Silent Night	Firestone Presents Your Christmas Favorites, Volume 7 (Firestone CSLP 7015)

PRICE, LLOYD
45s

Label, Number	Title (A Side/B Side)	Year	VG	VG+	NM
Double-L 728	Merry Christmas Mama/Auld Lang Syne	1963	3.00	6.00	12.00

PRICE, RAY
45s

Label, Number	Title (A Side/B Side)	Year	VG	VG+	NM
Columbia 45046	Jingle Bells/Happy Birthday to You, Our Lord	1969	—	3.00	6.00
Step One 381	For Christmas/With Christmas Near	1991	—	—	3.00
Albums					
Columbia CS 9861	Ray Price's Christmas Album	1969	3.00	6.00	12.00

Label, Number		Title (A Side/B Side)	Year	VG	VG+	NM

On Various-Artists Collections

Amazing Grace	Wonderful World of Christmas, The, Album Two (Capitol Special Markets SL-8025)
God Rest Ye Merry, Gentlemen	Sounds of Christmas (Columbia Special Products P 12474)
It Came Upon the Midnight Clear	Joy of Christmas, The, Featuring Marty Robbins and His Friends (Columbia Special Products C 11087)
Jingle Bells	Christmas Greetings, Vol. 4 (Columbia Special Products P 11987)
	Down-Home Country Christmas, A (Columbia Special Products P 14992)
Little Drummer Boy	Country Style Christmas, A (Columbia Musical Treasury 3P 6316)
	Nashville's Greatest Christmas Hits, Volume II (Columbia PC 44413)
Lord's Prayer, The	Country Christmas Favorites (Columbia Special Products C 10876)
	We Wish You a Country Christmas (Columbia Special Products P 14991)
O Come, All Ye Faithful	Country Style Christmas, A (Columbia Musical Treasury 3P 6316)
O Little Town of Bethlehem	Nashville's Greatest Christmas Hits (Columbia PC 44412)
Silent Night, Holy Night	Merry Christmas (Columbia Musical Treasury 3P 6306)

PRIDE, CHARLEY
45s

Label, Number		Title (A Side/B Side)	Year	VG	VG+	NM
RCA PB-13359		Let It Snow, Let It Snow, Let It Snow/Peace on Earth	1982	—	2.00	4.00
— B-side by Razzy Bailey						
RCA PB-13667		Let It Snow, Let It Snow, Let It Snow/O Holy Night	1983	—	2.00	4.00
RCA Victor 47-9933		Christmas in My Home Town/Santa and the Kids	1970	2.00	4.00	8.00
RCA Victor 447-0935		Christmas In My Home Town/Santa and the Kids	1972	—	2.00	4.00
— Gold Standard Series						

Albums

RCA Victor ANL1-1934		Christmas in My Home Town	1976	2.00	4.00	8.00
— Reissue of LSP-4406						
RCA Victor LSP-4406		Christmas in My Home Town	1970	3.00	6.00	12.00

On Various-Artists Collections

Christmas and Love	Happy Holidays, Volume 13 (RCA Special Products DPL1-0319)
Christmas in My Home Town	Brightest Stars of Christmas, The (RCA Special Products DPL1-0086)
	Country Christmas (Time-Life STL-109)
	Time-Life Treasury of Christmas, The (Time-Life STL-107)
	Very Merry Christmas, A, Volume VII (RCA Special Products DPL1-0049)
Christmas Without Mary	Country Christmas, A, Volume 4 (RCA CPL1-7012)
Let It Snow, Let It Snow, Let It Snow	Country Christmas (Time-Life STL-109)
	Country Christmas, A (RCA CPL1-4396)
	Family Christmas Collection, The (Time-Life STL-131)
Out of the East	Christmas with Colonel Sanders (RCA Victor PRS-291)
	Old Fashioned Christmas, An (Reader's Digest RDA 216-A)
Santa and the Kids	Country Christmas, A, Volume 3 (RCA CPL1-5178)

PRIMA, LOUIS
45s

Label, Number		Title (A Side/B Side)	Year	VG	VG+	NM
Buena Vista 446		Jolly Holiday/Supercalifragilisticexpialidocious	1965	3.75	7.50	15.00
— With Gia Maione						
Buena Vista 454		Santa, How Come Your Eyes Are Green	1966	3.00	6.00	12.00
		When Last Year They Were Blue/Senor Santa Claus				
Columbia 39614		Shake Hands with Santa/Eleanor	1951	3.75	7.50	15.00

PRIME TIME
On Various-Artists Collections

All I Need for Christmas Is Your Love	Total Experience Christmas, A (Total Experience TEL8-5707)

PRINCE
12-Inch Singles

Label, Number		Title (A Side/B Side)	Year	VG	VG+	NM
Warner Bros. 20291		I Would Die 4 U/Another Lonely Christmas	1984	3.75	7.50	15.00
— Oversized picture label with die-cut picture cover						

45s

Warner Bros. 29121		I Would Die 4 U/Another Lonely Christmas	1984	—	2.00	4.00
Warner Bros. 29121	PS	I Would Die 4 U/Another Lonely Christmas	1984	—	2.00	4.00

PRINCE, JAMES
45s

Z 3		Christmas Time/Too Late for Christmas	1963	2.00	4.00	8.00

PRINE, JOHN
45s

Oh Boy 001		I Saw Mommy Kissing Santa Claus/Silver Bells	198?	2.50	5.00	10.00
— Red vinyl						
Oh Boy 001	PS	I Saw Mommy Kissing Santa Claus/Silver Bells	198?	3.00	6.00	12.00

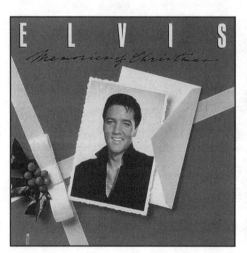

(Top left) Elvis Presley's Christmas music has been repackaged in many forms over the years. This 1970 release, the third collection to be called *Elvis' Christmas Album,* marked the first LP appearance of "If Every Day Was Like Christmas." (Top right) An all-new Elvis holiday album, *Elvis Sings the Wonderful World of Christmas,* greeted fans a year later. (Bottom left) *Memories of Christmas,* a posthumous release, contained, among other things, the full-length, nearly eight-minute-long version of "Merry Christmas Baby." (Bottom right) "Another Lonely Christmas," one the many non-LP B-side Prince released, was hidden on the flip of "I Would Die 4 U."

Label, Number		Title (A Side/B Side)	Year	VG	VG+	NM

PRITCHARD FAMILY WITH THE AAA CHOIR
45s

Label, Number		Title (A Side/B Side)	Year	VG	VG+	NM
Starr 42777		Noisy World Be Quiet/(Instrumental)	19??	—	2.00	4.00

PROMENADERS, THE
45s

Label, Number		Title (A Side/B Side)	Year	VG	VG+	NM
Promenade 1024		I Saw Mommy Kissing Santa Claus/White Christmas	198?	—	—	3.00
— B-side by Suzy Williams						

PROSEN, SID
45s

Label, Number		Title (A Side/B Side)	Year	VG	VG+	NM
Big 666		If I Were Really Santa Claus/(Instrumental)	19??	—	2.00	4.00

PROVINE, DOROTHY
On Various-Artists Collections

Label, Number		Title (A Side/B Side)	Year	VG	VG+	NM
Let It Snow, Let It Snow, Let It Snow		We Wish You a Merry Christmas (Warner Bros. W 1337)				

PUCKETT, GARY
On Various-Artists Collections

Label, Number		Title (A Side/B Side)	Year	VG	VG+	NM
O Holy Night		Very Merry Christmas, A, Volume IV (Columbia Special Products CSS 1464)				

PUNSTERS, THE
7-Inch Extended Plays

Label, Number		Title (A Side/B Side)	Year	VG	VG+	NM
Rosebud 001	PS	Boardwalk Santa/In Her Disarray//We're Drunk Again/Oh!Sarah	1980	2.00	4.00	8.00
Rosebud 001		Boardwalk Santa/In Her Disarray//We're Drunk Again/Oh!Sarah	1980	2.00	4.00	8.00

PURE GOLD
45s

Label, Number		Title (A Side/B Side)	Year	VG	VG+	NM
Green Dolphin 11489		(Please Chase My) Christmas Blues/I'm Your Santa Claus, Baby	1989	—	2.50	5.00

PUREZONE
45s

Label, Number		Title (A Side/B Side)	Year	VG	VG+	NM
Paw Print 5182		Santa Claus/Winter Dawn	19??	—	2.50	5.00

PUTNAM, MARK
45s

Label, Number		Title (A Side/B Side)	Year	VG	VG+	NM
Avocado 44	PS	On Christmas Day/(Instrumental)	19??	—	2.50	5.00
Avocado 44		On Christmas Day/(Instrumental)	19??	—	2.50	5.00

Q

QUACKERS, THE
45s

Label, Number		Title (A Side/B Side)	Year	VG	VG+	NM
Step One 396		Jolly Old Saint Nicholas/Up On The Housetop	1992	—	2.50	5.00

QUALEY, DAVID
On Various-Artists Collections

Label, Number		Title (A Side/B Side)	Year	VG	VG+	NM
Jesu, Joy of Man's Desiring		Winter's Solstice, A (Windham Hill WH-1045)				

QUE, JOHNNIE
45s

Label, Number		Title (A Side/B Side)	Year	VG	VG+	NM
Rhino 099		Rockabilly Christmas/(Instrumental)	198?	—	2.50	5.00
Rhino 099	PS	Rockabilly Christmas/(Instrumental)	198?	—	2.50	5.00

QUEEN
12-Inch Singles

Label, Number		Title (A Side/B Side)	Year	VG	VG+	NM
EMI 12QUEEN 5		Thank God It's Christmas// Man on the Prowl/Keep Passing the Open Windows	1984	6.25	12.50	25.00
— U.K. import						

45s

Label, Number		Title (A Side/B Side)	Year	VG	VG+	NM
EMI QUEEN 5		Thank God It's Christmas// Man on the Prowl/Keep Passing the Open Windows	1984	2.50	5.00	10.00

Label, Number		Title (A Side/B Side)	Year	VG	VG+	NM
EMI QUEEN 5	PS	Thank God It's Christmas// Man on the Prowl/Keep Passing the Open Windows	1984	2.50	5.00	10.00
— Above record and sleeve are U.K. imports						
Parlophone QUEENDJ 22		A Winter's Tale/Thank God It's Christmas	1995	10.00	20.00	40.00
— U.K. import; jukebox-only pressing						
On Various-Artists Collections						
Thank God It's Christmas		Christmas Rock Album, The (Priority SL 9465)				

QUICK TONES
45s
Pryor Platters 100		The Elf Party/Writer's Resolution	19??	—	2.50	5.00

QUINN, CARMEL
45s
Columbia 40611		The Story of the Magi/Santa's Coming	1955	3.00	6.00	12.00
GP 554	PS	The Story of the Magi/The Solitary Life	19??	—	2.00	4.00

QUINTO SISTERS, THE
45s
Columbia 43166		A Holly Jolly Christmas/Confidence	1964	2.50	5.00	10.00

R

R.E.M.
45s
Fan Club REM 92		Where's Captain Kirk?/Toyland	1992	3.75	7.50	15.00
Fan Club REM 92	PS	Where's Captain Kirk?/Toyland	1992	3.75	7.50	15.00
— Any of three variations of a gray sleeve						
Fan Club REM 92	PS	Where's Captain Kirk?/Toyland	1992	3.75	7.50	15.00
— White sleeve						
Fan Club REM 94		Sex Bomb/Christmas in Tunisia	1994	2.50	5.00	10.00
Fan Club REM 94	PS	Sex Bomb/Christmas in Tunisia	1994	3.75	7.50	15.00
— Picture sleeve also included a magnet, stamps and sticker						
Fan Club REM 1993		Silver Bells/Christmas Time Is Here	1993	3.75	7.50	15.00
Fan Club REM 1993	PS	Silver Bells/Christmas Time Is Here	1993	3.75	7.50	15.00
Fan Club U-23518M		Parade of the Wooden Soldiers/See No Evil	1988	12.50	25.00	50.00
— Green vinyl						
Fan Club U-23518M	PS	Parade of the Wooden Soldiers/See No Evil	1988	12.50	25.00	50.00
Fan Club 122589		Good King Wenceslas/Academy Fight Song	1989	12.50	25.00	50.00
Fan Club 122589	PS	Good King Wenceslas/Academy Fight Song	1989	12.50	25.00	50.00
— Fold-out poster sleeve						
Fan Club 122590		Ghost Reindeer in the Sky/Summertime	1990	7.50	15.00	30.00
Fan Club 122590	PS	Ghost Reindeer in the Sky/Summertime	1990	7.50	15.00	30.00
Fan Club 122591		Baby Baby/Christmas Griping	1991	7.50	15.00	30.00
Fan Club 122591	PS	Baby Baby/Christmas Griping	1991	7.50	15.00	30.00
On Various-Artists Collections						
Deck the Halls		Winter Warnerland (Warner Bros. PRO-A-3328)				

RABBITT, EDDIE
45s
Capitol Nashville S7-19347		Rockin' Around the Christmas Tree/ Have Yourself a Merry Little Christmas	1996	—	—	3.00

On Various-Artists Collections
Have Yourself a Merry Little Christmas	Christmas for the 90's, Volume 2 (Capitol Nashville 1P 8118)
Rockin' Around the Christmas Tree	Christmas for the 90's, Volume 1 (Capitol Nashville 1P 8117)

RADIO CITY MUSIC HALL ORCHESTRA
Albums
Continental CR-1004		Merry Christmas New York from the Radio City Music Hall	1972	3.00	6.00	12.00
RCA Victor LOP-1010	M	Christmas Holidays at Radio City Music Hall	1958	5.00	10.00	20.00
— With gatefold and 10-page bound-in booklet with fold-open poster of the Rockettes						
RCA Victor LSO-1010	S	Christmas Holidays at Radio City Music Hall	1958	10.00	20.00	40.00
— Same as above, but in "Living Stereo"						

Label, Number	Title (A Side/B Side)	Year	VG	VG+	NM
On Various-Artists Collections					
Medley: Hark! The Herald Angels Sing/Adeste Fideles	Gift from Your RCA Victor Record Dealer, A (RCA Victor SP-45-35)				
Nativity, The (Medley)	For a Musical Merry Christmas, Vol. Two (RCA Victor PRM 189)				
	Merry Christmas (RCA Victor PRM-168)				
	Happy Holidays, Vol. III (RCA Victor PRS-255)				
	60 Christmas Classics (Sessions DVL2-0723)				

RADUDES, THE
45s

Label, Number	Title (A Side/B Side)	Year	VG	VG+	NM
Radude 101	Christmas in Malibu/(Instrumental)	19??	3.00	6.00	12.00

RAE, RONIE
45s

Label, Number	Title (A Side/B Side)	Year	VG	VG+	NM
Goody Bear 101	Santa's Little Helper/King Of The Wild Reindeer	19??	—	2.00	4.00

RAFEL'S SON
45s

Label, Number	Title (A Side/B Side)	Year	VG	VG+	NM
QCA 440	If Flowers Bloomed On Christmas Day/Rudolph Pouts	1977	—	2.50	5.00

RAFFI
Albums

Label, Number	Title (A Side/B Side)	Year	VG	VG+	NM
MCA 10043	Raffi's Christmas Album	1990	3.75	7.50	15.00
— *Reissue of Shoreline LP*					
Shoreline SL-0226	Raffi's Christmas Album	1983	2.50	5.00	10.00
Shoreline R 154088	Raffi's Christmas Album	198?	3.75	7.50	15.00
— *Same as above, but BMG Direct Marketing edition*					

RAIN DOLLS, THE
12-Inch Singles

Label, Number	Title (A Side/B Side)	Year	VG	VG+	NM
AVI 242	Disco Santa Claus/Santa's Theme	1978	2.50	5.00	10.00
45s					
AVI 241	Disco Santa Claus/Santa's Theme	1978	—	2.50	5.00

RAINBOWS, THE
45s

Label, Number	Title (A Side/B Side)	Year	VG	VG+	NM
Ronnie 202	The Christmas Song/Love Me	19??	2.50	5.00	10.00
— *B-side by the Mellow Moods*					

RAINSFORD, WILLIE
45s

Label, Number		Title (A Side/B Side)	Year	VG	VG+	NM
Candy 1035	DJ	Christmas Shoes/There'll Be Rain, Dear This Christmas	197?	—	2.00	4.00

RAINWATER, MARVIN
45s

Label, Number	Title (A Side/B Side)	Year	VG	VG+	NM
Ralph Himself 17094	Little Ralph The Robot (Poem)/Little Ralph The Robot (Song)	19??	—	2.00	4.00

RALEY, HUGH WILSON
45s

Label, Number	Title (A Side/B Side)	Year	VG	VG+	NM
NSD 254	Erin, The Excellent Elf/Let's Put Christ Back Into Christmas	1986	—	—	3.00

RALKE, DON
45s

Label, Number	Title (A Side/B Side)	Year	VG	VG+	NM
Stardisc 100	Keep Christmas In Your Heart/Crackerjack Christmas	19??	2.50	5.00	10.00
Young CJC-1	Crackerjack Christmas/Keep Christmas In Your Heart	19??	2.00	4.00	8.00

RALSTON, BOB
Albums

Label, Number		Title (A Side/B Side)	Year	VG	VG+	NM
RCA Camden CAL-994	M	Christmas Hymns and Carols	196?	3.00	6.00	12.00
RCA Camden CAS-994	S	Christmas Hymns and Carols	196?	3.75	7.50	15.00

RAMBLERS, THE
45s

Label, Number	Title (A Side/B Side)	Year	VG	VG+	NM
Almont 315	Surfin' Santa/Silly Little Boy	1964	6.25	12.50	25.00

Label, Number		Title (A Side/B Side)	Year	VG	VG+	NM
RAMONES, THE						
12-Inch Singles						
Beggars Banquet BEG 201T		Merry Christmas (I Don't Want to Fight Tonight) Extended/I Wanna Live	1987	5.00	10.00	20.00
— U.K. import						
45s						
Beggars Banquet BEG-201		Merry Christmas (I Don't Want to Fight Tonight)/I Wanna Live	1987	—	3.00	6.00
Beggars Banquet BEG-201	PS	Merry Christmas (I Don't Want to Fight Tonight)/I Wanna Live	1987	—	3.00	6.00
— Above record and sleeve are U.K. imports						
RAND, CHARLES						
Albums						
Premier XM-10	M	Christmas Organ in the Ken Griffin Style	196?	3.00	6.00	12.00
Premier XMS-10	S	Christmas Organ in the Ken Griffin Style	196?	3.75	7.50	15.00
— Same as above, but in stereo						
RANDALL, JOSH						
45s						
Texan 106		Christmas at Home/They'll Be Here (Before Mornin')	19??	—	2.00	4.00
RANDOLPH, BOOTS						
45s						
Monument 1176		Sleigh Ride/White Christmas	1969	2.00	4.00	8.00
Monument 1937		Sleigh Ride/White Christmas	1976	—	2.00	4.00
— Golden Series						
Monument 8632		Sleigh Ride/White Christmas	1974	—	2.50	5.00
7-Inch Extended Plays						
Monument SMN-361		Sleigh Ride/Rudolph The Red-Nosed Reindeer// White Christmas/I'll Be Home For Christmas	19??	3.00	6.00	12.00
Albums						
Monument SLP 18127		Boots and Stockings	1969	3.75	7.50	15.00
RANDOLPH, WILLIAM						
45s						
Holiday Hits 904		Silent Night/The First Noel	195?	3.00	6.00	12.00
RAT PACK, THE						
45s						
Raynard 8796		Frosty Rudolph With Bells/I Need You	19??	3.00	6.00	12.00
RATHBONE, BASIL						
On Various-Artists Collections						
Christmas Spirit, The		Stingiest Man in Town, The (Columbia CL 950)				
I Wear a Chain		Stingiest Man in Town, The (Columbia CL 950)				
Mankind Should Be My Business		Stingiest Man in Town, The (Columbia CL 950)				
RATHBONE, BASIL, AND JOHNNY DESMOND						
On Various-Artists Collections						
Humbug		Stingiest Man in Town, The (Columbia CL 950)				
RATHBONE, BASIL, AND ROBERT WRIGHT						
On Various-Artists Collections						
One Little Boy		Stingiest Man in Town, The (Columbia CL 950)				
Spirit Theme		Stingiest Man in Town, The (Columbia CL 950)				
RAVE-UPS, THE						
12-Inch Singles						
Epic EAS 1909		Respectfully King Of Rain//Train To Nowhere/ The Night Before Christmas (Hey Baby)	1989	2.50	5.00	10.00
RAVEN, EDDY						
45s						
Elektra 47233	DJ	Blue Christmas/White Christmas	1981	—	2.50	5.00
— B-side by Mel Tillis						
On Various-Artists Collections						
Blue Christmas		Christmas Tradition, A (Warner Bros. 25630)				
Santa Claus Is Coming for Christmas (Why Can't You)		Country Christmas, A, Volume 4 (RCA CPL1-7012)				

Label, Number		Title (A Side/B Side)	Year	VG	VG+	NM
Thank God for Kids		Christmas for the 90's, Volume 1 (Capitol Nashville 1P 8117)				
White Christmas		Christmas for the 90's, Volume 2 (Capitol Nashville 1P 8118)				

RAVENS, THE
45s

Label, Number		Title (A Side/B Side)	Year	VG	VG+	NM
Mercury 70505		White Christmas/Silent Night	1954	50.00	100.00	200.00
— Pink label						
Mercury 70505		White Christmas/Silent Night	1954	25.00	50.00	100.00
— Black label						
Savoy 1540		White Christmas/Silent Night	1958	5.00	10.00	20.00

RAVENSCROFT, THURL (UNCREDITED)
45s

Label, Number		Title (A Side/B Side)	Year	VG	VG+	NM
Mercury Nashville 852 110-7		You're a Mean One, Mr. Grinch (same on both sides)	1995	—	2.00	4.00
— Green vinyl						

On Various-Artists Collections

You're a Mean One, Mr. Grinch	How the Grinch Stole Christmas (Mercury Nashville 528 439-1)	

RAVERS, THE
45s

Label, Number		Title (A Side/B Side)	Year	VG	VG+	NM
Zombie/Ariola 7683		(It's Gonna Be a) Punk Rock Christmas/Silent Night	1977	2.00	4.00	8.00
Zombie/Ariola 7683	PS	(It's Gonna Be a) Punk Rock Christmas/Silent Night	1977	2.50	5.00	10.00

RAWLS, LOU
45s

Label, Number		Title (A Side/B Side)	Year	VG	VG+	NM
Capitol 2026		Little Drummer Boy/A Child with a Toy	1967	2.00	4.00	8.00
Capitol S7-18908		What Are You Doing New Year's Eve?/	1995	—	—	3.00
		Have Yourself a Merry Little Christmas				

Albums

Label, Number		Title (A Side/B Side)	Year	VG	VG+	NM
Capitol T 2790	M	Merry Christmas, Ho, Ho, Ho	1967	3.75	7.50	15.00
Capitol ST 2790	S	Merry Christmas, Ho, Ho, Ho	1967	3.00	6.00	12.00

On Various-Artists Collections

Christmas Song, The	Yule Struttin' — A Blue Note Christmas (Blue Note 1P 8119)
Have Yourself a Merry Little Christmas	Christmas Carousel (Capitol SQBE-94406)
	Christmas Songs, The (Capitol SLB-57074)
Little Drummer Boy	I'll Be Home for Christmas (Pickwick SPC-1009)
Santa Claus Is Comin' to Town	Magic of Christmas, The (Capitol SWBB-93810)

RAY AND CLOVER
45s

Label, Number		Title (A Side/B Side)	Year	VG	VG+	NM
Tim/Kerr 9370		Santa Claus Is Back In Town/I'm Mad At The Fat Man	1993	2.00	4.00	8.00
— B-side by Poison Idea; picture disc						

RAY, ANNITA
45s

Label, Number		Title (A Side/B Side)	Year	VG	VG+	NM
Rage 59-3		I Want You With Me Christmas/Take Off Like The Wind	19??	—	2.00	4.00

RAY, CHUCK, AND THE GANG
45s

Label, Number		Title (A Side/B Side)	Year	VG	VG+	NM
Intra State 27		Roses In December/Tinker Town	19??	—	2.50	5.00

RAYNOR, J.C. & DONNA JO
45s

Label, Number		Title (A Side/B Side)	Year	VG	VG+	NM
RTF 101		A Christmas Letter To Daddy/My Christmas Came Early	1977	—	2.00	4.00
RTF 101	PS	A Christmas Letter To Daddy/My Christmas Came Early	1977	—	2.00	4.00

RAYNOR, JIM
45s

Label, Number		Title (A Side/B Side)	Year	VG	VG+	NM
Caldwell 415		Thank You For Listening This Christmas/Christmas Medley	19??	—	3.00	6.00

RAYONE AND THE PENGUINS
45s

Label, Number		Title (A Side/B Side)	Year	VG	VG+	NM
Moonlight 1001		Willie The Penguin/(B-side unknown)	19??	—	2.50	5.00

RCA VICTOR SALON ORCHESTRA
45s

Label, Number		Title (A Side/B Side)	Year	VG	VG+	NM
RCA Victor 47-2974		Jingle Bells Fantasy/The Night Before Christmas	1949	5.00	10.00	20.00

Label, Number		Title (A Side/B Side)	Year	VG	VG+	NM
REAL PROS, THE						
45s						
Cinema 7352		The Santa Beat/Can't Help It	197?	—	2.50	5.00
REBA						
On Various-Artists Collections						
Whole World Is Colored with Love, The		On This Christmas Night (Songbird MCA-3184)				
REBROFF, IVAN						
Albums						
CBS Masterworks IM 38658		Christmas with Ivan Rebroff	1983	2.50	5.00	10.00
RECORD GUILD OF AMERICA, THE						
45s						
Record Guild 1003		Jingle Bells/Auld Lang Syne	19??	—	2.50	5.00
RECTOR, HANK						
45s						
Starlite 1133		Santa Be a Pal/A Picture of Christmas at Home	19??	2.50	5.00	10.00
RED AUNTS						
On Various-Artists Collections						
Little Drummer Bitch		Happy Birthday, Baby Jesus (Sympathy For The Record Industry SFTRI 271)				
RED CAR AND THE BLUE CAR, THE						
45s						
Virgin 1394		Home For Christmas Day/Home For Christmas Day (Karaoke Version)	1991	—	2.00	4.00
Virgin 1394	PS	Home For Christmas Day/Home For Christmas Day (Karaoke Version)	1991	—	2.00	4.00
RED HOT CHILI PEPPERS						
45s						
EMI S7-18210		Deck the Halls/Knock Me Down	1994	—	2.50	5.00
— *Red vinyl*						
RED RED MEAT						
45s						
Sub Pop 376		There's a Star Above the Manger Tonight/Welcome Christmas	1996	—	—	2.50
Sub Pop 376	PS	There's a Star Above the Manger Tonight/Welcome Christmas	1996	—	—	2.50
— *With insert*						
RED RIVER DAVE						
45s						
Decca 29680		The Night Before Christmas, Caramba/ When Davy Crockett Met San Antonio Rose	1955	3.75	7.50	15.00
TNT 1017		The Night Before Christmas, Caramba!/ When Davy Crockett Met the San Antonio Rose	1955	5.00	10.00	20.00
REDBONE, LEON						
Albums						
August AS 8890		Christmas Island	1988	3.75	7.50	15.00
REDDEN, CHUCK						
45s						
Deep South 716		Beneath Your Christmas Tree/I Remember New Year's Eve	1982	—	2.00	4.00
REDDING, OTIS						
Also see OTIS AND CARLA.						
45s						
Atco 6631		White Christmas/Merry Christmas, Baby	1968	2.50	5.00	10.00
Atco 7069		White Christmas/Merry Christmas, Baby	1976	—	2.50	5.00
Atco 7321		White Christmas/Merry Christmas, Baby	1980	—	2.00	4.00
Atco 99955		White Christmas/Merry Christmas, Baby	1982	—	2.00	4.00
On Various-Artists Collections						
Merry Christmas Baby		Jingle Bell Rock (Time-Life SRNR-XM)				

Label, Number		Title (A Side/B Side)	Year	VG	VG+	NM
REDMOND, JOHN						
45s						
Coastline 1		'Round The Crib at Christmas/Christmas Presents	19??	—	2.50	5.00
Coastline 1	PS	'Round The Crib at Christmas/Christmas Presents	19??	—	2.50	5.00
REDUCERS, THE						
45s						
Rave On (no #)		Nothing for Christmas/Auld Lang Syne	19??	—	2.00	4.00
Rave On (no #)	PS	Nothing for Christmas/Auld Lang Syne	19??	—	2.00	4.00
REED, JERRY						
45s						
RCA JK-13666	DJ	Christmas Time's a-Coming (same on both sides)	1983	—	2.00	4.00
RCA PB-13666		Christmas Time's a-Coming/The Best I Ever Had	1983	—	2.50	5.00
On Various-Artists Collections						
Christmas Time's a-Coming		Country Christmas, A, Volume 2 (RCA AYL1-4809)				
REED, JIMMY						
45s						
RRG 44001		Christmas Present Blues/Crying Blind	19??	2.00	4.00	8.00
REED, LOU						
On Various-Artists Collections						
Holiday I.D.		Winter Warnerland (Warner Bros. PRO-A-3328)				
REED, PAUL, AND CHORUS						
45s						
Columbia JZSP 76341/0	DJ	That Man Over There/The Big Clown Balloons	1963	2.00	4.00	8.00
— B-side by "Orchestra and Chorus"; both from the play "Here's Love"						
REED, ROSEY						
45s						
Say So 552		Santa Baby (same on both sides)	19??	—	2.00	4.00
Say So 552	PS	Santa Baby (same on both sides)	19??	—	2.00	4.00
REELS, THE						
12-Inch Singles						
Mercury 6235 014		You Got Soul/Neon Rainbow//The Bombs Dropped on Xmas/ According to My Heart/Band of Gold	1980	5.00	10.00	20.00
— European import						
REESE, DON						
45s						
Action XYZ-1		Muley The One Eared Mule (same on both sides)	19??	2.50	5.00	10.00
REESE, LLOYD, AND THE SOLID ROCK CHORUS						
45s						
Verve 10461		Sweet Little Lord Jesus/NiÒo Chiquito	1966	2.50	5.00	10.00
REEVES, DEL						
45s						
Koala 329		White Christmas/White Christmas (Second Version)	1980	—	2.00	4.00
United Artists 50115		Christmas Is Lonely/Sajo	1966	2.00	4.00	8.00
REEVES, DIANNE						
On Various-Artists Collections						
Merrier Christmas, A		Yule Struttin' — A Blue Note Christmas (Blue Note 1P 8119)				
REEVES, JACK						
45s						
Pacific Challenger 9701		The Meaning of Christmas/The Birth of Christ	19??	—	2.00	4.00
REEVES, JIM						
45s						
RCA Victor 47-8252		An Old Christmas Card/Señor Santa Claus	1963	3.75	7.50	15.00
RCA Victor 47-8252	PS	An Old Christmas Card/Señor Santa Claus	1963	10.00	20.00	40.00
RCA Victor 47-8719		Snowflake/Take My Hand, Precious Lord	1965	2.00	4.00	8.00

Label, Number		Title (A Side/B Side)	Year	VG	VG+	NM
RCA Victor 74-0859		Blue Christmas/Snowflake	1972	—	2.50	5.00
RCA Victor 447-0884		An Old Christmas Card/Señor Santa Claus	1972	—	2.00	4.00
— Gold Standard Series						
RCA Victor 447-0885		Snowflake/Take My Hand, Precious Lord	1972	—	2.00	4.00
— Gold Standard Series						
Albums						
RCA Victor ANL1-1927		Twelve Songs of Christmas	1976	2.00	4.00	8.00
— Reissue of LSP-2758						
RCA Victor LPM-2758	M	Twelve Songs of Christmas	1963	3.75	7.50	15.00
RCA Victor LSP-2758	S	Twelve Songs of Christmas	1963	5.00	10.00	20.00
On Various-Artists Collections						
Blue Christmas		Blue Christmas (Welk Music Group WM-3002)				
		Old Fashioned Christmas, An (Reader's Digest RDA 216-A)				
C-H-R-I-S-T-M-A-S		Time-Life Treasury of Christmas, The, Volume Two (Time-Life STL-108)				
Jingle Bells		For a Musical Merry Christmas, Vol. Two (RCA Victor PRM 189)				
		Happy Holidays, Volume 19 (RCA Special Products DPL1-0689)				
		Time-Life Treasury of Christmas, The (Time-Life STL-107)				
Mary's Little Boy Child		Happy Holidays, Volume IV (RCA Victor PRS-267)				
		Music to Trim Your Tree By (RCA Victor PRM 225)				
		Old Fashioned Christmas, An (Reader's Digest RDA 216-A)				
O Come, All Ye Faithful		Christmas Festival of Songs and Carols, Volume 2 (RCA Victor PRM-195)				
Old Christmas Card, An		Christmas Through the Years (Reader's Digest RDA-143)				
		Country Christmas (Time-Life STL-109)				
		Joyous Noel (Reader's Digest RDA-57A)				
		Time-Life Treasury of Christmas, The, Volume Two (Time-Life STL-108)				
Silent Night		Time-Life Treasury of Christmas, The (Time-Life STL-107)				
Silver Bells		Family Christmas Collection, The (Time-Life STL-131)				
White Christmas		Christmas Eve with Colonel Sanders (RCA Victor PRS-256)				

REEVES, RAY
45s

Label, Number		Title (A Side/B Side)	Year	VG	VG+	NM
Aquarian 608		A Little Boy's Christmas Prayer/(B-side unknown)	19??	2.00	4.00	8.00

REGALS, THE
45s

Label, Number		Title (A Side/B Side)	Year	VG	VG+	NM
MGM 11869		There'll Always Be a Christmas/ When You're Home with the Ones You Love	1954	10.00	20.00	40.00

REGAN, DENISE
45s

Label, Number		Title (A Side/B Side)	Year	VG	VG+	NM
Dee Gee 3005		A Date with Santa Claus/Hole in the Stocking	1965	5.00	10.00	20.00
Dee Gee 3005		A Date with Santa Claus/Hole in the Stocking	1965	2.50	5.00	10.00

REGAN, PHIL
45s

Label, Number		Title (A Side/B Side)	Year	VG	VG+	NM
RCA Victor 47-3936		Christmas Story/Leprechaun Lullaby	1950	3.75	7.50	15.00

REGAN, TOMMY
45s

Label, Number		Title (A Side/B Side)	Year	VG	VG+	NM
Tell Star 5001		Santa Twist/(B-side unknown)	1962	3.00	6.00	12.00

REGENCY CHOIR, THE
45s

Label, Number		Title (A Side/B Side)	Year	VG	VG+	NM
Columbia 43937		The Bells Of Christmas/Three Wise Men, Wise Men Three	1966	2.00	4.00	8.00
Columbia JZSP 116425/6	DJ	The Bells Of Christmas/Three Wise Men, Wise Men Three	1966	2.50	5.00	10.00
On Various-Artists Collections						
Jesus Garcia		Have a Happy Holiday (Columbia Special Products CSS 1432)				
O Come All Ye Faithful		It's Christmastime! (Columbia Special Products CSM 429)				
O Little Town of Bethlehem		It's Christmastime! (Columbia Special Products CSM 429)				
Silent Night		It's Christmastime! (Columbia Special Products CSM 429)				

REGOS, EUGENIA
45s

Label, Number		Title (A Side/B Side)	Year	VG	VG+	NM
Flair 1024		I'm Gonna Write a Letter to Santa Claus/ I Wanna Be a Hollywood Cowboy	1953	5.00	10.00	20.00

REIND DEARS, THE
45s

Label, Number		Title (A Side/B Side)	Year	VG	VG+	NM
Limp 013		Xmas (Is Going to Bring Me...)/White Christmas	1978	2.00	4.00	8.00
Limp 013	PS	Xmas (Is Going to Bring Me...)/White Christmas	1978	2.00	4.00	8.00

Label, Number		Title (A Side/B Side)	Year	VG	VG+	NM
RELLA, CINDY						
45s						
Drum Boy 112		Bring Me A Beatle for Christmas/Cla-wence	1964	3.00	6.00	12.00
RENO AND SMILEY						
45s						
King 5814		Christmas Reunion/The True Meaning Of Christmas	1963	2.00	4.00	8.00
Albums						
King 874	M	The True Meaning of Christmas	1963	25.00	50.00	100.00
RENO, JOHNNY, AND HIS SOLID SENDERS						
45s						
Miracle 812		Boogie Woogie Santa Claus/Blues Before Christmas	19??	2.50	5.00	10.00
RESER, HARRY						
On Various-Artists Collections						
Santa Claus Is Coming to Town		Stash Christmas Album, The (Stash 125)				
RESIDENTS, THE						
45s						
Ralph RR 7812		Santa Dog '78/Fire	1978	5.00	10.00	20.00
Ralph RR 7812	PS	Santa Dog '78/Fire	1978	5.00	10.00	20.00
RETA, ALITA & MARILYN						
45s						
CCP 1002		Santa Claus Junior/Pee Wee The Pink Pine Tree	1976	—	2.00	4.00
— B-side by the Pee Wee Children's Chorus						
REVERE, PAUL, AND THE RAIDERS						
45s						
Hitbound X-2		Jingle Bell Rock/Jingle Bells	1983	3.00	6.00	12.00
— B-side by Mike Love and Dean Torrence						
Hitbound X-2	PS	Jingle Bell Rock/Jingle Bells	1983	5.00	10.00	20.00
— B-side by Mike Love and Dean Torrence						
Albums						
Columbia CL 2755	M	A Christmas Present...And Past	1967	3.75	7.50	15.00
Columbia CS 9555	S	A Christmas Present...And Past	1967	3.75	7.50	15.00
REY, LITTLE BOBBY						
45s						
Original Sound 08		Rockin' "J" Bells/Corrido de Auld Lang Syne	1959	6.25	12.50	25.00
Original Sound 4529		Rockin' "J" Bells/Corrido De Auld Lang Syne	197?	—	2.00	4.00
— Reissue						
REYNOLDS, DEBBIE						
On Various-Artists Collections						
There's No Place Like Home		Christmas Song, The, And Other Favorites (Columbia Special Products P 12446)				
We Wish You a Merry Christmas		Christmas Greetings, Vol. 4 (Columbia Special Products P 11987)				
		Joy of Christmas, The (Columbia Special Products P 12042)				
		Merry Christmas (Columbia Musical Treasury 3P 6306)				
		Ronco Presents A Christmas Gift (Columbia Special Products P 12430)				
RG & E MIXED CHORUS						
7-Inch Extended Plays						
Lifetime 2737		Joy to the World/O Little Town of Bethlehem/The First Noel// O Come All Ye Faithful/Deck the Halls/Silent Night	1958	2.50	5.00	10.00
RHEIMS, ROBERT						
45s						
Rheims 101		Silent Night/O Come All Ye Faithful	1959	2.50	5.00	10.00
Rheims 101	PS	Silent Night/O Come All Ye Faithful	1959	3.75	7.50	15.00
— Sleeve calls the B-side "Adeste Fidelis"						
Albums						
Rheims LP-6006	M	Merry Christmas in Carols	1958	3.75	7.50	15.00
Rheims LP-6008	M	We Wish You a Merry Christmas	1959	3.75	7.50	15.00
Rheims LP-6010	M	For the Whole Family at Christmas	1961	3.00	6.00	12.00
Rheims ST-7706	S	Merry Christmas in Carols	1958	5.00	10.00	20.00
Rheims ST-7708	S	We Wish You a Merry Christmas	1959	5.00	10.00	20.00
Rheims ST-7710	S	For the Whole Family at Christmas	1961	3.75	7.50	15.00

Label, Number	Title (A Side/B Side)	Year	VG	VG+	NM

On Various-Artists Collections

Label, Number	Title (A Side/B Side)	Year	VG	VG+	NM
Hark the Herald Angels Sing	Best of Christmas Vol. 2 (Mistletoe MLP-1221)				
Medley: Joy to the World/ O Little Town of Bethlehem	Best of Christmas Vol. 2 (Mistletoe MLP-1221)				

RHODES KIDS, THE
45s

Label, Number	Title (A Side/B Side)	Year	VG	VG+	NM
GRC 2042	Santa Loves Rock 'n' Roll Music/A Carpenter, a Mother and a King	1974	—	2.00	4.00

RICE, BOBBY G.
45s

Label, Number	Title (A Side/B Side)	Year	VG	VG+	NM
Metromedia BMBO-0168	My Christmas Wish for You/Holidays Are Happy Days	1973	—	2.50	5.00

RICE, LORRAINE
45s

Label, Number	Title (A Side/B Side)	Year	VG	VG+	NM
Cuca 1300	Happy Holidays/If Jesus Came To Your House	19??	2.00	4.00	8.00

RICE, MILDRED
45s

Label, Number	Title (A Side/B Side)	Year	VG	VG+	NM
Ricca 4152	A Note to Santa/Merry Christmas to You	19??	—	2.00	4.00

RICH, CHARLIE
On Various-Artists Collections

Label, Number	Title (A Side/B Side)	Year	VG	VG+	NM
Christmas Greetings	Christmas Greetings From RCA Victor And Groove Recording Artists (RCA Victor SP-45-128)				
God Rest Ye Merry Gentlemen	Down-Home Country Christmas, A (Columbia Special Products P 14992)				
	RFD Christmas (Columbia Special Products P 15427)				
O Holy Night	Nashville's Greatest Christmas Hits, Volume II (Columbia PC 44413)				
	RFD Christmas (Columbia Special Products P 15427)				
White Christmas	Christmas Trimmings (Columbia Special Products P 12795)				

RICHARD, BELTON
45s

Label, Number	Title (A Side/B Side)	Year	VG	VG+	NM
Swallow 10189	Another Lonely Christmas/Cajun Stripper	198?	—	2.00	4.00
Swallow 10236	Please Come Home For Christmas/Blue Christmas	198?	—	2.00	4.00

RICHARD, CLIFF
12-Inch Singles

Label, Number	Title (A Side/B Side)	Year	VG	VG+	NM
EMI 12EMP 31	Remember Me/Another Christmas Day/Brave New World	1987	3.75	7.50	15.00
— U.K. import with gold embossed sleeve					
EMI 12EMT 31	Remember Me/Another Christmas Day/Brave New World	1987	2.50	5.00	10.00
— U.K. import with poster sleeve					
EMI 12EMX 78	Mistletoe and Wine/Marmaduke/Little Town	1988	3.75	7.50	15.00
EMI 12XMAS 90	Saviour's Day/Oh Boy Medley	1990	2.50	5.00	10.00
EMI 12EMP 218	This New Year/Scarlet Ribbons/We Don't Talk	1991	3.00	6.00	12.00

45s

Label, Number	Title (A Side/B Side)	Year	VG	VG+	NM
Columbia DB 8293	All My Love/Sweet Little Jesus Boy	1967	2.50	5.00	10.00
— U.K. import					
EMI EM 31	Remember Me/Another Christmas Day	1987	—	2.50	5.00
EMI EM 31 PS	Remember Me/Another Christmas Day	1987	—	2.50	5.00
— Record and sleeve are U.K. imports					
EMI EMP 78	Mistletoe and Wine/Marmaduke	1988	—	2.50	5.00
EMI EMP 78 PS	Mistletoe and Wine/Marmaduke	1988	—	2.50	5.00
— Record and sleeve are U.K. imports; with poster/calendar sleeve					
EMI EMS 78	Mistletoe and Wine/Marmaduke/True Love Ways	1988	—	2.00	4.00
EMI EMS 78 PS	Mistletoe and Wine/Marmaduke/True Love Ways	1988	—	2.00	4.00
— Record and sleeve are U.K. imports					
EMI XMAS P90	Saviour's Day/Oh Boy Medley	1990	—	3.00	6.00
EMI XMAS P90 PS	Saviour's Day/Oh Boy Medley	1990	—	3.00	6.00
— Record and sleeve are U.K. imports; envelope sleeve with five photos					
EMI XMAS 91	Twelve Days of Christmas/Mistletoe and Wine/ The Holly and the Ivy (Acapella)	1991	—	3.00	6.00
— One record of a two-45 set					
EMI XMAS 91 PS	Twelve Days of Christmas/Mistletoe and Wine/ The Holly and the Ivy (Acapella)	1991	—	3.00	6.00
— Sleeve for both records of XMAS 91 (the other record is not Christmas-related); record and sleeve are U.K. imports					
EMI EM 218	This New Year/Scarlet Ribbons	1991	—	2.00	4.00
— With etched autograph on one side					
EMI EM 218 PS	This New Year/Scarlet Ribbons	1991	—	2.00	4.00
— Record and sleeve are U.K. imports					

Label, Number		Title (A Side/B Side)	Year	VG	VG+	NM
Uni 55145		The Day I Met Marie/Sweet Little Jesus Boy	1969	3.00	6.00	12.00
— A-side is not a Christmas song						

RICHARDS, BARRY
45s

Epic 9564		Baby Sittin' Santa/Kissin' Doll	1962	7.50	15.00	30.00

RICHARDS, BILLIE, AND PAUL SOLES
On Various-Artists Collections

We're a Couple of Misfits	Rudolph the Red-Nosed Reindeer (Decca DL 4815)

RICHARDS, KEITH
45s

Rolling Stones 19311		Run Rudolph Run/The Harder They Come	1978	5.00	10.00	20.00
Rolling Stones 19311	DJ	Run Rudolph Run (same on both sides)	1978	2.50	5.00	10.00

RICHARDS, KEITH, ORCHESTRA WITH DOODLEBUG AND THE HAMPSTERS
No, not Keith "Rolling Stones" Richards.
45s

Tiger 151		There's A Hole In My Christmas Stocking (Children's Version)/	198?	—	2.00	4.00
		There's A Hole In My Christmas Stocking				

RICHARDS, TOM
45s

Rama 26		Christmas Dreaming/When Santa Comes This Year	1953	10.00	20.00	40.00

RICHMOND, RUSTY
45s

Sarg 125		Santa's Here To Stay/You Ought To Know	1956	3.75	7.50	15.00

RICKS, JIMMY
45s

Signature 12051		The Christmas Song/Love Is the Thing	1960	5.00	10.00	20.00

RIDDLE, NELSON
Albums

Avon 10170		Avon Wishes You a Happy Holiday and a Joyous New Year	1970	5.00	10.00	20.00
— Given to Avon salespeople						

On Various-Artists Collections

Cantique de Noel	Have Yourself a Merry Little Christmas (Reprise R 50001)
Happy Holiday	All-Time Christmas Favorites (Capitol Special Markets SL-6931)
	Let's Celebrate Christmas (Capitol Special Markets SL-6923)

RIDGEWOOD, CLIFTON
45s

Era 114		Little Drummer Boy/Little Drummer Boy (Disco)	197?	—	2.50	5.00

RIFFMASTER
45s

Dancin' Record (# unknown)		I've Been Good/Reindeer Song	19??	2.50	5.00	10.00

RIFLE SPORT
45s

Big Money Inc. 012		Little Drummer Boy/Shanghaied	19??	—	2.50	5.00
— Red vinyl						
Big Money Inc. 012	PS	Little Drummer Boy/Shanghaied	19??	—	2.50	5.00

RIGHTEOUS BROTHERS, THE
On Various-Artists Collections

Righteous Brothers Show, The	For Christmas Seals...A Matter of Life and Breath (Decca Custom Style F)

RINGWALD, MOLLY
On Various-Artists Collections

First Noel, The	Disney's Christmas All-Time Favorites (Disneyland 1V 8150)

Label, Number		Title (A Side/B Side)	Year	VG	VG+	NM
RIOS, AUGIE						
45s						
Metro 20010		Donde Esta Santa Claus?/Ol' Fatso	1958	10.00	20.00	40.00
MGM 12966		Feliz Navidades/Gypsy Boy	1960	5.00	10.00	20.00
MGM 13292		Donde Esta Santa Claus?/Ol' Fatso	1964	3.00	6.00	12.00
RITCHARD, CYRIL						
On Various-Artists Collections						
I'm Naïve (reprise)		Dangerous Christmas of Red Riding Hood, The (ABC-Paramount 536)				
Snubbed		Dangerous Christmas of Red Riding Hood, The (ABC-Paramount 536)				
We Wish the World a Happy Yule		Dangerous Christmas of Red Riding Hood, The (ABC-Paramount 536)				
RITCHIE, JEAN						
Albums						
Tradition TLP 1031		Carols of All Seasons	1959	5.00	10.00	20.00
RITENOUR, LEE						
On Various-Artists Collections						
White Christmas		GRP Christmas Collection, A (GRP 9574)				
RITTER, TEX						
45s						
Capitol F1264		Merry Christmas Polka/Christmas Carols	1950	5.00	10.00	20.00
Capitol F2957		Is There a Santa Claus/Ole Tex Kringle	1954	3.75	7.50	15.00
Capitol F3903		Here Was a Man/It Came Upon the Midnight Clear	1959	3.75	7.50	15.00
RIVERS, BOB, COMEDY CORP						
45s						
Critique PR 2119	DJ	Wreck The Malls/The Twelve Pains Of Christmas	1987	—	2.50	5.00
Critique PR 2135	DJ	I'm Dressing Up Like Santa	1987	—	2.50	5.00
		(When I Get Out on Parole) (same on both sides)				
Critique 99263		The Twelve Pains of Christmas/A Message from the King	1988	—	2.50	5.00
Critique 99263	PS	The Twelve Pains of Christmas/A Message from the King	1988	—	2.50	5.00
Albums						
Critique 90671		Twisted Christmas	1987	3.00	6.00	12.00
RIVERS, MAVIS						
On Various-Artists Collections						
Medley: Away in a Manger/Hark! The Herald Angels Sing		Have Yourself a Merry Little Christmas (Reprise R 50001)				
RIVERS, ROSEMARY						
45s						
LC'S 102		Soon It Will Be Christmas/I'm a Lover	19??	—	3.00	6.00
ROBBIN, BILL, AND THE BLUE JAYS						
45s						
Pink 708		Rockin' Bells/White Christmas	1960	5.00	10.00	20.00
ROBBINS, MARTY						
Albums						
Columbia CL 2735	M	Christmas with Marty Robbins	1967	12.50	25.00	50.00
Columbia CS 9535	S	Christmas with Marty Robbins	1967	7.50	15.00	30.00
Columbia Special Products C10980	S	Christmas with Marty Robbins	1972	3.75	7.50	15.00

— *Stereo reissue; "Distributed by Apex Rendezvous, Inc." on back cover*

On Various-Artists Collections

Christmas Kisses	Country Style Christmas, A (Columbia Musical Treasury 3P 6316)
Christmas Prayer	Country Christmas (Time-Life STL-109)
	Joy of Christmas, The, Featuring Marty Robbins and His Friends (Columbia Special Products C 11087)
Christmas Time Is Here Again	Country Style Christmas, A (Columbia Musical Treasury 3P 6316)
	Merry Christmas from... (Reader's Digest RD4-83)
Hark! The Herald Angels Sing	Christmas Greetings from Nashville (Columbia PC 39467)
	Country Christmas (Columbia CS 9888)
	Country Style Christmas, A (Columbia Musical Treasury 3P 6316)
	Down-Home Country Christmas, A (Columbia Special Products P 14992)
	Joy of Christmas, The, Featuring Marty Robbins and His Friends (Columbia Special Products C 11087)
	Nashville's Greatest Christmas Hits (Columbia PC 44412)

Label, Number	Title (A Side/B Side)	Year	VG	VG+	NM
Joy of Christmas, The	Joy of Christmas, The, Featuring Marty Robbins and His Friends (Columbia Special Products C 11087)				
Little Stranger (In a Manger)	Joy of Christmas, The, Featuring Marty Robbins and His Friends (Columbia Special Products C 11087)				
O Little Town of Bethlehem	Country Christmas Favorites (Columbia Special Products C 10876)				
	Home for Christmas (Columbia Musical Treasury P3S 5608)				
	Home for Christmas (Realm 2V 8101)				
	Joy of Christmas, The, Featuring Marty Robbins and His Friends (Columbia Special Products C 11087)				
	Joy to the World (30 Classic Christmas Melodies) (Columbia Special Products P3 14654)				
	We Wish You a Country Christmas (Columbia Special Products P 14991)				

ROBERTINO
45s

Label, Number	Title (A Side/B Side)	Year	VG	VG+	NM
Four Corners 101	Santo Natale/Caro Gesu Bambino	1963	2.00	4.00	8.00

ROBERTS, BILL, AND THE WAYNE SINGERS
45s

Label, Number	Title (A Side/B Side)	Year	VG	VG+	NM
Accent 1266	Christmas Is For Everyone/Have A Heart	1967	2.00	4.00	8.00

ROBERTS, DEREK
45s

Label, Number	Title (A Side/B Side)	Year	VG	VG+	NM
Roulette 4656	There Won't Be Any Snow (Christmas In The Jungle)/A World Without Sunshine	1965	2.50	5.00	10.00

ROBERTS, KAYTON AND IVA LEE
45s

Label, Number	Title (A Side/B Side)	Year	VG	VG+	NM
Stoneway 1135	Silent Night/Opryland Swing	197?	—	2.50	5.00

ROBERTS, KENNY
45s

Label, Number	Title (A Side/B Side)	Year	VG	VG+	NM
Coral 60884	Sleighbell Polka/Elfie the Elf	1952	3.75	7.50	15.00
Coral 64105	He'll Be Coming Down the Chimney/Grandfather Kringle	1951	3.75	7.50	15.00

ROBERTS, LYNN
45s

Label, Number	Title (A Side/B Side)	Year	VG	VG+	NM
Ocean State DMS-3 — B-side by Bob Carroll	I Want My Santa Claus/Dreaming of Christmas	1982	—	2.00	4.00

ROBERTS, PADDY
45s

Label, Number	Title (A Side/B Side)	Year	VG	VG+	NM
London 9573	...And A Happy New Year/Got 'n' Idea	1962	3.00	6.00	12.00

ROBERTSON, DON, AND LOU DINNING
45s

Label, Number	Title (A Side/B Side)	Year	VG	VG+	NM
Jimmy McHugh 401 — B-side by the Mitchell Boy Choir	Let's Have An Old Fashioned Christmas/Ol' Kris Kringle	198?	—	—	3.00

ROBERTSON, ROBBIE
On Various-Artists Collections

Christmas Must Be Tonight	Scrooged (A&M SP-3921)				

ROBIN AND THE MERRY MEN
45s

Label, Number	Title (A Side/B Side)	Year	VG	VG+	NM
Mohawk 130	Mr. Santa, Bring Me a Doll/Ellen	1960	3.75	7.50	15.00

ROBIN SISTERS, THE
45s

Label, Number	Title (A Side/B Side)	Year	VG	VG+	NM
Polaris 100	Chimney Top Twist/Santa's Little Workshop	1962	3.75	7.50	15.00

ROBIN, TINA
45s

Label, Number	Title (A Side/B Side)	Year	VG	VG+	NM
Coral 62055	Winter Wonderland Cha Cha/I've Got My Love To Keep Me Warm	1958	3.00	6.00	12.00

ROBINSON, CARSON
45s

Label, Number	Title (A Side/B Side)	Year	VG	VG+	NM
RCA Victor 47-2870	Jingle Bells/Paddy Dear	1949	3.75	7.50	15.00

Label, Number	Title (A Side/B Side)	Year	VG	VG+	NM
7-Inch Extended Plays					
RCA Victor 547-0111	Jingle Bells/Paddy Dear//Golden Slippers/Turkey In The Straw	195?	3.00	6.00	12.00

ROBINSON, REVEREND CLEOPHUS
45s

Collectables 90122	Silent Night/Loves Me Like A Rock	1995	—	—	3.00
— B-side by the Dixie Hummingbirds; reissue					
Peacock 1789	Silent Night/I'm Not Tired Yet	1958	3.75	7.50	15.00
Peacock 3044	Go Tell It On The Mountain/Just Ask Him	1964	2.50	5.00	10.00
Peacock 3071	Silent Night/Amen	1965	2.50	5.00	10.00

ROBINSON, ROSCOE
45s

Gerri 002	'Tis Yuletide/Don't Forget the Soldiers	197?	—	2.50	5.00

ROBINSON, SMOKEY, AND THE MIRACLES
Also see THE MIRACLES.

On Various-Artists Collections

Medley: Deck the Halls/Bring a Torch, Jeannette, Isabella	Jingle Bell Rock (Time-Life SRNR-XM) Motown Christmas, A (Motown 795V2)
Go Tell It on the Mountain	Jingle Bell Rock (Time-Life SRNR-XM)
God Rest Ye Merry Gentlemen	Motown Christmas, A (Motown 795V2)
It's Christmas Time	Motown Christmas, A (Motown 795V2)
Jingle Bells	Motown Christmas, A (Motown 795V2)

ROBINSON, SUGAR CHILE
45s

Capitol F1259	Christmas Boogie/Rudolph the Red-Nosed Reindeer	1950	5.00	10.00	20.00

ROBINSON, TONY, AND THE ANGEL VOICES
45s

Nico Polo 0057		Christmas Wrapping/The Choral Wrap	19??	—	3.00	6.00
Nico Polo 0057	PS	Christmas Wrapping/The Choral Wrap	19??	—	3.00	6.00
— Record and sleeve are U.K. imports						

ROCHELLE, RENEE
45s

PBM 7801	A Christmas Story "On Hudson Bay"/Holly Jolly Christmas	1978	—	2.00	4.00

ROCHES, THE
45s

Warner Bros. 29815	The Hallelujah Chorus/Second Family	1982	5.00	10.00	20.00
Albums					
MCA 10020	We Three Kings	1990	3.75	7.50	15.00

ROCK, GEORGE, SEXTETTE
45s

Dyna 107	I Left The Light On For Santa/God Looks Like	196?	2.50	5.00	10.00

ROCKET FROM THE CRYPT
On Various-Artists Collections

Cancel Christmas	Happy Birthday, Baby Jesus (Sympathy For The Record Industry SFTRI 271)

ROCKIN' SIDNEY
45s

Goldband 1183	Soul Christmas (Part 1)/Soul Christmas (Part 2)	1966	2.00	4.00	8.00

ROCKIN' STOCKIN', THE
45s

Sun 350	Rockin' Lang Syne/Yuleville U.S.A.	1960	7.50	15.00	30.00
Sun 1960	Rockin' Lang Syne/Yuleville U.S.A.	19??	3.75	7.50	15.00
— Reissue with green and red print on a white label with original Sun logo					

On Various-Artists Collections

Yuleville, U.S.A.	Rockin' Christmas — The '50s (Rhino RNLP-066)

Label, Number		Title (A Side/B Side)	Year	VG	VG+	NM
ROCKY FELLERS, THE						
45s						
Scepter 1245		Santa Santa/Great Big World	1962	5.00	10.00	20.00
— A-side is a very early Neil Diamond composition						
Scepter 1245	DJ	Santa Santa/Santa's Grove	1963	3.00	6.00	12.00
— Promo reissue with new B-side. All-white label (no black oval)						
Scepter 1245	DJ	Santa Santa (same on both sides)	196?	2.00	4.00	8.00
— Promo reissue; white label with mid-1960s Scepter Records logo (black oval)						
RODGERS, ANTON; ALBERT FINNEY						
On Various-Artists Collections						
Thank You Very Much		Scrooge (Columbia Masterworks S 30258)				
RODGERS, JIMMIE						
45s						
Dot 16795		The Chipmunk Song (Christmas Don't Be Late)/In the Snow	1965	2.00	4.00	8.00
Roulette 4205		It's Christmas Once Again/Wistful Willie	1959	5.00	10.00	20.00
Albums						
Dot DLP 3657	M	Christmas with Jimmie	1965	3.00	6.00	12.00
Dot DLP 25657	S	Christmas with Jimmie	1965	3.75	7.50	15.00
Roulette R 25095	M	It's Christmas Once Again	1959	7.50	15.00	30.00
Roulette SR 25095	S	It's Christmas Once Again	1959	12.50	25.00	50.00
On Various-Artists Collections						
It Came Upon the Midnight Clear		Philco Album of Holiday Music, The (Columbia Special Products CSM 431)				
Twelve Days of Christmas, The		12 Days of Christmas, The (Pickwick SPC-1021)				
We Three Kings of Orient Are		Very Merry Christmas, A (Columbia Special Products CSS 563)				
ROGERS, ERIC, CHORALE AND ORCHESTRA						
Albums						
London Phase 4 SP 44027		The Glory of Christmas	196?	3.00	6.00	12.00
ROGERS, JESSE						
45s						
MGM 11369		An Old-Fashioned Christmas/Red, White and Blue	1952	5.00	10.00	20.00
RCA Victor 48-0100		Blue Christmas/Here Comes Santa Claus	1949	12.50	25.00	50.00
— Originals on green vinyl						
ROGERS, KENNY						
Also see KENNY ROGERS AND DOLLY PARTON.						
45s						
Liberty 1438		Kentucky Homemade Christmas/Carol of the Bells	1981	—	2.50	5.00
Liberty 1438	PS	Kentucky Homemade Christmas/Carol of the Bells	1981	—	3.00	6.00
Liberty 4065	DJ	Christmas Everyday//	198?	—	3.00	6.00
		Kentucky Homemade Christmas/Carol Of The Bells				
RCA PB-13944		The Christmas Song/Medley: Winter Wonderland-Sleigh Ride	1984	—	2.00	4.00
— B-side by Dolly Parton						
Reprise 22750		Christmas in America/Joy to the World	1989	—	—	3.00
Reprise 22750	PS	Christmas in America/Joy to the World	1989	—	—	3.00
Albums						
Liberty LN-10240		Christmas	198?	2.00	4.00	8.00
— Reissue of LOO 51115						
Liberty LOO-51115		Christmas	1981	2.50	5.00	10.00
Reprise 25973		Christmas in America	1989	3.00	6.00	12.00
On Various-Artists Collections						
Christmas Song, The		Christmas Treasury of Classics from Avon, A (RCA Special Products DPL1-0716)				
Silent Night		Mistletoe and Memories (RCA 8372-1-R)				
		Stars of Christmas, The (RCA Special Products DPL1-0842)				
White Christmas		Rocking Christmas Stocking, A (Capitol SPRO 9303/4/5/6)				
ROGERS, KENNY, AND DOLLY PARTON						
Also see DOLLY PARTON, KENNY ROGERS.						
45s						
RCA 5352-7-R		Christmas Without You/I Believe in Santa Claus	1987	—	—	3.00
— B-side by Dolly Parton						
RCA 9070-7-R		Christmas Without You/Medley: Winter Wonderland-Sleigh Ride	1989	—	—	3.00
— B-side by Dolly Parton						
RCA PB-13945		The Greatest Gift of All/White Christmas	1984	—	2.00	4.00
RCA PB-14261		Christmas Without You/A Christmas to Remember	1985	—	—	3.00
RCA PB-14261	PS	Christmas Without You/A Christmas to Remember	1985	—	2.00	4.00

Label, Number		Title (A Side/B Side)	Year	VG	VG+	NM
Albums						
RCA Victor ASL1-5307		Once Upon a Christmas	1984	2.50	5.00	10.00

ROGERS, LEE
45s
| D-Town 1062 | | You Won't Have To Wait Till Xmas/My One And Only | 19?? | — | 2.50 | 5.00 |

ROGERS, ROY, AND DALE EVANS
45s
Capitol 2022		Merry Christmas My Darling/Sleigh Ride-Jingle Bells	1967	2.50	5.00	10.00
RCA Victor 48-0128		Christmas on the Plains/Wonderful Christmas Night	1949	12.50	25.00	50.00
— Originals on green vinyl						

Albums
| Capitol T 2818 | M | Christmas Is Always | 1967 | 7.50 | 15.00 | 30.00 |
| Capitol ST 2818 | S | Christmas Is Always | 1967 | 7.50 | 15.00 | 30.00 |

On Various-Artists Collections
| I'll Be Home for Christmas | | Sound of Christmas, The, Vol. 3 (Capitol Creative Products SL-6680) | | | | |
| Medley: Sleigh Ride/Jingle Bells | | Joys of Christmas (Capitol Creative Products SL-6610) | | | | |

ROGERS, TRUDY BUCK
45s
| TBR & Company 101 | | The Christmas Mouse/Blessed Baby Jesus | 19?? | 2.00 | 4.00 | 8.00 |

ROHAN, JOHN
45s
| Canuck 102 | | It's That Time Again/There Will Always Be A Christmas | 19?? | — | — | 3.00 |
| Canuck 102 | PS | It's That Time Again/There Will Always Be A Christmas | 19?? | — | — | 3.00 |

ROMAN, DICK
45s
| Harmon 1011 | | Christmas Village/Climb Every Mountain | 19?? | 2.00 | 4.00 | 8.00 |

ROMAN, LULU
On Various-Artists Collections
| We Three Kings of Orient Are | | Merry Christmas (Rainbow Sound R-5032-LPS) | | | | |

ROMANO, DON
45s
| Merry-Go-Round 104 | | Christmas Rings A Bell/Happy New Year | 19?? | 2.00 | 4.00 | 8.00 |

ROMEOS, THE
45s
| Columbia AE7 1222 | DJ | Jingle Bells Jam/Seriously Affected | 198? | 2.00 | 4.00 | 8.00 |
| Columbia AE7 1222 | PS | Jingle Bells Jam/Seriously Affected | 198? | 2.00 | 4.00 | 8.00 |

RONALD, DAN
45s
| Cuca 1060 | | Little Drummer Boy/Silent Night | 196? | 3.00 | 6.00 | 12.00 |

RONETTES, THE
45s
| Pavillion 03333 | | I Saw Mommy Kissing Santa Claus/Rudolph the Red-Nosed Reindeer | 1982 | — | 2.50 | 5.00 |
| — B-side by The Crystals | | | | | | |

On Various-Artists Collections
Frosty the Snowman		Christmas Gift for You from Phil Spector, A (Philles PHLP-4005)				
		Phil Spector's Christmas Album (Apple SW 3400)				
		Phil Spector: Back to Mono 1958-1969 (Phil Spector/Abkco 7118-1)				
I Saw Mommy Kissing Santa Claus		Christmas Gift for You from Phil Spector, A (Philles PHLP-4005)				
		Phil Spector's Christmas Album (Apple SW 3400)				
		Phil Spector: Back to Mono 1958-1969 (Phil Spector/Abkco 7118-1)				
Sleigh Ride		Christmas EP (Philles X-EP)				
		Christmas Gift for You from Phil Spector, A (Philles PHLP-4005)				
		Phil Spector's Christmas Album (Apple SW 3400)				
		Phil Spector: Back to Mono 1958-1969 (Phil Spector/Abkco 7118-1)				

ROOT BOY SLIM AND THE SEX CHANGE BAND
45s
| Joe*Tel 4972 | | Xmas At K-Mart/Too Much Jawbone | 1978 | 2.00 | 4.00 | 8.00 |
| Joe*Tel 4972 | PS | Xmas At K-Mart/Too Much Jawbone | 1978 | 2.00 | 4.00 | 8.00 |

Label, Number		Title (A Side/B Side)	Year	VG	VG+	NM
ROS, EDMUNDO						
45s						
London 1153		Noche Buena (Christmas Eve)/Happy Bird	1951	3.75	7.50	15.00
ROSE, DAVID						
45s						
MGM SK-50105	S	The Night They Invented Christmas/Gigi	1958	3.75	7.50	15.00
Albums						
Capitol ST 2853		Christmas Album	1968	3.00	6.00	12.00
MGM E-3469	M	Merry Christmas to You	1956	6.25	12.50	25.00
— Yellow label						
MGM E-3469	M	Merry Christmas to You	1960	3.75	7.50	15.00
— Black label						

On Various-Artists Collections

Carol of the Bells	Christmas — The Season of Music (Capitol Creative Products SL-6679)
	Zenith Presents Christmas, A Gift of Music Vol. 3 (Capitol Creative Products SL-6659)
Christmas Song, The	Christmas Carousel (Capitol SQBE-94406)
Christmas Tree, The	Christmas, A Gift of Music (Capitol Special Markets SL-6687)
	Zenith Presents Christmas, A Gift of Music Vol. 4 (Capitol Creative Products SL-6687)
Little Drummer Boy	All-Time Christmas Favorites (Capitol Special Markets SL-6931)
	Best of Christmas, The, Vol. II (Capitol SM-11834)
	Christmas, A Gift of Music (Capitol Special Markets SL-6687)
	Zenith Presents Christmas, A Gift of Music Vol. 4 (Capitol Creative Products SL-6687)

Label, Number	Title (A Side/B Side)	Year	VG	VG+	NM
ROSE, THERESA					
45s					
Song In The Night 259	Santa, Don't Forget My Mommy/Lillies	19??	—	2.50	5.00
ROSELLI, JIMMY					
45s					
United Artists 1659	Buon Natale (Means Merry Christmas To You)/Christmas	1966	—	3.00	6.00
— "Silver Spotlight Series"					

ROSS, ELINOR
On Various-Artists Collections

Gesu Bambino   Joy to the World (30 Classic Christmas Melodies) (Columbia Special Products P3 14654)

Label, Number	Title (A Side/B Side)	Year	VG	VG+	NM
ROSS, JERIS					
45s					
Santa's Land 106	Hiding Behind The Christmas Tree/Joy, The Snow Flake	198?	—	2.00	4.00
ROSSI, STEVE					
45s					
Roulette 4773	Christmas Story/The Night Before Christmas	1967	2.00	4.00	8.00
ROTARY CONNECTION					
45s					
Cadet Concept 7009	Silent Night Chant/Peace At Least	1968	3.00	6.00	12.00
Albums					
Cadet Concept LPS 318	Peace	1969	3.75	7.50	15.00
On Various-Artists Collections					
Christmas Love	Have a Merry Chess Christmas (Chess/MCA CH-25210)				
ROTH, CHERYL					
45s					
Echo Mountain 111185	GB The Cosmic Snowball (same on both sides)	1985	—	—	3.00
ROUSSEAU, JACK					
45s					
Gone 5045	Christmas in the Snow/Piney	1958	3.75	7.50	15.00
ROVERS, THE					
45s					
Attic 275	Grandma Got Run Over by a Reindeer/Merry Bloody Christmas	198?	—	2.50	5.00

Label, Number		Title (A Side/B Side)	Year	VG	VG+	NM

ROWLAND, DAVE, AND SUGAR
45s
Elektra 47234	DJ	Winter Wonderland/Rudolph the Red-Nosed Reindeer	1981	2.00	4.00	8.00

— B-side by Mel and Nancy (Tillis and Sinatra)

ROY C
45s
Alaga 1005	A Merry Black Christmas/I Don't Want To Worry	19??	—	2.50	5.00

ROYAL COLLEGE OF MUSIC CHAMBER CHOIR AND BRASS ENSEMBLE
Albums
CBS Special Products DP 17891	Carols for Christmas	1984	3.00	6.00	12.00
CBS Special Products DP 18699	Carols for Christmas II	1985	3.00	6.00	12.00

ROYAL GUARDSMEN, THE
45s
Laurie 112		Snoopy's Christmas/The Smallest Astronaut	197?	—	2.00	4.00

— B-side by Barry Winslow; reissue

Laurie 3416		Snoopy's Christmas/It Kinda Looks Like Christmas	1967	2.50	5.00	10.00
Laurie 3416	PS	Snoopy's Christmas/It Kinda Looks Like Christmas	1967	5.00	10.00	20.00

Albums
Laurie LLP 2042	M	Snoopy and His Friends	1967	6.25	12.50	25.00

— With "Merry Snoopy's Christmas" poster still attached to back cover

Laurie LLP 2042	M	Snoopy and His Friends	1967	3.75	7.50	15.00

— With "Merry Snoopy's Christmas" poster missing. Contains two Christmas songs: The Story of Snoopy's Christmas/Snoopy's Christmas; It Kinda Looks Like Christmas

Laurie SLLP 2042	S	Snoopy and His Friends	1967	7.50	15.00	30.00

— With "Merry Snoopy's Christmas" poster still attached to back cover

Laurie SLLP 2042	S	Snoopy and His Friends	1967	5.00	10.00	20.00

— With "Merry Snoopy's Christmas" poster missing

ROYAL MALE CHOIR OF HOLLAND, THE
Albums
Epic LC 3074	Christmas Carols	195?	5.00	10.00	20.00

ROYAL PHILHARMONIC ORCHESTRA
45s
RCA Victor 47-7648	Hallelujah Chorus/And the Glory of the Lord	1959	2.50	5.00	10.00

On Various-Artists Collections
Angels We Have Heard on High	Christmas Through the Years (Reader's Digest RDA-143)
	Joyous Music for Christmas Time (Reader's Digest RD 45-M)
Away in a Manger	Joyous Music for Christmas Time (Reader's Digest RD 45-M)
Deck the Halls with Boughs of Holly	Joyous Music for Christmas Time (Reader's Digest RD 45-M)
God Rest Ye Merry, Gentlemen	Christmas Through the Years (Reader's Digest RDA-143)
	Joyous Music for Christmas Time (Reader's Digest RD 45-M)
Hallelujah Chorus	Christmas in New York (RCA Victor PRM-257)
	Christmas in the Air (RCA Special Products DPL1-0133)
	Christmas Programming from RCA Victor (RCA Victor SP-33-66)
	Family Christmas Collection, The (Time-Life STL-131)
	For a Musical Merry Christmas, Volume 3 (RCA Victor PRM-221)
	Merry Christmas (RCA Victor PRM-168)
	60 Christmas Classics (Sessions DVL2-0723)
Hark! The Herald Angels Sing	Christmas Through the Years (Reader's Digest RDA-143)
	Joyous Music for Christmas Time (Reader's Digest RD 45-M)
It Came Upon a Midnight Clear	Joyous Music for Christmas Time (Reader's Digest RD 45-M)
Joy to the World	Joyous Music for Christmas Time (Reader's Digest RD 45-M)
O Come, All Ye Faithful	Joyous Music for Christmas Time (Reader's Digest RD 45-M)
O Holy Night	Joyous Music for Christmas Time (Reader's Digest RD 45-M)
O Little Town of Bethlehem	Joyous Music for Christmas Time (Reader's Digest RD 45-M)
Pastoral Symphony	Old Fashioned Christmas, An (Reader's Digest RDA 216-A)
Twelve Days of Christmas, The	Christmas Through the Years (Reader's Digest RDA-143)
	Joyous Music for Christmas Time (Reader's Digest RD 45-M)
We Three Kings of Orient Are	Christmas Through the Years (Reader's Digest RDA-143)
	Joyous Music for Christmas Time (Reader's Digest RD 45-M)

ROYAL SCOTS DRAGOON GUARDS, THE
45s
RCA GB-13276	The Little Drummer Boy/Amazing Grace	1982	—	2.00	4.00

— Gold Standard Series

RCA Victor 74-0861	The Little Drummer Boy/Christmas Festival	1972	—	2.50	5.00

Label, Number		Title (A Side/B Side)	Year	VG	VG+	NM
ROYALS, THE						
45s						
Vagabond 444		Christmas Party/White Christmas	1963	12.50	25.00	50.00
Vagabond 444		Christmas Party/White Christmas	1963	25.00	50.00	100.00
— *Red vinyl*						
ROZA, LITA						
45s						
London 1398		The Little Boy That Santa Claus Forgot/Saint Nicholas Waltz	1953	3.00	6.00	12.00
RUBBISH, JONNY						
45s						
United Artists 36479	DJ	Santa's Alive/Policeman (I Got Pulled Over By A)	1978	2.50	5.00	10.00
— *U.K. import*						
RUBY, SUNSHINE						
45s						
RCA Victor 47-5474		I Wanna Do Something for Santa Claus/Too Fat for the Chimney	1953	5.00	10.00	20.00
RUCKER, BIG DADDY						
45s						
GME 1326		Christmas in the Ghetto/Just Do Your Thing	19??	2.50	5.00	10.00
RUDI AND THE RAIN DEARZ						
45s						
Tinsel 8		Santa's New Bag/I Stole Away On Christmas Day	19??	2.00	4.00	8.00
— *B-side by Pretty Polly Pinecone*						
RUDOLF'S NIGHTMARE						
45s						
Handsome 001		Silent Night/Twelve Days Of Xmas	19??	2.00	4.00	8.00
Handsome 001	PS	Silent Night/Twelve Days Of Xmas	19??	2.50	5.00	10.00
RUDOLPH AND THE GANG						
45s						
Yuletide 12033		Here Comes Fatty Claus/Comink Zee Clauski Fattnick	198?	5.00	10.00	20.00
RUFF, BUFF, ELMO & STUFFY (SANTA'S GNOMES)						
45s						
Santa's Land 102		Dear Santa/I Can Hardly Wait for Christmas	19??	—	2.00	4.00
— *B-side by Little Jo*						
RUGOLO, PETE, AND HIS ORCHESTRA						
45s						
Columbia 40369		Jingle Bells Mambo/Theme From The Lombardo Ending	1954	2.50	5.00	10.00
RUMBEL, NANCY						
On Various-Artists Collections						
Medley: Patapan/Noel Nouvelet		Narada: The Christmas Collection (Narada N-63902)				
RUMBLES LTD., THE						
45s						
Dad's 103		The Wildest Christmas/Santa Claus Is Coming To Town	1968	3.75	7.50	15.00
Dad's 103	PS	The Wildest Christmas/Santa Claus Is Coming To Town	1968	3.00	6.00	12.00
RUN-D.M.C.						
45s						
Profile 5235		Christmas in Hollis/Let the Jingle Bells Rock	1988	—	2.00	4.00
— *B-side by Sweet Tee; red vinyl*						
Albums						
Profile PRO-1419	(2)	Together Forever: Greatest Hits 1983-1991	1991	3.75	7.50	15.00
— *Contains one Christmas song:* Christmas in Hollis						
On Various-Artists Collections						
Christmas in Hollis		Very Special Christmas, A (A&M SP-3911)				

(Top left) Alternative band Red Red Meat put out this somewhat scarce holiday single on Sub Pop in the fall of 1996. (Top right) A decade after it first hit the market, Bob Rivers' *Twisted Christmas* remains a radio favorite during the Christmas season. Readily available in other formats, the LP is no longer easy to find. (Bottom left) Kenny Rogers and Dolly Parton followed up their "Islands in the Stream" with a Christmas album of both solo and duet material, *A Christmas To Remember,* which featured "Christmas Without You." (Bottom right) Rotary Connection, a mixed-race late 1960s band featuring Minnie Riperton, made this holiday LP in 1969. After years in short supply, original copies appeared in cut-out bins in the early 1990s, which has helped moderate its value.

Label, Number		Title (A Side/B Side)	Year	VG	VG+	NM

RUPPE, MORGAN, AND LISA CARRIE
45s

Hummingbird 109		Old Time Christmas/The Meaning of Christmas	19??	—	2.00	4.00

RUSSELL, AL
45s

Okeh 6845		I Don't Want to Be Alone for Christmas/I Love Each Move You Make	1951	30.00	60.00	120.00

RUSSELL, BOB & THE MUSIC CITY CHORALE
45s

Holiday Hits 903		The Christmas Song/I'll Be Home For Christmas	195?	3.00	6.00	12.00

RUSSELL, LEON
45s

Shelter 7328		Slipping Into Christmas/Christmas in Chicago	1972	—	2.50	5.00
Shelter 7328	PS	Slipping Into Christmas/Christmas In Chicago	1972	6.25	12.50	25.00

RYDELL, BOBBY/CHUBBY CHECKER
45s

Cameo 205		Jingle Bell Rock/Jingle Bell Imitations	1961	3.75	7.50	15.00
Cameo 205	PS	Jingle Bell Rock/Jingle Bell Imitations	1961	6.25	12.50	25.00

Albums

Cameo C 1013	M	Bobby Rydell/Chubby Checker	1961	7.50	15.00	30.00

— *Contains three Christmas songs:* Jingle Bell Rock; Jingle Bells Imitations; What Are You Doing New Year's Eve

S

SABATINO, BOBBY
45s

Gold Mine 711		I'm Gonna Hang Up Mommy's Stocking/Funny Little Snow Man	19??	2.50	5.00	10.00

SABERS, THE
45s

Cal-West 847		Cool, Cool Christmas/Always and Forever	19??	—	2.50	5.00

SACCHARINE TRUST
45s

SST 006.9		A Christmas Cry (same on both sides)	198?	3.00	6.00	12.00

SACCO, MARIA
45s

Mlay 328		Santa's Letter/Santa's On His Way	19??	2.00	4.00	8.00

— *B-side by Tommy Mossburg*

SACCO, TONY
45s

Weber 172		The Jolly Fat Man (In The Santa Claus Suit)/ Hark The Herald Angels Sing	19??	—	2.50	5.00

SADLER, SSGT. BARRY
45s

RCA Victor 47-9008		I Won't Be Home This Christmas/A Woman Is a Weepin' Willow Tree	1966	2.00	4.00	8.00

SAGAL, KATEY
On Various-Artists Collections

Starlight	Starlight Christmas, A (MCA 10066)

ST. CHARLES CHILDREN'S CHORUS
On Various-Artists Collections

Christmas Morn Is Dawning	Christmas in Saint Louis ((no label) TS77-558/9)

Label, Number		Title (A Side/B Side)	Year	VG	VG+	NM
ST. FRANCIS BOTTLE BAND, THE						
45s						
(no label) 2543		Joy to the World/We Wish You a Merry Christmas/	19??	2.50	5.00	10.00
		Away in a Manger/Christmas Tree/Silent Night//				
— B-side has no Christmas songs						
(no label) 2543	PS	The St. Francis Bottle Band	19??	2.50	5.00	10.00
ST. JOHN, MICHAEL						
45s						
Sterling 752		Christmas Is Christmas All Over the World/(Instrumental)	19??	—	2.00	4.00
SAINT LOUIS COUNTY COMMUNITY CHORUS						
On Various-Artists Collections						
Angels We Have Heard on High		Christmas in Saint Louis ((no label) TS77-558/9)				
ST. LOUIS SYMPHONY						
On Various-Artists Collections						
March of the Toys		Family Christmas Collection, The (Time-Life STL-131)				
Nutcracker: Dance of the Reed-Pipes		Family Christmas Collection, The (Time-Life STL-131)				
ST. MARGARET'S ALL BOYS CHOIR, THE						
45s						
Cricket CX9		Silent Night/O' Come All Ye Faithful	195?	2.00	4.00	8.00
— 7-inch 78 rpm single						
Cricket CX9	PS	Silent Night/O' Come All Ye Faithful	195?	2.00	4.00	8.00
— 7-inch 78 rpm single						
Cricket CX10		Jingle Bells/It Came Upon A Midnight Clear	195?	2.00	4.00	8.00
— 7-inch 78 rpm single						
Cricket CX10	PS	Jingle Bells/It Came Upon A Midnight Clear	195?	2.00	4.00	8.00
— 7-inch 78 rpm single						
ST. NICK						
45s						
Warner Bros. 49877		Jingle Bells (Laughing All the Way)/Gesundheit-The Last Recital	1981	2.50	5.00	10.00
— B-side by the Just For Laughs Players						
WEA 100194		Jingle Bells (Laughing All the Way)/Gesundheit-The Last Recital	198?	—	3.00	6.00
WEA 100194	PS	Jingle Bells (Laughing All the Way)/Gesundheit-The Last Recital	198?	—	3.00	6.00
— Import release						
ST. PATRICK'S CATHEDRAL CHOIR						
45s						
Roulette 4204		Carol of the Bells/Carol of the Drum	1959	3.00	6.00	12.00
Albums						
Roulette R 25142	M	Sings Christmas Songs (Volume 2)	1960	3.75	7.50	15.00
On Various-Artists Collections						
Joy to the World		Philco Album of Holiday Music, The (Columbia Special Products CSM 431)				
ST. THOMAS CHOIR						
On Various-Artists Collections						
In Dulci Jubilo		Magic of Christmas, The (Columbia Musical Treasury P3S 5806)				
SAINTS, THE						
45s						
Angela 103		White Christmas/Please Come Home For Christmas	19??	—	3.00	6.00
SALAS BROTHERS, THE						
45s						
Faro 625		Donde Esta Santa Claus/One Like Mine	1966	2.00	4.00	8.00
SALEM TRAVELERS, THE						
On Various-Artists Collections						
Merry Christmas to You		Have a Merry Chess Christmas (Chess/MCA CH-25210)				
SALERNO, JOHN						
45s						
Polytech 1023		Christmas in the Sun/Seasoned Smiles	1987	—	—	3.00

Label, Number		Title (A Side/B Side)	Year	VG	VG+	NM
SALES, SOUPY						
45s						
Reprise 244		Santa Claus Is Surfin' to Town/Santa Claus Is Comin' to Town	1963	7.50	15.00	30.00
SALSOUL ORCHESTRA, THE						
45s						
Salsoul 2052		We Wish You a Merry Christmas/Merry Christmas All	1976	—	2.50	5.00
Salsoul 2052	PS	We Wish You a Merry Christmas/Merry Christmas All	1976	—	3.00	6.00
Salsoul 2077		The Little Drummer Boy/Christmas Time	1978	—	2.50	5.00
Salsoul 2155		Deck The Halls/The Salsoul Christmas Suite	1981	—	2.00	4.00
Albums						
Salsoul CA-1001		Christmas Jollies	198?	2.00	4.00	8.00
— Reissue						
Salsoul CA-1004		Christmas Jollies II	198?	2.00	4.00	8.00
— Reissue						
Salsoul SZS 5507		Christmas Jollies	1976	3.00	6.00	12.00
Salsoul 8547		Christmas Jollies II	1981	3.00	6.00	12.00
On Various-Artists Collections						
Sleigh Ride		Happy Holidays, Volume 17 (RCA Special Products DPL1-0555)				
SALVATORE, BOBBY						
45s						
IPG 1012		Stick 'Em Up Santa/Big Al	1963	3.75	7.50	15.00
SAM I AM						
45s						
Oblong 12-25		Santa Claus Is Dead/(Take That) Fascist Groove Thang	1989	2.00	4.00	8.00
SAMMES, MIKE, SINGERS						
On Various-Artists Collections						
Do You Hear What I Hear		Disney's Christmas All-Time Favorites (Disneyland 1V 8150)				
		Disney's Christmas Favorites (Disneyland 2506)				
Little Drummer Boy		Disney's Christmas Favorites (Disneyland 2506)				
Rudolph the Red-Nosed Reindeer		Disney's Christmas Favorites (Disneyland 2506)				
SAMPSON, JANA, AND RANDALL PARR						
45s						
Rock-It 501		(Merry Christmas) From Lisa Marie/	1979	3.00	6.00	12.00
		(We've Got) Christmas On Our Mind				
— Colored vinyl, round						
Rock-It 501		(Merry Christmas) From Lisa Marie/	1979	—	3.00	6.00
		(We've Got) Christmas On Our Mind				
— Black vinyl						
Rock-It 2001		(Merry Christmas) From Lisa Marie/	1979	6.25	12.50	25.00
		(We've Got) Christmas On Our Mind				
— Colored vinyl, Santa-shaped						
Rock-It 2001		(Merry Christmas) From Lisa Marie/	1979	6.25	12.50	25.00
		(We've Got) Christmas On Our Mind				
— Colored vinyl, bell-shape						
SAN FERNANDO VALLEY MALE CHORUS, THE						
45s						
Commander 1001		Christmas Madonna/Silent Night	19??	—	3.00	6.00
SAN SEBASTIAN STRINGS, THE						
45s						
Warner Bros. 7754		And Every Day Was Christmas/Sunset Colors	1973	—	2.50	5.00
SANBORN SINGERS, THE						
On Various-Artists Collections						
Jingle Bells		Sounds of Christmas (Columbia Special Products P 12474)				
O Little Town of Bethlehem		Sounds of Christmas (Columbia Special Products P 12474)				
SANBORN, DAVID						
45s						
Warner Bros 29943		Rain on Christmas/Back Again	1982	—	2.00	4.00

Label, Number	Title (A Side/B Side)	Year	VG	VG+	NM
SANDERS, RAY					
45s					
Stadium 1115	Christmas Letter/Missing Christmas Card	1964	2.00	4.00	8.00
SANDERS, WES					
45s					
T-O-S 113	Mommie Married Santa Claus/Away In The Manger	19??	—	2.00	4.00
SANDLER AND YOUNG					
45s					
Capitol 2333	I Sing Noel/Santa Claus Is Coming to Town	1968	—	3.00	6.00
P.I.P. 6514	Medley: I Believe-Ave Maria/(B-side unknown)	1975	—	2.00	4.00
Albums					
Capitol ST 2967	The Christmas World of Sandler and Young	1968	3.00	6.00	12.00
True Value 1	Happy Holidays, Album Eleven	1975	2.50	5.00	10.00
— Sold only at True Value Hardware stores					
True Value 2	Happy Holidays! Album Twelve	1976	2.50	5.00	10.00
— Sold only at True Value Hardware stores					

On Various-Artists Collections

Adeste Fideles	Happy Holidays, Album 6 (Capitol Creative Products SL-6669)
	Joys of Christmas (Capitol Creative Products SL-6610)
Christmas Song, The	Christmas Sounds of Music, The (Capitol Creative Products SL-6643)
	Magic of Christmas, The (Capitol SWBB-93810)
Do You Hear What I Hear	Christmas Day (Pickwick SPC 1010)
	Happy Holidays, Album 6 (Capitol Creative Products SL-6669)
	Sound of Christmas, The, Vol. 3 (Capitol Creative Products SL-6680)
Hark the Herald Angels Sing	I'll Be Home for Christmas (Pickwick SPC-1009)
Have Yourself a Merry Little Christmas	Happy Holidays, Vol. 5 (Capitol Creative Products SL-6627)
	Joys of Christmas (Capitol Creative Products SL-6610)
I Sing Noel	Christmas — The Season of Music (Capitol Creative Products SL-6679)
	Happy Holidays, Vol. 5 (Capitol Creative Products SL-6627)
	Zenith Presents Christmas, A Gift of Music Vol. 3 (Capitol Creative Products SL-6659)
Jingle Bells	Christmas, A Gift of Music (Capitol Special Markets SL-6687)
	Zenith Presents Christmas, A Gift of Music Vol. 4 (Capitol Creative Products SL-6687)
Mister Santa	Best of Christmas, The, Vol. I (Capitol SM-11833)
	Happy Holidays, Album Seven (Capitol Creative Products SL-6730)
O Holy Night	Little Drummer Boy, The (Capitol/Pickwick SPC-3462)
Santa Claus Is Coming to Town	Christmas Carousel (Capitol SQBE-94406)

SANDS, ROBERT
On Various-Artists Collections

Boar's Head Carol, The	Life Treasury of Christmas Music, The (Project/Capitol TL 100)
Golden Carol of the Three	Life Treasury of Christmas Music, The (Project/Capitol TL 100)
Wise Men, The	

Label, Number		Title (A Side/B Side)	Year	VG	VG+	NM
SANDS, TONY						
45s						
Lost Gold LGRX-1		Star of Bethlehem/Little White Slippers	1989	—	—	3.00
Lost Gold LGRX-1	PS	Star of Bethlehem/Little White Slippers	1989	—	—	3.00
SANETTES, THE						
45s						
Ohn-J 1001		Merry Christmas/Blessings From Above	1964	2.50	5.00	10.00
SANTA CLAUS						
45s						
Capitol F1260		Do You Believe in Santa Claus/Gabby the Gobbler	1950	5.00	10.00	20.00
— B-side by Ken Carson						
Capitol 2335		What Santa Wants for Christmas/Jingle Bells	1968	2.00	4.00	8.00
Capitol/Bozo CASF-3084	PS	Santa Claus and Sparky Sing...	195?	3.75	7.50	15.00
Capitol/Bozo F32029		Do You Believe In Santa Claus?/I Don't Want A Lot For Christmas	195?	3.00	6.00	12.00
— B-side by Sparky; this 45 is the entire contents of Album CASF-3084						
Albums						
Capitol T 2836		Santa's Own Christmas	1967	3.75	7.50	15.00

SANTA CLAUS AND CHILD
On Various-Artists Collections

All I Want for Christmas...	Christmas in Saint Louis ((no label) TS77-558/9)

The Spector of Christmas Past

Generally hailed as among the two or three best rock-related Christmas albums ever, *A Christmas Gift For You From Phil Spector* has been released in the U.S. many times with three distinct covers. (Top) The original cover on Philles Records. Look carefully to notice the misspelled "Marshmellow World"! (Middle) The second cover, retitled *Phil Spector's Christmas Album*, was on four different 1970s and 1980s reissues. (Bottom) Probably the rarest cover in LP size, this composite was used to house the Christmas album on the 1991 box set *Back To Mono*.

A Rare Christmas

Holiday Hits

(Top) Among the first 45s to have picture sleeves were children's records. Sometimes, some of those were hits, too; Jimmy Boyd's "I Saw Mommy Kissing Santa Claus" hit #1 in the holiday season of 1952. By the way, the hole in the middle was in the sleeve when it came out; the 78 rpm version does not have the hole. (Bottom) The Eagles' "Please Come Home For Christmas" not only was the highest charting Christmas single of the 1970s, it was the only 45 by this band to be issued in the U.S. with a picture sleeve.

The Colorful Season

It's not uncommon for holiday 45s to come out in colored vinyl versions, particularly the Christmasy colors of red and green. Top row: Original RCA Red Seal pressing of "Sleigh Ride" by the Boston Pops Orchestra; "Christmas Song" by Jethro Tull. Bottom row: "Twas the Night After Christmas," the B-side of "Redneck 12 Days of Christmas" by Jeff Foxworthy; "Silent Night" by Garth Brooks.

More red and green holiday 45s. Top row: "Christmas (Baby Please Come Home)" by Dion; "Jingle Bell Rock" by Daryl Hall and John Oates (green version is pictured; it also came out on red vinyl).
Bottom row: "C-H-R-I-S-T-M-A-S" by Eddy Arnold, original RCA country series version from 1949; "Christmas Is a Special Day" by Fats Domino.

High Time for a Holiday

(Top) In 1971, the drugged-out comedy duo of Cheech and Chong came out with their non-LP holiday track, "Santa Claus And His Old Lady," which actually stands out as one of their most enduring routines. This sleeve is fairly scarce. (Bottom) Deck the halls with boughs of ganja? This unique cover was on one of at least two albums celebrating a *Reggae Christmas*.

Santa Claus and his Old Lady
CHEECH AND CHONG
ODE 66021

Reggae Christmas *The Joe Gibbs Family of Artists*

Christmas Comeback

In the 1980s, the arrival of the compact disc helped spur sales of Christmas records to new heights. Two of the most influential works of the decade, both of which are getting scarce on vinyl, were (top) *Mannheim Steamroller Christmas*, which has spawned two sequels and dozens of sound-alikes, and (bottom) *A Very Special Christmas*, which united 15 artists to benefit Special Olympics. It remains a consistent seller on CD and helped revive pop artists' interest in holiday music.

Vinyl Lives On

Not many Christmas albums of the 1990s come out on vinyl, but here are two exceptions. (Top) The 1995 picture disc from *How The Grinch Stole Christmas*, the soundtrack of the TV show available for the first time since 1966. (Bottom) *Christmas on Death Row*, a 1996 collection of material from the controversial rap/R&B label Death Row.

Label, Number		Title (A Side/B Side)	Year	VG	VG+	NM
SANTA CLAUS & HIS BAND						
45s						
Little Tots 113		The Coming Of Santa Claus/Christmas Morning	195?	2.50	5.00	10.00
— B-side by Mother and the Little Tots; 78 rpm 7-inch record						
SANTA CLAUS AND HIS HELPERS						
45s						
Columbia 40577		Santa's Laughing Song/Santa, The Happy Wanderer	1955	3.75	7.50	15.00
Columbia 40577	PS	Santa's Laughing Song/Santa, The Happy Wanderer	1955	6.25	12.50	25.00
SANTA MERRIE						
45s						
San-Mer 11		Merry Santa Merrie/A Little Boy's Christmas	19??	—	2.00	4.00
San-Mer 11	PS	Merry Santa Merrie/A Little Boy's Christmas	19??	—	2.00	4.00
SANTA SCHWARTZ						
45s						
Rotten Rat 1009		'Tis The Season To Make Money/Jingle Bones	19??	5.00	10.00	20.00
SANTA'S DISCO BAND						
12-Inch Singles						
Magic Disc MDD-506		Santa Claus Is Coming To Town Disco/Xmas Medley	1977	2.50	5.00	10.00
45s						
Magic Disc 215		Santa Claus Is Coming To Town/Joy	1977	—	2.50	5.00
— B-side by Mary Love						
SANTA'S HELPERS						
Albums						
Design SDLPX-30	S	All I Want for Christmas Are My Two Front Teeth	196?	3.00	6.00	12.00
SANTA'S PIXIE HELPERS						
45s						
Pri 320		The Animal's Christmas Song/The Christmas Song Cha Cha Cha?	198?	—	2.50	5.00
Pri 320	PS	The Animal's Christmas Song/The Christmas Song Cha Cha Cha?	198?	—	2.50	5.00
SANTO AND JOHNNY						
45s						
Canadian American 120		Twistin' Bells/Bullseye!	1960	4.00	8.00	16.00
Canadian American 120	PS	Twistin' Bells/Bullseye!	1960	10.00	20.00	40.00
Canadian American 132		Twistin' Bells/Christmas Day	1961	5.00	10.00	20.00
— B-side by Linda Scott						
SAQQARA DOGS, THE						
45s						
Black AFTP001		Splatterdance/Merry Xmas Blues	1986	5.00	10.00	20.00
— B-side by the Celibate Rifles						
SARDUCCI, FATHER GUIDO						
45s						
Warner Bros. 49627		I Won't Be Twisting This Christmas/Parco Mac Arthur	1980	2.00	4.00	8.00
Warner Bros 49627	PS	I Won't Be Twisting This Christmas/Parco Mac Arthur	1980	2.50	5.00	10.00
SARGE, MARIA & ELIJAH						
45s						
North Side 103		Jesus Loves Me/A Cabbage Patch Doll on Christmas Eve	198?	—	3.00	6.00
— B-side by Christian Holiday						
SATURDAY'S CHILDREN						
45s						
Dunwich 144		The Christmas Song/Deck Five	1967	2.00	4.00	8.00
SAVOY, MARK						
45s						
Swallow 10240		Silver Bells/She Made Me Lose My Mind	19??	—	2.00	4.00

Label, Number	Title (A Side/B Side)	Year	VG	VG+	NM

SAWYER BROWN
45s
Capitol B-44282 — It Wasn't His Child/Falling Apart at the Heart — 1988 — — — 2.00 — 4.00
On Various-Artists Collections
Blue Christmas — Christmas for the 90's, Volume 1 (Capitol Nashville 1P 8117)
Please Come Home for Christmas — Christmas for the 90's, Volume 2 (Capitol Nashville 1P 8118)

Label, Number	Title (A Side/B Side)	Year	VG	VG+	NM
SAWYER BROWN					
45s					
Capitol B-44282	It Wasn't His Child/Falling Apart at the Heart	1988	—	2.00	4.00

On Various-Artists Collections
Blue Christmas — Christmas for the 90's, Volume 1 (Capitol Nashville 1P 8117)
Please Come Home for Christmas — Christmas for the 90's, Volume 2 (Capitol Nashville 1P 8118)

SAXON, SKY, AND FIREWALL
On Various-Artists Collections
Christmas in the Courtroom — Stuff This in Your Stocking! Elves in Action (Veebltronics/Skyclad 68)

SCHAFER, DAN
45s

Label, Number	Title (A Side/B Side)	Year	VG	VG+	NM
Tortoise Int'l. TB-11292	New Year's Eve/Baby, Now That I've Found You	1977	—	2.00	4.00

SCHARFF, WALTER
On Various-Artists Collections
Overture — Dangerous Christmas of Red Riding Hood, The (ABC-Paramount 536)

SCHIAVONE SISTERS, THE
45s

Label, Number	Title (A Side/B Side)	Year	VG	VG+	NM
De-Lite 510	Granny Claus/Christmas Child (O' Bambino)	1968	2.00	4.00	8.00

SCHLAMME, MARTHA
Albums

Label, Number		Title (A Side/B Side)	Year	VG	VG+	NM
Vanguard VRS 497	M	Chansons de Noel	1956	7.50	15.00	30.00

SCHNEIDER, JOHN
45s

Label, Number	Title (A Side/B Side)	Year	VG	VG+	NM
Scotti Bros. 02606	Katey's Christmas Card/Silent Night, Holy Night	1981	—	3.00	6.00
Scotti Bros. 03369	Katey's Christmas Card/Silent Night, Holy Night	1982	—	2.00	4.00

Albums

Label, Number	Title (A Side/B Side)	Year	VG	VG+	NM
Scotti Brothers FZ 37617	White Christmas	1981	2.50	5.00	10.00
Scotti Brothers 3Z 37617	White Christmas	198?	2.00	4.00	8.00

— *Budget-line reissue with new prefix*
On Various-Artists Collections
Please Come Home for Christmas — Tennessee Christmas (MCA 5620)
Tennessee Christmas (MCA S45-17046)

SCHOOL, DANNY
45s

Label, Number	Title (A Side/B Side)	Year	VG	VG+	NM
Ford 135	Christmas Rings A Bell/Happy New Year	1964	2.50	5.00	10.00

SCHOPPA, KELLY
45s

Label, Number	Title (A Side/B Side)	Year	VG	VG+	NM
Bellaire 5131	Merry Texas Christmas/Holiday Love	198?	—	2.00	4.00
NSD 226	Ooh, Christmas Tree (Not The Traditional)/White Christmas	1986	—	—	3.00

SCHREINER, ALEXANDER
On Various-Artists Collections
Christians Awake — Merry Christmas from... (Reader's Digest RD4-83)

SCHROEDER-SHEKER, THERESE
On Various-Artists Collections
Salve Regina — Winter's Solstice II, A (Windham Hill WH-1077)

SCHULMERICH "CARILLON AMERICANA"
On Various-Artists Collections
Oh, Come All Ye Faithful — Decca 38170 (title unknown) (Decca DL 38170)

SCHULZ, CHARLES M. – See SOUNDTRACKS: "CHARLIE BROWN CHRISTMAS, A"

SCHUMANN, WALTER (THE VOICES OF...)
45s

Label, Number		Title (A Side/B Side)	Year	VG	VG+	NM
Capitol CDF-9016	(4)	Christmas In The Air	1951	12.50	25.00	50.00

— *Contains four records (F95017, F95018, F95019, F95020) and box*

Label, Number	Title (A Side/B Side)	Year	VG	VG+	NM
Capitol F1841	White Christmas/Winter Wonderland	1951	3.75	7.50	15.00
Capitol F95017	Christmas in the Air!/Adeste Fideles	1951	2.50	5.00	10.00

— *"Part 1" and "Part 8" of album CDF-9016*

Label, Number	Title (A Side/B Side)	Year	VG	VG+	NM
Capitol F95018	Silent Night/Carol of the Bells//Winter Wonderland	1951	2.50	5.00	10.00
— "Part 2" and "Part 7" of album CDF-9016					
Capitol F95019	White Christmas/Mary, Mary	1951	2.50	5.00	10.00
— "Part 3" and "Part 6" of album CDF-9016					
Capitol F95020	Patapan//Wonderful Counselor/Wolcum Yole	1951	2.50	5.00	10.00
— "Part 4" and "Part 5" of album CDF-9016					
RCA Victor 47-5542	The Sound of Christmas/Magic Is the Earth	1953	5.00	10.00	20.00
RCA Victor 47-5922	Calypso Christmas/Christmas Tree	1954	3.75	7.50	15.00
RCA Victor 47-6318	The First Snowfall/Christmas Gift	1955	3.00	6.00	12.00
RCA Victor LPM-1141/LPT-6702 DJ	Christmas Chopsticks/Pearls On Velvet	1955	3.00	6.00	12.00
— B-side by Glenn Miller (non-Christmas song); promo-only record using the numbers of the LPs from which the songs were taken					

7-Inch Extended Plays

Label, Number	Title (A Side/B Side)	Year	VG	VG+	NM
RCA Victor 547-0702	Sleigh Ride/God Rest Ye Merry, Gentlemen/The Christmas Song// C-H-R-I-S-T-M-A-S/Go Tell It On The Mountain/Christmas Chopsticks	1955	2.00	4.00	8.00
RCA Victor 547-0703	Rudolph The Red-Nosed Reindeer/What Child Is This/Rise Up Shepherd And Foller// Parade Of The Wooden Soldiers/Lully, Lully, Lu/Christmas Gift	1955	2.00	4.00	8.00
RCA Victor 547-0704	The First Snowfall/Fum, Fum, Fum/Christmas Tree// Christmas In Killarney/The First Noel/Frosty The Snowman/Hark! The Herald Angels Sing	1955	2.00	4.00	8.00
RCA Victor EPC-1141 (3)	The Voices Of Christmas	1955	7.50	15.00	30.00
— Contains three records (547-0702, 547-0703, 547-0704) and box					

Albums

Label, Number	Title (A Side/B Side)	Year	VG	VG+	NM
Pickwick PCX-1003 M	The Christmas Voices of Walter Schumann	196?	3.75	7.50	15.00
— Reissue of Capitol material					
Pickwick SPCX-1003 R	The Christmas Voices of Walter Schumann	196?	2.50	5.00	10.00
RCA Victor LPM-1141 M	The Voices of Christmas	1955	5.00	10.00	20.00

On Various-Artists Collections

Lully Lully Lu	Family Christmas Collection, The (Time-Life STL-131)
What Child Is This?	Joyous Noel (Reader's Digest RDA-57A)

SCHUMANN-HEINK, ERNESTINE
On Various-Artists Collections

Silent Night (German)	Joyous Noel (Reader's Digest RDA-57A)

SCHUUR, DIANE
On Various-Artists Collections

Christmas Song, The	GRP Christmas Collection, A (GRP 9574)

SCHWEIG, ARWIN
45s

Label, Number	Title (A Side/B Side)	Year	VG	VG+	NM
True North 2014	A Star And A Stable/Christmas Angel	19??	—	2.00	4.00

SCOFIELD, JOHN
On Various-Artists Collections

Chipmunk Christmas	Yule Struttin' — A Blue Note Christmas (Blue Note 1P 8119)

SCOOBY DOO AND FRIENDS
Albums

Label, Number	Title (A Side/B Side)	Year	VG	VG+	NM
Peter Pan 8214	Exciting Christmas Stories	1978	3.75	7.50	15.00
— With voices from the TV series: Don Messick, Casey Kasem, Frank Welker, Heather North, Pat Stevens.					

SCOTT, BILLY
45s

Label, Number	Title (A Side/B Side)	Year	VG	VG+	NM
Lamon 10114	Merry Christmas/A Night To Remember	1983	—	2.00	4.00

SCOTT, J. ANTHONY
45s

Label, Number	Title (A Side/B Side)	Year	VG	VG+	NM
Cinnamon Toast 322	Whistling Christmas/Laura Lee	19??	—	2.50	5.00

SCOTT, JACK
45s

Label, Number	Title (A Side/B Side)	Year	VG	VG+	NM
Groove 58-0027	There's Trouble Brewin'/Jingle Bell Slide	1963	5.00	10.00	20.00
Ponie 7021-11	There's Trouble Brewin'/Jingle Bell Slide	197?	—	2.00	4.00

On Various-Artists Collections

Christmas Greetings	Christmas Greetings From RCA Victor And Groove Recording Artists (RCA Victor SP-45-128)
There's Trouble Brewin'	Jingle Bell Rock (Time-Life SRNR-XM)

Label, Number		Title (A Side/B Side)	Year	VG	VG+	NM

SCOTT, LINDA
45s

| Canadian American 132 | | Christmas Day/Twistin' Bells | 1961 | 5.00 | 10.00 | 20.00 |
| — B-side by Santo and Johnny | | | | | | |

SCOTT, MABEL
45s

| Hollywood 1023 | | Boogie Woogie Santa Claus/How I Hate To See Christmas | 1954 | 7.50 | 15.00 | 30.00 |

On Various-Artists Collections

| Boogie Woogie Santa Claus | | Merry Christmas Baby (Christmas Music for Young Lovers) (Hollywood HLP 501) Merry Christmas Baby (Gusto/Hollywood K-5018-X) | | | | |

SCOTT, MARK, TEENS
45s

| Challenge 9177 | | Christmas/Christmas Eve | 1962 | 3.00 | 6.00 | 12.00 |

SCOTT, OLIVER
45s

Total Experience 2435		Joy to the World /The Christmas Song (Chestnuts Roasting on an Open Fire)	1985	—	2.00	4.00
— B-side by the Gap Band						
Total Experience 2435		Joy To The World/The Christmas Song	1985	—	2.00	4.00
— B-side by Charlie Wilson						

On Various-Artists Collections

| Joy to the World | | Total Experience Christmas, A (Total Experience TEL8-5707) | | | | |

SCOTT, SHEREE
45s

| Robbins 105 | | Twinkle Toes (The Littlest Reindeer)/Our Christmas Day | 1959 | 10.00 | 20.00 | 40.00 |

SCOTT, TOM
On Various-Artists Collections

| Have Yourself a Merry Little Christmas | GRP Christmas Collection, A (GRP 9574) | | | | | |

SCOTTLAND
45s

Shadow SL 100		Credit Card Christmas/Outside In	1988	2.00	4.00	8.00
— All copies have stickers affixed to the labels with the correct titles; the records were pressed with the labels reversed!						
Shadow SL 100	PS	Credit Card Christmas/Outside In	1988	2.00	4.00	8.00

SCREAMIN' KENNY
45s

| Sashay 212 | | Blue Lights On My Christmas Tree/Holiday | 19?? | — | 2.50 | 5.00 |

SCREAMING TRIBESMEN
12-Inch Singles

| Survival 656491-6 | | Ayla//Santa's Little Helper/A Stand Alone | 1990 | 5.00 | 10.00 | 20.00 |

SCROOGE BROTHERS, THE
Albums

| Rhino RNEP 70514 | EP | Commercial Christmasland | 1987 | 2.00 | 4.00 | 8.00 |

SEA LARKS, THE
45s

| Jolt 333 | | Christmas On The Prairie/Christmas For Little Folks | 195? | 5.00 | 10.00 | 20.00 |

SECORD, JOHN
45s

| Code Of West 1561 | | Christmas Candle (same on both sides) | 19?? | — | 2.00 | 4.00 |

SECRET WEAPON
On Various-Artists Collections

| I'm Coming Home | | Winter Warnerland (Warner Bros. PRO-A-3328) | | | | |

Label, Number		Title (A Side/B Side)	Year	VG	VG+	NM

SEDAKA, NEIL
On Various-Artists Collections

Christmas Greetings		Christmas Greetings From RCA Victor And Groove Recording Artists (RCA Victor SP-45-128)				
New Year's Greetings		Christmas Greetings From RCA Victor And Groove Recording Artists (RCA Victor SP-45-128)				

SEEGER, PEGGY, BARBARA AND PENNY
Albums

Folkways FC-7053	10	American Folk Songs for Christmas	195?	12.50	25.00	50.00
Scholastic SC 7553	M	American Folk Songs for Christmas	1966	5.00	10.00	20.00
— Reissue of Folkways material						

SEEGER, PETE
Albums

Folkways FA 2311	M	Traditional Christmas Carols	1956	7.50	15.00	30.00
Folkways FTS 32311	R	Traditional Christmas Carols	1967	3.00	6.00	12.00
Philips PHM 2-300	(2) M	The Story of the Nativity	1963	5.00	10.00	20.00
Philips PHS 2-300	(2) S	The Story of the Nativity	1963	6.25	12.50	25.00

SEGER, BOB
45s

Cameo 444		Sock It To Me, Santa/Florida Time	1966	7.50	15.00	30.00

On Various-Artists Collections

Little Drummer Boy, The		Very Special Christmas, A (A&M SP-3911)				

SEGER, GARY
45s

Tax Records 319		The Christmas Equalization Act/The British Are Coming	1976	—	3.00	6.00

SELDON, ELDON
45s

Country Pride 191		Alfie the Elf/Where Have All The Christians Gone	19??	—	2.00	4.00

SELF, JIMMY DEAN
45s

Nor-Va-Jak 1333		An Old Christmas Card/Blue Christmas	1960	3.75	7.50	15.00

SENATOR BOBBY
45s

Parkway 137		Mellow Yellow/White Christmas	1967	2.50	5.00	10.00
— A-side by "Senator Bobby & Senator McKinley"; B-side by "Bobby the Poet" (Dylan impersonation)						

SENIOR CONCERT ORCHESTRA, THE
On Various-Artists Collections

Auld Lang Syne	Joyous Christmas, Volume 2 (Columbia Special Products CSS 808)
Christmas Fantasy: Jingle Bells/Silent Night/Adeste Fideles	Joyous Christmas, Volume 4 (Columbia Special Products CSS 1485)
Christmas Is Forever (Medley)	Joyous Christmas, Volume 4 (Columbia Special Products CSS 1485)
Dance of the Sugar-Plum Fairy	Joyous Christmas, Volume V (Columbia Special Products C 10398)
Danse des Mirlitons (from The Nutcracker)	Joyous Christmas, Volume 6 (Columbia Special Products C 11083)
Go Tell It on the Mountain	Joyous Christmas, Volume V (Columbia Special Products C 10398)
Let It Snow! Let It Snow! Let It Snow!	Joyous Christmas, Volume 2 (Columbia Special Products CSS 808)
Medley: Deck the Halls/We Three Kings of Orient Are/ I Heard the Bells on Christmas Day	Joyous Christmas, Volume V (Columbia Special Products C 10398)
Medley: God Rest Ye Merry Gentlemen/O Tannenbaum	Joyous Christmas, Volume 2 (Columbia Special Products CSS 808)
Medley: Good King Wenceslas/ Away in a Manger	Joyous Christmas, Volume V (Columbia Special Products C 10398)
Medley: Hark! The Herald Angels Sing/ Deck the Hall with Boughs of Holly	Joyous Christmas, Volume 2 (Columbia Special Products CSS 808)
Medley: Jolly Old St. Nicholas/ O Tannenbaum/ Angels from the Realms of Glory	Joyous Christmas, Volume V (Columbia Special Products C 10398)
Old-Fashioned Christmas (Medley)	Joyous Christmas, Volume 6 (Columbia Special Products C 11083)
Petersburg Sleighride	Joyous Christmas, Volume 6 (Columbia Special Products C 11083)
Rudolf the Red-Nosed Reindeer	Joyous Christmas, Volume 2 (Columbia Special Products CSS 808)
Waltz of the Flowers (from The Nutcracker)	Joyous Christmas, Volume 4 (Columbia Special Products CSS 1485)
Yuletide Greetings (Medley)	Joyous Christmas, Volume 6 (Columbia Special Products C 11083)

Label, Number	Title (A Side/B Side)	Year	VG	VG+	NM
SENTACRUZ, DANIEL, ENSEMBLE					
45s					
EMI 4194	Christmas Carol/Lullaby	1975	—	2.00	4.00
SENTINALS, THE					
45s					
Era 3097	Christmas Eve/Latin Soul	1962	7.50	15.00	30.00
SERIOUS BROTHERS, THE					
45s					
Tune Town 101	It's Another Joyful Elvis Presley Christmas/(B-side unknown)	1988	4.00	8.00	12.00
SESAME STREET DOO WAHS, THE					
45s					
Sesame Street 22112	Counting The Days/Christmas Sing-A-Long	197?	—	2.50	5.00
— B-side by the Sesame Street Muppets & Cast					

SESAME STREET FESTIVAL ORCHESTRA
On Various-Artists Collections
Sesame Street Christmas Overture   Merry Christmas from Sesame Street (CRA CTW 25516)

SEVILLE, DAVID, AND THE CHIPMUNKS – See CHIPMUNKS, THE, DAVID SEVILLE AND

SEYMOUR'S HEARTBEAT TRUMPET					
7-Inch Extended Plays					
Heartbeat 711	Jingle Bells/O Come All Ye Faithful/Deck The Halls//	1960	2.00	4.00	8.00
	O Tannenbaum/The First Noel/Silent Night				
Sunny 531	Jingle Bells/O Come All Ye Faithful/Deck The Halls//	19??	2.00	4.00	8.00
	O Tannenbaum/The First Noel/Silent Night				

SHADOWFAX
On Various-Artists Collections
Petite Aubade   Winter's Solstice, A (Windham Hill WH-1045)

SHAMBLIN, MICHAEL					
45s					
Heart of Dixie 0117	Thank God For Christmas/(B-side unknown)	198?	—	—	3.00
SHANE, DESIREE					
45s					
Rollins 87	Jingle Bell Disco/Santa Can I Count On You	197?	—	2.50	5.00
SHANTONS, THE					
45s					
Jay-Mar 1292	The Christmas Song/Santa Claus Is Coming To Town	1960	50.00	100.00	200.00
SHARI					
45s					
Robinn 100	Ev'ry Day Is Christmas/April Fool	19??	—	2.00	4.00

SHARPE, CATHY
On Various-Artists Collections
North Pole Rock   Rockin' Christmas — The '50s (Rhino RNLP-066)

SHAW, ARTIE					
45s					
Decca 27243	White Christmas/Jingle Bells	1951	3.75	7.50	15.00
SHAW, ELEANOR					
45s					
Tin Pan Alley 45-516	I Can't Wait Until Next Christmas / Kindness	19??	3.00	6.00	12.00
SHAW, JOAN					
45s					
Jaguar 3010	I Want A Man For Christmas/Most Of All	1954	3.00	6.00	12.00

Label, Number	Title (A Side/B Side)	Year	VG	VG+	NM

SHAW, ROBERT, CHORALE
Also see ATLANTA SYMPHONY ORCHESTRA (SHAW).

Albums

Label, Number		Title (A Side/B Side)	Year	VG	VG+	NM
RCA Victor Red Seal LM-1112	M	Christmas Hymns and Carols	1952	10.00	20.00	40.00
RCA Victor Red Seal LM-1711	M	Christmas Hymns and Carols Volume II	1954	7.50	15.00	30.00
RCA Victor Red Seal LM-2139	M	Christmas Hymns and Carols, Volume 1	1957	5.00	10.00	20.00

— Original cover has "LM-2139" with "RCA Victor" in box on upper right

Label, Number		Title (A Side/B Side)	Year	VG	VG+	NM
RCA Victor Red Seal LM-2139	M	Christmas Hymns and Carols, Volume 1	1958	4.00	8.00	16.00

— Second cover has "LM-2139" in lower left corner; small "RE" is on front cover

Label, Number		Title (A Side/B Side)	Year	VG	VG+	NM
RCA Victor Red Seal LM-2684	M	The Many Moods of Christmas	1963	3.00	6.00	12.00
RCA Victor Red Seal LSC-2684	S	The Many Moods of Christmas	1963	3.75	7.50	15.00

On Various-Artists Collections

And the Glory of the Lord	American Family Album of Favorite Christmas Music, The (RCA Red Seal VCS-7060)
Angels We Have Heard on High	American Family Album of Favorite Christmas Music, The (RCA Red Seal VCS-7060)
	Christmas Festival of Songs and Carols, Volume 2 (RCA Victor PRM-195)
	For a Musical Merry Christmas (RCA Victor PR-149A)
	Happy Holidays, Volume IV (RCA Victor PRS-267)
Away in a Manger	American Family Album of Favorite Christmas Music, The (RCA Red Seal VCS-7060)
Behold the Lamb of God	American Family Album of Favorite Christmas Music, The (RCA Red Seal VCS-7060)
Carol of the Bells	Happy Holidays, Volume 19 (RCA Special Products DPL1-0689)
Christ Was Born on Christmas Day	Family Christmas Collection, The (Time-Life STL-131)
Deck the Halls	American Family Album of Favorite Christmas Music, The (RCA Red Seal VCS-7060)
First Noel, The	American Family Album of Favorite Christmas Music, The (RCA Red Seal VCS-7060)
	Joyous Noel (Reader's Digest RDA-57A)
For Unto Us a Child Is Born	American Family Album of Favorite Christmas Music, The (RCA Red Seal VCS-7060)
Glory to God	American Family Album of Favorite Christmas Music, The (RCA Red Seal VCS-7060)
God Rest You Merry, Gentlemen	American Family Album of Favorite Christmas Music, The (RCA Red Seal VCS-7060)
Hallelujah Chorus	American Family Album of Favorite Christmas Music, The (RCA Red Seal VCS-7060)
	Time-Life Treasury of Christmas, The, Volume Two (Time-Life STL-108)
Hark! The Herald Angels Sing	American Family Album of Favorite Christmas Music, The (RCA Red Seal VCS-7060)
	Joyous Noel (Reader's Digest RDA-57A)
I Saw Three Ships	Very Merry Christmas, A, Volume VI (RCA Special Products PRS-427)
It Came Upon the Midnight Clear	American Family Album of Favorite Christmas Music, The (RCA Red Seal VCS-7060)
Joy to the World	Joyous Noel (Reader's Digest RDA-57A)
Lift Up Your Heads	American Family Album of Favorite Christmas Music, The (RCA Red Seal VCS-7060)
Medley: Carol of the Bells/Deck the Halls	Time-Life Treasury of Christmas, The (Time-Life STL-107)
Medley: Carol of the Bells/Lo, How a Rose E'er Blooming/ Go Tell It on the Mountain	Happy Holidays, Volume 15 (RCA Special Products DPL1-0453)
Medley: Christmas Hymn/Hark! The Herald Angels Sing	Brightest Stars of Christmas, The (RCA Special Products DPL1-0086)
Medley: Coventry Carol/ Shepherd's Carol	Family Christmas Collection, The (Time-Life STL-131)
Medley: Good Christian Men, Rejoice/ Silent Night/Patapan/ O Come, All Ye Faithful	60 Christmas Classics (Sessions DVL2-0723)
Medley: I Saw Three Ships/ O Tannenbaum/Allon, Gay, Gay Bergeres/The Holly and the Ivy	Happy Holidays, Vol. 20 (RCA Special Products DPL1-0713)
Medley: Joy to the World/Angels We Have Heard on High	Henry Mancini Selects Great Songs of Christmas (RCA Special Products DPL1-0148)
	Time-Life Treasury of Christmas, The (Time-Life STL-107)
Medley: Joy to the World/It Came Upon a Midnight Clear	Christmas in New York (RCA Victor PRM-257)
Medley: O Come All Ye Faithful/Angels We Have Heard on High	Christmas in California (RCA Victor PRS-276)
	Christmas in New York Volume 2 (RCA Victor PRS-270)
Medley: O Come All Ye Faithful/ Away in a Manger/ God Rest Ye Merry, Gentlemen	Happy Holidays, Volume 13 (RCA Special Products DPL1-0319)
	Christmastime in Carol and Song (RCA PRM-271)
Medley: O Little Town of Bethlehem/ The First Noel	Very Merry Christmas, A, Volume 5 (RCA Special Products PRS-343)
Medley: Wassail Song/Deck the Halls	Happy Holidays, Volume 14 (RCA Special Products DPL1-0376)
Medley: We Three Kings of Orient Are/Hark, the Herald Angels Sing	Time-Life Treasury of Christmas, The, Volume Two (Time-Life STL-108)
O Come, All Ye Faithful	American Family Album of Favorite Christmas Music, The (RCA Red Seal VCS-7060)
	Very Merry Christmas, A, Volume VII (RCA Special Products DPL1-0049)
O Come, O Come, Emmanuel	American Family Album of Favorite Christmas Music, The (RCA Red Seal VCS-7060)
O Little Town of Bethlehem	American Family Album of Favorite Christmas Music, The (RCA Red Seal VCS-7060)
O Sanctissima	RCA Victor Presents Music for the Twelve Days of Christmas (RCA Victor PRS-188)
Overture (Sinfonia)	American Family Album of Favorite Christmas Music, The (RCA Red Seal VCS-7060)
Pastoral Symphony (Pifa)	American Family Album of Favorite Christmas Music, The (RCA Red Seal VCS-7060)
Silent Night	American Family Album of Favorite Christmas Music, The (RCA Red Seal VCS-7060)
So Blest a Sight	Family Christmas Collection, The (Time-Life STL-131)
Twelve Days of Christmas, The	Time-Life Treasury of Christmas, The, Volume Two (Time-Life STL-108)
Wassail Song	For a Musical Merry Christmas, Vol. Two (RCA Victor PRM 189)
We Three Kings	Happy Holidays, Vol. III (RCA Victor PRS-255)
	Music to Trim Your Tree By (RCA Victor PRM 225)

Label, Number		Title (A Side/B Side)	Year	VG	VG+	NM
SHEA, GEORGE BEVERLY						
45s						
RCA Victor 47-5408		O Holy Night/Go Tell It on the Mountain	1953	3.75	7.50	15.00
RCA Victor 47-5409		O Little Town of Bethlehem/Thou Didst Leave Thy Throne	1953	3.75	7.50	15.00
RCA Victor 47-5410		Silent Night/Away in a Manger	1953	3.75	7.50	15.00
RCA Victor 47-5411		I Wonder As I Wander/There's a Song in the Air	1953	3.75	7.50	15.00
RCA Victor 47-5904		Put Christ Back Into Christmas/Happy Birthday, Gentle Savior	1954	3.75	7.50	15.00
RCA Victor 47-6315		Christmas, Christmas/Sleep Precious Babe	1955	3.75	7.50	15.00
RCA Victor 47-8123		Greenwillow Christmas/He Is No Stranger	1962	3.00	6.00	12.00
Albums						
RCA Camden CAL-850	M	Christmas with George Beverly Shea	196?	3.00	6.00	12.00
RCA Camden CAS-850	S	Christmas with George Beverly Shea	196?	3.00	6.00	12.00
RCA Victor LPM-2064	M	Christmas Hymns	1959	3.75	7.50	15.00
RCA Victor LSP-2064	S	Christmas Hymns	1959	5.00	10.00	20.00
On Various-Artists Collections						
Go Tell It on the Mountain		Joyous Noel (Reader's Digest RDA-57A)				
Joy to the World		Merry Christmas (RCA Victor PRM-168)				
O Holy Night		Country Style Christmas, A (Columbia Musical Treasury 3P 6316)				
O Little Town of Bethlehem		Christmas Programming from RCA Victor (RCA Victor SP-33-66)				
		Happy Holidays, Vol. 20 (RCA Special Products DPL1-0713)				
		October Christmas Sampler 59-40-41 (RCA Victor SPS-33-54)				
SHEARER, CHARLIE						
45s						
Puzzle 110586		Reindeer Don't Run Over Grandma/Granny's Ten Feet Tall	1986	—	3.00	6.00
SHELDON, JACK						
45s						
Griffin 509		It's A California Christmas/Twenty Years	197?	—	2.50	5.00
SHELDON, LINN						
45s						
Cosmic 707		Boofo Goes Where Santa Goes/Rabbits Have A Christmas	19??	—	2.50	5.00
SHELTON, ANNE						
45s						
Buena Vista 476		It Won't Be Long 'Til Christmas/The Christmas Star	1969	2.00	4.00	8.00
Buena Vista 476	PS	It Won't Be Long 'Til Christmas/The Christmas Star	1969	2.50	5.00	10.00
SHELTON, RICKY VAN						
Albums						
Columbia FC 45269		Ricky Van Shelton Sings Christmas	1989	3.00	6.00	12.00
SHENANDOAH						
45s						
Capitol Nashville S7-19344		There's a Way in the Manger/	1996	—	—	3.00
		The Christmas Song (Chestnuts Roasting on an Open Fire)				
SHEPPARD, T.G.						
45s						
Hitsville 6048		May I Spend Every New Year's Eve with You/	1976	—	2.00	4.00
		I'll Always Remember That Song				
SHERMAN, ALLAN						
45s						
Warner Bros. 5406		The Twelve Gifts of Christmas/	1963	6.25	12.50	25.00
		You Went the Wrong Way, Old King Louie				
Albums						
Warner Bros. W 1569	M	For Swingin' Livers Only!	1964	3.00	6.00	12.00
— *Contains one Christmas song:* Twelve Gifts of Christmas, The						
Warner Bros. WS 1569	S	For Swingin' Livers Only!	1964	3.75	7.50	15.00
On Various-Artists Collections						
Twelve Gifts of Christmas, The		Dr. Demento Presents the Greatest Novelty Records of All Time Volume VI: Christmas (Rhino RNLP 825)				
SHERMAN, BOBBY						
45s						
Metromedia 204		Goin' Home (Sing a Song of Christmas Cheer)/	1970	—	3.00	6.00
		Love's What You're Gettin' for Christmas				
Metromedia 204	PS	Goin' Home (Sing a Song of Christmas Cheer)/	1970	2.00	4.00	8.00
		Love's What You're Gettin' for Christmas				

Label, Number		Title (A Side/B Side)	Year	VG	VG+	NM
Albums						
Metromedia MD 1038		Bobby Sherman Christmas Album	1970	3.75	7.50	15.00
On Various-Artists Collections						
Love's What You're Getting for Christmas		Joyous Songs of Christmas, The (Columbia Special Products C 10400)				

SHERMAN, JOE
45s

World Artists 1015		I Saw A Star/The Stolen Hours	1963	2.00	4.00	8.00
World Artists 1015	PS	I Saw A Star/The Stolen Hours	1963	2.50	5.00	10.00

SHERWIN TRIO, THE
45s

Sahara 105		Christmas Train/Born In Bethlehem	19??	—	2.50	5.00

SHILOH PENTECOSTAL CHOIR
45s

Paramount 0250		It's Christmas Again/Baby Boy	1973	—	2.50	5.00
Paramount 0251		No Room in the Inn/Creation	1973	—	2.50	5.00

SHINER, MERVIN
45s

Coral 61080		I Dreamt That I Was Santa Claus/ Don't Wait Until the Night Before Christmas	1953	3.75	7.50	15.00
Decca 28504		I Saw Mommy Kissing Santa Claus/ Snowy White Snow-Jingle Bells	1952	3.75	7.50	15.00
Decca 46280		Santa, Santa Don't Be Mad At Me/Fee Fi Fiddle	1950	3.75	7.50	15.00

SHINETTE, CAROL
45s

Optune 263		Christmas Is For The One You Love/Christmas Time	19??	2.00	4.00	8.00

SHIRLEY AND SQUIRRELY
45s

GRT 105		A Squirrely Christmas/Deck The Halls	1976	2.00	4.00	8.00

SHIRLEY, DANNY
45s

Amor 1005		Christmas Needs Love To Be Christmas/(B-side unknown)	1984	—	2.00	4.00

SHITBIRDS
On Various-Artists Collections

Christmas Is a Comin' (May God Bless You)	Happy Birthday, Baby Jesus (Sympathy For The Record Industry SFTRI 271)				

SHOO AND THE RAINDROPS
45s

Avenue D 16		Jingle Bell Stomp/Even Now	19??	—	2.50	5.00
— B-side by Shoo & The Jumpin' Tones						

SHOOK, JACK, AND DOTTIE DILLARD
45s

Coral 64066		There's No Place Like Home At Christmas/Blue Christmas	1950	3.75	7.50	15.00

SHORE, DINAH
7-Inch Extended Plays

Chevrolet 2886/7		You Meet The Nicest People/Jingle Bells// Silent Night/The Coventry Carol	1960	2.50	5.00	10.00
— 7-inch 33 1/3 rpm, small hole record from Capitol Custom Services						
Chevrolet 2886/7	PS	Season's Best	1960	2.50	5.00	10.00
RCA Victor EPA-4119		Opening/You Meet the Nicest People/Have Yourself a Merry Little Christmas//Christmas Party/Happy Christmas Little Friend/Closing	1957	3.00	6.00	12.00
RCA Victor EPA-4119	PS	You Meet the Nicest People at Christmas	1957	3.00	6.00	12.00

On Various-Artists Collections

Coventry Carol, The	Christmas — The Season of Music (Capitol Creative Products SL-6679)				
	Magic of Christmas, The (Capitol SWBB-93810)				
	Sound of Christmas, The, Vol. 3 (Capitol Creative Products SL-6680)				
	Zenith Presents Christmas, A Gift of Music Vol. 3 (Capitol Creative Products SL-6659)				
Happy Christmas Little Friend	Family Christmas Collection, The (Time-Life STL-131)				

Label, Number		Title (A Side/B Side)	Year	VG	VG+	NM
Silent Night		Christmas America (Capitol Special Markets SL-6884)				
		Christmas Carousel (Capitol SQBE-94406)				
		Happy Holidays, Vol. 5 (Capitol Creative Products SL-6627)				
		Joys of Christmas (Capitol Creative Products SL-6610)				
		Let's Celebrate Christmas (Capitol Special Markets SL-6923)				
		Sound of Christmas, The (Capitol Creative Products SL-6515)				
		Very Merry Christmas, A, Volume VIII (Capitol Special Markets SL-6954)				
Twelve Days of Christmas, The		Great Songs of Christmas, The, Album Five (Columbia Special Products CSP 238M)				
What Child Is This		American Christmas, An (Capitol Special Markets CP-68)				
		Wonderful World of Christmas, The, Album Two (Capitol Special Markets SL-8025)				

SHRUNKEN HEAD
45s

Label, Number		Title (A Side/B Side)	Year	VG	VG+	NM
Noise Werks 6602		What Child Is This/Less Out Of You	1994	—	2.00	4.00

SHURFINE SINGERS, THE
45s

Label, Number		Title (A Side/B Side)	Year	VG	VG+	NM
Josie 969		Go Tell It on the Mountain/Silent Night & The 11 O'Clock News	1966	2.50	5.00	10.00

SIDEBOTTOM, FRANK
7-Inch Extended Plays

Label, Number		Title (A Side/B Side)	Year	VG	VG+	NM
In Tape IT 041		Christmas Is Really Fantastic/Oh Come All Ye Faithful//	1987	—	2.50	5.00
		Mull Of Timperley/Christmas Medley				
In Tape IT 041	PS	(title unknown)	1987	—	2.50	5.00
— Both record and sleeve are U.K. imports						

SIGERSON, DAVITT
On Various-Artists Collections

Label, Number		Title (A Side/B Side)	Year	VG	VG+	NM
It's a Big Country		Christmas Record, A (Ze/Passport PB 6020)				

SIGLER, BUNNY
45s

Label, Number		Title (A Side/B Side)	Year	VG	VG+	NM
Philadelphia Int'l. 3582		Jingle Bells (Part 1)/Jingle Bells (Part 2)	1975	—	2.50	5.00

SILBERMAN, BENEDICT, ORCHESTRA AND CHORUS
45s

Label, Number		Title (A Side/B Side)	Year	VG	VG+	NM
Palette 5037		The Chipmunk Song/Lovers of Paris	1959	2.50	5.00	10.00

SILVERSTEIN, STEVE
On Various-Artists Collections

Label, Number		Title (A Side/B Side)	Year	VG	VG+	NM
D'Amour Je Suis de Sheriter		Christmas in San Francisco (Embarcadero Center EC-101)				

SIMEONE, HARRY, CHORALE
45s

Label, Number		Title (A Side/B Side)	Year	VG	VG+	NM
Kapp 628		O Bambino (One Cold and Blessed Winter)/	1964	2.00	4.00	8.00
		Sing of a Merry Christmas				
Kapp 628	PS	O Bambino (One Cold and Blessed Winter)/	1964	3.00	6.00	12.00
		Sing of a Merry Christmas				
Kapp 711		The Little Drummer Boy/Hallelujah	1965	2.00	4.00	8.00
— Re-recording of 1958 hit						
MCA 65030		The Little Drummer Boy/O Bambino	1973	—	2.00	4.00
— Black label with rainbow; this contains the 1965 Kapp re-recording of the A-side						
MCA 65030		The Little Drummer Boy/O Bambino	1980	—	—	3.00
— Blue label with rainbow; this contains the 1965 Kapp re-recording of the A-side						
Mercury 72065		Do You Hear What I Hear?/March of the Angels	1962	2.00	4.00	8.00
— Maroon label						
Mercury 72065		Do You Hear What I Hear?/March of the Angels	1962	2.00	4.00	8.00
— Black label						
Omni Sound 1002		Calypso Noel/Love Came Down	19??	—	2.00	4.00
20th Century 2434		The Little Drummer Boy/Oh Holy Night	1979	—	2.00	4.00
20th Fox 121		The Little Drummer Boy/Die Lorelei	1958	5.00	10.00	20.00
— Original pressings have light blue labels with no "Original Version" on label						
20th Fox 121		The Little Drummer Boy/Die Lorelei	1959	3.75	7.50	15.00
— Second pressings have light blue labels with "Original Version" in a box and a brief outline of the song on label						
20th Fox 121		The Little Drummer Boy/Die Lorelei	196?	2.50	5.00	10.00
— Reissue with black label and gold trim						
20th Fox 121	PS	The Little Drummer Boy/Die Lorelei	1959	6.25	12.50	25.00
20th Fox 429		The Little Drummer Boy/O Holy Night	1963	2.00	4.00	8.00
20th Fox 6429		The Little Drummer Boy/O Holy Night	1964	—	3.00	6.00
20th Fox 6429	PS	The Little Drummer Boy/O Holy Night	1964	2.00	4.00	8.00

Label, Number		Title (A Side/B Side)	Year	VG	VG+	NM
Albums						
Diplomat XS 1018		The Little Drummer Boy	196?	3.00	6.00	12.00
— Abridged reissue of 20th Fox material						
Kapp KL 1450	M	O Bambino/The Little Drummer Boy	1965	3.00	6.00	12.00
Kapp KS 3450	S	O Bambino/The Little Drummer Boy	1965	3.75	7.50	15.00
Mercury MG 20820	M	Wonderful Songs of Christmas	1963	3.75	7.50	15.00
Mercury SR 60820	S	Wonderful Songs of Christmas	1963	5.00	10.00	20.00
Mistletoe MLP-1201	S	The Little Drummer Boy	1973	2.00	4.00	8.00
— Reissue of TFS 3100 with same contents						
20th Century T-580		The Little Drummer Boy	1978	2.50	5.00	10.00
— Another reissue of TFS 3100						
20th Fox FOX-3002	M	Sing We Now of Christmas	1959	6.25	12.50	25.00
20th Fox TFM 3100	M	The Little Drummer Boy	1963	3.00	6.00	12.00
— Reissue of FOX-3002 with same contents						
20th Fox TFS 3100	S	The Little Drummer Boy	1963	3.75	7.50	15.00
— Same as above, but in stereo ("The Little Drummer Boy" is mono)						

On Various-Artists Collections

Carol of the Bells	Christmas Through the Years (Reader's Digest RDA-143)
Christmas Is	Great Songs of Christmas, The, Album Seven (Columbia Special Products CSS 547)
	WHIO Radio Christmas Feelings (Sound Approach/CSP P 16366)
Little Drummer Boy, The	Best of Christmas (Mistletoe MLP-1209)
	Billboard Greatest Christmas Hits, 1955-Present (Rhino R1 70636)
	Christmas Through the Years (Reader's Digest RDA-143)
	Happy Holidays, Vol. 23 (MCA Special Products 15042)
	Happy Holidays, Volume 18 (RCA Special Products DPL1-0608)
	Popular Christmas Classics (Capitol Special Markets SL-8100)
	Time-Life Treasury of Christmas, The (Time-Life STL-107)
	12 Hits of Christmas (United Artists UA-LA669-R)
Night Before Christmas Song, The	Let's Celebrate Christmas (Capitol Special Markets SL-6923)
O Holy Night	Best of Christmas (Mistletoe MLP-1209)
Rudolph the Red-Nosed Reindeer	Great Songs of Christmas, The, Album Seven (Columbia Special Products CSS 547)

SIMMONS, TED
On Various-Artists Collections

Gospel According to St. Luke	Christmas in Saint Louis ((no label) TS77-558/9)
Gospel According to St. Matthew and St. Luke	Christmas in Saint Louis ((no label) TS77-558/9)

SIMMONS, VESSIE
45s

Label, Number	Title (A Side/B Side)	Year	VG	VG+	NM
Simco 123	Christmas Party Rap (Part 1)/Christmas Party Rap (Part 2)	198?	—	2.00	4.00

SIMMS, LU ANN
45s

Label, Number	Title (A Side/B Side)	Year	VG	VG+	NM
Columbia 170	I Dreamt That I Was Santa Claus/I Just Can't Wait 'Til Christmas	1953	3.00	6.00	12.00
Columbia 40089	I Dreamt That I Was Santa Claus/I Just Can't Wait 'Til Christmas	1953	3.75	7.50	15.00

On Various-Artists Collections

Here Comes Santa Claus	Columbia 40109 (title unknown) (Columbia 4-40109)

SIMON AND GARFUNKEL
45s

Label, Number		Title (A Side/B Side)	Year	VG	VG+	NM
Columbia JZSP 116469	DJ	7 O'Clock News-Silent Night (same on both sides)	1966	6.25	12.50	25.00
— Promo-only Christmas release for radio stations						
Albums						
Columbia CL 2563	M	Parsley, Sage, Rosemary and Thyme	1966	3.75	·7.50	15.00
— Contains one Christmas song: 7 O'Clock News/Silent Night						
Columbia CS 9363	S	Parsley, Sage, Rosemary and Thyme	1966	2.50	5.00	10.00
— Same as above, but in stereo						
Columbia C5X 37587	(5)	Collected Works	1981	7.50	15.00	30.00
— Contains one Christmas song: 7 O'Clock News/Silent Night						

On Various-Artists Collections

Star Carol, The	Very Merry Christmas, A (Columbia Special Products CSS 563)

SIMON, FRED
On Various-Artists Collections

Simple Psalm	Winter's Solstice II, A (Windham Hill WH-1077)

SIMON, FRED, AND TRAUT/RODBY
On Various-Artists Collections

Christmas Song, The	Jazzy Wonderland, A (Columbia 1P 8120)

Label, Number	Title (A Side/B Side)	Year	VG	VG+	NM

SIMPSON, RED
45s
Capitol 3778	Truckin' Trees for Christmas/Blue Blue Christmas	1973	—	3.00	6.00

On Various-Artists Collections
Truckin' Trees for Christmas	Country Christmas (Time-Life STL-109)				

SINACORE, BENNY
45s
Tin Pan Alley 125/126	You Broke the Heart That Loved You/Christmas Won't Be the Same	196?	3.00	6.00	12.00
— Red vinyl					

SINATRA FAMILY, THE – See "VARIOUS ARTISTS COMPILATIONS"

SINATRA, FRANK
45s
Capitol F2954	White Christmas/The Christmas Waltz	1954	5.00	10.00	20.00
Capitol 2954	White Christmas/The Christmas Waltz	1962	2.50	5.00	10.00
— Also known to exist without the "F" prefix on orange and yellow swirl label					
Capitol F3900	Mistletoe and Holly/The Christmas Waltz	1957	3.75	7.50	15.00
— "The Christmas Waltz" here is a different version than that on Capitol 2954.					
Capitol PRO 1707/8 DJ	Mistletoe and Holly (with spoken intro)/Mistletoe and Holly	1960	25.00	50.00	100.00
— Christmas Seals record for 1960, with Sinatra introducing the song					
Capitol S7-18204	Jingle Bells/I'll Be Home for Christmas	1994	—	2.50	5.00
— Red vinyl					
Columbia 1-924	Remember Me in Your Dreams/Let It Snow, Let It Snow, Let It Snow	1950	15.00	30.00	60.00
— Microgroove 33 1/3 rpm single					
Columbia 6-924	Remember Me in Your Dreams/Let It Snow, Let It Snow, Let It Snow	1950	7.50	15.00	30.00
Columbia 38256	Silent Night/Adeste Fideles	1950	5.00	10.00	20.00
— From 45 box set B-167					
Columbia 38257	Jingle Bells/White Christmas	1950	5.00	10.00	20.00
— From 45 box set B-167					
Columbia 38258	O Little Town of Bethlehem/It Came Upon a Midnight Clear	1950	5.00	10.00	20.00
— From 45 box set B-167					
Columbia 38259	Have Yourself a Merry Little Christmas/Santa Claus Is Comin' to Town	1950	5.00	10.00	20.00
— From 45 box set B-167					
Columbia 39069	Remember Me in Your Dreams/Let It Snow, Let It Snow, Let It Snow	1950	3.75	7.50	15.00
— Reissue of Columbia 6-924					
Columbia JZSP 116427/8 DJ	White Christmas/Have Yourself A Merry Little Christmas	1966	12.50	25.00	50.00
Reprise 243	Have Yourself a Merry Little Christmas/How Shall I Send Thee?	1963	5.00	10.00	20.00
— B-side by Les Baxter					
Reprise 0314	I Heard the Bells on Christmas Day/The Little Drummer Boy	1964	5.00	10.00	20.00
Reprise 0314 PS	I Heard the Bells on Christmas Day/The Little Drummer Boy	1964	12.50	25.00	50.00
Reprise 0317	We Wish You the Merriest/Go Tell It on the Mountain	1964	10.00	20.00	40.00
— By Frank Sinatra/Bing Crosby/Fred Waring					
Reprise 0317 PS	We Wish You the Merriest/Go Tell It on the Mountain	1964	15.00	30.00	60.00
— By Frank Sinatra/Bing Crosby/Fred Waring					
Reprise 0790	Whatever Happened to Christmas?/I Wouldn't Trade Christmas	1968	3.00	6.00	12.00
— B-side by The Sinatra Family					
Reprise 1342	A Baby Just Like You/Christmas Mem'ries	1975	2.50	5.00	10.00
Reprise 1342 PS	A Baby Just Like You/Christmas Mem'ries	1975	10.00	20.00	40.00
— Blue printing, released with promo copies only					
Reprise 1342 PS	A Baby Just Like You/Christmas Mem'ries	1975	5.00	10.00	20.00
— Red and black printing, released with stock copies					

7-Inch Extended Plays
Capitol EAP 1-894	Jingle Bells/The Christmas Song//Mistletoe and Holly/I'll Be Home for Christmas	1957	3.00	6.00	12.00
Capitol EAP 1-894 PS	A Jolly Christmas from Frank Sinatra, Vol. 1	1957	3.00	6.00	12.00
Capitol EAP 2-894	The Christmas Waltz/Have Yourself a Merry Little Christmas//The First Noel/Hark the Herald Angels Sing	1957	3.00	6.00	12.00
Capitol EAP 2-894 PS	A Jolly Christmas from Frank Sinatra, Vol. 2	1957	3.00	6.00	12.00
Capitol EAP 3-894	O Little Town of Bethlehem/Adeste Fideles//It Came Upon a Midnight Clear/Silent Night	1957	3.00	6.00	12.00
Capitol EAP 3-894 PS	A Jolly Christmas from Frank Sinatra, Vol. 3	1957	3.00	6.00	12.00
Columbia B-167 (4)	Christmas Songs by Sinatra	1950	37.50	75.00	150.00
— Includes records 38256, 38257, 38258 and 38259 plus box					
Columbia B-10321	(contents unknown)	1957	7.50	15.00	30.00
Columbia B-10321 PS	Christmas Dreaming Vol. 1	1957	10.00	20.00	40.00
Columbia B-10322	(contents unknown)	1957	7.50	15.00	30.00
Columbia B-10322 PS	Christmas Dreaming, Vol. 2	1957	10.00	20.00	40.00

Label, Number		Title (A Side/B Side)	Year	VG	VG+	NM
Albums						
Capitol W 894	M	A Jolly Christmas from Frank Sinatra	1957	10.00	20.00	40.00
— Original mono with gray label						
Capitol W 894	M	A Jolly Christmas from Frank Sinatra	1958	7.50	15.00	30.00
— Black colorband label						
Capitol T 894	M	The Sinatra Christmas Album	196?	5.00	10.00	20.00
— Reissue of A Jolly Christmas with Frank Sinatra with same contents; some copies have this cover and "A Jolly Christmas" labels						
Capitol SM-894	R	The Sinatra Christmas Album	197?	2.00	4.00	8.00
— Reissue in rechanneled stereo; any color label						
Columbia CL 1032		Christmas Dreaming	1957	20.00	40.00	80.00
Columbia CL 2542	10	Christmas with Sinatra	1955	15.00	30.00	60.00
— "House Party Series" release						
Columbia CL 6019	10	Christmas Songs by Sinatra	1948	25.00	50.00	100.00
— With "gingerbread man" cover						
Columbia CL 6019	10	Christmas Songs by Sinatra	1949	20.00	40.00	80.00
— With green vinylite cover						
Columbia PC 40707		Christmas Dreaming	1987	7.50	15.00	30.00
— Reissue of CL 1032 with an extra track						
Harmony HL 7400	M	Have Yourself a Merry Little Christmas	1967	7.50	15.00	30.00
Harmony HS 11200	R	Have Yourself a Merry Little Christmas	1967	5.00	10.00	20.00
Mobile Fidelity 1-135	M	A Jolly Christmas from Frank Sinatra	1984	7.50	15.00	30.00
— Audiophile reissue under the original title						

On Various-Artists Collections

Christmas Waltz, The	Sinatra Family Wish You a Merry Christmas, The (Reprise FS-1026)
Have Yourself a Merry Little Christmas	Have Yourself a Merry Little Christmas (Reprise R 50001)
It Came Upon a Midnight Clear	Happy Holiday (Mistletoe 1243)
	Rocking Christmas Stocking, A (Capitol SPRO 9303/4/5/6)
Mistletoe and Holly	Happy Holiday (Mistletoe 1243)
Silent Night	Rocking Christmas Stocking, A (Capitol SPRO 9303/4/5/6)
Whatever Happened to Christmas?	Many Moods of Christmas, The (Columbia Special Products P 12013)
	Sinatra Family Wish You a Merry Christmas, The (Reprise FS-1026)
White Christmas	Christmas Album, A (Columbia PC 39466)
	Christmas Is... (Columbia Special Products P 11417)

SINATRA, FRANK, AND BING CROSBY
On Various-Artists Collections

Christmas Song, The	Happy Holiday (Mistletoe 1243)
Jingle Bells	Happy Holiday (Mistletoe 1243)

SINATRA, FRANK; BING CROSBY; FRED WARING
On Various-Artists Collections

Go Tell It on the Mountain	12 Songs of Christmas (Reprise F-2022)
We Wish You the Merriest	12 Songs of Christmas (Reprise F-2022)

SINATRA, FRANK, AND FRED WARING
On Various-Artists Collections

I Heard the Bells on Christmas Day	12 Songs of Christmas (Reprise F-2022)
Little Drummer Boy, The	12 Songs of Christmas (Reprise F-2022)
Old-Fashioned Christmas, An	12 Songs of Christmas (Reprise F-2022)

SINATRA, FRANK, FRANK JR., NANCY AND TINA (THE FAMILY)
On Various-Artists Collections

Bells of Christmas, The (Greensleeves)	Sinatra Family Wish You a Merry Christmas, The (Reprise FS-1026)
I Wouldn't Trade Christmas	Sinatra Family Wish You a Merry Christmas, The (Reprise FS-1026)
Twelve Days of Christmas, The	Sinatra Family Wish You a Merry Christmas, The (Reprise FS-1026)

SINATRA, FRANK, JR.
On Various-Artists Collections

Some Children See Him	Sinatra Family Wish You a Merry Christmas, The (Reprise FS-1026)

SINATRA, NANCY
45s

Label, Number		Title (A Side/B Side)	Year	VG	VG+	NM
Elektra 47234	DJ	Rudolph the Red-Nosed Reindeer/Winter Wonderland	1981	2.00	4.00	8.00
— As "Mel (Tillis) and Nancy"; B-side by Dave Rowland and Sugar						
Reprise 0880		It's Such a Lonely Time of the Year/Kids	1969	2.50	5.00	10.00

On Various-Artists Collections

It's Such a Lonely Time of Year	Sinatra Family Wish You a Merry Christmas, The (Reprise FS-1026)
Kids	Sinatra Family Wish You a Merry Christmas, The (Reprise FS-1026)

Label, Number		Title (A Side/B Side)	Year	VG	VG+	NM
SINATRA, TINA						
On Various-Artists Collections						
Santa Claus Is Comin' to Town		Sinatra Family Wish You a Merry Christmas, The (Reprise FS-1026)				
SINATRA, TINA AND NANCY						
On Various-Artists Collections						
O Bambino		Sinatra Family Wish You a Merry Christmas, The (Reprise FS-1026)				
(One Cold and Blessed Winter)						
SINCLAIR, JERRY, PROJECT						
45s						
Rainbow Valley SW025		Happy Birthday Jesus//(B-side unknown)	19??	—	2.00	4.00
SINGER, EDDIE						
45s						
EBS 111		Santa's Trucker Buddies/If Santa Had One Boot	197?	—	2.50	5.00
SINGERS, THE						
45s						
Date 1540		That's What Christmas Is/Johnny's Noel	1966	2.00	4.00	8.00
SINGING DOGS, THE, DON CHARLES PRESENTS						
45s						
RCA PA-10129		Jingle Bells/Oh! Susanna	1976	3.00	6.00	12.00
— Black label, dog near top						
45s						
RCA Victor 47-6344		Oh! Susannah//Pat-a-Cake/Three Blind Mice/Jingle Bells	1955	3.75	7.50	15.00
RCA Victor 47-6344	PS	Oh! Susannah//Pat-a-Cake/Three Blind Mice/Jingle Bells	1955	6.25	12.50	25.00
RCA Victor 48-1020		Jingle Bells/Oh! Susannah	1971	—	2.50	5.00
— First reissue; "Jingle Bells" lengthened to 1:47 on this and future issues						
RCA Victor F2NW-7846/7	DJ	Pearl's Jingle Bells/Caesar's Pat-A-Cake/King's Three Blind Mice//Dolly's Oh! Susanna (Fast)/ Dolly's Oh! Susanna (Slow)	1955	10.00	20.00	40.00
— Banded version for radio use ("Jingle Bells" is 1:15)						
RCA Victor PA-10129		Jingle Bells/Oh! Susannah	1974	—	2.00	4.00
— First issue of PA-10129 has tan or brown (also possibly orange) labels						
On Various-Artists Collections						
Jingle Bells		Christmas Through the Years (Reader's Digest RDA-143)				
SINGING NUNS, THE						
No relation to the "Dominique" lady.						
Albums						
SN 001	S	O Bambino	197?	3.00	6.00	12.00
SIPE, P.W., AND THE COUNTRY FOLKS						
45s						
Mohawk 14462		Christmas Comes And Goes/He Led Them Through	19??	2.50	5.00	10.00
SISTERS, THE						
45s						
Del-Fi 4302		Happy New Year, Baby/Ooh Poo Pah Doo	1964	2.50	5.00	10.00
SITES, BETTIE						
45s						
Celestial 1011		Christmas Moon/Christmas Angel	196?	2.50	5.00	10.00
— B-side by Dan Williams						
6 FEET DEEP						
On Various-Artists Collections						
Frosty the Snowman		Christmas on Death Row (Death Row/Interscope INT2-90108)				
Have Yourself a Merry Little Christmas		Christmas on Death Row (Death Row/Interscope INT2-90108)				
6 O'CLOCK NEWS						
45s						
6 o'clock News 2112		Run Run Rudolph/Whenever I See Your Face	19??	—	2.00	4.00
6 o'clock News 2112	PS	Run Run Rudolph/Whenever I See Your Face	19??	—	2.00	4.00

(Top left) This wasn't the first time that Santa Claus purported to tell his own story of Christmas, but this was a whole album's worth, released by Capitol in 1967. (Top right) *Sing We Now of Christmas,* from 1959, was the original name of the Harry Simeone Chorale LP that contained "The Little Drummer Boy," recorded the year before. (Bottom left) The first 12-inch LP of Frank Sinatra's *Christmas Dreaming,* with Columbia tracks recorded mostly in the 1940s, came out in 1957 to compete with *A Jolly Christmas with Frank Sinatra,* which Capitol issued the same year. (Bottom right) The original picture sleeve from The Singing Dogs' 1955 single. "Jingle Bells," part of the B-side medley, was rediscovered by a New York DJ in 1970 and became so popular that RCA released a lengthened version of the song the next Christmas season. It has since become a camp classic.

Label, Number		Title (A Side/B Side)	Year	VG	VG+	NM
SIX TRUMPETS, THE						
45s						
Nashboro 707		Jesus Christ, The Baby/My Jesus He's Pleased	1961	2.50	5.00	10.00
Nashboro 839		New Born King/Nobody But You Lord	1964	2.50	5.00	10.00
SIZEMORE, KEN						
45s						
Ranwood 1009		Why Is It Always Christmas/That's What Christmas Means To Me	1974	—	2.00	4.00
SKAGGS, RICKY, AND JAMES TAYLOR						
45s						
Epic AE7 2569	DJ	New Star Shining (same on both sides)	1986	—	—	3.00
Epic AE7 2569	PS	New Star Shining	1986	—	—	3.00
SKELTON, RED						
45s						
Columbia J-1973	DJ	The Little Christmas Tree (Part 1)/The Little Christmas Tree (Part 2)	195?	3.00	6.00	12.00
On Various-Artists Collections						
Little Christmas Tree, The, Part One/Part Two		First Christmas Record for Children (Harmony HS 14554)				
SKUNKS, THE						
45s						
Arvee 585		Smitty's Christmas Toy Piano/Smitty's Toy Piano	1959	3.75	7.50	15.00
SKYLINERS, THE						
45s						
Classic Artists 123		You're My Christmas Present/Another Lonely New Year's Eve	1990	—	2.50	5.00
SLADE						
12-Inch Singles						
Polydor POSPX 780		Merry Xmas Everybody (Extended)/Don't Blame Me	1985	3.00	6.00	12.00
— U.K. import						
RCA PT 40550		Santa Claus Is Coming to Town/ Auld Lang Syne/You'll Never Walk Alone	1985	5.00	10.00	20.00
— Second 12-inch in a U.K. two-pack (the other is RCA PT 40450)						
RCA RCAT 455		All Join Hands/My Oh My/Here's To...(The New Year)/ Merry Xmas Everybody (Live and Kickin')	1984	5.00	10.00	20.00
45s						
Polydor POSP 780		Merry Xmas Everybody/Don't Blame Me	1985	—	2.00	4.00
— Yet another reissue						
Polydor POSP 780	PS	Merry Xmas Everybody/Don't Blame Me	1985	—	2.00	4.00
— Both record and sleeve are U.K. imports						
Polydor 2058 422		Merry Xmas Everybody/Don't Blame Me	1973	—	2.50	5.00
— U.K. import; original issue with regular Polydor label						
Polydor 2058 422		Merry Xmas Everybody/Don't Blame Me	1980	—	2.00	4.00
— Reissue with green background and "holly leaf" label						
Polydor 2058 422	PS	Merry Xmas Everybody/Don't Blame Me	1980	—	2.00	4.00
— Photo of group on sleeve; both record and sleeve are U.K. imports						
RCA 291		(And Now the Waltz) C'est La Vie/Merry Xmas Everybody	1982	—	2.00	4.00
RCA 291	PS	(And Now the Waltz) C'est La Vie/Merry Xmas Everybody	1982	—	2.00	4.00
— Both record and sleeve are U.K. imports						
RCA 373		My Oh My/Merry Xmas Everybody (live)/ Keep Your Hands Off My Power Supply	1983	—	2.00	4.00
RCA 373	PS	My Oh My/Merry Xmas Everybody (live)/ Keep Your Hands Off My Power Supply	1983	—	2.00	4.00
— Both record and sleeve are U.K. imports						
RCA PB 40549		Santa Claus Is Coming to Town/Auld Lang Syne/ You'll Never Walk Alone	1985	—	3.00	6.00
— Second 45 (no picture sleeve) in a U.K. two-pack (the other is RCA PB 40449)						
Receiver BOYZ 4		Merry Xmas Everybody/Don't Blame Me	1989	—	2.00	4.00
Receiver BOYZ 4	PS	Merry Xmas Everybody/Don't Blame Me	1989	—	2.00	4.00
— Both record and sleeve are U.K. imports						
Warner Bros. 7759		Merry Christmas Everybody/Don't Blame Me	1973	2.50	5.00	10.00
SLEIGH, BOB & THE CHRISTMAS ALLSTARS						
45s						
Bulrush A2		(I Wanna Be) The Fairy (On The Christmas Tree)/Christmas Day	19??	—	2.00	4.00
— U.K. import						

Label, Number		Title (A Side/B Side)	Year	VG	VG+	NM
SLOPPY SECONDS						
45s						
Taang! 68		Lonely Christmas//Conned Again/Hooray For Santa Claus	199?	—	3.00	6.00
— *Combination red and clear vinyl*						
Taang! 68	PS	Lonely Christmas//Conned Again/Hooray For Santa Claus	199?	—	3.00	6.00
SLOW MOTION						
45s						
RK 1024		Christmas Charade/Maybe	19??	—	2.50	5.00
SMALL, DANNY						
45s						
United Artists 542		On Christmas Day/Theme from Taras Bulba (The Wishing Star)	1962	3.00	6.00	12.00
SMALL, MILLIE						
45s						
Atlantic 2266		Bring It On Home to Me/I've Fallen in Love with a Snowman	1965	2.50	5.00	10.00

SMART, CHARLES, AND JAMES BLADES
On Various-Artists Collections
While Shepherds Watched Their Flocks Magic of Christmas, The (Columbia Musical Treasury P3S 5806)

SMECK, ROY						
Albums						
"X" LPA-3016	10	Christmas in Hawaii	195?	37.50	75.00	150.00
SMITH, ARTHUR						
45s						
MGM 10847		Merry Christmas, Everyone/Guitar Jingle Bells	1950	3.75	7.50	15.00
SMITH, BOB						
45s						
Clet 8389		Lonely at Christmas//(B-side unknown)	19??	2.00	4.00	8.00
SMITH, BUCKLEY						
45s						
Hoss 105		Busy Busy Santa Clause/Christmas Every Day	19??	—	2.50	5.00

SMITH, CARL
On Various-Artists Collections
Silent Night Country Christmas (Columbia CS 9888)
Country Christmas Favorites (Columbia Special Products C 10876)
Country Style Christmas, A (Columbia Musical Treasury 3P 6316)
We Wish You a Country Christmas (Columbia Special Products P 14991)

SMITH, CONNIE
On Various-Artists Collections
First Noel, The Country Style Christmas, A (Columbia Musical Treasury 3P 6316)
O Come All Ye Faithful Nashville's Greatest Christmas Hits (Columbia PC 44412)
What Child Is This Country Style Christmas, A (Columbia Musical Treasury 3P 6316)
Merry Christmas (Columbia Musical Treasury 3P 6306)

SMITH, CONNIE, AND WILLIE NELSON
On Various-Artists Collections
Silent Night, Holy Night Nashville Christmas Album, The (Epic PE 40418)

SMITH, DALE						
45s						
Bolo 726		When Christmas Bells Are Ringing/Christmas Story	1961	2.50	5.00	10.00
SMITH, DAVID LEROY						
45s						
Master 1002		Sounds Of Christmas/Join We The Angels	19??	—	2.00	4.00
SMITH, DON						
45s						
VJ International 1224		Black Christmas/Don't 'Cha Walk On Me	197?	—	3.00	6.00

Label, Number		Title (A Side/B Side)	Year	VG	VG+	NM
SMITH, E.B.						
45s						
Talmu 315		Magic of Christmas/The Little Drummer Boy	19??	—	3.00	6.00
SMITH, ETHEL						
45s						
Decca 24142		White Christmas/Jingle Bells	1950	3.00	6.00	12.00
— *Side 7 and 8 of "Album No. 9-92"*						
Decca 24734		Silent Night/Adeste Fideles	1950	3.00	6.00	12.00
— *Side 1 and 2 of "Album No. 9-92"*						
Decca 24735		Hark, The Herald Angels Sing/O, Little Town Of Bethlehem	1950	3.00	6.00	12.00
— *Side 3 and 4 of "Album No. 9-92"*						
Decca 24736		It Came Upon A Midnight Clear/O, Holy Night	1950	3.00	6.00	12.00
— *Side 5 and 6 of "Album No. 9-92"*						
7-Inch Extended Plays						
Decca 9-92	(4)	Christmas Songs	1950	12.50	25.00	50.00
— *Contains 4 records (24142, 24734, 24735, 24736) plus box*						
Decca ED 558 (91127)		Silent Night/Adeste Fideles// Hark! The Herald Angels Sing/O Little Town of Bethlehem	195?	2.50	5.00	10.00
Decca ED 558 (91128)		It Came Upon a Midnight Clear/O Holy Night// White Christmas/Jingle Bells	195?	2.50	5.00	10.00
Decca ED 558	PS	Christmas Music	195?	3.75	7.50	15.00
— *Cover for 2-EP set*						
Albums						
Decca DL 8187	M	Christmas Music	1955	5.00	10.00	20.00
On Various-Artists Collections						
O Little Town of Bethlehem		Thank You for Opening Your Christmas Club with Us (Decca 34211)				
SMITH, GREGG, SINGERS						
Albums						
Turnabout QTV 34710	Q	The World Rejoices	1977	3.75	7.50	15.00
SMITH, HUEY "PIANO"						
Albums						
Ace LP-1027	M	'Twas the Night Before Christmas	1962	75.00	150.00	300.00
SMITH, JACK						
45s						
Fifth Street 1119		Next Christmas Day/Ozark Mountains	19??	—	2.50	5.00
SMITH, JIMMY						
Albums						
Verve V 8604	M	Christmas '64	1964	5.00	10.00	20.00
Verve V6 8604	S	Christmas '64	1964	3.75	7.50	15.00
SMITH, KATE						
45s						
RCA Victor 47-9007		Christmas Eve in My Home Town/Happy Birthday, Dear Christ Child	1966	2.50	5.00	10.00
Albums						
RCA Victor LPM-3607	M	The Kate Smith Christmas Album	1966	3.00	6.00	12.00
RCA Victor LSP-3607	S	The Kate Smith Christmas Album	1966	3.75	7.50	15.00
On Various-Artists Collections						
Christmas Eve in My Home Town		Christmas Through the Years (Reader's Digest RDA-143) Happy Holidays, Volume 17 (RCA Special Products DPL1-0555) Old Fashioned Christmas, An (Reader's Digest RDA 216-A)				
I Heard the Bells on Christmas Day		Joyous Noel (Reader's Digest RDA-57A)				
It's Beginning to Look Like Christmas		Happy Holidays, Volume IV (RCA Victor PRS-267)				
Medley: Deck the Halls/Joy to the World/It Came Upon the Midnight Clear		Christmas Through the Years (Reader's Digest RDA-143)				
O Holy Night		Happy Holidays, Vol. 20 (RCA Special Products DPL1-0713) Carols and Candlelight (Columbia Special Products P 12525) Christmas with Colonel Sanders (RCA Victor PRS-291)				
Silver Bells		60 Christmas Classics (Sessions DVL2-0723) Christmas in New York (RCA Victor PRM-257) Christmas in the Air (RCA Special Products DPL1-0133) Happy Holidays, Volume 14 (RCA Special Products DPL1-0376) Henry Mancini Selects Great Songs of Christmas (RCA Special Products DPL1-0148) Time-Life Treasury of Christmas, The (Time-Life STL-107)				

Label, Number		Title (A Side/B Side)	Year	VG	VG+	NM

SMITH, KEELY
45s
Dot 16147		Christmas Island/Silent Night	1960	3.75	7.50	15.00
Albums						
Dot DLP-3345	M	A Keely Christmas	1961	6.25	12.50	25.00
Dot SLP-25345	S	A Keely Christmas	1961	7.50	15.00	30.00
On Various-Artists Collections						
First Noel, The		Have Yourself a Merry Little Christmas (Reprise R 50001)				

SMITH, MEL
45s
Epic 657687		Another Blooming Christmas/Ho! Ho! Ho! Hoedown	1991	—	2.00	4.00
Epic 657687	PS	Another Blooming Christmas/Ho! Ho! Ho! Hoedown	1991	—	2.00	4.00
— Both record and sleeve are U.K. imports						

SMITH, MEL & KIM WILDE
45s
10 Records TEN 2		Rockin' Around The Christmas Tree/Deck The Blooming Halls	19??	2.00	4.00	8.00
10 Records TEN 2	PS	Rockin' Around The Christmas Tree/Deck The Blooming Halls	19??	2.00	4.00	8.00
— Both record and sleeve are U.K. imports						

SMITH, SHUGGY RAY
45s
| Pzazz 019 | | Papa And Santa Claus/The Hitch Hiking Hippie | 1968 | 2.00 | 4.00 | 8.00 |

SMITH, WARREN
45s
| Warner Bros. 5125 | | Dear Santa/The Meaning of Christmas | 1959 | 6.25 | 12.50 | 25.00 |

SMITHEREENS, THE
45s
| Capitol S7-18206 | | Rudolph, the Red Nosed Reindeer/A Girl Like You | 1994 | — | 2.50 | 5.00 |
| — Red vinyl | | | | | | |

SMOKING POPES
45s
Capitol 7PRO-11335/6	DJ	Pure Imagination/O Holy Night	1996	—	—	3.00
Capitol 7PRO-11335/6	PS	Egg Nog	1996	—	—	3.00
— Sleeve is a single sheet of paper in a plastic bag; 1,500 pressed						

SMOTHERS BROTHERS, THE
45s
Smothers Inc. 79151		The Christmas Bunny Part 1/The Christmas Bunny Part 2	1969	6.25	12.50	25.00
Smothers Inc. 79151	PS	The Christmas Bunny Part 1/The Christmas Bunny Part 2	1969	12.50	25.00	50.00
Albums						
Mercury MG 21051	M	Mom Always Liked You Best!	1965	3.00	6.00	12.00
— Contains one Christmas track: Santa Claus						
Mercury SR 61051	S	Mom Always Liked You Best!	1965	3.75	7.50	15.00

SNEED, DON, AND COMPANY
45s
| Cascade 2001 | | Santa's a Hippie/In Yesterday | 196? | — | 3.00 | 6.00 |

SNOOP DOGGY DOGG FEATURING NATE DOGG
On Various-Artists Collections
Santa Claus Goes Straight to the Ghetto Christmas on Death Row (Death Row/Interscope INT2-90108)

SNOW, HANK
45s
RCA Victor 47-5340		Christmas Roses/Reindeer Boogie	1953	3.75	7.50	15.00
RCA Victor 47-9030		Christmas Cannonball/God Is My Santa Claus	1966	2.50	5.00	10.00
RCA Victor 74-0459		Blue Christmas/Nestor, The Long Eared Christmas Donkey	1971		*Unreleased*	
RCA Victor PB-10136		A Letter to Santa Claus/Christmas Roses	1974	—	2.50	5.00
RCA Victor PB-10459		Blue Christmas/Nestor, The Long Eared Christmas Donkey	1975	—	2.50	5.00
7-Inch Extended Plays						
RCA Victor EPA 472		Frosty the Snowman/Silent Night//	1953	5.00	10.00	20.00
		Christmas Roses/The Reindeer Boogie				
RCA Victor EPA 472	PS	A Country Christmas with Hank Snow	1953	5.00	10.00	20.00

Label, Number		Title (A Side/B Side)	Year	VG	VG+	NM
Albums						
RCA Victor LPM-3826	M	Christmas with Hank Snow	1967	7.50	15.00	30.00
RCA Victor LSP-3826	S	Christmas with Hank Snow	1967	10.00	20.00	40.00
On Various-Artists Collections						
Reindeer Boogie		Country Christmas (Time-Life STL-109)				

SNOW, WHITNEY
45s

Tower 380		The Christmas Angels Sing/Whitey, the Snow White Lamb	1967	2.50	5.00	10.00
— B-side by Justin Wilson						

SNOWMEN, THE
45s

Slack ODB-1		Hokey Cokey/Don't Go Short	1981	1.00	—	5.00
Slack ODB-1	PS	Hokey Cokey/Don't Go Short	1981	—	2.50	5.00
— Both record and sleeve are U.K. imports						

SNUG HARBOR
45s

Airplayn 0001		Every Christmas Eve/What A Way To End The Day	19??	—	2.50	5.00
Airplayn 0001	PS	Every Christmas Eve/What A Way To End The Day	19??	—	2.50	5.00

SOAPS AND HEARTS ENSEMBLE, THE
45s

RCA 62979		Merry Christmas Wherever You Are// O Come All Ye Faithful/Joy to the World	1994	—	—	3.00
— B-side by Martha Byrne						
RCA 62979	PS	Merry Christmas Wherever You Are// O Come All Ye Faithful/Joy to the World	1994	—	—	3.00

SOCIETY THREAT
45s

Airborne 10012		It's Christmas, Yes It Is/(Instrumental)	19??	2.00	4.00	8.00

SOCIETY'S CHILDREN
45s

Atco 6538		White Christmas/I'll Let You Know	1967	3.00	6.00	12.00

SOELVGUTTENE BOYS CHOIR
On Various-Artists Collections

Deilig Er Den Himmel Bla	Christmas in Norway (Capitol T 10377)
Deilig Er Jorden	Christmas in Norway (Capitol T 10377)
Du Gronne Glitrende Tre Goddag	Christmas in Norway (Capitol T 10377)
Jeg Synger Julekvad	Christmas in Norway (Capitol T 10377)
Kimer, I Klokker	Christmas in Norway (Capitol T 10377)
O Du Herlige	Christmas in Norway (Capitol T 10377)

SON OF PETE
45s

Beserkley 5746		Silent Knight/Disco Party, Part 2	1976	—	2.00	4.00
— This record is completely blank on both sides!						
Beserkley 5746	PS	Silent Knight/Disco Party, Part 2	1976	—	2.00	4.00

SONGSMITHS, THE
45s

Tag 7011		What Is The Meaning Of Christmas/Que Es Navidad	19??	—	2.00	4.00

SONICS, THE
45s

Etiquette 22		Don't Believe in Christmas/Christmas Spirit	1965	7.50	15.00	30.00
— B-side by the Wailers						

SONNIER, JO-EL
45s

Goldband 1242		Merry Christmas Tonight/Coming For Christmas	197?	—	2.50	5.00
— B-side by Charles Page						

Label, Number		Title (A Side/B Side)	Year	VG	VG+	NM
SONNY						
45s						
Specialty 733		One Little Answer/Comin' Down the Chimney	1974	—	3.00	6.00
— As "Sonny Bono and Little Tootsie"						
SOSEBEE, TOMMY						
45s						
Coral 64107		Winter Wonderland/New Year Bells	1951	3.75	7.50	15.00
SOUL COMFORTERS, THE						
45s						
Hollywood 1042		White Christmas/Silent Night	1955	7.50	15.00	30.00
SOUL DUO, THE						
45s						
Shiptown 132		Just A Sad Xmas/Can't Nobody Love Me	19??	—	3.00	6.00
SOUL SEARCHERS, THE						
45s						
Songbird 1187		Christmas In Vietnam/Lord, Help Me	197?	—	3.00	6.00
SOUL STIRRERS, THE						
45s						
Checker 5007		Christmas Joy/I Know I'll Be Free	19??	3.00	6.00	12.00
Chess 5056		Christmas Means Love/(B-side unknown)	19??	3.75	7.50	15.00
On Various-Artists Collections						
Christmas Means Love		Have a Merry Chess Christmas (Chess/MCA CH-25210)				
SOULFUL STRINGS						
Albums						
Cadet LPS-814		The Magic of Christmas	1969	3.00	6.00	12.00
SOUNDS OF CHRISTMAS, THE						
45s						
RCA Victor 8727-7-R		Dance Of The Sugar Plum Fairy/Coventry Carol	1988	—	—	3.00
SOUP BEAN HOLLER GIRLS						
45s						
BFI 133		Christmas Is For Kids (same on both sides)	19??	—	2.00	4.00
SOUTHERN CALIFORNIA MORMON CHOIR, THE						
Albums						
Capitol T 2590	M	The Southern California Mormon Choir Sings the Songs of Christmas	1966	3.00	6.00	12.00
Capitol ST 2590	S	The Southern California Mormon Choir Sings the Songs of Christmas	1966	3.75	7.50	15.00
SOUTHERN CROSS						
45s						
Suma 1001		Santa's In A Semi/Ain't It Sad	19??	—	3.00	6.00
SOUTHERN PACIFIC						
On Various-Artists Collections						
Run Rudolph Run		Christmas Tradition, A, Volume II (Warner Bros. 25762)				
SOUTHLAND CORPORATION, THE						
45s						
Southland 10882		A Blast From The Past/A Holiday Message	1982	—	2.50	5.00
— B-side is a message from John P. Thompson						
Southland 10882	PS	A Blast From The Past/A Holiday Message	1982	—	2.50	5.00
SOUTHWEST HIGH SCHOOL CHOIR						
45s						
Columbia 41295		God's Christmas Tree/Great Somebody	1958	3.00	6.00	12.00

Label, Number		Title (A Side/B Side)	Year	VG	VG+	NM
SOVINE, EDDY						
45s						
Trumpet 606		Santa's On His Way/Our Country	19??	2.50	5.00	10.00
SOVINE, RED						
45s						
Chart 5231		Santa Claus Is a Texas Cowboy/The Legend of the Christmas Rose	1974	—	2.50	5.00
Gusto 9015		Christmas Is For Kids/What Does Christmas Look Like	1978	—	2.00	4.00
MGM 10782		Christmas Alone/Dear Mister Santa Claus	1950	3.75	7.50	15.00
SPACE KIDS, THE						
45s						
Laurie 3475		Take a Ride on Santa's Rocket/(Instrumental)	1968	2.00	4.00	8.00
SPARKY						
45s						
Capitol F1204		I Don't Want a Lot for Christmas/Frosty the Snowman	1950	3.75	7.50	15.00
Capitol/Bozo CASF-3084	PS	Santa Claus and Sparky Sing...	195?	3.75	7.50	15.00
— B-side by Santa Claus						
Capitol/Bozo F32029		I Don't Want A Lot For Christmas/Do You Believe In Santa Claus?	195?	3.00	6.00	12.00
— B-side by Santa Claus; this 45 is the entire contents of Album CASF-3084						
SPARROW ARTISTS						
45s						
Sparrow SGL CMAS	DJ	The Christmas Story/Christmas ID's	1987	—	2.00	4.00
— Artists on this disc: Michael Card, Scott Wesley Brown, Margaret Becker, Steve Camp, Richard Souther, Steven Curtis Chapman, Geoff Moore, Rick Florian (White Heart), Deniece Williams, Steve Green and Billy Smiley (White Heart).						
SPECIAL EFX						
On Various-Artists Collections						
Silent Night		GRP Christmas Collection, A (GRP 9574)				
SPECTOR, PHIL						
45s						
Chrysalis 3202		Sleigh Ride/Winter Wonderland//White Christmas/ Christmas (Baby Please Come Home)	1987	3.75	7.50	15.00
— Also known as "The Phil Spector Christmas Mix"						
Chrysalis 3202	PS	The Phil Spector Christmas Mix	1987	3.75	7.50	15.00
— Sleeve and record are U.K. imports; songs meld into one another on each side						
Pavillion AE7 1354	DJ	Phil Spector's Christmas Medley (same on both sides)	1981	3.75	7.50	15.00
— Promo-only sampler from the Pavillion reissue of Phil Spector's Christmas Album						
SPECTOR, PHIL, AND ARTISTS						
On Various-Artists Collections						
Silent Night		Christmas Gift for You from Phil Spector, A (Philles PHLP-4005)				
		Phil Spector's Christmas Album (Apple SW 3400)				
		Phil Spector: Back to Mono 1958-1969 (Phil Spector/Abkco 7118-1)				
SPECTRUM						
45s						
Blackbury 5002		Funky Christmas (Boogie All The Way)/Beautiful Woman	1978	2.00	4.00	8.00
SPELMAN, MARION						
On Various-Artists Collections						
Soon 'Twill Be Christmas Eve		Ten Tunes of Christmas (Candee 50-50)				
There's No Time Like Christmas Time		Ten Tunes of Christmas (Candee 50-50)				
SPENCER, JON, BLUES EXPLOSION						
45s						
Sub Pop 180		Big Yule Log Boogie/My Christmas Wish	1992	12.50	25.00	50.00
— Mispress on clear lilac vinyl; labels claim this is "Max Gomez Love"/"Assassin" by Wolverton Bros.						
Sub Pop 180		Big Yule Log Boogie/My Christmas Wish	1992	5.00	10.00	20.00
— Green vinyl						
Sub Pop 180	PS	Big Yule Log Boogie/My Christmas Wish	1992	5.00	10.00	20.00

Label, Number		Title (A Side/B Side)	Year	VG	VG+	NM
SPIELMAN, FRED						
On Various-Artists Collections						
Concerto Inferno		Stingiest Man in Town, The (Columbia CL 950)				
SPINA, VIC						
45s						
VM 1002		Doo Wopp Santa Claus/One Summer Night	19??	2.00	4.00	8.00
SPINAL TAP						
45s						
Enigma 1143		Christmas With The Devil/Christmas With The Devil (Scratch Mix)	1984	—	3.00	6.00
Enigma 1143	PS	Christmas With The Devil/Christmas With The Devil (Scratch Mix)	1984	2.50	5.00	10.00
Albums						
MCA 10514	PD	Break Like the Wind	1992	3.75	7.50	15.00
— Picture disc (only U.S. vinyl version of this LP). Contains one Christmas song: Christmas with the Devil						
SPINNING WIG HATS, THE						
45s						
Lyntone 16928		Christmas In New Zealand (one-sided)	199?	3.00	6.00	12.00
— Flexidisc						
SPIRO, ROBERT						
On Various-Artists Collections						
Angel Gabriel, The		Life Treasury of Christmas Music, The (Project/Capitol TL 100)				
God Rest You Merry		Life Treasury of Christmas Music, The (Project/Capitol TL 100)				
Here We Come a-Wassailing		Life Treasury of Christmas Music, The (Project/Capitol TL 100)				
SPISAK, RAY						
45s						
Rite 1000		Hurrah For Santa/Ridem Santa	19??	2.00	4.00	8.00
SPITALNY, PHIL						
45s						
RCA Victor 47-3875		God Rest Ye Merry, Gentlemen/Carol of the Bells	1950	3.75	7.50	15.00
RCA Victor 47-3876		The First Noel/'Twas the Night Before Christmas	1950	3.75	7.50	15.00
RCA Victor 47-3877		Adeste Fideles/Hark the Herald Angels Sing	1950	3.75	7.50	15.00
SPITTING IMAGE						
45s						
Virgin 921		Santa Claus Is On The Dole/1st Atheist Tabernacle Choir	1986	2.00	4.00	8.00
Virgin 921	PS	Santa Claus Is On The Dole/1st Atheist Tabernacle Choir	1986	2.00	4.00	8.00
— Both record and sleeve are U.K. imports						
SPLIT ENZ						
45s						
Fan Club (no #)	DJ	Merry Christmas from Split Enz	1982	2.50	5.00	10.00
— Green vinyl for members of fan club						
SPORTSMEN QUARTET, THE						
45s						
Capitol F90017		Silent Night/Wassail, Wassail	1949	2.50	5.00	10.00
Capitol F90018		We Three Kings Of Orient Are/O Little Town Of Bethlehem	1949	2.50	5.00	10.00
Capitol F90019		Good King Wenceslas/Away In A Manger	1949	2.50	5.00	10.00
7-Inch Extended Plays						
Capitol CCF 9005	(3)	Carols At Christmas	1949	8.75	17.50	35.00
— Contains 3 records (F90017, F90018, F90019) plus box						
SPORTSMEN, THE						
45s						
Key 507		Reindeer Rock/The Only Thing I Want For Christmas	1955	5.00	10.00	20.00
Ronroy 1004		Santa's Toy Express/On This Silent Night	1962	2.00	4.00	8.00
SPRINGSTEEN, BRUCE						
45s						
Columbia AE7 1332	DJ	Santa Claus Is Coming to Town (same on both sides)	1981	5.00	10.00	20.00
Columbia AE7 1332	PS	Santa Claus Is Coming to Town (same on both sides)	1981	6.25	12.50	25.00
Columbia 05728		My Hometown/Santa Claus Is Coming to Town	1985	—	2.00	4.00
Columbia 05728	PS	My Hometown/Santa Claus Is Coming to Town	1985	—	2.00	4.00

Label, Number		Title (A Side/B Side)	Year	VG	VG+	NM
Columbia 06432		War/Merry Christmas Baby	1986	—	2.00	4.00
Columbia 06432	PS	War/Merry Christmas Baby	1986	—	2.00	4.00
Columbia 08414		My Hometown/Santa Claus Is Coming to Town	1985	—	—	3.00

— *Gray label reissue; many copies of this were issued with Columbia 05728 picture sleeves*

On Various-Artists Collections

Merry Christmas Baby		Very Special Christmas, A (A&M SP-3911)				
Santa Claus Is Comin' to Town		In Harmony 2 (Columbia PC 37461)				

SQUEEZE
45s

Label, Number		Title (A Side/B Side)	Year	VG	VG+	NM
A&M AMS 7495		Christmas Day/Going Crazy	1979	2.00	4.00	8.00
— *Black vinyl*						
A&M AMS 7495		Christmas Day/Going Crazy	1979	3.00	6.00	12.00
— *White vinyl*						
A&M AMS 7495	PS	Christmas Day/Going Crazy	1979	2.00	4.00	8.00

— *Both record and sleeve are U.K. imports*

SQUIER, BILLY
45s

Label, Number		Title (A Side/B Side)	Year	VG	VG+	NM
Capitol A-5037		My Kinda Lover/Christmas Is the Time to Say "I Love You"	1981	—	2.00	4.00
— *A-side is not a Christmas song*						
Capitol A-5037	PS	My Kinda Lover/Christmas Is the Time to Say "I Love You"	1981	—	2.50	5.00
Capitol B-5303		Christmas Is the Time to Say "I Love You"/White Christmas	1983	—	2.50	5.00
Capitol B-5303	PS	Christmas Is the Time to Say "I Love You"/White Christmas	1983	—	3.00	6.00
Capitol SPRO 9870	DJ	Christmas Is The Time To Say I Love You/White Christmas	1983	2.00	4.00	8.00
— *Has the same picture sleeve as B-5303*						
Capitol S7-18207		Christmas Is the Time to Say "I Love You"/Everybody Wants You	1994	—	2.00	4.00
— *Green vinyl*						
Capitol S7-57890		Christmas Is the Time to Say "I Love You"/Christmas Blues	1992	—	2.50	5.00
— *B-side by Canned Heat*						

On Various-Artists Collections

Christmas Is the Time to Say I Love You		Christmas Rock Album, The (Priority SL 9465)				
White Christmas		Christmas Rock Album, The (Priority SL 9465)				

SQUIRE, CHRIS, AND ALAN WHITE
45s

Label, Number		Title (A Side/B Side)	Year	VG	VG+	NM
Atlantic K11695		Run with the Fox/(B-side unknown)	1981	—	2.50	5.00
— *U.K. import*						

SQUIRES, ROSEMARY
On Various-Artists Collections

My Favorite Things		Old Fashioned Christmas, An (Reader's Digest RDA 216-A)				

SQUIRRELS, THE
45s

Label, Number		Title (A Side/B Side)	Year	VG	VG+	NM
Cameo 284		Grandma's House/The Girl That I'll Adore	1963	2.50	5.00	10.00
— *B-side by the Philadelphia Minstrels*						

SQUIRTGUN
45s

Label, Number		Title (A Side/B Side)	Year	VG	VG+	NM
Squirtgun 41807M		Blue Christmas (same on both sides)	1995	—	2.50	5.00
— *Blue vinyl*						

STAFFORD, JO
45s

Label, Number		Title (A Side/B Side)	Year	VG	VG+	NM
Capitol F1262		White Christmas/Silent Night	1950	3.75	7.50	15.00
Capitol PRO 2756	DJ	Christmas Is The Season/Merry Christmas	1964	2.50	5.00	10.00
Capitol 54-90042		Silent Night/White Christmas	1949	3.75	7.50	15.00
Columbia 39893		Christmas Roses/Chow, Willy	1952	3.75	7.50	15.00
— *With Frankie Laine*						
Columbia 40103		The Christmas Blues/What Good Am I Without You	1953	3.75	7.50	15.00

Albums

Label, Number		Title (A Side/B Side)	Year	VG	VG+	NM
Columbia CL 691	M	Happy Holiday	1955	15.00	30.00	60.00

On Various-Artists Collections

Christmas Song, The		Spirit of Christmas, The (Columbia Special Products CSP 249)				
O Little Town of Bethlehem		Christmas to Remember, A, Vol. 3 (Capitol Creative Products SL-6681)				
		Have Yourself a Merry Little Christmas (Reprise R 50001)				
		Sound of Christmas, The (Capitol Creative Products SL-6515)				

Label, Number		Title (A Side/B Side)	Year	VG	VG+	NM
Santa Claus Is Comin' to Town		Best of Christmas, The, Vol. I (Capitol SM-11833)				
Silent Night		Magic of Christmas, The (Capitol SWBB-93810)				
		Philco Album of Holiday Music, The (Columbia Special Products CSM 431)				
Winter Weather		Many Moods of Christmas, The (Columbia Special Products P 12013)				
Winter Wonderland		Christmas Carousel (Capitol SQBE-94406)				
		Christmas Is... (Columbia Special Products P 11417)				

STAFFORD, JO, AND GORDON MACRAE
7-Inch Extended Plays

Label, Number		Title (A Side/B Side)	Year	VG	VG+	NM
Capitol EAP 1-9021		Songs Of Christmas Part 1/Songs Of Christmas Part 2	195?	2.50	5.00	10.00
Capitol EAP 1-9021	PS	Songs Of Christmas	195?	2.50	5.00	10.00

STAMEY, CHRIS, GROUP
45s

Label, Number		Title (A Side/B Side)	Year	VG	VG+	NM
Coyote 8699		Christmas Time/Occasional Shivers	1986	2.50	5.00	10.00
— Green vinyl						
Coyote 8699	PS	Christmas Time/Occasional Shivers	1986	2.50	5.00	10.00
— Actually a plain white sleeve with gold sticker						

STAN & DOUG
45s

Label, Number	Title (A Side/B Side)	Year	VG	VG+	NM
Golden Crest 550	Christmas Goose (Snowbird)/Christmas Medley	1970	2.00	4.00	8.00

STANKUS, TOM "T-BONE"
45s

Label, Number	Title (A Side/B Side)	Year	VG	VG+	NM
Ransom 2205	Christmas Is Coming/Hardcore Granola	19??	5.00	10.00	20.00

STANLEY BROTHERS, THE
45s

Label, Number	Title (A Side/B Side)	Year	VG	VG+	NM
Starday 413	Christmas Is Near/Holiday Pickin'	1958	5.00	10.00	20.00

STANTE, TONI
45s

Label, Number	Title (A Side/B Side)	Year	VG	VG+	NM
Parkway 970	Donde Esta Santa Claus/It's My Life	1965	2.50	5.00	10.00

STAPLE SINGERS, THE
45s

Label, Number	Title (A Side/B Side)	Year	VG	VG+	NM
Riverside 4540	There Was a Star/The Virgin Mary Had One Son	1962	3.00	6.00	12.00
Stax 0084	Who Took the Merry Out of Christmas/(Instrumental)	1970	2.00	4.00	8.00

STAPLES, MARK
45s

Label, Number	Title (A Side/B Side)	Year	VG	VG+	NM
Mark Staples 9547	A Mining City Christmas/Our Lady Of the Rockies	1984	—	2.00	4.00

STAPLES, MAVIS
45s

Label, Number		Title (A Side/B Side)	Year	VG	VG+	NM
Warner Bros PRO-S-3878	DJ	Christmas Vacation (same on both sides)	1989	—	2.50	5.00

STAPLETON, CYRIL
45s

Label, Number		Title (A Side/B Side)	Year	VG	VG+	NM
London 1895		I Saw Three Ships/Christmas Island	1959	2.50	5.00	10.00
Albums						
Richmond S 30057	S	Children's Christmas Album	196?	3.75	7.50	15.00

STAR WARS INTERGALACTIC DROID CHOIR & CHORALE, THE – See MECO.

STARDUST, ALVIN
45s

Label, Number		Title (A Side/B Side)	Year	VG	VG+	NM
Chrysalis ALV 3	PS	So Near To Christmas/Alright - OK// Clock On The Wall/Show You The Way	1983	—	3.00	6.00
— Two-record set						
Chrysalis ALV 3		So Near To Christmas/Alright - OK/ Clock On The Wall/Show You The Way	1983	—	3.00	6.00
— Sleeve for two-record set; both of above are U.K. imports						
Chrysalis 2835		So Near To Christmas/Alright - OK	1984	—	3.00	6.00
Chrysalis 2835	PS	So Near To Christmas/Alright - OK	1984	—	3.00	6.00
— Both record and sleeve are U.K. imports						

Label, Number		Title (A Side/B Side)	Year	VG	VG+	NM
Honey Bee Honey 13		Christmas/Executive	1989	—	3.00	6.00
Honey Bee Honey 13	PS	Christmas/Executive	1989	—	3.00	6.00
— Both record and sleeve are U.K. imports						

STARETTES
45s
| Venett 101 | DJ | Fifi The Christmas Fawn/Little Christmas Bells | 1962 | 3.00 | 6.00 | 12.00 |

STARK, DONNA
45s
| RCI 2348 | | Christmas Day Is Near/Set Me Free | 1980 | — | 2.00 | 4.00 |

STARMAN
45s
Eva-Tone 83318		Noel Noel	19??	—	2.50	5.00
— Flexidisc						
Eva-Tone 83318	PS	Noel Noel	19??	—	2.50	5.00

STARR, BOBBY
45s
| Continental Arts 575 | | Jake The Flake/(B-side unknown) | 19?? | — | 2.50 | 5.00 |

STARR, SUSI Q, AND JOHNNY HENDERSON
45s
| Coors DC-6 | | Santa's Bringing Daddy Home (same on both sides) | 198? | — | 2.00 | 4.00 |

STARS OF FAITH
45s
| Vee Jay 915 | | Go Where I Send Thee/Poor Little Jesus Boy | 1962 | 2.50 | 5.00 | 10.00 |

STATES, THE
45s
| States 13331 | | This Christmas/I've Got An Angel | 19?? | — | 3.00 | 6.00 |
| States 13331 | PS | This Christmas/I've Got An Angel | 19?? | — | 3.00 | 6.00 |

STATESMEN QUARTET, THE
45s
| Capitol F40263 | | White Christmas/Santa Claus Song | 1949 | 3.75 | 7.50 | 15.00 |

STATLER BROTHERS, THE
45s
Mercury 55046		I Believe in Santa's Cause/Who Do You Think	1978	—	2.00	4.00
Mercury 76130		I Never Spend A Christmas That I Don't Think Of You/ Who Do You Think?	1981	—	2.00	4.00
Mercury 884 320-7		Christmas Eve (Kodia's Theme)/Mary's Sweet Smile	1985	—	—	3.00

7-Inch Extended Plays
| Mercury DJ 577 | DJ | I Never Spend a Christmas That I Don't Think of You/ Jingle Bells//Away in a Manger/The Carols Those Kids Used to Sing | 1978 | — | 3.00 | 6.00 |
| Mercury DJ 577 | PS | A Very Merry Christmas from the Statler Brothers | 1978 | 2.00 | 4.00 | 8.00 |

Albums
| Mercury SRM-1-5012 | | Christmas Card | 1978 | 2.50 | 5.00 | 10.00 |
| Mercury 824 785-1 | | Christmas Present | 1985 | 2.50 | 5.00 | 10.00 |

On Various-Artists Collections
| Carols Those Kids Used to Sing | | Country Christmas (Time-Life STL-109) | | | | |

STATON, JOHNNY, AND THE FEATHERS
45s
| Classic Artists 117 | | Happy Holiday/More Than Enough For Me | 1989 | — | 2.50 | 5.00 |
| *— B-side by the Jaguars* | | | | | | |

STATON, MERRILL, CHOIR
On Various-Artists Collections
| Winter Song, The | | Happy Holidays, Volume II (Columbia Special Products CSM 348) | | | | |
| | | Spirit of Christmas, The (Columbia Special Products CSP 249) | | | | |

Label, Number		Title (A Side/B Side)	Year	VG	VG+	NM
STATUES, THE						
45s						
Holiday 1026	DJ	White Christmas/Get Off My Roof	197?	3.00	6.00	12.00
— B-side by Jerry and the Landsliders						
Liberty 55292		White Christmas/Jeannie with the Light Brown Hair	1960	6.25	12.50	25.00
STEADMAN, GERRY & HIS ENCHANTED MOUNTAIN						
45s						
Gateway 1009		Christmas Teddy Bear/Holiday Rock	19??	—	3.00	6.00
STEELE, SAUNDRA						
45s						
United Artists X1331		First Christmas/(Instrumental)	1979	—	3.00	6.00
STEELEYE SPAN						
45s						
Chrysalis 2007		Gaudete/The Holly and the Ivy	1972	—	2.50	5.00
Chrysalis 2007	PS	Gaudete/The Holly and the Ivy	1972	—	2.50	5.00
— Above record and sleeve are U.K. imports						
Chrysalis 2008		Gaudete/Royal Forester	1972	—	3.00	6.00
Chrysalis 2102		Gaudete/Royal Forester	1974	—	2.50	5.00
Chrysalis 2129		The Boar's Head Carol/Gaudete/Some Rival	1976	—	2.50	5.00
Chrysalis 2129	PS	The Boar's Head Carol/Gaudete/Some Rival	1976	—	2.50	5.00
— Above record and sleeve are U.K. imports						

STEIN, IRA, AND RUSSELL WALDER
On Various-Artists Collections

Engravings II	Winter's Solstice, A (Windham Hill WH-1045)
Medieval Memory II	Winter's Solstice II, A (Windham Hill WH-1077)

STERILLES, THE
On Various-Artists Collections

I Got a Lot of Toys for Christmas	Stuff This in Your Stocking! Elves in Action (Veebltronics/Skyclad 68)

STERN, ISAAC
On Various-Artists Collections

Ave Maria	Best of the Great Songs of Christmas (Album 10) (Columbia Special Products CSS 1478)
	Joy to the World (30 Classic Christmas Melodies) (Columbia Special Products P3 14654)
Ave Maria (Bach-Gounod)	Great Songs of Christmas, The, Album Four (Columbia Special Products CSP 155M)
Ave Maria (Schubert)	Great Songs of Christmas, The, Album Three (Columbia Special Products CSP 117)

Label, Number		Title (A Side/B Side)	Year	VG	VG+	NM
STERN, KITTY & BOB						
45s						
Yuletide 121		Merry Christmas (And A Happy New Year) (same on both sides)	19??	2.00	4.00	8.00

STEVE & EYDIE – See STEVE LAWRENCE AND EYDIE GORME.

STEVENS, CONNIE
On Various-Artists Collections

Away in a Manger	We Wish You a Merry Christmas (Warner Bros. W 1337)

Label, Number		Title (A Side/B Side)	Year	VG	VG+	NM
STEVENS, DODIE						
45s						
Dot 16166		Merry, Merry Christmas Baby/Jingle Bells	1960	5.00	10.00	20.00

On Various-Artists Collections

Merry, Merry Christmas Baby	Jingle Bell Rock (Time-Life SRNR-XM)
	Rockin' Little Christmas (MCA 25084)

Label, Number		Title (A Side/B Side)	Year	VG	VG+	NM
STEVENS, RAY						
45s						
MCA 52738		Santa Claus Is Watching You/Armchair Quarterback	1985	—	2.00	4.00
MCA 52738	PS	Santa Claus Is Watching You/Armchair Quarterback	1985	—	2.00	4.00
Mercury 72058		Santa Claus Is Watching You/Loved and Lost	1962	3.75	7.50	15.00
Mercury 72058	PS	Santa Claus Is Watching You/Loved and Lost	1962	6.25	12.50	25.00
NRC 063		Happy Blue Year/White Christmas	1960	6.25	12.50	25.00

On Various-Artists Collections

Greatest Little Christmas Ever Wuz	Happy Holidays, Vol. 23 (MCA Special Products 15042)
	Tennessee Christmas (MCA 5620)

Label, Number	Title (A Side/B Side)	Year	VG	VG+	NM

STEVENS, RISE
On Various-Artists Collections

Friendly Beasts, The	Favorite Christmas Carols from the Voice of Firestone (Firestone MLP 7005)				
Medley: Away in the Manger/It Came Upon a Midnight Clear	Firestone Presents Your Favorite Christmas Carols, Volume 2 (Firestone MLP 7006)				
O Come, O Come, Emmanuel	Firestone Presents Your Favorite Christmas Carols, Volume 2 (Firestone MLP 7006)				
O Holy Night	Favorite Christmas Carols from the Voice of Firestone (Firestone MLP 7005)				
Silent Night	Favorite Christmas Carols from the Voice of Firestone (Firestone MLP 7005)				
What Child Is This	Favorite Christmas Carols from the Voice of Firestone (Firestone MLP 7005)				

STEVENS, RISE; BRIAN SULLIVAN; FIRESTONE CHORUS
On Various-Artists Collections

Angels We Have Heard on High	Firestone Presents Your Favorite Christmas Carols, Volume 2 (Firestone MLP 7006)				
Joy to the World	Firestone Presents Your Favorite Christmas Carols, Volume 2 (Firestone MLP 7006)				

STEVENS, SHAKIN'
12-Inch Singles

Epic TA 6769	Merry Christmas Everyone//Blue Christmas/With My Heart	1985	3.75	7.50	15.00
— U.K. import					

45s

Epic EPCA 6769	Merry Christmas Everyone/With My Heart	1985	—	3.00	6.00
— U.K. import					

STEVENSON, B.W.
45s

MCA 41151	A Special Wish/Holding a Special Place for You	1979	—	2.00	4.00

On Various-Artists Collections

Special Wish, A	On This Christmas Night (Songbird MCA-3184)				

STEVIE, HOWIE
45s

Jamie 1393	If You Knew How Long I've Been So Good ForChristmas Part 1/ If You Knew How Long I've Been So Good For Christmas Part 2	1970	—	3.00	6.00
Pal 1101	If You Knew How Long I've Been So Good for Christmas/ If You Knew How Long I've Been So Good For Christmas	1969	2.00	4.00	8.00
— B-side by Steve Howard					

STEWART, CARA
45s

Iris 2001	Christmas Will Be Here Before You Know It/ I Spent My Last Three Dollars For An Irish Sweepstakes Ticket	198?	—	—	3.00

STEWART, HARRY
45s

Capitol F2618	The Night Before Christmas/Oh Oh Don't Ever Go	1953	3.75	7.50	15.00

STEWART, MIKE; THE SANDPIPERS, MITCHELL MILLER & ORCHESTRA
45s

Golden R68	Rudolph The Red-Nosed Reindeer/The Reindeer Dance	195?	2.00	4.00	8.00
— Yellow 7-inch 78 rpm record					
Golden R68 PS	Rudolph The Red-Nosed Reindeer/The Reindeer Dance	195?	2.00	4.00	8.00

STEWART, VERNON
45s

Blu-J 304	Christmas Tree In Heaven/Down To The Blues	196?	2.00	4.00	8.00

STIFF LITTLE FINGERS
45s

Chrysalis 2405	At the Edge//Running Bear/White Christmas	1979	—	3.00	6.00
— Tracks 1 and 2 are not Christmas songs					
Chrysalis 2405	At the Edge//Silly Encores	1979	—	3.00	6.00
— Sleeve and record are U.K. imports					

STING
12-Inch Singles

A&M 12164	Russians/Gabriel's Message/I Burn for You (Live)	1985	—	3.00	6.00
— Tracks 1 and 3 are not Christmas songs					

Label, Number		Title (A Side/B Side)	Year	VG	VG+	NM
45s						
A&M 2799		Russians/Gabriel's Message	1985	—	—	3.00
— A-side is not a Christmas song						
A&M 2799	PS	Russians/Gabriel's Message	1985	—	—	3.00
On Various-Artists Collections						
Gabriel's Message		Very Special Christmas, A (A&M SP-3911)				

STOCKWELL, SHIRLEY
45s

Stardisc 11063		The Christmas Wish/(Instrumental)	198?	—	2.00	4.00

STOKOWSKI, LEOPOLD
On Various-Artists Collections

Dance of the Sugar Plum Fairy	For a Musical Merry Christmas (RCA Victor PR-149A)	

STOMPERS, THE
45s

Gone 5120		Stompin' Round the Christmas Tree/Forgive Me	1961	37.50	75.00	150.00

STONE, CLIFFIE
45s

Capitol F1265		Christmas Waltz/Here Comes Santa Claus	1950	3.75	7.50	15.00
Capitol F3585		Rudolph the Red-Nosed Reindeer/Jingle Bells	1956	3.75	7.50	15.00

STONE, WALTER, AND THE TRADEWINDS
45s

Popularity 679		Christmas Time Again/I've Got Love	197?	—	2.00	4.00

STONEMANS, THE
Albums

MGM SE-4613		A Stoneman Christmas	1968	3.00	6.00	12.00

STOOKEY, NOEL PAUL
Albums

Warner Bros. BS 2674		One Night Stand	1973	2.50	5.00	10.00
— Contains one Christmas song: Jingle Bells						

STOOKEY, NOEL PAUL, AND THE BODYWORKS BAND
45s

Benson 5616	DJ	For Christmas (same on both sides)	198?	—	2.00	4.00
Benson 5616	PS	For Christmas (same on both sides)	198?	—	2.00	4.00

STORDAHL, AXEL
Albums

Decca DL 8933	M	Christmas in Scandinavia	1960	3.75	7.50	15.00
Decca DL 78933	S	Christmas in Scandinavia	1960	5.00	10.00	20.00
On Various-Artists Collections						
Deilig er Jorden		Decca 38170 (title unknown) (Decca DL 38170)				
Glade Jul		Decca 38170 (title unknown) (Decca DL 38170)				

STORMER
45s

Rockwoodz 101		Yule Tide Fever/Be Mine For Christmas	1981	—	2.00	4.00
Rockwoodz 101	PS	Yule Tide Fever/Be Mine For Christmas	1981	—	2.00	4.00

STORY, LIZ
On Various-Artists Collections

Greensleeves	Winter's Solstice, A (Windham Hill WH-1045)	

STORYTELLERS, THE
45s

Classic Artists 137		Christmas Time Is Coming/White Christmas	1990	—	2.50	5.00
— B-side by The Storytellers and Vicky Tafoya						

Label, Number		Title (A Side/B Side)	Year	VG	VG+	NM
STOTT, WALLY						
45s						
Warner Bros PRO 119/20		Happy Holiday/White Christmas	196?	3.75	7.50	15.00
— Promo-only single from the "Holiday Inn" movie						
STRAIT, GEORGE						
45s						
MCA S45-17234	DJ	Merry Christmas Strait to You/White Christmas	1986	5.00	10.00	20.00
— Promo only on red vinyl						
MCA S45-17451	DJ	For Christ's Sake, It's Christmas/When It's Christmas Time in Texas	1987	3.75	7.50	15.00
— Promo only on white vinyl						
Albums						
MCA 5800		Merry Christmas Strait to You	1986	2.50	5.00	10.00
MCA R 134172		Merry Christmas Strait to You	1986	3.00	6.00	12.00
— Same as above, but BMG Direct Marketing version						
On Various-Artists Collections						
Frosty the Snowman		Happy Holidays, Vol. 23 (MCA Special Products 15042)				
Santa Claus Is Coming to Town		Country Christmas (Time-Life STL-109)				
When It's Christmas Time in Texas		Country Christmas (Time-Life STL-109)				
STRASSER, SHAWN						
45s						
Antique 1401		Getting Ready For Christmas/Hey, Mister Santa Claus	19??	2.00	4.00	8.00
STRATTON, BERT						
45s						
Gallery II 008	DJ	Tiny Christmas Heart (same on both sides)	1986	—	—	3.00
STREET CORNER SINGERS, THE						
45s						
Atlantic 89008		Rudolph The Red-Nosed Reindeer/Hark!	1988	—	—	3.00
Atlantic 89008	PS	Rudolph The Red-Nosed Reindeer/Hark!	1988	—	—	3.00
STREET PAJAMA						
45s						
Street Pajama 101		Mrs. Claus' Angst/What Crime Am I Payin' For Now	1984	—	3.00	6.00
Street Pajama 101	PS	Mrs. Claus' Angst/What Crime Am I Payin' For Now	1984	—	3.00	6.00
STREET, JOYE						
45s						
Reena 1052		Make This A Good Christmas/What I Really Want For Christmas	198?	—	2.00	4.00
STREET, MEL						
45s						
GRT 109		Old Christmas Card/You Cared Enough To Send Me The Very Best	1976	—	2.00	4.00
STREETSINGERS						
45s						
Entree 5001		I'll Be Home For Christmas/Don't Call Me	19??	—	2.50	5.00
STREISAND, BARBRA						
45s						
Columbia 43896		Sleep in Heavenly Peace (Silent Night)/Gounod's Ave Maria	1966	2.50	5.00	10.00
Columbia 43896	PS	Sleep in Heavenly Peace (Silent Night)/Gounod's Ave Maria	1966	5.00	10.00	20.00
Columbia 44350		Jingle Bells?/White Christmas	1967	7.50	15.00	30.00
Columbia 44350	PS	Jingle Bells?/White Christmas	1967	10.00	20.00	40.00
Columbia 44351		Have Yourself a Merry Little Christmas/The Best Gift	1967	2.50	5.00	10.00
Columbia 44351	PS	Have Yourself a Merry Little Christmas/The Best Gift	1967	5.00	10.00	20.00
Columbia 44352		My Favorite Things/The Christmas Song	1967	7.50	15.00	30.00
Columbia 44352	PS	My Favorite Things/The Christmas Song	1967	10.00	20.00	40.00
Columbia 44354		I Wonder As I Wander/The Lord's Prayer	1967	7.50	15.00	30.00
Albums						
Columbia CL 2757	M	A Christmas Album	1967	6.25	12.50	25.00
Columbia CS 9557	S	A Christmas Album	1967	3.00	6.00	12.00
— Originals have red labels with "360 Sound" at the bottom of the label						
Columbia CS 9557	S	A Christmas Album	197?	2.00	4.00	8.00
— Later pressings have orange labels with "Columbia" circling the label						

Label, Number	Title (A Side/B Side)	Year	VG	VG+	NM

On Various-Artists Collections

Best Gift, The	Season's Greetings from Barbra Streisand...And Friends (Columbia Special Products CSS 1075)				
Christmas Song, The	Very Merry Christmas, A, Volume IV (Columbia Special Products CSS 1464)				
	Christmas Is... (Columbia Special Products P 11417)				
	Collection of Christmas Favorites, A (Columbia Special Products P 14988)				
	Season's Greetings from Barbra Streisand...And Friends (Columbia Special Products CSS 1075)				
Gounod's Ave Maria	It's Christmas Time! (Columbia Special Products P 14990)				
	Great Songs of Christmas, The, Album Six (Columbia Special Products CSM 388)				
	Season's Greetings from Barbra Streisand...And Friends (Columbia Special Products CSS 1075)				
Have Yourself a Merry Little Christmas	Christmas Greetings, Vol. 3 (Columbia Special Products P 11383)				
	Joyous Songs of Christmas, The (Columbia Special Products C 10400)				
I Wonder As I Wander	That Christmas Feeling (Columbia Special Products P 11853)				
Jingle Bells?	Christmas Album, A (Columbia PC 39466)				
Lord's Prayer, The	Great Songs of Christmas, The, Album Seven (Columbia Special Products CSS 547)				
O Little Town of Bethlehem	Christmas Greetings (Columbia Special Products CSS 1499)				
	Great Songs of Christmas, The, Album Eight (Columbia Special Products CSS 888)				
	Many Moods of Christmas, The (Columbia Special Products P 12013)				
	Season's Greetings from Barbra Streisand...And Friends (Columbia Special Products CSS 1075)				
Silent Night	Best of the Great Songs of Christmas (Album 10) (Columbia Special Products CSS 1478)				
	Christmas Greetings, Vol. 4 (Columbia Special Products P 11987)				
	Great Songs of Christmas, The, Album Six (Columbia Special Products CSM 388)				
	Great Songs of Christmas, The, Album Eight (Columbia Special Products CSS 888)				
	Season's Greetings from Barbra Streisand...And Friends (Columbia Special Products CSS 1075)				
	WHIO Radio Christmas Feelings (Sound Approach/CSP P 16366)				
White Christmas	Ronco Presents A Christmas Gift (Columbia Special Products P 12430)				
	WHIO Radio Christmas Feelings (Sound Approach/CSP P 16366)				

STRICKLAND, WILLIE
45s

Starlite 527	A Christmas Medley/The Wish (A Christmas Story)	1978	—	2.00	4.00
— B-side by Dick Valicenti					

STRIDELLS, THE
45s

Curtom 1949	I Remember Christmas/Mix It Up	1969	—	3.00	6.00

STRIDER, GENE
45s

Ford 100	On Christmas Day/Happy New Year	198?	—	—	3.00

STRONG, NOLAN, AND THE DIABLOS
45s

Pyramid 159	White Christmas/Danny Boy	19??	3.75	7.50	15.00

STRUNK, JUD
45s

Ad-Media 6416	The Santa Song/A Special Christmas Tree	1969	2.50	5.00	10.00
Ad-Media 6416 PS	The Santa Song/A Special Christmas Tree	1969	3.75	7.50	15.00

STRYPER
45s

Enigma 061	Winter Wonderland/Reason For The Season	1984	2.00	4.00	8.00

STUARTI, ENZO
Albums

Mistletoe MLP-1237	Comin' Home for Christmas	1978	2.50	5.00	10.00

On Various-Artists Collections

O Come All Ye Faithful	Happy Holiday (Mistletoe 1243)				
O Holy Night	Happy Holiday (Mistletoe 1243)				

STUCKEY, NAT
45s

Paula 288	Blue Christmas/How Can Christmas Be Merry	1967	2.00	4.00	8.00
Paula 1295	Blue Christmas/How Can Christmas Be Merry	198?	—	2.00	4.00

Label, Number		Title (A Side/B Side)	Year	VG	VG+	NM
STUERMER, DARYL						
On Various-Artists Collections						
Little Drummer Boy		GRP Christmas Collection, A (GRP 9574)				
STURR, JIMMY						
Albums						
Starr R-BS-116	(2)	Polka Christmas in My Home Town	1979	3.75	7.50	15.00
STYNE, JULE, AND BOB MERRILL						
45s						
Amp RRH		An Open End Interview With The Composers Of "The Dangerous Christmas Of Red Riding Hood"	196?	—	2.50	5.00
SUBWAY SERENADE						
45s						
Ave D 4		White Christmas/ What Are You Doing New Year's Eve?	19??	—	3.00	6.00
SUGARPLUM GANG, THE						
12-Inch Singles						
PlumCrazy PCR 1224		A Visit From St. Nicholas (The Christmas Rap)/A Visit From St. Nicholas (Radio Version) / A Visit From St. Nicholas (Instrumental)	1983	2.00	4.00	8.00
SUICIDE						
On Various-Artists Collections						
Hey Lord		Christmas Record, A (Ze/Passport PB 6020)				
SULLIVAN, BRIAN						
On Various-Artists Collections						
Deck the Hall		Firestone Presents Your Favorite Christmas Carols, Volume 2 (Firestone MLP 7006)				
First Noel, The		Favorite Christmas Carols from the Voice of Firestone (Firestone MLP 7005)				
It Came Upon the Midnight Clear		Favorite Christmas Carols from the Voice of Firestone (Firestone MLP 7005)				
Medley: We Three Kings of Orient Are/ God Rest Ye Merry, Gentlemen		Firestone Presents Your Favorite Christmas Carols, Volume 2 (Firestone MLP 7006)				
O Come, All Ye Faithful		Favorite Christmas Carols from the Voice of Firestone (Firestone MLP 7005)				
O Little Town of Bethlehem		Favorite Christmas Carols from the Voice of Firestone (Firestone MLP 7005)				
SULLIVAN, ED, PRESENTS						
45s						
Columbia 44720		Good King Wenceslas/Jingle Bells	1968	—	3.00	6.00
Columbia JZSP 135543/4	DJ	Rudolph, The Red-Nosed Reindeer/ The Little Drummer Boy/Jingle Bells/O Holy Night	1968	—	3.00	6.00
On Various-Artists Collections						
Good King Wenceslas		Joy to the World (30 Classic Christmas Melodies) (Columbia Special Products P3 14654)				
I Saw Mommy Kissing Santa Claus		Very Merry Christmas, A, Volume 3 (Columbia Special Products CSS 997)				
SULLIVAN, JERI						
45s						
Accent 1391		Let's Have An Old Fashioned Christmas/Christian Jamboree	197?	—	2.50	5.00
SUMMER, DONNA						
45s						
Casablanca 858 366-7		Melody of Love/The Christmas Song	1994	—	—	3.00
— A-side is not a Christmas song						
Casablanca 858 366-7	PS	Melody of Love/The Christmas Song	1994	—	—	3.00
SUMMERS, ANDREW ROWAN						
Albums						
Folkways FA-2002	10	Christmas Carols	195?	12.50	25.00	50.00
Folkways FC 7502	M	Christmas Carols	196?	3.75	7.50	15.00
SUMMERS, J.B.						
45s						
Gotham 209		I Want A Present For Christmas/My Baby Left Me	1952	6.25	12.50	25.00
SUMMERS, SUSAN, AND CHOIR						
45s						
Toni 100		Christmas Is Coming/Lollipops & Gumdrops	19??	—	2.00	4.00

Label, Number		Title (A Side/B Side)	Year	VG	VG+	NM
SUN, JOE						
45s						
Elektra 47229		Silent Night/Wings of My Victory	1981	—	2.50	5.00
Elektra 47232	DJ	Silent Night/Oh Holy Night	1981	—	2.50	5.00
— B-side by Helen Cornelius						
SUNNY						
45s						
Key-Loc 1010		I Want To Come Home For Christmas/(B-side unknown)	19??	2.00	4.00	8.00
SUNNY, BUDDY & MARIE						
45s						
(no label) 2731		Why Isn't It Christmas Yet?/The Star Spangled Barnyard	19??	—	2.00	4.00
— B-side by Sunny Lewis						
SUNSHINE						
45s						
Light 617		Joy To The World/Over In Bethlehem	1973	—	2.00	4.00
SUPREMES, THE						
45s						
Motown 1085		Children's Christmas Song/Twinkle, Twinkle Little Me	1965	3.75	7.50	15.00
Motown 1085	DJ	Twinkle Twinkle Little Me/Children's Christmas	1965	6.25	12.50	25.00
— Promo only on red vinyl						
Albums						
Motown M 638	M	Merry Christmas	1965	7.50	15.00	30.00
Motown MS 638	S	Merry Christmas	1965	10.00	20.00	40.00
Motown 5252ML		Merry Christmas	1982	2.50	5.00	10.00
— Reissue of MS 638 with same contents						

On Various-Artists Collections

Children's Christmas Song	Motown Christmas, A (Motown 795V2)
the World	Motown Christmas, A (Motown 795V2)
My Favorite Things	Jingle Bell Rock (Time-Life SRNR-XM)
	Motown Christmas, A (Motown 795V2)
Silver Bells	Motown Christmas, A (Motown 795V2)
Twinkle, Twinkle Little Me	Time-Life Treasury of Christmas, The, Volume Two (Time-Life STL-108)
White Christmas	Motown Christmas, A (Motown 795V2)

Label, Number		Title (A Side/B Side)	Year	VG	VG+	NM
SURF BOYS, THE						
45s						
Scepter 12180		Stuck in the Chimney/I Told Santa Claus I Want You	1966	6.25	12.50	25.00
SURF, SAMMY						
45s						
620 1001		Because It's Christmas/Twinkle Toes	19??	—	3.00	6.00
SURFARIS, THE						
45s						
Decca 31561		A Surfer's Christmas List/Santa's Speed Shop	1963	7.50	15.00	30.00

On Various-Artists Collections

Surfer's Christmas List, A	Rockin' Little Christmas (MCA 25084)

Label, Number	Title (A Side/B Side)	Year	VG	VG+	NM
SURREAL MCCOYS					
45s					
Diesel Only 244	Honky Tonk Christmas/Woke Up	199?	2.00	4.00	8.00

Label, Number		Title (A Side/B Side)	Year	VG	VG+	NM
SUTHERLAND, JOAN						
45s						
London 9807		The Twelve Days of Christmas/The Holly and the Ivy	1965	2.00	4.00	8.00
Albums						
London 5943	M	Joy of Christmas	196?	3.00	6.00	12.00

On Various-Artists Collections

Ave Maria	Great Songs of Christmas, Album Nine (Columbia Special Products CSS 1033)
Joy to the World	Magic of Christmas, The (Columbia Musical Treasury P3S 5806)
Twelve Days of Christmas, The	Great Songs of Christmas, Album Nine (Columbia Special Products CSS 1033)

 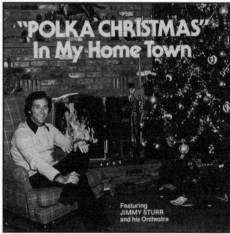

(Top left) Only 1,500 copies were pressed in 1996 of this Smoking Popes promo of the *Willy Wonka and the Chocolate Factory* song "Pure Imagination" backed with "O Holy Night." (Top right) Fresh off their pseudo-documentary movie, Spinal Tap recorded "Christmas with the Devil" in 1984 on this scarce Enigma single. The song finally appeared on LP in 1991. (Bottom left) Jo Stafford was past her hit-making prime when *Happy Holiday* was released on Columbia in 1955, but it is sought after by collectors of female vocalists. (Bottom right) Multiple Grammy winner Jimmy Sturr released this two-record set for polka-ing around the Christmas tree in 1979.

Label, Number		Title (A Side/B Side)	Year	VG	VG+	NM
SVENSON, OLE						
45s						
Hamilton 50014		I Vant a Christmas Drum/Yingle Yingle Yumping Beans	1959	3.00	6.00	12.00
SWAN SILVERTONES, THE						
45s						
Vee-Jay 869		Great Day In December/The Lord's Prayer	1958	15.00	30.00	60.00
On Various-Artists Collections						
Go Tell It on the Mountain		Mahalia (Jackson) and Friends at Christmastime (Columbia Special Products P 11804)				
SWAN, DOTTIE						
45s						
Southern Artists 2028		Red, White & Blue Christmas/Words From A Song	19??	—	2.50	5.00
SWANS, THE						
45s						
Ballad 1007		Happy/The Santa Claus Boogie	1955	150.00	300.00	600.00
SWANSON, BRAD, AND HIS WHISPERING ORGAN SOUND						
45s						
Thunderbird 525	DJ	Rudolph The Red Nose Reindeer/Jingle Bells	19??	—	3.00	6.00
SWANSON, JACK						
45s						
Abbey 15057		New Year Bells/Take Your Tears	19??	2.00	4.00	8.00
SWEET TEE						
45s						
Profile 5235		Let the Jingle Bells Rock/Christmas in Hollis	1988	—	2.00	4.00
— B-side by Run-D.M.C.						
SWEETHEARTS OF THE RODEO						
On Various-Artists Collections						
Jingle Bell Rock		Nashville Christmas Album, The (Epic PE 40418)				
SWINGING EMBERS, THE						
45s						
Ace 644		Winter Wonderland/I'm So Lonely	1961	3.75	7.50	15.00
SYLVIA						
On Various-Artists Collections						
Reflections		Country Christmas, A, Volume 2 (RCA AYL1-4809)				
SYLVIA, MARGO – See TUNE WEAVERS.						
SYLVIAN, DAVID						
On Various-Artists Collections						
Forbidden Colours		Merry Christmas, Mr. Lawrence (MCA 6125)				
SZA'VEE, MISS						
45s						
Soular 501		A Prayer For Christmas/Jingling Bells	19??	—	—	3.00
Soular 501	PS	A Prayer For Christmas/Jingling Bells	19??	—	2.00	4.00

T

Label, Number		Title (A Side/B Side)	Year	VG	VG+	NM
T. REX						
45s						
Lyntone (# unknown)		Christmas Time/Wanna Spend My Christmas with You/Christmas/Everybody Knows It's Christmas	1972	10.00	20.00	40.00
— Fan-club flexidisc						

Label, Number		Title (A Side/B Side)	Year	VG	VG+	NM
Lyntone (# unknown)	PS	Christmas Time/Wanna Spend My Christmas with You/ Christmas/Everybody Knows It's Christmas	1972	10.00	20.00	40.00
— Brown envelope and letter with above flexi; both are U.K. imports						
Marc On Wax SBOLAN 12PD		Christmas Bop/Shy Boy//Ride A White Swan (live)	1983	2.00	4.00	8.00
— U.K.-only picture disc						

TABBYNACLE CHOIR, THE
45s

DDD 101		Caterwaul Of The Bells/Meowy Chrismouse (Medley)	198?	—	2.50	5.00
DDD 101	PS	Caterwaul Of The Bells/Meowy Chrismouse (Medley)	198?	2.00	4.00	8.00

TALBOYS, LEE
45s

Royalty 110		Alvie The Elf/Christmastime In Snowland// Alvie The Elf/Christmastime In Snowland (Sing-a-Long)	1979	—	2.00	4.00
— 33 1/3 rpm 7-inch record						
Royalty 110	PS	Alvie The Elf/Christmastime In Snowland// Alvie The Elf/Christmastime In Snowland (Sing-a-Long)	1979	—	2.00	4.00

TATE, DANNY
45s

Charisma S7-19350		Lovin' Little Christmas/Christmas Forever	1996	—	—	3.00
— B-side on EMI by Freddie Jackson						

TATE, SNUKY
On Various-Artists Collections

Santa's Agent   (untitled) (Flexipop 15)

TAVARES, ERNIE, TRIO
45s

Dootone 325		I'm Alone Tonight/It's Christmas	1953	37.50	75.00	150.00
— B-side by the Bonairs						

TAYLOR, BILLY
On Various-Artists Collections

Bright Star in the East   Merry Christmas from David Frost and Billy Taylor (Bell 6053)
Joy to the World   Merry Christmas from David Frost and Billy Taylor (Bell 6053)
We Need Peace and We Need Love   Merry Christmas from David Frost and Billy Taylor (Bell 6053)

TAYLOR, CHARLES
On Various-Artists Collections

Christmas Message, A   Mahalia (Jackson) and Friends at Christmastime (Columbia Special Products P 11804)

TAYLOR, JOHNNIE
45s

Columbia AE7 1153	DJ	God Is Standing By/God Is Amazing	1977	2.00	4.00	8.00
— B-side by Deniece Williams; promo with "Suggested Christmas Programming" on label						

TAYLOR, LITTLE JOHNNY
45s

Galaxy 743		Please Come Home For Christmas/Miracle Maker	1965	2.00	4.00	8.00
Ichiban 169		Christmas Is Here Again/Ugly Man	1988	—	3.00	6.00
Ichiban 174		Christmas Is Here Again/I Enjoy You	1989	—	3.00	6.00

TAYLOR, R.B.
45s

Aurum 102		Christmas In Arizona/Bruce, Eye In The Sky	198?	—	2.00	4.00

TAYLOR, RAY
45s

Crescent Hill 503		Let Me Live 'Till Christmas/She'll Leave You In The Cold	19??	—	2.50	5.00

TEAGARDEN, JACK, AND JOHNNY MERCER
On Various-Artists Collections

Christmas Night in Harlem   Stash Christmas Album, The (Stash 125)

Label, Number		Title (A Side/B Side)	Year	VG	VG+	NM

TEBALDI, RENATA
On Various-Artists Collections

Ave Maria (Bach-Gounod)		Time-Life Treasury of Christmas, The, Volume Two (Time-Life STL-108)				

TEE, RICHARD
On Various-Artists Collections

Jingle Bells		Jazzy Wonderland, A (Columbia 1P 8120)				

TEMPLE, SEBASTIAN
45s

Capitol 5313		A Great Day in Bethlehem/A Perfect Family	1964	2.00	4.00	8.00

TEMPTATIONS, THE
45s

Gordy 1654		Silent Night/Everything for Christmas	1982	—	3.00	6.00
Gordy 1713		Silent Night/Everything for Christmas	1983	—	2.50	5.00
Gordy 7082		Silent Night/Rudolph, the Red-Nosed Reindeer	1968	2.50	5.00	10.00
Motown Yesteryear 690		Silent Night/Everything For Christmas	198?	—	2.00	4.00

Albums

Gordy GS 951		The Temptations' Christmas Card	1970	6.25	12.50	25.00
Gordy 998		Give Love at Christmas	1980	3.75	7.50	15.00
Motown 5279ML		Give Love at Christmas	1983	2.50	5.00	10.00
— Reissue of Gordy 998 with same contents						

On Various-Artists Collections

Little Drummer Boy, The		Motown Christmas, A (Motown 795V2)				
My Christmas Tree		Jingle Bell Rock (Time-Life SRNR-XM)				
		Motown Christmas, A (Motown 795V2)				
Rudolph, the Red-Nosed Reindeer		Jingle Bell Rock (Time-Life SRNR-XM)				
		Motown Christmas, A (Motown 795V2)				
Silent Night		Motown Christmas, A (Motown 795V2)				

TERMINATORS OF ENDEARMENT
45s

Subterranean 64		Stranger In The Manger/Santa's Gone Surfin'	1987	—	2.50	5.00
Subterranean 64	PS	Stranger In The Manger/Santa's Gone Surfin'	1987	—	2.50	5.00

TERRY, AL
45s

Feature 1079		Will Christmas Be A Happy Day For Me/Santa Claus Is On His Way	19??	—	2.50	5.00

TEX, JOE
45s

Dial 4068		I'll Make Everyday Christmas (For My Woman)/Don't Give Up	1967	2.50	5.00	10.00

TEXAS BOYS CHOIR, THE
45s

Derrick 900		I Believe In Christmas/Jingles	19??	—	2.50	5.00

THA DOGG POUND
On Various-Artists Collections

I Wish		Christmas on Death Row (Death Row/Interscope INT2-90108)				

THACKRAY, JAKE
45s

Dot 17055		Remember Bethlehem/Joseph	1967	2.00	4.00	8.00

THARPE, SISTER ROSETTA
45s

Decca 48328		In Bethlehem/When Jesus Was Born	1954	3.00	6.00	12.00

THEBOM, BLANCHE
On Various-Artists Collections

Virgin's Slumber Song, The		Joyous Noel (Reader's Digest RDA-57A)				

THEE HEADCOATEES
45s

Damaged Goods DAMGOOD 12 PD		Santa Claus/Evil Thing	198?	2.50	5.00	10.00
— U.K. import picture disc						

Label, Number		Title (A Side/B Side)	Year	VG	VG+	NM

THEY MIGHT BE GIANTS
45s

Elektra 64578		O Tannenbaum/Christmas Cards	1993	—	—	3.00
— Green vinyl						
Elektra 64578	PS	O Tannenbaum/Christmas Cards	1993	—	—	3.00

THIELMANS, TOOTS
45s

Command 4107		Jingle Bells/Sleigh Ride	1967	—	3.00	6.00
— B-side by Al Casamenit						

THIRD PARTY, THE
45s

Scepter 12340		What Do You Want For Christmas?/Everybody	1971	3.00	6.00	12.00

THOMAS SISTERS, THE
45s

Chief 101		Donde Esta Santa Claus?/Down By The River Side	19??	—	2.50	5.00

THOMAS, B.J.
45s

MCA 41134	God Bless the Children/On This Christmas Night	1979	—	2.00	4.00

On Various-Artists Collections

First Noel, The	Nashville's Greatest Christmas Hits, Volume II (Columbia PC 44413)
God Bless the Children	On This Christmas Night (Songbird MCA-3184)
On This Christmas Night	On This Christmas Night (Songbird MCA-3184)

THOMAS, BUELL
45s

Dalton 102	Shepherds & Kings/My Christmas Star	19??	—	2.00	4.00
— B-side by Jean Doran					
Dootone 316	Santa Claus Walks Just Like Daddy/You're My Christmas	1953	7.50	15.00	30.00
— B-side by Gerri Goodley					
Dootone 318	Green Christmas/For My Bride At Christmas Time	1953	7.50	15.00	30.00

THOMAS, CARLA
45s

Atlantic 2212	Gee Whiz, It's Christmas/All I Want for Christmas Is You	1963	3.75	7.50	15.00
Gusto 816	All I Want For Christmas Is You/Gee Whiz, It's Christmas	1979	2.50	5.00	10.00
— A Canadian import ($5) from 1986 exists on King					
Stax 206	All I Want for Christmas Is You/Winter Snow	1966	3.00	6.00	12.00

On Various-Artists Collections

Gee Whiz, It's Christmas	Jingle Bell Rock (Time-Life SRNR-XM)

THOMAS, DANNY
45s

Myrrh 124		Christmas Year/It's Sad To Be Lonely At Christmas	1972	—	2.50	5.00
RCA Victor 47-9342		The First Christmas/Christmas Story	1967	2.50	5.00	10.00
RCA Victor 47-9342	PS	The First Christmas/Christmas Story	1967	2.50	5.00	10.00

THOMAS, HARRY
45s

Northwest 101	Deacon's Christmas Eve/(B-side unknown)	19??	4.50	9.00	18.00

THOMAS, RUFUS
45s

Stax 0187	That Makes Merry Christmas Baby/I'll Be Your Santa Claus	1973	—	3.00	6.00
Stax 1073	I'll Be Your Santa Claus/Christmas Comes Once A Year	197?	—	2.50	5.00
— B-side by Albert King; reissue					

THOMAS, SEAN BARNEY, FEATURING J. FLEX
On Various-Artists Collections

Party 4 Da Homies	Christmas on Death Row (Death Row/Interscope INT2-90108)

THOMPSON, HANK
45s

Capitol 5310	Mr. and Mrs. Snowman/I'd Like to Have an Elephant for Christmas	1964	2.50	5.00	10.00
Capitol 5535	Little Christmas/Gonna Wrap My Heart in Angel Ribbons	1965	2.50	5.00	10.00

Label, Number		Title (A Side/B Side)	Year	VG	VG+	NM
Albums						
Capitol T 2154	M	It's Christmas Time	1963	5.00	10.00	20.00
Capitol ST 2154	S	It's Christmas Time	1963	6.25	12.50	25.00
On Various-Artists Collections						
Silver Bells		Christmas Stocking (Capitol NP 90494)				

THOMPSON, SLIM, AND THE FAT CATS
45s

Label, Number		Title (A Side/B Side)	Year	VG	VG+	NM
Recent 2044		Santa's Rockabilly Christmas/ Santa Must Have Lost His Way Last Night	19??	—	3.00	6.00
Recent 4370		Waldo, The Friendly Elf/(B-side unknown)	19??	—	2.50	5.00

THOMPSON, SONNY
45s

Label, Number	Title (A Side/B Side)	Year	VG	VG+	NM
Club 51 148	Not On A Christmas Tree/Sonny Claus Blues	19??	5.00	10.00	20.00

— Reissue of Miracle 148 (on 78 only)

THOMSEN, MARK
45s

Label, Number	Title (A Side/B Side)	Year	VG	VG+	NM
Pre-Show 831029	Noel/New Beginning	1983	—	—	3.00

THORNTON, BUDDY
45s

Label, Number	Title (A Side/B Side)	Year	VG	VG+	NM
Four Star 1668	Ole Santa Claus Is Coming to Town/Lonely Christmas Eve	1954	5.00	10.00	20.00

THOROGOOD, GEORGE, AND THE DESTROYERS
12-Inch Singles

Label, Number		Title (A Side/B Side)	Year	VG	VG+	NM
EMI America SPRO-9293/4	DJ	Rock And Roll Christmas/New Year's Eve Party	1983	2.00	4.00	8.00

— Promo only on red vinyl

45s

Label, Number		Title (A Side/B Side)	Year	VG	VG+	NM
EMI America 8187		Rock And Roll Christmas/New Year's Eve Party	1983	—	2.50	5.00
EMI America 8187	PS	Rock And Roll Christmas/New Year's Eve Party	1983	—	3.00	6.00
EMI S7-17647		Rock And Roll Christmas/New Year's Eve Party	1993	—	2.50	5.00

— Red vinyl

THREE ACES AND A JOKER
45s

Label, Number	Title (A Side/B Side)	Year	VG	VG+	NM
Xmas 3711	Sleigh Bell Rock/Rockin' & Rollin' With Santa	19??	2.00	4.00	8.00

— B-side by the Hepsters; reissue of rare R&B sides

On Various-Artists Collections

Label, Number	Title (A Side/B Side)	Year	VG	VG+	NM
Sleigh Bell Rock	Rockin' Christmas — The '50s (Rhino RNLP-066)				

THREE BLONDE MICE
45s

Label, Number	Title (A Side/B Side)	Year	VG	VG+	NM
Atco 6324	Ringo Bells/The 12 Days of Christmas	1964	7.50	15.00	30.00

THREE COURGETTES, THE
On Various-Artists Collections

Label, Number	Title (A Side/B Side)	Year	VG	VG+	NM
Christmas Is Coming	Christmas Record, A (Ze/Passport PB 6020)				

THREE STOOGES, THE
45s

Label, Number	Title (A Side/B Side)	Year	VG	VG+	NM
Little Golden 559	All I Want For Christmas Is My Two Front Teeth/ I Got A Cold For Christmas	19??	3.00	6.00	12.00

On Various-Artists Collections

Label, Number	Title (A Side/B Side)	Year	VG	VG+	NM
Wreck the Halls with Boughs of Holly	Dr. Demento Presents the Greatest Novelty Records of All Time Volume VI: Christmas (Rhino RNLP 825)				

THREE SUNS, THE
45s

Label, Number	Title (A Side/B Side)	Year	VG	VG+	NM
RCA Victor 47-3057	Adeste Fideles/Santa Claus Is Coming to Town	1949	2.50	5.00	10.00
RCA Victor 47-3058	Winter Wonderland/White Christmas	1949	2.50	5.00	10.00
RCA Victor 47-3059	Jingle Bells/Silent Night	1949	2.50	5.00	10.00
RCA Victor 47-3924	Sleigh Ride/I'll Find You	1949	3.75	7.50	15.00
RCA Victor 47-4323	Sleigh Ride/Uncle Mistletoe	1951	3.75	7.50	15.00

Label, Number		Title (A Side/B Side)	Year	VG	VG+	NM
7-Inch Extended Plays						
RCA Victor EPA-250		White Christmas/Winter Wonderland//Silent Night/Jingle Bells	195?	3.00	6.00	12.00
RCA Victor EPA-250	PS	The Three Suns Present Your Christmas Favorites	195?	3.00	6.00	12.00
RCA Victor WP 250	(3)	Your Christmas Favorites	1949	10.00	20.00	40.00
— Three records (47-3057, 47-3058, 47-3059) plus box						
Albums						
RCA Camden CAL-633	M	The Sound of Christmas	1964	3.00	6.00	12.00
RCA Camden CAS-633(e)	R	The Sound of Christmas	1964	3.00	6.00	12.00
RCA Victor LPM-52	10	Christmas Favorites	1951	12.50	25.00	50.00
RCA Victor LPM-1132	M	Sounds of Christmas	1955	7.50	15.00	30.00
RCA Victor LPM-2054	M	A Ding Dong Dandy Christmas!	1959	5.00	10.00	20.00
RCA Victor LSP-2054	S	A Ding Dong Dandy Christmas!	1959	7.50	15.00	30.00
RCA Victor LPM-3056	10	Christmas Party	1952	12.50	25.00	50.00
On Various-Artists Collections						
Ding Dong Dandy Christmas		Christmas Programming from RCA Victor (RCA Victor SP-33-66)				
It Came Upon the Midnight Clear		Joyous Noel (Reader's Digest RDA-57A)				
O Little Town of Bethlehem		For a Musical Merry Christmas, Volume 3 (RCA Victor PRM-221)				
Santa Claus Is Coming to Town		October Christmas Sampler 59-40-41 (RCA Victor SPS-33-54)				

THREE WISE MEN, THE
Band is actually XTC.

45s						
Virgin 642		Thanks For Christmas/Countdown To Christmas Party Time	1983	2.50	5.00	10.00
Virgin 642	PS	Thanks For Christmas/Countdown To Christmas Party Time	1983	2.50	5.00	10.00
— Record and sleeve are U.K. imports						

THRONHILL, CLAUDE, AND HIS ORCHESTRA
On Various-Artists Collections

Snowfall		Remembering Christmas with the Big Bands (RCA Special Products DPM1-0506)

THROWING MUSES
On Various-Artists Collections

Santa		Winter Warnerland (Warner Bros. PRO-A-3328)

TIJUANA VOICES

45s						
P.I.P. 8907		Tijuana Christmas/Deck The Halls	197?	—	2.00	4.00
Albums						
Pickwick SPCX-1005		Tijuana Voices Sing Merry Christmas	1970	3.00	6.00	12.00

TIL, SONNY
Also see THE ORIOLES.

45s						
RCA Victor 74-0606		Crying in the Chapel/What Are You Doing New Year's Eve	1971	2.00	4.00	8.00

TILLIS, MEL

45s						
Elektra 47233	DJ	White Christmas/Blue Christmas	1981	—	2.50	5.00
— B-side by Eddy Raven						
Elektra 47234	DJ	Rudolph the Red-Nosed Reindeer/Winter Wonderland	1981	2.00	4.00	8.00
— As "Mel and Nancy" (Sinatra); B-side by Dave Rowland and Sugar						

TILLOTSON, JOHNNY

45s						
MGM 13633		Christmas Country Style/Christmas Is the Best of All	1966	2.50	5.00	10.00
Albums						
MGM E-4402	M	The Christmas Touch	1966	5.00	10.00	20.00
MGM SE-4402	S	The Christmas Touch	1966	6.25	12.50	25.00

TIMBUK 3

12-Inch Singles						
I.R.S. L33-17427	DJ	All I Want for Christmas/ Medley: Blue Christmas-I Want You x 3	1987	3.75	7.50	15.00
45s						
I.R.S. 53221		All I Want for Christmas/Medley: Blue Christmas-I Love You x 3	1987	—	3.00	6.00
I.R.S. 53221	PS	All I Want for Christmas/Medley: Blue Christmas-I Love You x 3	1987	—	3.00	6.00

Label, Number		Title (A Side/B Side)	Year	VG	VG+	NM
TIMMONS, CY						
45s						
Erewhon 1003		Once Upon A Christmas Tree/It's Christmas	1980	—	2.50	5.00
TINGSTAD, ERIC, AND NANCY RUMBEL						
On Various-Artists Collections						
It Came Upon a Midnight Clear		Narada: The Christmas Collection (Narada N-63902)				
TINT OF DARKNESS, A						
45s						
Starfire 120		Jingle Bells (KMEL)//	1979	2.00	4.00	8.00
		Jingle Bells (Steve Hardy's Beach Party)/So Much In Love (Rated X)				
— Yellow vinyl						
Starfire 120	PS	Jingle Bells (KMEL)//	1979	2.00	4.00	8.00
		Jingle Bells (Steve Hardy's Beach Party)/So Much In Love (Rated X)				
TINY TIM						
45s						
Victim 1001		Rudolph The Red-Nosed Reindeer/White Christmas	198?	3.00	6.00	12.00
TIPPERARY BRASS, THE						
45s						
Teiger 506		Santa Claus Is Coming To Town/Christmas Medley	19??	—	2.00	4.00
TIPPINS, LITTLE CATHY						
45s						
Fantasy 577		It's Christmas Eve And We're Alone/La Pinata	196?	3.00	6.00	12.00
— B-side by Los Ninos De Mexico						
TIRZAH						
45s						
Squire 18119		Sock It To Me Santa/Patch Pockets, Lollipops & Puppy Love	19??	—	2.50	5.00
TODAY GENERATION, THE						
45s						
Christmas '70 111070		That Day Of The Year/Turkey Lurkey Time	1970	—	3.00	6.00
— B-side by Trudy Love						
TODD, PAUL						
45s						
K-tel 160		Christmas Is for Children/We Wish You A Merry Christmas	1989	—	—	3.00
K-tel 160	PS	Christmas Is for Children/We Wish You A Merry Christmas	1989	—	—	3.00
TOLMAN, RUSS, AND THE NORTH POLE MEN						
On Various-Artists Collections						
Happy Birthday		Stuff This in Your Stocking! Elves in Action (Veebltronics/Skyclad 68)				
TOMLINSON, MICHAEL						
45s						
Desert Rain 3202		If You're There/Yellow Windows	19??	—	2.00	4.00
Desert Rain 3202	PS	If You're There/Yellow Windows	19??	—	2.00	4.00
TOMPALL AND THE GLASER BROTHERS						
45s						
Elektra 47230	DJ	Silver Bells/Please Come Home for Christmas	1981	—	2.50	5.00
— B-side by Johnny Lee						
TONSBERG CHORAL CHOIR						
Albums						
Harmony Music LP-18	M	Christmas Songs from Norway	196?	3.75	7.50	15.00
TONY AND MACK						
45s						
Golden Crest 744		Christmas Tree Park/Christmas In Paree	19??	—	2.00	4.00
Golden Crest 744	PS	Christmas Tree Park/Christmas In Paree	19??	—	2.00	4.00

Label, Number		Title (A Side/B Side)	Year	VG	VG+	NM
TONY AND THE DAYDREAMS						
45s						
Planet 1054		Christmas Lullaby/Handin' Hand	1961	50.00	100.00	200.00
TOONE, GENE, AND CHAPTER IV						
45s						
Wand 11293		Baby Boy (Part 1)/Baby Boy (Part 2)	1975	—	2.50	5.00
TOREADOR BRASS, THE						
Albums						
Harmony HS-11352		Toreador Christmas	1968	3.00	6.00	12.00
TORME, MEL						
45s						
Columbia 43167		Every Day's a Holiday/One Little Snowflake	1964	3.00	6.00	12.00
Columbia 43167	DJ	Every Day's a Holiday/One Little Snowflake	1964	3.75	7.50	15.00
— Promo only on green vinyl						
Columbia 45283		The Christmas Song/(B-side unknown)	1970	—	3.00	6.00
Albums						
Verve V-8593	M	Verve's Choice — The Best of Mel Torme	1964	3.00	6.00	12.00
Verve V6-8593	S	Verve's Choice — The Best of Mel Torme	1964	3.75	7.50	15.00
— Contains one Christmas song: Christmas Song, The						
On Various-Artists Collections						
Christmas Song, The		Happy Holidays, Vol. 20 (RCA Special Products DPL1-0713)				
		Merry Christmas from... (Reader's Digest RD4-83)				
		Old-Fashioned Christmas, An (Longines Symphonette LS 214)				
		Very Merry Christmas, A, Volume IV (Columbia Special Products CSS 1464)				
TORRES, JUDY						
45s						
Profile 5242		Christmas Time Won't Be The Same This Year/(Instrumental)	1988	—	2.00	4.00
— Green vinyl						
TOSH AND THE JIVESTERS						
45s						
Broadway 112		Merry Christmas (Betcha My Boots)/	19??	2.00	4.00	8.00
		That Fascinatin', Procrastinatin' Gal Of Mine				
TOWNE CHOIR, THE						
45s						
Capitol 5538		African Noel/Papa Noel	1965	2.00	4.00	8.00
TOWNE, SKIP, AND FRIENDS						
12-Inch Singles						
Charmed Life CL 33 AD		O, Come All Ye Faithful/Georg Friedrich's Party//	1988	—	3.00	6.00
		Hallelujah Dance/Messiah Mix				
TOWNSEND, BOB						
45s						
Minaret 106		Christmas Message From Space/The Night Before New Year's	1962	2.50	5.00	10.00
TOZZI, GEORGIO, AND ROSALIND ELLIS						
On Various-Artists Collections						
Silent Night		Christmas Programming from RCA Victor (RCA Victor SP-33-66)				
		October Christmas Sampler 59-40-41 (RCA Victor SPS-33-54)				
TRACEY, WREG						
45s						
Anna 1126		All I Want for Christmas (Is Your Love)/Take Me Back	1960	10.00	20.00	40.00
TRACTORS, THE						
45s						
Arista 12771		The Santa Claus Boogie/Swingin' Home for Christmas	1994	—	2.00	4.00
TRAINOR, FRANK						
45s						
Wyndblough 001		Rhonda The Reindeer's Magical Tail//Hurry Up/The House Is Dark	1986	—	2.00	4.00

Label, Number		Title (A Side/B Side)	Year	VG	VG+	NM
TRAPP FAMILY SINGERS, THE						
7-Inch Extended Plays						
Decca 94004		Angelus Ad Pastores/In Mativitate Domini/	195?	2.50	5.00	10.00
		The Christmas Nightingale//Angels We Have Heard On High/From				
		Heaven High/Bring Your Torches, Jeannette, Isabella/Quittez, Pasteurs				
— "Gold Label Series" record						
Decca 94005		Puer Natus Est Nobis/Pastorale//Pastores A Belen/	195?	2.50	5.00	10.00
		Bethlehem/Christmas Rose				
— "Gold Label Series" record						
Decca 94006		Ave Maria/Quem Pastores Laudavere/Beata Viscera//	195?	2.50	5.00	10.00
		I Sing Of A Maiden/El Rorro/Senex Puerum Portabat				
— "Gold Label Series" record						
7-Inch Extended Plays						
Decca ED 1200	(3)	Christmas With The Trapp Family Singers	195?	8.75	17.50	35.00
— 3 records (94004, 94005, 94006) plus box						
Albums						
RCA Camden CAL-209	M	The Trapp Family Singers Present Christmas and Folk Songs	195?	5.00	10.00	20.00
On Various-Artists Collections						
Jesus, Jesus, Rest Your Head		Happy Holidays, Vol. 23 (MCA Special Products 15042)				
TRASHMEN, THE						
45s						
Garrett 4013		Dancing with Santa/Real Live Doll	1964	6.25	12.50	25.00
Garrett 4013	PS	Dancing with Santa/Real Live Doll	1964	37.50	75.00	150.00
Sundazed 112		Dancing with Santa/Real Live Doll	1996	—	—	2.00
— Red vinyl						
Sundazed 112	PS	Dancing with Santa/Real Live Doll	1996	—	—	2.00
TRAVELERS, THE						
45s						
Andex 2011		I'll Be Home for Christmas/Katie the Kangaroo	1958	7.50	15.00	30.00
TRAVELING WILBURYS (NELSON WILBURY, I.E., GEORGE HARRISON)						
On Various-Artists Collections						
Holiday I.D.		Winter Warnerland (Warner Bros. PRO-A-3328)				
TRAVIS, RANDY						
45s						
Warner Bros PRO-S-2842	DJ	White Christmas Makes Me Blue/Sleigh Ride	1987	—	2.00	4.00
— B-side by Mark O'Connor						
Warner Bros. 22766		Oh, What a Silent Night/Winter Wonderland	1989	—	2.00	4.00
Warner Bros. 27707		An Old Time Christmas/How Do I Wrap My Heart Up for Christmas	1988	—	2.50	5.00
Warner Bros. 27707	PS	An Old Time Christmas/How Do I Wrap My Heart Up for Christmas	1988	—	2.50	5.00
Warner Bros. 28556		White Christmas Makes Me Blue/Pretty Paper	1986	—	2.00	4.00
Albums						
Warner Bros. 25972		An Old-Fashioned Christmas	1989	3.00	6.00	12.00
On Various-Artists Collections						
Holiday I.D.		Winter Warnerland (Warner Bros. PRO-A-3328)				
How Do I Wrap My Heart Up		Winter Warnerland (Warner Bros. PRO-A-3328)				
for Christmas						
White Christmas Makes Me Blue		Christmas Tradition, A (Warner Bros. 25630)				
TREACHEROUS THREE, THE						
45s						
Atlantic 89593		Santa's Rap/At Christmas Time	1984	—	2.00	4.00
— B-side by Luther (later known as Luther Vandross)						
TREADWELL, IRENE						
45s						
Jay Dee 782		Church Bells Are Ringing on Christmas Morning/	1953	5.00	10.00	20.00
		Dear Santa Bring Back My Daddy to Me				
TREECE, RONNIE, AND ANN SAVAGE						
45s						
Round Eye 103		Jingle's Dream/Twelve Days Of Christmas	19??	2.00	4.00	8.00

Label, Number		Title (A Side/B Side)	Year	VG	VG+	NM
TRENT, CARL						
45s						
Golden Voice 708		Jingle Bell Trucker/Don't Say That You Can't Love Me	197?	—	3.00	6.00
TREVOR, VAN						
45s						
Band Box 373	DJ	Christmas In The Country/PSA Announcements	1966	2.50	5.00	10.00
Claridge 305		Christmas in Washington Square/Melting Snow	1965	3.75	7.50	15.00
TRIBBLE, MARK						
45s						
Paloma 92787	DJ	The Year I Saw Santa Claus (same on both sides)	1987	—	—	3.00
TRINA, MARGUERITE						
45s						
Bella 19		The Rocking Tree/The Brat	1959	3.00	6.00	12.00
TRIPP, PAUL						
45s						
Musicor 1125		An Old-Fashioned Christmas/I've Got a Date with Santa	1965	3.00	6.00	12.00
TRITT, TRAVIS						
45s						
Warner Bros. 18703		Santa Looked a Lot Like Daddy/Winter Wonderland	1992		2.00	4.00
TROPICAL WAVES						
12-Inch Singles						
Arapaima (no #)		Christmas In The Island/It's Nearly Christmas Day	198?	3.00	6.00	12.00
TRUTH						
45s						
Paragon 45042		Here We Come A Caroling/Caroling Caroling// Do You Hear What I Hear?	198?	—	—	3.00
TSUNAMI						
45s						
Simple Machine 014 — B-side by Velocity Girl		Could Have Been Christmas/Merry Christmas, I Love You	199?	—	3.00	6.00
Simple Machine 014 — B-side by Velocity Girl	PS	Could Have Been Christmas/Merry Christmas, I Love You	199?	—	3.00	6.00
TUBB, ERNEST						
45s						
Decca 28453		Merry Texas Christmas, You All/Blue Snowflakes	1952	3.75	7.50	15.00
Decca 28946		I'm Trimming My Christmas Tree with Teardrops/ We Need God for Christmas	1953	3.75	7.50	15.00
Decca 29350		I'll Be Walkin' the Floor This Christmas/Lonely Christmas Eve	1954	3.75	7.50	15.00
Decca 31334		Christmas Is Just Another Day for Me/ Rudolph the Red-Nosed Reindeer	1961	3.00	6.00	12.00
Decca 31866		Who's Gonna Be Your Santa Claus/Blue Christmas Tree	1965	2.50	5.00	10.00
Decca 46186		White Christmas/Blue Christmas	1949	3.75	7.50	15.00
Decca 46268		Christmas Island/Christmas	1950	5.00	10.00	20.00
MCA 65024 — Black label with rainbow		White Christmas/Blue Christmas	1973	—	2.00	4.00
MCA 65024 — Blue label with rainbow		White Christmas/Blue Christmas	1980	—	—	3.00
7-Inch Extended Plays						
Decca ED 2089		(contents unknown)	195?	3.00	6.00	12.00
Decca ED 2089	PS	White Christmas	195?	3.00	6.00	12.00
Decca 74518 — 33 1/3 stereo jukebox pressing (contents unknown)		Blue Christmas	1964	3.75	7.50	15.00
Albums						
Decca DL 4518	M	Blue Christmas	1963	6.25	12.50	25.00
Decca DL 5497	10	Sing a Song of Christmas	1954	37.50	75.00	150.00
Decca DL 74518 — Same as DL 4518, but in stereo	S	Blue Christmas	1963	7.50	15.00	30.00
On Various-Artists Collections						
Blue Christmas		Blue Christmas (Welk Music Group WM-3002)				
I'll Be Walkin' the Floor This Christmas		Country Christmas (Time-Life STL-109)				

Label, Number	Title (A Side/B Side)	Year	VG	VG+	NM

TUBES, THE
45s

Tubes 12682XS	Tubular Holiday	1982	12.50	25.00	50.00
— Fan club flexidisc					
Tubes 833502XS	Happy Holidaze	1983	12.50	25.00	50.00
— Fan club flexidisc					

TUCKER, LITTLE TOMMY
45s

Laurie 3077	(All I Want For Christmas Is) My Two Front Teeth/ Mister Cuddly Wuddly	1960	3.75	7.50	15.00
— Also released as "Little Tommy"					

TUCKER, RICHARD
On Various-Artists Collections

Lord's Prayer, The	Best of the Great Songs of Christmas (Album 10) (Columbia Special Products CSS 1478)
	Great Songs of Christmas, The, Album Five (Columbia Special Products CSP 238M)
	Joyous Christmas, Volume V (Columbia Special Products C 10398)
	Merry Christmas from... (Reader's Digest RD4-83)
O Little Town of Bethlehem	Great Songs of Christmas, The, Album Five (Columbia Special Products CSP 238M)
	Magnavox Album of Christmas Music (Columbia Special Products CSQ 11093)

TUCKER, TANYA
45s

Liberty S7-57895	Winter Wonderland/What Child Is This	1992	—	2.00	4.00

On Various-Artists Collections

Away in a Manger	RFD Christmas (Columbia Special Products P 15427)
	Ronco Presents A Christmas Gift (Columbia Special Products P 12430)
Silent Night	RFD Christmas (Columbia Special Products P 15427)
Silver Bells	Down-Home Country Christmas, A (Columbia Special Products P 14992)
What Child Is This	Christmas for the 90's, Volume 2 (Capitol Nashville 1P 8118)
Winter Wonderland	Christmas for the 90's, Volume 1 (Capitol Nashville 1P 8117)

TUCKER, TOMMY
45s

MGM 10854	Christmas In Killarney/Jing-A-Ling	1950	3.75	7.50	15.00

TUCSON, ARIZONA BOYS CHORUS
45s

United Artists 682	Sing Noel/Sleep, Little Tiny King	1963	3.00	6.00	12.00
United Artists 783	African Noel/Sleep, Little Tiny King	1964	2.50	5.00	10.00

TUNE WEAVERS, THE
45s

Classic Artists 107	Merry, Merry Christmas Baby/What Are You Doing New Year's Eve	1988	—	2.00	4.00
— As "Margo Sylvia and Tune Weavers"					

TURKISH COMPOSERS
45s

Turkey TIO		The Story Of Santa Claus/Turkey, The Bible Land	19??	—	—	3.00
Turkey TIO	PS	The Story Of Santa Claus/Turkey, The Bible Land	19??	—	—	3.00

TURNER, IKE AND TINA
45s

Warner Bros. 5493	Ooh Poop A Doo/Merry Christmas Baby	1964	3.00	6.00	12.00
— A-side is not a Christmas song					

TURNER, MCCOY
On Various-Artists Collections

I'll Be Home for Christmas	God Rest Ye Merry, Jazzmen (Columbia FC 37551)

TURNER, SAMMY
45s

Verve 10465	A Child Was Born/Come to Me Comf'tably	1966	7.50	15.00	30.00

TURNER, TITUS
45s

Okeh 6929	Christmas Morning/Be Sure You Know	1952	7.50	15.00	30.00

Label, Number		Title (A Side/B Side)	Year	VG	VG+	NM
TURTLE ISLAND STRING QUARTET						
On Various-Artists Collections						
Chorale #220		Winter's Solstice II, A (Windham Hill WH-1077)				
TUTTLE, WESLEY						
45s						
Capitol F1266		What I Want for Christmas/White Christmas	1950	3.75	7.50	15.00
TWEETY & SWEETY (THE PARAKEET & THE CANARY)						
45s						
Storz 101		Deck The Cage (With Boughs Of Holly)/Silent Night, Holy Night	19??	2.50	5.00	10.00
23 SKIDOO						
45s						
Mercury 72874		The New Year's Song/Courtesy	1968	2.50	5.00	10.00
TWIGGY						
45s						
Spartan TWIG 1		Winter Wonderland/Needles And Pins	198?	2.50	5.00	10.00
Spartan TWIG 1	PS	Winter Wonderland/Needles And Pins	198?	2.50	5.00	10.00
— Above record and sleeve are U.K. imports						
TWISTIN' KINGS						
45s						
Motown 1022		Xmas Twist/White House Twist	1961	10.00	20.00	40.00
TWITTY, CONWAY						
45s						
Warner Bros. 29129		White Christmas/Happy the Christmas Clown	1984	—	2.50	5.00
Warner Bros. 29129	PS	White Christmas/Happy the Christmas Clown	1984	—	2.50	5.00
Albums						
Warner Bros. 23971		Merry Twistmas	1983	5.00	10.00	20.00
TWO MISTER F'S, THE						
45s						
Mercury 5741		Mrs. Santa Claus/Say a Prayer	1951	3.75	7.50	15.00
2.3 CHILDREN						
45s						
Penguin 2303		Christmas In The City/Santa's Just An Anagram For Satan	198?	2.50	5.00	10.00
Penguin 2303	PS	Christmas In The City/Santa's Just An Anagram For Satan	198?	2.50	5.00	10.00
220 VOLT						
12-Inch Singles						
Epic 07500		Heavy Xmas (Maxi-Version)/Heavy Xmas (Single)	1987	3.00	6.00	12.00
TYCOON						
45s						
Starlight 27		White Christmas/Silent Night	19??	—	2.50	5.00
TYLER, WINK						
45s						
Buzz 500		Merry Christmas You Two/(B-side unknown)	19??	—	2.00	4.00

U

Label, Number		Title (A Side/B Side)	Year	VG	VG+	NM
U.K. CENTERFOLDS, THE						
12-Inch Singles						
Oops OOPS3		Wet 'n' Wild (7" Mix)/Wet 'n' Wild (12" Remix)/ Wet 'n' Wild (Techno Mix)//Get Your Tits Out for Christmas (7" Mix)/ Get Your Tits Out for Christmas (Hard, Funky & Long Mix)	1995	2.00	4.00	8.00
— B-side by Grab This						

Label, Number		Title (A Side/B Side)	Year	VG	VG+	NM
U.K. SUBS						
12-Inch Singles						
Fall Out FALL 12 044		Hey! Santa/Captain Scarlet//Thunderbird/Street Legal	198?	4.50	9.00	18.00
— European import						
U.S. ARM BAND						
45s						
Nocturne 111		Rudolph, The Red-Nosed Reindeer/Jingle Bells	19??	2.50	5.00	10.00
— Yellow label						
Nocturne 111		Rudolph, The Red-Nosed Reindeer/Jingle Bells	19??	2.50	5.00	10.00
— White label						
Nocturne 111	PS	Rudolph, The Red-Nosed Reindeer/Jingle Bells	19??	2.50	5.00	10.00
U2						
On Various-Artists Collections						
Christmas (Baby Please Come Home)		Very Special Christmas, A (A&M SP-3911)				
UGGAMS, LESLIE						
45s						
MGM 11626		My Stocking Is Empty/This Is Santa Claus	1953	5.00	10.00	20.00
— As "Leslie 'Uggams' Crayne"						
MGM 11868		Uncle Santa/The Fat, Fat Man	1954	5.00	10.00	20.00
On Various-Artists Collections						
It's Beginning to Look Like Christmas		Very Merry Christmas, A, Volume 3 (Columbia Special Products CSS 997)				
Reminder Spot		For Christmas Seals...A Matter of Life and Breath (Decca Custom Style E)				
ULANO, SAM						
45s						
MGM SK-37		Santa & The Doodle-Li-Boop/The Story Of Santa Claus	1954	2.50	5.00	10.00
MGM SK-37	PS	Santa & The Doodle-Li-Boop/The Story Of Santa Claus	1954	5.00	10.00	20.00
UNIQUES, THE						
45s						
Clifton 62		After New Year's Eve/Kiss, Kiss, Kiss	19??	2.00	4.00	8.00
Demand 1994		Merry Christmas, Darling/I Wanna Chance	198?	2.00	4.00	8.00
— B-side by the Vows; green vinyl "collector's issue"						
Demand 2936		Merry Christmas Darling/Rockin' Rudolph	1963	12.50	25.00	50.00
Demand 3950		Merry Christmas Darling (And A Happy New Year Too)/Times Change	1963	7.50	15.00	30.00
Dot 16533		Merry Christmas Darling/Times Change	1963	6.25	12.50	25.00
Paula 255		Please Come Home for Christmas/(Instrumental)	1966	3.00	6.00	12.00
UNTAMED YOUTH, THE						
45s						
Norton 45-004		Santa's Gonna Shut 'Em Down/Santa's Midnight Run	1989	—	2.00	4.00
Norton 45-004	PS	Santa's Gonna Shut 'Em Down/Santa's Midnight Run	1989	—	2.00	4.00
USHER						
12-Inch Singles						
LaFace 73008-24131-1		Comin' For X-Mas/(B-side unknown)	1995	2.00	4.00	8.00

V

Label, Number		Title (A Side/B Side)	Year	VG	VG+	NM
VAGABONDS, THE						
45s						
Campus 127		A Sunday Kind Of Christmas/Buon Natale	19??	5.00	10.00	20.00
VALE, JERRY						
45s						
Columbia 44280		Santa Mouse/Silent Night, Holy Night	1967	—	3.00	6.00
Columbia JZSP 79175/6	DJ	Silent Night, Holy Night/Oh Holy Night	1963	2.50	5.00	10.00
Columbia JZSP 111776	DJ	Blue Christmas (same on both sides)	1965	2.50	5.00	10.00

Label, Number		Title (A Side/B Side)	Year	VG	VG+	NM
Albums						
Columbia CL 2225	M	Christmas Greetings	1964	3.00	6.00	12.00
Columbia CS 9025	S	Christmas Greetings	1964	3.75	7.50	15.00
On Various-Artists Collections						
(There's No Place Like) Home for the Holidays		Merry Christmas (Columbia Musical Treasury 3P 6306)				
Have Yourself a Merry Little Christmas		Home for Christmas (Columbia Musical Treasury P3S 5608)				
		Home for Christmas (Realm 2V 8101)				
Home for the Holidays		Great Songs of Christmas, The, Album Seven (Columbia Special Products CSS 547)				
It Came Upon the Midnight Clear		Have a Happy Holiday (Columbia Special Products CSS 1432)				
O Come, All Ye Faithful		Great Songs of Christmas, The, Album Seven (Columbia Special Products CSS 547)				
O Holy Night		Merry Christmas from... (Reader's Digest RD4-83)				
		Philco Album of Holiday Music, The (Columbia Special Products CSM 431)				
		Spirit of Christmas, The (Columbia Special Products CSP 249)				
White Christmas		Collection of Christmas Favorites, A (Columbia Special Products P 14988)				

VALENTIN, DAVE
On Various-Artists Collections

Santa Claus Is Coming to Town		GRP Christmas Collection, A (GRP 9574)				

VALENTINE, DICKIE
45s

London 1620		Christmas Island/Christmas Alphabet	1955	3.00	6.00	12.00

VALENTINE, JUDY
45s

Epic 9004		A Ride in Santa's Sleigh/She Was Five and He Was Ten	1953	5.00	10.00	20.00

VALENTINES, THE
45s

Rama 186		Christmas Prayer/K-I-S-S Me	1955	100.00	200.00	400.00
— *Blue label*						
Rama 186		Christmas Prayer/K-I-S-S Me	1955	10.00	20.00	40.00
— *Red label*						
Roulette 58		Christmas Prayer/Nature's Creation	196?	2.50	5.00	10.00
— *"Golden Goodies Series"*						

VALICENTI, DICK
45s

Starlite 527		The Wish (A Christmas Story)/A Christmas Medley	1978	—	2.00	4.00
— *B-side by Willie Strickland*						

VALLEY YOUTH CHORALE, THE
45s

Felsted 8693		The Little Bell/Do You Hear What I Hear	1963	2.00	4.00	8.00

VAN DYKES, THE
45s

Baldwin 8308		Christmas Forever/Christmas Forever (Reprise)	1983	—	3.00	6.00

VAN HORNE, RANDY
45s

Everest 19391		Jingle Bells/What Are You Doing New Year's Eve	1960	3.00	6.00	12.00

VANCE, VINCE, AND THE VALIANTS
45s

Valiant 92689		All I Want For Christmas Is You/Exceptional Man	1989	—	2.00	4.00
Valiant 92689	PS	All I Want For Christmas Is You/Exceptional Man	1989	—	2.00	4.00

VANDA, CINDY
45s

Grand Prize 5225		Santa On His 1990 Harley/Christmas It's Christmas	1989	—	2.00	4.00

VANDALS, THE
Albums

Kung Fu 78762		Christmas with the Vandals: Oi to the World!	1996	2.50	5.00	10.00

Label, Number		Title (A Side/B Side)	Year	VG	VG+	NM
VANDEPITTE, DAWN						
45s						
Buddah 550		Christmas Isn't Christmas/(B-side unknown)	1976	—	2.50	5.00
VANDROSS, LUTHER						
45s						
Atlantic 89593		At Christmas Time/Santa's Rap	1984	—	2.00	4.00
— As "Luther"; B-side by the Treacherous Three						
Epic 78466		I Can Make It Better/A Kiss for Christmas	1996	—	—	3.00
— A-side is not a Christmas song						
VANE, SYBIL						
45s						
Island PR7 6902-7		White Christmas/Disgruntled Christmas	1994	2.00	4.00	8.00
— B-side by Local H; green vinyl						
VANELLI, JOHNNY						
45s						
Little Apples 2801		Phroomf/Santa's Ride	1965	3.00	6.00	12.00
VAUGHN, BILLY						
Albums						
Dot DLP 3148	M	Christmas Carols	1958	3.75	7.50	15.00
Dot DLP 25899		Have Yourself a Merry Merry Christmas	1968	3.00	6.00	12.00
On Various-Artists Collections						
White Christmas		12 Days of Christmas, The (Pickwick SPC-1021)				
VEE, BOBBY						
45s						
Liberty 55517		A Not-So-Merry Christmas/Christmas Vacation	1962	7.50	15.00	30.00
— This record's existence has been questioned						
Liberty 56149		Electric Trains and You/In and Out of Love	1969	—	3.00	6.00
Albums						
Liberty LRP-3267	M	Merry Christmas from Bobby Vee	1962	7.50	15.00	30.00
Liberty LST-7267	S	Merry Christmas from Bobby Vee	1962	10.00	20.00	40.00
Sunset SUM-1186	M	The Christmas Album	1967	3.00	6.00	12.00
— Reissue of Liberty album with two fewer tracks and shuffled order						
Sunset SUS-5186	S	The Christmas Album	1967	3.00	6.00	12.00
— Same as above, but in stereo						
VELOCITY GIRL						
45s						
Simple Machine 014		Merry Christmas, I Love You/Could Have Been Christmas	199?	—	3.00	6.00
— B-side by Tsunami						
Simple Machine 014	PS	Merry Christmas, I Love You/Could Have Been Christmas	199?	—	3.00	6.00
— B-side by Tsunami						
VELOURS, THE						
45s						
Clifton 1987		Old Fashion Christmas/I Wish You Love	19??	—	3.00	6.00
VELVET SOUNDS, THE						
45s						
Cosmopolitan 530/531		Hanging Up Christmas Stockings/Sing A Song Of Christmas Cheer	19??	—	3.00	6.00
VENTURES, THE						
45s						
Dolton 312		Sleigh Ride/Snow Flakes	1965	3.75	7.50	15.00
EMI S7-18212		Jingle Bell Rock/Jingle Bells	1994	—	2.50	5.00
— Red vinyl						
EMI SPRO 19949	DJ	Rudolf The Red-Nosed Reindeer/Depression	1994	—	2.50	5.00
— B-side by Johnny and the Dwellers						
EMI SPRO 19949	PS	Rudolf The Red-Nosed Reindeer/Depression	1994	—	2.50	5.00
Albums						
Dolton BLP-2038	M	The Ventures' Christmas Album	1965	7.50	15.00	30.00
Dolton BST-8038	S	The Ventures' Christmas Album	1965	5.00	10.00	20.00

Label, Number	Title (A Side/B Side)	Year	VG	VG+	NM

On Various-Artists Collections

Sleigh Ride	Jingle Bell Rock (Time-Life SRNR-XM)				

VERA, RICKY, AND STEVE ALLEN
45s

Coral 61098	How Can Santa Come to Puerto Rico/Can I Wait Up for Santa Claus	1953	7.50	15.00	30.00

VERNON, MARIE
45s

Allied 5012	I Want You For Christmas/Christmas Tree Waltz	195?	3.75	7.50	15.00

VIBRA CORPORATION
12-Inch Singles

Passport PSC-7910	Snow White Rock Christmas/I Wish It Could Be Christmas Everyday	1977	2.00	4.00	8.00

45s

Passport 7910	Snow White Rock Christmas/I Wish It Could Be Christmas Everyday	1977	—	2.50	5.00

VICKERS, VIC
45s

La Lousianne 8153	The Christmas Mouse/Christmas In Cajun Country	198?	—	2.50	5.00

VICTOR, RAY
45s

Accent 1235	Sleigh Ride/Noche De Invierno	196?	2.00	4.00	8.00

VIDEOCRAFT CHORUS
On Various-Artists Collections

Most Wonderful Day of the Year, The	Rudolph the Red-Nosed Reindeer (Decca DL 4815)
We Are Santa's Elves	Rudolph the Red-Nosed Reindeer (Decca DL 4815)

VIDEOCRAFT ORCHESTRA AND BURL IVES
On Various-Artists Collections

Overture and A Holly Jolly Christmas	Rudolph the Red-Nosed Reindeer (Decca DL 4815)

VIENNA BOYS CHOIR
On Various-Artists Collections

Still, Still	Spirit of Christmas, The (Capitol Creative Products SL-6516)
Stille Nacht, Heilige Nacht (Silent Night)	Spirit of Christmas, The (Capitol Creative Products SL-6516)

VIENNA CHOIR BOYS
Albums

RCA Red Seal ARL1-3437	Britten: A Ceremony of Carols/Seven English Christmas Carols	1979	2.50	5.00	10.00

On Various-Artists Collections

Ding Dong Merrily on High	Family Christmas Collection, The (Time-Life STL-131)
In Dulci Jubilo	Time-Life Treasury of Christmas, The, Volume Two (Time-Life STL-108)
Joy to the World	Family Christmas Collection, The (Time-Life STL-131)
Medley: Christmas Is Coming/Adeste Fideles/Angels We Have Heard on High	Firestone Presents Your Favorite Christmas Music, Volume 6 (Firestone MLP 7014)
Medley: Fum, Fum, Fum/O Come, Little Children/Deck the Hall	Firestone Presents Your Favorite Christmas Music, Volume 6 (Firestone MLP 7014)
Medley: Jingle Bells/Ding Dong! Merrily on High/The Bells of Christmas	Firestone Presents Your Christmas Favorites, Volume 7 (Firestone CSLP 7015)
Medley: Joy to the World/The First Noel/Hark! The Herald Angels Sing	Firestone Presents Your Christmas Favorites, Volume 7 (Firestone CSLP 7015)
O Tannenbaum	Firestone Presents Your Favorite Christmas Music, Volume 6 (Firestone MLP 7014)
Silent Night	Firestone Presents Your Favorite Christmas Music, Volume 6 (Firestone MLP 7014)
While Shepherds Watched Their Flocks	Firestone Presents Your Christmas Favorites, Volume 7 (Firestone CSLP 7015)

VINCENT & PESCI
45s

Mainstream 5531	Can You Fix The Way I Talk For Christmas?/Little People Blues	1972	2.50	5.00	10.00

VINCENT, JOANNE
45s

Gale 103	Santa And His Sleigh/Red, Red Rover	19??	2.00	4.00	8.00

Label, Number		Title (A Side/B Side)	Year	VG	VG+	NM

VINE, EMMA, AND THE EMOTIONALS
On Various-Artists Collections

Oh Santa		Stuff This in Your Stocking! Elves in Action (Veebltronics/Skyclad 68)				

VINTON, BOBBY
45s

Bobby Vinton 100		Santa Must Be Polish/Santa Claus Is Coming to Town	1987	—	—	3.00
Bobby Vinton 100	PS	Santa Must Be Polish/Santa Claus Is Coming to Town	1987	—	—	3.00
Epic 9741		The Bell That Couldn't Jingle/Dearest Santa	1964	2.50	5.00	10.00
Epic 10689		Christmas Eve in My Home Town/The Christmas Angel	1970	—	3.00	6.00
Epic 50169		Christmas Eve in My Home Town/The Christmas Angel	1975	—	2.50	5.00

7-Inch Extended Plays

Epic EG 7215		Silver Bells/White Christmas//O Holy Night/The Christmas Song	1963	2.50	5.00	10.00
Epic EG 7215	PS	Songs of Christmas	1963	2.50	5.00	10.00

Albums

Epic LN 24122	M	A Very Merry Christmas	1964	3.00	6.00	12.00
Epic BN 26122	S	A Very Merry Christmas	1964	3.75	7.50	15.00

On Various-Artists Collections

Christmas Chopsticks	Very Merry Christmas, A, Volume 3 (Columbia Special Products CSS 997)
Christmas Eve in My Home Town	Happy Holidays, Vol. 21 (RCA Special Products DPL1-0739)
	Merry Christmas (Columbia Musical Treasury 3P 6306)
Dearest Santa	Spirit of Christmas, The (Columbia Special Products CSP 249)
Do You Hear What I Hear	Gift of Christmas, The, Vol. 1 (Columbia Special Products CSS 706)
	Very Merry Christmas, A (Columbia Special Products CSS 563)
White Christmas	Wondrous Winter: Songs of Winter, Songs of Christmas
	(Columbia Special Products CSS 708/9)

VIOLINAIRES, THE
45s

Jewel 222		Little Jesus Boy/White Christmas	1973	5.00	10.00	20.00

VISE SQUAD, THE
45s

Vise Recording 02		Jada's Christmas Song/Open Up Your Heart	19??	2.50	5.00	10.00

VO-CALS, THE
45s

Silhouette 517		Santa Claus Serenade/Wild Honey	19??	2.00	4.00	8.00

VOICES OF CHRISTMAS
Albums

Crown CMX 900	M	The Little Drummer Boy	196?	3.00	6.00	12.00
Custom CS 9	S	The Little Drummer Boy	196?	3.00	6.00	12.00
— Same contents as Crown LP						
Yuletide Series YS-219	S	The Little Drummer Boy	197?	2.50	5.00	10.00
— Reissue of Custom LP						

On Various-Artists Collections

Caroling, Caroling	Christmas — The Season of Music (Capitol Creative Products SL-6679)
	Zenith Presents Christmas, A Gift of Music Vol. 3 (Capitol Creative Products SL-6659)
First Noel, The	Christmas Carousel (Capitol SQBE-94406)
	Christmas with Glen Campbell and the Hollywood Pops Orchestra
	(Capitol Creative Products SL-6699)
	Magic of Christmas, The (Capitol SWBB-93810)
Happy Holiday	Happy Holidays, Vol. 5 (Capitol Creative Products SL-6627)
Hark the Herald Angels Sing	20 Christmas Favorites (Yulesong SY-0220)
I Heard the Bells on Christmas Day	Christmas with Glen Campbell and the Hollywood Pops Orchestra
	(Capitol Creative Products SL-6699)
	Christmas, A Gift of Music (Capitol Special Markets SL-6687)
	Zenith Presents Christmas, A Gift of Music Vol. 4 (Capitol Creative Products SL-6687)
Little Drummer Boy	20 Christmas Favorites (Yulesong SY-0220)
Winter Wonderland	Joys of Christmas (Capitol Creative Products SL-6610)

VOICES OF MARYMAR
45s

Accent 1105		Silent Night/Joy To The World//	196?	2.50	5.00	10.00
		Hark The Herald Angels Sing/The First Noel				

VOICES OF THE LITTLE FLOWER, THE
45s

Decca 32059		Christmas All Year Round/The Little Pine Tree	1966	2.00	4.00	8.00

(Top left) They Might Be Giants, an idiosyncratic alternative duo, released a couple of spottily distributed singles on Elektra in 1993, including their take on this traditional holiday favorite. (Top right) Thanks to Sundazed Records, a reissue label that still believes in the 45, the Trashmen's very rare "Dancin' with Santa" picture sleeve re-emerged in 1996. (Bottom left) A cool song with a cool sleeve, this 1989 Norton Records 45 is sought-after by car-music collectors. (Bottom right) A perennial on country radio, this is the scarce original sleeve for Vince Vance and the Valiants' "All I Want for Christmas Is You," also from 1989.

Label, Number		Title (A Side/B Side)	Year	VG	VG+	NM

VOICES, THE
45s

Cash 1016		Santa Claus Baby/Santa Claus Boogie	1955	20.00	40.00	80.00
Cash 1016		Santa Claus Boogie/Santa Claus Baby	197?	—	2.50	5.00
— Reproduction						
Specialty 754		Santa Claus Boogie/Santa Claus Baby	197?	3.75	7.50	15.00
— Red vinyl						

VOLZ, GREG X.
45s

(no label) 20738	DJ	Hark The Herald Angels Sing/(B-side unknown)	1987	—	2.00	4.00

W

WACHTER, EMIL, WITH FRED AHRENS, ELMER DREHMAN AND GEORGE FRANGOULIS
On Various-Artists Collections

Scrooge from A Christmas Carol   Christmas in Saint Louis ((no label) TS77-558/9)

WADDELL, KAREEM
45s

Hitt 185		Oh, The Man In The Moon Is Santa Claus/Hap, Hap, Happy New Year	19??	2.50	5.00	10.00

WADDILL, HUGH
45s

Lin 5028		Keep the Christ in Christmas/Silver Bells	1962	3.00	6.00	12.00

WADE, MARION
45s

Servicemaster 14006		Christmas Message//Silent Night/Come All Ye Faithful	198?	—	2.00	4.00
— Green vinyl						

WAGNER, BOB
45s

Ace 669		Lonely Christmas Again/Blue Evening	1962	3.00	6.00	12.00

WAGNER, LARRY, AND HIS ORCHESTRA
45s

Pinky 801		It's Time To Sing/The Christmas Gift Of Love	19??	—	3.00	6.00

WAGNER, ROGER, CHORALE
On Various-Artists Collections

Adeste Fideles	Little Drummer Boy, The (Capitol/Pickwick SPC-3462)
Carol of the Bells	Christmas Songs, The, Volume II (Capitol SL-57065)
Gesu Bambino	Spirit of Christmas, The (Capitol Creative Products SL-6516)
	Very Merry Christmas, A, Volume VIII (Capitol Special Markets SL-6954)
Good King Wenceslas	Christmas Carousel (Capitol SQBE-94406)
	Merry Christmas (Columbia Musical Treasury 3P 6306)
Hark! The Herald Angels Sing	Christmas to Remember, A, Vol. 3 (Capitol Creative Products SL-6681)
It Came Upon a Midnight Clear	Christmas Songs, The (Capitol SLB-57074)
Jingle Bells	Magic of Christmas, The (Capitol SWBB-93810)
Joy to the World	Christmas Day (Pickwick SPC 1010)
	Joys of Christmas (Capitol Creative Products SL-6610)
Joy to the World (Introducing: Sing We Now of Christmas/ O Tannenbaum/O Holy Night)	Zenith Presents Christmas, A Gift of Music (Capitol Creative Products SL-6544)
Little Drummer Boy	Christmas Stocking (Capitol NP 90494)
O Holy Night	Christmas to Remember, A (Capitol Creative Products SL-6573)
O Tannenbaum	Happy Holidays, Vol. 5 (Capitol Creative Products SL-6627)
We Three Kings	Christmas to Remember, A (Capitol Creative Products SL-6573)
What Child Is This	Christmas Songs, The (Capitol SLB-57074)
Yule Medley	Sound of Christmas, The, Vol. 3 (Capitol Creative Products SL-6680)

Label, Number		Title (A Side/B Side)	Year	VG	VG+	NM
WAIFS, THE						
45s						
Sycamore 100		A Letter To Santa Claus/Whiplash	19??	2.00	4.00	8.00
— B-side by Alabam						
WAILERS, THE						
45s						
Etiquette 22		Christmas Spirit/Don't Believe in Christmas	1965	7.50	15.00	30.00
— B-side by the Sonics						
WAITRESSES, THE						
45s						
Collectables 4949		Christmas Wrapping/I Know What Boys Like	1994	—	—	3.00
— First U.S. stock 45 release						
Polydor PRO ???	DJ	Christmas Wrapping (same on both sides)	1981	5.00	10.00	20.00
— Stock copy does not exist						
Ze WIP 6763		Christmas Wrapping/Christmas Fever	1981	5.00	10.00	20.00
— B-side by Charlelie Couture; U.K. import						
Ze WIP 6821		Christmas Wrapping/Hangover 1-1-83	1982	2.50	5.00	10.00
— U.K. pressing with punch-out center intact						
Ze WIP 6821	PS	Christmas Wrapping/Hangover 1-1-83	1982	2.50	5.00	10.00
Albums						
Polydor PX1-507	EP	I Could Rule the World If I Could Only Get the Parts	1982	2.50	5.00	10.00
— Contains one Christmas song: Christmas Wrapping						
On Various-Artists Collections						
Christmas Wrapping		Christmas Record, A (Ze/Passport PB 6020)				
		Christmas Rock Album, The (Priority SL 9465)				
WAKELY, JIMMY						
Also see MARGARET WHITING AND JIMMY WAKELY.						
45s						
Capitol F2644		It's Christmas/Thanks	1953	3.75	7.50	15.00
Capitol F90040		Christmas Polka/If Santa Claus Could Bring You Back To Me	1949	3.75	7.50	15.00
Shasta 106		That's Santa Claus/Lonely Is The Hunter	196?	2.50	5.00	10.00
Shasta 124		Swinging Jingle Bells/Silver Bells	196?	2.50	5.00	10.00
Albums						
Capitol H-9004	10	Christmas on the Range	1950	37.50	75.00	150.00
Dot DLP-25734	S	Christmas with Jimmy Wakely	1966	6.25	12.50	25.00
Dot DLP-3754	M	Christmas with Jimmy Wakely	1966	5.00	10.00	20.00
On Various-Artists Collections						
Winter Wonderland		12 Days of Christmas, The (Pickwick SPC-1021)				
WALCOTT, MIGUEL						
45s						
Kanika 8501		It's Nearly Christmas Day/Christmas In The Islands	1985	2.00	4.00	8.00
WALKER, ALBERTINA						
45s						
Gospel 1119		The Christmas Song/Silent Night	19??	2.00	4.00	8.00
WALKER, CLINT						
45s						
Warner Bros. 5133		Silver Bells/Love at Home	1959	3.00	6.00	12.00
On Various-Artists Collections						
Silver Bells		We Wish You a Merry Christmas (Warner Bros. W 1337)				
WALKER, GARY						
45s						
Jin 195		Santa's Got A Brand New Bag/Losing My Mind Over You	196?	2.50	5.00	10.00
WALLACE, CEDRIC, ORCHESTRA						
45s						
Derby 786		White Christmas/Lonely Christmas	1952	3.75	7.50	15.00

Label, Number	Title (A Side/B Side)	Year	VG	VG+	NM

WALLACE, DOC
45s

Ace 20618	Rockin Reindeer/The Ugliest Little Christmas Tree	19??	—	—	3.00
— B-side by Roger Kirby					

WALLACH, ELI
On Various-Artists Collections

Reminder Spot	For Christmas Seals...A Matter of Life and Breath (Decca Custom Style E)				

WALLER, FATS
On Various-Artists Collections

Swingin' Them Jingle Bells	Stash Christmas Album, The (Stash 125)				
Winter Weather	Remembering Christmas with the Big Bands (RCA Special Products DPM1-0506)				

WALLETS, THE
45s

Spiffola 334	'Twas The Night Before Christmas/ A Visit To The Temple Of A Slow Poke	198?	2.50	5.00	10.00

WALSH, BILLY J.
45s

Christmas Ranch 84101	My Gift Is For You/Heaven	1984	—	2.00	4.00

WALTERS, BARBARA
On Various-Artists Collections

Reminder Spot	For Christmas Seals...A Matter of Life and Breath (Decca Custom Style E)				

WALTONS, THE – See "VARIOUS ARTISTS COMPILATIONS" ("WALTONS' CHRISTMAS ALBUM, THE")

WALUNAS, ART, AND HIS ORCHESTRA
45s

MSK 728	Christmas Tree Polka/Silver Bells	19??	—	2.00	4.00

WARD, BILLY, AND HIS DOMINOES
45s

King 1281	Christmas in Heaven/Ringing In a Brand New Year	1953	25.00	50.00	100.00
King 6016	O Holy Night/What Are You Doin' New Year's Eve	1965	5.00	10.00	20.00
King 6106	O Holy Night/What Are You Doin' New Year's Eve	1967	3.75	7.50	15.00

On Various-Artists Collections

Christmas in Heaven	Merry Christmas Baby (Gusto/Hollywood K-5018-X)				

WARD, BOB
45s

(no label) 13868	Merry Christmas At The Hammond Organ	19??	2.00	4.00	8.00

WARD, JOE
45s

Gusto 814	Nuttin' For Christmas/Christmas Time's A Coming	1979	—	2.00	4.00
— B-side by Mac Wiseman					
King 4854	Nuttin' for Xmas/Christmas Questions	1955	3.00	6.00	12.00

WARDETTES, THE
45s

Pongo-Britt 45	Santa Is A Dirty Old Man/Jangle Bells	198?	—	3.00	6.00
— B-side by the Fumblers					

WARE, OZIE, WITH DUKE ELLINGTON
On Various-Artists Collections

Santa Claus Bring My Man Back	Stash Christmas Album, The (Stash 125)				

WARFIELD, SANDRA, WITH JAMES McKRACKEN
On Various-Artists Collections

Little Drummer Boy	Joy to the World (30 Classic Christmas Melodies) (Columbia Special Products P3 14654)				

Label, Number		Title (A Side/B Side)	Year	VG	VG+	NM

WARINER, STEVE
On Various-Artists Collections

Noel, Noel		Country Christmas, A (RCA CPL1-4396)				
Tennessee Christmas		Tennessee Christmas (MCA 5620)				
		Tennessee Christmas (MCA S45-17046)				

WARING, FRED, AND THE PENNSYLVANIANS
45s

Capitol F3901		Christmas Was Meant for Children/	1958	3.00	6.00	12.00
		I Heard the Bells on Christmas Day				
Decca 23642		Twas the Night Before Christmas (Part 1)/	1950	3.00	6.00	12.00
		Twas the Night Before Christmas (Part 2)				

— *Sides 1 and 2 of "Album No. 9-67"*

| Decca 23643 | | Silent Night/Oh Gathering Clouds | 1950 | 3.00 | 6.00 | 12.00 |

— *Sides 3 and 4 of "Album No. 9-67"*

| Decca 23644 | | Adeste Fideles/Cantique De Noel | 1950 | 3.00 | 6.00 | 12.00 |

— *Sides 5 and 6 of "Album No. 9-67"*

| Decca 23645 | | The First Noel/O Little Town of Bethlehem// | 1950 | 3.00 | 6.00 | 12.00 |
| | | Carol of the Bells/Beautiful Saviour | | | | |

— *Sides 7 and 8 of "Album No. 9-67"*

| Decca 24500 | | White Christmas/Twelve Days Of Christmas | 195? | 3.00 | 6.00 | 12.00 |

— *78 originally released in 1948*

| Decca 24500 | | White Christmas/Twelve Days Of Christmas | 1960 | 2.00 | 4.00 | 8.00 |

— *Also known to exist on color bars label*

| Decca 27283 | | When Angels Sang Of Peace/ | 1950 | 3.00 | 6.00 | 12.00 |
| | | The Christmas Song (Merry Christmas To You) | | | | |

— *Sides 1 and 2 of "Album No. 9-97"*

| Decca 27284 | | A Musical Christmas Card/O Christmas Tree// | 1950 | 3.00 | 6.00 | 12.00 |
| | | Kentucky Wassailsong/Parade Of The Wooden Soldiers | | | | |

— *Sides 3 and 4 of "Album No. 9-97"*

| Decca 27285 | | Heigh Ho the Holly/See Amid the Winter's Snow// | 1950 | 3.00 | 6.00 | 12.00 |
| | | Behold That Star/Carol of the Bells | | | | |

— *Sides 5 and 6 of "Album No. 9-97"*

| Decca 27286 | | Jingle Bells (Part 1)/Jingle Bells (Part 2) | 1950 | 3.00 | 6.00 | 12.00 |

— *Sides 7 and 8 of "Album No. 9-97"*

Decca 27292		This Was A Real Nice Christmas/You'll Never Walk Alone	1950	3.00	6.00	12.00
Decca 28970		Winter Wonderland/Snow, Snow	1953	3.00	6.00	12.00
Decca 29351		Rudolph the Red-Nosed Reindeer/	1954	3.00	6.00	12.00
		Santa Claus Is Comin' to Town				
Decca 88023		A Visit From St. Nicholas Part 1/A Visit From St. Nicholas Part 2	195?	3.00	6.00	12.00
Decca 88023	PS	A Visit From St. Nicholas Part 1/A Visit From St. Nicholas Part 2	195?	5.00	10.00	20.00
Reprise 0315		It's Christmas Time Again/Christmas Candles	1964	3.00	6.00	12.00

— *With Bing Crosby*

| Reprise 0316 | | The 12 Days of Christmas/Do You Hear What I Hear | 1964 | 2.50 | 5.00 | 10.00 |

7-Inch Extended Plays

Capitol EAP 1-896		(contents unknown)	1957	3.00	6.00	12.00
Capitol EAP 1-896	PS	Now Is the Caroling Season (Part 1)	1957	3.00	6.00	12.00
Capitol EAP 2-896		O Christmas Tree/Silver Bells/Angels We Have Heard on High/	1957	3.00	6.00	12.00
		In Sweetest Jubilee/I Heard the Bells on Christmas Day/The Christmas Song				
Capitol EAP 2-896	PS	Now Is the Caroling Season (Part 2)	1957	3.00	6.00	12.00
Capitol EAP 3-896		(contents unknown)	1957	3.00	6.00	12.00
Capitol EAP 3-896	PS	Now Is the Caroling Season (Part 3)	1957	3.00	6.00	12.00
Decca 9-67	(4)	'Twas the Night Before Christmas	1950	12.50	25.00	50.00

— *Contains 4 records (23642, 23643, 23644, 23645) and box*

| Decca 9-74 | (3) | The Song of Christmas | 1950 | 10.00 | 20.00 | 40.00 |

— *Includes records and box*

| Decca 9-97 | (4) | (title unknown) | 195? | 12.50 | 25.00 | 50.00 |

— *Contains 4 records (27283, 27284, 27285, 27286) and box*

Decca ED 678 (91329)		When Angels Sang Of Peace/The Christmas Song//	195?	2.50	5.00	10.00
		Medley: A Musical Christmas Card-O Christmas Tree-The Sleigh/				
		Medley: Kentucky Wassail Song-Parade of the Wooden Soldiers				
Decca ED 678 (91330)		Medley: Heigh Ho The Holly-See Amid The Winter's	195?	2.50	5.00	10.00
		Snow/Medley: Behold That Star-Carol Of The Bells//Jingle Bells				
Decca ED 678	PS	Christmas Time	195?	2.50	5.00	10.00

— *Cover for 2-EP set*

Decca ED 2546		(contents unknown)	195?	3.00	6.00	12.00
Decca ED 2546	PS	Christmas Time	195?	3.00	6.00	12.00
Decca ED 2656		(contents unknown)	195?	3.00	6.00	12.00
Decca ED 2656	PS	Christmas Songs	195?	3.00	6.00	12.00

Albums

| Capitol STBB-347 | (2) | Christmas Magic | 1970 | 3.75 | 7.50 | 15.00 |

— *Collects ST 1260 and ST 1610 in one package (abridged)*

Label, Number		Title (A Side/B Side)	Year	VG	VG+	NM
Capitol T 896	M	Now Is the Caroling Season	1957	5.00	10.00	20.00
— Originals have gray labels						
Capitol T 896	M	Now Is the Caroling Season	1959	3.75	7.50	15.00
— First reissue: Black label with colorband, "Capitol" logo at 9 o'clock						
Capitol T 896	M	Now Is the Caroling Season	1962	3.00	6.00	12.00
— Second reissue: Black label with colorband, "Capitol" logo at 12 o'clock						
Capitol ST 896	S	Now Is the Caroling Season	1959	3.75	7.50	15.00
— Black label with colorband, "Capitol" logo at 9 o'clock						
Capitol ST 896	S	Now Is the Caroling Season	1962	3.00	6.00	12.00
— Black label with colorband, "Capitol" logo at 12 o'clock						
Capitol T 1260	M	The Sounds of Christmas	1959	3.75	7.50	15.00
— Originals have black label with colorband and "Capitol" logo at 9 o'clock						
Capitol ST 1260	S	The Sounds of Christmas	1959	5.00	10.00	20.00
— Originals have black label with colorband and "Capitol" logo at 9 o'clock						
Capitol T 1610	M	The Meaning of Christmas	1961	3.75	7.50	15.00
Capitol ST 1610	S	The Meaning of Christmas	1961	5.00	10.00	20.00
Capitol SM-1610		The Meaning of Christmas	197?	2.00	4.00	8.00
— Reissue of ST 1610						
Decca DL 4809	M	A-Caroling We Go	1966	3.00	6.00	12.00
Decca DLP 5021	10	'Twas the Night Before Christmas	1949	12.50	25.00	50.00
Decca DL 8084	M	Song of Christmas	1954	6.25	12.50	25.00
Decca DL 8171	M	'Twas the Night Before Christmas	1955	5.00	10.00	20.00
Decca DL 8172	M	Christmas Time	1955	5.00	10.00	20.00
Decca DL 74809	S	A-Caroling We Go	1966	3.75	7.50	15.00
— Same as 4809, but in stereo						
Decca DL 78171	R	'Twas the Night Before Christmas	196?	3.00	6.00	12.00
Decca DL 78172		RChristmas Time	196?	3.00	6.00	12.00
MCA 15009		A-Caroling We Go	1973	2.50	5.00	10.00
— Reissue of DL 74809; black label with rainbow						
MCA 15009		A-Caroling We Go	1980	2.00	4.00	8.00
— Blue label with rainbow						
MCA 15011		Christmas Time	1973	2.50	5.00	10.00
— Reissue of DL 78172; black label with rainbow						
MCA 15011		Christmas Time	1980	2.00	4.00	8.00
— Blue label with rainbow						
MCA 15016		'Twas the Night Before Christmas	1973	2.50	5.00	10.00
— Reissue of DL 78171; black label with rainbow						
MCA 15016		'Twas the Night Before Christmas	1980	2.00	4.00	8.00
— Blue label with rainbow						

On Various-Artists Collections

Caroling, Caroling	Old-Fashioned Christmas, An (Longines Symphonette LS 214)
Do You Hear What I Hear	12 Songs of Christmas (Reprise F-2022)
Hanover Winter Song	Old Fashioned Christmas, An (Reader's Digest RDA 216-A)
O Come, O Come Emmanuel	Magic of Christmas, The (Columbia Musical Treasury P3S 5806)
Ring Those Christmas Bells	Happy Holidays, Album 6 (Capitol Creative Products SL-6669)
Rudolph the Red-Nosed Reindeer	Old Fashioned Christmas, An (Reader's Digest RDA 216-A)
Santa Claus Is Coming to Town	Old Fashioned Christmas, An (Reader's Digest RDA 216-A)
Silver Bells	Happy Holidays, Vol. 5 (Capitol Creative Products SL-6627)
	Magic of Christmas, The (Capitol SWBB-93810)
	Merry Christmas with Nat King Cole/Fred Waring and the Pennsylvanians (Capitol Special Markets SL-6883)
Sleigh Ride	All-Time Christmas Favorites (Capitol Special Markets SL-6931)
	Christmas to Remember, A (Capitol Creative Products SL-6573)
	Happy Holly Days (Capitol Creative Products SL-6761)
	Merry Christmas with Nat King Cole/Fred Waring and the Pennsylvanians (Capitol Special Markets SL-6883)
	Very Merry Christmas, A, Volume VIII (Capitol Special Markets SL-6954)
	Zenith Presents Christmas, A Gift of Music (Capitol Creative Products SL-6544)
Twelve Days of Christmas, The	12 Songs of Christmas (Reprise F-2022)
'Twas the Night Before Christmas	Christmas Through the Years (Reader's Digest RDA-143)
	Time-Life Treasury of Christmas, The (Time-Life STL-107)
When Angels Sang of Peace	12 Songs of Christmas (Reprise F-2022)
White Christmas	12 Songs of Christmas (Reprise F-2022)
	Christmas America (Capitol Special Markets SL-6884)
	Christmas Carousel (Capitol SQBE-94406)
	Happy Holidays, Vol. 5 (Capitol Creative Products SL-6627)
	Merry Christmas with Nat King Cole/Fred Waring and the Pennsylvanians (Capitol Special Markets SL-6883)
	Sound of Christmas, The (Capitol Creative Products SL-6515)
Winter Wonderland	Merry Christmas with Nat King Cole/Fred Waring and the Pennsylvanians (Capitol Special Markets SL-6883)

WARNER BROS. MALE CHORUS
On Various-Artists Collections

Star Carol, The	We Wish You a Merry Christmas (Warner Bros. W 1337)

Label, Number	Title (A Side/B Side)	Year	VG	VG+	NM

WARNER BROS. STARS
On Various-Artists Collections

Deck the Halls	We Wish You a Merry Christmas (Warner Bros. W 1337)				
We Wish You a Merry Christmas	We Wish You a Merry Christmas (Warner Bros. W 1337)				

WARNER, SANDY
45s

Signature 12018	All I Want For Christmas Is Your Love/ Girl With The Long Black Hair	1960	2.50	5.00	10.00

WARNKE, MIKE
On Various-Artists Collections

Christmas Song, A	On This Christmas Night (Songbird MCA-3184)				

WAS (NOT WAS)
On Various-Artists Collections

Christmas Time in the Motor City	Christmas Record, A (Ze/Passport PB 6020)				

WASHINGTON, BABY
45s

Liberty 1393	Silent Night/Merry Christmas Baby	1980	—	2.50	5.00
— B-side by Charles Brown					
Sue 149	Silent Night/White Christmas	1967	5.00	10.00	20.00
Veep 1274	Silent Night/White Christmas	1967	5.00	10.00	20.00

WASHINGTON, DINAH
45s

Mercury 70263	Silent Night/The Lord's Prayer	1953	4.00	8.00	16.00
Mercury 71557	Ol' Santa/The Light	1959	3.00	6.00	12.00

WASHINGTON, GROVER, JR.
On Various-Artists Collections

Blue Christmas	Jazzy Wonderland, A (Columbia 1P 8120)				

WATKINS, SAMMY, AND THE HI-TONES
45s

MorSam 28333	It's One Day Closer To Christmas/Somebody's Heart	19??	2.00	4.00	8.00

WATSON, BOBBY, AND HORIZON
On Various-Artists Collections

Vauncing Chimes	Yule Struttin' — A Blue Note Christmas (Blue Note 1P 8119)				

WATSON, DALE
45s

Penny Ellen 2001	What's A Christmas Without An Angel/ Christmas Just Ain't Christmas Without You	198?	—	—	3.00
— B-side by James Intveld; green vinyl					
Penny Ellen 2001 PS	What's A Christmas Without An Angel/ Christmas Just Ain't Christmas Without You	198?	—	—	3.00
— B-side by James Intveld					

WATSON, DOC
45s

Poppy XW370	New Born King/Peace in the Valley	1973	—	2.00	4.00

WATSON, LEO
45s

Coral 61738	Jingle Bells/Sonny Boy	1956	2.50	5.00	10.00

WATSON, PAT
45s

Spirit SP-1	It's Christmas Time/Oh What A Planet	1986	—	—	3.00
Spirit SP-1 PS	It's Christmas Time/Oh What A Planet	1986	—	—	3.00

WAVERLY CONSORT, THE
Albums

Columbia Masterworks M 34554	A Renaissance Christmas Celebration	1977	3.00	6.00	12.00

Label, Number		Title (A Side/B Side)	Year	VG	VG+	NM
WAYNE, BERNIE						
45s						
20th Century Fox 559		Christmas Is Over/Christmas Is Over	1964	2.00	4.00	8.00
— B-side by the Hushtones						
WAYNE, BOBBY						
45s						
Mercury 70268		Snow, Snow, Beautiful Snow/The Jones Boy	1953	3.75	7.50	15.00
WAYNE, BUDDY						
45s						
Gardena 132		Artificial Christmas/Heartbreak Ahead	1962	3.00	6.00	12.00
WAYNE, CHUCK						
45s						
Pumpkin 1001		A Christmas Gift/A Christmas Gift	1984	—	—	3.00
— B-side by Helen Merrill						
WAYNE, DICK, AND THE SATELLITES						
45s						
Hart-Van 16011	DJ	I Know There Is A Santa Claus/Tears Come Easy To My Eyes	198?	—	2.00	4.00
WAYNE, DOTTIE						
45s						
Vee Jay 482		Silent Night/Little Church Bell	1962	3.75	7.50	15.00
WAYNE, JERRY						
45s						
Playtime 40101		Jingle Bells/Good King Wenceslas	195?	—	3.00	6.00
Playtime 40101	PS	Jingle Bells/Good King Wenceslas	195?	3.00	6.00	12.00
On Various-Artists Collections						
Good King Wenceslas		Child's Christmas, A (Harmony HS 14563)				
Jingle Bells		Child's Christmas, A (Harmony HS 14563)				
WE FIVE						
45s						
A&M XMAS 1	DJ	My Favorite Things/The 12 Days Of Christmas	1968	3.00	6.00	12.00
— B-side by the Baja Marimba Band						
A&M XMAS 1	PS	My Favorite Things/The 12 Days Of Christmas	1968	3.75	7.50	15.00
— B-side by the Baja Marimba Band						
On Various-Artists Collections						
My Favorite Things		Something Festive! (A&M SP-19003)				
WEATHER GIRLS, THE						
45s						
ARC 04299		Dear Santa (Bring Me a Man This Christmas) (Part 1 & 2)	1983	—	2.50	5.00
WEAVER, CHARLEY						
45s						
Columbia 41504		Xmas in Mt. Idy/ Happy New Year, Happy New Year (Come to the Party, Do)	1959	3.75	7.50	15.00
WEAVER, J. C.						
45s						
Wild Turkey 7721		I Hope You Have A Merry Christmas/Christmas Time	19??	—	2.00	4.00
WEAVER, PATTY						
45s						
Re Se 101		Christmas Is .../You're All I Want For Christmas	1976	—	2.50	5.00
WEAVERS, THE						
45s						
Decca 27783		We Wish You a Merry Christmas/One for the Little Bitty Baby	1951	3.75	7.50	15.00
— Sides 1 and 2 of "Album No. 9-284"						
Decca 27817		The Seven Blessings of Mary/The Twelve Days of Christmas	1951	3.75	7.50	15.00
— Sides 3 and 4 of "Album No. 9-284"						

Label, Number		Title (A Side/B Side)	Year	VG	VG+	NM
Decca 27818		Go Tell It on the Mountain/Poor Little Jesus	1951	3.75	7.50	15.00
— Sides 5 and 6 of "Album No. 9-284"						
Decca 27819		Lulloo Lullay-It's Almost Day/	1951	3.75	7.50	15.00
		Burgundian Carol-God Rest Ye Merry Gentlemen				
— Sides 7 and 8 of "Album No. 9-284"						
7-Inch Extended Plays						
Decca 9-284	(4)	We Wish You a Merry Christmas	1951	18.75	37.50	75.00
— Four records (27783, 27817, 27818, 27819) plus box						
Albums						
Decca DL-5373	10	We Wish You a Merry Christmas	1952	25.00	50.00	100.00
Vanguard VRS 9010	M	The Weavers at Carnegie Hall	1957	10.00	20.00	40.00
— Contains one Christmas song: Go Where I Send Thee						

WEBB, JACK

7-Inch Extended Plays						
RCA Victor 547-0342		The Christmas Story (Part 1)/The Christmas Story (Part 4)	1953	3.00	6.00	12.00
RCA Victor 547-0343		The Christmas Story (Part 2)/The Christmas Story (Part 3)	1953	3.00	6.00	12.00
RCA Victor EPB 3199	PS	The Christmas Story	1953	3.75	7.50	15.00
— Cover for 2-EP set						
Albums						
RCA Victor LPM-3199	10	Dragnet — The Christmas Story	1954	37.50	75.00	150.00

WEBB, JOYCE

45s						
International 556		Santa Claus, You're Really Doin' Fine/	196?	3.00	6.00	12.00
		Christmas Ain't No Time To Be Alone				

WEBBER SISTERS, THE

12-Inch Singles						
Black Eagle CW-17		Jolly Christmas/Christmas Message	198?	—	3.00	6.00

WEBER, HENRY

45s						
Mercury 5514		Christmas Carols (Part 1)/Christmas Carols (Part 2)	1950	3.75	7.50	15.00

WECHTER, JULIUS, AND THE BAJA MARIMBA BAND
Also see BAJA MARIMBA BAND.

On Various-Artists Collections

God Rest Ye Merry, Gentlemen	Magic of Christmas, The (Columbia Musical Treasury P3S 5806)
	Something Festive! (A&M SP-19003)
Twelve Days of Christmas	Something Festive! (A&M SP-19003)

WEEDE, ROBERT; BASIL RATHBONE
On Various-Artists Collections

I Wear a Chain	Stingiest Man in Town, The (Columbia CL 950)

WEINER SANGERKNABEN

Albums						
Capitol T 10164	M	Christmas in Austria	196?	3.75	7.50	15.00

WELCH CHORALE, THE

Albums						
Vanguard VRS 428	M	A Music Box of Christmas Carols	1954	5.00	10.00	20.00
— With Music Boxes from the Bornand Collection...also see "Carolers, The"						

WELK, LAWRENCE

45s						
(no label) (no #)		Season's Greetings From Your Dodge Dealer	196?	2.00	4.00	8.00
— Cardboard record						
Coral 61081		Angel on the Christmas Tree/Are My Ears On Straight	1953	3.75	7.50	15.00
— With Sara Berner						
Coral 61095		Christmas Carols (Part 1)/Christmas Carols (Part 2)	1953	3.00	6.00	12.00
Coral 61745		Ring Those Christmas Bells/Let's Have an Old-Fashioned Christmas	1956	2.50	5.00	10.00
Coral 61746		Christmas Waltz/Santa from Santa Fe	1956	3.00	6.00	12.00
— With the Lennon Sisters						
Coral 61914		Merry Christmas from Our House to Your House/	1957	3.00	6.00	12.00
		Santa Claus Is Here Again				
— With the Lennon Sisters						

Label, Number		Title (A Side/B Side)	Year	VG	VG+	NM
Coral 62053		Outer Space Santa/ All Around The Merry Christmas Tree	1958	3.00	6.00	12.00
— As "Lawrence Welk's Little Band"						
Coral 98054	DJ	Christmas Carols (Part 1)/Christmas Carols (Part 2)	19??	2.00	4.00	8.00
— "Merry Christmas from Lawrence Welk" custom label						
Dot 16017		Christmas Moon/Peppy the Peppermint Bear	1959	3.00	6.00	12.00
— With the Lennon Sisters						
Mercury 5735		Merry Christmas Polka/Julida Polka	1951	3.75	7.50	15.00
Mercury 70738		Merry Christmas Polka/Laughing Polka	1955	3.00	6.00	12.00
Ranwood 1091		Christmas In Los Angeles/Carol Of The Bells	1980	—	2.00	4.00
— By "The Lawrence Welk Christmas Chorale"						
7-Inch Extended Plays						
Coral EC 82032 (83068)		(contents unknown)	1956	2.50	5.00	10.00
Coral EC 82032 (83069)		Santa Claus Is Comin' To Town/Winter Wonderland// Christmas Dreaming (A Little Early This Year)/ The Twelve Gifts Of Christmas	1956	2.50	5.00	10.00
Coral EC 82032	PS	Jingle Bells	1956	3.00	6.00	12.00
— Cover for 2-EP set						
Albums						
Coral CRL 57093	M	Merry Christmas from Lawrence Welk	1956	5.00	10.00	20.00
Coral CRL 57186	M	Jingle Bells	1957	5.00	10.00	20.00
Coral CRL 757093	R	Merry Christmas from Lawrence Welk	196?	3.00	6.00	12.00
— Same as CRL 57093, but in rechanneled stereo						
Coral CRL 757186	R	Jingle Bells	1957	3.00	6.00	12.00
Dot DLP 3397	M	Silent Night and 13 Other Best-Loved Christmas Songs	1961	3.00	6.00	12.00
Dot DLP 25397	S	Silent Night and 13 Other Best-Loved Christmas Songs	1961	3.75	7.50	15.00
Pickwick SPC-1019		The Christmas Song	197?	2.50	5.00	10.00
— Reissue of Coral LP "Jingle Bells" with shuffled running order						
Sunnyvale SVL-1015		Silent Night and 13 Other Best-Loved Christmas Songs	1978	2.00	4.00	8.00
— Same contents as Dot 25397						

On Various-Artists Collections

Blue Christmas	Blue Christmas (Welk Music Group WM-3002)
Christmas in Los Angeles	Blue Christmas (Welk Music Group WM-3002)
I'll Be Home for Christmas	12 Days of Christmas, The (Pickwick SPC-1021)

Medley: Hark! The Herald Angels
  Sing/Good King Wenceslas/It Came
  Upon a Midnight Clear
	Great Songs of Christmas, Album Nine (Columbia Special Products CSS 1033)

Rudolph, the Red-Nosed Reindeer	Magic of Christmas, The (Columbia Musical Treasury P3S 5806)
Santa Claus Is Comin' to Town	Christmas Through the Years (Reader's Digest RDA-143)
	Old-Fashioned Christmas, An (Longines Symphonette LS 214)
Silent Night	Thank You for Opening Your Christmas Club with Us (Decca 34211)
Silver Bells	Home for the Holidays (MCA MSM-35007)
Twelve Gifts of Christmas, The	Best of Christmas Vol. 2 (Mistletoe MLP-1221)
Winter Wonderland	Best of Christmas Vol. 2 (Mistletoe MLP-1221)
	WHIO Radio Christmas Feelings (Sound Approach/CSP P 16366)

WELKER, FRANK
45s

Label, Number		Title (A Side/B Side)	Year	VG	VG+	NM
Down The Hall 6757		A Totally Ridiculous 12 Days Of Christmas/ Ronald Reagan's Night Before Christmas	198?	—	3.00	6.00
Down The Hall 6757	PS	A Totally Ridiculous 12 Days Of Christmas/ Ronald Reagan's Night Before Christmas	198?	—	3.00	6.00

WELLS, ARLENE
45s

Label, Number		Title (A Side/B Side)	Year	VG	VG+	NM
(no label) 1000		Holly Jolly Christmas/Favorite Things	19??	—	2.00	4.00
— Plays at 33 1/3 rpm						

WELLS, KITTY
45s

Label, Number		Title (A Side/B Side)	Year	VG	VG+	NM
Decca 31441		Christmas Ain't Like Christmas Anymore/ Dancer (With the Light Up On His Tail)	1962	2.50	5.00	10.00
Albums						
Decca DL 4349	M	Christmas Day with Kitty Wells	1962	3.00	6.00	12.00
Decca DL 74349	S	Christmas Day with Kitty Wells	1962	3.75	7.50	15.00

WELLS, KITTY, AND JOHNNY WRIGHT
45s

Label, Number		Title (A Side/B Side)	Year	VG	VG+	NM
Decca 32604		There Won't Be Any Tree This Christmas/White Christmas	1969	—	2.50	5.00

Label, Number	Title (A Side/B Side)	Year	VG	VG+	NM
WELLS, LORRAINE					
45s					
Mar-Vel 105	Santa Claus Has Moved To Indiana/ I Found Romance When I Danced With You	19??	2.50	5.00	10.00
— B-side by George Sabo					
WENTZ, BILL					
45s					
Lamon 10129	Christmas In Dixie/(B-side unknown)	198?	—	2.50	5.00
WERNER, OLAV					
On Various-Artists Collections					
Det Kimer Nu Til Julefest	Christmas in Norway (Capitol T 10377)				
Et Barn Er Fodt I Bethlehem	Christmas in Norway (Capitol T 10377)				
Glade Jul	Christmas in Norway (Capitol T 10377)				
Her Kommer Dine Arme Sma	Christmas in Norway (Capitol T 10377)				
Jeg Er Sa Glad Hver Julekveld	Christmas in Norway (Capitol T 10377)				
O Jul Med Din Glede	Christmas in Norway (Capitol T 10377)				
WESS, FRANK					
On Various-Artists Collections					
Merry Christmas	Merry Christmas from David Frost and Billy Taylor (Bell 6053)				
WESSON, JIM					
On Various-Artists Collections					
Medley: Jingle Bells/We Wish You a Merry Christmas	Merry Christmas (Rainbow Sound R-5032-LPS)				
WEST COAST, THE					
45s					
Dee Jay 201	Christmas Time/(What Are You Doing) New Year's Eve	198?	—	2.50	5.00
WEST, CHRISTOPHER, MEDALLION ORCHESTRA					
45s					
Kapp 963	Some Other Tree/Adeste Fideles	1968	2.00	4.00	8.00
WEST, DOTTIE					
45s					
RCA Victor 48-1012	Six Weeks Every Summer (Christmas Every Day)/ Wish I Didn't Love You Anymore	1971	—	2.50	5.00
On Various-Artists Collections					
You Are My Christmas Carol	Happy Holidays, Volume 16 (RCA Special Products DPL1-0501)				
WESTERN WIND, THE					
Albums					
Musical Heritage Society MHS 4077	Christmas in the New World	1979	3.00	6.00	12.00
Nonesuch 79053	An Old-Fashioned Christmas: Caroling with the Western Wind	1983	2.50	5.00	10.00
WESTMINSTER BRASS ENSEMBLE					
On Various-Artists Collections					
O Beauteous Heavenly Light	Old Fashioned Christmas, An (Reader's Digest RDA 216-A)				
WESTPHALIAN CHORUS ENSEMBLE					
Albums					
Nonesuch H-71242	Michael Praetorius: Polytonal Christmas Music	197?	3.00	6.00	12.00
WHALUM, KIRK					
On Various-Artists Collections					
Go Tell It on the Mountain	Jazzy Wonderland, A (Columbia 1P 8120)				
WHAM!					
12-Inch Singles					
Epic TA 4949	Last Christmas (Pudding Mix)/Everything She Wants	1984	5.00	10.00	20.00
— U.K. import					
45s					
Columbia CS7 2591 DJ	Last Christmas (6:43)/Last Christmas (4:24)	1986	2.50	5.00	10.00

Label, Number		Title (A Side/B Side)	Year	VG	VG+	NM
Epic (no #)		Merry Xmas from Wham!	1984	5.00	10.00	20.00
— Fan club single, no sleeve; U.K. import						
Epic GA 4949		Last Christmas/Everything She Wants	1984	—	2.50	5.00
Epic GA 4949	PS	Last Christmas/Everything She Wants	1984	2.00	4.00	8.00
— Gatefold sleeve; sleeve and record are U.K. imports						

Albums

Label, Number		Title (A Side/B Side)	Year	VG	VG+	NM
Columbia OC 40285		Music from the Edge of Heaven	1986	2.50	5.00	10.00
— With "removable sticker" list of song titles still on front cover. Contains one Christmas song: Last Christmas (long version)						

WHIPPLE, REX
45s

Label, Number	Title (A Side/B Side)	Year	VG	VG+	NM
Romax 100	Night That Santa Cried/Little Orphan Boy	19??	2.00	4.00	8.00

WHISPERS, THE
45s

Label, Number	Title (A Side/B Side)	Year	VG	VG+	NM
Solar YB-11449	Happy Holidays to You/Try and Make It Better	1978	—	3.00	6.00

Albums

Label, Number	Title (A Side/B Side)	Year	VG	VG+	NM
Solar 60451	Happy Holidays to You	1985	3.00	6.00	12.00

WHISTLE
12-Inch Singles

Label, Number	Title (A Side/B Side)	Year	VG	VG+	NM
Select 62279	Santa Is A B-Boy//Santa Is A B-Boy(Instrumental)/ Santa Is A B-Boy (A Cappella)	1986	2.00	4.00	8.00

WHITE LIGHTNIN'
45s

Label, Number		Title (A Side/B Side)	Year	VG	VG+	NM
PUN 34647		(Every Day's) Christmas In Vegas/Call Me Nick	19??	—	3.00	6.00
PUN 34647	PS	(Every Day's) Christmas In Vegas/Call Me Nick	19??	—	3.00	6.00

WHITE NIGHTS, THE
45s

Label, Number		Title (A Side/B Side)	Year	VG	VG+	NM
White Night 16308		Santa Claus Loves To Rock-N-Roll (same on both sides)	1985	—	2.00	4.00
White Night 16308	PS	Santa Claus Loves To Rock-N-Roll (same on both sides)	1985	—	2.00	4.00

WHITE, JAMES
On Various-Artists Collections

Label, Number	Title (A Side/B Side)	Year	VG	VG+	NM
Christmas with Satan	Christmas Record, A (Ze/Passport PB 6020)				

WHITE, JOHNNY
45s

Label, Number	Title (A Side/B Side)	Year	VG	VG+	NM
Verve 10187	The Christmas Seal Song/Seal Boogie	1959	3.75	7.50	15.00

WHITE, PAUL
45s

Label, Number	Title (A Side/B Side)	Year	VG	VG+	NM
Country Jubilee 0101	Elvis, Christmas Won't Be Christmas Without You/(B-side unknown)	1977	3.00	6.00	12.00
Spin Check (no #)	Merry Christmas Elvis/I'm So Lonesome I Could Cry	1978	3.00	6.00	12.00

WHITE, ROBERT, AND THE CANDY MOUNTAIN BOYS
45s

Label, Number	Title (A Side/B Side)	Year	VG	VG+	NM
Nashville 5151	It's Hillbilly Christmas (Every Saturday)/Picture In The Wallet	196?	2.00	4.00	8.00

WHITE, YOLANDA
45s

Label, Number	Title (A Side/B Side)	Year	VG	VG+	NM
Decca 31340	My Brother Wants a Doll for Christmas/ What I Want for Christmas (Is Six More Years)	1961	5.00	10.00	20.00

WHITE. L.E., AND LOLA JEAN DILLON
45s

Label, Number	Title (A Side/B Side)	Year	VG	VG+	NM
Ho-Ho 20445	The Big One/What A Day I've Had	19??	—	2.00	4.00

WHITEHOUSE, BILL (RUFUS)
45s

Label, Number	Title (A Side/B Side)	Year	VG	VG+	NM
Independent Sound 101	Two More Days 'Till Christmas/Elvis, From Us To You	1978	—	3.00	6.00

WHITFIELD, DAVID
45s

Label, Number	Title (A Side/B Side)	Year	VG	VG+	NM
London 1508	Santo Natale/Adeste Fideles	1954	3.75	7.50	15.00

Label, Number	Title (A Side/B Side)	Year	VG	VG+	NM

WHITING, MARGARET, AND JIMMY WAKELY
Also see JIMMY WAKELY.
45s

Capitol F1255	Silver Bells/Christmas Candy	1950	5.00	10.00	20.00
Capitol F3905	Silver Bells/Christmas Candy	1958	3.00	6.00	12.00

On Various-Artists Collections

Silver Bells	Best of Christmas, The, Vol. II (Capitol SM-11834)				
	Popular Christmas Classics (Capitol Special Markets SL-8100)				

WHITLEY, KEITH
45s

RCA 3711-7-R	There's a New Kid in Town/A Christmas Letter	1990	—	2.00	4.00
RCA 5050-7-R	A Christmas Letter/Santa Are You Coming to Atlanta	1986	—	—	3.00
— B-side by Pake McEntire					
RCA PB-14238	A Christmas Letter/If You Think I'm Crazy Now	1985	—	2.00	4.00

On Various-Artists Collections

Christmas Letter, A	Country Christmas, A, Volume 4 (RCA CPL1-7012)				

WHITMAN, SLIM
45s

Cleveland Int'l. 03370	Where Is the Christ in Christmas/Sleep My Child	1982	—	2.00	4.00
Epic 50957	Where Is the Christ in Christmas/	1980	—	2.00	4.00
	Sleep My Child (All Through the Night)				

Albums

Cleveland Int'l. JE 36847	Christmas with Slim Whitman	1980	3.00	6.00	12.00
Columbia Special Products P 16323	Christmas with Slim Whitman	198?	2.50	5.00	10.00
Epic PE 36847	Christmas with Slim Whitman	1981	2.00	4.00	8.00
— Reissue of Cleveland Int'l. JE 36847					

On Various-Artists Collections

Winter Wonderland	Nashville's Greatest Christmas Hits, Volume II (Columbia PC 44413)				

WHITNEY, JILL
45s

Coral 61082	Little Johnny Jingle Bells/Ragamuffin Doll	1953	3.75	7.50	15.00

WHITNEY, TY
45s

20th Fox 448	Surfin' Santa Claus/Winner's Wonderland	1963	7.50	15.00	30.00

WHITTAKER, ROGER
Albums

Capitol Nashville C1 594058	World's Most Beautiful Christmas Songs	1990	3.75	7.50	15.00
— Available on vinyl through Columbia House only					
RCA Victor ANL1-2933	The Roger Whittaker Christmas Album	1978	3.00	6.00	12.00

On Various-Artists Collections

Christmas Is Here Again	Happy Holidays, Volume 16 (RCA Special Products DPL1-0501)				
	Happy Holidays, Volume 18 (RCA Special Products DPL1-0608)				
Ding Dong Merrily on High	Time-Life Treasury of Christmas, The (Time-Life STL-107)				
God Rest Ye Merry, Gentlemen	Time-Life Treasury of Christmas, The, Volume Two (Time-Life STL-108)				
Hallelujah It's Christmas	Happy Holidays, Volume 17 (RCA Special Products DPL1-0555)				
Holly and the Ivy, The	Time-Life Treasury of Christmas, The, Volume Two (Time-Life STL-108)				
Home for Christmas	Happy Holidays, Volume 19 (RCA Special Products DPL1-0689)				
Little Drummer Boy, The	Time-Life Treasury of Christmas, The, Volume Two (Time-Life STL-108)				
O Tannenbaum	Family Christmas Collection, The (Time-Life STL-131)				
Rocking	Time-Life Treasury of Christmas, The (Time-Life STL-107)				
Silent Night	Happy Holidays, Vol. 20 (RCA Special Products DPL1-0713)				
Tiny Angels	Happy Holidays, Volume 17 (RCA Special Products DPL1-0555)				
Twelve Days of Christmas, The	Stars of Christmas, The (RCA Special Products DPL1-0842)				
	Time-Life Treasury of Christmas, The (Time-Life STL-107)				
We Wish You a Merry Christmas	Family Christmas Collection, The (Time-Life STL-131)				

WHO, THE
Albums

Decca DXSW 7205	(2)	Tommy		1969	10.00	20.00	40.00
— With booklet. Contains one Christmas song: Christmas							
Decca DXSW 7205	(2) DJ	Tommy		1969	50.00	100.00	200.00
— White label promo							
MCA 10005	(2)	Tommy		1973	3.75	7.50	15.00
— Same contents as Decca release; black labels with rainbow							

Label, Number		Title (A Side/B Side)	Year	VG	VG+	NM
MCA 10005	(2)	Tommy	1978	3.00	6.00	12.00
— Tan labels						
MCA 10005	(2)	Tommy	1980	2.50	5.00	10.00
— Blue labels with rainbow						

WHORF, MIKE
45s

Omnisound 1025		The Man With A Hundred Names/Christmas In A Small Town	198?	—	2.50	5.00
— B-side by Rick Peoples						

WICKER, GINNY
45s

Sky Bow 3088		Christmas In Heaven/(B-side unknown)	19??	—	2.00	4.00

WICKES, MARY
On Various-Artists Collections

Christmas Memory, A	Christmas in Saint Louis ([no label] TS77-558/9)

WIGGINS, ROY
45s

Gusto 123		Blue Christmas/Little Drummer Boy	197?	—	2.50	5.00
— B-side by Vic Jordan						

WIGHT, ART
45s

REV 200-69	Pickin' Fights For Christmas/Three Cigarettes	19??	2.00	4.00	8.00

WIGHT, BLAIS, AND CAROLYN WARD
45s

Sandy Cedarbark Music	Lilacs in November/Don't Wait to Give Your Love to Me at Christmas	19??	—	2.50	5.00

WILD ROSE
On Various-Artists Collections

Jingle Bell Rock	Christmas for the 90's, Volume 1 (Capitol Nashville 1P 8117)
Star of Bethlehem	Christmas for the 90's, Volume 2 (Capitol Nashville 1P 8118)

WILDER BROTHERS, THE
45s

Wing 90039	I Want a Goat for Christmas/That Old Chimney	1955	3.75	7.50	15.00

WILDER, JO; GINO CONFORTI; JOE ROSS
On Various-Artists Collections

Twelve Days to Christmas	She Loves Me (MGM E 4118OC-2)

WILLIAMS BROTHERS, THE
On Various-Artists Collections

Holiday Season, The	Christmas with Andy Williams and the Williams Brothers (Columbia Special Products C 10105)
Kay Thompson's Jingle Bells	Christmas with Andy Williams and the Williams Brothers (Columbia Special Products C 10105)
Medley: Deck the Halls/To Santa Claus' House We Go/God Rest Ye Merry Gentlemen/Good King Wenceslas/ Hark the Herald Angels Sing/ O Come All Ye Faithful	Christmas with Andy Williams and the Williams Brothers (Columbia Special Products C 10105)
Medley: O Little Town of Bethlehem/ Joy to the World	Christmas with Andy Williams and the Williams Brothers (Columbia Special Products C 10105)

WILLIAMS, ANDY
45s

Label, Number		Title (A Side/B Side)	Year	VG	VG+	NM
Cadence 1282		Christmas Is a Feeling in Your Heart/ The Wind, The Sand and The Stars	1955	3.75	7.50	15.00
Columbia AE7 1108	DJ	It's the Most Wonderful Time of the Year/ Kay Thompson's Jingle Bells	1976	2.50	5.00	10.00
— Special radio promo for Christmas Seals. Also contains public service announcements for Christmas Seals by Williams on each side.						
Columbia AE7 1108	PS	It's the Most Wonderful Time of the Year/ Kay Thompson's Jingle Bells	1976	2.50	5.00	10.00
Columbia 10054	PS	Christmas Present/The Lord's Prayer	1974	—	2.50	5.00
Columbia 10054		Christmas Present/The Lord's Prayer	1974	—	2.00	4.00

Label, Number		Title (A Side/B Side)	Year	VG	VG+	NM
Columbia 42894		The Christmas Song (Chestnuts Roasting On An Open Fire)/ White Christmas	1963	2.00	4.00	8.00
— Stock copy or black vinyl promo						
Columbia 42894	DJ	The Christmas Song (Chestnuts Roasting On An Open Fire)/ White Christmas	1963	3.00	6.00	12.00
— Promo only on green vinyl						
Columbia 43458		Do You Hear What I Hear/Some Children See Him	1965	2.00	4.00	8.00
Columbia 44709		The Christmas Song (Chestnuts Roasting On An Open Fire)/ It's The Most Wonderful Time Of The Year	1968	—	3.00	6.00
Columbia JZSP 76322/3	DJ	Away In A Manger/O Holy Night	1963	2.50	5.00	10.00
Columbia JZSP 111911/2	DJ	Have Yourself A Merry Little Christmas/The Bells Of St. Mary's	1966	2.00	4.00	8.00
— Yellow label						
Columbia JZSP 111911/2	DJ	Have Yourself A Merry Little Christmas/The Bells Of St. Mary's	1966	2.00	4.00	8.00
— White label						

Albums

Label, Number		Title	Year	VG	VG+	NM
Columbia CL 2087	M	The Andy Williams Christmas Album	1963	3.00	6.00	12.00
Columbia CL 2420	M	Merry Christmas	1965	3.00	6.00	12.00
Columbia CS 8887	S	The Andy Williams Christmas Album	1963	3.00	6.00	12.00
— Same as 2087, but in stereo						
Columbia CS 9220	S	Merry Christmas	1965	3.00	6.00	12.00
— Same as 2420, but in stereo						
Columbia C 33191		Christmas Present	1974	2.50	5.00	10.00

On Various-Artists Collections

Away in a Manger	Christmas with Andy Williams and the Williams Brothers (Columbia Special Products C 10105)
Bells of St. Mary, The	60 Christmas Classics (Sessions DVL2-0723)
Carol of the Bells	Christmas Trimmings (Columbia Special Products P 12795)
	Ronco Presents A Christmas Gift (Columbia Special Products P 12430)
	WHIO Radio Christmas Feelings (Sound Approach/CSP P 16366)
Do You Hear What I Hear	Best of the Great Songs of Christmas (Album 10) (Columbia Special Products CSS 1478)
	Great Songs of Christmas, The, Album Six (Columbia Special Products CSM 388)
First Noel, The	Christmas with Andy Williams and the Williams Brothers (Columbia Special Products C 10105)
	It's Christmas Time! (Columbia Special Products P 14990)
Hark the Herald Angels Sing	Silent Night... (Columbia Special Products P 14989)
	60 Christmas Classics (Sessions DVL2-0723)
I Heard the Bells on Christmas Day	Christmas Song, The, And Other Favorites (Columbia Special Products P 12446)
It's the Most Wonderful Time of the Year	Christmas Album, A (Columbia PC 39466)
	Christmas with Andy Williams and the Williams Brothers (Columbia Special Products C 10105)
	Great Songs of Christmas, The, Album Eight (Columbia Special Products CSS 888)
	Stars of Christmas, The (RCA Special Products DPL1-0842)
	That Christmas Feeling (Columbia Special Products P 11853)
Let It Snow! Let It Snow! Let It Snow!	Many Moods of Christmas, The (Columbia Special Products P 12013)
Lord's Prayer, The	60 Christmas Classics (Sessions DVL2-0723)
Mary's Little Boy	60 Christmas Classics (Sessions DVL2-0723)
O Holy Night	Christmas Is... (Columbia Special Products P 11417)
	Christmas with Andy Williams and the Williams Brothers (Columbia Special Products C 10105)
	Great Songs of Christmas, The, Album Five (Columbia Special Products CSP 238M)
O Little Town of Bethlehem	Christmas Greetings, Vol. 4 (Columbia Special Products P 11987)
Silent Night, Holy Night	Christmas with Andy Williams and the Williams Brothers (Columbia Special Products C 10105)
Sleigh Ride	Joyous Songs of Christmas, The (Columbia Special Products C 10400)
Song for the Christmas Tree (The Twelve Days of Christmas)	Christmas with Andy Williams and the Williams Brothers (Columbia Special Products C 10105)
White Christmas	Carols and Candlelight (Columbia Special Products P 12525)

WILLIAMS, CLARENCE'S, BLUE FIVE
On Various-Artists Collections

Santa Claus Blues	Stash Christmas Album, The (Stash 125)

WILLIAMS, DAN
45s

Label, Number		Title	Year	VG	VG+	NM
Celestial 1011		Christmas Moon/Christmas Angel	196?	2.50	5.00	10.00
— B-side by Bettie Sites						

WILLIAMS, DENIECE
45s

Label, Number		Title	Year	VG	VG+	NM
Columbia AE7 1153	DJ	God Is Amazing/God Is Standing By	1977	2.00	4.00	8.00
— B-side by Johnnie Taylor; promo with "Suggested Christmas Programming" on label						
MCA 53707		Do You Hear What I Hear?/Every Moment	1989	—	—	3.00
Sparrow S7-18215		Do You Hear What I Hear/Silent Night	1994	—	2.50	5.00
— B-side by Bebe and Cece Winans; green vinyl						

WILLIAMS, DIANA
45s

Label, Number		Title	Year	VG	VG+	NM
Little Gem 1022		One More Christmas/Goodbye Bing, Elvis and Guy	1977	—	3.00	6.00

Label, Number		Title (A Side/B Side)	Year	VG	VG+	NM
WILLIAMS, DICKY						
45s						
Bad 1004		It's Christmas Again/I Truly Love You	198?	—	2.00	4.00
WILLIAMS, HANK, JR.						
45s						
Elektra 47231	DJ	Little Drummer Boy/The Christmas Song	1981	2.00	4.00	8.00
— B-side by Sonny Curtis						
WILLIAMS, HORACE, AND CHOKER CAMPBELL						
45s						
Magic City 002		Santa Goofed/I'm Going Christmas Shopping	196?	15.00	30.00	60.00
WILLIAMS, KENNY						
45s						
Ben Mor 1001		An Old Fashioned Christmas (Part 1)/ An Old Fashioned Christmas (Part 2)	19??	3.00	6.00	12.00
WILLIAMS, MAYNARD						
45s						
MCA 65032		Christmas Dream/Lonely Without You	1974	—	2.00	4.00
WILLIAMS, ROGER						
45s						
Kapp KJB-87		White Christmas/Winter Wonderland	196?	2.00	4.00	8.00
Kapp 299		Adeste Fideles/Hark the Herald Angels Sing	1959	2.50	5.00	10.00
Kapp 300		Mary's Little Boy Child/Winter Wonderland	1959	2.50	5.00	10.00
Kapp 440		Santa Claus, Santa Claus (We Love You)/Jingle Bells	1961	2.50	5.00	10.00
Albums						
Kapp KL 1164	M	Christmas Time	1959	3.00	6.00	12.00
On Various-Artists Collections						
Medley: O Holy Night/Joy to the World/ It Came Upon a Midnight Clear		Happy Holidays, Vol. 23 (MCA Special Products 15042)				
O Holy Night		Home for the Holidays (MCA MSM-35007)				
We Three Kings of Orient Are		Magic of Christmas, The (Columbia Musical Treasury P3S 5806)				
WILLIAMS, SMUGGY						
45s						
Soul Staff 106		Christmas 'Round The Corner/I Couldn't Sleep Last Night	19??	2.00	4.00	8.00
WILLIAMS, SUZY						
45s						
Promenade 1024		I Saw Mommy Kissing Santa Claus/White Christmas	198?	—	—	3.00
— B-side by the Promenaders						
WILLIAMS, VICTORIA						
45s						
Singles Only 459		What A Wonderful World/Have Yourself A Merry Little Christmas	199?	—	2.00	4.00
Singles Only 459	PS	What A Wonderful World/Have Yourself A Merry Little Christmas	199?	—	2.00	4.00
WILLIAMSON, BRUCE						
45s						
Lamon 10087		I Saw Mommy Kissing Santa Claus/(B-side unknown)	198?	—	2.00	4.00
WILLIAMSON, CHRIS						
45s						
Olivia 944		Hard Candy Christmas/The Christmas Song	198?	—	2.00	4.00
WILLIAMSON, SONNY BOY						
45s						
Trumpet 145		Sonny Boy's Christmas Blues/Pontiac Blues	195?	20.00	40.00	80.00
WILLIE B.						
45s						
La Lousianne 8062		Santa In Bayou Land/Put Christ Back Into Christmas	197?	—	2.50	5.00

Label, Number		Title (A Side/B Side)	Year	VG	VG+	NM
WILLIO AND PHILLIO						
45s						
Wizard 102		All Winter Long//Hail to Thee O Christmas Tree/	19??	—	2.50	5.00
		The Christmas Roundelay				
Wizard 102	PS	All Winter Long//Hail to Thee O Christmas Tree/	19??	—	2.50	5.00
		The Christmas Roundelay				
On Various-Artists Collections						
I Wish It Could Be Christmas		Disney's Christmas All-Time Favorites (Disneyland 1V 8150)				
All Year Long						
WILLIS "THE GUARD" & VIGORISH						
Later recorded as "Buckner and Garcia."						
45s						
Handshake 5308		Merry Christmas In The NFL/(Instrumental)	1980	2.00	4.00	8.00
WILLIS SISTERS, THE						
45s						
Renown 126		Doodley Duck/It's Christmas Again	1960	3.00	6.00	12.00
WILLIS, DONALD						
45s						
Sparkette 1001		Rock And Roll Christmas/The Guiding Light	1958	5.00	10.00	20.00
WILLS, BOB						
45s						
MGM 11082		Silver Bells/Last Goodbye	1951	5.00	10.00	20.00
WILLS, COKE, AND THE TEXANS						
45s						
ICA 104		Santa's Going Country/Christmas Eve On The Prairie	19??	2.00	4.00	8.00
WILLS, TOMMY						
45s						
Juke 2020		Blue Christmas/What Are You Doing New Year's Eve	19??	—	3.00	6.00
WILSON SISTERS, THE						
45s						
King 5724		Little Klinker/All I Want For Christmas Is My Two Front Teeth	1962	2.00	4.00	8.00
King 5724	PS	Little Klinker/All I Want For Christmas Is My Two Front Teeth	1962	5.00	10.00	20.00
WILSON, ANN AND NANCY						
45s						
Capitol 44488		Here Is Christmas	1989	—	—	—
— Stock copy on cassette only; may be on a promo 45 with a different number, but we haven't confirmed this.						
WILSON, CARNIE & WENDY						
45s						
SBK S7-17648		Hey Santa!/Have Yourself a Merry Little Christmas	1993	—	2.50	5.00
— Green vinyl						
WILSON, CHARLIE						
45s						
Total Experience 2435		The Christmas Song/Joy To The World	1985	—	2.00	4.00
— B-side by Oliver Scott						
WILSON, DICK						
45s						
Silver Leaf 101		Merry Christmas/I Miss All The Songs	19??	—	2.00	4.00
Silver Leaf 200		Merry Christmas To You Dear Holy-One/I Miss All The Songs	19??	—	2.00	4.00
WILSON, JACKIE						
45s						
Brunswick 55254		Silent Night/Oh Holy Night	1963	3.00	6.00	12.00
Albums						
Brunswick BL 54112	M	Merry Christmas from Jackie Wilson	1963	7.50	15.00	30.00
Brunswick BL 754112	S	Merry Christmas from Jackie Wilson	1963	10.00	20.00	40.00

Label, Number	Title (A Side/B Side)	Year	VG	VG+	NM

WILSON, JIM
45s

Mercury 70755	Round, Round the Christmas Tree/Daddy, Who Is Santa Claus	1955	3.00	6.00	12.00

WILSON, JOEMY
Albums

Dargason DM-105	Gifts II: Traditional Christmas Carols	1987	2.50	5.00	10.00

WILSON, JUSTIN
45s

Project 5001	Randolph The Rouge Nosed Reindeer/Santa	1966	3.75	7.50	15.00
Tower 299	Santa Claus Gonna Brought Himself to Town/	1966	3.00	6.00	12.00
	Randolph the Rouge-Nosed Reindeer				
Tower 380	Whitey, the Snow White Lamb/When Christmas Angels Sing	1967	2.50	5.00	10.00
— B-side by Whitney Snow					

WILSON, NANCY
45s

Capitol 5084	That's What I Want for Christmas/	1963	2.50	5.00	10.00
	What Are You Doing New Year's Eve				
Capitol 6275	That's What I Want For Christmas/	19??	—	2.50	5.00
	What Are You Doing New Year's Eve?				
— Starline reissue					

On Various-Artists Collections

Christmas Waltz, The	Best of Christmas, The, Vol. II (Capitol SM-11834)
	Christmas Songs, The, Volume II (Capitol SL-57065)
	Happy Holidays, Album 6 (Capitol Creative Products SL-6669)
	I'll Be Home for Christmas (Pickwick SPC-1009)
	Joys of Christmas (Capitol Creative Products SL-6610)
	Sound of Christmas, The, Vol. 2 (Capitol Creative Products SL-6534)
That's What I Want for Christmas	Holiday Magic (Capitol Creative Products SL-6728)
	Magic of Christmas, The (Capitol SWBB-93810)

WILSON, NANCY, AND KIMIKO ITOH
On Various-Artists Collections

Silent Night	Jazzy Wonderland, A (Columbia 1P 8120)

WILSON, STAN
45s

Cavalier 831	Greensleeves/The St. James Infirmary	19??	3.00	6.00	12.00

WINANS, BEBE AND CECE
45s

Capitol B-44261	Heaven/Silent Night, Holy Night	1988	—	—	3.00
Capitol B-44477	Mean Time/Silent Night, Holy Night	1989	—	—	3.00
Sparrow S7-18215	Silent Night/Do You Hear What I Hear	1994	—	2.50	5.00
— B-side by Deniece Williams; green vinyl					

WINANS, THE
45s

Qwest 28154	The Real Meaning of Christmas/How Can You Live Without Christ?	1987	—	2.00	4.00

WINE, TONI
45s

Colpix 715	My Boyfriend's Coming Home for Christmas/What a Pity	1963	3.75	7.50	15.00

WING AND A PRAYER FIFE AND DRUM CORPS
45s

Wing & A Prayer 76	A Holiday Gift/(B-side unknown)	1976	2.00	4.00	8.00

WINSBY, MILT
45s

Redic 2939	It's Christmas Time Again/(B-side unknown)	19??	2.50	5.00	10.00

WINSTON, GEORGE
45s

Windham Hill WS-0005		Variations on the Kanon by Johann Pachelbel/Carol of the Bells	1984	—	2.50	5.00
Windham Hill WS-0005	PS	Variations on the Kanon by Johann Pachelbel/Carol of the Bells	1984	—	2.50	5.00

Label, Number		Title (A Side/B Side)	Year	VG	VG+	NM
Albums						
Windham Hill WD 1025		December	1982	3.00	6.00	12.00

WINTER, PAUL
Albums

Living Music LM-12		Wintersong	1986	2.50	5.00	10.00

WINTERGARTEN, RICHARD
45s

Pulstrak 103		I Remember Christmas/I Remember Christmas (Instrumental)	1986	—	—	3.00
Pulstrak 103	PS	I Remember Christmas/I Remember Christmas (Instrumental)	1986	—	—	3.00
Sceneville 102		The Little Christmas Tree/I Remember Christmas (Instrumental)	1986	—	—	3.00
Sceneville 102	PS	The Little Christmas Tree/I Remember Christmas (Instrumental)	1986	—	—	3.00

WINTERHALTER, HUGO
45s

Columbia 1-401		Blue Christmas/You're All I Want For Christmas	1949	5.00	10.00	20.00
— Microgroove 33 1/3 rpm, 7-inch single (small hole)						
RCA Victor 447-0875		White Christmas/Blue Christmas	196?	2.00	4.00	8.00
— Reissue; black label, dog on top						
RCA Victor 47-3937		White Christmas/Blue Christmas	1950	3.75	7.50	15.00
RCA Victor 47-7397		Rudolph the Red-Nosed Reindeer Cha Cha/ The Christmas Song Cha Cha	1958	2.50	5.00	10.00
RCA Victor 47-7642		Rudolph the Red-Nosed Reindeer Cha Cha/Sleigh Ride	1959	2.50	5.00	10.00
Albums						
RCA Camden CAL-449	M	Christmas Magic	1958	3.75	7.50	15.00
On Various-Artists Collections						
Carol of the Bells		For a Musical Merry Christmas, Vol. Two (RCA Victor PRM 189) 60 Christmas Classics (Sessions DVL2-0723)				

WINTERS, JUNE
45s

Mercury 5502		Christmas in My Heart/Charms for Sale	1950	3.75	7.50	15.00

WISEMAN, MAC
45s

Gusto 814		Christmas Time's A Coming/Nuttin' For Christmas	1979	—	2.00	4.00
— B-side by Joe Ward						

WITHERS, BILL
45s

Sussex 247		Let Us Love/The Gift of Giving	1972	—	2.50	5.00
Sussex 247	PS	Let Us Love/The Gift of Giving	1972	2.00	4.00	8.00

WITHERSPOON, JIMMY
On Various-Artists Collections

Christmas Blues		Merry Christmas Baby (Christmas Music for Young Lovers) (Hollywood HLP 501) Merry Christmas Baby (Gusto/Hollywood K-5018-X)				

WIXELL, INGVAR
Albums

Capitol T 10485	M	Christmas Music of Sweden	1965	3.00	6.00	12.00
Capitol DT 10485	R	Christmas Music of Sweden	1965	3.00	6.00	12.00
Capitol SP-10485	R	Christmas Music of Sweden	1969	2.50	5.00	10.00
— Reissue with new prefix and label						
Capitol SM-10485	R	Christmas Music of Sweden	197?	2.00	4.00	8.00
— Reissue with new prefix and label						

WIZZARD
45s

Harvest 05517		I Wish It Could Be Christmas Everyday/Rob Roy's Nightmare	1973	3.00	6.00	12.00
Harvest 05517	PS	I Wish It Could Be Christmas Everyday/Rob Roy's Nightmare	1973	5.00	10.00	20.00
— European (non-U.K.) import						
Harvest 5079		I Wish It Could Be Christmas Everyday/Rob Roy's Nightmare	1973	3.00	6.00	12.00
Harvest 5079	PS	I Wish It Could Be Christmas Everyday/Rob Roy's Nightmare	1973	3.00	6.00	12.00
— Gatefold sleeve; Harvest logo stuck over Warner Bros. logo						
Warner Bros. K 16336		I Wish It Could Be Christmas Everyday/Rob Roy's Nightmare	1973	3.75	7.50	15.00
— Original U.K. pressing						

Label, Number		Title (A Side/B Side)	Year	VG	VG+	NM
Warner Bros. K 16336	PS	I Wish It Could Be Christmas Everyday/Rob Roy's Nightmare	1973	3.75	7.50	15.00

— Gatefold sleeve; both sleeve and record withdrawn and moved to Harvest

WOELLER, DAVID
45s

Playboy 50015		Hotel Christmas/(B-side unknown)	1972	—	3.00	6.00

WOLFE, RICHARD, CHILDREN'S CHORUS
45s

RCA Victor SPS-45-279	DJ	A Merry Christmas Wish/A Merry Christmas Song!	1970	—	3.00	6.00

— B-side by Living Strings and Living Voices

WONDER, STEVIE
45s

Tamla 54142		Some Day at Christmas/The Miracles of Christmas	1966	3.75	7.50	15.00
Tamla 54214		What Christmas Means to Me/Bedtime for Toys	1971	—	3.00	6.00

Albums

Tamla T-281	M	Someday at Christmas	1967	7.50	15.00	30.00
Tamla TS-281	S	Someday at Christmas	1967	10.00	20.00	40.00

On Various-Artists Collections

Ave Maria (Schubert)	Motown Christmas, A (Motown 795V2)
One Little Christmas Tree	Motown Christmas, A (Motown 795V2)
Someday at Christmas	Motown Christmas, A (Motown 795V2)
What Christmas Means to Me	Motown Christmas, A (Motown 795V2)

WOOD, GLORIA
45s

Greeting 2001		Christmas Ride/Christmas Angel	19??	2.50	5.00	10.00

— B-side by the Mellowmen

WOODDELL, WOODY, AND THE BAILEY SISTERS
45s

Dome 1055		Elfie The Elf/Christmas Isn't Christmas	19??	—	2.50	5.00

WOODYETTES, THE
45s

Decca 30482		Jimminy Christmas/The Woody Woodpecker Song	1957	3.75	7.50	15.00

WOOLEY, SHEB
45s

MGM 12733		Santa and the Purple People Eater/Star of Love	1958	5.00	10.00	20.00
MGM 12733	PS	Santa and the Purple People Eater/Star of Love	1958	10.00	20.00	40.00

WOOLPIT CAROLLERS
45s

Warner Bros K 16867		The Wind Is Blowing/Without Santa	1976	2.00	4.00	8.00

— B-side by John Halsey and Friend; U.K. import

WORKSHOP, THE
45s

Era 3191		Presidential Christmas Shopping/New Year's Happening	1967	2.00	4.00	8.00

WORLD'S GREATEST JAZZBAND, THE
45s

World Jazz WJSS3		Silent Night/Jingle Bells	1972	—	2.00	4.00
World Jazz WJSS3	PS	Silent Night/Jingle Bells	1972	—	2.00	4.00
World Jazz WJSS5		Joy To The World/Winter Wonderland	1972	—	2.00	4.00
World Jazz WJSS5	PS	Joy To The World/Winter Wonderland	1972	—	2.00	4.00

WRENCH, ALLEN, AND MATT NAKED
45s

Road Whore 14414		Allen Wrench Is Coming To Town/Punk Sex Bomb	198?	2.50	5.00	10.00

WRIGHT, BETTY, AND FAMILY
45s

Ms. B 4504		A Christmas To Remember/2nd Chapter Of The Book Of Matthew	1988	—	—	3.00

Label, Number		Title (A Side/B Side)	Year	VG	VG+	NM
WRIGHT, GEORGE						
Albums						
Dot DLP 3479	M	Christmas Time	1962	3.00	6.00	12.00
Dot DLP 25479	S	Christmas Time	1962	3.75	7.50	15.00
Hifi R705	M	Music for Christmas	195?	3.75	7.50	15.00
Hifi R706	M	Merry Christmas	195?	3.75	7.50	15.00
On Various-Artists Collections						
God Rest Ye Merry Gentlemen		12 Days of Christmas, The (Pickwick SPC-1021)				
WRIGHT, MARTHA						
On Various-Artists Collections						
Holly and the Ivy, The		Firestone Presents Your Christmas Favorites, Volume 3 (Firestone MLP 7008)				
Silver Bells		Firestone Presents Your Christmas Favorites, Volume 3 (Firestone MLP 7008)				
WRIGHT, RUBY						
45s						
Candee 502		This Is Christmas/(B-side unknown)	196?	5.00	10.00	20.00
Candee EP-50-50		Christmas Is A Birthday Time//Have A Merry Merry	196?	2.00	4.00	8.00
		Merry Merry Christmas/The Happy Time				
— B-side by Ruth Lyons						
Fraternity 787		Let's Light the Christmas Tree/Merry Merry Christmas	1957	3.75	7.50	15.00
King 1288		Santa's Little Sleigh Bells/Toodle Oo To You	1953	5.00	10.00	20.00
On Various-Artists Collections						
Christmas Is a Birthday Time		Ten Tunes of Christmas (Candee 50-50)				
Have a Merry Merry Merry Merry		Ten Tunes of Christmas (Candee 50-50)				
Christmas						
Let's Light the Christmas Tree		Ten Tunes of Christmas (Candee 50-50)				
WRIGHT, STEVE						
45s						
Lin 5024		Silver Bells/Keep The Christ In Christmas	1960	7.50	15.00	30.00
WRIGHTSON, EARL						
On Various-Artists Collections						
O Come All Ye Faithful		Great Songs of Christmas, The, Album Two (Columbia Special Products XTV 86100/1)				
O Holy Night		Great Songs of Christmas, The (Columbia Special Products XTV 69406/7)				
Silent Night		Great Songs of Christmas, The, Album Two (Columbia Special Products XTV 86100/1)				
WYATT, DANNY						
45s						
Ruby 270		Christmas In Kentucky/You Broke A Date, Vow And Heart	195?	3.75	7.50	15.00
WYATT, JOANNA						
45s						
Curb 03481		The Little Drummer Boy/Dancing in Rio	1982	—	2.00	4.00
WYCKOFF, GERRY						
45s						
Buffalo 45005		Christmas Day Was A Hundred Years Ago/	198?	—	2.00	4.00
		Christmas Day Was A Hundred Years Ago (Instrumental)				
WYCOFF, MICHAEL						
45s						
RCA PB-13366		The Christmas Song/Love Is So Easy	1982	—	2.00	4.00
RCA PB-13366	PS	The Christmas Song/Love Is So Easy	1982	—	2.00	4.00
RCA PB-13697		You Are Everything/The Christmas Song	1983	—	2.00	4.00
WYMAN, KAREN						
On Various-Artists Collections						
Have Yourself a Merry Little Christmas		Christmas in Saint Louis ((no label) TS77-558/9)				
WYNETTE, TAMMY						
45s						
Epic AS 60	DJ	White Christmas/One Happy Christmas	1973	2.00	4.00	8.00
— 1973 Christmas Seals promotional record						
Epic AS 60	PS	White Christmas/One Happy Christmas	1973	2.50	5.00	10.00
Epic 10690		One Happy Christmas/(Merry Christmas) We Must Be Having One	1970	2.00	4.00	8.00
Albums						
Epic E 30343		Christmas with Tammy	1970	3.75	7.50	15.00

Label, Number		Title (A Side/B Side)	Year	VG	VG+	NM

On Various-Artists Collections

(Merry Christmas) We Must Be Having One	Country Style Christmas, A (Columbia Musical Treasury 3P 6316)
Away in a Manger	Country Christmas Favorites (Columbia Special Products C 10876)
	Happy Holidays, Album Nine (Columbia Special Products P 11793)
	Nashville's Greatest Christmas Hits (Columbia PC 44412)
	We Wish You a Country Christmas (Columbia Special Products P 14991)
Blue Christmas	Blue Christmas (Welk Music Group WM-3002)
Count Your Blessings Instead of Sheep	Christmas Greetings (Columbia Special Products CSS 1499)
	Country Christmas (Columbia CS 9888)
	Home for Christmas (Columbia Musical Treasury P3S 5608)
	Home for Christmas (Realm 2V 8101)
It Came Upon a Midnight Clear	Magic of Christmas, The (Columbia Musical Treasury P3S 5806)
	Nashville's Greatest Christmas Hits, Volume II (Columbia PC 44413)
Joy to the World	Country Style Christmas, A (Columbia Musical Treasury 3P 6316)
	Joy of Christmas, The, Featuring Marty Robbins and His Friends
	(Columbia Special Products C 11087)
One Happy Christmas	Country Christmas (Time-Life STL-109)
Silent Night, Holy Night	Christmas Greetings from Nashville (Columbia PC 39467)
White Christmas	Country Christmas (Time-Life STL-109)
	Country Style Christmas, A (Columbia Musical Treasury 3P 6316)
	Merry Christmas (Columbia Musical Treasury 3P 6306)
	We Wish You a Country Christmas (Columbia Special Products P 14991)

WYNETTE, TAMMY, AND THE O'KANES
On Various-Artists Collections

Away in a Manger	Nashville Christmas Album, The (Epic PE 40418)

X

XTC – See THREE WISE MEN.

Y

YANKOVIC, "WEIRD AL"
45s

Rock N Roll 06588		Christmas At Ground Zero/One of Those Days	1986	—	2.50	5.00
Rock N Roll 06588	PS	Christmas At Ground Zero/One of Those Days	1986	—	2.50	5.00

YANKOVIC, FRANKIE
45s

Columbia 39594		Christmas Chopsticks/The Merry Christmas Polka	1951	3.00	6.00	12.00
Columbia 42010		Kringleville Polka/You And Me	1960	2.50	5.00	10.00
Columbia 43173		There'll Always Be a Santa Claus/	1964	2.00	4.00	8.00
		Jing-a-Ling (Christmas Time Is Here Again)				
Smash 888 196-7		Old Fashioned Christmas Polka/Christmas Chimes	1986	—	—	3.00

Albums

Columbia CL 2253	M	Christmas Party	1964	3.00	6.00	12.00
Columbia CS 9053	S	Christmas Party	1964	3.75	7.50	15.00
Smash 830 396-1		Christmas Memories	198?	2.50	5.00	10.00

YARBROUGH AND PEOPLES
On Various-Artists Collections

Christmas Dreams	Total Experience Christmas, A (Total Experience TEL8-5707)

YARBROUGH, GLENN
45s

Stanyan 34	Simple Christmas/A Hand To Hold At Christmas	1974	—	2.50	5.00
— B-side by Rod McKuen					

Label, Number		Title (A Side/B Side)	Year	VG	VG+	NM
YEARWOOD, TRISHA						
45s						
MCA 54940		It Wasn't His Child/Reindeer Boogie	1994	—	—	3.00
YEAWORTHS, THE						
45s						
RCA Victor 47-8480		The Ballad of the Christmas Donkey/Oky Doky Tokyo	1964	3.00	6.00	12.00
YELLO						
12-Inch Singles						
4th & B'Way 448 018-1	DJ	Jingle Bells (Single Version)/Jingle Bells (Movie Version)//Jingle Bells (Santa Club Mix)	1995	2.50	5.00	10.00
YIN AND YAN						
45s						
Gull 26		The 12 Days Of Christmas/Breakfast Conversations	1975	2.00	4.00	8.00
— U.K. import						
YOAKAM, DWIGHT						
45s						
Reprise 28156		Santa Claus Is Back in Town/Christmas Eve With The Babylonian Cowboys: Jingle Bells	1987	—	2.50	5.00
Reprise 28156	PS	Santa Claus Is Back in Town/Christmas Eve With The Babylonian Cowboys: Jingle Bells	1987	—	2.50	5.00
On Various-Artists Collections						
Santa Claus Is Back in Town		Christmas Tradition, A, Volume II (Warner Bros. 25762) Country Christmas (Time-Life STL-109)				
YOBS, THE						
45s						
Fresh 41		Yobs On 45/The Ballad Of The Warrington	1982	2.00	4.00	8.00
Fresh 41	PS	Yobs On 45/The Ballad Of The Warrington	1982	2.50	5.00	10.00
— Sleeve and record are U.K. imports						
NEMS NES 114		Run Rudolph Run/The Worm Song	1977	2.00	4.00	8.00
NEMS NES 114	PS	Run Rudolph Run/The Worm Song	1977	2.50	5.00	10.00
— Sleeve and record are U.K. imports						
Safari YULE 1		Rub-a-Dum-Dum/Another Christmas	1981	2.00	4.00	8.00
Safari YULE 1	PS	Rub-a-Dum-Dum/Another Christmas	1981	2.50	5.00	10.00
— Sleeve and record are U.K. imports						
Yob 79		Silent Night/Stille Nacht	1978	2.00	4.00	8.00
Yob 79	PS	Silent Night/Stille Nacht	1978	2.50	5.00	10.00
— Sleeve and record are U.K. imports						
Albums						
Safari RUDE 1		Christmas Album	1980	5.00	10.00	20.00
— U.K. import						
YORGESSON, YOGI						
45s						
Capitol F781		I Yust Go Nuts At Christmas/Yingle Bells	1949	5.00	10.00	20.00
Capitol F1831		Christmas Party/I Was Santa at the Schoolhouse	1951	3.75	7.50	15.00
Capitol F2978		Be Kind to the Street Corner Santa/I Give Up, What Is It	1954	3.75	7.50	15.00
Capitol F3904		I Yust Go Nuts at Christmas/Yingle Bells	1958	3.75	7.50	15.00
Capitol S7-57891		I Yust Go Nuts at Christmas/Nuttin' for Christmas	1992	—	2.50	5.00
— B-side by Stan Freberg						
7-Inch Extended Plays						
Capitol EAP 1-461		I Yust Go Nuts At Christmas/Yingle Bells//The Christmas Story/ I Was Santa Claus At the Schoolhouse (for the P.T.A.)	195?	3.75	7.50	15.00
Capitol EAP 1-461	PS	Yingle Bells	195?	3.75	7.50	15.00
On Various-Artists Collections						
I Yust Go Nuts at Christmas		Christmas Through the Years (Reader's Digest RDA-143) Dr. Demento Presents the Greatest Novelty Records of All Time Volume VI: Christmas (Rhino RNLP 825)				
YOUNG AMERICANS, THE						
On Various-Artists Collections						
Ding Dong Merrily on High		Firestone Presents Your Favorite Christmas Music, Volume 4 (Firestone MLP 7011)				
Masters in This Hall		Firestone Presents Your Favorite Christmas Music, Volume 4 (Firestone MLP 7011)				
Medley: Away in a Manger/Silent Night/Coventry Carol		Firestone Presents Your Favorite Christmas Music, Volume 4 (Firestone MLP 7011)				

Label, Number	Title (A Side/B Side)	Year	VG	VG+	NM
Medley: Here We Come a-Caroling/ Deck the Halls/God Rest You Merry, Gentlemen/O Little Town of Bethlehem	Firestone Presents Your Favorite Christmas Music, Volume 4 (Firestone MLP 7011)				
Medley: We Three Kings of Orient Are/Hark! The Herald Angels Sing	Firestone Presents Your Favorite Christmas Music, Volume 4 (Firestone MLP 7011)				

YOUNG, ANN
45s

Class 805 DJ	Souvenirs Of Christmas/Once A Fool	19??	—	2.50	5.00
— B-side by Bobby Grabeau					

YOUNG, BILLY
45s

Joyja 001	What Is Christmas/Love Clause	19??	—	3.00	6.00

YOUNG, FARON
45s

Capitol F2629	You're an Angel on My Christmas Tree/ I'm Gonna Tell Santa Claus on You	1953	3.75	7.50	15.00
Step One 455	White Christmas/The Christmas Song	199?	—	2.50	5.00
— Red vinyl					

YOUNG, LORETTA
7-Inch Extended Plays

Decca ED 549 (91133)	The Littlest Angel Part 1/The Littlest Angel Part 2	195?	2.50	5.00	10.00
Decca ED 549 (91134)	The Littlest Angel Part 3/The Littlest Angel Part 4	195?	2.50	5.00	10.00
Decca ED 549	The Littlest Angel	195?	2.50	5.00	10.00
— Cover for 2-EP set					

YOUNG, PAUL
45s

CBS DA 4972	Everything Must Change/Give Me My Freedom// Everything Must Change (Instrumental)/ Christmas Message/I Close My Eyes And Count To Ten (Live)	1984	—	3.00	6.00
— Double pack of 45s					
CBS DA 4972 PS	Everything Must Change/Give Me My Freedom// Everything Must Change (Instrumental)/ Christmas Message/I Close My Eyes And Count To Ten (Live)	1984	—	3.00	6.00
— Sleeve and records are U.K. imports					

YOUNG, VICTOR & HIS SINGING STRINGS – See CLARK DENNIS.

YOUNGSTERS, THE
45s

Empire 109	Christmas In Jail/Dreamy Eyes	1956	15.00	30.00	60.00

On Various-Artists Collections

Christmas in Jail	Rockin' Christmas — The '50s (Rhino RNLP-066)				

YULETIDE CHORISTERS
On Various-Artists Collections

That Christmas Feeling	Happy Holidays, Vol. 22 (RCA Special Products DPL1-0777)				

YUTAKA
On Various-Artists Collections

This Christmas	GRP Christmas Collection, A (GRP 9574)				

Z

ZABKA, STAN, 'S ORCHESTRA
45s

Palladium 605	(Christmas Time) Chimes/Chimes (Theme)	19??	—	3.00	6.00
— Green and silver labels					
Palladium 605	(Christmas Time) Chimes/Chimes (Theme)	19??	—	3.00	6.00
— Red and white labels					

Label, Number	Title (A Side/B Side)	Year	VG	VG+	NM
ZAHND, RICKY, AND THE BLUE JEANERS					
45s					
Columbia 4-263	(I'm Getting) Nuttin' For Christmas/ Something Barked On Christmas Morning	1955	3.75	7.50	15.00
— Yellow-label Children's Series edition					
Columbia 40576	(I'm Getting) Nuttin' For Christmas/ Something Barked On Christmas Morning	1955	3.75	7.50	15.00
On Various-Artists Collections					
(I'm Gettin') Nuttin' for Christmas	Child's Christmas, A (Harmony HS 14563)				
Something Barked on Christmas Morning	Child's Christmas, A (Harmony HS 14563)				
ZAMFIR					
Albums					
Philips 822 571-1	Christmas with Zamfir	198?	2.50	5.00	10.00
ZAMORA, PAUL					
45s					
Rockin G 930	It's Christmas Time (English)/ (Spanish)	1987	—	—	3.00
ZEBRA					
45s					
Blue Thumb 109	Christmas Morning (Part 1)/Christmas Morning (Part 2)	1969	2.50	5.00	10.00
ZEE, KATHY AND JIMMY					
45s					
Willette 121	Santa Claus Rock & Roll/(B-side unknown)	196?	5.00	10.00	20.00
ZICKLIN					
45s					
Jam 1225	Something Special Xmas Season/Don't Talk To Strangers	19??	—	3.00	6.00
ZIMBALIST, EFREM, JR.					
45s					
Warner Bros. 5126	Adeste Fideles// Deck the Halls with Boughs of Holly/Caroling, Caroling	1959	3.00	6.00	12.00
— B-side by The Guitars Inc.					
Warner Bros. 5126 PS	Adeste Fideles// Deck the Halls with Boughs of Holly/Caroling, Caroling	1959	5.00	10.00	20.00
On Various-Artists Collections					
Adeste Fideles	We Wish You a Merry Christmas (Warner Bros. W 1337)				
ZIRCONS, THE					
45s					
Cool Sound 1030	Silver Bells/You Are My Sunshine	1964	7.50	15.00	30.00
ZOLT'S SECOND FOUNDATION					
45s					
Trafic 87212	Christmas On The Moon/Tu Vois Cette Etoile Qui Eclate	1987	—	—	3.00
Trafic 87212 PS	Christmas On The Moon/Tu Vois Cette Etoile Qui Eclate	1987	—	—	3.00
— Fold-out poster sleeve					
ZUKER, DONNA					
45s					
Fable 603	I Think It's Almost Christmas Time/My Christmas Prayer	19??	—	3.00	6.00
— B-side by Jesse Hodges					
ZZ TOP					
On Various-Artists Collections					
Holiday I.D.	Winter Warnerland (Warner Bros. PRO-A-3328)				

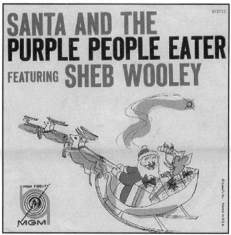

(Top left) New-wave band The Waitresses lives on through "Christmas Wrapping." This sleeve is taken from a UK issue from late 1982. A US promo 45 exists from the early 1980s, but it wasn't commercially released on 7-inch here until 1994. (Top right) In 1958, the year that "The Purple People Eater" was so popular, Sheb Wooley had him meet the bearded fat man in this sequel. This is a very difficult sleeve to find. (Bottom left) Ho, ho, ho, baby! Dwight Yoakam's version of "Santa Claus Is Back in Town" from 1987 can stand alongside Elvis' original without blushing. (Bottom right) In the early days of Warner Bros. Records, many of their releases were by actors on their TV shows, such as this obscure holiday 45 from Efrem Zimbalist, Jr. of "77 Sunset Strip."

Title		Label, Number	Year	VG	VG+	NM

Original Cast Recordings

Albums

Title		Label, Number	Year	VG	VG+	NM
Annie		Columbia Masterworks JS 34712	1977	2.50	5.00	10.00
— *Original labels have "Columbia" circling the perimeter of the label. Contains one Christmas song: New Deal for Christmas, A (McArdle, Andrea; Reid Shelton; Sandy Faison; Raymond Thorne)*						
Annie		CBS Masterworks JS 34712	197?	2.00	4.00	8.00
— *Later labels have "CBS Masterworks" circling the perimeter of the label. Contents are the same.*						
Annie's Christmas		Columbia CC 38361	1982	3.00	6.00	12.00
— *Based on the characters in the "Annie" Broadway play*						
Side 1: Deck the Halls with Boughs of Holly; Angels We Have Heard on High						
Side 2: Jolly Old St. Nicholas; We Wish You a Merry Christmas						
Best Little Whorehouse in Texas, The		MCA 3049	1978	3.00	6.00	12.00
— *Contains one Christmas song: Hard Candy Christmas (Blair, Pamela, et al.)*						
Best Little Whorehouse in Texas, The		MCA 37218	1980	2.00	4.00	8.00
— *Reissue of MCA 3049 with same contents*						
I Love My Wife		Atlantic SD 19107	1977	2.50	5.00	10.00
— *Contains one Christmas song: Lovers on Christmas Eve*						
Mame	S	Columbia Masterworks KOS 3000	1966	5.00	10.00	20.00
Mame	M	Columbia Masterworks KOL 6600	1966	3.75	7.50	15.00
— *Contains one Christmas song: We Need a Little Christmas (Lansbury, Angela; Frankie Michaels; Jane Connell; and Sab Shimono)*						
She Loves Me	(2) M	MGM E 4118OC-2	1963	10.00	20.00	40.00
She Loves Me	(2) S	MGM SE 4118OC-2	1963	12.50	25.00	50.00
— *Contains one Christmas song: Twelve Days to Christmas (Wilder, Jo; Gino Conforti; Joe Ross)*						

Soundtracks

45s

Title		Label, Number	Year	VG	VG+	NM
Amahl and the Night Visitors (Side 1)/ Amahl and the Night Visitors (Side 8)		RCA Red Seal 49-3836	1952	2.00	4.00	8.00
— *Red vinyl; part of RCA Red Seal WDM-1701*						
Amahl and the Night Visitors (Side 2)/ Amahl and the Night Visitors (Side 7)		RCA Red Seal 49-3837	1952	2.00	4.00	8.00
— *Red vinyl; part of RCA Red Seal WDM-1701*						
Amahl and the Night Visitors (Side 3)/ Amahl and the Night Visitors (Side 6)		RCA Red Seal 49-3838	1952	2.00	4.00	8.00
— *Red vinyl; part of RCA Red Seal WDM-1701*						
Amahl and the Night Visitors (Side 4)/ Amahl and the Night Visitors (Side 5)		RCA Red Seal 49-3839	1952	2.00	4.00	8.00
— *Red vinyl; part of RCA Red Seal WDM-1701*						
Charlie Brown Christmas, A		Charlie Brown 401	1977	—	2.50	5.00
— *7-inch, 33 1/3, edited (12-minute) and at times revised version of the TV special*						
Charlie Brown Christmas, A	PS	Charlie Brown 401	1977	—	2.50	5.00
— *24-page booklet with slot in back for record*						

7-Inch Extended Plays

Title		Label, Number	Year	VG	VG+	NM
Amahl and the Night Visitors	(4)	RCA Red Seal WDM 1701	1952	10.00	20.00	40.00
— *Soundtrack of the 1951 NBC-TV production; includes 4 red vinyl 45s (49-3836 through 49-3839) and box*						
Frosty the Snowman		Disneyland 253	1976	—	2.50	5.00
— *Not the original soundtrack, but placed here to avoid confusion (we hope); actually a recitation of the 1970s children's book based on the song*						
Side 1: Frosty the Snowman (Story and Song)						
Side 2: Frosty the Snowman (Story and Song); Frosty the Snowman (Groce, Larry)						
Frosty the Snowman	PS	Disneyland 253	1976	—	3.00	6.00
— *24-page "Little Golden Book & Record" with slot inside back cover for record*						
White Christmas (Part 1)		Decca ED 819 (# unknown)	1954	2.50	5.00	10.00
— *Contents unknown*						
White Christmas (Part 2)		Decca ED 819 (# unknown)	1954	2.50	5.00	10.00
— *Contents unknown*						
White Christmas (Part 3)		Decca ED 819 (# unknown)	1954	2.50	5.00	10.00
— *Contents unknown*						
White Christmas	PS	Decca ED 819	1954	2.50	5.00	10.00
— *Box for 3-EP set*						

Title		Label, Number	Year	VG	VG+	NM

Albums

Title		Label, Number	Year	VG	VG+	NM
Amahl and the Night Visitors	10	RCA Red Seal LM-1701	1952	12.50	25.00	50.00
— Soundtrack of the 1951 NBC-TV production						
Amahl and the Night Visitors	M	RCA Red Seal LM-1701	1952	10.00	20.00	40.00
— Soundtrack of the 1951 NBC-TV production; 12-inch record in hinged box with booklet						
Amahl and the Night Visitors	M	RCA Red Seal LM-2762	1964	3.75	7.50	15.00
— Soundtrack of the 1963 NBC Opera Company TV production						
Amahl and the Night Visitors	S	RCA Red Seal LSC-2762	1964	3.75	7.50	15.00
— Same as above, but in stereo; large "RCA Victor" and dog at top of label						
Amahl and the Night Visitors	S	RCA Red Seal LSC-2762	1969	3.00	6.00	12.00
— Stereo reissue on red label without dog; no bar code on back cover						
Amahl and the Night Visitors	S	RCA Red Seal LSC-2762	198?	2.50	5.00	10.00
— Stereo reissue on red label without dog; with bar code on back cover						
Best Little Whorehouse in Texas, The		MCA 6112	1982	2.50	5.00	10.00
— Contains one Christmas song: Hard Candy Christmas (Parton, Dolly)						
Best Little Whorehouse in Texas, The		MCA 1499	1987	2.00	4.00	8.00
— Reissue of MCA 6112						
Charlie Brown Christmas, A		Charlie Brown 3701	1977	5.00	10.00	20.00
— Complete soundtrack with dialogue, plus music by Vince Guaraldi; includes 12-page bound-in booklet with script and illustrations. Also see "Guaraldi, Vince, Trio."						
Side 1: Charlie Brown Christmas, A (Part 1)						
Side 2: Charlie Brown Christmas, A (Part 2)						
Christmas Raccoons, The		Starland Music 1031	1982	3.00	6.00	12.00
— Story record with Rich Little, Rita Coolidge and Rupert Holmes as the star voices						
Christmas That Almost Wasn't, The	M	RCA Camden CAL-1086	1966	6.25	12.50	25.00
Christmas That Almost Wasn't, The	S	RCA Camden CAS-1086	1966	7.50	15.00	30.00
— Soundtrack to movie. Album is not banded, but these are the songs:						
Side 1: Christmas That Almost Wasn't, The; Kids Get All the Breaks; Why Can't Every Day Be Christmas?; Christmas Is Coming; Hustle Bustle; I'm Bad; Name of the Song Is Prune, The; What Are Children Like?; Why Can't Every Day Be Christmas?						
Side 2: Time for Christmas; I've Got a Date with Santa; Santa Claus Bound; Nothing to Do But Wait; Why Can't Every Day Be Christmas?; Christmas That Almost Wasn't, The						
Claymation Christmas Celebration		Atlantic 81922	1988	3.00	6.00	12.00
— Soundtrack to TV special.						
Side 1: Rudolph the Red-Nosed Reindeer; Good King Swing; We Three Kings Bop; God Rest Ye; Carol of the Bells; Silent Night Jazzy Night						
Side 2: Noel; Hark!; Up on the Housetop; Joy!; Waffle, Waddle, Wallow, Wassle;Angels We Have Heard on High						
Dangerous Christmas of Red Riding Hood, The	M	ABC-Paramount 536	1965	3.75	7.50	15.00
Dangerous Christmas of Red Riding Hood, The	S	ABC-Paramount S-536	1965	6.25	12.50	25.00
— Music from a television special.						
Side 1: Overture (Scharff, Walter); We Wish the World a Happy Yule (Ritchard, Cyril); My Red Riding Hood (Minnelli, Liza); Snubbed (Ritchard, Cyril); Woodsman's Serenade/Granny's Gulch/Along the Way (Damone, Vic, and Liza Minnelli); I'm Naïve (Minnelli, Liza)						
Side 2: Red Riding Hood Improvisation; I'm Naïve (reprise); We're Gonna Howl Tonight (Animals, The); Ding-a-Ling, Ding-a-Ling (Minnelli, Liza, and Cyril Ritchard); Poor Mouse; Granny/Along the Way (reprise) (Damone, Vic; Liza Minnelli; Cyril Ritchard); We Wish the World a Happy Yule (reprise) (Damone, Vic; Liza Minnelli; Cyril Ritchard)						
84 Charing Cross Road		Varese Sarabande STV 81306	1987	3.00	6.00	12.00
— Contains one Christmas song: Christmas Gift, 1949 (Sussex Carol)						
Fenwick		Fenwick FLP-621	1968	5.00	10.00	20.00
— Soundtrack to TV special; packaged in oversize (13 1/2 x 13 1/2) sleeve with color cartoon booklet; made especially for Motorola. Unbanded record; narration surrounds the following songs:						
Side 1: Fenwick Theme Introduction; Santa's Workshop; Fenwick (Reprise)						
Side 2: What a Land, Santa Land!; Keep Thy Faith, Children (Bryant, Anita)						
For the First Time	M	RCA Red Seal LM-2338	1959	3.75	7.50	15.00
For the First Time	S	RCA Red Seal LSC-2338	1959	5.00	10.00	20.00
— "Shaded dog" and smaller RCA Victor lettering						
For the First Time	S	RCA Red Seal LSC-2338	1965	3.75	7.50	15.00
— "White dog" and larger RCA Victor lettering						
For the First Time	S	RCA Red Seal LSC-2338	1969	3.00	6.00	12.00
— No dog Contains one Christmas song: Ave Maria (Schubert) (Lanza, Mario)						
Frosty the Snowman		MGM SE-4733	1970	15.00	30.00	60.00
Frosty's Winter Wonderland		Disneyland 1368	1976	5.00	10.00	20.00
— Soundtrack to TV special. Unbanded record; narration (by Andy Griffith) and story (Jackie Vernon, Shelley Winters, Dennis Day, Paul Frees) surround the following songs:						
Side 1: Overture; Frosty the Snowman (Griffith, Andy)						
Side 2: Frosty the Snowman (Griffith, Andy); Winter Wonderland						

Title		Label, Number	Year	VG	VG+	NM
Gaily, Gaily		United Artists UAS 5202	1969	6.25	12.50	25.00

— *Contains one Christmas song:* Christmas Eve on Skid Row (Mercouri, Melina)

Heidi's Song		K-Tel NU 5310	1982	3.00	6.00	12.00

— *Contains one Christmas song:* Christmas-y Day, A (Hall, Sandie)

Holiday Inn		Decca DL 4256	1962	6.25	12.50	25.00

— *Contains the following Christmas songs:* Happy Holiday; White Christmas; Let's Start the New Year Right (all by Crosby, Bing)

Holiday Inn		MCA 25205	1987	2.00	4.00	8.00

— *Reissue of Decca LP*

How the Grinch Stole Christmas	M	Leo LE-901	1966	12.50	25.00	50.00
How the Grinch Stole Christmas	S	Leo LES-901	1966	17.50	35.00	70.00
How the Grinch Stole Christmas		Mercury Nashville 528 439-1	1995	3.00	6.00	12.00

— *Picture disc*
    Side 1: How the Grinch Stole Christmas (Karloff, Boris, narrator)
    Side 2: Welcome Christmas; Trim Up the Tree; You're a Mean One, Mr. Grinch (Ravenscroft, Thurl); Welcome Christmas

How the Grinch Stole Christmas		Random House/Scholastic 0-394-05008-8	1975	3.75	7.50	15.00

— *Not the original soundtrack, but placed here to avoid confusion (we hope). B-side is a condensation of Folkways FC-7750 (1956).*
    Side 1: How the Grinch Stole Christmas (Mostel, Zero)
    Side 2: Bring a Torch; Friendly Beasts, The; Mary Had a Baby; Come and Sing; Gently, the Maiden; Fum-Fum-Fum; Simple Birth, The; Haidom-Haidom; O Christmas Tree; Bagpipers' Carol; Saint Basil; Little Bitty Baby; Twelve Days of Christmas (all by Mills, Alan)

Irma La Douce	S	Columbia Masterworks OS 2029	1960	10.00	20.00	40.00

— *Contains one Christmas song:* Christmas Child (The Cast)

Irma La Douce	M	Columbia Masterworks OL 5560	1960	7.50	15.00	30.00
Mame		Warner Bros. W 2773	1974	3.75	7.50	15.00

— *Contains one Christmas song:* We Need a Little Christmas (Ball, Lucille, and Cast)

Meet Me in St. Louis	M	Decca DL 8498	1957	7.50	15.00	30.00

— *B-side of LP is "The Harvey Girls." Contains one Christmas song:* Have Yourself a Merry Little Christmas (Garland, Judy)

Meet Me in St. Louis		AEI 3101	1978	3.00	6.00	12.00

— *Reissue of Decca LP*

Merry Christmas, Mr. Lawrence		MCA 6125	1983	2.50	5.00	10.00

— *Music by Ryuichi Sakamoto. David Bowie stars in the movie, but does not sing on the LP.*
    Side 1: Merry Christmas, Mr. Lawrence; Batavia; Germination; Hearty Breakfast, A; Before the War; Seed and the Sower, The; Brief Encounter, A; Ride Ride Ride (Celliers' Brother's Song);Fight, The
    Side 2: Father Christmas; Dismissed!; Assembly; Beyond Reason; Sowing the Seed; 23rd Psalm; Last Regrets; Ride Ride Ride (Reprise); Seed, The; Forbidden Colours (Sylvian, David)

Rudolph the Red-Nosed Reindeer	M	Decca DL 4815	1964	15.00	30.00	60.00
Rudolph the Red-Nosed Reindeer	M	Decca DL 34327	1965	10.00	20.00	40.00

— *Custom products reissue*

Rudolph the Red-Nosed Reindeer	S	Decca DL 74815	1964	20.00	40.00	80.00
Rudolph the Red-Nosed Reindeer		MCA 15003	1973	5.00	10.00	20.00

— *Reissue of Decca album*
    Side 1: Overture and A Holly Jolly Christmas (Videocraft Orchestra and Burl Ives); Jingle, Jingle, Jingle (Francis, Stan); We Are Santa's Elves (Videocraft Chorus); There's Always Tomorrow (Orenstein, Janet); We're a Couple of Misfits (Richards, Billie, and Paul Soles); Silver and Gold (Ives, Burl); Most Wonderful Day of the Year, The (Videocraft Chorus); Holly Jolly Christmas, A (Ives, Burl); Rudolph the Red-Nosed Reindeer (Ives, Burl With Videocraft Chorus)
    Side 2: Rudolph the Red-Nosed Reindeer; I Heard the Bells on Christmas Day; There's Always Tomorrow; Jingle, Jingle, Jingle; We're a Couple of Misfits; Silver and Gold; We Are Santa's Elves; Most Wonderful Day of the Year, The; Holly Jolly Christmas, A; Christmas Medley (all by Decca Concert Orchestra)

Santa Claus Is Comin' to Town		MGM SE-4732	1970	15.00	30.00	60.00
Santa Claus The Movie		EMI America SJ-17177	1985	2.50	5.00	10.00

    Side 1: Main Title: Every Christmas Eve & Santa's Theme (Jones, Aled); Arrival of the Elves (Mancini, Henry); Making Toys (Ambrosian Children's Choir); Christmas Rhapsody (Mancini, Henry); It's Christmas Again (Ambrosian Children's Choir); March of the Elves (Mancini, Henry); Patch, Natch! (Ambrosian Singers)
    Side 2: It's Christmas All Over the World (Easton, Sheena); Shouldn't Do That (Kaja); Sleigh Ride Over Manhattan (Mancini, Henry); Sad Patch (Mancini, Henry); Patch Versus Santa(Mancini, Henry); Thank You, Santa (Ambrosian Children's Choir)

Say One for Me	M	Columbia CL 1337	1959	10.00	20.00	40.00
Say One for Me	S	Columbia CS 8147	1959	20.00	40.00	80.00

— *Contains one Christmas song:*
    Side 2, Song 7: Secret of Christmas, The (Crosby, Bing)

Scrooge		Columbia Masterworks S 30258	1970	10.00	20.00	40.00

Title	Label, Number	Year	VG	VG+	NM
Scrooge	Columbia Special Products P 14077	1977	3.00	6.00	12.00

— *Special Products reissue*
    Side 1: Overture; Christmas Carol, A; Christmas Children (Collings, David; Richard Beaumont; Karen Scargill); I Hate People (Finney, Albert); Father Christmas; See the Phantoms (Guinness, Alec); December the 25th (Naismith, Laurence); Happiness (Neve, Suzanne); You . . .You (Finney, Albert)
    Side 2: I Like Life (More, Kenneth; Albert Finney); Beautiful Day, The (Beaumont, Richard); Happiness (Reprise) (Neve, Suzanne; Albert Finney); Thank You Very Much (Rodgers, Anton; Albert Finney); I'll Begin Again (Finney, Albert); I Like Life (Reprise) (Finney, Albert); Medley: Father Christmas/Thank You Very Much (Finney, Albert); Christmas Carol, A (Finney, Albert)

Scrooged	A&M SP-3921	1988	2.50	5.00	10.00

— *Includes the following Christmas songs:* We Three Kings of Orient Are (Davis, Miles; Larry Carlton; David Sanborn; and Paul Shaffer); Christmas Must Be Tonight (Robertson, Robbie); Christmas Song, The (Cole, Natalie)

Stingiest Man in Town, The	Columbia CL 950	1956	5.00	10.00	20.00

— *Music from a television play first aired on The Alcoa Hour*

Stingiest Man in Town, The	Columbia Special Products P 12637	1975	2.50	5.00	10.00

— *Reissue of Columbia LP; same contents*
    Side 1: Christmas Carol, A (Four Lads, The); Old Fashioned Christmas, An (Desmond, Johnny); Humbug (Rathbone, Basil, and Johnny Desmond); Stingiest Man in Town, The (Four Lads, The); Christmas Carol, A (Four Lads, The); I Wear a Chain (Weede, Robert; Basil Rathbone); Spirit Theme (Rathbone, Basil; Robert Wright); Golden Dreams (Damone, Vic; Patrice Munsel); It Might Have Been (Damone, Vic; Patrice Munsel)
    Side 2: Christmas Carol, A/The Christmas Spirit (Four Lads, The); Yes, There Is a Santa Claus (Madigan, Betty); One Little Boy (Rathbone, Basil; Robert Wright); Old Fashioned Christmas, An (Desmond, Johnny); Birthday Party of the King (Desmond, Johnny); Christmas Carol, A (Four Lads, The); I Wear a Chain (Rathbone, Basil); Concerto Inferno (Spielman, Fred); Mankind Should Be My Business (Rathbone, Basil); Christmas Spirit, The (Rathbone, Basil); One Little Boy (Green, Martyn; Basil Rathbone); Yes, There Is a Santa Claus (Madigan, Betty); Christmas Carol, A (Four Lads, The)

Tommy	(2) Polydor PD 2 9502	1975	5.00	10.00	20.00

— *Contains one Christmas song:* Christmas (Ann-Margret, Alison Dowling and Oliver Reed)

'Twas the Night Before Christmas	Disneyland 1367	1976	5.00	10.00	20.00

— *Soundtrack to TV special. Unbanded record; narration (by Joel Grey) and story (Tammy Grimes, John McGiver, George Gobel) surround the following songs:*
    Side 1: Overture; Christmas Chimes; Give Your Heart a Try (Gobel, George)
    Side 2: Even a Miracle Needs a Hand (Grey, Joel); Even a Miracle Needs a Hand (Grimes, Tammy); Christmas Chimes

When Harry Met Sally. . .	Columbia SC 45319	1989	3.00	6.00	12.00

— *Contains one Christmas song:* Winter Wonderland (Connick, Harry, Jr.)

White Christmas	Decca DL 8083	1954	12.50	25.00	50.00
Yes, Georgio	London PDV 9001	1982	2.50	5.00	10.00

— *Contains one Christmas song:* Ave Maria (Schubert) (Pavarotti, Luciano)

Various Artists Collections

45s

Christmas Messages	DJ	Elektra 47254	1981	3.75	7.50	15.00

— *From Mel Tillis; Sonny Curtis; Dave Rowland; Helen Cornelius; Joe Sun; and Tompall and the Glaser Brothers*

Happy Christmas From The Stars		Black Levis 2570/1	198?	3.00	6.00	12.00

— *Flexidisc; greetings from Abba, ABC, Adam Ant, Bananarama, Bucks Fizz, Captain Sensible, Culture Club, Duran Duran, Fun Boy Three, Haircut 100, Imagination, The Jam, Madness, Mari Wilson, Musical Youth, Piranhas, Police, Steve Strange, Toyah, Ultravox*

Holiday Greetings from Warner Bros.	DJ	Warner Bros. PRO 653	1976	2.50	5.00	10.00

— *Promotional item with messages from WB sales/promotion staff to radio stations*

Holiday Greetings from Warner Bros.	PS	Warner Bros. PRO 653	1976	2.50	5.00	10.00
Seasons Greetings from United Artists	DJ	United Artists 50118	1966	5.00	10.00	20.00

— *Holiday greetings and IDs from (Side 1:) Ferrante & Teicher, Pat Cooper, Al Caiola, Jimmy Roselli; (Side 2:) Jackie Vernon, Anthony & The Imperials, Bobby Goldsboro, Jimmy McGriff, Del Reeves*

Silent Night/The 12 Days Of Christmas		Robin Hood 1006	195?		3.00	6.00

— *No artist credited on label*

Silent Night/The 12 Days Of Christmas	PS	Robin Hood 1006	195?		3.00	6.00
Spirit of Christmas		Alitha (no #)	198?		3.00	6.00

— *Flexidisc of greetings and samplers from the label. With Sue Raney, The Escorts, Barbara Jean English, and The Pastors.*

White Christmas/Oh Little Town Of Bethlehem		Robin Hood 1003	195?		3.00	6.00

— *No artist credited on label*

White Christmas/Oh Little Town Of Bethlehem	PS	Robin Hood 1003	195?		3.00	6.00

7-Inch Extended Plays

American Christmas, An	Capitol Special Markets CP-68	1974		3.00	6.00

    Side 1: Hark the Herald Angels Sing/It Came Upon a Midnight Clear (Crosby, Bing); What Child Is This (Shore, Dinah).
    Side 2: Hymn to Christmas, A (Hollywood Pops Orchestra)

Title		Label, Number	Year	VG	VG+	NM
American Christmas, An	PS	Capitol Special Markets CP-68	1974	2.00	4.00	8.00
Christmas EP	DJ	Philles X-EP	1963	25.00	50.00	100.00

Side 1: Sleigh Ride (Ronettes, The); Bells of St. Mary, The (Bob B. Soxx and the Blue Jeans)
Side 2: Christmas (Baby Please Come Home) (Love, Darlene); Santa Claus Is Coming to Town (Crystals, The).
The above two tracks may be in reverse order; we're not sure.

Christmas EP	PS	Philles X-EP	1963	100.00	200.00	400.00

— Sleeve for above promo-only record

Christmas Greetings From RCA Victor And Groove Recording Artists	DJ	RCA Victor SP-45-128	1963	12.50	25.00	50.00

Side 1: Christmas Greetings, in order, from Ann-Margret; Arnold, Eddy; Bare, Bobby; Cooke, Sam; Davis, Skeeter; Hirt, Al; Mancini, Henry; March, Peggy; Nero, Peter; Rich, Charlie; Scott, Jack; Sedaka, Neil
Side 2: New Year's Greetings, in order, from Ann-Margret; Arnold, Eddy; Bare, Bobby; Cooke, Sam; Davis, Skeeter; Hamilton, George, IV; Hirt, Al; Leonetti, Tommy; Mancini, Henry; March, Peggy; Nero, Peter; Sedaka, Neil

Christmas Greetings From The Entire Columbia Record Family	DJ	Columbia JZSP 58623/4	1960	12.50	25.00	50.00

— No picture sleeve
Side 1: Christmas Greetings from the Entire Columbia Record Family; Christmas Greetings from Ray Conniff & The Singers
Side 2: Medley: Jolly Old St. Nicholas/The Little Drummer Boy (Conniff, Ray)

Columbia 40109 (title unknown)		Columbia 4-40109	1953	3.00	6.00	12.00

Side 1: White Christmas (Godfrey, Arthur); Winter Wonderland (Davis, Sammy, Jr.)
Side 2: Here Comes Santa Claus (Simms, Lu Ann); Christmas Song, The (LaRosa, Julius)

Flexipop 15 (untitled)		Flexipop 15	198?	3.75	7.50	15.00

— Flexidisc
Side 1: Yuletown Throw Down (Rapture) (Blondie Co-Starring Freddie)
Side 2: Christmas Song, The (Brattles, The); Santa's Agent (Tate, Snuky)

Gift from Your RCA Victor Record Dealer, A		RCA Victor SP-45-35	1958	2.50	5.00	10.00

Side 1: God Rest Ye Merry, Gentlemen (Como, Perry); Good King Wenceslas (Ames Brothers, The)
Side 2: Silent Night (Belafonte, Harry); Hark! The Herald Angels Sing/Adeste Fideles (Radio City Music Hall Orchestra)

Gift from Your RCA Victor Record Dealer, A	PS	RCA Victor SP-45-35	1958	5.00	10.00	20.00

— Sleeve is labeled "Merry Christmas from Your RCA Victor Record Dealer"

"Holiday Greetings" Voice Tracks	DJ	Columbia JZSP 111921/2	1966	15.00	30.00	60.00

— Greetings from (Side 1:) Jimmy Dean, Jerry Vale (2), Andy Williams, Patti Page (2); (Side 2:) Percy Faith (3), Ray Conniff (4)

Merriest Time!, The		Sesac 35	195?	2.00	4.00	8.00

Side 1: Wild Bells (Honey Dreamers, The); Jangle Waltz (Maltby, Richard)
Side 2: Skater's Holiday (Maltby, Richard); Merry Bells, The (Henderson, Skitch)

Merriest Time!, The	PS	Sesac 35	195?	2.00	4.00	8.00

— Cover for above EP

Merry Christmas (Part 1)		Coral EC 82003 (# unknown)	195?	3.75	7.50	15.00
Merry Christmas (Part 2)		Coral EC 82003 (# unknown)	195?	3.75	7.50	15.00
Merry Christmas	PS	Coral EC 82003	195?	3.75	7.50	15.00

— Cover for 2-EP set

Merry Christmas And A Happy New Year	DJ	Modern Radio 102	19??		3.00	6.00

Side 1: Santa Baby (Kitt, Eartha); Story of Christmas, The (Madigan, Betty)
Side 2: I Got a Cold for Christmas (Ames Brothers, The); Night After Christmas, The (Homer and Jethro)

Merry Christmas And A Happy New Year	PS	Modern Radio 102	19??		3.00	6.00

— Cover for above promo record

Santa's Hit Parade		Columbia Record Club D-17	195?	2.50	5.00	10.00

— Available only through the Columbia Record Club
Side 1: Rudolph, the Red-Nosed Reindeer (Autry, Gene); Suzy Snowflake (Clooney, Rosemary)
Side 2: Frosty the Snow Man (Autry, Gene); Night Before Christmas, The (Clooney, Rosemary)

Santa's Hit Parade	PS	Columbia Record Club D-17	195?	5.00	10.00	20.00
Seasonings		Sunspot 1033	19??	—	2.00	4.00

Side 1: Jamie's Letter; Santa and Bobby; Papa and Tony; Neighbors; Warm Hugs; Holiday Salute
Side 2: Mistletoe; Runaway; Worried Helen; The Xmas Story; Grandma's Gift; The Bell Ringer

Seasonings	PS	Sunspot 1033	19??		2.00	4.00

— Above sleeve and record are public service announcements from the Seventh-Day Adventist Church

Tennessee Christmas	DJ	MCA S45-17046	1985		3.00	6.00

Side 1: One Bright Star (Larson, Nicolette); Please Come Home for Christmas (Schneider, John)
Side 2: Tennessee Christmas (Wariner, Steve); Christmas in the Caribbean (Buffett, Jimmy)

Tennessee Christmas	PS	MCA S45-17046	1985		3.00	6.00

— Cover for above promo record

Thank You for Opening Your Christmas Club with Us		Decca 34211	1963	2.50	5.00	10.00

— 7-inch 33 1/3 rpm single with small hole; distributed by various banks
Side 1: Jingle Bells (Four Aces); O Little Town of Bethlehem (Smith, Ethel); O Come All Ye Faithful (Kaye, Sammy)
Side 2: Silent Night (Welk, Lawrence); Adeste Fideles (Ames Brothers, The); Ave Maria (McGuire Sisters, The)

Title		Label, Number	Year	VG	VG+	NM
Thank You for Opening Your Christmas Club with Us	PS	Decca 34211	1963	3.00	6.00	12.00
We Wish You a Merry Christmas		RCA Victor PRS-277	1968	2.00	4.00	8.00

— *Distributed only through Radio Shack stores*
Side 1: Jingle Bells (Andrews, Julie); It Came Upon a Midnight Clear (Damone, Vic)
Side 2: Joy to the World (Jones, Jack); We Wish You a Merry Christmas (Anderson, Marian)

| We Wish You a Merry Christmas | PS | RCA Victor PRS-277 | 1968 | 2.50 | 5.00 | 10.00 |

— *Sleeve says the number is "68-1968"*

Albums

| All-Time Christmas Favorites | | Capitol Special Markets SL-6931 | 1973 | 3.00 | 6.00 | 12.00 |

— *Sold only at Sylvania dealers*
Side 1: Happy Holiday (Riddle, Nelson); Christmas Waltz, The (Lee, Peggy); Medley: Hark the Herald Angels Sing/It Came Upon a Midnight Clear (Crosby, Bing); Have Yourself a Merry Little Christmas (Campbell, Glen); Sleigh Ride (Waring, Fred, and the Pennsylvanians)
Side 2: Little Drummer Boy (Rose, David); First Noel, The (Fitzgerald, Ella); Medley: We Wish You a Merry Christmas/Silver Bells (Crosby, Bing); My Favorite Things (Ford, Tennessee Ernie); Joy to the World (Cole, Nat King)

| American Family Album of Favorite Christmas Music, The | (2) | RCA Red Seal VCS-7060 | 1970 | 3.75 | 7.50 | 15.00 |

Side 1: Nutcracker, The: Christmas Tree Scene/Dance of the Sugar-Plum Fairy; Sleigh Ride (Mozart); Hansel and Gretel: Overture/Dream Pantomime (all by Boston Pops Orchestra [Fiedler])
Side 2: White Christmas; Sleigh Ride; Parade of the Wooden Soldiers; Winter Wonderland; Rudolph, the Red-Nosed Reindeer; Santa Claus Is Comin' to Town (all by Boston Pops Orchestra [Fiedler])
Side 3 (*all are excerpts from Handel's "Messiah" with the Robert Shaw Chorale*): Overture (Sinfonia); And the Glory of the Lord; For Unto Us a Child Is Born; Pastoral Symphony (Pifa); Glory to God; Behold the Lamb of God; Lift Up Your Heads; Hallelujah Chorus
Side 4 (all by the Robert Shaw Chorale): Silent Night; Away in a Manger; O Come, All Ye Faithful; Hark! The Herald Angels Sing;It Came Upon the Midnight Clear; God Rest You Merry, Gentlemen; First Noel, The; O Little Town of Bethlehem; Angels We Have Heard on High; O Come, O Come, Emmanuel; Deck the Halls

| Best of Christmas | | Mistletoe MLP-1209 | 1974 | 2.50 | 5.00 | 10.00 |

Side 1: Rudolph the Red-Nosed Reindeer (Autry, Gene); Little Drummer Boy (Simeone, Harry, Chorale); 'Twas the Night Before Christmas (Liberace); This Time of the Year (Benton, Brook); Jingle Bell Rock (Helms, Bobby)
Side 2: Up on the House Top (Autry, Gene); O Holy Night (Simeone, Harry, Chorale); You're All I Want for Christmas (Benton, Brook); Christmas Song, The (Liberace); Jingle Bells (Helms, Bobby)

| Best of Christmas Vol. 2 | | Mistletoe MLP-1221 | 1975 | 2.50 | 5.00 | 10.00 |

Side 1: Chipmunk Song, The (Chipmunks, The, David Seville and); Hark the Herald Angels Sing (Rheims, Robert); Santa Claus Is Coming to Town (Ferrante and Teicher); Winter Wonderland (Welk, Lawrence); Ave Maria (Liberace)
Side 2: (All I Want for Christmas Is) My Two Front Teeth (Chipmunks, The, David Seville and); Medley: Joy to the World/O Little Town of Bethlehem (Rheims, Robert); Silent Night Medley (Ferrante and Teicher); Twelve Gifts of Christmas, The (Welk, Lawrence); O Holy Night (Liberace)

| Best of Christmas, The | | RCA Victor CPL1-7013 | 1985 | 2.50 | 5.00 | 10.00 |

Side 1: Christmas in Dixie (Alabama); Light of the Stable (Judds, The); Silent Night, Holy Night (Jennings, Waylon, and Jessi Colter); Blue Christmas (Conley, Earl Thomas)
Side 2: It's Christmas (Milsap, Ronnie); Hard Candy Christmas (Parton, Dolly); Silver Bells (Presley, Elvis); Pretty Paper (Nelson, Willie)

| Best of Christmas, The, Vol. I | | Capitol SM-11833 | 1978 | 2.50 | 5.00 | 10.00 |

Side 1: Christmas Song, The (Cole, Nat King); I Like a Sleighride (Lee, Peggy); White Christmas (Gleason, Jackie); Mister Santa (Sandler and Young); Christmas Is for Children (Campbell, Glen)
Side 2: I'll Be Home for Christmas (Martino, Al); Santa Claus Is Comin' to Town (Stafford, Jo); I Wish You a Merry Christmas (Crosby, Bing); Let It Snow! Let It Snow! Let It Snow! (Martin, Dean); Winter Wonderland (Newton, Wayne)

| Best of Christmas, The, Vol. II | | Capitol SM-11834 | 1978 | 2.50 | 5.00 | 10.00 |

Side 1: Do You Hear What I Hear (Crosby, Bing); Christmas Waltz, The (Wilson, Nancy); Little Drummer Boy, The (Rose, David); Have Yourself a Merry Little Christmas (Lettermen, The); Rudolph, the Red-Nosed Reindeer (Martin, Dean)
Side 2: Star Carol, The (Ford, Tennessee Ernie); Silver Bells (Whiting, Margaret, and Jimmy Wakely); I Saw Mommy Kissing Santa Claus (Gleason, Jackie); Caroling, Caroling (Cole, Nat King); Silent Night (Fitzgerald, Ella)

| Best of the Great Songs of Christmas (Album 10) | | Columbia Special Products CSS 1478 | 1970 | 3.00 | 6.00 | 12.00 |

— *Sold only at Goodyear tire dealers*
Side 1: First Noel, The (Davidson, John); Carol of the Bells (New York Philharmonic [Bernstein]; Joy to the World (Moffo, Anita); Lord's Prayer, The(Tucker, Richard); Away in a Manger (Jackson, Mahalia); Ave Maria (Stern, Isaac); Silent Night (Streisand, Barbra)
Side 2: Happiest Christmas, The (Clark, Petula); Christmas Song, The (Bennett, Tony); Little Drummer Boy, The (Faith, Percy); Do You Hear What I Hear (Williams, Andy); Toyland (Day, Doris); Night Before Christmas, The (Lawrence, Steve); We Wish You a Merry Christmas (Conniff, Ray)

| Billboard Greatest Christmas Hits, 1935-1954 | | Rhino R1 70637 | 1989 | 3.75 | 7.50 | 15.00 |

Side 1: White Christmas (Crosby, Bing); Let It Snow! Let It Snow! Let It Snow! (Monroe, Vaughn); Rudolph, the Red-Nosed Reindeer (Autry, Gene); Christmas Song, The (Cole, Nat King)
1946 recording (alternate take with no string section); (All I Want for Christmas Is) My Two Front Teeth (Jones, Spike, and His City Slickers)
Side 2: I Saw Mommy Kissing Santa Claus (Boyd, Jimmy); Christmas Island (Andrews Sisters, The, and Guy Lombardo); Silent Night (Crosby, Bing); Here Comes Santa Claus(Autry, Gene); Santa Baby (Kitt, Eartha)

Title	Label, Number	Year	VG	VG+	NM
Billboard Greatest Christmas Hits, 1955-Present	Rhino R1 70636	1989	3.75	7.50	15.00

Side 1: Jingle Bell Rock (Helms, Bobby); Rockin' Around the Christmas Tree (Lee, Brenda); Chipmunk Song, The (Chipmunks, The, David Seville and); Little Drummer Boy, The (Simeone, Harry, Chorale) *Stereo re-recording;* Mary's Boy Child (Belafonte, Harry)
Side 2: Blue Christmas (Presley, Elvis); Nuttin' for Christmas (Gordon, Barry, with Art Mooney); Please Come Home for Christmas (Brown, Charles); White Christmas (Drifters, The); Grandma Got Run Over by a Reindeer (Elmo & Patsy) *1983 re-recording*

| Bing Crosby and Rosemary Clooney: White Christmas | Holiday/Collector's Gold 598 | 1980 | 2.50 | 5.00 | 10.00 |

— *Crosby recordings are from a radio broadcast*
Side 1: White Christmas (Crosby, Bing); Adeste Fideles (Crosby, Bing); Rudolph, the Red-Nosed Reindeer (Crosby, Bing); Away in a Manger (Crosby, Bing); O Little Town of Bethlehem (Crosby, Bing, and Frank Sinatra); Silent Night (Crosby, Bing)
Side 2: Christmas Song, The; It Came Upon a Midnight Clear; Have Yourself a Merry Little Christmas; Little Drummer Boy; Jingle Bells (all by Clooney, Rosemary)

| Blue Christmas | DJ | Welk Music Group WM-3002 | 1984 | 20.00 | 40.00 | 80.00 |

— *Promo only; compiled by the publisher of "Blue Christmas" and other holiday tunes for radio use*
Side 1: Blue Christmas (Presley, Elvis); Blue Christmas (Living Voices); Blue Christmas (Atkins, Chet); Blue Christmas (Nelson, Willie); Blue Christmas (Gilley, Mickey); Blue Christmas (Welk, Lawrence); Blue Christmas (Reeves, Jim); Blue Christmas (Tubb, Ernest); Blue Christmas (Wynette, Tammy); Blue Christmas (Gleason, Jackie)
Side 2: Blue Christmas (Campbell, Glen); Blue Christmas (Beach Boys, The); Blue Christmas (Davis, Danny, and the Nashville Brass); Blue Christmas (Mathis, Johnny); Blue Christmas(Haggard, Merle); Christmas Is (Como, Perry); Mele Kalikimaka (Crosby, Bing); Ding-a-Ling the Christmas Bell (Anderson, Lynn); Christmas in Los Angeles (Welk, Lawrence); Brazilian Sleighride (Faith, Percy)

| Brightest Stars of Christmas, The | RCA Special Products DPL1-0086 | 1974 | 10.00 | 20.00 | 40.00 |

— *Sold only at JCPenney department stores*
Side 1: We Wish You a Merry Christmas (Philadelphia Orchestra [Ormandy]); Here Comes Santa Claus (Presley, Elvis); Winter Wonderland (Davis, Danny, and the Nashville Brass); Home for the Holidays (Como, Perry); Medley: It Came Upon a Midnight Clear/ Away in a Manger/The First Noel (Mancini, Henry)
Side 2: Jingle Bells (Andrews, Julie); Joy to the World (Ames, Ed); Sleigh Ride (Boston Pops Orchestra [Fiedler]); Christmas in My Home Town (Pride, Charley); Medley: Christmas Hymn/ Hark! The Herald Angels Sing (Shaw, Robert, Chorale); Silent Night (Franchi, Sergio)

| Broadway Christmas Songs | Broadway BLP-XMAS-1001 | 19?? | 3.00 | 6.00 | 12.00 |

— *Performed by anonymous musicians*
Side 1: O Come All Ye Faithful; Deck the Halls; Joy to the World; It Came Upon a Midnight Clear; Hark the Herald Angels Sing; First Noel, The; Silent Night, Holy Night; O Little Town of Bethlehem
Side 2: God Rest Ye Merry Gentlemen; Jingle Bells; O Holy Night; Away in a Manger; Auld Lang Syne; O Christmas Tree

| Carols and Candlelight | Columbia Special Products P 12525 | 1974 | 2.50 | 5.00 | 10.00 |

— *Sold only at Goodyear tire dealers*
Side 1: Joy to the World (Kostelanetz, Andre); O Holy Night (Smith, Kate); First Noel, The (Davidson, John); What Child Is This? (Andrews, Julie); Go Tell It on the Mountain (Jackson, Mahalia); Silent Night (Belafonte, Harry); O Come All Ye Faithful (Bernstein, Leonard)
Side 2: I'll Be Home for Christmas (Day, Doris); Moonlight in Vermont (Getz, Stan); Christmas Is (Faith, Percy); Christmas Song (Lawson, Yank, and Bob Haggart); Medley: I Love the Winter Weather/I've Got My Love to Keep Me Warm (Bennett, Tony); Snowfall (Light, Enoch); White Christmas (Williams, Andy)

| Celebrate the Season with Tupperware | RCA Special Products DPL1-0803 | 1987 | 7.50 | 15.00 | 30.00 |

— *Sold only at Tupperware parties*
Side 1: Sleigh Ride (Boston Pops Orchestra [Fiedler]); White Christmas (Parton, Dolly); Medley: Caroling, Caroling/The First Noel/Hark! The Herald Angels Sing/Silent Night (Como, Perry); Let It Snow! Let It Snow! Let It Snow! (Mathis, Johnny); Santa Claus (I Still Believe in You) (Alabama)
Side 2: Christmas Song, The (Cole, Nat King); Winter Wonderland (Murray, Anne); Feliz Navidad (Feliciano, Jose); I'll Be Home for Christmas (Presley, Elvis); Medley: What Are You Doing New Year's Eve/Auld Lang Syne (Mancini, Henry)

| Child's Christmas, A | Harmony HS 14563 | 197? | 3.00 | 6.00 | 12.00 |

Side 1: 'Twas the Night Before Christmas (Carney, Art); Rudolph, the Red-Nosed Reindeer (Autry, Gene); Parade of the Wooden Soldiers (Heatherton, Ray); (I'm Gettin') Nuttin' for Christmas (Zahnd, Ricky); Twelve Days of Christmas, The (Ives, Burl)
Side 2: Something Barked on Christmas Morning (Zahnd, Ricky); March of the Christmas Toys (Ferrer, Jose); Jingle Bells (Wayne, Jerry); Good King Wenceslas (Wayne, Jerry)

| Christmas — The Season of Music | Capitol Creative Products SL-6679 | 1970 | 3.00 | 6.00 | 12.00 |

Side 1: Carol of the Bells (Rose, David); I Sing Noel (Sandler and Young); First Noel, The (Fitzgerald, Ella); Winter Wonderland(Martin, Dean); Holly and the Ivy, The (Hollywood Pops Orchestra); Coventry Carol, The (Shore, Dinah)
Side 2: Little Drummer Boy, The (Korean Orphan Choir); Sing We Now of Christmas (Ford, Tennessee Ernie); What Child Is This (Lettermen, The); Jesu, Joy of Man's Desiring (Hollywood Pops Orchestra); Caroling, Caroling (Voices of Christmas); O Tannenbaum (Hollywood Bowl Symphony Orchestra)

| Christmas Album, A | Columbia PC 39466 | 1984 | 2.50 | 5.00 | 10.00 |

Side 1: White Christmas (Sinatra, Frank); It's the Most Wonderful Time of the Year (Williams, Andy); Sleigh Ride (Mathis, Johnny); Winter Wonderland (Miller, Mitch); Christmas Song, The (Bennett, Tony)
Side 2: Jingle Bells? (Streisand, Barbra); Joy to the World (Faith, Percy); O Come, All Ye Faithful (Nabors, Jim); Deck the Halls with Boughs of Holly (Mormon Tabernacle Choir); Have Yourself a Merry Little Christmas (Goulet, Robert); We Wish You a Merry Christmas (Kostelanetz, Andre)

| Christmas Album, The | (2) | Columbia C2 30763 | 1972 | 3.75 | 7.50 | 15.00 |
| Christmas America | | Capitol Special Markets SL-6884 | 1973 | 3.00 | 6.00 | 12.00 |

Side 1: Christmas America — Part One (Hollywood Pops Orchestra); White Christmas (Waring, Fred, and the Pennsylvanians); Christmas Song, The (Cole, Nat King); Hark, the Herald Angels Sing (Fitzgerald, Ella); Winter Wonderland (Martin, Dean); Over the River and Through the Woods (Hollywood Pops Orchestra)
Side 2: There's No Place Like Home (Campbell, Glen); Christmas Waltz, The (Lee, Peggy); My Favorite Things (Ford, Tennessee Ernie); Have Yourself a Merry Little Christmas (Crosby, Bing); Silent Night (Shore, Dinah); Christmas America — Part Two (Hollywood Pops Orchestra)

Title		Label, Number	Year	VG	VG+	NM
Christmas America, Album Two		Capitol Special Markets SL-6950	1974	3.00	6.00	12.00

Side 1: Christmas America - Suite No. 1 (Hollywood Pops Orchestra); Christmas Wishes (Murray, Anne); Santa Claus and Popcorn (Haggard, Merle); It Must Be Getting Close to Christmas (Campbell, Glen); Medley: Hark the Herald Angels Sing/It Came Upon a Midnight Clear (Crosby, Bing); Silent Night (Newton, Wayne)
Side 2: Hymn to Christmas, A (Hollywood Pops Orchestra); First Noel, The (Cole, Nat King); What Will the New Year Bring (Fargo, Donna); Mr. and Mrs. Snowman (Clark, Roy); O Holy Night (Lettermen, The); Christmas America - Suite No. 2 (Hollywood Pops Orchestra)

Title		Label, Number	Year	VG	VG+	NM
Christmas As It Happened	DJ	Mennonite Hour TR4H-5299/5300	1966	3.00	6.00	12.00

— "A series of seven 'newscasts' of the memorable events leading up to the birth of Jesus Christ"; tracks have locked grooves; possibly issued without a cover
Side 1: Day 1 Promo; Day 1 Newscast; Day 2 Promo; Day 2 Newscast; Day 3 Promo; Day 3 Newscast; Day 4 Promo; Day 4 Newscast
Side 2: Day 5 Promo; Day 5 Newscast; Day 6 Promo; Day 6 Newscast; Christmas Day Promo; Christmas Day Wrap Up

Title		Label, Number	Year	VG	VG+	NM
Christmas Carol, A/Music of Christmas	M	MGM E3222	1955	7.50	15.00	30.00

— Expanded version of 10-inch LP (see "Barrymore, Lionel")
Side 1: Christmas Carol, A (Barrymore, Lionel, as Ebenezer Scrooge)
Side 2: Medley: Deck the Halls/I Saw Three Ships; God Rest Ye Merry Gentlemen; While Shepherds Watched Their Flocks; Angels We Have Heard on High; Away in a Manger; O Holy Night; In the Bleak Mid-Winter; What Child Is This?; Coventry Carol (all by Canterbury Choir, The)

Title		Label, Number	Year	VG	VG+	NM
Christmas Carousel	(2)	Capitol SQBE-94406	1972	3.75	7.50	15.00

— Available only through the Capitol Record Club
Side 1: Let It Snow! Let It Snow! Let It Snow (Martin, Dean); Jingle Bells (Hollyridge Strings, The); O Come All Ye Faithful (Martino, Al); Snowbird (Murray, Anne);Good King Wenceslas (Wagner, Roger, Chorale)
Side 2: Caroling, Caroling (Cole, Nat King); Silent Night (Shore, Dinah); O Harken Ye (Ford, Tennessee Ernie); Silver Bells (Newton, Wayne); Christmas Song, The (Rose, David)
Side 3: First Noel, The (Voices of Christmas); Winter Wonderland (Stafford, Jo); There's No Place Like Home (Campbell, Glen); Little Drummer Boy (Lee, Peggy); Have Yourself a Merry Little Christmas (Rawls, Lou)
Side 4: Medley: What Child Is This/The Holly and the Ivy (Crosby, Bing); O Little Town of Bethlehem (Fitzgerald, Ella); White Christmas (Waring, Fred, and the Pennsylvanians); Santa Claus Is Coming to Town (Sandler and Young); Star Carol, The (Lee, Peggy)

Title		Label, Number	Year	VG	VG+	NM
Christmas Classics (Golden Archive Series)		Rhino R1 70192	1988	3.75	7.50	15.00
Christmas Country		Elektra 5E-554	1981	3.00	6.00	12.00
Christmas Day		Pickwick SPC 1010	197?	3.00	6.00	12.00

Side 1: Deck the Halls (Lee, Peggy); O Come All Ye Faithful (Martino, Al); Christmas Day (Beach Boys, The); God Rest Ye Merry Gentlemen (Ford, Tennessee Ernie); White Christmas (Lee, Peggy)
Side 2: Do You Hear What I Hear (Sandler and Young); Away in a Manger (Cole, Nat King); O Little Town of Bethlehem (Lombardo, Guy); Joy to the World (Wagner, Roger, Chorale); Silent Night (Fitzgerald, Ella)

Title		Label, Number	Year	VG	VG+	NM
Christmas Day in the Country		Columbia Special Products P 11887	1973	2.50	5.00	10.00
Christmas Eve with Colonel Sanders		RCA Victor PRS-256	1967	5.00	10.00	20.00

— Sold only at Kentucky Fried Chicken restaurants
Side 1: White Christmas (Reeves, Jim); O Little Town of Bethlehem (Kerr, Anita, Singers); Medley: Up on the Housetop/Jingle Bells (Cramer, Floyd); Medley: Hark! The Herald Angels Sing/Good King Wenceslas/God Rest Ye Merry, Gentlemen (Hugo and Luigi Children's Chorus); O Come, All Ye Faithful (Atkins, Chet); Medley: Winter Wonderland/Silver Bells (Mancini, Henry)
Side 2: Joy to the World (Damone, Vic); I Heard the Bells on Christmas Day (Atkins, Chet); Little Drummer Boy, The (Luboff, Norman, Choir); Christmas Festival, A (Medley) (Boston Pops Orchestra [Fiedler])

Title		Label, Number	Year	VG	VG+	NM
Christmas Festival of Songs and Carols	M	RCA Victor PRM-170	1964	3.00	6.00	12.00
Christmas Festival of Songs and Carols	S	RCA Victor PRS-170	1964	3.75	7.50	15.00

— Above two sold only at JCPenney department stores

Title		Label, Number	Year	VG	VG+	NM
Christmas Festival of Songs and Carols, Volume 2	M	RCA Victor PRM-195	1965	3.00	6.00	12.00
Christmas Festival of Songs and Carols, Volume 2	S	RCA Victor PRS-195	1965	3.75	7.50	15.00

— Above two sold only at JCPenney department stores
Side 1: Medley: We Wish You a Merry Christmas/Jingle Bells (Hugo and Luigi Children's Chorus); Little Drummer Boy (Atkins, Chet); Sleigh Ride(Melachrino Strings, The); Christmas Song, The (Ames Brothers, The); O Come, All Ye Faithful (Reeves, Jim); White Christmas (Luboff, Norman, Choir)
Side 2: O Holy Night (Lanza, Mario); Nutcracker, The: Overture/Dance of the Sugar Plum Fairy (Boston Pops Orchestra [Fiedler]); Angels We Have Heard on High (Shaw, Robert, Chorale); Medley: Hark! The Herald Angels Sing/O Little Town of Bethlehem/Silent Night (Gary, John)

Title		Label, Number	Year	VG	VG+	NM
Christmas for the 90's, Volume 1		Capitol Nashville 1P 8117	1990	3.75	7.50	15.00

— Available on vinyl through Columbia House only
Side 1: Rockin' Around the Christmas Tree (Rabbitt, Eddie); Blue Christmas (Sawyer Brown); Winter Wonderland (Tucker, Tanya); Jingle Bell Rock (Wild Rose); I'll Be Home for Christmas (Bogguss, Suzy)
Side 2: God Rest Ye Merry, Gentlemen (Brooks, Garth); Little Drummer Boy, The (Gatlin Brothers, The); Christmas Song, The (Campbell, Glen); Silver Bells (Dalton, Lacy J.); Thank God for Kids (Raven, Eddy)

Title		Label, Number	Year	VG	VG+	NM
Christmas for the 90's, Volume 2		Capitol Nashville 1P 8118	1990	3.75	7.50	15.00

— Available on vinyl through Columbia House only
Side 1: Star of Bethlehem (Wild Rose); Silent Night (Brooks, Garth); First Noel, The (Bogguss, Suzy); O Holy Night (Campbell, Glen); Have Yourself a Merry Little Christmas (Rabbitt, Eddie)
Side 2: Away in a Manger (Dalton, Lacy J.); Do You Hear What I Hear (Gatlin Brothers, The); What Child Is This (Tucker, Tanya); White Christmas (Raven, Eddy); Please Come Home for Christmas (Sawyer Brown)

(Top left) "A Charlie Brown Christmas," the TV special, basically in its entirety, appears on this lavish children's record from 1977. It also includes a 12-page booklet with the complete text and numerous Charles M. Schulz illustrations. (Top right) This spoken-word recording by the former Tevye from *Fiddler on the Roof* was done with Dr. Seuss' blessing and released through Scholastic Book Services in 1975. (Bottom left) Many collectible Christmas various-artists sets have an Elvis Presley track on them. This one, available through Tupperware in 1987, has his "I'll Be Home for Christmas" and can fetch up to $30 Near Mint. (Bottom right) The Columbia House record club made dozens of exclusive vinyl pressings in the early 1990s, of which this, *Christmas for the 90's, Volume 1,* was one. Among its tracks is one by Garth Brooks.

Title		Label, Number	Year	VG	VG+	NM
Christmas Gift for You from Phil Spector, A	M	Philles PHLP-4005	1963	37.50	75.00	150.00

— *First pressings have blue and black labels*
    Side 1: White Christmas (Love, Darlene); Frosty the Snowman (Ronettes, The); Bells of St. Mary's, The (Bob B. Soxx and the Blue Jeans); Santa Claus Is Coming to Town (Crystals, The); Sleigh Ride (Ronettes, The); Marshmallow World, A (Love, Darlene)
    Side 2: I Saw Mommy Kissing Santa Claus (Ronettes, The); Rudolph, the Red-Nosed Reindeer (Crystals, The); Winter Wonderland (Love, Darlene); Parade of the Wooden Soldiers (Crystals, The); Christmas (Baby Please Come Home) (Love, Darlene); Here Comes Santa Claus (Bob B. Soxx and the Blue Jeans); Silent Night (Spector, Phil, and Artists)

Title		Label, Number	Year	VG	VG+	NM
Christmas Gift for You from Phil Spector, A	M	Philles PHLP-4005	1964	20.00	40.00	80.00

— *Second pressings have yellow and red labels*

Title		Label, Number	Year	VG	VG+	NM
Christmas Gift for You from Phil Spector, A	M	Phil Spector/Rhino RNLP 70235	1987	3.00	6.00	12.00

— *Reissue of above album*

Title		Label, Number	Year	VG	VG+	NM
Christmas Gift for You from Phil Spector, A	M	Phil Spector/Abkco D1-4005	1989	5.00	10.00	20.00

— *Still another reissue of above LP*

Title		Label, Number	Year	VG	VG+	NM
Christmas Greetings		Columbia Special Products CSS 1433	1970	2.50	5.00	10.00

    Side 1: O Come All Ye Faithful (Goulet, Robert); Hark! The Herald Angels Sing (Layton, Eddie); Here We Come a-Caroling (New Christy Minstrels, The); Away in a Manger (Griffin, Ken); Medley: Good Christian Men Rejoice/O Holy Night (Philadelphia Brass Ensemble)
    Side 2: Medley: March of the Toys/Toyland (Kostelanetz, Andre); Jingle Bells (Ives, Burl); Good King Wenceslas (Byrd, Charlie); Joy to the World (Conniff, Ray); Hallelujah Chorus (Mormon Tabernacle Choir)

Title		Label, Number	Year	VG	VG+	NM
Christmas Greetings		Columbia Special Products CSS 1499	1970	2.50	5.00	10.00

— *Sold only at A&P grocery stores*
    Side 1: Deck the Hall with Boughs of Holly (Conniff, Ray); Sleigh Ride (Kostelanetz, Andre); Christmas Spirit, The (Cash, Johnny); White Christmas (Mathis, Johnny); Happy Holiday (Lawrence, Steve, and Eydie Gorme); O Little Town of Bethlehem (Streisand, Barbra)
    Side 2: Santa Claus Is Comin' to Town (Miller, Mitch); Twelve Days of Christmas, The (Mormon Tabernacle Choir); Count Your Blessings Instead of Sheep (Wynette, Tammy); God Rest Ye Merry, Gentlemen (Faith, Percy); O Come All Ye Faithful (Goulet, Robert); Hark! The Herald Angels Sing (Jackson, Mahalia)

Title		Label, Number	Year	VG	VG+	NM
Christmas Greetings, Vol. 2		Columbia Special Products C 10???	1971	2.50	5.00	10.00

— *Sold only at A&P grocery stores*

Title		Label, Number	Year	VG	VG+	NM
Christmas Greetings, Vol. 3		Columbia Special Products P 11383	1972	2.50	5.00	10.00

— *Sold only at A&P grocery stores*
    Side 1: Skater's Waltz (Kostelanetz, Andre); Medley: We Wish You a Merry Christmas/Silent Night/O Come All Ye Faithful/Jingle Bells/Where Is Love (Bennett, Tony); It Came Upon a Midnight Clear (Carr, Vikki); Blue Christmas (Cash, Johnny); Christmas Song, The (Burnett, Carol); O Holy Night (Mathis, Johnny); Ave Maria(Moffo, Anna)
    Side 2: Have Yourself a Merry Little Christmas (Streisand, Barbra); Joy to the World (Philadelphia Orchestra [Ormandy]); Mr. Mistletoe (Anderson, Lynn); Greensleeves (Lindsay, Mark); Toyland (Day, Doris); Here's to You (Grant, Cary)

Title		Label, Number	Year	VG	VG+	NM
Christmas Greetings, Vol. 4		Columbia Special Products P 11987	1973	3.00	6.00	12.00

— *Sold only at A&P grocery stores*
    Side 1: We Wish You a Merry Christmas (Reynolds, Debbie); Secret of Christmas, The (Andrews, Julie); Deck the Hall with Boughs of Holly (Mann, Johnny, Singers); O Little Town of Bethlehem (Williams, Andy); Silent Night, Holy Night (Streisand, Barbra); Twelve Days of Christmas, The (Mormon Tabernacle Choir)
    Side 2: What Child Is This? (Carr, Vikki); White Christmas (Bennett, Tony); Joy to the World (Faith, Percy); O Come, All Ye Faithful (Merrill, Robert); Jingle Bells (Price, Ray);Auld Lang Syne (Lombardo, Guy)

Title		Label, Number	Year	VG	VG+	NM
Christmas Greetings from Nashville		Columbia PC 39467	1984	2.50	5.00	10.00

    Side 1: Winter Wonderland (Nelson, Willie); Jingle Bells (Jones, George); Santa Claus Is Coming to Town (Haggard, Merle); White Christmas (Gilley, Mickey); Don't Wish Me Merry Christmas (Anderson, Lynn); Rudolph, the Red-Nosed Reindeer (Autry, Gene)
    Side 2: O Holy Night (Gatlin, Larry, and the Gatlin Brothers); Silent Night, Holy Night (Wynette, Tammy); Joy to the World (Cash, Johnny); Hark! The Herald Angels Sing (Robbins, Marty); East Tennessee Christmas (Atkins, Chet)

Title		Label, Number	Year	VG	VG+	NM
Christmas Greetings from Nashville		RCA Victor CPL1-0262	1973	3.00	6.00	12.00
Christmas Hits from Warner Bros.	DJ	Warner Bros. 8467/8	1959	12.50	25.00	50.00
Christmas in California		RCA Victor PRS-276	1968	3.00	6.00	12.00

— *Available only from Bank of America*
    Side 1: Deck the Halls (Damone, Vic); Sleigh Ride (Boston Pops Orchestra [Fiedler]); Here Comes Santa Claus (Hirt, Al); Let It Snow, Let It Snow, Let It Snow (Ames, Ed); Medley: Jingle Bells/Winter Wonderland (Nero, Peter); I'll Be Home for Christmas (Cantrell, Lana)
    Side 2: Good King Wenceslas (Gould, Morton); O Little Town of Bethlehem (Mancini, Henry); Medley: O Come All Ye Faithful/Angels We Have Heard on High (Shaw, Robert, Chorale); Star in the East, A (Belafonte, Harry); Medley: Hark the Herald Angels Sing/God Rest Ye Merry Gentlemen/The First Noel (Luboff, Norman, Choir); Ave Maria (Price, Leontyne)

Title		Label, Number	Year	VG	VG+	NM
Christmas in Italy	M	Capitol T 10093	196?	3.75	7.50	15.00
Christmas in Italy	R	Capitol SM-10093	197?	2.50	5.00	10.00

    Side 1: E Nato Gesu (Coro di Allune della piccola Casa San Giuseppe); Buon Natale (Coro di Allune della piccola Casa San Giuseppe); Pastorale(Guarino, Gian Mario, Orchestra diretta da); Presepe(Guarino, Gian Mario, Orchestra diretta da); Notte Sacra (Cordova e Coro, Alvaro); Bianco Natale
    Side 2: La Ninna Nanna a Gesu (Lipparini, R., tenor); La Stella di Betlemme (Coro di Allune della piccola Casa San Giuseppe); Alla Luce d'una Stella (Capella Musicale della Basilica di San Francisco in Assisi); Campane di Natale (Capella Musicale della Basilica di San Francisco in Assisi); Cantico d'Amore; Dolce Risveglio (Coro di Allune della piccola Casa San Giuseppe)

Title		Label, Number	Year	VG	VG+	NM
Christmas in New York	M	RCA Victor PRM-257	1967	3.00	6.00	12.00

Title		Label, Number	Year	VG	VG+	NM

Christmas in New York   S   RCA Victor PRS-257   1967   3.75   7.50   15.00
- Side 1: Silver Bells (Smith, Kate); Christmas Song, The (Mancini, Henry); Little Drummer Boy, The (Gould, Morton); Rudolph the Red-Nosed Reindeer (Boston Pops Orchestra [Fiedler]); White Christmas (Luboff, Norman, Choir); Santa Claus Is Coming to Town (Damone, Vic)
- Side 2: What Child Is This (Ames, Ed); Medley: Joy to the World/It Came Upon a Midnight Clear (Shaw, Robert, Chorale); Silent Night (Anderson, Marian); First Noel, The (Lanza, Mario); Hallelujah Chorus (Royal Philharmonic Orchestra [Beecham]); O Holy Night (Peerce, Jan)

Christmas in New York Volume 2   RCA Victor PRS-270   1968   3.00   6.00   12.00
- Side 1: Deck the Halls (Damone, Vic); Sleigh Ride (Boston Pops Orchestra [Fiedler]; Here Comes Santa Claus (Hirt, Al); Let It Snow! Let It Snow! Let It Snow! (Ames, Ed); Medley: Winter Wonderland/Jingle Bells (Nero, Peter); I'll Be Home for Christmas (Cantrell, Lana)
- Side 2: Good King Wenceslas (Gould, Morton); O Little Town of Bethlehem (Mancini, Henry); Medley: O Come, All Ye Faithful/Angels We Have Heard on High (Shaw, Robert, Chorale); Star in the East, A (Belafonte, Harry); Medley: Hark! The Herald Angels Sing/God Rest Ye Merry, Gentlemen/The First Noel (Luboff, Norman, Choir); Ave Maria (Price, Leontyne)

Christmas in Norway   M   Capitol T 10377   196?   3.75   7.50   15.00
- Side 1: Jeg Er Sa Glad Hver Julekveld (Werner, Olav); Kimer, I Klokker (Soelvguttene Boys Choir); Et Barn Er Fodt I Bethlehem (Werner, Olav); Jeg Synger Julekvad (Soelvguttene Boys Choir); Her Kommer Dine Arme Sma (Werner, Olav); Du Gronne Glitrende Tre Goddag (Soelvguttene Boys Choir)
- Side 2: Glade Jul (Werner, Olav); Deilig Er Den Himmel Bla (Soelvguttene Boys Choir); O Jul Med Din Glede (Werner, Olav); Deilig Er Jorden (Soelvguttene Boys Choir); Det Kimer Nu Til Julefest (Werner, Olav); O Du Herlige (Soelvguttene Boys Choir)

Christmas in Saint Louis   (no label) TS77-558/9   1977   3.75   7.50   15.00
— *Record is not banded, but here are the titles and artists:*
- Side 1: Introduction (Fender, Harry); I Hear America Singing (M.A.C. Apollos and Orchestra); Dedication (Danforth, William H.); Christmas Caroling Song (Executive Committee, St. Louis Christmas Carols Association); Gospel According to St. Matthew and St. Luke (Simmons, Ted); Angels We Have Heard on High (Saint Louis County Community Chorus); Gospel According to St. Luke (Simmons, Ted);How Far Is It to Bethlehem? (Lindenwood Colleges Madrigal Singers); Christmas Morn Is Dawning (St. Charles Children's Chorus); Scrooge from A Christmas Carol (Wachter, Emil, with Fred Ahrens, Elmer Drehmanand George Frangoulis)
- Side 2: Jingle Bells (Fender, Harry); Santa's Clause (Carney, Jack, and Harry Fender); Do You Hear What I Hear? (Moolah Chanters El Koran); All I Want for Christmas . . . (Santa Claus and Child); Santa Claus Is Coming to Town (Lester Family, The); Greetings to St. Louis City (Conway, James F.); Silver Bells (Groom, Suzanne); Greetings to St. Louis County (McNary, Gene); We Wish You a Merry Christmas (Dierdorf, Dan/Jeff Severson/St. Louis Football Cardinals); Christmas Memory, A (Wickes, Mary); Have Yourself a Merry Little Christmas (Wyman, Karen)

Christmas in San Francisco   Embarcadero Center EC-101   1974   3.75   7.50   15.00
— *Featuring members of the San Francisco, Oakland and San Jose Symphonies, the San Francisco and Western Operas, etc.; not all tracks have artists identified.*
- Side 1: Montage: The Sounds of Christmas in San Francisco; On This Day; Magnificat: Gloria: Sicut Erat in Principio; Silent Night (Grace Cathedral Boys' and Men's Choir); La Volta (Campbell, Jeanette); Noel, Joseph Est Bien Marie; Noel Etranger (Fenstermaker, John); O Come Emmanuel (Grace Cathedral Men's Choir)
- Side 2: Sing a Song of Christmas; Posida-s (Guerrero, Juan); Allegro from Sonata No. 4 for Flute and Continuo; Il est ne le Divin Enfant (Le Choeur de Notre Dame des Victoires); D'Amour Je Suis de Sheriter (Silverstein, Steve); Hallelujah Chorus; Grace Cathedral Bells

Christmas in the Air   RCA Special Products DPL1-0133   1975   2.50   5.00   10.00
- Side 1: Hallelujah Chorus (Royal Philharmonic Orchestra [Beecham]); Silent Night (Martin, Tony); Silver Bells (Smith, Kate); Angels We Have Heard on High (Fox, Virgil); Away in a Manger (Franchi, Sergio)
- Side 2: Christmas Song, The (Maye, Marilyn); Deck the Halls (Damone, Vic); Medley: We Three Kings/Good King Wenceslas (MacKenzie, Gisele); Medley: The First Noel/O Come, All Ye Faithful/O Holy Night (Gary, John)

Christmas in the Stars: Star Wars Christmas Album   RSO RS-1-3093   1980   3.75   7.50   15.00
— *Concept album with Meco, Anthony Daniels as C3PO, Maury Yeston, Ron McBrien and John Bongiovi (later Jon Bon Jovi!)*
- Side 1: Christmas in the Stars; Bells, Bells, Bells; Odds Against Christmas, The; What Can You Get a Wookiee for Christmas (When He Already Owns a Comb?); R2-D2 We Wish You a Merry Christmas
- Side 2: Sleigh Ride; Merry, Merry Christmas; Christmas Sighting, A ('Twas the Night Before Christmas); Meaning of Christmas, The

Christmas Is...   Columbia Special Products P 11417   1972   3.00   6.00   12.00
— *Sold only at Goodyear tire dealers*
- Side 1: Christmas Is... (Hillside Singers, The); Winter Wonderland (Stafford, Jo); White Christmas (Sinatra, Frank); Have Yourself a Merry Little Christmas (Garland, Judy); What Child Is This? (Carr, Vikki); Santa Claus Is Comin' to Town (Bennett, Tony); Christmas Song, The (Streisand, Barbra)
- Side 2: It's Beginning to Look Like Christmas (Crosby, Bing); I'll Be Home for Christmas (Day, Doris); O Holy Night (Williams, Andy); Jingle Bells (Mills Brothers, The); Silver Bells (Page, Patti); Merry Christmas Darling (Carpenters); Silent Night, Holy Night (Andrews, Julie); Christmas Is... (Reprise) (Hillside Singers, The)

Christmas Memories Played on Antique Musical Boxes   Classic Christmas CC 1934   1977   2.50   5.00   10.00
From anonymous sources.
- Side 1: O Tannenbaum; O Sanctissima; Silent Night; Among Shepherds; Holy City, The; Among Shepherds; Every Year Anew; O Come Little Children
- Side 2: O Tannenbaum; O Come Little Children; See the Conquering Hero; Cloister Bells; Ave Maria (Bach-Gounod); Adeste Fideles; Monastery Bells

Christmas Night in Bethlehem: The Midnight Ceremony at St. Catherine's Church   ABC Dunhill DS-55002   1968   3.75   7.50   15.00
— *Recording of the 1967 midnight Mass in the Holy Land; with 24-page booklet*
- Side 1: Matins:Christus Natus Est Nobis/Jesus Redemptor/Lesson; Silent Night; Midnight Mass: Dominus Dixit Ad Me/Kyrie/Gloria
- Side 2: Midnight Mass Continued: De Gradual/Alleluia/The Gospel/Credo/Offertory/Preface/Sanctus/Benedictus/Agnus Dei; Adeste Fideles; Jesus Redemptor; Bells

Title	Label, Number	Year	VG	VG+	NM
Christmas on Death Row	Death Row/Interscope INT2-90108	1996	3.75	7.50	15.00

Side 1: Santa Claus Goes Straight to the Ghetto (Snoop Doggy Dogg featuring Nate Dogg); Christmas Song, The (Danny Boy); I Wish (Tha Dogg Pound); Silver Bells (Michel'le)

Side 2: Peaceful Christmas (Danny Boy); Christmas in the Ghetto (O.F.T.B.); Silent Night (B.G.O.T.I. and 6 Feet Deep & Guess); Be Thankful (Nate Dogg)

Side 3: On This Glorious Day (816); Frosty the Snowman (6 Feet Deep); O Holy Night (B.G.O.T.I.); Party 4 Da Homies (Thomas, Sean Barney, featuring J. Flex)

Side 4: White Christmas (Guess); This Christmas (Danny Boy); Have Yourself a Merry Little Christmas (6 Feet Deep); Christmas Everyday (Guess)

| Christmas Programming from RCA Victor   DJ | RCA Victor SP-33-66 | 1959 | 250.00 | 500.00 | 1,000. |

— Promo-only collection; has been counterfeited, but originals have color covers

Side 1: Home for the Holidays Presumably the re-recording (Como, Perry); White Christmas (Klein, John); Rudolph, the Red-Nosed Reindeer (Boston Pops Orchestra [Fiedler]); Silent Night (Tozzi, Giorgio, and Rosalind Ellis); Blue Christmas (Esquivel); Santa Claus Is Comin' to Town (Hunter, Ralph)

Side 2: Ding Dong Dandy Christmas (Three Suns, The); I'll Be Home for Christmas (Presley, Elvis); O Christmas Tree (Lanza, Mario); Hallelujah Chorus (Royal Philharmonic Orchestra); Winter Wonderland (Melachrino, George, Orchestra); O Little Town of Bethlehem(Shea, George Beverly)

| Christmas Rap | Profile 1247 | 1987 | 2.50 | 5.00 | 10.00 |
| Christmas Record, A | Ze/Passport PB 6020 | 1982 | 5.00 | 10.00 | 20.00 |

Side 1: Things Fall Apart (Cristina); Hey Lord (Suicide); Christmas Is Coming (Three Courgettes, The); Christmas with Satan (White, James)

Side 2: Christmas Wrapping (Waitresses, The); Christmas on Riverside Drive (Darnell, August); It's a Holiday (Material with Nona Hendryx); Christmas Time in the Motor City (Was [Not Was]); It's a Big Country (Sigerson, Davitt)

| Christmas Rock Album, The | Priority SL 9465 | 1986 | 3.75 | 7.50 | 15.00 |

Side 1: White Christmas (Squier, Billy); Thank God It's Christmas (Queen); Father Christmas (Kinks, The); Run Rudolph Run (Edmunds, Dave); Silent Night (Bishop, Elvin)

Side 2: Merry Christmas, Baby (Beach Boys, The); Step Into Christmas (John, Elton); Christmas Is the Time to Say I Love You (Squier, Billy); Christmas Wrapping (Waitresses, The); All I Want for Christmas Is You (Foghat)

| Christmas Song, The, And Other Favorites | Columbia Special Products P 12446 | 1974 | 2.50 | 5.00 | 10.00 |

Side 1: Silver Bells (Mathis, Johnny); I Heard the Bells on Christmas Day (Williams, Andy); Ring Christmas Bells (Conniff, Ray); Sleigh Ride (Lawrence, Andre);Christmas Song, The (Burnett, Carol)

Side 2: Little Drummer Boy (Faith, Percy); Deck the Hall with Boughs of Holly (Mann, Johnny, Singers); Santa Claus Is Coming to Town (Lawrence, Steve, and Eydie Gorme); There's No Place Like Home (Reynolds, Debbie); Twelve Days of Christmas, The (Mormon Tabernacle Choir)

| Christmas Songs, The | (2) | Capitol SLB-57074 | 1988 | 3.75 | 7.50 | 15.00 |

Side 1: Christmas Song, The (Cole, Nat King); Little Drummer Boy, The (Lettermen, The); Away in a Manger (Gentry, Bobbie); Joy to the World (Hollywood Bowl Symphony Orchestra [Dragon]); Happy Holiday (Lee, Peggy); Silent Night (Newton, Wayne); It Came Upon a Midnight Clear (Wagner, Roger, Chorale)

Side 2: I'll Be Home for Christmas (Campbell, Glen); Rudolph, the Red-Nosed Reindeer (Martin, Dean); Let It Snow! Let It Snow! Let It Snow! (Horne, Lena); Have Yourself a Merry Little Christmas (Rawls, Lou); I Wish You a Merry Christmas (Crosby, Bing); Hark! The Herald Angels Sing (Fitzgerald, Ella); O Tannenbaum (Kenton, Stan); God Rest Ye Merry, Gentlemen (Ford, Tennessee Ernie)

Side 3: Deck the Hall (Hollywood Bowl Symphony Orchestra [Newman]); Do You Hear What I Hear (Crosby, Bing); Angels We Have Heard on High (Fitzgerald, Ella); Twelve Days of Christmas, The (Ford, Tennessee Ernie); Silver Bells (Haggard, Merle); Jingle Bells (Mann, Johnny, Singers); O Come All Ye Faithful (Martino, Al); Here Comes Santa Claus (Lombardo, Guy, and the Royal Canadians)

Side 4: Santa Claus Is Coming to Town (Beach Boys, The); White Christmas (Martin, Dean); O Holy Night (Crosby, Bing); O Little Town on Bethlehem (Cole, Nat King); Sleigh Ride (Ferrante and Teicher); Winter Wonderland (Horne, Lena); What Child Is This (Wagner, Roger, Chorale)

| Christmas Songs, The, Volume II | Capitol SL-57065 | 1989 | 3.00 | 6.00 | 12.00 |

Side 1: Joy to the World (Murray, Anne); Star Carol, The (Ford, Tennessee Ernie); Sing We Noel (Kingston Trio, The); First Noel, The (Fitzgerald, Ella); We Three Kings of Orient Are (Beach Boys, The)

Side 2: Baby, It's Cold Outside (Martin, Dean); Christmas Waltz, The (Wilson, Nancy); Carol of the Bells (Wagner, Roger, Chorale); I've Got My Love to Keep Me Warm (Ferrante and Teicher); Frosty the Snowman (Jan and Dean)

| Christmas Sounds of Music, The | Capitol Creative Products SL-6643 | 1969 | 3.00 | 6.00 | 12.00 |

— Sold only at B.F. Goodrich tire dealers

Side 1: There's No Place Like Home; Have Yourself a Merry Little Christmas; Silent Night, Holy Night; Night Before Christmas, The (all by Campbell, Glen)

Side 2: Christmas Song, The (Sandler and Young); Away in a Manger (Gentry, Bobbie); White Christmas (Lettermen, The); O Little Town of Bethlehem (Fitzgerald, Ella); Scarlet Ribbons (Gentry, Bobbie); O Holy Night (Lettermen, The)

| Christmas Stocking | M | Capitol NP 90494 | 1965 | 3.75 | 7.50 | 15.00 |
| Christmas Stocking | S | Capitol SNP 90494 | 1965 | 3.75 | 7.50 | 15.00 |

— Above two available only through the Capitol Record Club

Side 1: Christmas Song, The (Cole, Nat King); Deck the Halls (Dunstedter, Eddie); God Rest Ye Merry, Gentlemen (Martin, Dean); Santa Claus Is Comin' to Town (Lee, Peggy); Jingle Bells (Lombardo, Guy); Little Drummer Boy (Wagner, Roger, Chorale)

Side 2: White Christmas (Martino, Al); Silver Bells (Thompson, Hank); Rudolph, the Red-Nosed Reindeer (Martin, Dean); Santa's Gonna Come in a Stagecoach Cover misidentifies song as "Santa's Comin in a Stage Coach"; label has correct title (Owens, Buck); We Wish You a Merry Christmas (Kingston Trio, The); O Tannenbaum (Hollywood Bowl Symphony Orchestra [Dragon])

Title	Label, Number	Year	VG	VG+	NM
Christmas Through the Years (5) Reader's Digest RDA-143		1984	5.00	10.00	20.00

— Available only through Reader's Digest magazine by mail order

Side 1: Sleigh Ride (Boston Pops Orchestra [Fiedler]); Have Yourself a Merry Little Christmas (Como, Perry); Little Drummer Boy, The (Simeone, Harry, Chorale); Christmas Eve in My Home Town (Smith, Kate); Silver Bells (Como, Perry); Silent Night (Crosby, Bing)

Side 2: (There's No Place Like) Home for the Holidays *Original 1954 recording* (Como, Perry); White Christmas (Martin, Freddy); Let It Snow! Let It Snow! Let It Snow! (Monroe, Vaughn); Christmas Song, The (Como, Perry); Jolly Old St. Nicholas (Ames Brothers, The); Rudolph the Red-Nosed Reindeer (Crosby, Bing)

Side 3: Mary's Boy Child (Belafonte, Harry); Carol of the Bells (Simeone, Harry, Chorale); Santa Claus Is Comin' to Town (Welk, Lawrence); Christmas in Killarney (Day, Dennis); Family Christmas, A *Released on 45 as "A Crosby Christmas"* (Crosby, Bing); Frosty the Snow Man (Lombardo, Guy)

Side 4: Marshmallow World, A (Crosby, Bing); Here Comes Santa Claus (Fisher, Eddie); It's Beginning to Look Like Christmas (Como, Perry); I Saw Mommy Kissing Santa Claus (Jones, Spike, and His City Slickers); Jingle Bell Rock (Helms, Bobby); Nuttin' for Christmas (Freberg, Stan)

Side 5: O Holy Night (Lettermen, The); I Wish It Could Be Christmas Forever (Como, Perry); Medley: Deck the Halls/Joy to the World/It Came Upon the Midnight Clear (Smith, Kate); Away in a Manger (Ames, Ed); Do You Hear What I Hear? (Crosby, Bing)

Side 6: Christmas Waltz (Lettermen, The); Old Christmas Card, An (Reeves, Jim); Christmas Is (Fireside Singers, The); Pretty Paper (Orbison, Roy); Jingle Bells (Singing Dogs, The, Don Charles Presents); Rockin' Around the Christmas Tree (Lee, Brenda); Feliz Navidad (Feliciano, Jose)

Side 7: Adeste Fideles (Crosby, Bing); O Little Town of Bethlehem (Haymes, Dick); Blue Christmas (Morgan, Russ); Winter Wonderland (Como, Perry); 'Twas the Night Before Christmas (Waring, Fred, and the Pennsylvanians)

Side 8: I'll Be Home for Christmas (Crosby, Bing); Christmas Dreaming (A Little Early This Year) (Haymes, Dick); Jingle Bells (Miller, Glenn); (All I Want for Christmas Is) My Two Front Teeth (Jones, Spike, and the City Slickers); Merry Christmas Polka, The (Martin, Freddy); I Yust Go Nuts at Christmas (Yorgeson, Yogi)

Side 9 (all by McCarthy, John, Chorale): Here We Come a-Caroling; What Child Is This?; Angels from the Realms of Glory; O Christmas Tree; I Saw Three Ships; Holly and the Ivy, The; O Sanctissima; We Wish You a Merry Christmas

Side 10 (all by Royal Philharmonic Orchestra): Hark! The Herald Angels Sing; We Three Kings of Orient Are; Twelve Days of Christmas, The; God Rest Ye Merry, Gentlemen; Angels We Have Heard on High

| Christmas to Remember, A | Capitol Creative Products SL-6573 | 1968 | 3.00 | 6.00 | 12.00 |

— Sold only at Montgomery Ward stores

Side 1: Hark! The Herald Angels Sing (Hollywood Bowl Symphony Orchestra); Away in a Manger (Cole, Nat King); Happy Holiday (Lee, Peggy); I'll Be Home for Christmas (Martino, Al); Little Drummer Boy, The (Lettermen, The); O Holy Night (Wagner, Roger, Chorale)

Side 2: First Noel, The (Ford, Tennessee Ernie); Rudolph, the Red-Nosed Reindeer (Lombardo, Guy); We Three Kings (Wagner, Roger, Chorale); O Come All Ye Faithful (Martino, Al); Sleigh Ride (Waring, Fred, and the Pennsylvanians); Deck the Hall (Hollywood Bowl Symphony Orchestra)

| Christmas to Remember, A, Vol. 2 | Capitol Creative Products SL-66?? | 1969 | 3.00 | 6.00 | 12.00 |

— Sold only at Montgomery Ward stores

| Christmas to Remember, A, Vol. 3 | Capitol Creative Products SL-6681 | 1970 | 2.50 | 5.00 | 10.00 |

— Sold only at Montgomery Ward stores

Side 1: Christmas Song, The (Lettermen, The); Santa Claus Is Coming to Town (Hollyridge Strings, The); Little Drummer Boy (Lee, Peggy); Hang Your Wishes on the Tree (Baxter, Les); White Christmas (Martino, Al)

Side 2: O Come All Ye Faithful (Fitzgerald, Ella); Joy to the World (Ford, Tennessee Ernie); Medley: Away in a Manger/Silent Night/Caroling, Caroling (Hollywood Pops Orchestra); O Little Town of Bethlehem (Stafford, Jo); Hark! The Herald Angels Sing (Wagner, Roger, Chorale)

| Christmas Tradition, A | Warner Bros. 25630 | 1987 | 3.00 | 6.00 | 12.00 |

Side 1: White Christmas Makes Me Blue (Travis, Randy); Carpenter, A Mother and a King, A (Forester Sisters, The); Colorado Christmas (Nitty Gritty Dirt Band, The); Silent Night (Everly Brothers, The); Have Yourself a Merry Little Christmas (Gayle, Crystal)

Side 2: It Came Upon a Midnight Clear (Highway 101); Cowboys' Christmas Ball, The (Murphey, Michael Martin); Light of the Stable (Harris, Emmylou); Blue Christmas (Raven, Eddy); Sleigh Ride (O'Connor, Mark)

| Christmas Tradition, A, Volume II | Warner Bros. 25762 | 1988 | 2.50 | 5.00 | 10.00 |

Side 1: Rockin' Around the Christmas Tree (Flores, Rosie); Silver Bells (Horn, Jim); Blue Christmas (Highway 101); Santa Claus Is Coming to Town (Murphey, Michael Martin);O Little Town of Bethlehem (McCarters, The)

Side 2: Jingle Bells (A-Strings, The); Run Rudolph Run (Southern Pacific); Santa Claus Is Back in Town (Yoakam, Dwight); I'll Be Home for Christmas (Forester Sisters, The); What Child Is This (O'Connor, Mark)

| Christmas Treasury of Classics from Avon, A | RCA Special Products DPL1-0716 | 1985 | 2.50 | 5.00 | 10.00 |

— Sold only through Avon dealers

Side 1: Medley: Winter Wonderland/Sleigh Ride (Parton, Dolly); Come Dear Children 'Round and 'Round the Christmas Tree (Crosby, Bing); First Noel, The (Cole, Nat King);Deck the Halls (Andrews, Julie); Twelve Days of Christmas, The (Denver, John, and the Muppets)

Side 2: Home for the Holidays (Como, Perry); Silver Bells (Presley, Elvis); Joy to the World (Murray, Anne); Feliz Navidad (Feliciano, Jose); Christmas Song, The(Rogers, Kenny)

| Christmas Trimmings | Columbia Special Products P 12795 | 1975 | 2.50 | 5.00 | 10.00 |

Side 1: Deck the Halls with Boughs of Holly (Mann, Johnny, Singers); White Christmas (Rich, Charlie); Do You Hear What I Hear (Bryant, Anita); It's Christmas Time All Over the World(Davis, Sammy, Jr.); Christmas Song, The (Bennett, Tony); Twelve Days of Christmas, The (Mormon Tabernacle Choir)

Side 2: O Holy Night (Mathis, Johnny); O Come All Ye Faithful (Andrews, Julie); Carol of the Bells (Williams, Andy); What Child Is This (Carr, Vikki); God Rest Ye Merry Gentlemen (Goulet, Robert); Joy to the World (Philadelphia Orchestra [Ormandy])

| Christmas with Andy Williams and the Williams Brothers | Columbia Special Products C 10105 | 1971 | 2.50 | 5.00 | 10.00 |

Side 1: It's the Most Wonderful Time of the Year (Williams, Andy); Kay Thompson's Jingle Bells (Williams Brothers, The); Song for the Christmas Tree (The Twelve Days of Christmas) (Williams, Andy); Holiday Season, The (Williams Brothers, The); First Noel, The (Williams, Andy)

Side 2: Silent Night, Holy Night (Williams, Andy); Medley: O Little Town of Bethlehem/Joy to the World (Williams Brothers, The); Away in a Manger (Williams, Andy); Medley: Deck the Halls/To Santa Claus' House We Go/God Rest Ye Merry Gentlemen/Good King Wenceslas/Hark the Herald Angels Sing/O Come All Ye Faithful (Williams Brothers, The); O Holy Night (Williams, Andy)

Title	Label, Number	Year	VG	VG+	NM
Christmas with Colonel Sanders	RCA Victor PRS-291	1969	5.00	10.00	20.00

— *Sold only at Kentucky Fried Chicken restaurants*
Side 1: Out of the East (Pride, Charley); Sleigh Ride (Boston Pops Orchestra [Fiedler]); Have Yourself a Merry Little Christmas (Gary, John); Good King Wenceslas (Gould, Morton); O Holy Night (Smith, Kate); Mary's Boy Child (Belafonte, Harry)
Side 2: Jingle Bell Rock (Atkins, Chet); Merry Christmas Neighbor (Greene, Lorne; Michael Landon; Dan Blocker); My Favorite Things (Nero, Peter); First Noel, The (Franchi, Sergio); I'll Be Home for Christmas (Cantrell, Lana);Carol for Another Christmas (Mancini, Henry)

Christmas with Eddy Arnold/ Christmas with Henry Mancini	RCA Special Products DPL1-0079	1974	3.00	6.00	12.00

Side 1: Jolly Old St. Nicholas (Arnold, Eddy); Medley: God Rest Ye Merry, Gentlemen/Deck the Halls/Hark! The Herald Angels Sing (Mancini, Henry); Silent Night (Arnold, Eddy); Little Drummer Boy, The (Mancini, Henry); It Came Upon a Midnight Clear (Arnold, Eddy)
Side 2: I Heard the Bells on Christmas Day (Arnold, Eddy); Medley: We Three Kings of Orient Are/O Come, All Ye Faithful/Joy to the World (Mancini, Henry); Up on the Housetop (Arnold, Eddy); Christmas Song, The (Mancini, Henry); O Little Town of Bethlehem (Arnold, Eddy)

Christmas with Glen Campbell and the Hollywood Pops Orchestra	Capitol Creative Products SL-6699	1971	3.00	6.00	12.00
Christmas with Glen Campbell and the Hollywood Pops Orchestra	Capitol Special Markets SL-6699	197?	2.50	5.00	10.00

Side 1: There's No Place Like Home (Campbell, Glen); Holly and the Ivy, The (Hollywood Pops Orchestra); It Must Be Getting Close to Christmas (Campbell, Glen); First Noel, The (Voices of Christmas); Silent Night (Campbell, Glen)
Side 2: Medley: Jingle Bells/Up on the House Top/Jolly Old St. Nicholas (Hollywood Pops Orchestra); I'll Be Home for Christmas (Campbell, Glen); I Heard the Bells on Christmas Day (Voices of Christmas); Adeste Fideles (Hollywood Pops Orchestra); Night Before Christmas, The (Campbell, Glen)

Christmas with Johnny Mathis and Percy Faith	Columbia Special Products P 11805	1973	2.50	5.00	10.00

Side 1 (all by Percy Faith): O Come, All Ye Faithful; It Came Upon the Midnight Clear; Good King Wenceslas; O Holy Night; Joy to the World
Side 2 (all by Johnny Mathis): Sleigh Ride; What Child Is This; Jingle Bell Rock; Silver Bells; Silent Night

Christmas, A Gift of Music	Capitol Special Markets SL-6687	197?	3.00	6.00	12.00

— *Reissue of "Zenith Presents Christmas, A Gift of Music, Vol. 4"*

Christmastime in Carol and Song	M	RCA PRM-271	1968	5.00	10.00	20.00
Christmastime in Carol and Song	S	RCA PRS-271	1968	3.00	6.00	12.00

Side 1: Deck the Halls (Damone, Vic); Sleigh Ride (Boston Pops Orchestra [Fiedler]); Here Comes Santa Claus (Hirt, Al); Let It Snow! Let It Snow! Let It Snow! (Ames, Ed); Medley: Winter Wonderland/Jingle Bells (Nero, Peter); I'll Be Home for Christmas (Cantrell, Lana)
Side 2: Good King Wenceslas (Gould, Morton); O Little Town of Bethlehem (Mancini, Henry); Medley: O Come, All Ye Faithful/Angels We Have Heard on High (Shaw, Robert, Chorale); Star in the East, A (Belafonte, Harry); Medley: Hark! The Herald Angels Sing/God Rest Ye Merry Gentlemen/The First Noel (Luboff, Norman, Choir); Ave Maria (Schubert) (Price, Leontyne)

Christmastime in Carol and Song	RCA PRS-289	1969	3.00	6.00	12.00

Side 1: Medley: Joy to the World/Jingle Bells/Away in a Manger/We Wish You a Merry Christmas (Fiedler, Arthur); Carol of the Bells (Fiedler, Arthur); Go Tell It on the Mountain (Lawrence, Steve); Silent Night (Fiedler, Arthur); Hurry Home for Christmas (Lawrence, Steve, and Eydie Gorme); I Wonder As I Wander (Price, Leontyne)
Side 2: Medley: Here We Come a-Caroling/O Christmas Tree/I Saw Three Ships (Fiedler, Arthur); It Came Upon a Midnight Clear (Gorme, Eydie); Nutcracker Suite Excerpts: Overture/Russian Dance/Dance of the Sugar-Plum Fairy/Dance of the Reed Flutes (Fiedler, Arthur); Ave Maria (Bach-Gounod) (Price, Leontyne); Little Drummer Boy, The (Fiedler, Arthur)

Collection of Christmas Favorites, A	Columbia Special Products P 14988	1979	2.50	5.00	10.00

Side 1: My Favorite Things (Bennett, Tony); Joy to the World (Nabors, Jim); Christmas Song, The (Streisand, Barbra); O Holy Night (Jackson, Mahalia); Happy Holidays (Faith, Percy)
Side 2: God Rest You Merry Gentlemen (Crosby, Bing); White Christmas (Vale, Jerry); Little Drummer Boy (Conniff, Ray, Singers); Sleigh Ride (Kostelanetz, Andre); Angels We Have Heard on High (Goulet, Robert, and Carol Lawrence)

Cool Yule	Rhino RNLP-70073	1985	3.00	6.00	12.00
Cool Yule, Volume 2	Rhino R1 70193	1988	3.00	6.00	12.00
Country Christmas	Columbia CS 9888	1968	3.75	7.50	15.00

Side 1: Hark! The Herald Angels Sing (Robbins, Marty); Joy to the World (Chuck Wagon Gang, The); I Heard the Bells on Christmas Day (Cash, Johnny); Count Your Blessings Instead of Sheep (Wynette, Tammy); Blue Christmas (Jackson, Stonewall); It Came Upon the Midnight Clear (Dean, Jimmy)
Side 2: Do You Hear What I Hear? (Bryant, Anita); O Holy Night (Ives, Burl); Silent Night (Smith, Carl); Blue Snowfall (Morgan, George); Rudolph, the Red-Nosed Reindeer (Autry, Gene)

Country Christmas		Epic PE 36823	1980	2.50	5.00	10.00
Country Christmas	M	King 811	1962	25.00	50.00	100.00
Country Christmas	(3)	Time-Life STL-109	1988	5.00	10.00	20.00

— *Available from Time-Life by mail order only; boxed set*
Side 1: Country Christmas (Lynn, Loretta); Santa Claus Is Coming to Town (Strait, George); I'll Be Home for Christmas (Presley, Elvis); Rudolph, the Red-Nosed Reindeer (Autry, Gene); Jingle Bells (Nelson, Willie); Santa's Gonna Come in a Stagecoach (Owens, Buck); If We Make It Through December (Haggard, Merle); Pretty Paper (Orbison, Roy); Christmas Prayer (Robbins, Marty)
Side 2: Mr. and Mrs. Santa Claus (Jones, George, and Tammy Wynette); Christmas Time's a-Comin' (Monroe, Bill); Carols Those Kids Used to Sing (Statler Brothers, The); Away in a Manger (McEntire, Reba); Tennessee Christmas (Alabama); Old Toy Trains (Miller, Roger); I Can't Have a Merry Christmas, Mary (Without You) (Lewis, Jerry Lee); Old Christmas Card, An (Reeves, Jim)

Title	Label, Number	Year	VG	VG+	NM

Side 3: Blue Christmas (Presley, Elvis); Christmas Boogie (Davis Sisters, The); Jingle Bell Rock (Atkins, Chet); Christmas in My Home Town (Pride, Charley); One Happy Christmas (Wynette, Tammy); I'll Be Walkin' the Floor This Christmas (Tubb, Ernest); Blue Christmas Lights (Owens, Buck); Christmas Time in the Valley (Fender, Freddy); Friendly Beasts, The (Louvin Brothers, The)
Side 4: Santa Looked a Lot Like Daddy (Owens, Buck); Santa Claus Is Back in Town (Yoakam, Dwight); It Won't Seem Like Christmas (Lynn, Loretta); What a Merry Christmas This Could Be (Nelson, Willie); If Every Day Was Like Christmas (Presley, Elvis); It Came Upon the Midnight Clear (Louvin Brothers, The); Here Comes Santa Claus (Autry, Gene); Truckin' Trees for Christmas (Simpson, Red)
Side 5: When It's Christmas Time in Texas (Strait, George); Santa! Don't Pass Me By (Fender, Freddy); Nuttin' for Christmas (Homer and Jethro); Reindeer Boogie (Snow, Hank); It's Christmas (Milsap, Ronnie); My Mom and Santa Claus (Jones, George); White Christmas(Wynette, Tammy); Little Drummer Boy, The (Cash, Johnny)
Side 6: Christmas in Dixie (Alabama); Let It Snow, Let It Snow, Let It Snow (Pride, Charley); C-H-R-I-S-T-M-A-S *Stereo re-recording*(Arnold, Eddy); Lonely Christmas Call (Gilley, Mickey); Hard Candy Christmas (Parton, Dolly);Winter Wonderland (Atkins, Chet); Goin' Home for Christmas (Haggard, Merle); Silent Night (McEntire, Reba)

Title	Label, Number	Year	VG	VG+	NM
Country Christmas, A	RCA CPL1-4396	1982	2.50	5.00	10.00
Country Christmas, A	RCA AYL1-4812	1983	2.00	4.00	8.00

Side 1: Let It Snow, Let It Snow, Let It Snow (Pride, Charley); Every Time I Hear Blue Christmas (I Get the Christmas Blues) (Everette, Leon); Christmas Is Just a Song for Us This Year (Mandrell, Louise, and R.C. Bannon); Peace on Earth (A Song for All Seasons)(Bailey, Razzy)
Side 2: Christmas in Dixie (Alabama); Fall Softly Snow (Brown, Jim Ed, and Helen Cornelius); Noel, Noel (Wariner, Steve); Pretty Paper (Nelson, Willie). AYL1-4812 is a reissue of CPL1-4396.

Title	Label, Number	Year	VG	VG+	NM
Country Christmas, A, Volume 2	RCA AYL1-4809	1983	3.00	6.00	12.00

Side 1: White Christmas (Conley, Earl Thomas); Hard Candy Christmas (Parton, Dolly); Christmas Time's a-Coming (Reed, Jerry); Winter Wonderland (Arnold, Eddy)
Side 2: Reflections (Sylvia); Silver Bells (Presley, Elvis); I've Got What You Want for Christmas (Mandrell, Louise); Christmas in Dixie (Alabama)

Title	Label, Number	Year	VG	VG+	NM
Country Christmas, A, Volume 3	RCA CPL1-5178	1984	2.50	5.00	10.00

Side 1: It's Christmas (Milsap, Ronnie); Santa and the Kids (Pride, Charley); Blue Christmas (Conley, Earl Thomas); Light of the Stable (Judds, The)
Side 2: Rockin' Little Christmas (Allen, Deborah); Christmas in Dixie (Alabama); Santa, Please (Medley, Bill); Silent Night, Holy Night (Jennings, Waylon, and Jessi Colter)

Title	Label, Number	Year	VG	VG+	NM
Country Christmas, A, Volume 4	RCA CPL1-7012	1985	2.50	5.00	10.00

Side 1: Medley: Winter Wonderland/Sleigh Ride (Parton, Dolly); Christmas Without Mary (Pride, Charley); Christmas Started with a Child (Bruce, Ed); Who Is This Babe (Judds, The)
Side 2: Christmas Letter, A (Whitley, Keith); Santa Are You Coming to Atlanta (McEntire, Pake); Santa Claus Is Coming for Christmas (Why Can't You) (Raven, Eddy); California Christmas(Kanter, Hillary)

Title	Label, Number	Year	VG	VG+	NM
Country Christmas Favorites	Columbia 3C 36088	1979	2.00	4.00	8.00
Country Christmas Favorites	Columbia Special Products C 10876	1972	2.50	5.00	10.00

Side 1: Soon It Will Be Christmas Day (Anderson, Lynn); Hark! The Herald Angels Sing (Chuck Wagon Gang, The); Little Drummer Boy, The (Cash, Johnny); Silver Bells (Page, Patti); Silent Night, Holy Night (Smith, Carl)
Side 2: Away in a Manger (Wynette, Tammy); O Little Town of Bethlehem (Robbins, Marty); Go Tell It on the Mountain (Nabors, Jim); Blue Snowfall (Morgan, George); Lord's Prayer, The(Price, Ray)

Title	Label, Number	Year	VG	VG+	NM
Country Style Christmas, A (3)	Columbia Musical Treasury 3P 6316	1975	3.75	7.50	15.00

Side 1: O Come, All Ye Faithful (Price, Ray); Joy to the World (Wynette, Tammy); It Came Upon the Midnight Clear (Dean, Jimmy); Hark! The Herald Angels Sing (Robbins, Marty); First Noel, The (Smith, Connie)
Side 2: What Child Is This (Smith, Connie); O Holy Night (Shea, George Beverly); Do You Hear What I Hear (Bryant, Anita); O Little Town of Bethlehem (Ives, Burl); Silent Night, Holy Night (Smith, Carl)
Side 3: Mr. Mistletoe (Anderson, Lynn); Winter Wonderland (Arnold, Eddy); Blue Christmas (Jackson, Stonewall); Santa Claus Is Comin' to Town (Davis, Skeeter); Little Drummer Boy (Price, Ray)
Side 4: Jingle Bells (Cash, Johnny); Soon It Will Be Christmas Day (Anderson, Lynn); Christmas Song, The (McCoy, Charlie); White Christmas (Wynette, Tammy); Christmas Time Is Here Again (Robbins, Marty)
Side 5: Have Yourself a Merry Little Christmas (Dean, Jimmy); Spirit of Christmas, The (Anderson, Lynn); Home for the Holidays (Nabors, Jim); I Heard the Bells on Christmas Day (Cash, Johnny); Blue Snowfall (Morgan, George)
Side 6: Christmas Kisses (Robbins, Marty); Deck the Halls (Atkins, Chet); Jingle Bell Rock (Anderson, Lynn); Christmas Cheer (McCoy, Charlie); (Merry Christmas) We Must Be Having One (Wynette, Tammy)

Title	Label, Number	Year	VG	VG+	NM
Decca 38170 (title unknown)	Decca DL 38170	196?	3.00	6.00	12.00

Side 1: We Wish You a Merry Christmas (Columbus Boychoir); Glade Jul (Stordahl, Axel); First Noel, The (Haymes, Dick); Cantique de Noel (Lopez, Vincent); Hark! The Herald Angels Sing (Four Aces); Medley: Joy to the World/God Rest Ye Merry, Gentlemen/Away in a Manger (Bradley, Owen); Angels We Have Heard on High (Columbus Boychoir)
Side 2: Deck the Hall (Columbus Boychoir); It Came Upon a Midnight Clear (Haymes, Dick); Oh, Come All Ye Faithful (Schulmerich "Carillon Americana"); Silent Night (Four Aces); Deilig er Jorden (Stordahl, Axel); Oh, Little Town of Bethlehem (Haymes, Dick); Jingle Bells (Four Aces)

Title	Label, Number	Year	VG	VG+	NM
Disney's Christmas All-Time Favorites	Disneyland 1V 8150	1981	3.75	7.50	15.00

Side 1: Chipmunk Song, The (Chip 'n' Dale and Donald Duck); Joy to the World (Groce, Larry); Twelve Days of Christmas, The (Mickey Mouse/Donald Duck/Goofy/Minnie Mouse/Chip 'n' Dale/Clarabelle Cow/Larry Groce); White Christmas (Groce, Larry); Frosty the Snowman (Groce, Larry); I Wish It Could Be Christmas All Year Long (Willio and Phillio); Away in a Manger (Groce, Larry); Here Comes Santa Claus (Mickey Mouse/Donald Duck/Goofy/Larry Groce); Jingle Bells (Children's Chorus); Deck the Halls (Groce, Larry)
Side 2: Sleigh Ride (Mickey Mouse/Donald Duck/Goofy/Larry Groce); Here We Come a-Caroling (Groce, Larry); Do You Hear What I Hear (Sammes, Mike, Singers); O Christmas Tree (Groce, Larry); Santa Claus Is Coming to Town (Groce, Larry); First Noel, The (Ringwald, Molly); Silver Bells (Groce, Larry); Have Yourself a Merry Little Christmas (Groce, Larry); Winter Wonderland (Groce, Larry); Silent Night (Groce, Larry)

Title	Label, Number	Year	VG	VG+	NM
Disney's Christmas Favorites	Disneyland 2506	1979	3.00	6.00	12.00

Side 1: White Christmas (Groce, Larry); Rudolph the Red-Nosed Reindeer (Sammes, Mike, Singers); We Wish You a Merry Christmas (Children's Chorus); Winter Wonderland (Groce, Larry); Jolly Old Saint Nicholas (Children's Chorus); Do You Hear What I Hear? (Sammes, Mike, Singers); O Christmas Tree (Groce, Larry)
Side 2: Frosty the Snow Man (Groce, Larry); Jingle Bells (Children's Chorus); Deck the Halls (Groce, Larry); Little Drummer Boy (Sammes, Mike, Singers); Santa Claus Is Coming to Town (Groce, Larry); Silent Night (Groce, Larry)

(Top left) This 1980 *Star Wars*-inspired item was masterminded by Meco, featured the original voice of C3PO, and included a pre-fame Jon Bon Jovi as one of the singers. (Top right) This 1986 album on Priority is worth finding. Among other once-rare tracks, "Thank God It's Christmas" by Queen made its US debut here. (Bottom left) What better way to spend the holidays than with the Kentucky Fried Chicken icon? This 1969 album marked the premiere of "Out of the East" by Charley Pride. (Bottom right) This otherwise ordinary Disney LP contains one true oddity: "The First Noel" sung by a very young Molly Ringwald!

Title	Label, Number	Year	VG	VG+	NM
Dr. Demento Presents the Greatest Novelty Records of All Time Volume VI: Christmas	Rhino RNLP 825	1985	3.75	7.50	15.00

Side 1: All I Want for Christmas Is My Two Front Teeth (Jones, Spike, and the City Slickers); Twelve Gifts of Christmas, The (Sherman, Allan); I Want a Hippopotamus for Christmas (Peevey, Gayla); Santa and the Satellite (Buchanan and Goodman); Christmas Carol, A (Lehrer, Tom); Green Chritma (Freberg, Stan)

Side 2: Grandma Got Run Over by a Reindeer (Elmo and Patsy); I Yust Go Nuts at Christmas (Yorgesson, Yogi); Nuttin' for Christmas (Freberg, Stan); Wreck the Halls with Boughs of Holly (Three Stooges, The); I'm a Christmas Tree (Fischer, Wild Man [with Dr. Demento]); Santa Claus and His Old Lady (Cheech and Chong)

Title	Label, Number	Year	VG	VG+	NM
Down-Home Country Christmas, A	Columbia Special Products P 14992	1979	2.00	4.00	8.00
Down-Home Country Christmas, A	SeaShell P 14992	1981	2.00	4.00	8.00

— *Reissue of Columbia Special Products P 14992*

Side 1: Jingle Bells (Price, Ray); Spirit of Christmas, The (Cash, Johnny); O Come All Ye Faithful (Nabors, Jim); Have Yourself a Merry Little Christmas (Dean, Jimmy); Soon It Will Be Christmas Day (Anderson, Lynn)

Side 2: Hark! The Herald Angels Sing (Robbins, Marty); Silver Bells (Tucker, Tanya); God Rest Ye Merry Gentlemen (Rich, Charlie); What Child Is This (Miller, Jody); Joy to the World (Chuck Wagon Gang, The)

Title	Label, Number	Year	VG	VG+	NM
Family Christmas Collection, The (5)	Time-Life STL-131	1990	7.50	15.00	30.00

— *Available from Time-Life via mail order only*

Side 1: Deck the Halls (Damone, Vic); Frosty the Snowman (Como, Perry); Jolly Old St. Nicholas (Arnold, Eddy); Sleigh Ride (Philadelphia Orchestra [Ormandy]); Bells of Christmas, The (Andrews, Julie); Ding Dong Merrily on High (Vienna Choir Boys); O Little Town of Bethlehem (Franchi, Sergio)

Side 2: Wintertime and Christmastime (Gary, John); Medley: Coventry Carol/Shepherd's Carol (Shaw, Robert, Chorale); Rudolph the Red-Nosed Reindeer (Martino, Al); First Noel, The (Ames, Ed); Medley: In Dulci Jubilo/Angels We Have Heard on High (Philadelphia Singers and Concerto Soloists Chamber Orchestra of Philadelphia); O Tannenbaum (Whittaker, Roger)

Side 3: March of the Toys (St. Louis Symphony); God Rest Ye Merry Gentlemen (Como, Perry); White Christmas (Presley, Elvis); Ave Maria (Bach-Gounod) (Domingo, Placido); Let It Snow! Let It Snow! Let It Snow! (Pride, Charley); Here Comes Santa Claus (Fisher, Eddie); Hark! The Herald Angels Sing (Gary, John)

Side 4: Jesu, Joy of Man's Desiring (Luboff, Norman, Choir); Fantasia on "I Saw Three Ships" (Galway, James); What a Merry Christmas This Could Be (Nelson, Willie); Wexford Carol, The (Andrews, Julie); Twelve Days of Christmas, The (Como, Perry); Carol of the Bells (Philadelphia Orchestra [Ormandy])

Side 5: Christmas Song, The (Gary, John); Silver Bells (Reeves, Jim); It's Christmas (Milsap, Ronnie); Little Drummer Boy, The (Luboff, Norman, Choir); Happy Christmas Little Friend (Shore, Dinah); It Came Upon the Midnight Clear (Arnold, Eddy); Hallelujah Chorus (Royal Philharmonic Orchestra and Chorus)

Side 6: Jingle Bells (Ames Brothers, The); Winter Wonderland (Martin, Dean); I'll Be Home for Christmas (Presley, Elvis); Greensleeves (Augustana Choir, The); Nutcracker: Dance of the Sugar-Plum Fairy (Boston Pops Orchestra [Fiedler]); O Holy Night (Lanza, Mario); Fall Softly Snow (Brown, Jim Ed, and Helen Cornelius)

Side 7: Go Tell It on the Mountain (Philadelphia Orchestra [Smith]); Toyland (Como, Perry); He's Too Fat for the Chimney (MacKenzie, Gisele); I Heard the Bells on Christmas Day (Crosby, Bing); Holly and the Ivy, The (Canadian Brass, The); So Blest a Sight (Shaw, Robert, Chorale); Star in the East, A (Belafonte, Harry)

Side 8: Joy to the World (Vienna Choir Boys); Nutcracker: Dance of the Reed-Pipes (St. Louis Symphony); In the Bleak Midwinter (Augustana Choir, The); Happy Holidays (Alabama); Here We Come a-Wassailing (Hunter, Ralph, Choir); Jingle Bell Rock (Arnold, Eddy); Away in a Manger (Andrews, Julie)

Side 9: Christ Was Born on Christmas Day (Shaw, Robert, Chorale); Adeste Fideles (Domingo, Placido); Blue Christmas (Conley, Earl Thomas); We Three Kings (Leibert, Dick); Lully Lully Lu (Schumann, Walter); If Every Day Was Like Christmas (Presley, Elvis)

Side 10: Santa Claus Is Comin' to Town (Damone, Vic); Good King Wenceslas (Philadelphia Orchestra [Ormandy]); Have Yourself a Merry Little Christmas (Gary, John); Greatest Gift of All, The (Greenwood, Lee); Do You Hear What I Hear (Como, Perry); Medley: O Come, O Come Emmanuel/I Wonder As I Wander (Canadian Brass, The); Silent Night (Philadelphia Orchestra [Ormandy]); We Wish You a Merry Christmas (Whittaker, Roger)

Title	Label, Number	Year	VG	VG+	NM
Family Christmas Favorites from Bing Crosby and the Columbus Boychoir	Decca DL 34487	1967	3.75	7.50	15.00

— *Sold only at Safeway grocery stores*

Side 1: Christmas Song, The (Crosby, Bing); Away in a Manger (Crosby, Bing); O Come All Ye Faithful (Columbus Boychoir); Twelve Days of Christmas, The (Crosby, Bing); Jingle Bells (Columbus Boychoir); Deck the Halls (Crosby, Bing)

Side 2: Rudolph, the Red-Nosed Reindeer (Crosby, Bing); I Saw Three Ships (Crosby, Bing); Silent Night (Columbus Boychoir); Angels We Have Heard on High (Crosby, Bing); We Three Kings of Orient Are (Crosby, Bing); I Wish You a Merry Christmas (Columbus Boychoir)

Title		Label, Number	Year	VG	VG+	NM
Favorite Christmas Carols from the Voice of Firestone	M	Firestone MLP 7005	1962	3.75	7.50	15.00

— *Sold only at Firestone tire dealers; actually Volume 1 of the "Firestone Presents..." series*

Side 1: Medley: Joy to the World/Away in a Manger/ We Three Kings of Orient Are/Hark! The Herald Angels Sing (Firestone Chorus); What Child Is This (Stevens, Rise); O Come, All Ye Faithful (Sullivan, Brian); Medley: A Virgin Unspotted/God Rest You Merry, Gentlemen/Deck the Hall (Firestone Chorus); O Little Town of Bethlehem (Sullivan, Brian); O Holy Night (Stevens, Rise)

Side 2: It Came Upon the Midnight Clear (Sullivan, Brian); Friendly Beasts, The (Stevens, Rise); Medley: Here We Come a-Wassailing/Good King Wenceslas/O Christmas Tree (Firestone Chorus); First Noel, The (Sullivan, Brian); Silent Night (Stevens, Rise); Medley: Jingle Bells/Up on the House-Top/Jolly Old St. Nicholas/We Wish You a Merry Christmas (Firestone Chorus)

Title		Label, Number	Year	VG	VG+	NM
Firestone Presents Your Favorite Christmas Carols, Volume 2	M	Firestone MLP 7006	1963	3.75	7.50	15.00

Title		Label, Number	Year	VG	VG+	NM
Firestone Presents Your Favorite Christmas Carols, Volume 2	S	Firestone SLP 7006	1963	4.00	8.00	16.00

— *Above two sold only at Firestone tire dealers*

    Side 1: Medley: O Holy Night/O Come All Ye Faithful (Columbus Boychoir and Firestone Chorus); O Come, O Come, Emmanuel (Stevens, Rise, and Firestone Chorus); Medley: Hark! The Herald Angels Sing/The First Noel (Columbus Boychoir); Medley: We Three Kings of Orient Are/God Rest Ye Merry, Gentlemen (Sullivan, Brian, and Firestone Chorus); Angels We Have Heard on High (Stevens, Rise; Brian Sullivan; Firestone Chorus); Carol of the Bells (Columbus Boychoir)
    Side 2: Hallelujah Chorus (Firestone Chorus); Deck the Hall (Sullivan, Brian, and Firestone Chorus); Medley: Away in the Manger/It Came Upon a Midnight Clear (Stevens, Rise, and Firestone Chorus); Joy to the World (Stevens, Rise; Brian Sullivan; Firestone Chorus); Medley: Silent Night/O Little Town of Bethlehem/ Jingle Bells (Columbus Boychoir and Firestone Chorus); Twelve Days of Christmas, The (The Entire Company)

Title		Label, Number	Year	VG	VG+	NM
Firestone Presents Your Christmas Favorites, Volume 3	M	Firestone MLP 7008	1964	3.75	7.50	15.00
Firestone Presents Your Christmas Favorites, Volume 3	S	Firestone SLP 7008	1964	4.00	8.00	16.00

— *Above two sold only at Firestone tire dealers*

    Side 1: Medley: Hark! The Herald Angels Sing/It Came Upon a Midnight Clear/Joy to the World (Columbus Boychoir and Firestone Chorus); Gesu Bambino (Peters, Roberta); Panis Angelicus (Corelli, Franco); Holly and the Ivy, The (Wright, Martha); Go Tell It on the Mountain (MacRae, Gordon); Medley: Here We Come a-Wassailing/God Rest You Merry, Gentlemen/Bring a Torch, Jeanette, Isabella/Good King Wenceslas (Columbus Boychoir and Firestone Chorus)
    Side 2: O Holy Night (Corelli, Franco); Little Drummer Boy, The (Columbus Boychoir and Firestone Chorus); Ave Maria (Peters, Roberta); Sleigh Ride (MacRae, Gordon); Silver Bells (Wright, Martha); White Christmas (MacRae, Gordon, and Martha Wright)

Title		Label, Number	Year	VG	VG+	NM
Firestone Presents Your Favorite Christmas Music, Volume 4	M	Firestone MLP 7011	1965	3.00	6.00	12.00
Firestone Presents Your Favorite Christmas Music, Volume 4	S	Firestone SLP 7011	1965	3.75	7.50	15.00

— *Above two sold only at Firestone tire dealers*

    Side 1: Medley: Here We Come a-Caroling/Deck the Halls/God Rest You Merry, Gentlemen/O Little Town of Bethlehem (Young Americans, The); Angels We Have Heard on High (McCracken, James); I Wonder As I Wander (Kirsten, Dorothy); Medley: We Three Kings of Orient Are/Hark! The Herald Angels Sing (Young Americans, The); It Came Upon a Midnight Clear (Damone, Vic); Ding Dong Merrily on High (Young Americans, The); Christmas Song, The (Andrews, Julie)
    Side 2: Joy to the World (Kirsten, Dorothy); Ave Maria (McCracken, James); Medley: Away in a Manger/Silent Night/ Coventry Carol (Young Americans, The); Rocking (Little Jesus, Sweetly Sleep) (Andrews, Julie); Masters in This Hall (Young Americans, The); Have Yourself a Merry Little Christmas (Damone, Vic); Bells of Christmas, The (Andrews, Julie)

Title		Label, Number	Year	VG	VG+	NM
Firestone Presents Your Favorite Christmas Music, Volume 5	M	Firestone MLP 7012	1966	3.00	6.00	12.00
Firestone Presents Your Favorite Christmas Music, Volume 5	S	Firestone SLP 7012	1966	3.75	7.50	15.00

— *Above two sold only at Firestone tire dealers*

    Side 1: Joy to the World (Andrews, Julie); Irish Carol (Andrews, Julie); O Little Town of Bethlehem (Previn, Andre); Deck the Halls (Andrews, Julie); Angels from the Realms (Andrews, Julie); Away in a Manger (Andrews, Julie)
    Side 2: Bells of Christmas, The; It Came Upon the Midnight Clear; Sunny Bank (I Saw Three Ships); God Rest You Merry, Gentlemen; Wexford Carol; Jingle Bells (all by Andrews, Julie)

Title		Label, Number	Year	VG	VG+	NM
Firestone Presents Your Favorite Christmas Music, Volume 6	M	Firestone MLP 7014	1967	2.50	5.00	10.00
Firestone Presents Your Favorite Christmas Music, Volume 6	S	Firestone SLP 7014	1967	3.00	6.00	12.00

— *Above two sold only at Firestone tire dealers*

    Side 1: Medley: Christmas Is Coming/Adeste Fideles/Angels We Have Heard on High (Vienna Choir Boys); First Noel, The (Peters, Roberta); O Tannenbaum (Vienna Choir Boys); O Little Town of Bethlehem (Jones, Jack); And the Glory of the Lord (Firestone Chorus); Hark the Herald Angels Sing (Peters, Roberta, and Jack Jones)
    Side 2: This Is That Time of the Year (Jones, Jack); Medley: Fum, Fum, Fum/O Come, Little Children/Deck the Hall (Vienna Choir Boys); Dance of the Christmas Doll (Leighton, Bernie); I Heard the Bells on Christmas Day (Firestone Chorus); Alleluia (Mozart) (Peters, Roberta); Silent Night (Vienna Choir Boys); Medley: Christmas Is Coming/We Wish You a Merry Christmas (Peters, Roberta, and Jack Jones with the Vienna Choir Boys)

Title	Label, Number	Year	VG	VG+	NM
Firestone Presents Your Christmas Favorites, Volume 7	Firestone CSLP 7015	1968	3.00	6.00	12.00

— *Sold only at Firestone tire dealers*

    Side 1: Medley: Joy to the World/The First Noel/Hark! The Herald Angels Sing (Vienna Choir Boys and Firestone Chorus); Rise Up, Shepherd, and Follow (Gary, John, and Firestone Chorus); O Holy Night (Price, Leontyne); Good Christian Men, Rejoice (Gedda, Nicolai, and Firestone Chorus); While Shepherds Watched Their Flocks (Vienna Choir Boys); I Still Believe in Christmas (Carr, Vikki, and Firestone Chorus)
    Side 2: Medley: Jingle Bells/Ding Dong! Merrily on High/The Bells of Christmas (Vienna Choir Boys and Firestone Chorus); Ave Maria (Gedda, Nicolai); He Shall Feed His Flock (Price, Leontyne); It Came Upon the Midnight Clear (Gary, John, and Firestone Chorus); Medley: Jolly Old St. Nicholas/Up on the House Top (Carr, Vikki, and Firestone Chorus); Silent Night (Price, Leontyne; Nicolai Gedda; Vienna Choir Boys; Firestone Chorus)

Title	Label, Number	Year	VG	VG+	NM
First Christmas Record for Children	Harmony HS 14554	197?	3.00	6.00	12.00

    Side 1: Here Comes Santa Claus (Day, Doris); I Saw Mommy Kissing Santa Claus (Boyd, Jimmy); Littlest Snowman, The (Keeshan, Bob [Captain Kangaroo]); Suzy Snowflake (Clooney, Rosemary); 'Twas the Night Before Christmas, Part One/Part Two (Heatherton, Ray)
    Side 2: Jingle Bells (Godfrey, Arthur); Little Christmas Tree, The, Part One/Part Two (Skelton, Red); He'll Be Coming Down the Chimney (Autry, Gene); Santa Claus Is Comin' to Town (Hannon, Bob); C-H-R-I-S-T-M-A-S (Clooney, Rosemary)

Title		Label, Number	Year	VG	VG+	NM
For a Musical Merry Christmas	M	RCA Victor PR-149A	1963	3.00	6.00	12.00

— *Sold only at Acme Markets (Mid-Atlantic states)*

Side 1: Good King Wenceslas (Ames Brothers, The); O Little Town of Bethlehem (Lanza, Mario); Little Drummer Boy, The (Hugo and Luigi Children's Chorus); We Wish You a Merry Christmas (Anderson, Marian); Silent Night (Fisher, Eddie); Twelve Days of Christmas, The (Hunter, Ralph, Choir)

Side 2: Angels We Have Heard on High (Shaw, Robert, Chorale); Dance of the Sugar Plum Fairy (Stokowski, Leopold); Gesu Bambino (Peerce, Jan); Christmas Festival (Boston Pops Orchestra [Fiedler])

Title		Label, Number	Year	VG	VG+	NM
For a Musical Merry Christmas, Vol. Two	M	RCA Victor PRM 189	1965	3.00	6.00	12.00
For a Musical Merry Christmas, Vol. Two	S	RCA Victor PRS 189	1965	3.75	7.50	15.00

— *Above two sold only at B.F. Goodrich tire dealers*

Side 1: Sleigh Ride (Boston Pops Orchestra [Fiedler]; Wassail Song (Shaw, Robert, Chorale); Carol of the Bells (Winterhalter, Hugo); Little Drummer Boy, The (Hugo and Luigi); We Three Kings of Orient Are (MacKenzie, Gisele); Let There Be Peace on Earth (Luboff, Norman, Choir)

Side 2: White Christmas (Melachrino Strings, The); Jingle Bells (Reeves, Jim); Medley: Hark! The Herald Angels Sing/ God Rest Ye Merry, Gentlemen (Henderson, Skitch); Medley: Silent Night/O Holy Night/O Come All Ye Faithful (Radio City Music Hall Orchestra)

Title		Label, Number	Year	VG	VG+	NM
For a Musical Merry Christmas, Volume 3	M	RCA Victor PRM-221	1966	3.00	6.00	12.00
For a Musical Merry Christmas, Volume 3	S	RCA Victor PRS-221	1966	3.75	7.50	15.00

— *Above two sold only at B.F. Goodrich tire dealers*

Side 1: Christmas Song, The (Gary, John); Little Drummer Boy (Atkins, Chet); Christmas Festival (Boston Pops Orchestra [Fiedler])

Side 2: Santa Claus Is Comin' to Town (Ames Brothers, The); Rudolph, the Red-Nosed Reindeer (Hines, Mimi); O Holy Night (Lanza, Mario); O Little Town of Bethlehem (Three Suns, The); Silent Night (Living Voices); Hallelujah Chorus (Royal Philharmonic Orchestra [Beecham])

Title		Label, Number	Year	VG	VG+	NM
For Christmas Seals . . . A Matter of Life and Breath	DJ	Decca Custom Style E	1968	5.00	10.00	20.00

— *Promo-only album for Christmas Seals*

Side 1: Joel Grey Reminder Show, The (Grey, Joel)

Side 2: Reminder Spots by (in order) Uggams, Leslie; MacRae, Gordon; Lawrence, Carol; Goulet, Robert; Dean, Jimmy; Cristal, Linda; Field, Sally;Cambridge, Godfrey; Curtis, Tony; Bain, Barbara/Martin Landau; Fabian; Barry, Ken; Duff, Howard; Alexander, Ben; Meyerson, Bess; Palmer, Betsy; Karloff, Boris; Walters, Barbara; Ford, Glenn; Wallach, Eli; Powell, Jane

Title		Label, Number	Year	VG	VG+	NM
For Christmas Seals . . . A Matter of Life and Breath	DJ	Decca Custom Style F	1968	6.25	12.50	25.00

— *Promo-only album for Christmas Seals; four five-minute programs*

Side 1: George Hamilton IV Show, The (Hamilton, George, IV); Tony Bennett Show, The (Bennett, Tony)

Side 2: Herb Alpert and the Tijuana Brass Show, The (Alpert, Herb, and the Tijuana Brass); Righteous Brothers Show, The (Righteous Brothers, The)

Title	Label, Number	Year	VG	VG+	NM
From Under the Christmas Tree	Capitol Creative Products SL-6589	1968	3.00	6.00	12.00
Funky Christmas	Cotillion SD 9911	1976	3.75	7.50	15.00
Gift of Christmas, The, Vol. 1	Columbia Special Products CSS 706	1968	3.00	6.00	12.00

— *A product of First Financial Marketing*

Side 1: Joy to the World (Conniff, Ray); That Old Christmas Spirit (Lawrence, Steve); O Tannenbaum (Philadelphia Brass Ensemble); First Noel, The (Bryant, Anita); Silent Night, Holy Night (Dean, Jimmy); Christmas Song, The (Day, Doris)

Side 2 Deck the Halls (Glad Singers, The); Santo Natale (Page, Patti); God Rest Ye Merry Gentlemen (Miller, Mitch); Do You Hear What I Hear (Vinton, Bobby); Twelve Days of Christmas, The (Luboff, Norman, Choir); Hallelujah Chorus (Philadelphia Orchestra [Ormandy]) *With the Temple University Choir*

Title		Label, Number	Year	VG	VG+	NM
Glory of Christmas, The	(3)	Columbia Musical Treasury P3S 5356	196?	3.75	7.50	15.00

— *Performed by anonymous musicians*

Side 1: Carol of the Bells; I Saw Three Ships; For Unto Us a Child Is Born; Here We Come a-Caroling; Jingle Bells; What Child Is This?; O Tannenbaum; Hark the Herald Angels Sing

Side 2: We Wish You a Merry Christmas; Caroling, Caroling; O Holy Night; Patapan; Christmas Song, The; We Three Kings of Orient Are; Peter and the Wolf (Excerpt); Ave Maria (Schubert)

Side 3: Twelve Days of Christmas, The; Adeste Fideles; Away in a Manger; God Rest Ye Merry, Gentlemen; Toyland; Good King Wenceslas; Come, Dear Children; In Dulci Jubilo

Side 4: Deck the Hall with Boughs of Holly; It Came Upon the Midnight Clear; Glory to God in the Highest; O Little Town of Bethlehem; Nutcracker Suite (Excerpt); Gesu Bambino; Prayer from "Hansel and Gretel"; Silent Night, Holy Night

Side 5: White Christmas; Little Drummer Boy, The; First Noel, The; Rudolph, the Red-Nosed Reindeer; Joseph Dearest, Joseph Mine; When Christmas Comes; Holy City, The; Do You Hear What I Hear?

Side 6: Joy to the World; Angels We Have Heard on High; Silver Bells; Some Children See Him; Santa Claus Is Comin' to Town; O Come, O Come Emmanuel; I'll Be Home for Christmas; Hallelujah Chorus

Title	Label, Number	Year	VG	VG+	NM
God Rest Ye Merry, Jazzmen	Columbia FC 37551	1981	3.00	6.00	12.00

Side 1: Have Yourself a Merry Little Christmas (Gordon, Dexter, Quartet); I'll Be Home for Christmas (Turner, McCoy); Christmas Song, The (Blythe, Arthur, Quartet)

Side 2: Our Little Town (Heath Brothers, The); God Rest Ye Merry, Gentlemen (D'Rivera, Pasquito, and John Miller); We Three Kings of Orient Are (Marsalis, Wynton, Quintet)

Title	Label, Number	Year	VG	VG+	NM
Golden Glow of Christmas, The, Vol. 1	Columbia Special Products C 10925	1972	3.00	6.00	12.00

Title		Label, Number	Year	VG	VG+	NM
Goodyear Presents The Great Songs of Christmas		RCA Special Products DPL1-0285	1977	2.50	5.00	10.00

— Sold only at Goodyear tire dealers

Side 1: Christmas Song, The (Como, Perry); Sleigh Ride (Philadelphia Orchestra [Ormandy]); Toyland (Como, Perry); Santa Claus Is Comin' to Town (Philadelphia Orchestra [Smith]); Home for the Holidays (Como, Perry); White Christmas (Philadelphia Orchestra [Smith])

Side 2: Joy to the World (Philadelphia Orchestra [Ormandy]); O Holy Night (Como, Perry); Go Tell It on the Mountain (Philadelphia Orchestra [Smith]); Ave Maria (Como, Perry); It Came Upon a Midnight Clear (Philadelphia Orchestra [Page]); Carol Medley: Caroling, Caroling/The First Noel/Hark! The Herald Angels Sing/Silent Night (Como, Perry); We Wish You a Merry Christmas (Philadelphia Orchestra [Ormandy])

| Great Songs of Christmas, The | M | Columbia Special Products XTV 69406/7 | 1961 | 3.75 | 7.50 | 15.00 |

— Sold only at Goodyear tire dealers

Side 1: Silent Night (Mormon Tabernacle Choir); O Little Town of Bethlehem (Farrell, Eileen); O Come All Ye Faithful/ Jesu Bambino (Faith, Percy); What Child Is This (Miller, Mitch); O Holy Night (Wrightson, Earl); Unto Us a Child Is Born (New York Philharmonic [Bernstein])

Side 2: Medley: Ring, Christmas Bells/The First Noel/We Wish You a Merry Christmas (De Vol, Frank); Twelve Days of Christmas, The (Ives, Burl); Carol of the Bells (Mormon Tabernacle Choir); Medley: God Rest Ye Merry, Gentlemen/We Three Kings/Deck the Halls (Luboff, Norman, Choir); Sleigh Ride (Kostelanetz, Andre)

| Great Songs of Christmas, The | M | Columbia Special Products XTV 69406/7 | 1962 | 3.00 | 6.00 | 12.00 |

— Reissue with no reference to Goodyear on the cover

| Great Songs of Christmas, The, Album Two | M | Columbia Special Products XTV 86100/1 | 1962 | 3.75 | 7.50 | 15.00 |

— Sold only at Goodyear tire dealers

Side 1: Hark! The Herald Angels Sing (Faith, Percy); O Little Town of Bethlehem (Mormon Tabernacle Choir); It Came Upon the Midnight Clear (Farrell, Eileen); Coventry Carol (Farrell, Eileen); Away in a Manger (Kostelanetz, Andre); Joy to the World (Faith, Percy); First Noel, The (Eddy, Nelson); Sleep, Holy Babe (Farrell, Eileen); Holly and the Ivy, The (Luboff, Norman, Choir); O Come All Ye Faithful (Wrightson, Earl); Silent Night (Wrightson, Earl)

Side 2: Deck the Hall with Boughs of Holly (Philadelphia Orchestra [Ormandy]); God Rest Ye Merry, Gentlemen (Previn, Andre); Angels We Have Heard on High (Mormon Tabernacle Choir); Good King Wenceslas (Mormon Tabernacle Choir); Medley: Dance of the Sugar Plum Fairy/Waltz of the Flowers (New York Philharmonic [Bernstein]); Medley: Toyland/March of the Toys (Kostelanetz, Andre); Medley: O Tannenbaum/Here We Come a-Caroling (Luboff, Norman, Choir); Jingle Bells (Eddy, Nelson)

| Great Songs of Christmas, The, Album Three | M | Columbia Special Products CSP 117 | 1963 | 3.75 | 7.50 | 15.00 |

— Sold only at Goodyear tire dealers. The number listed is on the jacket; on the record, the number is "XTV 86656/7"

Side 1: O Little Town of Bethlehem (Philadelphia Orchestra [Ormandy]); Silent Night (Andrews, Julie); Medley: I Saw Three Ships/Here We Come a-Caroling (Faith, Percy); Medley: It Came Upon the Midnight Clear/Away in the Manger (Miller, Mitch); Ave Maria (Schubert) (Stern, Isaac)

Side 2: Panis Angelicus (Goulet, Robert); Joy to the World (Mormon Tabernacle Choir); O Tannenbaum (Faith, Percy); Medley: Snow in the Street/Joseph Dearest, Joseph Mine (New Christy Minstrels, The); Carol of the Bells (New York Philharmonic [Bernstein]); Medley: Hark the Herald Angels Sing/A La Nanita Nana (Luboff, Norman, Choir); Medley: The Holly and the Ivy/We Wish You a Merry Christmas (Previn, Andre); We Three Kings of Orient Are (Mormon Tabernacle Choir); Wassail, Wassail (New Christy Minstrels, The)

| Great Songs of Christmas, The, Album Four | M | Columbia Special Products CSP 155M | 1964 | 3.75 | 7.50 | 15.00 |
| Great Songs of Christmas, The, Album Four | S | Columbia Special Products CSP 155S | 1964 | 4.50 | 9.00 | 18.00 |

— Sold only at Goodyear tire dealers

Side 1: Silent Night (Martin, Mary); O Little Town of Bethlehem (Mormon Tabernacle Choir); O Come All Ye Faithful (Goulet, Robert); Joy to the World (Philadelphia Orchestra [Ormandy]); Good King Wenceslas (Faith, Percy); What Child Is This (Brothers Four, The); Holy, Holy, Holy (Jackson, Mahalia); Abide with Me (Jackson, Mahalia); Ave Maria (Bach-Gounod) (Stern, Isaac)

Side 2: Toyland (Day, Doris); Shepherd Boy, The (New Christy Minstrels, The); Deck the Hall with Boughs of Holly (Mormon Tabernacle Choir); First Noel, The (Miller, Mitch); Hark! The Herald Angels Sing (Previn, Andre); God Rest Ye Merry, Gentlemen (Brothers Four, The); Coventry Carol (Miller, Mitch); O Come Little Children (Philadelphia Orchestra [Ormandy]); Go Tell It on the Mountain (Brothers Four, The) Sing Hosanna, Hallelujah (New Christy Minstrels, The)

| Great Songs of Christmas, The, Album Five | M | Columbia Special Products CSP 238M | 1965 | 3.00 | 6.00 | 12.00 |
| Great Songs of Christmas, The, Album Five | S | Columbia Special Products CSP 238S | 1965 | 3.75 | 7.50 | 15.00 |

— Sold only at Goodyear tire dealers;

Side 1: O Holy Night (Williams, Andy); It Came Upon the Midnight Clear (Kostelanetz, Andre); Caroling, Caroling (Alberghetti, Anna Maria); Jolly Old St. Nicholas (Chevalier, Maurice); Little Drummer Boy (Philadelphia Orchestra [Ormandy]); Star Carol, The (Alberghetti, Anna Maria); We Three Kings of Orient Are (Philadelphia Orchestra [Ormandy]); Medley: Hark! The Herald Angels Sing/Angels We Have Heard (Kostelanetz, Andre); Silent Night (Chevalier, Maurice); Lord's Prayer, The (Tucker, Richard)

Side 2: Sleigh Ride (Lawrence, Steve, and Eydie Gorme); Twelve Days of Christmas, The (Shore, Dinah); O Little Town of Bethlehem (Tucker, Richard); Lo, How a Rose E'er Blooming (Carroll, Diahann); Some Children See Him (Carroll, Diahann); Medley: O Come, All Ye Faithful/The First Noel (Kaye, Danny); Silver Bells (Day, Doris); Medley: Jingle Bells/It's Christmas Time All Over the World (Davis, Sammy, Jr.)

| Great Songs of Christmas, The, Album Six | M | Columbia Special Products CSM 388 | 1966 | 3.00 | 6.00 | 12.00 |

Title		Label, Number	Year	VG	VG+	NM
Great Songs of Christmas, The, Album Six	S	Columbia Special Products CSS 388	1966	3.75	7.50	15.00

— *Sold only at Goodyear tire dealers*
Side 1: Silent Night (Streisand, Barbra); Do You Hear What I Hear (Williams, Andy); Christmas Song, The (Mathis, Johnny); Medley: Holiday of Love/Caroling, Caroling (King Family, The); Jesu, Joy of Man's Desiring (Casals, Pablo); Medley: O Little Town of Bethlehem/It Came Upon the Midnight Clear (King Family, The); O Come, All Ye Faithful (Peerce, Jan); Ave Maria (Streisand, Barbra)
Side 2: Frosty the Snowman (Conniff, Ray); We Need a Little Christmas (New Christy Minstrels, The); Let It Snow! Let It Snow! Let It Snow! (Lawrence, Steve, and Eydie Gorme); Hark! The Herald Angels Sing (Conniff, Ray); Noel Nouvelet (Peerce, Jan); March of the Kings (Mormon Tabernacle Choir); Deck the Halls with Boughs of Holly (Mormon Tabernacle Choir); White World of Winter, The (Crosby, Bing); Il Est Ne (New Christy Minstrels, The); Still, Still, Still (Mormon Tabernacle Choir); Away in a Manger (Jackson, Mahalia); We Wish You a Merry Christmas (Conniff, Ray)

Great Songs of Christmas, The, Album Seven	Columbia Special Products CSS 547	1967	3.00	6.00	12.00

— *Sold only at Goodyear tire dealers*
Side 1: Santa Claus Is Coming to Town (Bennett, Tony); Toyland (Howes, Sally Ann); This Christmas I Spend with You (Goulet, Robert); Deck the Hall with Boughs of Holly (Cleveland Orchestra [Szell]); Do You Hear What I Hear (Carroll, Diahann); Christmas Song, The (Bennett, Tony); 'Twas the Night Before Christmas (Lawrence, Steve); God Rest Ye Merry, Gentlemen (Brothers Four, The); First Noel, The (Davidson, John); Lord's Prayer, The (Streisand, Barbra)
Side 2: Rudolph the Red-Nosed Reindeer (Simeone, Harry, Chorale); Home for the Holidays (Vale, Jerry); O Little Town of Bethlehem (Howes, Sally Ann); Let Me Be the First (To Wish You a Merry Christmas) (Lawrence, Steve); Patapan (Cleveland Orchestra [Szell]); O Come, All Ye Faithful (Vale, Jerry); Here We Come a-Caroling (New Christy Minstrels, The); Hark, the Herald Angels Sing (Davidson, John); Christmas Is (Simeone, Harry, Chorale); Silent Night (New Christy Minstrels, The)

Great Songs of Christmas, The, Album Eight	Columbia Special Products CSS 888	1968	3.00	6.00	12.00

Side 1: It's the Most Wonderful Time of the Year (Williams, Andy); Christmas Waltz, The (Goulet, Robert, and Carol Lawrence); Here Comes Santa Claus (Conniff, Ray); I've Got My Love to Keep Me Warm/I Love Winter Weather (Bennett, Tony); Have Yourself a Merry Little Christmas (Faith, Percy); Marshmallow World, A (Mathis, Johnny); Little Drummer Boy, The (Faith, Percy); Sleigh Ride (New Christy Minstrels, The)
Side 2: O Little Town of Bethlehem (Streisand, Barbra); On Christmas Night All Christians Sing (Newley, Anthony); It Came Upon a Midnight Clear (Howes, Sally Ann); Medley: March of the Kings/Hark! The Herald Angels Sing (Merrill, Robert); Little Jesus, Sweetly Sleep (Newley, Anthony); Ave Maria (Moffo, Anna); Mary's Little Boy Child (Brothers Four, The); What Child Is This (Bennett, Tony); Joy to the World (Moffo, Anna); Silent Night (Streisand, Barbra)

Great Songs of Christmas, Album Nine	Columbia Special Products CSS 1033	1969	3.00	6.00	12.00

— *Version 1 has a 10 1/2-inch flap on right inner gatefold (part of record is exposed)*

Great Songs of Christmas, Album Nine	Columbia Special Products CSS 1033	1969	3.00	6.00	12.00

— *Sold only at Goodyear tire dealers; version 2 has a 12 1/4-inch flap on right inner gatefold (record is completely covered)*
Side 1: Happiest Christmas, The (Clark, Petula); Secret of Christmas, The (Crosby, Bing); Twelve Days of Christmas, The (Sutherland, Joan); First Noel, The (Francis, Connie); Medley: O Come All Ye Faithful/God Rest Ye Merry, Gentlemen (Kiley, Richard); Medley: Hark! The Herald Angels Sing/Good Kng Wenceslas/It Came Upon a Midnight Clear (Welk, Lawrence); In Dulci Jubilo (London Symphony Orchestra/Roger Wagner Chorale); O Holy Night (Mantovani); Silent Night, Holy Night (Clark, Petula)
Side 2: Winter Wonderland (Horne, Lena); Skater's Waltz (Mantovani); O Little Town of Bethlehem (Francis, Connie); Panis Angelicus (Kiley, Richard); Jingle Bells (Horne, Lena); O Sanctissima (London Symphony Orchestra/Roger Wagner Chorale); Christmas Tale for Children, A (Horowitz, Vladimir); Ave Maria (Sutherland, Joan)

GRP Christmas Collection, A	GRP 9574	1988	3.00	6.00	12.00

Side 1: Little Drummer Boy (Stuermer, Daryl); Have Yourself a Merry Little Christmas (Scott, Tom); Carol of the Bells (Benoit, David); Christmas Song, The (Schuur, Diane); Santa Claus Is Coming to Town (Valentin, Dave); White Christmas (Ritenour, Lee)
Side 2: This Christmas (Yutaka); God Rest Ye Merry, Gentlemen (Corea, Chick, Elektric Band); Sleigh Ride (Daniels, Eddie); What Child Is This (Egan, Mark); Silent Night (Special EFX); Some Children See Him (Grusin, Dave)

Hallmark Presents: The Best Loved Christmas Carols		1985			

— *See "London Symphony Orchestra"*

Hallmark Presents: Carols of Christmas	Hallmark 629 XPR	1989	3.00	6.00	12.00

— *With the Mormon Tabernacle Choir, Sarah Vaughan and Samuel Ramey; sold only at Hallmark Cards dealers*
Side 1: O Come, All Ye Faithful; O Little Town of Bethlehem; March of the Toys; Deck the Halls; Do You Hear What I Hear?; Hallelujah Chorus
Side 2: Bless This Day; White Christmas/Happy Holidays Medley; We Three Kings; What Child Is This?; O Holy Night

Hallmark Presents: Christmas — Listen to the Joy	Hallmark 626 XPR	1986	2.50	5.00	10.00

— *With Placido Domingo, The London Symphony Orchestra, The Vienna Choir Boys; sold only at Hallmark Cards dealers*
Side 1: We Three Kings of Orient Are; Away in a Manger; I Wonder As I Wander; Do You Hear What I Hear; Jesu, Joy of Man's Desiring; Adeste Fideles
Side 2: Little Drummer Boy; Gift of Love, The; Good Christian Men Rejoice; I Heard the Bells on Christmas Day; It Came Upon the Midnight Clear; O Little Town of Bethlehem

Hallmark Presents: Songs for the Holidays	Hallmark 627 XPR	1987	2.50	5.00	10.00

— *With Peter Hoffmann, Deborah Sasson, The London Symphony Orchestra and Chorus; sold only at Hallmark Cards dealers*
Side 1: Sleigh Ride; Silver Bells; Holly and the Ivy, The; Silent Night; O Tannenbaum; O Holy Night
Side 2: Home for the Holidays; Christmas Hymn; Christmas Song, The; Carol of the Bells; Ave Maria; Here We Come a Wassailing

Happy Birthday, Baby Jesus	10	Sympathy For The Record Industry SFTRI 271	1993	2.50	5.00	10.00

Side 1: Christmas Is a Comin' (May God Bless You) (Shitbirds); Brand New Bike (Junkyard Dogs); Night Before Christmas, The (Claw Hammer); I Wish It Could Be Christmas Everyday (Devil Dogs); Cancel Christmas (Rocket from the Crypt)
Side 2: Run, Run, Rudolph (Humpers); Santa Claus Never Forgets (Jackknife); Christmas (Baby Please Come Home) (New Bomb Turks); Little Drummer Bitch (Red Aunts); Mr. Blue X-mas (Cut Your Head on Christmas) (Evans, Monsieur Jeffrey, with Ross Johnson and the AMF)

Title		Label, Number	Year	VG	VG+	NM
Happy Holiday		Mistletoe 1243	1978	2.50	5.00	10.00

    Side 1: Have Yourself a Merry Little Christmas (Clooney, Rosemary); White Christmas (Crosby, Bing) *Radio broadcast;* O Holy Night (Stuarti, Enzo); Mistletoe and Holly (Sinatra, Frank) *TV broadcast;* O Come All Ye Faithful (Stuarti, Enzo); Silent Night (Monte, Lou)

    Side 2: Rudolph, the Red-Nosed Reindeer (Crosby, Bing); Count Your Blessings (Clooney, Rosemary); Jingle Bells (Sinatra, Frank, and Bing Crosby) *From broadcast;* Silver Bells (Monte, Lou); It Came Upon a Midnight Clear (Sinatra, Frank); Christmas Song, The (Sinatra, Frank, and Bing Crosby) *From broadcast*

Title		Label, Number	Year	VG	VG+	NM
Happy Holidays	M	Columbia Special Products CSP 2??M	1965	3.75	7.50	15.00
Happy Holidays	S	Columbia Special Products CSP 2??S	1965	3.75	7.50	15.00

— *Sold only at True Value Hardware stores*

Title		Label, Number	Year	VG	VG+	NM
Happy Holidays, Volume 1		RCA Special Products DPL1-0411	1979	3.00	6.00	12.00

— *Sold only at V&S Variety Stores; for contents, see "Happy Holidays, Volume 14"*

Title		Label, Number	Year	VG	VG+	NM
Happy Holidays, Volume II	M	Columbia Special Products CSM 348	1966	3.75	7.50	15.00
Happy Holidays, Volume II	S	Columbia Special Products CSS 348	1966	3.00	6.00	12.00

— *Sold only at True Value Hardware stores*

    Side 1: Sleigh Ride (Kostelanetz, Andre); Let It Snow! Let It Snow! Let It Snow! (Day, Doris); When Lights Are Low (Bennett, Tony); I Wonder As I Wander (Faith, Percy); Go Tell It on the Mountain (New Christy Minstrels, The); Skaters' Waltz (DeVol, Frank)

    Side 2: Winter Song, The (Staton, Merrill, Choir); Pretty Snowflakes (Page, Patti); Holly and the Ivy, The (Luboff, Norman, Choir); Snowfall (Beneke, Tex); Our Winter Love (Bryant, Anita); You'd Be So Nice to Come Home To (Conniff, Ray)

Title		Label, Number	Year	VG	VG+	NM
Happy Holidays, Vol. III		RCA Victor PRS-255	1967	3.75	7.50	15.00

— *Sold only at True Value Hardware stores*

    Side 1: We Wish You a Merry Christmas (Hugo and Luigi Children's Chorus); Sleigh Ride (Boston Pops Orchestra [Fiedler]); Medley: Hark! The Herald Angels Sing/God Rest Ye Merry, Gentlemen (Henderson, Skitch); Little Drummer Boy, The (Atkins, Chet); O Little Town of Bethlehem (Franchi, Sergio); We Three Kings (Shaw, Robert, Chorale)

    Side 2 Silent Night (Ames, Ed); White Christmas (Mancini, Henry); My Favorite Things (Henderson, Florence); The Nativity (Medley) (Radio City Music Hall Orchestra)

Title		Label, Number	Year	VG	VG+	NM
Happy Holidays, Volume IV		RCA Victor PRS-267	1968	3.75	7.50	15.00

— *Sold only at True Value Hardware stores*

    Side 1: It's Beginning to Look Like Christmas (Smith, Kate); Jingle Bells (Gould, Morton); Santa Claus Is Comin' to Town (Damone, Vic); Medley: Silver Bells/Winter Wonderland (Cramer, Floyd); Little Drummer Boy, The (Hugo and Luigi Children's Chorus); Christmas Song, The (Living Strings)

    Side 2: Angels We Have Heard on High (Shaw, Robert, Chorale); Mary's Little Boy Child (Reeves, Jim); Jolly Old St. Nicholas (Atkins, Chet); Christmas Festival, A (Medley) (Boston Pops Orchestra [Fiedler])

Title		Label, Number	Year	VG	VG+	NM
Happy Holidays, Vol. 5		Capitol Creative Products SL-6627	1969	3.00	6.00	12.00

— *Sold only at True Value Hardware stores*

    Side 1: Silver Bells (Waring, Fred, and the Pennsylvanians); Have Yourself a Merry Little Christmas (Sandler and Young); Happy Holiday (Voices of Christmas); I'll Be Home for Christmas (Martino, Al); Caroling, Caroling (Cole, Nat King); White Christmas (Waring, Fred, and the Pennsylvanians)

    Side 2: O Come All Ye Faithful (Ford, Tennessee Ernie); O Holy Night (Lettermen, The); Hark! The Herald Angels Sing (Hollywood Bowl Symphony Orchestra); I Sing Noel (Sandler and Young); O Little Town of Bethlehem (Fitzgerald, Ella); O Tannenbaum (Wagner, Roger, Chorale); Silent Night (Shore, Dinah)

Title		Label, Number	Year	VG	VG+	NM
Happy Holidays, Album 6		Capitol Creative Products SL-6669	1970	3.00	6.00	12.00

— *Sold only at True Value Hardware stores*

    Side 1: Ring Those Christmas Bells (Waring, Fred, and the Pennsylvanians); Christmas Song, The (Hollyridge Strings, The); Hang Your Wishes on the Tree (Baxter, Les); Do You Hear What I Hear (Sandler and Young); I Like a Sleighride (Lee, Peggy); Medley: Jingle Bells/Up on the House Top/Jolly Old St. Nicholas (Hollywood Pops Orchestra)

    Side 2: Christmas Waltz, The (Wilson, Nancy); Adeste Fideles (Sandler and Young); Hark! The Herald Angels Sing (Korean Orphan Choir, The); Santa Claus' Party (Baxter, Les); Medley: Silent Night/The First Noel (James, Sonny); Medley: Toyland/March of the Toys/We Wish You a Merry Christmas (Hollywood Pops Orchestra)

Title		Label, Number	Year	VG	VG+	NM
Happy Holidays, Album Seven		Capitol Creative Products SL-6730	1971	3.00	6.00	12.00

— *Sold only at True Value Hardware stores*

    Side 1: Sing We Now of Christmas (Ford, Tennessee Ernie); Christmas Song, The (Hollywood Pops Orchestra); Mister Santa (Sandler and Young); We Three Kings (New Sounds of Christmas, The); Christmas Carousel (Lee, Peggy)

    Side 2: We Wish You a Merry Christmas/You're All I Want for Christmas (Martino, Al); Cradle in Bethlehem, A (Cole, Nat King); Child's Christmas Medley, A (New Sounds of Christmas, The); Silent Night (Lettermen, The); O Come All Ye Faithful (Fitzgerald, Ella)

Title		Label, Number	Year	VG	VG+	NM
Happy Holidays, Album 8		Columbia Special Products C 11086	1972	2.50	5.00	10.00

— *Sold only at True Value Hardware stores*

    Side 1: Hark! The Herald Angels Sing (Philadelphia Orchestra [Ormandy]); Rudolph, the Red-Nosed Reindeer (Anderson, Lynn); Twelve Days of Christmas, The (Ives, Burl); O Holy Night (Mathis, Johnny); Deck the Hall (Nero, Peter)

    Side 2: I Heard the Bells (Mormon Tabernacle Choir); O Come, All Ye Faithful (Nabors, Jim); Coventry Carol, The (Byrd, Charlie); My Favorite Things (Bennett, Tony); Jingle Bells (Conniff, Ray)

Title		Label, Number	Year	VG	VG+	NM
Happy Holidays, Album Nine		Columbia Special Products P 11793	1973	2.50	5.00	10.00

— *Sold only at True Value Hardware stores*

    Side 1: Joy to the World (Biggs, E. Power); It Came Upon the Midnight Clear (Bryant, Anita); Winter Wonderland (Lawrence, Steve, and Eydie Gorme); God Rest Ye Merry, Gentlemen (Faith, Percy); Away in a Manger (Wynette, Tammy)

    Side 2: Silver Bells (Goulet, Robert); First Noel, The (Davidson, John); Sleigh Ride (New Christy Minstrels, The); O Tannenbaum (Philadelphia Brass Ensemble); Silent Night, Holy Night (Miller, Mitch)

Title		Label, Number	Year	VG	VG+	NM
Happy Holidays, Album Ten		Columbia Special Products P 12344	1974	2.50	5.00	10.00

— *Sold only at True Value Hardware stores*

Title		Label, Number	Year	VG	VG+	NM
Happy Holidays, Album Eleven			1975			

— *See "Sandler and Young"*

Title		Label, Number	Year	VG	VG+	NM
Happy Holidays! Album Twelve			1976			

— *See "Sandler and Young"*

`397`

Title	Label, Number	Year	VG	VG+	NM
Happy Holidays, Volume 13	RCA Special Products DPL1-0319	1978	2.50	5.00	10.00

— *Sold only at True Value Hardware stores*
Side 1: Home for the Holidays (Como, Perry); Medley: Here We Come a-Caroling/O Christmas Tree/I Saw Three Ships (Boston Pops Orchestra [Fiedler]); Christmas Song, The (Mancini, Henry); Ave Maria (Schubert) (Price, Leontyne); Jingle Bells (Andrews, Julie)
Side 2: It Came Upon a Midnight Clear (Philadelphia Orchestra [Ormandy]); Medley: O Come All Ye Faithful/Away in a Manger/God Rest Ye Merry, Gentlemen (Shaw, Robert, Chorale); Christmas and Love (Pride, Charley); Medley: Hark! The Herald Angels Sing/O Little Town of Bethlehem/Silent Night (Gary, John); Santa Claus Is Comin' to Town (Davis, Danny, and Nashville Brass)

| Happy Holidays, Volume 14 | RCA Special Products DPL1-0376 | 1979 | 2.50 | 5.00 | 10.00 |

— *Sold only at True Value Hardware stores*
Side 1: Christmas Song, The (Como, Perry); Winter Wonderland (Boston Pops Orchestra [Fiedler]); Little Drummer Boy, The (Luboff, Norman, Choir); White Christmas (Gary, John); I'll Be Home for Christmas (Cantrell, Lana)
Side 2: Joy to the World (Philadelphia Orchestra [Ormandy]); Time to Be Jolly, A (Crosby, Bing); Silver Bells (Smith, Kate); Medley: Wassail Song/Deck the Halls (Shaw, Robert, Chorale); O Holy Night (Peerce, Jan)

| Happy Holidays, Volume 15 | RCA Special Products DPL1-0453 | 1980 | 2.50 | 5.00 | 10.00 |

— *Sold only at True Value Hardware stores*
Side 1: There Is No Christmas Like a Home Christmas (Como, Perry); Santa Claus Is Comin' to Town (Boston Pops Orchestra [Fiedler]); Sunny Bank (Andrews, Julie); Do You Hear What I Hear (Gary, John); Medley: We Three Kings of Orient Are/O Come All Ye Faithful/Joy to the World (Mancini, Henry)
Side 2: Hark! The Herald Angels Sing (Philadelphia Orchestra [Ormandy]); Silver Bells (Jones, Jack); White Christmas (Cantrell, Lana); Medley: Carol of the Bells/Lo, How a Rose E'er Blooming/Go Tell It on the Mountain (Shaw, Robert, Chorale); Mary's Boy Child (Belafonte, Harry)

| Happy Holidays, Volume 16 | RCA Special Products DPL1-0501 | 1981 | 2.50 | 5.00 | 10.00 |

— *Sold only at True Value Hardware stores*
Side 1: Medley: It Came Upon a Midnight Clear/Away in a Manger/The First Noel (Mancini, Henry); Deck the Halls (Andrews, Julie); Silent Night (Mantovani); Angels We Have Heard on High (Philadelphia Orchestra [Ormandy]); Christmas Is Here Again (Whittaker, Roger)
Side 2: 'Twas the Night Before Christmas (Greene, Lorne); Sleigh Ride (Fitzgerald, Ella); Christ Is Born (Como, Perry); You Are My Christmas Carol (West, Dottie); Ave Maria (Bach-Gounod) (Domingo, Placido)

| Happy Holidays, Volume 17 | RCA Special Products DPL1-0555 | 1982 | 2.50 | 5.00 | 10.00 |

— *Sold only at True Value Hardware stores*
Side 1: Hallelujah It's Christmas (Whittaker, Roger); Dialog and Songs/It's Beginning to Look a Lot Like Christmas (Chipmunks, The); Sleigh Ride (Salsoul Orchestra, The); Pretty Paper (Nelson, Willie); Silver Bells (Murray, Anne)
Side 2: Love Is a Christmas Rose (Como, Perry); Carol for Another Christmas (Mancini, Henry); Silent Night (Arnold, Eddy); Christmas Eve in My Home Town (Smith, Kate); Tiny Angels (Whittaker, Roger)

| Happy Holidays, Volume 18 | RCA Special Products DPL1-0608 | 1983 | 2.50 | 5.00 | 10.00 |

— *Sold only at True Value Hardware stores*
Side 1: Christmas Is... (Jones, Jack); Winter Wonderland (Murray, Anne); Sleigh Ride (Mozart) (Boston Pops Orchestra [Fiedler]); Twelve Days of Christmas, The (Belafonte, Harry); If Every Day Was Like Christmas (Presley, Elvis)
Side 2: Christmas Is Here Again (Whittaker, Roger); Little Drummer Boy, The (Simeone, Harry, Chorale); O Holy Night (Cole, Nat King); Christmas Is the Warmest Time of the Year (Ames, Ed); I Wish It Could Be Christmas Forever (Como, Perry)

| Happy Holidays, Volume 19 | RCA Special Products DPL1-0689 | 1984 | 2.50 | 5.00 | 10.00 |

— *Sold only at True Value Hardware stores*
Side 1: Home for Christmas (Whittaker, Roger); Carol of the Bells (Shaw, Robert, Chorale); Merry Christmas Darling *Original 1970 rendition* (Carpenters); Do You Hear What I Hear (Crosby, Bing); White Christmas (Boston Pops Orchestra [Fiedler])
Side 2: Joy to the World (Andrews, Julie); What a Merry Christmas This Could Be (Nelson, Willie); Silver Bells (Luboff, Norman, Choir); Christmas Song, The (Lee, Peggy); Jingle Bells (Reeves, Jim)

| Happy Holidays, Vol. 20 | RCA Special Products DPL1-0713 | 1985 | 3.00 | 6.00 | 12.00 |

— *Sold only at True Value Hardware stores*
Side 1: Little Drummer Boy, The (Crosby, Bing); Medley: Deck the Halls/Joy to the World/It Came Upon a Midnight Clear (Smith, Kate); Silent Night (Whittaker, Roger); Christmas Song, The (Torme, Mel); Blue Christmas (Presley, Elvis); The Great Songs of Christmas (Medley) (Mantovani); Ave Maria (Bach-Gounod) (Franchi, Sergio)
Side 2: Sleigh Ride (Carpenters); Toyland (Como, Perry); It's Christmas (Milsap, Ronnie); O Little Town of Bethlehem (Shea, George Beverly); Medley: I Saw Three Ships/O Tannenbaum/Allon, Gay, Gay Bergeres/The Holly and the Ivy (Shaw, Robert, Chorale); I Wonder As I Wander (Price, Leontyne); O Holy Night (Lanza, Mario)

| Happy Holidays, Vol. 21 | RCA Special Products DPL1-0739 | 1986 | 3.00 | 6.00 | 12.00 |

— *Sold only at True Value Hardware stores*
Side 1: Have Yourself a Merry Little Christmas (Galway, James); Christmas Toast, A (Crosby, Bing); Angels from the Realm of Glory (Andrews, Julie); Good King Wenceslas (Ames Brothers, The); Silver Bells (Presley, Elvis); Santa Claus Is Comin' to Town (Dorsey, Tommy)
Side 2: Happy Holidays (Alabama); God Rest Ye Merry, Gentlemen (Cole, Nat King); I Wonder As I Wander (Canadian Brass, The); Hurry Home for Christmas (Lawrence, Steve, and Eydie Gorme); Christmas Eve in My Home Town (Vinton, Bobby); Jingle Bells (Miller, Glenn, and His Orchestra)

| Happy Holidays, Vol. 22 | RCA Special Products DPL1-0777 | 1987 | 2.50 | 5.00 | 10.00 |

— *Sold only at True Value Hardware stores*
Side 1: Medley: Here We Come a-Caroling/We Wish You a Merry Christmas/God Rest Ye Merry, Gentlemen (Como, Perry); That Christmas Feeling (Yuletide Choristers); Away in a Manger (Andrews, Julie); Silver Bells (Milsap, Ronnie); Have Yourself a Merry Little Christmas (Carpenters); O Holy Night (Lettermen, The)
Side 2: White Christmas (Parton, Dolly); Flying Home for Christmas (Living Voices); Homecoming Christmas (Alabama); Little Drummer Boy, The (Gayle, Crystal); Feliz Navidad (Feliciano, Jose); Silent Night (Fitzgerald, Ella)

| Happy Holidays, Vol. 23 | MCA Special Products 15042 | 1988 | 3.00 | 6.00 | 12.00 |

— *Sold only at True Value Hardware stores; appears to be the last one on vinyl LP*
Side 1: Santa Claus Is Coming to Town (Lynn, Loretta); It's Christmas Time (Oak Ridge Boys, The); Merry Christmas Baby (Berry, Chuck); This Christmas (Jets, The); Frosty the Snowman (Strait, George); Greatest Little Christmas Ever Wuz (Stevens, Ray)
Side 2: Winter Wonderland (Andrews Sisters, The); Jesus, Jesus, Rest Your Head (Trapp Family Singers, The); Little Drummer Boy, The *Stereo re-recording* (Simeone, Harry, Chorale); Jingle Bell Rock (Lee, Brenda); Medley: O Holy Night/Joy to the World/It Came Upon a Midnight Clear (Williams, Roger); White Christmas (Crosby, Bing)

Title	Label, Number	Year	VG	VG+	NM

Happy Holly Days — Capitol Creative Products SL-6761 — 1971 — 2.50 — 5.00 — 10.00
- Side 1: Medley: God Rest Ye Merry Gentlemen/Jingle Bells/Good King Wenceslas (101 Strings); Caroling, Caroling (Cole, Nat King); Medley: We Wish You a Merry Christmas/Silver Bells (Martino, Al); Little Drummer Boy (Lettermen, The); Sleigh Ride (Waring, Fred, and the Pennsylvanians)
- Side 2: Little Altar Boy (Campbell, Glen); Christmas Waltz, The (Lee, Peggy); Twelve Days of Christmas, The (New Sounds of Christmas, The); Away in a Manger (Fitzgerald, Ella); Hark, the Herald Angels Sing (Hollywood Bowl Symphony Orchestra)

Have a Happy Holiday — Columbia Special Products CSS 1432 — 1970 — 2.50 — 5.00 — 10.00
- Side 1: Twelve Days of Christmas, The (Mormon Tabernacle Choir); Deck the Hall with Boughs of Holly (Miller, Mitch, and the Gang); Silent Night, Holy Night (Bryant, Anita); Happy Holiday (Faith, Percy); Let It Snow! Let It Snow! Let It Snow! (Lawrence, Steve, and Eydie Gorme)
- Side 2: Adoramus Te (Conniff, Ray); We Wish You a Merry Christmas (Kostelanetz, Andre); It Came Upon the Midnight Clear (Vale, Jerry); You're All I Want for Christmas (Laine, Frankie); Jesus Garcia (Regency Choir, The)

Have a Jewish Christmas . . .? — M — Tower T-5081 — 1967 — 3.75 — 7.50 — 15.00
— *Comedy sketches narrated by Lennie Weinrib and acted by Christine Nelson, Benny Rubin, Reginald X. Carlisle and Naomi Lewis*
- Side 1: Problem, The; Christmas Cards; Christmas Trees; Tanta and the Tree
- Side 2: Santa Claus; Christmas Machers; Party, The;Shut Up, Irving!

Have a Merry Chess Christmas — Chess/MCA CH-25210 — 1988 — 3.00 — 6.00 — 12.00
- Side 1: Run, Rudolph, Run (Berry, Chuck); Hey Santa Claus (Moonglows, The); Merry Christmas Baby (Berry, Chuck); Love for Christmas (Gems, The); Christmas Means Love (Soul Stirrers, The)
- Side 2: Christmas Ain't Christmas, New Year's Ain't New Year's Without the One You Love (O'Jays, The); Blue Christmas (Meditation Singers, The); Santa Claus Is Coming to Town (Lewis, Ramsey, Trio); Merry Christmas to You (Salem Travelers, The); Christmas Love (Rotary Connection)

Have Yourself a Merry Little Christmas — M — Reprise R 50001 — 1963 — 6.25 — 12.50 — 25.00
— *Wreath cover; titled on back cover "Top Hollywood Stars Want You to..."*

Have Yourself a Merry Little Christmas — M — Reprise R 50001 — 1963 — 6.25 — 12.50 — 25.00
— *Christmas tree cover; titled "Frank Sinatra and His Friends Want You to..."*

Have Yourself a Merry Little Christmas — S — Reprise R9-50,001 — 1963 — 7.50 — 15.00 — 30.00
— *Christmas tree cover; titled "Frank Sinatra and His Friends Want You to..."*
- Side 1: Have Yourself a Merry Little Christmas (Sinatra, Frank); O Little Town of Bethlehem (Stafford, Jo); Vision of Sugar Plums, A (May, Billy); What Child Is This (McGuire Sisters, The); First Noel, The (Smith, Keely); Deck the Halls (Hi-Lo's, The); Jingle Bells (Davis, Sammy, Jr.)
- Side 2: Medley: Go Tell It On the Mountain/How Shall I Send Thee/Carol of the Bells/Joy to the World (Baxter, Les); Medley: Away in a Manger/Hark! The Herald Angels Sing (Rivers, Mavis); Adeste Fideles (Monte, Lou); Cantique de Noel (Riddle, Nelson); It Came Upon a Midnight Clear (Clooney, Rosemary); Peace on Earth and Silent Night (Martin, Dean)

Have Yourself a Merry Little Christmas — Rhino R1 70911 — 198? — 3.00 — 6.00 — 12.00

Henry Mancini Selects Great Songs of Christmas — RCA Special Products DPL1-0148 — 1975 — 2.50 — 5.00 — 10.00
— *Sold only at Goodyear tire dealers*
- Side 1: Have Yourself a Merry Little Christmas (Mancini, Henry); Santa Claus Is Comin' to Town (Carpenters); Medley: Joy to the World/Angels We Have Heard on High (Shaw, Robert, Chorale); Irish Carol (Andrews, Julie); Silent Night (Como, Perry); O Holy Night (Mantovani); Ave Maria (Schubert) (Price, Leontyne)
- Side 2: Jingling Brass (Davis, Danny, Nashville Brass); Christmas Is the Warmest Time of the Year (Ames, Ed); White Christmas (Mancini, Henry); Sleigh Ride (Fitzgerald, Ella); Christmas Song, The (Gary, John); Silver Bells (Smith, Kate); Christmas Toast, A (Crosby, Bing); Medley: What Are You Doing New Year's Eve/Auld Lang Syne (Mancini, Henry)

Hillbilly Holiday — Rhino R1 70195 — 1988 — 3.00 — 6.00 — 12.00

Holiday Magic — Capitol Creative Products SL-6728 — 1971 — 3.00 — 6.00 — 12.00
- Side 1: I Like a Sleighride (Lee, Peggy); That's What I Want for Christmas (Wilson, Nancy); My Favorite Things (Ford, Tennessee Ernie); Christmas Carousel (Lee, Peggy); Have Yourself a Merry Little Christmas (Campbell, Glen)
- Side 2: Christmas Song, The (Lettermen, The); Away in a Manger (Gentry, Bobbie); There's No Place Like Home (Campbell, Glen); Remember Me at Christmas (Newton, Wayne); O Come All Ye Faithful (Martino, Al)

Holiday Magic — Capitol Special Markets SL-6728 — 197? — 2.50 — 5.00 — 10.00
— *Same as above, but reissue on renamed label*

Home for Christmas — (3) — Columbia Musical Treasury P3S 5608 — 1971 — 3.75 — 7.50 — 15.00
- Side 1: Hallelujah Chorus (Mormon Tabernacle Choir); I Heard the Bells on Christmas Day (Cash, Johnny); God Rest Ye Merry, Gentlemen (Brothers Four, The); Have Yourself a Merry Little Christmas (Vale, Jerry); Good King Wenceslas (Faith, Percy); Jingle Bells (Conniff, Ray)
- Side 2: White Christmas (Bennett, Tony); Count Your Blessings Instead of Sheep (Wynette, Tammy); I'll Be Home for Christmas (Mathis, Johnny); Away in a Manger (Farrell, Eileen); Glory to God in the Highest (London Pops Orchestra); What Child Is This (Davidson, John)
- Side 3: O Little Town of Bethlehem (Robbins, Marty); O Tannenbaum (Philadelphia Brass Ensemble); Rudolph, the Red-Nosed Reindeer (Autry, Gene) *Rechanneled stereo;* Twelve Days of Christmas, The (Ives, Burl) *Rechanneled stereo;* O Holy Night (Kostelanetz, Andre); Silent Night, Holy Night (Bryant, Anita)
- Side 4: Ave Maria (Schubert) (Philadelphia Orchestra [Ormandy]); Little Drummer Boy, The (Page, Patti); Holly and the Ivy, The (Biggs, E. Power); Go Tell It on the Mountain (Jackson, Mahalia); First Noel, The (Byrd, Charlie); Here Comes Santa Claus (Conniff, Ray)
- Side 5: Silver Bells (Day, Doris); Joseph Dearest, Joseph Mine (London Pops Orchestra); It Came Upon the Midnight Clear (Philadelphia Orchestra [Ormandy]); Santa Claus Is Comin' to Town (Davidson, John); We Wish You a Merry Christmas (Kostelanetz, Andre); Carol of the Bells (New York Philharmonic)
- Side 6: Hark the Herald Angels Sing (Philadelphia Orchestra [Ormandy]); We Three Kings of Orient Are (London Pops Orchestra); Do You Hear What I Hear? (Nabors, Jim); Holy City, The (Ford, Rita); Christmas Song, The (Goulet, Robert); Joy to the World (Faith, Percy)

Title		Label, Number	Year	VG	VG+	NM
Home for Christmas	(2)	Realm 2V 8101	1977	3.75	7.50	15.00

Side 1: White Christmas (Bennett, Tony); Have Yourself a Merry Little Christmas (Vale, Jerry); Jingle Bells (Conniff, Ray); Count Your Blessings Instead of Sheep (Wynette, Tammy); I'll Be Home for Christmas (Mathis, Johnny); Rudolph, the Red-Nosed Reindeer (Autry, Gene) *Reprocessed stereo*
Side 2: Little Drummer Boy, The (Page, Patti); Here Comes Santa Claus (Conniff, Ray); Silver Bells (Day, Doris); Santa Claus Is Comin' to Town (Davidson, John); Do You Hear What I Hear (Nabors, Jim); Christmas Song, The (Goulet, Robert)
Side 3: I Heard the Bells on Christmas Day (Cash, Johnny); God Rest Ye Merry, Gentlemen (Brothers Four, The); Good King Wenceslas (Faith, Percy); What Child Is This (Davidson, John); O Little Town of Bethlehem (Robbins, Marty); Holy City, The (Ford, Rita's, Music Boxes) *Reprocessed stereo*
Side 4: Silent Night, Holy Night (Bryant, Anita); First Noel, The (Boyd, Charlie); We Wish You a Merry Christmas (Kostelanetz, Andre); Twelve Days of Christmas, The (Ives, Burl) *Reprocessed stereo;* Joy to the World (Faith, Percy); Go Tell It on the Mountain (Jackson, Mahalia)

| Home for the Holidays | | MCA MSM-35007 | 1978 | 3.00 | 6.00 | 12.00 |

— Sold only at Firestone dealers (add 50% for sticker that says "Season's Greetings Firestone")
Side 1: Hark the Herald Angels Sing (Boone, Pat, Family); Medley: God Rest Ye Merry Gentlemen/It Came Upon a Midnight Clear/The First Noel (Jones, Jack); It's Beginning to Look a Lot Like Christmas (Crosby, Bing); Jingle Bells (Brady Bunch, The); I'll Be Home for Christmas (Fountain, Pete); Adeste Fideles (Atlanta Symphony Orchestra [Shaw])
Side 2: Santa Claus Is Coming to Town (Lynn, Loretta); Silver Bells (Welk, Lawrence); Jesu Bambino (Liberace); Silent Night (Boone, Pat, Family); O Little Town of Bethlehem (Ives, Burl); O Holy Night (Williams, Roger); Hallelujah Chorus (Atlanta Symphony Orchestra [Shaw])

| I'll Be Home for Christmas | | Pickwick SPC-1009 | 197? | 2.50 | 5.00 | 10.00 |

Side 1: Rudolph, the Red-Nosed Reindeer (Martin, Dean); Caroling, Caroling (Cole, Nat King); Christmas Song, The (Lee, Peggy); Twelve Days of Christmas, The (Ford, Tennessee Ernie); Silver Bells (Martino, Al)
Side 2: Little Drummer Boy (Rawls, Lou); Hark the Herald Angels Sing (Sandler and Young); Jingle Bells (Lombardo, Guy); I'll Be Home for Christmas (Beach Boys, The); Christmas Waltz, The (Wilson, Nancy)

| In Harmony 2 | | Columbia PC 37461 | 1981 | 3.75 | 7.50 | 15.00 |

— Contains one Christmas song:
Side 2, Song 5: Santa Claus Is Comin' to Town (Springsteen, Bruce)

| It's Christmas Time! | | Columbia Special Products P 14990 | 1979 | 2.00 | 4.00 | 8.00 |

Side 1: First Noel, The (Williams, Andy); It Came Upon the Midnight Clear (Andrews, Julie); God Rest Ye Merry Gentlemen (Brothers Four, The); Ave Maria (Streisand, Barbra); We Three Kings of Orient Are (Miller, Mitch)
Side 2: O Come All Ye Faithful (Bryant, Anita); What Child Is This (Mathis, Johnny); Santo Natale (Page, Patti); Coventry Carol (Newley, Anthony); We Wish You a Merry Christmas (Conniff, Ray)

| It's Christmas Time! | | SeaShell P 14990 | 1981 | 2.00 | 4.00 | 8.00 |

— Reissue of Columbia Special Products P 14990

| It's Christmastime! | M | Columbia Special Products CSM 429 | 1966 | 3.00 | 6.00 | 12.00 |

— Sold only at A&P grocery stores
Side 1: Jingle Bells (Beneke, Tex, Ray Eberle and the Modernaires); First Noel, The (Farrell, Eileen); Medley: Deck the Halls/Good King Wenceslas (Lanin, Lester); Twelve Days of Christmas, The (Jesus and Mary Choral Group, The); O Tannenbaum (Biggs, E. Power)
Side 2: Joy to the World (Kostelanetz, Andre); O Come All Ye Faithful (Regency Choir, The); O Holy Night (Jesus and Mary Choral Group, The); O Little Town of Bethlehem (Regency Choir, The); Silent Night (Regency Choir, The)

| Ital Christmas | | Top Ranking (no #) | 197? | 6.25 | 12.50 | 25.00 |

— Jamaican import
Side 1: Broke Pocket Christmas (Miller, Jacob "Killer"); Ahameric Ismas (High, Ray "Weather Man"); Silver Bells (Miller, Jacob "Killer"); Bionic Christmas (High, Ray "Weather Man")
Side 2: All I Want for Ismas (Miller, Jacob "Killer"); Ismas Drew (High, Ray "Weather Man"); Twelve Days of Ismas (Miller, Jacob "Killer"); Twelve Days at G.P. (High, Ray "Weather Man"); Deck the Halls (Miller, Jacob "Killer"); Rock This Christmas Rocker (High, Ray "Weather Man")

| Jazzy Wonderland, A | | Columbia 1P 8120 | 1990 | 3.75 | 7.50 | 15.00 |

— Available on vinyl through Columbia House only
Side 1: This Christmas (Connick, Harry, Jr. and Branford Marsalis); Santa Claus Is Comin' to Town (DeFrancesco, Joe, and Dwight Sills); Silent Night (Wilson, Nancy, and Kimiko Itoh); Blue Christmas (Washington, Grover, Jr.); Little Drummer Boy, The (Lundberg, Karl, and Full Circle); Some Children See Him (Marsalis, Branford, and Harry Connick, Jr.); White Christmas (Bennett, Tony)
Side 2: Winter Wonderland (Marsalis, Wynton); Go Tell It on the Mountain (Whalum, Kirk); This Is Christmas (Marsalis, Ellis); Jingle Bells (Tee, Richard); Christmas Song, The (Simon, Fred, and Traut/Rodby); Little Drummer Boy, The (Jordan, Marlon, and Delfeayo Marsalis); O Come All Ye Faithful (Croft, Monte, and Terence Blanchard)

Jingle Bell Jazz	M	Columbia CL 1893	1962	5.00	10.00	20.00
Jingle Bell Jazz	S	Columbia CS 8693	1962	3.75	7.50	15.00
Jingle Bell Jazz		Harmony KH 32529	1973	3.00	6.00	12.00

— Reissue of CS 8693 with one track changed

| Jingle Bell Jazz | | Columbia PC 36803 | 1980 | 2.50 | 5.00 | 10.00 |

— Reissue of Harmony KH 32529 on the "Jazz Odyssey" series
Side 1: Jingle Bells (Ellington, Duke); White Christmas (Hampton, Lionel); Winter Wonderland (Hamilton, Chico); Christmas Song, The (McRae, Carmen); Rudolph, the Red-Nosed Reindeer (Poindexter, Pony); We Three Kings of Orient Are (Horn, Paul)
Side 2: Santa Claus Is Comin' to Town (Brubeck, Dave, Quartet); Deck Us All with Boston Charlie (Lambert, Hendricks and Ross); Deck the Halls (Hancock, Herbie); If I Were a Bell (Manhattan Jazz All-Stars, The); Rockin' Around the Christmas Tree (Morris, Marlowe); Blue Xmas (To Whom It May Concern) (Davis, Miles)

| Jingle Bell Rock | (2) | Time-Life SRNR-XM | 1987 | 5.00 | 10.00 | 20.00 |

— Available from Time-Life by mail order only; boxed set
Side 1: Jingle Bell Rock (Helms, Bobby); Run Rudolph Run (Berry, Chuck); Merry Christmas Baby (Redding, Otis); Go Tell It on the Mountain (Robinson, Smokey, and the Miracles); My Favorite Things (Supremes, The); White Christmas (Drifters, The)
Side 2: Man with All the Toys, The (Beach Boys, The); Jingle Bells (Booker T. and the MG's); Rudolph, the Red-Nosed Reindeer (Temptations, The); Gee Whiz, It's Christmas (Thomas, Carla); Someday at Christmas (Jackson Five, The); Frosty the Snowman (Jan and Dean); Christmas Song, The (King Curtis)

400

Title	Label, Number	Year	VG	VG+	NM

Side 3: Rockin' Around the Christmas Tree (Lee, Brenda); Medley: Deck the Halls/Bring a Torch (Robinson, Smokey, and the Miracles); It's Christmas (Marvin and Johnny); My Christmas Tree (Temptataions, The); Sleigh Ride (Ventures, The); Christmas Ain't Christmas Without the One You Love (O'Jays, The)
Side 4: I Saw Mommy Kissing Santa Claus (Jackson Five, The); There's Trouble Brewin' (Scott, Jack); Merry, Merry Christmas Baby (Stevens, Dodie); Winter Wonderland (Franklin, Aretha); This Christmas (Hathaway, Donnie); Step Into Christmas (John, Elton)

Joy of Christmas, The   Columbia Special Products P 12042   1973   3.00   6.00   12.00
— Sold only at Strawbridge & Clothier stores (Philadelphia area)
Side 1: Joy to the World (Philadelphia Orchestra [Ormandy]); Sleigh Ride (New Christy Minstrels, The); God Rest You Merry, Gentlemen (Goulet, Robert); Kissin' by the Mistletoe (Franklin, Aretha); Deck the Halls (Faith, Percy)
Side 2: Jingle Bells (Ellington, Duke); First Noel, The (Davidson, John); Go Tell It on the Mountain (Jackson, Mahalia); What Child Is This (Byrd, Charlie); We Wish You a Merry Christmas (Reynolds, Debbie)

Joy of Christmas, The, Featuring   Columbia Special Products   1972   3.75   7.50   15.00
Marty Robbins and His Friends   C 11087
Side 1: Joy of Christmas, The; O Little Town of Bethlehem; Little Stranger (In a Manger); Hark! The Herald Angels Sing; Christmas Prayer, A (all by Robbins, Marty)
Side 2: Soon It Will Be Christmas Day (Anderson, Lynn); It Came Upon the Midnight Clear (Price, Ray); Joy to the World (Wynette, Tammy); First Noel, The (Chuck Wagon Gang, The); Silent Night, Holy Night (Cash, Johnny)

Joy to the World   (3)   Columbia Special Products   1978   5.00   10.00   20.00
(30 Classic Christmas Melodies)   P3 14654
— Box set; produced for Murray Hill Records
Side 1: For Unto Us a Child Is Born (Philadelphia Orchestra [Ormandy]); It Came Upon a Midnight Clear (Jackson, Mahalia); What Child Is This? (Brothers Four, The); We Three Kings of Orient Are (Biggs, E. Power); O Come All Ye Faithful (Nabors, Jim)
Side 2: God Rest You Merry, Gentlemen (Goulet, Robert); Away in a Manger (Farrell, Eileen); Good King Wenceslas (Sullivan, Ed, Presents); Noel We Sing (Biggs, E. Power); O Holy Night (Davidson, John)
Side 3: Go Tell It on a Mountain (Nabors, Jim); Holly and the Ivy, The (Biggs, E. Power); Gesu Bambino (Ross, Elinor); O Little Town of Bethlehem (Robbins, Marty); O Tannenbaum (Philadelphia Orchestra [Ormandy])
Side 4: Panis Angelicus (Goulet, Robert); First Noel, The (Douglas, Mike); Ave Maria (Stern, Isaac); Hark! The Herald Angels Sing (Luboff, Norman, Choir); Hallelujah Chorus (Philadelphia Orchestra [Ormandy])
Side 5: Jingle Bells (Page, Patti); Deck the Hall with Boughs of Holly (Philadelphia Brass Ensemble); Silver Bells (Davidson, John); Joy to the World (Nabors, Jim); Twelve Days of Christmas, The (Philadelphia Brass Ensemble)
Side 6: Little Drummer Boy (Warfield, Sandra, with James McKracken); Silent Night (Jackson, Mahalia); Here We Go A-Caroling (Philadelphia Orchestra [Ormandy]); White Christmas (Goulet, Robert); We Wish You a Merry Christmas (Kostelanetz, Andre)

Joyful Sound of Christmas, The   RCA Record Club CSP-0601   1969   3.75   7.50   15.00
— Available only through the RCA Record Club
Side 1: (There's No Place Like) Home for the Holidays (Living Strings); Frosty the Snow Man (Klein, John); Winter Wonderland (Living Voices); Have Yourself a Merry Little Christmas (Living Strings); Santa Claus Is Coming to Town (Living Voices)
Side 2: Christmas Song, The (Living Voices); Let It Snow! Let It Snow! Let It Snow! (Klein, John); Happy Holiday (Living Strings and Living Voices); Rudolph the Red-Nosed Reindeer (Leibert, Dick); Mary's Boy Child (Living Strings); White Christmas (Living Strings and Living Voices)

Joyous Christmas   Columbia Special Products CSS 5??   1967   3.00   6.00   12.00
— Produced for the Beneficial Finance System

Joyous Christmas, Volume 2   Columbia Special Products CSS 808   1968   3.00   6.00   12.00
— Produced for the Beneficial Finance System
Side 1: O Holy Night (Goulet, Robert); Medley: God Rest Ye Merry Gentlemen/O Tannenbaum (Senior Concert Orchestra, The); Joy to the World (Miller, Mitch); Rudolf the Red-Nosed Reindeer (Senior Concert Orchestra, The); Silver Bells (Mathis, Johnny); We Wish You a Merry Christmas (Gramercy [NYC] Boys' Club Choir); Medley: Hark! The Herald Angels Sing/Deck theHall with Boughs of Holly (Senior Concert Orchestra, The)
Side 2: Winter Wonderland (Lawrence, Steve, and Eydie Gorme); Ave Maria (Gounod) (Moye, Eugene, Jr., cello solo); I'll Be Home for Christmas (Day, Doris); Let It Snow! Let It Snow! Let It Snow! (Senior Concert Orchestra, The); 'Twas the Night Before Christmas (Cross, Milton J.); Silent Night (Mormon Tabernacle Choir); Auld Lang Syne (Senior Concert Orchestra, The)

Joyous Christmas, Volume 3   Columbia Special Products CSS 1???   1969   3.00   6.00   12.00
— Produced for the Beneficial Finance System

Joyous Christmas, Volume 4   Columbia Special Products CSS 1485   1970   3.00   6.00   12.00
— Produced for the Beneficial Finance System
Side 1: Joy to the World (Mormon Tabernacle Choir); Hark! The Herald Angels Sing (Davidson, John); Christmas Fantasy: Jingle Bells/Silent Night/Adeste Fideles (Senior Concert Orchestra, The); Sleigh Ride (Mathis, Johnny); Waltz of the Flowers (from The Nutcracker) (Senior Concert Orchestra, The); First Noel, The (Eddy, Nelson) Rechanneled stereo
Side 2: White Christmas (Day, Doris); Christmas Is Forever (Medley) (Senior Concert Orchestra, The); Rejoice Greatly (from Messiah) (Arlene, Bess); Toyland (Beneficial Singers, The); Little Drummer Boy, The (Cash, Johnny); Joyous Christmas (Beneficial Singers, The)

Joyous Christmas, Volume V   Columbia Special Products C 10398   1971   2.50   5.00   10.00
— Produced for the Beneficial Finance System
Side 1: Secret of Christmas, The (Crosby, Bing); Medley: Jolly Old St. Nicholas/O Tannenbaum/Angels from the Realms of Glory (Senior Concert Orchestra, The); Do You Hear What I Hear? (Carroll, Diahann); Medley: Deck the Halls/We Three Kings of Orient Are/I Heard the Bells on Christmas Day (Senior Concert Orchestra, The); Ave Maria (Schubert) (Moffo, Anna); Dance of the Sugar-Plum Fairy (Senior Concert Orchestra, The)
Side 2: Medley: We Wish You a Merry Christmas/Silent Night/O Come, All Ye Faithful/Jingle Bells (Bennett, Tony); Go Tell It on the Mountain (Senior Concert Orchestra, The); Angels We Have Heard on High (Goulet, Robert, and Carol Lawrence); Medley: Good King Wenceslas/Away in a Manger (Senior Concert Orchestra, The); Lord's Prayer, The (Tucker, Richard); Joyous Christmas (Beneficial Singers, The)

Title	Label, Number	Year	VG	VG+	NM
Joyous Christmas, Volume 6	Columbia Special Products C 11083	1972	2.50	5.00	10.00

— *Produced for the Beneficial Finance System*
 Side 1: Jingle Bells (Kaye, Danny); Toyland (Day, Doris); Old-Fashioned Christmas (Medley) (Senior Concert Orchestra, The); He's Got the Whole World in His Hands (Bryant, Anita); Petersburg Sleighride (Senior Concert Orchestra, The); Christmas Lullaby (Grant, Cary)
 Side 2: Just What I Wanted for Christmas (Crosby, Bing); Rockin' Around the Christmas Tree (Anderson, Lynn); Yuletide Greetings (Medley) (Senior Concert Orchestra, The); Medley: Merry Christmas/Dame, Get Up and Bake Your Pies/Christmas Is Coming (Biggs, E. Power); Joy to the World (Jackson, Mahalia); Deck the Hall with Boughs of Holly (Kaye, Danny); Danse des Mirlitons (from The Nutcracker) (Senior Concert Orchestra, The); Joyous Christmas (Beneficial Singers, The)

Joyous Music for Christmas Time	(4) M	Reader's Digest RD 45-M	1963	5.00	10.00	20.00
Joyous Music for Christmas Time	(4) S	Reader's Digest RD 45-S	1963	5.00	10.00	20.00

— *Available only through Reader's Digest magazine by mail order*
 Side 1: Joy to the World; O Little Town of Bethlehem; Deck the Halls with Boughs of Holly; Away in a Manger; God Rest You Merry, Gentlemen; Angels We Have Heard on High (all by Royal Philharmonic Orchestra)
 Side 2: O Come, All Ye Faithful; We Three Kings of Orient Are;Twelve Days of Christmas, The; O Holy Night; It Came Upon a Midnight Clear; Hark! The Herald Angels Sing (all by Royal Philharmonic Orchestra)
 Side 3: Christmas Suite for Orchestra (Winter Wonderland/Jingle Bells/Santa Claus Is Coming to Town/Rudolph the Red-Nosed Reindeer/White Christmas/Sleigh Ride/Skaters Waltz) (Benson, Richard, and His Orchestra)
 Side 4: First Noel, The; Good King Wenceslas; Ave Maria; O Come, O Come, Emmanuel; Christmas Is Coming; Carol of the Bells (all by Pearson, Leslie/John Paice/London Bell Ringers/Westminster Brass Ensemble)
 Side 5: And the Glory of the Lord Shall Be Revealed; Comfort Ye My People; Every Valley Shall Be Exalted; For Unto Us a Child Is Born; Pastoral Symphony; He Shall Feed His Flock; Come Unto Him; And He Shall Purify (all by London Philharmonic Orchestra)
 Side 6: Behold the Lamb of God; He Was Despised and Rejected of Men; The Trumpet Shall Sound; I Know That My Redeemer Liveth; Hallelujah (all by London Philharmonic Orchestra)
 Side 7: Stille Nacht, Heilige Nacht; Ihr Kinderlein Kommet; Es Ist ein Ros' Entsprungen; O Tannenbaum; Heiligste Nacht; Nun Singet und Seid Froh; Wie Schon Leuchtet der Morgenstern; Den die Hirten Lobten Sehre; O Du Frohliche, O Du Selige; Vom Himmel Hoch Da Komm Ich Her (all by Aeolian Kammerchor)
 Side 8: Guillo Pron Ton Tambourin; Quelle Est Cette Odeur Agreable?; Sus! Qu'on Se Reveille; Voici la Nouvelle; Marche des Rois; O Jesus, Nous Voici Comme Autrefois les Anges; Bethlehem: Dans cette etable; Durreau la Duree; Ding, Dong; Noel, Noel, Noel (all by Chanteurs de la Vierge)

Joyous Noel	(4)	Reader's Digest RDA-57A	1966	3.75	7.50	15.00

— *Available only through Reader's Digest magazine by mail order*
 Side 1: White Christmas (Gary, John); Deck the Halls (Ames Brothers, The); It Came Upon the Midnight Clear (Three Suns, The); Twelve Days of Christmas, The (Belafonte, Harry); C-H-R-I-S-T-M-A-S (Arnold, Eddy); Little Drummer Boy, The (Mancini, Henry)
 Side 2: I'll Be Home for Christmas (Como, Perry); Sleigh Ride (Melachrino Strings, The); Have Yourself a Merry Little Christmas (MacKenzie, Gisele); Christmas in Killarney (Day, Dennis); Silver Bells (Cramer, Floyd); God Rest Ye Merry, Gentlemen (Kerr, Anita, Singers)
 Side 3: Joy to the World (Shaw, Robert, Chorale); Away in a Manger (Lanza, Mario); Rise Up, Shepherd, an' Foller (Maynor, Dorothy); Holy City, The (Hines, Jerome); O Little Town of Bethlehem (Crooks, Richard); Ave Maria (Schubert) (Anderson, Marian)
 Side 4: O Christmas Tree (Lanza, Mario); Virgin's Slumber Song, The (Thebom, Blanche); Ave Maria (Bach-Gounod) (McCormack, John, and Fritz Kreisler); Hark! The Herald Angels Sing (Shaw, Robert, Chorale); Angel's Song (Anderson, Marian); Buon Natale (Christmastime in Rome) (Franchi, Sergio)
 Side 5: We Wish You a Merry Christmas (Greene, Lorne); Mary's Little Boy Chile (Belafonte, Harry); Winter Wonderland (Gary, John); What Child Is This? (Schumann, Walter); Frosty the Snowman (Monroe, Vaughn); Old Christmas Card, An (Reeves, Jim)
 Side 6: First Nowell, The (Shaw, Robert, Chorale); Christmas Song, The (Como, Perry); I Heard the Bells on Christmas Day (Smith, Kate); I Saw Three Ships (Lanza, Mario); Go Tell It on the Mountain (Shea, George Beverly); Do You Hear What I Hear? (Luboff, Norman, Choir)
 Side 7: Adeste Fideles (O Come, All Ye Faithful) (McCormack, John); Nazareth (Crooks, Richard); Cantique de Noel (O Holy Night) (Caruso, Enrico); Panis Angelicus (McCormack, John); Gesu Bambino (The Infant Jesus) (Martinelli, Giovanni); Silent Night (German) (Schumann-Heink, Ernestine); Silent Night (Melton, James)
 Side 8: Jingle Bells (Miller, Glenn); All I Want for Christmas (Jones, Spike, and the City Slickers); Santa Claus Is Comin' to Town (Ames Brothers, The); Rudolph the Red-Nosed Reindeer (Locklin, Hank); I Saw Mommy Kissing Santa Claus (Hines, Mimi); Parade of the Wooden Soldiers (Martin, Freddy)

Joyous Songs of Christmas, The	Columbia Special Products C 10400	1971	2.50	5.00	10.00

— *Sold only at Goodyear tire dealers*
 Side 1: We Need a Little Christmas (Faith, Percy); Christmas Song, The (Burnett, Carol); Winter Wonderland (Bennett, Tony); Love's What You're Getting for Christmas (Sherman, Bobby); Christmas Waltz, The (Lennon Sisters, The); Deck the Halls (Kaye, Danny); Joy to the World (Mormon Tabernacle Choir)
 Side 2: Have Yourself a Merry Little Christmas (Streisand, Barbra); Go Tell It on the Mountain (Nabors, Jim); Let It Snow! Let It Snow! Let It Snow! (Horne, Lena); Hark! The Herald Angels Sing (Philadelphia Orchestra [Ormandy])/Temple University Concert Choir; Sleigh Ride (Williams, Andy); Silver Bells (Mathis, Johnny); We Wish You a Merry Christmas (Conniff, Ray)

Joys of Christmas	Capitol Creative Products SL-6610	1969	3.00	6.00	12.00
Joys of Christmas	Capitol Special Markets SL-6610	197?	2.50	5.00	10.00

— *Reissue with revised label name*
 Side 1: Joy to the World (Wagner, Roger, Chorale); Adeste Fideles (Sandler and Young); Silent Night (Shore, Dinah); Do You Hear What I Hear (Crosby, Bing); Toyland/March of the Toys (Hollywood Pops Orchestra); O Little Town of Bethlehem (Korean Orphan Choir)
 Side 2: Winter Wonderland (Voices of Christmas); First Noel, The (Korean Orphan Choir); Christmas Waltz, The (Wilson, Nancy); Medley: Sleigh Ride/Jingle Bells (Rogers, Roy); Have Yourself a Merry Little Christmas (Sandler and Young); Medley: We Three Kings/We Wish You a Merry Christmas (Hollywood Pops Orchestra)

Let's Celebrate Christmas	Capitol Special Markets SL-6923	1973	3.00	6.00	12.00

 Side 1: Happy Holiday (Riddle, Nelson); White Christmas (Martin, Dean); Silent Night (Shore, Dinah); Night Before Christmas Song, The (Simeone, Harry, Chorale); Adeste Fideles (Hollywood Pops Orchestra)
 Side 2 Medley: Hark the Herald Angels Sing/ It Came Upon a Midnight Clear (Crosby, Bing); Scarlet Ribbons (Gentry, Bobbie); We Three Kings (New Sounds of Christmas, The); Blue Christmas (Campbell, Glen); Joy to the World (Cole, Nat King)

Title		Label, Number	Year	VG	VG+	NM
Life Treasury of Christmas Music, The	M	Project/Capitol TL 100	1963	5.00	10.00	20.00

— *Designed as a supplement to the Life Book of Christmas; selections performed by anonymous chorus and orchestra and Boy Choristers from the Church of the Transfiguration (NY) except as noted*

Side 1: Joy to the World (Baker, Walter); Jerusalem Gaude; Angel Gabriel, The (Spiro, Robert); Rocking Carol (Boy Choristers of the Church of the Transfiguration [NY]); Angels We Have Heard on High; Carol of the Bagpipers, The; Golden Carol of the Three Wise Men, The (Sands, Robert); Joy to the World

Side 2: Adeste Fideles (Baker, Walter); Hodie Christus Natus Est; Boar's Head Carol, The (Sands, Robert); Coventry Carol (Love, Shirley); Huron Indian Carol; Masters in This Hall; God Rest You Merry (Spiro, Robert); Deck the Halls; Here We Come a-Wassailing (Spiro, Robert); Patapan; Hark! The Herald Angels Sing (Baker, Walter)

| Little Drummer Boy, The | | Capitol/Pickwick SPC-3462 | 197? | 2.50 | 5.00 | 10.00 |

Side 1: Little Drummer Boy, The (Newton, Wayne); White Christmas (Martin, Dean); O Holy Night (Sandler and Young); What Child Is This (Martino, Al); Mrs. Santa Claus (Cole, Nat King)

Side 2: Jingle Bells (Hollyridge Strings, The); Adeste Fideles (Wagner, Roger, Chorale); It Came Upon a Midnight Clear (Fitzgerald, Ella); Silent Night (Lombardo, Guy)

| Magic of Christmas, The | (2) | Capitol SWBB-93810 | 1971 | 3.75 | 7.50 | 15.00 |

— *Available only through the Capitol Record Club*

Side 1: Jingle Bells (Wagner, Roger, Chorale); Happy Holiday (Lee, Peggy); Caroling, Caroling (Cole, Nat King); Night Before Christmas, The (Campbell, Glen); What Child Is This (Lettermen, The)

Side 2: My Favorite Things (Ford, Tennessee Ernie); O Little Town of Bethlehem (Fitzgerald, Ella); Rudolph, the Red-Nosed Reindeer (Newton, Wayne); O Holy Night (Martino, Al); Away in a Manger (Gentry, Bobbie)

Side 3: White Christmas (Martin, Dean); Silver Bells (Waring, Fred, and the Pennsylvanians); That's What I Want for Christmas (Wilson, Nancy); Christmas Dinner, Country Style (Crosby, Bing); We Three Kings of Orient Are (Beach Boys, The)

Side 4: Christmas Song, The (Sandler and Young); Coventry Carol, The (Shore, Dinah); Santa Claus Is Comin' to Town (Rawls, Lou); First Noel, The (Voices of Christmas); Silent Night (Stafford, Jo)

| Magic of Christmas, The | (2) | Columbia Musical Treasury P2M 5245 | 196? | 3.75 | 7.50 | 15.00 |

— *No artists mentioned*

Side 1: Deck the Hall with Boughs of Holly; Carol of the Bells; Away in a Manger; O Holy Night; Sleigh Ride; Here We Come a-Caroling; O Little Town of Bethlehem; Prayer from "Hansel and Gretel"; Joy to the World

Side 2: I Saw Three Ships; All Through the Night; White Christmas; Sleepers Awake!; Little Drummer Boy, The; We Three Kings of Orient Are; Jingle Bells; Greensleeves (What Child Is This?); Hallelujah Chorus

Side 3: We Wish You a Merry Christmas; Joseph Dearest, Joseph Mine; God Rest Ye Merry, Gentlemen; Twelve Days of Christmas, The; It Came Upon the Midnight Clear; Santa Claus Is Comin' to Town; Angels We Have Heard on High; Silent Night, Holy Night; First Noel, The

Side 4: O Come, All Ye Faithful; Silver Bells; Rudolph, the Red-Nosed Reindeer; Good King Wenceslas; Ave Maria (Schubert); Christmas Song, The; I'll Be Home for Christmas; Do You Hear What I Hear?; Hark! The Herald Angels Sing

| Magic of Christmas, The | (3) | Columbia Musical Treasury P3S 5806 | 1972 | 5.00 | 10.00 | 20.00 |

Side 1: Have Yourself a Merry Little Christmas (Aldrich, Ronnie); First Noel, The (Mathis, Johnny); It Came Upon a Midnight Clear (Wynette, Tammy); Good King Wenceslas (Biggs, E. Power); Jingo Jango (Kaempfert, Bert); Santa Claus Is Coming to Town (Ives, Burl); I Saw Three Ships (Mantovani)

Side 2: Silent Night, Holy Night (Philadelphia Orchestra [Ormandy]); Medley: O Tannenbaum/Jingle Bells (Last, James); Come, Dear Children (Burt, Alfred, Carols); I Heard the Bells on Christmas Day (Crosby, Bing); Little Drummer Boy, The (Lennon Sisters, The); Here We Come a-Caroling (Conniff, Ray); While Shepherds Watched Their Flocks (Smart, Charles, and James Blades)

Side 3: Here Comes Santa Claus (Conniff, Ray); Winter Wonderland (Alpert, Herb, and the Tijuana Brass); Rudolph, the Red-Nosed Reindeer (Welk, Lawrence); What Child Is This (Davidson, John); Sweet Little Jesus Boy (Jackson, Mahalia); Frosty the Snowman (Lombardo, Guy); O Come, All Ye Faithful (Goulet, Robert)

Side 4: Twelve Days of Christmas, The (Mantovani); For Unto Us a Child Is Born (Baxter, Terry); We Three Kings of Orient Are (Williams, Roger); Medley: Little Donkey/Do You Hear What I Hear? (Kallmann, Gunter); I'll Be Home for Christmas (Nabors, Jim); O Come, O Come Emmanuel (Waring, Fred, and the Pennsylvanians); Silver Bells (Page, Patti)

Side 5: Hark! The Herald Angels Sing (Faith, Percy); Sleigh Ride (Boston Pops Orchestra [Fiedler] *1970s re-recording;* Angels We Have Heard on High (Mormon Tabernacle Choir); In Dulci Jubilo (St. Thomas Choir); Christmas Song, The (Bennett, Tony); Coventry Carol (Byrd, Charlie); God Rest Ye Merry, Gentlemen (Wechter, Julius, and the Baja Marimba Band)

Side 6: We Wish You a Merry Christmas (Kostelanetz, Andre); White Christmas (Aldrich, Ronnie); Happy Holiday (Crosby, Bing); Bright, Bright the Holly Berries (Burt, Alfred, Carols); Joy to the World (Sutherland, Joan); Let It Snow! Let It Snow! Let It Snow! (Day, Doris); Carol of the Bells (New York Philharmonic [Bernstein])

| Magnavox Album of Christmas Music | Q | Columbia Special Products CSQ 11093 | 1972 | 5.00 | 10.00 | 20.00 |

— *Sold only at Magnavox dealers; yes, this is in quadraphonic!*

Side 1: It's Beginning to Look a Lot Like Christmas (Kostelanetz, Andre); I Love the Winter Weather/I've Got My Love to Keep Me Warm (Bennett, Tony); Jingle Bells (Page, Patti); Frosty the Snowman (Anderson, Lynn); Trepak (from Nutcracker Suite) (Nero, Peter)

Side 2: O Little Town of Bethlehem (Tucker, Richard); O Holy Night (Nero, Peter); Holly and the Ivy, The (Biggs, E. Power); I Wonder As I Wander (Faith, Percy); Panis Angelicus (Kiley, Richard)

| Mahalia (Jackson) and Friends at Christmastime | | Columbia Special Products P 11804 | 1973 | 3.00 | 6.00 | 12.00 |

— *Side 2 is all rechanneled stereo; Side 1 is true stereo*

Side 1: Silent Night; What Child Is This; Hark! The Herald Angels Sing; O Little Town of Bethlehem; Away in a Manger (all by Jackson, Mahalia)

Side 2: God Rest Ye Merry Gentlemen (Caravans, The); White Christmas (Original Five Blind Boys, The); Christmas Message, A (Taylor, Charles); Go Tell It on the Mountain (Swan Silvertones, The); Mary's Boy Child (Gospel Clefs, The)

| Many Moods of Christmas, The | | Columbia Special Products P 12013 | 1973 | 3.00 | 6.00 | 12.00 |

— *Sold only at Goodyear tire dealers*

Side 1: White Christmas (Fitzgerald, Ella); Christmasland (Bennett, Tony); Winter Weather (Stafford, Jo); O Little Town of Bethlehem (Streisand, Barbra); Christmas Waltz (Boone, Pat); Whatever Happened to Christmas? (Sinatra, Frank); Medley: Jingle Bells/It's Christmas Time All Over the World (Davis, Sammy, Jr.)

Side 2: Christmas Song, The (Beneke, Tex, in the Glenn Miller Style); Toyland (Day, Doris); Jingle Bell Rock (Fountain, Pete); Christmas Is (Crosby, Bing); O Come All Ye Faithful (Andrews, Julie); Let It Snow! Let It Snow! Let It Snow! (Williams, Andy); What Are You Doing New Year's Eve (Fitzgerald, Ella)

Title			Label, Number	Year	VG	VG+	NM
Merry Christmas		(3)	Columbia Musical Treasury 3P 6306	1975	3.75	7.50	15.00

Side 1: We Wish You a Merry Christmas (Reynolds, Debbie); Blue Christmas (Newton, Wayne); I Saw Mommy Kissing Santa Claus (Anderson, Lynn); 'Twas the Night Before Christmas (Brothers Four, The); Winter Wonderland (Miller, Mitch); Jingle Bells (Cash, Johnny)

Side 2: First Noel, The (Davidson, John); Christmas Comes to Us All Once a Year (Jackson, Mahalia); Christmas Eve in My Home Town (Vinton, Bobby); Christmas Bells (Page, Patti); God Rest Ye Merry, Gentlemen (Byrd, Charlie); Santa Claus Is Comin' to Town (Conniff, Ray)

Side 3: Let It Snow! Let It Snow! Let It Snow! (Martin, Dean); Do You Hear What I Hear (Bryant, Anita); Silver Bells (Goulet, Robert); White Christmas (Wynette, Tammy); (There's No Place Like) Home for the Holidays (Vale, Jerry); Good King Wenceslas (Wagner, Roger, Chorale)

Side 4: Out of the East (Baxter, Terry); O Little Town of Bethlehem (Kostelanetz, Andre); My Favorite Things (Bennett, Tony); What Child Is This (Smith, Connie); O Holy Night (Mathis, Johnny); It Came Upon a Midnight Clear (Philadelphia Orchestra [Ormandy])

Side 5: Unto Us a Child Is Born (Biggs, E. Power); Frosty the Snowman (Autry, Gene); Sleigh Ride (Boston Pops Orchestra [Fiedler]) *1970s re-recording;* I'll Be Home for Christmas (Day, Doris); Silent Night, Holy Night (Price, Ray); O Come All Ye Faithful (Martino, Al)

Side 6: There's No Place Like Home (Campbell, Glen); Joy to the World (Mormon Tabernacle Choir); Christmas Song, The (Nabors, Jim); Hark! The Herald Angels Sing (Faith, Percy); That Holiday Feeling (Lawrence, Steve, and Eydie Gorme); Auld Lang Syne (Lanin, Lester)

Title			Label, Number	Year	VG	VG+	NM
Merry Christmas	10		Coral CRL 56080	1952	20.00	40.00	80.00
Merry Christmas	M		King 680	1959	50.00	100.00	200.00
Merry Christmas			Rainbow Sound R-5032-LPS	198?	2.50	5.00	10.00

Side 1: I Heard the Bells on Christmas Day (Morris, Sue); God Rest Ye Merry Gentlemen (Elkins, Curtis); O Holy Night (Partridge, Judy); Christmas Spirit, The (Cline, Bob); Go Tell It on the Mountain (Dodge, Sue)

Side 2: What Child Is This? (Lea, Melva); Medley: Jingle Bells/We Wish You a Merry Christmas (Wesson, Jim); Angels We Have Heard on High (Dodge, Sue); Christmas Time Is the Best Time of the Year (McSpadden, Gary); We Three Kings of Orient Are (Roman, LuLu)

Title			Label, Number	Year	VG	VG+	NM
Merry Christmas	M		RCA Victor PRM-168	1964	3.00	6.00	12.00
Merry Christmas	S		RCA Victor PRS-168	1964	3.75	7.50	15.00

Side 1: Nativity, The: Silent Night/O Holy Night/O Come All Ye Faithful (Radio City Music Hall Orchestra); Overture; Marche (from The Nutcracker) Boston Pops Orchestra [Fiedler]); Hallelujah Chorus (Royal Philharmonic Orchestra)

Side 2: Home for the Holidays (Como, Perry); Little Drummer Boy, The (Atkins, Chet); Medley: Hark! The Herald Angels Sing/God Rest Ye Merry, Gentlemen (Henderson, Skitch); Joy to the World (Shea, George Beverly); Medley: Away in a Manger/The First Noel/It Came Upon a Midnight Clear (Klein, John); Let There Be Peace on Earth (Luboff, Norman, Choir)

Title			Label, Number	Year	VG	VG+	NM
Merry Christmas Baby (Christmas Music for Young Lovers)	M		Hollywood HLP 501	1956	30.00	60.00	120.00

Side 1: Merry Christmas Baby (Brown, Charles); Sleigh Ride (Glenn, Lloyd, Trio); Christmas Every Day (Moore, Johnny's, Blazers); Boogie Woogie Santa Claus (Scott, Mabel; Lonesome Christmas Part 1 (Fulson, Lowell); Christmas Dreams (Moore, Johnny's, Blazers)

Side 2: Christmas Eve Baby (Moore, Johnny's, Blazers); Christmas Letter (Moore, Johnny's, Blazers); Love for Christmas (Jackson Trio); Lonesome Christmas Part 2 (Fulson, Lowell); Christmas Blues (Witherspoon, Jimmy); Jingle Bell Hop (Jackson Trio)

Title			Label, Number	Year	VG	VG+	NM
Merry Christmas Baby			Gusto/Hollywood K-5018-X	1978	3.00	6.00	12.00

Side 1: Merry Christmas Baby (Brown, Charles); Christmas Every Day (Moore, Johnny's, Blazers); Boogie Woogie Santa Claus (Scott, Mabel); Christmas Eve Baby (Moore, Johnny's, Blazers); Christmas in Heaven (Ward, Billy, and His Dominoes); Christmas Tears (King, Freddy); Jingle Bell Hop (Jackson Trio); Christmas Dreams (Moore, Johnny's, Blazers)

Side 2: Lonesome Christmas Part 1 (Fulson, Lowell); I'll Be Home for Christmas (Jackson, Bull Moose); Sleigh Ride (Glenn, Lloyd, Trio); I Hear Jingle Bells (King, Freddy); Christmas Letter (Moore, Johnny's, Blazers); Love for Christmas (Jackson Trio); Christmas Blues (Witherspoon, Jimmy); Lonesome Christmas Part 2 (Fulson, Lowell)

Title			Label, Number	Year	VG	VG+	NM
Merry Christmas from . . .		(4)	Reader's Digest RD4-83	196?	5.00	10.00	20.00

— Available only through Reader's Digest magazine by mail order

Side 1: Hark the Herald Angels Sing (Luboff, Norman, Choir); Adeste Fideles (Farrell, Eileen); For Unto Us a Child Is Born (Philadelphia Orchestra [Ormandy]); Lord's Prayer, The (Tucker, Richard); Once in Royal David's City (Mormon Tabernacle Choir); Holy City, The (Eddy, Nelson); O Sanctissima (Philadelphia Orchestra [Ormandy])

Side 2: Joy to the World (Philadelphia Orchestra [Ormandy]); While Shepherds Watched Their Flocks (Mormon Tabernacle Choir); Christians Awake (Schreiner, Alexander); Break Forth, O Beauteous, Heavenly Light (Mormon Tabernacle Choir); O Come, O Come, Emmanuel (Mormon Tabernacle Choir); Hallelujah Chorus (Philadelphia Orchestra [Ormandy])

Side 3: O Little Town of Bethlehem (Luboff, Norman, Choir); It Came Upon a Midnight Clear (Mathis, Johnny); Deck the Halls (Biggs, E. Power); First Noel, The (Eddy, Nelson); O Tannenbaum (Luboff, Norman, Choir); O Holy Night (Vale, Jerry); Angels We Have Heard on High (Kostelanetz, Andre)

Side 4: Here We Come a-Caroling (Conniff, Ray); God Rest Ye Merry, Gentlemen (Goulet, Robert); Away in a Manger (Bryant, Anita); Good King Wenceslas (Faith, Percy); We Three Kings of Orient Are (Miller, Mitch); Silent Night (Byrd, Charlie); Silent Night (Gorme, Eydie)

Side 5: Christmas Song, The (Torme, Mel); Winter Wonderland (Murad, Jerry's, Harmonicats); I'll Be Home for Christmas (Brothers Four, The); Let It Snow, Let It Snow, Let It Snow (Lawrence, Steve, and Eydie Gorme); Blue Christmas (Mathis, Johnny); Sleigh Ride (Conniff, Ray)

Side 6: White Christmas (Goulet, Robert); Have Yourself a Merry Little Christmas (Day, Doris); Happy Holiday (Faith, Percy); Silver Bells (Day, Doris); Frosty the Snowman (Miller, Mitch); You're All I Want for Christmas (Laine, Frankie)

Side 7: Santa Claus Is Comin' to Town (Lawrence, Steve, and Eydie Gorme); Rudolph, the Red-Nosed Reindeer (Autry, Gene); Jingle Bells (Miller, Mitch); Christmas Time Is Here Again (Robbins, Marty); I Saw Mommy Kissing Santa Claus (Boyd, Jimmy); Here Comes Santa Claus (Autry, Gene)

Side 8: Twelve Days of Christmas, The (Miller, Mitch); Toyland (Day, Doris); Little Drummer Boy, The (New Christy Minstrels, The); Coventry Carol (Byrd, Charlie); What Child Is This (Miller, Mitch); Go Tell It on the Mountain (Jackson, Mahalia); Christmas Story, The (Ives, Burl)

Title		Label, Number	Year	VG	VG+	NM
Merry Christmas from David Frost and Billy Taylor		Bell 6053	1970	3.75	7.50	15.00

Side 1: Joy to the World (Taylor, Billy); Rise Up Shepherd (Crawford, Joseph); We Need Peace and We Need Love (Taylor, Billy); Wexford Carol (Granger, Gerri); Bright Star in the East (Taylor, Billy)
Side 2: Away in a Manger (Mitchell, Ella); Stable Down the Road (Mitchell, Ella, and Billy Taylor); Merry Christmas (Wess, Frank); Christmas Song (Granger, Gerri); Go Tell It on the Mountain (Mitchell, Ella, and Milt Grayson); House of Christmas, The (Frost, David); Go Tell It on the Mountain (Reprise)

Title		Label, Number	Year	VG	VG+	NM
Merry Christmas from Motown		Motown MS-681	1970	7.50	15.00	30.00
Merry Christmas from Sesame Street		CRA CTW 25516	1975	3.00	6.00	12.00

Side 1: Sesame Street Christmas Overture (Sesame Street Festival Orchestra); We Wish You a Merry Christmas (The Company); Deck the Halls Medley (The Company); I Hate Christmas (Oscar); Christmas Story, A (Mr. Hooper, Ernie and Bert); Have Yourself a Merry Little Christmas (Bert and Ernie); Twelve Days of Christmas, The (The Company)
Side 2: It's Beginning to Look a Lot Like Christmas Medley (Big Bird/Susan and Gordon/Bob/Grover); Night Before Christmas on Sesame Street, The (David); Saludo (aguinaldo) (Maria and Luis); Arrurrru (Maria and Luis); (All I Want for Christmas Is) My Two Front Teeth (The Count); Christmas Pageant, A (Bert/Ernie/Prairie Dawn/Herry Monster/Grover/Cookie Monster); Keep Christmas With You (All Through the Year) (The Company); We Wish You a Merry Christmas (reprise) (The Company)

Title		Label, Number	Year	VG	VG+	NM
Merry Christmas to You	M	Capitol T 9030	1955	12.50	25.00	50.00
Merry Christmas with Nat King Cole/ Fred Waring and the Pennsylvanians		Capitol Special Markets SL-6883	1973	2.50	5.00	10.00

Side 1: Christmas Song, The (Cole, Nat King); Silver Bells (Waring, Fred, and the Pennsylvanians); O Little Town of Bethlehem (Cole, Nat King); God Rest Ye Merry, Gentlemen (Cole, Nat King); White Christmas (Waring, Fred, and the Pennsylvanians); Caroling, Caroling (Cole, Nat King)
Side 2: Joy to the World (Cole, Nat King); Winter Wonderland (Waring, Fred, and the Pennsylvanians); Away in a Manger (Cole, Nat King); Cradle in Bethlehem, A (Cole, Nat King); Sleigh Ride (Waring, Fred, and the Pennsylvanians); Adeste Fideles (Cole, Nat King)

Title		Label, Number	Year	VG	VG+	NM
Mistletoe and Memories		RCA 8372-1-R	1988	3.75	7.50	15.00

Side 1: Santa Claus (I Still Believe in You) (Alabama); Blue Christmas (Oslin, K.T.); O Come All Ye Faithful (Presley, Elvis); Silent Night (Rogers, Kenny); White Christmas (Parton, Dolly)
Side 2: Silver Bells (Judds, The); It's Not Christmas (Milsap, Ronnie); This Time of Year (Johnson, Michael); In a Manger (Baillie and the Boys)

Title		Label, Number	Year	VG	VG+	NM
Motown Christmas, A	(2)	Motown 795V2	1973	5.00	10.00	20.00
Motown Christmas, A	(2)	Motown 5256ML2	1982	3.75	7.50	15.00

— Reissue with same contents

Title		Label, Number	Year	VG	VG+	NM
Motown Christmas, A	(2)	Motown R 271663	1983	4.00	8.00	16.00

— RCA Music Service edition

Side 1: Santa Claus Is Coming to Town (Jackson Five, The); What Christmas Means to Me (Wonder, Stevie); Rudolph, the Red-Nosed Reindeer (Temptations, The); My Favorite Things (Supremes, The); Deck the Halls/Bring a Torch, Jeannette, Isabella (Robinson, Smokey, and the Miracles); I Saw Mommy Kissing Santa Claus (Jackson Five, The)
Side 2: Ave Maria (Schubert) (Wonder, Stevie); Silent Night (Temptations, The); Little Christmas Tree (Jackson, Michael); God Rest Ye Merry Gentlemen (Robinson, Smokey, and the Miracles); Christmas Song, The (Jackson Five); Joy to the World (Supremes, The)
Side 3: Little Drummer Boy, The (Temptations, The); Silver Bells (Supremes, The); Someday at Christmas (Wonder, Stevie); Frosty the Snowman (Jackson Five, The); Jingle Bells (Robinson, Smokey, and the Miracles); My Christmas Tree (Temptations, The)
Side 4: White Christmas (Supremes, The); One Little Christmas Tree (Wonder, Stevie); Give Love on Christmas Day (Jackson Five, The); It's Christmas Time (Robinson, Smokey, and the Miracles); Children's Christmas Song (Supremes, The); Have Yourself a Merry Little Christmas (Jackson Five, The)

Title		Label, Number	Year	VG	VG+	NM
Music Box Melodies of Christmas		Pickwick SPC-1014	197?	2.50	5.00	10.00

— Also see "Ford, Rita." These, from anonymous sources, apparently are not from Ms. Ford's collection.
Side 1: Silent Night; O Sanctissima; Song of the Bells; First Noel, The; O Tannenbaum; Adeste Fideles
Side 2: Ave Maria; Hark! The Herald Angels Sing; Come All Ye Children; Rosary, The; Jingle Bells; Auld Lang Syne

Title		Label, Number	Year	VG	VG+	NM
Music to Trim Your Tree By	M	RCA Victor PRM 225	1966	3.00	6.00	12.00
Music to Trim Your Tree By	S	RCA Victor PRS 225	1966	3.75	7.50	15.00

Side 1: Deck the Halls (Damone, Vic); Sleigh Ride (Boston Pops Orchestra [Fiedler]); We Wish You a Merry Christmas (Anderson, Marian); Medley: The Coventry Carol/God Rest Ye Merry, Gentlemen (Atkins, Chet); Medley: Deck the Halls/Good King Wenceslas/It Came Upon the Midnight Clear/Under the Christmas Mistletoe (Leibert, Dick)
Side 2: Medley: Silent Night/Jingle Bells (Hugo and Luigi); White Christmas (Gary, John); Silver Bells (Hirt, Al); We Three Kings (Shaw, Robert, Chorale); Mary's Little Boy Child (Reeves, Jim); Do You Hear What I Hear? (Luboff, Norman, Choir)

Title		Label, Number	Year	VG	VG+	NM
Muzak Stimulus Progression Number Three: Christmas		Muzak S-2563	196?	3.00	6.00	12.00

— Instrumental versions by anonymous musicians
Side 1: O Holy Night; O Little Town of Bethlehem; O Come, O Come, Emmanuel; Medley: As with Gladness, Men of Old/It Came Upon the Midnight Clear; Hark the Herald Angels Sing; Joy to the World
Side 2: O Come, All Ye Faithful; Silent Night; We Three Kings of Orient Are; Medley: Once in Royal David's City/ Watchman, Tell Us of the Night; First Noel, The; Medley: Angels We Have Heard on High/Good Christian Men, Rejoice!

Title		Label, Number	Year	VG	VG+	NM
Narada: The Christmas Collection		Narada N-63902	1988	3.00	6.00	12.00

Side 1: Joy to the World (Mitchell, Bruce); Ukrainian Carol (Brewer, Spencer); What Child Is This (Buffett, Peter); It Came Upon a Midnight Clear (Tingstad, Eric, and Nancy Rumbel); Man from Ceasaria, The (Friedemann)
Side 2: O Holy Night (Lanz, David, and Paul Speer); Medley: Patapan/Noel Nouvelet (Rumbel, Nancy); Return of the Magi (Ellwood, William); God Rest Ye Merry Gentlemen (Doan, John); Away in a Manger (Darling, David); I Saw Three Ships (Arkenstone, David)

Title		Label, Number	Year	VG	VG+	NM
Nashville Christmas Album, The		Epic PE 40418	1986	2.50	5.00	10.00

Side 1: Silent Night, Holy Night (Smith, Connie, and Willie Nelson); O Little Town of Bethlehem (Gray, Mark); What Child Is This (Frickie, Janie); White Christmas (Haggard, Merle); Away in a Manger (Wynette, Tammy, and the O'Kanes)
Side 2: Jingle Bell Rock (Sweethearts of the Rodeo); Silver Bells (Jones, George, and Gene Watson); Pretty Paper (Conlee, John); Rockin' Around the Christmas Tree (Gilley, Mickey, and Libby Hurley); Winter Wonderland (McClain, Charly, and Wayne Massey)

Title	Label, Number	Year	VG	VG+	NM

Nashville's Greatest Christmas Hits   Columbia PC 44412   1988   2.50   5.00   10.00
     Side 1: Silent Night, Holy Night (Nelson, Willie); Sweet Baby Jesus (Gatlin, Larry, and the Gatlin Brothers Band); O Come All Ye
        Faithful (Smith, Connie); Hark! The Herald Angels Sing (Robbins, Marty); O Little Town of Bethlehem (Price, Ray)
     Side 2: Away in a Manger (Wynette, Tammy); White Christmas (Haggard, Merle); Joy to the World (Cash, Johnny); Silver
        Bells (Jones, George, and Gene Watson); Do You Hear What I Hear (Atkins, Chet)

Nashville's Greatest Christmas Hits, Volume 2   Columbia PC 44413   1988   2.50   5.00   10.00
     Side 1: Pretty Paper (Nelson, Willie); It Came Upon the Midnight Clear (Wynette, Tammy); O Holy Night (Rich, Charlie); First Noel,
        The (Thomas, B.J.); Let It Snow, Let It Snow, Let It Snow (Atkins, Chet)
     Side 2: Hallelujah Chorus (Gatlin, Larry, and the Gatlin Brothers Band); Soon It Will Be Christmas Day (Anderson, Lynn); I'll Be Home
        for Christmas (Gilley, Mickey); Winter Wonderland (Whitman, Slim); Little Drummer Boy, The (Price, Ray)

O. Henry's The Gift of the Magi   E.F. MacDonald EFMX-62   1962   5.00   10.00   20.00
— *Special album done by the E.F. MacDonald Company, Dayton, Ohio*
     Side 1: Gift of the Magi, The (Carradine, John)
     Side 2: Adeste Fideles (101 Strings); O Holy Night (Les Djinns [French Girls Choir]); Silent Night (101 Strings); Noel (101 Strings); He
        Is Born a Divine Child (Les Djinns [French Girls Choir]); Hark the Herald Angels Sing (101 Strings)

October 1960 Popular Stereo Sampler   DJ   RCA Victor SPS-33-96   1960   150.00   300.00   600.00
— *Promo-only collection. Contains one Christmas song:*
     Side 1, Song 5: Little Drummer Boy, The (Hugo and Luigi Children's Chorus)

October '61 Pop Sampler   DJ   RCA Victor SPS-33-141   1961   150.00   300.00   600.00
— *Promo-only collection. Contains one Christmas song:*
     Side 1, Song 5:Jingle Bells (Atkins, Chet)

October Christmas Sampler 59-40-41   DJ   RCA Victor SPS-33-54   1959   150.00   300.00   600.00
— *Promo-only collection*
     Side 1: Blue Christmas (Presley, Elvis); Have Yourself a Merry Little Christmas (MacKenzie, Gisele); White Christmas (Klein, John);
        Blue Christmas (Esquivel); Winter Wonderland (Melachrino, George, Orchestra); Santa Claus Is Coming to Town (Three
        Suns, The); Santa Claus Is Coming to Town (Hunter, Ralph)
     Side 2: O Little Town of Bethlehem (Shea, George Beverly); Home for the Holidays (Como, Perry); What a Friend We Have in
        Jesus (Johnson Family, The); Christmas Festival, A (Boston Pops Orchestra [Fiedler]); O Christmas Tree (Lanza, Mario);
        Silent Night (Tozzi, Georgio, and Rosalind Ellis)

Old-Fashioned Christmas, An   S   Longines Symphonette LS 214   196?   3.00   6.00   12.00
— *Record label has the number SYS 5422*
     Side 1: Sleigh Ride (Anderson, Leroy); Christmas Song, The (Torme, Mel); Caroling, Caroling (Waring, Fred, and the
        Pennsylvanians); Frosty the Snowman (Lee, Brenda); It's Beginning to Look Like Christmas (Kaye, Sammy)
     Side 2: Silver Bells (King, Wayne); Rudolph, the Red-Nosed Reindeer (Four Aces, The); I Saw Mommy Kissing Santa
        Claus (Lombardo, Guy); I Heard the Bells on Christmas Day (Crosby, Bing); Santa Claus Is Coming to Town (Welk, Lawrence)

Old Fashioned Christmas, An   (6)   Reader's Digest RDA 216-A   197?   5.00   10.00   20.00
— *Available only through Reader's Digest magazine by mail order*
     Side 1: Deck the Halls (Damone, Vic); O Come, All Ye Faithful (Fireside Singers, The); O Little Town of Bethlehem (Franchi, Sergio);
        Silent Night (Fireside Singers, The); Away in the Manger (Ames, Ed); Holly and the Ivy, The (Leibert, Dick)
     Side 2: Hark! The Herald Angels Sing (Fireside Singers, The); Mary's Little Boy Chile (Reeves, Jim); Ave Maria (Price, Leontyne);
        Panis Angelicus (Franchi, Sergio); Go Tell It on the Mountain (Fireside Singers, The); Children, Go Where I Send Thee
        (Fireside Singers, The)
     Side 3: Medley: Here We Come a-Caroling/O Christmas Tree/I Saw Three Ships (Fiedler, Arthur); First Noel, The (Fireside Singers,
        The); Angels We Have Heard on High (Fox, Virgil); God Rest Ye Merry Gentlemen (Crosby, Bing); We Three Kings of Orient
        Are (Fireside Singers, The); What Child Is This? (Coster, Janet)
     Side 4: Santa Claus Is Coming to Town (Waring, Fred, and the Pennsylvanians); Here Comes Santa Claus (Crosby, Bing with the
        Andrews Sisters); Rudolph the Red-Nosed Reindeer (Waring, Fred, and the Pennsylvanians); Frosty the Snowman
        (Lombardo, Guy); Parade of the Wooden Soldiers, The (Nalle, Billy); Christmas Eve in My Home Town (Smith, Kate)
     Side 5: Twelve Days of Christmas, The (Fireside Singers, The); Gather Around the Christmas Tree (McCarthy, John); It Came Upon
        the Midnight Clear (Damone, Vic); Good King Wenceslas (Fireside Singers, The); Medley: Tu Scendi Dalle Stelle/O
        Bambino (Franchi, Sergio); Little Drummer Boy, The (Fiedler, Arthur)
     Side 6: Carol of the Bells (Fireside Singers, The); Jingle Bells (Fireside Singers, The); Ding Dong! Merrily on High (Leibert, Dick);
        Silver Bells (Fireside Singers, The); I Heard the Bells on Christmas Day (Dixon, Reginald); We Wish You a Merry
        Christmas (Fireside Singers, The)
     Side 7: Christmas Song, The (Mancini, Henry); White Christmas (Como, Perry); My Favorite Things (Squires, Rosemary); Christmas
        Is . . . (Jones, Jack); Have Yourself a Merry Little Christmas (Garland, Judy); I'll Be Home for Christmas (Fireside Singers, The)
     Side 8: Let It Snow! Let It Snow! Let It Snow! (Fireside Singers, The); Winter Wonderland (Fireside Singers, The); Sleigh Ride (Dixon,
        Reginald); Hanover Winter Song (Waring, Fred, and the Pennsylvanians); Rags (Gold, Marty); Skater's Waltz (Philharmonic
        Pops Orchestra)
     Side 9: Blue Christmas (Reeves, Jim); Jolly Old St. Nicholas (Arnold, Eddy); Out of the East (Pride, Charley); Rockin' Around the
        Christmas Tree (Lee, Brenda); Jingle Bell Rock (Cramer, Floyd); C-H-R-I-S-T-M-A-S (Arnold, Eddy)
     Side 10: Joy to the World (Fireside Singers, The); Alleluia (Davies, William); O Holy Night (Fireside Singers, The); O Beauteous
        Heavenly Light (Westminster Brass Ensemble); Once in Royal David's City (Ambrosian Singers, The); Joy to the World (Fox,
        Virgil)
     Side 11: Dance of the Sugar Plum Fairy/Trepak/Waltz of the Flowers (New Symphony Orchestra of London); March of the Little Lead
        Soldiers (Orchestra de la Societe des Concerts, Symphonique de Paris); March of the Toys (Engel, Lehman, and His
        Orchestra); Toyland (Engel, Lehman, and His Orchestra)
     Side 12: For Unto Us a Child Is Born (London Philharmonic Orchestra and Chorus); Pastoral Symphony (Royal Philharmonic
        Orchestra); He Shall Feed His Flock Come Unto Him (London Philharmonic Orchestra and Chorus) *Soli: Norman Proctor,*
        Heather Harper; I Know That My Redeemer Liveth (London Philharmonic Orchestra and Chorus) *Soprano: Heather Harper;*
        Hallelujah Chorus (London Philharmonic Orchestra and Chorus)

On This Christmas Night   Songbird MCA-3184   1979   3.75   7.50   15.00
     Side 1: On This Christmas Night (Thomas, B.J.); Whole World Is Colored with Love, The (Reba); Born a Child in Bethlehem (Ford,
        Tennessee Ernie); Santa's Reindeer Ride (Grant, Amy); Special Wish, A (Stevenson, B.W.)
     Side 2: God Bless the Children (Thomas, B.J.); Gift of Love (Boones, The); Almost Christmastime (Meece, David); Star, The (Peek,
        Dan); Christmas Song, A (Warnke, Mike)

(Top left) On the heels of her success in *The Sound of Music,* Firestone got Julie Andrews to record 11 of the 12 songs on its 1966 Christmas album. A year later, RCA Victor issued an "official" Julie Andrews Christmas LP using the same recordings. (Top right) The most enduring of the custom Christmas series is True Value Hardware's *Happy Holidays.* The first edition was released in 1965, and except for 1977, it hasn't missed a holiday season since. Apparently the last one to be released on vinyl, however, was Volume 23 from 1988. (Bottom left) Once again, poor Bert gets the worst of it on the cover of this 1975 release. (Bottom right) Muzak for the masses: The subscription-only "environmental music" company issued this LP, possibly only as a promo, in the 1960s.

Title		Label, Number	Year	VG	VG+	NM
Original Amateur Hour	(2)	United Artists UXL 2	1960	10.00	20.00	40.00
25th Anniversary Album						

— *Contains one Christmas song:*
    Side 2, Song 4: I'll Be Home for Christmas (Lund, Art)

Title		Label, Number	Year	VG	VG+	NM
Peace on Earth	(2)	Capitol S?B?-585	1970	3.75	7.50	15.00
Phil Spector: Back to Mono 1958-1969	(5)	Phil Spector/Abkco 7118-1	1991	25.00	50.00	100.00

— *Box set; Sides 9 and 10 are the final vinyl reissue of (same as Side 1 and Side 2 of)* A Christmas Gift for You from Phil Spector

Title		Label, Number	Year	VG	VG+	NM
Phil Spector's Christmas Album	M	Apple SW 3400	1972	7.50	15.00	30.00

— *Reissue of A Christmas Gift for You from Phil Spector, PHLP-4005, with same contents*

Title		Label, Number	Year	VG	VG+	NM
Phil Spector's Christmas Album	M	Warner/Spector SP 9103	1974	5.00	10.00	20.00

— *Reissue of above album*

Title		Label, Number	Year	VG	VG+	NM
Phil Spector's Christmas Album	S	Pavillion PZ 37686	1981	3.75	7.50	15.00

— *Reissue of above album, but in true stereo*

Title		Label, Number	Year	VG	VG+	NM
Phil Spector's Christmas Album	S	Passport PB 3604	1984	3.00	6.00	12.00

— *Reissue of above album, also in true stereo*

Title		Label, Number	Year	VG	VG+	NM
Philco Album of Holiday Music, The		Columbia Special Products CSM 431	1966	3.75	7.50	15.00

— *Sold only at Philco dealers*
    Side 1: O Holy Night (Vale, Jerry); First Noel, The (Farrell, Eileen); White Christmas (Dean, Jimmy); Medley: O Little Town of Bethlehem/Deck the Hall with Boughs of Holly (Luboff, Norman, Choir); Silent Night (Stafford, Jo)
    Side 2: Joy to the World (St. Patrick's Cathedral Choir); It Came Upon the Midnight Clear (Rodgers, Jimmie); O Come, All Ye Faithful (Ferguson, Maynard); I Saw Three Ships (Burke Family Singers, The); Jingle Bells (Basie, Count)

Title	Label, Number	Year	VG	VG+	NM
Popular Christmas Classics	Capitol Special Markets SL-8100	1977	3.00	6.00	12.00

    Side 1: Christmas Song, The (Cole, Nat King) *Stereo recording;* Holly Jolly Christmas, A (Ives, Burl); Rudolph, the Red-Nosed Reindeer (Autry, Gene); Little Drummer Boy, The (Simeone, Harry, Chorale) *This is the original mono version;* Sleigh Ride (Anderson, Leroy)
    Side 2: Silver Bells (Whiting, Margaret, and Jimmy Wakely); Star Carol, The (Ford, Tennessee Ernie); White Christmas (Martin, Dean); Silent Night (Campbell, Glen); Do You Hear What I Hear (Crosby, Bing)

Title		Label, Number	Year	VG	VG+	NM
RCA Victor Presents Music for the	S	RCA Victor PRS-188	1965	3.00	6.00	12.00
Twelve Days of Christmas						

    Side 1: Twelve Days of Christmas, The (Hunter, Ralph, Choir); O Come, All Ye Faithful (Lanza, Mario); O Sanctissima (Shaw, Robert, Chorale); Christmas Festival, A (Medley) (Boston Pops Orchestra [Fiedler])
    Side 2: Christmas Song, The (Gary, John); Sleigh Ride (Melachrino Strings, The); Little Drummer Boy, The (Luboff, Norman, Choir); Jolly Old Saint Nicholas (Arnold, Eddy); Santa Claus Is Comin' to Town (Ames Brothers, The); Merry Christmas Neighbor (Greene, Lorne; Michael Landon; Dan Blocker)

Title	Label, Number	Year	VG	VG+	NM
Reggae Christmas, A	Real Authentic Sound RAS 3101	1984	3.00	6.00	12.00

    Side 1: We Wish You a Merry Christmas (Broggs, Peter/Don Carlos/Freddie McGregor/Smiley/Michigan/Glenice Spencer /Eek-A-Mouse/Pablo Black); Jingle Bells (Carlos, Don, and Glenise Spencer); Joy to the World (Lodge, June); Come All Ye Faithful (McGregor, Freddie)
    Side 2: Drummer Boy (Michigan and Smiley); Twelve Days of Christmas (Broggs, Peter); Silent Night (Black, Pablo); Feliz Navidad (McGregor, Freddie); Night Before Christmas, The (Eek-A-Mouse)

Title	Label, Number	Year	VG	VG+	NM
Reggae Christmas by The Joe Gibbs Family	Joe Gibbs Music 8077	1982	5.00	10.00	20.00
of Artists					

— *Includes Dennis Brown, Trinity, Mighty Diamonds, Culture, Sly & Robbie, June Lodge, Marcia Aitken, Jacob Miller, George Nooks, Cornell Campbell, Enos Mcleod and others on the following:*
    Side 1: Joy to the World; Deck the Halls; Christmas Is Coming; O Come Let Us Adore Him; O Come All Ye Faithful; Jingle Bells; Hark the Herald Angels Sing; Santa Claus Is Coming to Town; I'm Dreaming of a Black Christmas; Rudolph the Red-Nosed Reindeer; Christmas Breeze; First Noel, The; Joy to the World; We Wish You a Merry Christmas
    Side 2: On the Twelve Day of Ismus; We Three Kings; Deck the Halls; Winter Wonderland; O Little Town of Bethlehem

Title		Label, Number	Year	VG	VG+	NM
Remembering Christmas	M	RCA Special Products	1981	3.00	6.00	12.00
with the Big Bands		DPM1-0506				

    Side 1: Jingle Bells (Miller, Glenn, and His Orchestra); White Christmas (Kaye, Sammy, and His Orchestra); Silver Bells (Fontane Sisters, The); Parade of the Wooden Soldiers (Clinton, Larry, and His Orchestra); Winter Weather (Waller, Fats)
    Side 2: Winter Wonderland (Flanagan, Ralph, and His Orchestra); Snowfall (Thronhill, Claude, and His Orchestra); Greensleeves (What Child Is This) (New Glenn Miller Orchestra [McKinley]); Sleigh Ride (Martin, Freddy, and His Orchestra); Medley: What Are You Doing New Year's Eve/Auld Lang Syne (Mancini, Henry)

Title	Label, Number	Year	VG	VG+	NM
RFD Christmas	Columbia Special Products P 15427	1981	2.50	5.00	10.00

    Side 1: Joy to the World (Jones, George); First Noel, The (Miller, Jody); Away in a Manger (Tucker, Tanya); God Rest Ye Merry Gentlemen (Rich, Charlie); O Little Town of Bethlehem (James, Sonny)
    Side 2: O Holy Night (Rich, Charlie); Silent Night (Tucker, Tanya); O Come All Ye Faithful (Jones, George); What Child Is This (Miller, Jody); Soon It Will Be Christmas Day (Anderson, Lynn)

Title	Label, Number	Year	VG	VG+	NM
Rockin' Christmas — The '50s	Rhino RNLP-066	1984	3.75	7.50	15.00

    Side 1: Sleigh Bell Rock (Three Aces and a Joker); Dig That Crazy Santa Claus (McLollie, Oscar); Jingle Jangle (Penguins, The); Rockin' Santa Claus (Moods, The); Rockin' and Rollin' with Santa Claus (Hipsters, The); Christmas in Jail (Youngsters, The); Just a Lonely Christmas (Moonglows, The)
    Side 2: Jingle Bell Rock (Helms, Bobby); North Pole Rock (Sharpe, Cathy); Santa and the Satellite (Parts 1 and 2) (Buchanan and Goodman); Hey Santa Claus (Moonglows, The); Who Says There Ain't No Santa Claus (Holden, Ron); Yulesville, U.S.A. (Rockin' Stockin, The); It's Christmas (Marvin and Johnny)

Title	Label, Number	Year	VG	VG+	NM
Rockin' Christmas — The '60s	Rhino RNLP-067	1984	3.75	7.50	15.00
Rockin' Little Christmas	MCA 25084	1986	3.75	7.50	15.00

Title	Label, Number	Year	VG	VG+	NM
Rockin' Little Christmas	MCA R 154275	1986	3.75	7.50	15.00

— *BMG Music Service edition*
> Side 1: Rockin' Around the Christmas Tree (Lee, Brenda); Run Rudolph Run (Berry, Chuck); Hey Santa Claus (Moonglows, The); Merry, Merry Christmas Baby (Stevens, Dodie); Surfin' Santa (Byron, Lord Douglas); Love for Christmas (Gems, The)
> Side 2: Jingle Bell Rock (Helms, Bobby); Mambo Santa Mambo (Enchanters, The); I'm Gonna Lasso Santa Claus (Lee, Brenda); Merry Christmas Baby (Berry, Chuck); (Just a) Lonely Christmas (Moonglows, The); Surfer's Christmas List, A (Surfaris, The)

| Rocking Christmas Stocking, A | (2) Capitol SPRO 9303/4/5/6 | 1984 | 5.00 | 10.00 | 20.00 |

— *Promo only. Includes the following Christmas songs:*
> Side 1: Song 3, It Came Upon a Midnight Clear (Sinatra, Frank); Song 6, White Christmas (Rogers, Kenny)
> Side 2: Song 3, Silent Night (Sinatra, Frank); Song 5, Away in a Manger (Murray, Anne)
> Side 3: Song 3, Little Drummer Boy, The (Crosby, Bing); Song 6 First Noel, The (Cole, Nat King)
> Side 4: Song 3, O Tannenbaum (Cole, Nat King); Song 6 O Little Town of Bethlehem (Cole, Nat King)

| Ronco Presents A Christmas Gift | Columbia Special Products P 12430 | 1974 | 3.00 | 6.00 | 12.00 |

— *"Distributed Exclusively by Ronco Teleproducts"*
> Side 1: White Christmas (Streisand, Barbra); Santa Claus Is Coming to Town (Bennett, Tony); Away in a Manger (Tucker, Tanya); Go Tell It on the Mountain (Jackson, Mahalia); Carol of the Bells (Williams, Andy); Angels We Have Heard on High (Lawrence, Carol, and Robert Goulet); O Holy Night (Nilsson, Birgit); Joy to the World (Mormon Tabernacle Choir); White World of Winter, The (Crosby, Bing); Happy Holiday (Lawrence, Steve, and Eydie Gorme)
> Side 2: We Wish You a Merry Christmas (Reynolds, Debbie); Jingle Bells (Ellington, Duke); Christmas Song, The (Mathis, Johnny); What Child Is This (Carr, Vikki); Deck the Halls (Faith, Percy); Medley: March of the Kings/Hark! The Herald Angels Sing (Merrill, Robert); Little Drummer Boy, The (Conniff, Ray); Silent Night, Holy Night (Cash, Johnny); O Come All Ye Faithful (Andrews, Julie); It's Christmastime All Over the World (Davis, Sammy, Jr.)

| Sampler III | American Gramaphone AG-366 | 1984 | 3.00 | 6.00 | 12.00 |

— *Contains one Christmas song:*
> Side 2, Song 6: Good King Wenceslas (Mannheim Steamroller)

| Season's Greetings from Barbra Streisand... And Friends | Columbia Special Products CSS 1075 | 1969 | 5.00 | 10.00 | 20.00 |

— *Created exclusively for Maxwell House Coffee*
> Side 1: O Little Town of Bethlehem; Sleep in Heavenly Peace (Silent Night); Gounod's Ave Maria; Christmas Song, The; Best Gift, The (all by Streisand, Barbra)
> Side 2: O Holy Night (Nabors, Jim); Silver Bells (Day, Doris); Medley: The First Noel/It Came Upon the Midnight Clear/O Come, All Ye Faithful (Kostelanetz, Andre); Jingle Bells (Nabors, Jim); Toyland (Day, Doris); Medley: Hark! The Herald Angels Sing/Angels We Have Heard on High (Kostelanetz, Andre)

| Seasons Greetings (A Christmas Festival of Stars) | M Columbia CL 1394 | 1959 | 5.00 | 10.00 | 20.00 |
| Seasons Greetings (A Christmas Festival of Stars) | S Columbia CS 8189 | 1959 | 6.25 | 12.50 | 25.00 |

> Side 1: Seasons Greetings (Miller, Mitch); What Child Is This (Mathis, Johnny); Secret of Christmas, The (Crosby, Bing); Medley: The First Noel/Wassail, Wassail, All Over the Town/Hark! The Herald Angels Sing/God Rest Ye Merry Gentlemen (Luboff, Norman, Choir); Hallalujah Chorus (Faith, Percy)
> Side 2: Christmas Song, The (Mathis, Johnny); Star Carol, The (Hi-Los, The); Number One Day of Christmas (Kennedy, Ed); O Come All Ye Faithful (Miller, Mitch); Silent Night, Holy Night (Faith, Percy); Auld Lang Syne (Miller, Mitch)

| Shell's Wonderful World of Music | (2) Longines Symphonette LWSH-5/6 | 196? | 3.75 | 7.50 | 15.00 |

— *Assembled by the Longines Symphonette Society (anonymous artists) for Shell gas stations*
> Side 1: I'll Be Home for Christmas; Christmas Song, The; Babes in Toyland; White Christmas
> Side 2: First Noel, The; Twelve Days of Christmas, The; O Holy Night; It Came Upon a Midnight Clear; God Rest Ye Merry Gentlemen
> Side 3: Joy to the World; Dance of the Sugar Plum Fairies; Good King Wenceslaus; Away in a Manger; Medley: We Wish You a Merry Christmas/I Saw Three Ships/Christmas Is Coming
> Side 4: Silent Night; Medley: Deck the Halls with Boughs of Holly/Jingle Bells/Ave Maria/We Three Kings of Orient Are/Oh Come All Ye Faithful

| Shell's Wonderful World of Music, Vol. 2 | (2) Longines Symphonette LWSH-7/8 | 196? | 3.75 | 7.50 | 15.00 |

— *Assembled by the Longines Symphonette Society (anonymous artists) for Shell gas stations*
> Side 1: Santa Claus Is Comin' to Town; Away in a Manger; Babes in Toyland; What Child Is This; Let It Snow, Let It Snow
> Side 2: It's Beginning to Look a Lot Like Christmas; O Little Town of Bethlehem; O Holy Night; Oh Come, All Ye Faithful; Silver Bells
> Side 3: Christmas Song, The; Ave Maria (Schubert); God Rest Ye Merry Gentlemen; I'll Be Home for Christmas; First Noel, The
> Side 4: White Christmas; It Came Upon a Midnight Clear; Have Yourself a Merry Little Christmas; Joy to the World; Silent Night

| Silent Night . . . | Columbia Special Products P 14989 | 1979 | 2.00 | 4.00 | 8.00 |
| Silent Night . . . | SeaShell P 14989 | 1981 | 2.00 | 4.00 | 8.00 |

— *Reissue*
> Side 1: Silent Night, Holy Night (Andrews, Julie); Hark the Herald Angels Sing (Williams, Andy); Trepak from "Nutcracker Suite" (Nero, Peter); It Came Upon the Midnight Clear (Carr, Vikki); Oh Tannenbaum (Faith, Percy)
> Side 2: Do You Hear What I Hear (Mathis, Johnny); Mary's Little Boy Child (Jackson, Mahalia); Go Tell It on a Mountain (Conniff, Ray); What Child Is This (Davidson, John); Twelve Days of Christmas, The (New York Philharmonic)

| Sinatra Family Wish You a Merry Christmas, The | Reprise FS-1026 | 1969 | 12.50 | 25.00 | 50.00 |

> Side 1: I Wouldn't Trade Christmas (Sinatra, Frank, Frank Jr., Nancy and Tina [The Family]); It's Such a Lonely Time of Year (Sinatra, Nancy); Some Children See Him (Sinatra, Frank, Jr.); O Bambino (One Cold and Blessed Winter) (Sinatra, Tina and Nancy); Bells of Christmas, The (Greensleeves) (Sinatra, Frank, Frank Jr., Nancy and Tina [The Family])
> Side 2: Whatever Happened to Christmas? (Sinatra, Frank); Santa Claus Is Comin' to Town (Sinatra, Tina); Kids (Sinatra, Nancy); Christmas Waltz, The (Sinatra, Frank); Twelve Days of Christmas, The (Sinatra, Frank, Frank Jr., Nancy and Tina [The Family])

Title		Label, Number	Year	VG	VG+	NM
60 Christmas Classics	(4)	Sessions DVL2-0723	1985	5.00	10.00	20.00

— *Record 3 is numbered "P18827" and Record 4 is numbered "P18828"*

Side 1: Fanfare/Joy to the World (Mills, Frank); Medley: It Came Upon a Midnight Clear/Away in a Manger/The First Noel (Mancini, Henry); Sleigh Ride (Boston Pops Orchestra [Fiedler]); Sunny Bank (Andrews, Julie); Christmas Song, The (Gary, John); (There's No Place Like) Home for the Holidays (Living Strings)

Side 2: Wassail Song (Hunter, Ralph, Choir); Medley: Joy to the World/Oh Little Town of Bethlehem/Hark! The Herald Angels Sing (Luboff, Norman, Choir); Winter Wonderland (Davis, Danny, and the Nashville Brass); Let It Snow! Let It Snow! Let It Snow! (Ames, Ed); Good King Wenceslas (Gould, Morton); Medley: Ring Christmas Bells/We Wish You a Merry Christmas (Living Strings with Living Voices); Medley: Good Christian Men, Rejoice/Silent Night/Patapan/O Come, All Ye Faithful (Shaw, Robert, Chorale)

Side 3: Medley: Deck the Halls/It's Beginning to Look Like Christmas (Living Strings); I'll Be Home for Christmas (Cantrell, Lana); White Christmas (Boston Pops Orchestra [Fiedler]); Here Comes Santa Claus (Down Santa Claus Lane) (Fisher, Eddie); Pretty Paper (Nelson, Willie); Carol of the Bells (Winterhalter, Hugo); We Three Kings of Orient Are (McCarthy, John, Chorale); Hallelujah Chorus (Royal Philharmonic Orchestra [Beecham])

Side 4: Nativity, The (Radio City Music Hall Orchestra); God Rest You Merry, Gentlemen (Andrews, Julie); Do You Hear What I Hear (Ames, Ed); Cathedral Bells Are Ringing (Mills, Frank); Medley: The First Noel/O Come, All Ye Faithful/O Holy Night (Gary, John); Angels from the Realms (McCarthy, John, Chorale); Silent Night, Holy Night (Martin, Tony)

Side 5: Christmas Festival, A (Medley) (Boston Pops Orchestra [Fiedler]); White World of Winter, The (Crosby, Bing); Jingle Bells (Page, Patti); Medley: March of the Toys/Toyland (Kostelanetz, Andre); Mary's Little Boy (Williams, Andy); Medley: Wassail Song/The First Noel/O Christmas Tree/Green Needles (Living Voices); O Come, O Come Emmanuel (Philadelphia Orchestra [Ormandy])

Side 6: White Christmas (Bennett, Tony); While Shepherds Watched (London Symphony Orchestra); Medley: Jolly Old St. Nicholas/The Little Drummer Boy (Conniff, Ray); My Favorite Things (Martin, Mary); Coventry Carol (Miller, Mitch); Scarlet Ribbons (Browns, The); We Need a Little Christmas (Faith, Percy); Lord's Prayer, The (Williams, Andy)

Side 7: Happy Holidays (Faith, Percy); Winter Wonderland (Bennett, Tony); See Amid the Winter Snows (Andrews, Julie); Hark! The Herald Angels Sing (Williams, Andy); Twelve Days of Christmas, The (Conniff, Ray); Angels We Have Heard on High (Luboff, Norman, Choir); Ave Maria (Philadelphia Orchestra [Ormandy])

Side 8: Rudolph, the Red-Nosed Reindeer (Autry, Gene); What Child Is This? (Brothers Four, The); Christmas Eve in My Home Town (Living Strings); Secret of Christmas, The (Crosby, Bing); Santa Claus Is Comin' to Town (Bennett, Tony); Bells of St. Mary, The (Williams, Andy); O Sanctissima (Philadelphia Orchestra [Ormandy]); Medley: Let It Snow! Let It Snow! Let It Snow!/Count Your Blessings/We Wish You a Merry Christmas (Conniff, Ray)

| Something Festive! | | A&M SP-19003 | 1967 | 3.75 | 7.50 | 15.00 |

— *Sold only at B.F. Goodrich tire dealers*

Side 1: Winter Wonderland (Alpert, Herb, and the Tijuana Brass); Christmas Song, The (Mendes, Sergio, and Brasil '66); Raggedy Ann and Raggedy Andy (Minnelli, Liza); Twelve Days of Christmas (Wechter, Julius, and the Baja Marimba Band); My Favorite Things (We Five)

Side 2: Bell That Couldn't Jingle, The (Bacharach, Burt); It's the Most Wonderful Time (Jolly, Pete); Snow (Longet, Claudine); God Rest Ye Merry, Gentlemen (Wechter, Julius, and the Baja Marimba Band); Jingle Bell Rock (Alpert, Herb, and the Tijuana Brass)

| Soul Christmas | | Atco SD 33-269 | 1968 | 7.50 | 15.00 | 30.00 |
| Sound of Christmas, The | S | Capitol Creative Products SL-6515 | 1966 | 3.00 | 6.00 | 12.00 |

Side 1: Caroling, Caroling (Cole, Nat King); Silent Night (Shore, Dinah); Christmas Song, The (Hollyridge Strings, The); Do You Hear What I Hear (Crosby, Bing); O Little Town of Bethlehem (Stafford, Jo); Joy to the World (Hollywood Bowl Symphony Orchestra)

Side 2: Little Drummer Boy, The (Korean Orphan Choir, The); First Noel, The (Ford, Tennessee Ernie); White Christmas (Waring, Fred, and the Pennsylvanians); Medley: We Wish You a Merry Christmas/Silver Bells (Martino, Al); We Three Kings (Hollywood Bowl Symphony Orchestra); O Holy Night (Cole, Nat King)

| Sound of Christmas, The, Vol. 2 | | Capitol Creative Products SL-6534 | 1967 | 3.00 | 6.00 | 12.00 |

Side 1: Christmas Colors (Medley) (Hollywood Pops Orchestra); Virgin's Slumber Song, The (Ford, Tennessee Ernie); Christmas Song, The (Lee, Peggy); Deck the Hall (Cole, Nat King); Medley: What Child Is This/The Holly and the Ivy (Crosby, Bing); Caroling, Caroling (Hollywood Pops Orchestra)

Side 2: Christmas Waltz, The (Wilson, Nancy); Silent Night (Lettermen, The); Christmas Is for Children (Campbell, Glen); Dream of Toyland, A (Hollywood Pops Orchestra); Ave Maria (Bach-Gounod) (Corelli, Franco); God Rest Ye Merry, Gentlemen (Cole, Nat King); We Wish You a Merry Christmas (Hollywood Pops Orchestra)

| Sound of Christmas, The, Vol. 3 | | Capitol Creative Products SL-6680 | 1970 | 3.00 | 6.00 | 12.00 |

Side 1: I'll Be Home for Christmas (Rogers, Roy); Coventry Carol, The (Shore, Dinah); Yule Medley (Hollywood Pops Orchestra); Do You Hear What I Hear? (Sandler and Young); Hang Your Wishes on the Tree (Baxter, Les)

Side 2: Little Drummer Boy (Korean Orphan Choir); Yule Medley (Wagner, Roger, Chorale); Hark the Herald Angels Sing (Hollywood Bowl Symphony Orchestra); Mary's Little Boy (Lettermen, The); Silent Night (Fitzgerald, Ella)

| Sounds of Christmas | | Columbia Special Products P 12474 | 1974 | 3.00 | 6.00 . | 12.00 |

— *Sold only through Amway dealers*

Side 1: It Came Upon a Midnight Clear (Carr, Vikki); O Little Town of Bethlehem (Sanborn Singers, The); Angels We Have Heard on High (Faith, Percy); Silent Night, Holy Night (Mormon Tabernacle Choir); O Come, All Ye Faithful (Goulet, Robert); Deck the Hall with Boughs of Holly (Conniff, Ray)

Side 2: Little Drummer Boy, The (Conniff, Ray); Silver Bells (Mathis, Johnny); Jingle Bells (Sanborn Singers, The); God Rest Ye Merry, Gentlemen (Price, Ray); We Wish You a Merry Christmas (Mann, Johnny, Singers); Santa Claus Is Comin' to Town (Miller, Mitch)

| Spirit of Christmas, The | | Capitol Creative Products SL-6516 | 1966 | 3.75 | 7.50 | 15.00 |

Side 1: Christmas Waltz, The (Lettermen, The); White Christmas (Hollyridge Strings, The); Still, Still, Still (Vienna Boys Choir); O Come All Ye Faithful (Martino, Al); Don't Forget to Feed the Reindeer (Lee, Peggy); O Holy Night (Crosby, Bing)

Side 2: Christmas Song, The (Lettermen, The); Have Yourself a Merry Little Christmas (Hollyridge Strings, The); Stille Nacht, Heilige Nacht (Silent Night) (Vienna Boys Choir); Star Carol, The (Lee, Peggy); What Child Is This (Martino, Al); Gesu Bambino (Wagner, Roger, Chorale)

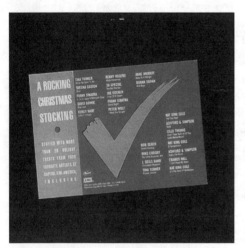 

(Top left) This Capitol Special Markets LP from 1977 is unusual because it features the original mono recording of "The Little Drummer Boy" by the Harry Simeone Chorale. Most compilations use the stereo re-recording from the 1960s. The two are audibly different, especially near the end. (Top right) Don't want to pay four figures for the Moonglows' Christmas 45? Find this 1986 album, and get both sides, plus other cool tracks from the MCA archives, for a fraction of that. (Bottom left) This Capitol two-record promo LP from 1984 mixes current hits of the day with holiday tunes from such artists as Nat King Cole and Frank Sinatra. Jarring, to say the least. (Bottom right) Among the middle-of-the-road artists on this 1967 compilation, there is a holiday tune from We Five.

Title		Label, Number	Year	VG	VG+	NM
Spirit of Christmas, The	M	Columbia Special Products CSP 249	1965	3.75	7.50	15.00

— *Sold only at A&P grocery stores*
  Side 1: Dearest Santa (Vinton, Bobby); Night Before Christmas Song, The (Clooney, Rosemary); O Holy Night (Vale, Jerry); Winter Wonderland (Lanin, Lester); Christmas Song, The (Stafford, Jo); Winter Song, The (Staton, Merrill, Choir)
  Side 2: Deck the Hall with Boughs of Holly (Faith, Percy); O Little Town of Bethlehem (Cole, Buddy); Medley: What Child Is This/The Twelve Days of Christmas/Baloo Lammy (Luboff, Norman, Choir); Star Carol, The (Hi-Lo's, The); Medley: We Three Kings of Orient Are/Good King Wenceslas/O Tannenbaum (De Vol, Frank); Medley: The First Noel/Hark! The Herald Angels Sing/O Come, All Ye Faithful/We Wish You a Merry Christmas (Conniff, Ray)

| Spirit of Christmas, The, Volume III | | Columbia Special Products CSS 1463 | 1970 | 3.00 | 6.00 | 12.00 |

  Side 1: What Child Is This? (Mathis, Johnny); Mary's Lullaby (Sleep Baby, Sleep) (Bryant, Anita); Toyland (Kostelanetz, Andre); Joy to the World (Jackson, Mahalia); Hallelujah Chorus (Faith, Percy)
  Side 2: Silent Night (Cash, Johnny); Happy Birthday, Jesus (Ives, Burl); We Three Kings of Orient Are (Conniff, Ray); (There's No Place Like) Home for the Holidays (Goulet, Robert); Twelve Days of Christmas, The (Mormon Tabernacle Choir)

| Starlight Christmas, A | | MCA 10066 | 1990 | 2.50 | 5.00 | 10.00 |

  Side 1: What a Christmas Feeling (Clewer, Janey); I'm All Lit Up Like a Christmas Tree (Clewer, Janey); Love Will Keep Us Warm This Year for Christmas (Medeiros, Glenn, and Janey Clewer); I'm Christmasing with You (LaBelle, Patti); Let's Build a Snowman (Lola the Ladybug and Myron the Moose)
  Side 2: I Cannot Forget (Jets, The); Christmas in the Air (Clewer, Janey); Ain't No Time for Diets (Clewer, Janey; Gene Moreford; and Don Shelton); Remember Christmas (Clewer, Janey); Starlight (Sagal, Katey); Christmas Lullaby (Clewer, Janey)

| Stars of Christmas, The | | RCA Special Products DPL1-0842 | 1988 | 5.00 | 10.00 | 20.00 |

— *Sold only through Avon dealers*
  Side 1: Beneath the Christmas Star (Collins, Judy); Let It Snow! Let It Snow! Let It Snow! (Mathis, Johnny); Santa Claus Is Comin' to Town (Pointer Sisters, The); Jingle Bells (Feliciano, Jose); Rockin' Around the Christmas Tree (Forester Sisters, The); White Christmas (Crosby, Bing)
  Side 2: It's the Most Wonderful Time of the Year (Williams, Andy); Twelve Days of Christmas, The (Whittaker, Roger); Merry Christmas Darling (Carpenters); If Every Day Was Like Christmas (Presley, Elvis); I Saw Three Ships (Galway, James); Silent Night (Rogers, Kenny)

| Stash Christmas Album, The | | Stash 125 | 1980 | 3.75 | 7.50 | 15.00 |

  Side 1: Merry Christmas (Hopkins, Lightnin'); Santa Claus Blues (Williams, Clarence's, Blue Five); Santa Claus Bring My Man Back (Ware, Ozie, with Duke Ellington); Santa Claus Came in the Spring (Dandridge, Putney, Swing Band); Santa Claus Is Coming to Town (Reser, Harry); Christmas Night in Harlem (Teagarden, Jack, and Johnny Mercer); Jingle Bells (Goodman, Benny)
  Side 2: Swingin' Them Jingle Bells (Waller, Fats); Merry Christmas Baby (Hampton, Lionel); Santa Claus Got Stuck in My Chimney (Fitzgerald, Ella); Cool Yule (Armstrong, Louis); 'Zat You, Santa Claus? (Armstrong, Louis); Christmas in New Orleans (Armstrong, Louis); Night Before Christmas, The (Armstrong, Louis)

| Stuff This in Your Stocking! Elves in Action | | Veebltronics/Skyclad 68 | 1990 | 3.00 | 6.00 | 12.00 |

  Side 1: I'll Be Home for Christmas (Hello Disaster); Merry Xmas Everybody! (French Lemon Samples); It's Christmas (And I Love You) (Electric Shoes, The); Father Christmas (Leonards, The); White Christmas (Dirty Dogs); Santa Claus (Pink Slip Daddy); Happy Birthday (Tolman, Russ, and the North Pole Men)
  Side 2: Oh Santa (Vine, Emma, and the Emotionals); I Believe in Father Christmas (Human Drama); I Got a Lot of Toys for Christmas (Sterilles, The); Christmas in the Courtroom (Saxon, Sky, and Firewall); God Rest Ye Merry, Gentlemen (Jigsaw Seen, The); Holiday Cheer (L-Status); Home for Christmas (Characters, The)

| Ten Tunes of Christmas | | Candee 50-50 | 195? | 5.00 | 10.00 | 20.00 |

— *Sold through "The 50-50 Club," a Cincinnati radio and TV show; all the artists have Cincinnati ties*
  Side 1: Hey Nonnie Nonnie (Lyons, Ruth, and the Dello-Larks); Soon 'Twill Be Christmas Eve (Spelman, Marion); Christmas Is Gettin' Mighty Close (Bonnie Lou *With Peter Grant*); Christmas Is a Birthday Time (Wright, Ruby); Have a Merry Merry Merry Merry Christmas (Wright, Ruby) *As "Ruby and the Angel Choir"*
  Side 2: Happy Time, The (Al' of Us); There's No Time Like Christmas Time (Spelman, Marion); It's Christmas-Time Again (Bonnie Lou); Sing a Song of Christmas (Braun, Bob); Let's Light the Christmas Tree (Wright, Ruby)

| Tennessee Christmas | | MCA 5620 | 1985 | 3.00 | 6.00 | 12.00 |
| Tennessee Christmas | | MCA R 134563 | 1985 | 3.00 | 6.00 | 12.00 |

— *RCA Music Service edition*
  Side 1: Away in a Manger (McEntire, Reba); Tennessee Christmas (Wariner, Steve); Please Come Home for Christmas (Schneider, John); One Bright Star (Larson, Nicolette); First Noel, The (Lynn, Loretta)
  Side 2: Greatest Little Christmas Ever Wuz (Stevens, Ray); Christmas Song, The (Lee, Brenda); Christmas in the Caribbean (Buffett, Jimmy); Christmas Is Paintin' the Town (Oak Ridge Boys, The); Winter Wonderland (Mandrell, Barbara)

| That Christmas Feeling | | Columbia Special Products P 11853 | 1973 | 3.00 | 6.00 | 12.00 |

— *Sold only at JCPenney department stores*
  Side 1: We Need a Little Christmas (Faith, Percy); Carol of the Bells (New York Philharmonic [Bernstein]); It's the Most Wonderful Time of the Year (Williams, Andy); God Rest Ye Merry, Gentlemen (Mathis, Johnny); Away in the Manger (Mormon Tabernacle Choir); O Bambino (One Cold and Blessed Winter) (New Christy Minstrels, The)
  Side 2: Here We Come a-Caroling (Conniff, Ray); I Wonder As I Wander (Streisand, Barbra); O Little Town of Bethlehem (Luboff, Norman, Choir); Home for the Holidays (Goulet, Robert); Medley: Hark! The Herald Angels Sing/We Three Kings of Orient Are (Philadelphia Orchestra [Ormandy]); It's Christmas Time All Over the World (Davis, Sammy, Jr.)

| Time-Life Treasury of Christmas, The | (3) | Time-Life STL-107 | 1986 | 5.00 | 10.00 | 20.00 |

— *Available from Time-Life by mail order only; boxed set*

| Time-Life Treasury of Christmas, The | (3) | Time-Life STL-107 | 1989 | 3.75 | 7.50 | 15.00 |

— *Available from Time-Life by mail order only; wide sleeve rather than box*
  Side 1: White Christmas (Crosby, Bing); Medley: Winter Wonderland/Sleigh Ride (Parton, Dolly); Little Drummer Boy, The (Simeone, Harry, Chorale) *Stereo re-recording*; O Little Town of Bethlehem (Previn, Andre); Twelve Days of Christmas, The (Whittaker, Roger); Hark, the Herald Angels Sing (Cole, Nat King); O Holy Night (Como, Perry)
  Side 2: Christmas Song, The (Carpenters); Medley: Carol of the Bells/Deck the Halls (Shaw, Robert, Chorale); 'Twas the Night Before Christmas (Waring, Fred, and the Pennsylvanians); Here Comes Santa Claus (Presley, Elvis); Santa's Beard (Beach Boys, The); Christmas in My Home Town (Pride, Charley); Away in a Manger (Ames, Ed); Silent Night (Reeves, Jim)

Title		Label, Number	Year	VG	VG+	NM

Side 3: Home for the Holidays (Como, Perry) *1958 re-recording;* Rudolph, the Red-Nosed Reindeer (Autry, Gene); Feliz Navidad (Feliciano, Jose); Good King Wenceslas (Gould, Morton, and the RCA Symphony Orchestra); Jingle Bell Rock (Helms, Bobby); Medley: Here We Come a-Caroling/O Tannenbaum/I Saw Three Ships (Boston Pops Orchestra [Fiedler]); Ave Maria (Schubert) (Price, Leontyne)

Side 4: Ding Dong Merrily on High (Whittaker, Roger); If Every Day Was Like Christmas (Presley, Elvis) *Mono version;* Rockin' Around the Christmas Tree (Lee, Brenda); Santa Claus Is Coming to Town (Como, Perry); Jingle Bells (Reeves, Jim); What Child Is This (Previn, Andre); Adeste Fideles (Pavarotti, Luciano)

Side 5: I'll Be Home for Christmas (Como, Perry); God Rest Ye Merry, Gentlemen (Andrews, Julie); Christmas in Dixie (Alabama); Do You Hear What I Hear (Crosby, Bing); Medley: Joy to the World/Angels We Have Heard On High (Shaw, Robert, Chorale); Blue Christmas (Campbell, Glen); It Came Upon a Midnight Clear (Philadelphia Orchestra [Page]); Have Yourself a Merry Little Christmas (Garland, Judy)

Side 6: Mary's Boy Child (Belafonte, Harry); Rocking (Whittaker, Roger); Let It Snow, Let It Snow, Let It Snow (Horne, Lena); First Noel, The (Franchi, Sergio); Silver Bells (Smith, Kate); Holly Jolly Christmas, A (Ives, Burl); It's Beginning to Look Like Christmas (Como, Perry, and the Fontane Sisters); We Wish You a Merry Christmas (Philadelphia Orchestra [Ormandy])

| Time-Life Treasury of Christmas, The, Volume Two | (3) | Time-Life STL-108 | 1987 | 5.00 | 10.00 | 20.00 |

— *Available from Time-Life by mail-order only; all known copies are boxed sets*

Side 1: Christmas Song, The (Cole, Nat King) *Stereo re-recording;* Jingle Bells (Crosby, Bing, and the Andrews Sisters); Little Drummer Boy, The (Whittaker, Roger); Sleigh Ride (Boston Pops Orchestra [Fiedler]); I Heard the Bells on Christmas Day (Belafonte, Harry); Up on the House Top (Arnold, Eddy); Irish Carol (Andrews, Julie); Jolly Old St. Nicholas (Atkins, Chet)

Side 2: Bless This House (Como, Perry); Medley: O Little Town of Bethlehem/It Came Upon a Midnight Clear (Canadian Brass, The); Christmas Is for Children (Campbell, Glen); Blue Christmas (Presley, Elvis); Frosty the Snowman (Foley, Red); Old Christmas Card, An (Reeves, Jim); In Dulci Jubilo (Vienna Choir Boys); O Come All Ye Faithful (Ames, Ed)

Side 3: Silent Night (Franchi, Sergio); There's No Christmas Like a Home Christmas (Como, Perry) *1968 re-recording;* Christmas Day (Beach Boys, The); Tennessee Christmas (Alabama); Home for Christmas (Gould, Morton, and the RCA Symphony Orchestra); Coventry Carol (Choir of King's College, Cambridge); Holly and the Ivy, The (Whittaker, Roger); O Holy Night (Pavarotti, Luciano)

Side 4: White Christmas (Como, Perry); Winter Wonderland (Andrews Sisters, The); I'll Be Home for Christmas (Crosby, Bing); Twelve Days of Christmas, The (Shaw, Robert, Chorale); Gifts They Gave, The (Belafonte, Harry); Toy Trumpet, The (Boston Pops Orchestra [Fiedler] with Al Hirt); God Rest Ye Merry, Gentlemen (Whittaker, Roger); Good King Wenceslas (Ames Brothers, The)

Side 5: Rudolph, the Red-Nosed Reindeer (Crosby, Bing); C-H-R-I-S-T-M-A-S (Reeves, Jim); Twinkle, Twinkle Little Me (Supremes, The); Jingle Bell Rock (Atkins, Chet); That Special Time of Year (Knight, Gladys, and the Pips); Pretty Paper (Nelson, Willie); Old Toy Trains (Miller, Roger); Medley: We Three Kings of Orient Are/Hark, the Herald Angels Sing (Shaw, Robert, Chorale)

Side 6: Medley: Here We Come a-Caroling/We Wish You a Merry Christmas (Como, Perry); Do You Hear What I Hear (Ames, Ed); Shepherds in the Field Abiding (Choir of King's College, Cambridge); Joy to the World (Andrews, Julie); O Come, O Come, Emmanuel (Fox, Virgil); Gesu Bambino (Pavarotti, Luciano); Ave Maria (Bach-Gounod) (Tebaldi, Renata); Hallelujah Chorus (Shaw, Robert, Chorale)

| Total Experience Christmas, A | | Total Experience TEL8-5707 | 1984 | 3.00 | 6.00 | 12.00 |

Side 1: This Christmas (Gap Band, The); Christmas Song, The (Gap Band, The); Christmas Won't Be Christmas Without My Baby (Ellis, Jonah); Christmas Dreams (Yarbrough and Peoples)

Side 2: All I Need for Christmas Is Your Love (Prime Time); Silent Night (Ford, Pennye, and Oliver Scott); Please Come Home for Christmas (Goodie); I Miss You Most of All at Christmas (Gap Band, The); Joy to the World (Scott, Oliver)

| 12 Days of Christmas, The | | Pickwick SPC-1021 | 1976 | 2.50 | 5.00 | 10.00 |

Side 1: Twelve Days of Christmas, The (Rodgers, Jimmie); Joy to the World (Boone, Pat); Oh Little Town of Bethlehem (Liberace); Silent Night (Mills Brothers, The); I'll Be Home for Christmas (Welk, Lawrence); Little Drummer Boy (Lennon Sisters, The)

Side 2: White Christmas (Vaughn, Billy); God Rest Ye Merry Gentlemen (Wright, George); It Came Upon a Midnight Clear (Guitar, Bonnie); Do You Hear What I Hear (Fisher, Eddie); Winter Wonderland (Wakely, Jimmy); We Wish You a Merry Christmas (Hollaran Singers)

| 12 Hits of Christmas | | United Artists UA-LA669-R | 1976 | 3.00 | 6.00 | 12.00 |

Side 1: Christmas Song, The (Cole, Nat King) *1961 stereo re-recording;* Rudolph the Red-Nosed Reindeer (Autry, Gene); Little Drummer Boy, The (Simeone, Harry, Chorale) *1960s stereo re-recording;* Jingle Bell Rock (Helms, Bobby); Chipmunk Song, The (Chipmunks, The, David Seville and); Rockin' Around the Christmas Tree (Lee, Brenda)

Side 2: I Saw Mommy Kissing Santa Claus (Boyd, Jimmy); Santa Baby (Kitt, Eartha); Here Comes Santa Claus (Autry. Gene); Sleigh Ride (Anderson, Leroy); All I Want for Christmas Is My Two Front Teeth (Jones, Spike, and His City Slickers); Do You Hear What I Hear (Crosby, Bing)

| 12 Songs of Christmas | M | Reprise F-2022 | 1964 | 5.00 | 10.00 | 20.00 |
| 12 Songs of Christmas | S | Reprise FS-2022 | 1964 | 3.75 | 7.50 | 15.00 |

Side 1: White Christmas (Waring, Fred, and the Pennsylvanians); It's Christmas Time Again (Crosby, Bing, and Fred Waring); Go Tell It on the Mountain (Sinatra, Frank; Bing Crosby; Fred Waring); Old-Fashioned Christmas, An (Sinatra, Frank, and Fred Waring); When Angels Sang of Peace (Waring, Fred, and the Pennsylvanians); Little Drummer Boy, The (Sinatra, Frank, and Fred Waring)

Side 2: I Heard the Bells on Christmas Day (Sinatra, Frank, and Fred Waring); Do You Hear What I Hear (Waring, Fred, and the Pennsylvanians); Secret of Christmas, The (Crosby, Bing, and Fred Waring); Twelve Days of Christmas, The (Waring, Fred, and the Pennsylvanians); Christmas Candles (Crosby, Bing, and Fred Waring); We Wish You the Merriest (Sinatra, Frank; Bing Crosby; Fred Waring)

| 20 Christmas Favorites | S | Yulesong SY-0220 | 197? | 2.50 | 5.00 | 10.00 |

Side 1: Little Drummer Boy (Voices of Christmas, The); Hark the Herald Angels Sing (Voices of Christmas, The); Good King Wenceslas (Organ & Chimes); It Came Upon a Midnight Clear (Organ & Chimes); God Rest Ye Merry Gentlemen (Organ & Chimes); Away in a Manger (Organ & Chimes); Jingle Bells (Evans, Robert); O Tannenbaum (Evans, Robert); 12 Days of Chrsitmas (Evans, Robert); O Little Town of Bethlehem (Evans, Robert)

Side 2: O Holy Night (Evans, Robert); Rudolph the Red-Nosed Reindeer (Evans, Robert); Twas the Night Before Christmas (Evans, Robert); O Come All Ye Faithful (Evans, Robert); Silent Night (Evans, Robert); First Noel, The (Christmas Strings, The); Deck the Halls (Christmas Strings, The); White Christmas (Christmas Strings, The); Joy to the World (Pipe Organ & Chimes); We Three Kings (Evans, Robert)

Title	Label, Number	Year	VG	VG+	NM
Very Merry Christmas, A	Columbia Special Products CSS 563	1967	5.00	10.00	20.00

— *Sold only at Grants stores*
- Side 1: Little Drummer Boy, The (Conniff, Ray); Jingle Bells (Dean, Jimmy); Santo Natale (Page, Patti); Star Carol, The (Simon and Garfunkel); O Holy Night (Mathis, Johnny); We Three Kings of Orient Are (Rodgers, Jimmie); Sweetest Dreams Be Thine (Bikel, Theodore)
- Side 2: Medley: The First Noel/It Came Upon a Midnight Clear/O Come All Ye Faithful (Kostelanetz, Andre); Touch Hands on Christmas Morning (Douglas, Mike); Der Tag, Der Ist So Freudenreich (Biggs, E. Power); Twelve Days of Christmas, The (Ives, Burl); God Rest Ye Merry, Gentlemen (Previn, Andre); Do You Hear What I Hear (Vinton, Bobby); Hallelujah Chorus (Mormon Tabernacle Choir)

Very Merry Christmas, A, Volume Two	Columbia Special Products CSS 788	1968	3.00	6.00	12.00

— *Sold only at Grants stores*
- Side 1: Joy to the World (Miller, Mitch); O Holy Night (Goulet, Robert); It Came Upon the Midnight Clear (Bryant, Anita); Sleigh Ride (Kostelanetz, Andre); Christmas Song, The (Lawrence, Steve); O Little Town of Bethlehem (Jackson, Mahalia); Here We Come a-Caroling (New Christy Minstrels, The)
- Side 2: Jingle Bells (Nabors, Jim); Have Yourself a Merry Little Christmas (Day, Doris); Silver Bells (Mathis, Johnny); We Need a Little Christmas (Henderson, Skitch); I Heard the Bells on Christmas Day (Cash, Johnny); White Christmas (Gorme, Eydie); Medley: What Child Is This/The Holly and the Ivy (Crosby, Bing); Silent Night (Mormon Tabernacle Choir)

Very Merry Christmas, A, Volume 3	Columbia Special Products CSS 997	1969	3.00	6.00	12.00

— *Sold only at Grants stores*
- Side 1: Do You Hear What I Hear (Goulet, Robert); It's Beginning to Look a Lot Like Christmas (Uggams, Leslie); Angels We Have Heard on High (Faith, Percy); I'll Be Home for Christmas (Mathis, Johnny); Real Meaning of Christmas, The (Conniff, Ray); Three Wise Men, Wise Men Three (Nabors, Jim); Christmas Chimes (Kostelanetz, Andre)
- Side 2: Christmas Lullaby (Grant, Cary); For Unto Us a Child Is Born (Philadelphia Orchestra [Ormandy]/Temple University Choir); Christmas Story (Ives, Burl); Silver Bells (Jackson, Mahalia); I Saw Mommy Kissing Santa Claus (Sullivan, Ed, Orchestra); Some Children See Him (Carroll, Diahann); What Child Is This (Miller, Mitch); Christmas Chopsticks (Vinton, Bobby)

Very Merry Christmas, A, Volume IV	Columbia Special Products CSS 1464	1970	3.75	7.50	15.00

— *Sold only at Grants stores*
- Side 1: That Holiday Feeling (Lawrence, Steve, and Eydie Gorme); O Holy Night (Puckett, Gary); Dance of the Sugar Plum Fairy/Dance of the Toy Flutes (Boston Pops Orchestra [Fiedler]); What Child Is This (Lindsay, Mark); Christmas Song, The (Torme, Mel); Best Gift, The (Streisand, Barbra)
- Side 2: I Heard the Bells on Christmas Day (Cash, Johnny); Have Yourself a Merry Little Christmas (Bennett, Tony); Winter Wonderland (Franklin, Aretha); Secret of Christmas, The (Crosby, Bing); Silent Night (Andrews, Julie); Christmas Medley (Hallelujah/Hark the Herald Angels Sing/Deck the Halls/Joy to the World) (Nero, Peter)

Very Merry Christmas, A, Volume 5	RCA Special Products PRS-343	1971	2.50	5.00	10.00

— *Sold only at Grants stores*
- Side 1: Home for the Holidays (Como, Perry) *1958 re-recording;* Medley: O Little Town of Bethlehem/The First Noel (Shaw, Robert, Chorale); Ballad of the Christmas Donkey, The (Ames, Ed); Sleigh Ride (Boston Pops Orchestra [Fiedler]); Sweet Little Jesus Boy (Gary, John); Santa Claus Is Comin' to Town (Arnold, Eddy)
- Side 2: Medley: Frosty the Snowman/Rudolph, the Red-Nosed Reindeer (Mancini, Henry); Christmas Is Coming (Belafonte, Harry); O Holy Night (Lanza, Mario); Medley: The Little Drummer Boy/Hark the Herald Angels Sing (Luboff, Norman, Choir); Medley: Here We Come a-Caroling/We Wish You a Merry Christmas (Como, Perry)

Very Merry Christmas, A, Volume VI	RCA Special Products PRS-427	1972	2.50	5.00	10.00

— *Sold only at Grants stores*
- Side 1: There Is No Christmas Like a Home Christmas (Como, Perry) *1968 re-recording;* Medley: Coventry Carol/God Rest Ye Merry, Gentlemen (Atkins, Chet); I Saw Three Ships (Shaw, Robert, Chorale); Twelve Days of Christmas, The (Belafonte, Harry); Christmas Festival Medley (Joy to the World/Deck the Halls/Jingle Bells/O Come All Ye Faithful) (Boston Pops Orchestra [Fiedler])
- Side 2: Medley: God Rest Ye Merry, Gentlemen/Deck the Halls/Hark the Herald Angels Sing (Mancini, Henry); Do You Hear What I Hear (Gary, John); Ave Maria (Schubert) (Price, Leontyne); I Heard the Bells on Christmas Day (Ames, Ed); Silent Night (Luboff, Norman, Choir); Little Drummer Boy, The (Como, Perry)

Very Merry Christmas, A, Volume VII	RCA Special Products DPL1-0049	1973	2.50	5.00	10.00

— *Sold only at Grants stores*
- Side 1: Toyland (Como, Perry); O Come All Ye Faithful (Shaw, Robert, Chorale); God Rest Ye Merry, Gentlemen (Andrews, Julie); What Child Is This (Ames, Ed); Hallelujah Chorus (Beecham, Sir Thomas)
- Side 2: Winter Wonderland (Boston Pops Orchestra [Fiedler]); Christmas in My Home Town (Pride, Charley); Good King Wenceslas (Gould, Morton); Jingling Brass (Davis, Danny); Santa Claus Is Coming to Town (Como, Perry)

Very Merry Christmas, A, Volume VIII	Capitol Special Markets SL-6954	1974	2.50	5.00	10.00

— *Sold only at Grants stores*
- Side 1: Do You Hear What I Hear (Crosby, Bing); Christmas Waltz, The (Lee, Peggy); Sleigh Ride (Waring, Fred, and the Pennsylvanians); It Came Upon a Midnight Clear (Ford, Tennessee Ernie); For Unto Us a Child Is Born (English Chamber Orchestra/ Ambrosian Singers)
- Side 2: Christmas Song, The (Cole, Nat King); Gesu Bambino (Wagner, Roger, Chorale); Blue Christmas (Campbell, Glen); Silent Night (Shore, Dinah); Christmas Medley for Children, A (Hollywood Pops Orchestra [Feller])

Very Special Christmas, A	A&M SP-3911	1987	3.75	7.50	15.00

— *Benefit album for Special Olympics*
- Side 1: Santa Claus Is Comin' to Town (Pointer Sisters, The); Winter Wonderland (Eurythmics); Do You Hear What I Hear (Houston, Whitney); Merry Christmas Baby (Springsteen, Bruce); Have Yourself a Merry Little Christmas (Pretenders); I Saw Mommy Kissing Santa Claus (Mellencamp, John Cougar); Gabriel's Message (Sting)
- Side 2: Christmas in Hollis (Run-D.M.C.); Christmas (Baby Please Come Home) (U2); Santa Baby (Madonna); Little Drummer Boy, The (Seger, Bob); Run Rudolph Run (Adams, Bryan); Back Door Santa (Bon Jovi); Coventry Carol (Moyet, Alison); Silent Night (Nicks, Stevie)

Title	Label, Number	Year	VG	VG+	NM

Waltons' Christmas Album, The — Columbia KC 33193 — 1974 — 3.75 — 7.50 — 15.00
— *Only one of the actors who appeared on the show appears on the album, thus it's listed under Various Artists rather than Soundtracks or under "Waltons, The." Throughout album, narrations by Earl Hamner.*
Side 1: Waltons Theme, The (Kellaway, Roger); First Noel, The (Holiday Singers, The); God Rest Ye Merry, Gentlemen (Holiday Singers, The); It Came Upon a Midnight Clear (Holiday Singers, The); Hark the Herald Angels Sing (Holiday Singers, The); Silent Night (Holiday Singers, The)
Side 2: Joy to the World (Holiday Singers, The); Grandpa's Christmas Wish (Geer, Will, and the Holiday Singers); O Come All Ye Faithful (Holiday Singers, The); O Little Town of Bethlehem (Holiday Singers, The); Spirit of Christmas (Kellaway, Roger)

We Wish You a Country Christmas — Columbia Special Products P 14991 — 1979 — 2.00 — 4.00 — 8.00
We Wish You a Country Christmas — SeaShell P 14991 — 1981 — 2.00 — 4.00 — 8.00
— *Reissue*
Side 1: White Christmas (Wynette, Tammy); O Holy Night (Nabors, Jim); Frosty the Snowman (Anderson, Lynn); Silent Night, Holy Night (Smith, Carl); It Came Upon a Midnight Clear (Dean, Jimmy)
Side 2: Away in a Manger (Wynette, Tammy); O Little Town of Bethlehem (Robbins, Marty); Go Tell It on the Mountain (Nabors, Jim); Blue Snowfall (Morgan, George); Lord's Prayer, The (Price, Ray)

We Wish You a Merry Christmas — Warner Bros. W 1337 — 1960 — 6.25 — 12.50 — 25.00
Side 1: Adeste Fideles (Zimbalist, Efrem, Jr.); Deck the Halls (Warner Bros. Stars); Away in a Manger (Stevens, Connie); Yulesville (Byrnes, Edd); Winter Wonderland (Brown, Peter); God Rest Ye Merry Gentlemen (Danton, Ray); Mele Kalikimaka (Ponce, Poncie)
Side 2: Santa Claus Is Coming to Town (Cole, Eddie); White Christmas (Conrad, Bob); Let It Snow, Let It Snow, Let It Snow (Provine, Dorothy); Silver Bells (Walker, Clint); Once in Royal David's City (Moore, Roger); Star Carol, The (Warner Bros. Male Chorus); It Came Upon a Midnight Clear (Hardin, Ty); We Wish You a Merry Christmas (Warner Bros. Stars)

We Wish You a Merry Christmas S — Warner Bros. WS 1337 — 1960 — 7.50 — 15.00 — 30.00
— *Same as above, but in stereo*

WHIO Radio Christmas Feelings — Sound Approach/CSP P 16366 — 1981 — 3.00 — 6.00 — 12.00
— *Sold by Elder Beerman Stores in the Dayton, Ohio area*
Side 1: Do You Hear What I Hear? (Goulet, Robert); Joy to the World (Conniff, Ray); We Three Kings (Byrd, Charlie); Let It Snow! Let It Snow! Let It Snow! (Lawrence, Steve, and Eydie Gorme); Christmas Song, The (Bennett, Tony); Happy Holiday (Faith, Percy); Sleep in Heavenly Peace (Silent Night) (Streisand, Barbra)
Side 2: Carol of the Bells (Williams, Andy); O Come, O Come, Emmanuel (Mormon Tabernacle Choir); Little Drummer Boy, The (Faith, Percy); Winter Wonderland (Welk, Lawrence); Christmas Is (Simeone, Harry, Chorale); White Christmas (Streisand, Barbra); We Wish You a Merry Christmas (Kostelanetz, Andre)

Winter Warnerland (2) — Warner Bros. PRO-A-3328 — 1988 — 10.00 — 20.00 — 40.00
— *Promo-only set; Record 1 is red vinyl, Record 2 is green vinyl*
Side 1: God Rest the House (Lorber, Jeff); Winter Wonderland (Good Question); Cold Chillin' Christmas (Cold Chillin' Juice Crew [Big Daddy Kane, MC Shan, Roxanne Shante]); Holiday I.D. (Traveling Wilburys [Nelson Wilbury, i.e., George Harrison]); Maybe This Could Be the Christmas (Cole, Gardner); Holiday I.D. (Ingram, James); Holiday I.D. (English) (Apollonia); Holiday I.D. (Spanish) (Apollonia)
Side 2: Once in a Blue Moon (PM); I'm Coming Home (Secret Weapon); Fais Do-Do (Lanois, Daniel); What Child Is This (O'Connor, Mark); Silver Bells (Horn, Jim); Christmas Medley (Herman, Pee-wee); Christmas Without You (Page, Tommy)
Side 3: Santa's Harley; Holiday I.D. (ZZ Top); Holiday I.D. (Bulletboys); Santa Claus Is Getting Down (Davis, Jesse Ed); Rudolph the Manic Reindeer (Los Lobos); Deck the Halls (R.E.M.); Medley: Angels We Have Heard on High/Gloria (Hugo Largo); Holiday I.D. (Reed, Lou); Blue Christmas (Dax, Danielle); Santa (Throwing Muses); Holiday I.D. (Haza, Ofra)
Side 4: 2000 Years of Love (54-40); I Believe in Father Christmas (Honeymoon Suite); Ways to Save Money at Christmas (Brown, Julie); Holiday I.D. (Cetera, Peter); Silent Night (Cetera, Peter); Holiday I.D. (Travis, Randy); How Do I Wrap My Heart Up for Christmas (Travis, Randy); Don't Drink and Drive, Duh (Herman, Pee-wee); Pee-wee Wilbury I.D. (Herman, Pee-wee); Santa's Jet

Winter's Solstice, A — Windham Hill WH-1045 — 1985 — 3.00 — 6.00 — 12.00
Side 1: Jesu, Joy of Man's Desiring (Qualey, David); Engravings II (Stein, Ira, and Russell Walder); New England Morning (Ackerman, William); High Plains (Christmas on the High-Line) (Aaberg, Philip); Nollaig (Oskay, Billy, and Micheal O Domhnaill)
Side 2: Greensleeves (Story, Liz); Bach Bouree (from the French Suite) (Anger, Darol, and Mike Marshall); Northumbrian Lullabye (Dalglish, Malcolm); Petite Aubade (Shadowfax); Tale of Two Cities, A (Isham, Mark)

Winter's Solstice II, A — Windham Hill WH-1077 — 1988 — 3.00 — 6.00 — 12.00
Side 1: Gift, The (Aaberg, Philip); 17th Century Canon (McCandless, Paul; James Matheson; Robin May); Prelude to Cello Suite #1 in G Major (Hedges, Michael); This Rush of Wings (Metamora); Sung to Sleep (Manring, Michael); Medley: E'en So, Lord Jesus Quickly Come/Dadme Albricias Hijos D'Eva (Sons of Eve Reward My Tidings) (Modern Mandolin Quartet); Bring Me Back a Song (Nightnoise)
Side 2: Salve Regina (Schroeder-Sheker, Therese); Chorale #220 (Turtle Island String Quartet); Simple Psalm (Simon, Fred); Flute Sonata in E minor, 3rd Movement (Higbie, Barbara, and Emily Klion); Come Life Shaker Life (Dalglish, Malcolm); Medieval Memory II (Stein, Ira, and Russel Walder); Abide the Winter (Ackerman, Will); By the Fireside (Mathieu, William Allaudin)

Wonderful World of Christmas, The, Album Two — Capitol Special Markets SL-8025 — 1976 — 2.50 — 5.00 — 10.00
Side 1: White Christmas (Haggard, Merle); Sweetest Song, The (Boone, Pat); What Child Is This (Shore, Dinah); Blue Christmas (Campbell, Glen); Medley: Noche De Pas (Silent Night)/Feliz Navidad a Todos (We Wish You a Merry Christmas) (Fender, Freddy); Santa Claus Is Coming to Town (Fargo, Donna)
Side 2: New Snow on the Roof (Campbell, Glen); Jingle Bells (Haggard, Merle); Away in a Manger (Lynn, Loretta); Amazing Grace (Price, Ray); Sing Silent Night (McCall, C.W.); Medley: It Came Upon a Midnight Clear/O Cone, All Ye Faithful (Dean, Jimmy)

Wondrous Winter: Songs of Winter, Songs of Christmas (2) — Columbia Special Products CSS 708/9 — 1968 — 3.75 — 7.50 — 15.00
— *Produced for NORM/A Step Ahead; record 1 has two tangential Christmas songs; record 2 is all Christmas songs*
Side 2: Song 1, My Favorite Things (Gorme, Eydie); Song 3, Overture to "The Nutcracker Suite" (New York Philharmonic [Bernstein])
Side 3: We Need a Little Christmas (Faith, Percy); Hallelujah Chorus (Philadelphia Orchestra [Ormandy]); O Come, All Ye Faithful (Jackson, Mahalia); White Christmas (Vinton, Bobby); Dance of the Sugar-Plum Fairy (New York Philharmonic [Bernstein])
Side 4: Medley: God Rest Ye Merry, Gentlemen/Hark! The Herald Angels Sing (Luboff, Norman, Choir); Away in a Manger (Bryant, Anita); O Holy Night (Douglas, Mike); I Heard the Bells on Christmas Day (Cash, Johnny); First Noel, The (Miller, Mitch)